THE CLAN DONALD

Rev. A. MACDONALD,

MINISTER OF KILLEARNAN.

AND THE

Rev. A. MACDONALD,

MINISTER OF KILTARLITY.

VOL I.

"The sovereignty of the Gael to the Clan Cholla,
It is right to proclaim it."

Inverness :
THE NORTHERN COUNTIES PUBLISHING COMPANY, Ltd.
1896.

TO

THE RIGHT HONOURABLE

THE LADY MACDONALD,

WIFE OF RONALD ARCHIBALD, LORD MACDONALD,

HEIR MALE OF JOHN MACDONALD OF ISLA,

EARL OF ROSS AND LORD OF THE ISLES, THIRTY-FIRST IN DESCENT FROM

SOMERLED,

KING OF THE ISLES AND LORD OF ARGYLL,

THIS FIRST VOLUME OF

THE CLAN DONALD

IS WITH MUCH RESPECT

DEDICATED

BY HER LADYSHIP'S CLANSMEN,

THE AUTHORS.

PREFACE.

This is the first of three volumes of the Clan
Donald History, undertaken at the request of
the Clan Donald Society. The large variety of
authorities to be consulted, illustrative matter
recently come to hand, and an Appendix more
voluminous than was at first anticipated, these,
along with other unexpected causes, have compelled the postponement of its publication beyond
the date at which it was first expected to
appear. It is hoped that, notwithstanding inevitable faults and failings, the manner in which
the work has so far been executed may prove
satisfactory to our Clan Donald readers, and that,
entering as it does to a large extent upon the
domain of Scottish History, it may also prove
acceptable to the public at large. That such
a work should have been mooted at this time of
day may appear superfluous to those who believe
that the subject has already been treated exhaustively throughout its wide extent. Such an
assumption is very wide of the mark. The late
Dr Skene, even in his earlier and less mature work
on "The Highlanders of Scotland," in which he
has occasion to refer at considerable length to

"Siol Chuinn," did not profess to write the history
of the Clan Donald; and Mr Donald Gregory—
than whom no more painstaking, thorough, or con-
scientious student of Scottish history ever lived—
wrote of this Clan only so far as to illustrate the
general history of the Highlands up to 1625. Mr
Charles Fraser-Mackintosh, in his erudite researches
regarding "The Last Macdonalds of Isla," *i.e.*, of
Dunnyveg, has only touched upon a part of the
stirring annals of that House. Mr Alexander
Mackenzie, M.J.I., is doubtless responsible for a
compilation entitled "The History of the Macdonalds and Lords of the Isles," drawn principally
from the pages of Skene, Gregory, the Clanranald
Book of 1819, Wood's Douglas's Peerage, and other
writers. It is clear, however, that a production
of this nature, based upon second-hand materials
rather than upon primary sources of historical
study, cannot, upon the most charitable view, be
regarded as a serious contribution to the literature
of the subject. Even as a compilation it is
defective in scope. Many Macdonald families
whose position was outstanding, and whose annals
abounded in most stirring events—such as Dunnyveg, Antrim, Ardnamurchan, Largie, and others—
have been passed over with a mere reference in this
"History of the Macdonalds and Lords of the Isles."

The period embraced in this volume extends from
the twelfth down to the middle of the sixteenth
century, the purpose being to trace the history of

the Lordship of the Isles not only to the fall of
the House of Isla in 1493, but also to record the
successive attempts made to restore it down to the
last move by Sir James Macdonald in 1545-6. While
writing the earlier chapters we felt embarrassed by
our remoteness from the great libraries of the South,
and consequently this part of the volume may have
to some extent suffered as regards thoroughness of
research. With respect to the bulk of the volume
these difficulties have been overcome. Through the
great kindness of Miss Yule, of Tarradale House, the
rich resources of the London Library were placed at
our disposal, while through the unwearied co-operation
of an accomplished Clanswoman, Miss Macdonell of
Keppoch, we have obtained many valuable extracts
from the Library of the British Museum. We also
spent much time among the various libraries of the
" Modern Athens," and obtained from a number of
sources information both interesting and fresh. To
Mr Morrison of the Public Library, Mr Clark of
the Advocates' Library, Dr Joseph Anderson of
the Society of Antiquaries Library, and to Mr
Maitland-Thomson of the Historical Department
of the Register House, we tender our sincerest
thanks for the facilities so kindly and courteously
afforded. The valuable private library of Beaufort
Castle, Inverness-shire, was with great kindness
opened up to us by Lord Lovat. Its varied
collection of club publications and other historical
works have proved of immense assistance, and we

beg to record our deep sense of his lordship's
courtesy and consideration.

In the course of our researches we have consulted
at first hand such repositories of historical lore as
the Annals of the Four Masters, The Annals of
Ulster, The Annals of Loch Cé, Hugh Macdonald's
MS., the Macdonald MS. of 1700, The Chronicle
of Man, Anecdotes of Olave the Black, The
Chartulary of Paisley, Haco's Expedition, Acts of
the Scottish Parliament, Rymer's Fœdera, Ayloffe's
Calendar of Ancient Charters, Rotuli Scotiæ,
Patent Roll, Anderson's Historical Documents of
Scotland, Robertson's Index of Charters, Register
of the Great Seal, Exchequer Rolls, Chamberlain
Rolls, Acts of the Lords of Council, Register
of the Privy Seal, Documents in State Paper Office,
with many other historical works written on the
Highlands of Scotland.

Mrs Ramsay of Kildalton very kindly lent us a
copy of "The Book of Islay," printed for private
circulation only, and containing much material for
our work, available mostly for the period embraced
in our second volume.

To the heads of the great Families of the Isles
who so readily responded to our request for help
we owe a deep debt of gratitude. Lord Macdonald
and the Chief of Clanranald, who have placed at
our disposal a mass of most valuable papers, have
conferred a very great obligation not only upon
us but through us upon the Clan in general, and

no effort will be spared to turn these documents—
relating to the sixteenth, seventeenth, and eighteenth
centuries—to the very best account. Lord Antrim's
courteous response to our enquiries as to historical
documents connected with his Family calls for our
warmest thanks.

Colonel Macdonald of Glenaladale and Æneas R.
Macdonald, Esq. of Morar, in proof of the great
interest they take in our work, have kindly furnished
us with historical documents of considerable interest
and value.   We record with sincere thanks the
interest displayed in our work by our friend and
countryman, Alexander Macdonald, Esq. of Balranald and Edenwood, head of the Clann Domhnuill
Herraich, who with his wonted kindness has furnished
us with valuable genealogical notes connected with
the ancient family of which he is the representative.
We beg also to acknowledge our obligations to
Captain Allan Macdonald of Waternish, head of the
house of Balfinlay, for the warm interest he has
manifested in us and in our work, as well as for
interesting historical materials available for our
second volume.   We desire to record with most
grateful recollections the aid and co-operation
rendered us by one of the warmest-hearted of
Clansmen and best of Highlanders, Alexander
Macdonald, Esq. of Treaslan, Portree.   For various
contributions towards this and the succeeding
volumes we have to acknowledge our indebtedness
to that genial and enthusiastic Clansman, Dr

Keith Norman Macdonald of Edinbane Hospital, Skye, the Orpheus of the Clan, whose volumes on the music and song of the Gael are the delight of all Highlanders.

Among others who have assisted us during the progress of this volume special reference is due to Charles Fraser-Mackintosh, Esq. of Drummond, lately M.P. for Inverness-shire, whose services, whether in the field of literature or politics, deserve the everlasting gratitude of every Highlander. We desire also to record our obligation to Dr C. R. Macdonald, County Medical Officer, Ayr, who kindly placed at our disposal papers left by his cultured father, the late Hugh Macdonald, Esq., Grandtully, whose memory as an indefatigable collector and writer of Clan Donald lore deserves honourable mention in any record of the Clan Cholla. We are much indebted to the kindness of a cultured young gentleman, D. Murray Rose, Esq., for many valuable suggestions as to sources of information, and for other assistance. Special acknowledgment is likewise due to Ranald W. Macdonald, Esq., of H.M. Customs, one of the secretaries of the Glasgow Macdonald Society, and John Macdonald, Esq., Newton-on-Ayr, formerly one of the secretaries of the Glasgow Macdonald Society, for help often asked and as often generously and ungrudgingly given. We have further to express our sense of the kindly help rendered us by Andrew Ross, Esq., S.S.C., Marchmont Herald, Edinburgh, and W. R. Macdonald, Esq., of the Scottish Metropolitan Life Assurance Company, Edinburgh. Last, but not least, we would record our gratitude to the venerable Miss L. C. R. Macdonell, Mavis Bank, Rothesay, daughter of that prince of Highlanders, the late Colonel Alexander Ranaldson Macdonell of Glengarry.

We trust that the illustrations, most of which are entirely new, will enhance the value of the volume and its interest to the Clan. In connection with these we have again to express our indebtedness to Miss Josephine M. Macdonell of Keppoch, who has contributed several animated battle scenes, and whose cordial assistance has ever been ungrudgingly bestowed. In conclusion, we must in justice express our obligations to the manager of the Northern Counties Printing and Publishing Company, Limited (Mr Livingston), whose valuable advice and unfailing urbanity have made the passage of this volume through the press most pleasant to remember.

July 7, 1896.

CONTENTS.

CHAPTER I.

INTRODUCTORY.

CHAPTER II.

DESCENT OF THE CLAN DONALD.

CHAPTER III.

SOMERLED MACGILLEBRIDE.—1100-1164.

CHAPTER IV.

THE DESCENDANTS OF SOMERLED.—1164-1266.

CHAPTER V.

BRUCE AND THE CLAN CHOLLA.—1284–1329.

CHAPTER VI.

THE GOOD JOHN OF ISLA.—1330–1386.

CHAPTER VII.

DONALD OF HARLAW.

CHAPTER VIII.

ALEXANDER DE ILE, EARL OF ROSS.—1425-1449.

CHAPTER IX.

JOHN DE ILE, EARL OF ROSS.

CHAPTER X.

DECLINE AND FALL OF THE HOUSE OF ISLA.—1462-1498.

CHAPTER XIV.

THE CHURCH AND EDUCATION.

APPENDICES.

CONTENTS.

ILLUSTRATIONS, &c.

LIST OF SUBSCRIBERS.

Macdonald of the Isles, The Right Hon. The Lady, Armadale Castle, Skye.

Atholl, His Grace The Duke of, Blair Castle, Blair-Atholl.

D'Oyley, The Most Hon. The Marchioness (*nee* Macdonald), Paris *(3 copies)*.

Antrim, The Right Hon. The Earl of, Glenarm Castle, Co. Antrim.

Lovat, The Right Hon. The Lord, Beaufort Castle, Inverness-shire.

Macdonald, The Hon. Hugh J. (heir to the British Barony of Macdonald of Earnscliffe), Winnipeg, Manitoba, Canada.

Macdonald of Clanranald, Admiral Sir Reginald, 1A Ovington Square, London *(3 copies)*.

Aylmer Morley, Mrs, Whiterdine, Founhope, Herefordshire.

Bain, James, Esq., chief librarian, Public Library, Toronto.

Barret, F. T., Esq., Mitchell Library, Glasgow.

Barron, James, Esq., *Courier* Office, Inverness.

Bethell, W., Esq., Rise Park, Hull.

Blair, Sheriff, Ardross Terrace, Inverness.

Buchanan, A. W., Esq., Polmont.

Cameron, Donald, Esq., Lochgorm, Inverness.

Cameron, Duncan, Esq., Fettes, Muir of Ord.

Cazenove, C. D., Esq., bookseller, London.

Clark, Colonel, of Ballindoun, Ballindoun House, Beauly.

Clark, G. T., Esq., London.

Cooke, Mrs, Raeburn, Boscombe, Bournemouth.

Cunninghame, John, Esq. of Balgownie, Culross.

Darroch, Duncan, Esq. of Torridon.

Dow, The Rev. John, Manse of Knockbain, Munlochy.

Drayton, Mrs, Gobborn Park, Lancs.

Ellice, C. H., Esq., Brompton, London.

Fletcher, J. Douglas, Esq. of Rosehaugh.

Gibson, The Rev. John Mackenzie, 22 Regent Terrace, Edinburgh.

Hay, Colin, Esq., Ardbeg, Islay.

Henderson, George, Esq., Ph.D., 192 Morningside Road, Edinburgh.

Macalister, Major C. B., of Glenbarr, Kintyre.

Macallister, James, Esq., wine merchant, Ballymena, Ireland.
MacConnell, Wm., Esq., Knockdolian, Colmonell, Ayrshire.
M'Crindle, John, Esq , Auchinlee, Ayr.
Macdonald, Alexander, Esq. of Balranald and Edenwood, Springfield, Fife.
Macdonald, The Rev. Alex., Napanse, Ontario, Canada.
Macdonald, A., Esq., Commercial Bank House, Thurso.
Macdonald, A. W., Esq., Invernevis, Fort-William.
Macdonald, Andrew, Esq., solicitor, Inverness.
Macdonald, A. R., Esq., Ord, Isleornsay, Skye.
Macdonald, Captain Allan, of Waternish, Fasach House, Portree (2 copies).
Macdonald, Allan, Esq., LL.D., Glenarm, Co. Antrim.
Macdonald, Andrew H., Esq., of Calrossie, Rogart Manse.
Macdonald, Angus, Esq., Cunambuntag, Benbecula.
Macdonald, Colonel, of Treaslan, Portree, Skye.
Macdonald, Charles, Esq., 247 Fifth Avenue, New York.
Macdonald, Charles, Esq., 17 Oswald Street, Glasgow.
Macdonald, Dr C. R., 7 Wellington Square, Ayr.
Macdonald, Charles D., Esq., Rosario, Argentine Republic.
Macdonald, The Rev. Colin, Rogart Manse, Sutherlandshire.
Macdonald, The Rev. Donald, minister of N. Uist, Lochmaddy.
Macdonald, The Rev. D. J., Killean Manse, Muasdale, Kintyre.
Macdonald, Donald, Esq. of Rammerscales, Locherbie.
Macdonald, D. T., Esq., Calmult, Michigan, U.S.A.
Macdonald, Duncan, Esq., 2 Heriot Row, Edinburgh.
Macdonald, E., Esq., 39 Donegal Place, Belfast.
Macdonald, The Rev. Finlay R., The Manse, Coupar-Angus.
Macdonald, Henry M., Esq., 34 Broad Street, New York City, U.S.A.
Macdonald, H. A., Esq., 370 Great Western Road, Glasgow.
Macdonald, Harry, Esq., Viewfield, Portree.
Macdonald, H. L., Esq. of Dunach, Dunach House, Oban.
Macdonald, The Rev. Fred. Charles, M.A., vicar of St Hilda's, Sunderland.
Macdonald, James, Esq., W.S., Edinburgh.
Macdonald, James, Esq., Moss Cottage, Benbecula.
Macdonald, J. J., Esq., 42 York Place, Edinburgh.
Macdonald, John, Esq., Keppoch, Roy-Bridge.
Macdonald, J. M., Esq., Harley Street, London.
Macdonald, Colonel John A., of Glenaladale, Glenfinan.
Macdonald, Dr Keith Norman, Gesto Hospital, Skye.
Macdonald, The Rev. Mosse, M.A., St Aidan's College, Birkenhead,

Macdonald, Peter, Esq., Carlton Place, Glasgow.

Macdonald, Admiral Robertson, Edinburgh.

Macdonald, R. M. Livingstone, Esq., Flodigarry, Skye.

Macdonald, Ronald Mosse, Esq., The Homestead, Datchet.

Macdonald, The Rev. R., minister of South Uist, Lochboisdale.

Macdonald, Roderick, Esq., 17 Oswald Street, Glasgow.

Macdonald, Stuart Hugh, Esq., The Homestead, Datchet.

Macdonald, T., Esq., H.M.B.'s Supreme Court, Shanghai, China.

Macdonald, The Rev. Thomas Mosse, M.A., Canon of Lincoln and Rector of Kersal.

Macdonald, W. R., Esq., 1 Forres Street, Edinburgh.

Macdonald, The Hon. W. J., Armadale House, Vancouver, British Columbia.

Macdonald, Wm. M., 2nd Batt. Q.O. Cameron Highlanders.

Macdonald, Miss, Barnfield Hill, Southampton.

Macdonald, Miss Jonë, of Milland Place, Sussex.

Macdonell, Dr. D., 17 Crumlea Road, Belfast.

Macdonnell, Hercules H. G., Esq., Barrister, 4 Roby Place, Kingstown, Ireland.

Macdonnell, James, Esq. of Kilsharvan and Murlough, Ireland.

Macdonnell, Colonel John, of Kilmore, County Antrim.

Macdonnell, The Very Rev. J. Cotter, D.D., Misterton Rectory, Lutterworth.

Macdonell, Miss L. C. R., of Glengarry, Mavis Bank, Rothesay.

Macdonell, Mrs, of Keppoch, 86 Cambridge Street, Eccleston Square, London.

MacDougall, E. A., Esq., 14 High Street, Eccleston Square, London, S.W.

MacDowall, The Rev. James, The Manse, Rosemarkie.

Macgregor, D. R., Esq., Melbourne, Victoria.

MacInnes, Lt.-Colonel John, Glendaruel, Argyleshire.

Mackay, Eneas, Esq., Stirling.

Mackay, John, Esq., C.E., Hereford (2 copies).

Mackay, Wm., Esq., solicitor, Inverness.

Mackenzie, Colonel Burton, of Kilcoy, Kilcoy Castle, Muir of Ord.

Mackenzie, H. H., Esq., Balelone, Lochmaddy.

Mackenzie, The Rev. K. A., LL.D., Manse of Kingussie.

Mackenzie, Thomas, Esq., Daluaine.

Mackenzie, W. Dalziel, Esq. of Farr, Inverness-shire.

Mackintosh, Charles Fraser, Esq. of Drummond.

Maclean, Alex. Scott, Esq., Greenock.

Maclean, Charles, Esq., Milton, South Uist, Lochboisdale.

MacLaverty, Græme A., Esq. of Chanting Hall, Hamilton.

Macleay, Murdo, Esq., Broom Cottage, Ullapool.

Macleod, Colonel John N., of Kintarbert and Saddell, Saddell Castle, Campbeltown.

Macleod, Norman, Esq., Gaelic bookseller, The Mound, Edinburgh.

Macrae, The Rev. Alex., Emmanuel School, Wandsworth Common, London, S.W.

Macrae, The Rev. G. W. B., Manse of Cross, Stornoway.

Macrae, John, Esq., late of Langash, North Uist.

Macquarrie, The Rev. A. J., Manse of Ferintosh.

Martin, Adam W., Esq., Knock, Belfast.

Martin, Major Martin, R.E., Howwood, Renfrewshire.

Mainwaring, Charles, Esq., Feugh Cottage, Banchory, Aberdeen.

Millar, Miss J. Macdonald, Courthill, Hermitage Gardens, Edinburgh.

Moreton, Lt.-Colonel A. H. Macdonald, Benbridge, Isle of Wight.

Morrison, Dr Alex. C., Lochside Cottage, Larkhall.

Noble, John, Esq., Inverness *(9 copies)*.

Pearson, Dr Archd., 4 Middleton Terrace, Ibrox, Glasgow.

Pender-Smith, Dr J., Dingwall.

Perrins, Mrs Dyson, Davenham, Malvern.

Pryor, Mrs, Armadale, Cecil Road, Boscombe, Bournemouth.

Rankin, The Rev. E. A., B.D., Kilmorack Manse, Beauly,

Rawlins, The Rev. J. Arthur, M.A., St. Andrew's Vicarage, Willesden, London.

Roberts, Mrs Vernon, Dunloskin, Kersal, Manchester.

Ryan, Mrs James, Glenomera, Ceylon.

Sinclair, The Ven. Wm. Macdonald, Archdeacon of London, The Chapter House, St. Paul's, London.

Sykes, Harold P., Esq., 2nd Dragoon Guards.

Tolmie, The Rev. A. M. C., M.A., The Manse, Campbeltown.

Yule, Miss A. F., Tarradale House, Muir of Ord.

THE CLAN DONALD.

CHAPTER I.

INTRODUCTORY.

Difficulties of the Subject.—Primitive Populations.—Picts and
Dalriads.—Union of Dalriada and Pictavia.—The Norse
Occupation.—Kingdom of Man and the Isles.—Traces of the
Norseman.—The Gall-Gael.

THE descent and early history of the Clan Donald,
like those of the other Highland clans, are involved
in much obscurity. From the materials at the
disposal of the historian, it is difficult, if not impossible, to weave anything like a clear, reliable, or
consistent narrative. Fact and fiction are so often
mixed up together, and tradition so frequently conflicts with what is regarded as authentic history,
that the task of the historian sometimes assumes
great, perhaps unmanageable, proportions. The
Clan Donald, however, occupy so conspicuous and
important a position in the annals of the country,
that any attempt to throw further light upon its
rise and history may be regarded as worthy of
commendation, even should it meet with but partial
success.

The origin of this Clan is bound up with some of
the most important questions of Scottish ethnology.
In order, therefore, to lead up to a more or less
clear conception of the subject, it seems desirable

1

that we should have recourse to the scanty materials available for the construction of a history of the early inhabitants of the country. The history of Great Britain, so far as it has been written, commences with the Roman occupation, about the middle of the first century. But archæologists, going back into the dim and hoary past, have found vestiges of a race that occupied the land at a period long prior to recorded time. Traces have been discovered of a prehistoric non-Aryan race, resembling the Iberians and the Aquitani, a race short statured, long skulled, dark haired, and dark complexioned; that lived in caves, and buried their dead in caves and chambered tombs; the representatives of the Stone Age, whose polished stone weapons of various kinds are the treasure and delight of the antiquary. They were probably the same race as the ancient tin miners of Cornwall, to whom Herodotus makes reference, and who, from their practice of carrying bags as receptacles for the metal, are supposed to have been the *fir-bolg* of Irish mythology. To them also do we owe the so-called Druidical circles; barrows, and other stone remains which are found scattered over European lands; silent witnesses of the oldest phase of religious culture of which our Western lands bear any trace.

Long before the historical period a new wave, a Celtic Aryan race, Gaidhels or Goidels, visited our island, and pushed the aboriginal race into the more distant and inaccessible mountainous regions to the north and west. They spoke a language which is in our day represented by the Manx Gaelic and the Gaelic of Scotland and Ireland. These in their turn were followed and pressed northwards and westward by another Celtic Aryan race, the Britons or

Brythons, whose language now survives only in Wales. The Gaidhels were probably bronze users, while the Brythonic invaders—as a later wave— were versed in the use of iron tools and weapons.

When the Romans came to Britain the country was more or less divided among the fore-mentioned races, and this continued very much the case until the close of the Roman occupation in 410 A.D.

Confining our attention to Scotland, we find that Roman historians make mention of two nations occupying that land in the second century, whom they denominate the Caledonii and the Meatae. These names in the course of time disappear, and are succeeded by the Picti and Attacotti. Such a variety of names is perplexing to the historian, but, notwithstanding much ingenuity displayed by various writers, there is every reason to believe that they are all applicable to the one Goedelic race, which, as already stated, followed the pre-historic race as the predominant occupiers of the North of Scotland. These people, properly designated as the Alban Gael, though territorially divided into two or more provinces, and speaking probably slightly different dialects of the same tongue, were yet in all racial characteristics one. The best authorities are agreed that they were homogeneous with the Cruithne of Ireland, where, as in Scotland, they succeeded the Firbolg, and that their language, around which such fierce controversy has been waged, was an archaic type of our modern Scottish Gaelic. The date of their advent to Scotland is of course a question of great obscurity, though in all probability it must have been some time between 500 and 300 B.C. During a period of nearly 400 years this brave race baffled in many a red field the mighty legionaries of Rome, and though time and again they were driven, by the force of numbers and superior discipline, to their native fastnesses, they remained unconquered.

For 200 years after the evacuation of Britain by the Romans, the history of Scotland is almost a blank, and when, in the beginning of the seventh century, the light of history again dawns upon us, we find four distinct peoples occupying as many different districts of our present Scotland. The Picts or Alban Gael have to all appearance absorbed and assimilated, or at any rate converted to their own speech and social customs, the non-Aryan people they found in the land, and are now the predominating race. The Britons occupy the region of Strathclyde, while two new races, the Angles and the Dalriadic Scots, have made settlements of their own. The Alban Gael occupied the country north of the Firth of Forth; the Britons the region of Strathclyde, and thence south to Cumberland; the Angles that from the Forth to the Humber; and the Scots of Dalriada the country afterwards known as Oirirghaidheal, Islay, a part of Mull and some of the lesser Southern Isles.[1] These four races are on the whole the materials out of which the modern Scottish nation has been formed, and it is clear that even the Lowland Scot has in him as much of the Celt as of the Teuton. As regards the Iberian or pre-historic population, it is probable that the type, though absorbed as to language and social life into the larger and more powerful organism of the Celt, yet in its physical characteristics still survives in the small, dark-haired, black-eyed

---

[1] *Vide* Map of Four Kingdoms in Skene's Celtic Scotland.

natives of parts of the north-west of Scotland, as it is also to be found in Wales, as well as in Ireland west of the Shannon. Every nation is more or less a blend of several nationalities; but nowhere is this more marked than in the Scottish Highlands, where there seems to be more of an admixture of races than in any country in Europe of the same size.

As already indicated, the Picts or Alban Gael occupied by far the greater portion of the country. To the north of the Firth of Forth they were divided into the Northern and Southern Picts; the former holding the country north of the Grampians, and the latter inhabiting the region from that mountain range south to the Firth of Forth. Not only so, but in the counties of Wigtown and Kirkcudbright there was a settlement of what were called the Niduarian Picts, and in the debateable region south of the Firth of Forth they had settlements in the neighbourhood of Edinburgh, and have left traces of their presence in the name of the Pentland Hills.

The founders of the Scottish kingdom of Dalriada were also an offshoot of the Goedelic branch of the Celtic tree. Both in Scotland and Ireland they are found appearing at a period subsequent to the Cruithne. The kingdoms of the Picts and of the Scots seem, in fact, to have been two collateral Gaelic nationalities, with well-defined dynasties and territories, embracing regions in both lands. Most writers are agreed that the colony of Irish Scots settled permanently in Argyll about the beginning of the sixth century. That for several centuries prior to that date there had been Irish immigrations to the Scottish coast on a greater or lesser scale seems highly probable. Indeed, when we bear in

mind the nearness of Kintyre to the North of
Ireland, intercourse must have been frequent in very
early times. During the Roman occupation mention
is frequently made by historians of the wandering
Irish, who, like the Scandinavians of later days,
infested the coastlands of Scotland, and at times
carried their predatory incursions into the heart of
the country. Irish historians have sometimes proved
imaginative guides in threading the mazes of these
early centuries. Yet there is nothing inherently
improbable in the statement that the first Dalriadic
settlers were brought over to Scotland in the middle
of the third century by Cairbre Riada ; meaning the
Ruadh or red-haired, after whom a territory in the
North of Ireland, the Routes and Glens, derives its
name.[1] The centre of these early settlements was
Kintyre, whose ancient name of Dalruadhain was a
form of the Irish Dalriada. The theory that the
King of the Alban Gaels or Picts, finding his
kingdom harassed by the Britons of Strathclyde on
the one hand, and the Angles on the other, invited
the Dalriads to Argyll, seems, all things considered,
a highly probable one. They were not destined,
however, to keep the peace long with any of the
neighbouring nationalities, and their future relations
with the Alban Gael is a long story of strife and
bloodshed.

When we come to the middle of the fifth century
we stand upon firmer historical ground. About that
time, perhaps a little later, Erc, King of Dalriada,
died, leaving three sons, Fergus, Lorn, and Angus.
A dispute arose as to the succession, when, according
to the Celtic law of Tanistry, Olchu, their father's
brother, assumed the sceptre, to the exclusion of

---

[1] According to the Annals of the Four Masters, in 506 A.D.

Fergus, the eldest son. Thereupon Fergus, with his two brothers, crossed the Irish Channel, after obtaining the blessing of St Patrick,[1] and landed on the coast of Argyll, with, it is said, only one hundred and fifty followers. From this period onwards the history of Argyll becomes the history of the Scots Dalriads, and from the fact that we find no record of opposition to their settlement, we may infer that the inhabitants must have been largely recruited from the same Irish stock in former times. The three brothers divided the country into three districts ; Lorn occupying the district which bears his name, as well as the greater portion of Argyll, while Angus acquired the lands of Islay and Jura, and Fergus, the eldest, possessed Kintyre, and on the death of Lorn succeeded him in his extensive dominions. All three were dependent upon the Irish kingdom of Dalriada. This subjection to the parent stock continued for more than sixty years, and until the time of Aidan, when finally, by the intervention of St Columba, it was agreed at the great Council of Drumceat to free the Scots Dalriads from paying the customary tribute, thus making them an independent nation. It was stipulated that in the time of war the Scots Dalriads must assist their Irish allies. Aidan thus became the first King of Dalriada, and held Court at Dunadd, which became the capital of the new kingdom, none of his predecessors having attained a higher dignity than that of Toiseach, or chief ruler of a tribe.

After the period at which we have now arrived, it is unnecessary to follow in detail, at anyrate at this stage of our work, the fortunes or the genealogies of the Dalriadic kings or their relations to

[1] Albanic Duan.

other Scottish nationalities.   During the period
leading up to the consolidation of Scottish Dalriada,
as well as for some time thereafter, there were the
usual internal broils ; Kintyre against Lorn, and
both, singly or together, against the Britons of
Strathclyde.   Much of the civil discord sprang from
the operation of the Celtic law of succession, in
which direct hereditary descent often conflicted with
the will and interests of the tribe.   In time the
descendants of Angus dropped out of sight, and his
family became extinct in the male line, but his
grand-daughter having married the grandson of
Fergus Mor, his possessions were added to those of
the reigning house of Dalriada.

The light of Scottish history waxes very dim
during the sixth, seventh, and eighth centuries, but
it seems to fail us altogether in the ninth, when
there is in truth a darkness that can be felt.   It
would appear, however, that up to the year 733 A.D.
there was no serious collision between the Dalriads
and their neighbours the Alban Gael.   But in that
year we find it recorded in the Annals of Ulster
that Angus Mac Fergus, the King of the Alban
Gael, invaded the territory of the Dalriads with a
powerful army, and, after a series of sanguinary
combats, defeated them.   He subdued them finally
in the year 741, and added Dalriada as a province
to his kingdom.   The Annals of Ulster of that year
record " the downfall of the Dalriads by Angus Mac
Fergus."   This Angus Mac Fergus was the greatest
of all the kings of the Alban Gael, if the Irish
Annals are to be relied on, and it was he who laid
the foundation of the future kingdom of present
Scotland.

From the year 741 A.D., when Dalriada became a province of the Northern Kingdom, to the year 843, Scottish history is intensely obscure. We are not disposed to adopt either of the extreme views that have been advanced by writers as to the circumstances leading to the elevation of Kenneth MacAlpin in that year to the throne of a united realm. On the one hand the older view, that his accession was the result of conquest, in the course of which the Pictish race was annihilated by the Dalriadic Scots, is an absurd and thrice-exploded historical fiction. The paternity of this view is undoubtedly to be traced to the monkish writers of St Andrews, who inserted it in their Register of that See in the year 1251, or 400 years after the pretended event. John of Fordun, that prince of fabulists, gave further currency to that and other myths in his Chronicle, which he finished about the year 1400 A.D. Other monkish writers followed in the same vein, and the more the ball of fable rolled the more it gathered volume, until it became at last a veritable planet in the ecclesiastical nebula.

From other sources, such as Nennius, the Saxon Chronicler of 891 A.D., the Welsh Triads, the Irish Annals, and the Albanic Duan, it seems undoubted that Kenneth MacAlpin's succession to the Pictish Kingdom was based on his descent from the Pictish sovereigns. Ungus, King of the Southern Picts, had a sister Ungusia, who married Aycha IV., King of Scots, and their son Alpin, who succeeded his father early in the ninth century, was thus connected in the female line with the royal house of Pictavia. Succession through a female was an acknowledged principle of Pictish descent, and when the throne of the Picts fell vacant, Kenneth, the

son of Alpin, laid claim to it. The Southern Picts
as a nation acquiesced in an arrangement which,
while it gave them a king of their own royal
lineage, made at the same time for peace and union
between races that had so much in common.

On the other hand we believe it to be equally
mistaken, to maintain, as Dr Skene has done, that,
when Kenneth MacAlpin ascended the united
throne, Dalriada had sunk into utter insignificance,
and ceased to have any existence as a separate
kingdom. It is difficult to speak definitely of a
time so historically dark, and we cannot say
whether Dalriada regained to the full extent its
former independence. But it seems clear that,
however depressed the fortunes of this kingdom
may have been, a royal descent was maintained
from father to son until the ruling family of Dalriada was able to provide a king for the new and
united realm of Alban.

If the Picts as a distinctive race seem to pass
out of history after 842 A.D., their disappearance is
apparent and not real. The King of the Dalriads
became the ruler of the united people, and the
Dalriads were consequently regarded as the governing and presumably the dominant race. The union
further welded together nations similar in language,
customs, and social institutions, nations that quickly
and easily amalgamated into one national system.
Yet, though the two races became one nation, the
actual fusion was only partial. The Picts of the
Central and Northern Highlands were little if at all
affected by the union politically,[1] socially, or racially,
and hence we may regard the Highlanders of Perth-

---

[1] The Picts north of the Grampians were not of course included in the
new Kingdom.

shire and the interior of Inverness-shire as the purest representatives of the ancient Gaelic stock of Caledonia. On the other hand, the Dalriads remained to a large extent a distinct people within their own territory of Oirthirghael.

The Islands as well as the Highlands of Scotland were in historic times originally inhabited by the primitive stock of Caledonia, the Picts, or Alban Gael, with probably an admixture in some districts of the prehistoric Iberian population. The Hebrides, however, owing to their insular position, were from the beginning of the ninth century subject to conditions which had a far-reaching effect upon their relations to the mainland of Scotland. Before the union of the Alban Gael and the Dalriadic Scots, and as far back as 794 A.D., we find from the Annals of Ulster that "the Islands of Britain were ravaged by the Gentiles." Indeed, we can gather from hints somewhat dark and vague that, long before they had effected permanent settlements in the Isles, these Gentiles or Scandinavian pirates, whose galleys swept the northern seas, were the scourge and terror of the Hebrideans. More definitely they were Danes and Norwegians, known in the Highlands under the designation respectively of *Dubhgall* and *Fionnghall*, or both together as *Lochlanaich*. The Western Isles, the theatre of their piratical ravages, came to be known to the Gael as *Innse-Gall*, or the Islands of the Strangers, to themselves as the Sudereys, or Southern Isles, to distinguish them from the Nordereys or Orkneys.

The Danes were earlier in the order of invasion, and the special animosity they displayed in the ruthless destruction of religious houses like Iona and Lindisfarne, and the consequent destruction of precious historical records, are traceable to well-known contemporary causes. The cruelties which the Emperor Charlemagne inflicted upon the Pagan inhabitants of Saxony and North Germany fired the Gothic nations with hatred towards Christianity, and explained the special form which the incursions of the Danes assumed. During the ninth century these sea rovers kept the Islands and the Western seaboard in a state of perpetual turmoil impossible either to conceive or describe.

> When watchfires burst across the main
> From Rona, and Uist, and Skye,
> To tell that the ships of the Dane
> And the red-haired slayer were nigh ;
> Our Islesmen rose from their slumbers,
> And buckled on their arms,
> But few, alas ! were their numbers
> To Lochlin's mailèd swarms ;
> And the blade of the bloody Norse
> Has filled the shores of the Gael
> With many a floating corse
> And many a widow's wail.

The Danes, however, never made settlements in the Scottish Isles, whose history for three hundred years, from about 800 A.D., is bound up with the Norwegian invasion. This invasion caused the erection of Norwegian kingdoms in Ireland and in the Western Isles. The Isle of Man and the Southern Isles of Scotland were the centre of the Norwegian settlements in the north-west of Europe. From these islands, which were peculiarly adapted as strongholds for the Vikings, whose strength lay in their large and well-built ships, the tide of invasion flowed in various directions, and the surviving records of the age derive much of their interest from the adventures of these kings of the sea.

In considering the origin of this Norwegian invasion, we find that it is largely accounted for by a political revolution which occurred in Norway. There, as elsewhere, the tendency of things has lain in the absorption of petty nationalities in a larger imperial unity. In or about the year 875 A.D., according to the sagas, Harold Harfager, or the Fair-haired, one of the greatest and bravest on the long roll of Scandinavian heroes, having suppressed the power of a number of minor chiefs, established himself as King of the whole of Norway. Many of the independent petty princes or jarls opposed his pretensions and disputed his title to the crown. Rather than submit to his rule, and fearing his vengeance, some of these princes took refuge in the Western Isles, and, uniting their forces there, they began to harass Harold's domains. Exasperated by these frequent incursions, Harold resolved to pursue his enemies to their retreat in the Western Isles. He prosecuted the campaign with great vigour, and his progress was so irresistible that in a short time he made a total conquest of Man, the Hebrides, Shetland and Orkney, including Caithness. It is difficult even now ; how much more so must it have been in that remote age ? to preserve the loyalty of a colony of diverse races so far from the imperial centre ; and the difficulty was continually arising during the Norwegian occupation of the Isles. The very next year after the conquest we find the Isles in open rebellion against the royal authority. The Norwegian sagas differ as to the details of the re-conquest of the Isles. According to some, such as the Zandnama, Harold dispatched a trusty cousin and councillor, the happy possessor of the euphonious name of Ketil Flatnose, to restore peace and

good government among his island subjects. This
the flat-nosed one very soon succeeded in doing, but
he accomplished more : he declared himself King of
the Isles. According to another and more probable
version of the story—the Laxœla-saga—Ketil
emigrated from Norway to the Isles, not as the
viceroy of Harold, but because, like the other minor
potentates of Norway, he was obnoxious to him and
unable to resist his power. All the accounts, however, agree in saying that Ketil exercised something
like supreme power in the Isles during the remainder
of his life. Flatnose was followed by a succession of
kings, though not of his own line, whose identity on
the broad plain of history is not easily discernible in
the absence of any law of hereditary succession to
guide us. To attempt to bring historical order out
of the chaos in which that succession is involved
passes the wit of man. Suffice it to say that these
kings or rulers of the Isles, with few interruptions,
followed one another, either from Norway or Orkney
or from Man or Ireland, until Man and the Isles
were finally added to Scotland by purchase in the
latter half of the thirteenth century. After the
defeat of Haco at Largs, and his subsequent death
at Kirkwall, in Orkney, his son and successor,
Magnus, entered into a treaty with Alexander III.
of Scotland, whereby the latter acquired Man and
the Isles for the sum of 400 merks sterling, with the
additional annual payment to Norway of 100 merks
sterling, to be paid in the Church of St Magnus in
Orkney.

It is difficult to give anything like a true or
faithful picture of the condition of the Western
Isles during the Norse occupation. It does not seem
at all clear that the character of the Celtic

population, or its social institutions any more than its language, underwent any palpable or material alteration. Some admixture of Teutonic blood may be inferred from the strongly-marked Scandinavian features sometimes seen in the inhabitants of the Hebrides, especially in the Island of Lewis. The native Celt largely predominated all along, but it is undoubted that the blood of the brave old Vikings courses through the veins of some of the best types of the Scottish Highlander. It is also permissible to think that this Teutonic strain, with its characteristic tenacity of purpose and sustained power of effort, combined with Celtic brilliancy and emotional fervour, differentiates the Highlanders of the West from more purely Celtic nations, and places them, both in war and peace, in the front rank of European races. Considering, however, that the Norsemen and the Celts of the Isles seem to have lived on terms of mutual friendship after the time of Harold Harfager, it is singular that the former did not leave a deeper or more permanent impression. The explanation probably is to be found very much in the words of Gregory, with whom in this matter we are disposed to agree, " that as in all cases of conquest the change in the population must have been most perceptible in the higher ranks, owing to the natural tendency of invaders to secure their new possessions where practicable by matrimonial alliances with the natives." In some respects, however, the Norseman has left his mark upon the Western Isles. While the language of the people was preserved unaffected by the invader, the place names both in the Isles and coastlands of Scotland bear extensive traces of his influence. The Celtic system of land tenure, which was purely tribal,

seems to have been largely modified, and the system
of rent borrowed from the Teuton meets us in the
farthing-lands, penny-lands, and merklands to be
found in ancient valuations and conveyances of
landed property. In the folk-lore of the Hebrides,
Lochlin and its kings frequently appear; and
altogether, in a variety of ways not affecting the
deeper or more characteristic life of the people, the
footprints of the Norseman are to be seen.

Before proceeding to consider the descent of the
Clan Donald, which we purpose doing in the next
chapter, it is necessary that we should take note of
a people called the Gall-Gael, whom we find in the
reign of Kenneth MacAlpin appearing as the allies
of the Scandinavian pirates, and joining them
everywhere in their depredations. The peculiar
combination of the word Gall, with Gael as the
qualitative part of the compound, is naturally
somewhat puzzling to the historian, especially as
the historical references to these people are neither
numerous nor distinct. The name Gall has always
been applied by the Gael to foreigners or strangers,
to men of different race and language from
themselves. It was first applied by them to the
Saxons of Northumbria. The name of Gall-Gael
was first applied by the Irish to the Picts of
Galloway, because the inhabitants of Galloway, being
of the Cruithne or Pictish race, and thus Celtic, had
for long been under the rule of the Saxon Gall of
Northumbria. Afterwards the name came to be
applied to Western Gaels, who, in their characteristic
modes of life, and possibly also through a fusion of
races, came to resemble the Scandinavians of the
Hebrides. They were Galls, that is strangers, in
the sense that they had no settled homes, and, as

DUN AONGHA'S, NORTH UIST.

DUN TORQUIL, NORTH UIST.

such, were sea rovers or pirates after the fashion of
the Scandinavians of *Innse-Gall*. But they we.e
also Gaels, recruited from various branches of the
Celtic race, from Pictavia, Dalriada, and Ireland. It
is clear therefore that the Gall-Gael were not a race
of Gaels bound together by ties of blood and kinship,
but Gaels whose bond of union was that they were
engaged in similar pursuits. But it seems necessary
also to state that the Gall-Gael apparently received
their name not alone because the Gael conformed to
the wild roving habits of the Norse Vikings, but
because the two were blended in one, and constituted
one band of sea robbers. This, we think, is clearly
proved by their being so often referred to as North-
men. There seems no evidence whatever to show,
notwithstanding the authority of Dr Skene, that the
Gall-Gael were a race of Celts with territorial
dignities or possessions. They were Gaelic pirates
banded with the Norwegians ; only this and nothing
more. They appear and flit before us for a time on
the stage of history, and disappear mysteriously
without leaving one trace of their identity, neither
territory nor pedigree, not even one name handed
down ; merry-dancers on the horizon, phantoms
which cross our threshold to ruffle the serenity
of our historical calm.

CHAPTER II.

DESCENT OF THE CLAN DONALD.

Rise of the Kingdom of Alban.—Rise and Growth of English
Influence.—Feudal Scotland.—Origin of the Clan Donald.—
Theories on the Subject.—The Dalriadic Origin.—Genealogy
of the Clan down to Somerled.

BEFORE introducing upon the historical stage the
dynasty of Celtic princes, known as the Kings and
Lords of the Isles, it will conduce to clearness of
historical perspective if we trace briefly the rise of
the kingdom of Alban, and its gradual development
into feudal Scotland. The period in Scottish history
covered by the ninth, tenth, and eleventh centuries
witnessed the growth of this larger imperial unity,
which commenced to be realised in the reign of
Kenneth MacAlpin. The new name of Alban, by
which the Kingdom of Scone came to be known in
the reign of Donald, the son of Constantine, does
not appear to have arisen from the addition of any
new territory acquired since the union of Pictavia
and Dalriada, and there seems to be no explanation
of the change, beyond the fact that we find it
recorded in the Irish Annals for the first time during
his reign. Thereafter, the Kings were no longer
designated *Reges Pictorum*, but *Ri Alban*, and in
the Pictish Chronicle Pictavia gives place to
Albania.

It does not appear that Northern Pictdom,
though reckoned nominally a province of Alban,
ever became fully incorporated with it while it

retained that name. The relationship between the Northern and Southern Picts after the accession of Kenneth MacAlpin is exceedingly difficult to define. It seems, however, a fair inference from the dim history of those ages that the division between the two peoples was not merely geographical. The union of Dalriada and Southern Pictavia would have been regarded with little favour by the Picts of the North, especially as the accession of the King of Dalriada to the Pictish throne gave the Scots the *prestige* of a dominant race, and had the effect of alienating two communities that were at first homogeneous. Furthermore, the inroads of the Scandinavian marauders all along the coastlands of the Northern Gael stimulated the exercise of the law of self-preservation; threw them back upon their own resources; consolidated their organic unity, and welded them more and more into a distinct and separate people. During the succeeding centuries, and until the unity of the Scottish realm was finally accomplished, the North presents a scene of conflict and confusion more intense, if possible, than is found in other parts of North Britain. The struggle for independence was long and persistent, and, though more than once compelled to yield to the invader, the Northern Gael was able to cast off the alien yoke and assert his ancient independence. Thus it was that, hemmed in on the one hand by Scandinavian incursions, and on the other by their neighbours and kinsmen from the South, we find the men of the North, now under the sway of the Norwegian Earls of Orkney, now under the Kings of Alban, and at intervals independent of both, under their own Mormaors. This state of matters continued until, finally, in the reign of David I., the province was ceded by conquest to the Scottish Crown.

We may now briefly indicate the extension of the Kingdom of Alban towards the South and East, and the causes that moulded it under one feudal monarchy. The history of Alban is parallel in many respects to that of the Northern Province. Besieged, on the one hand, by the Anglo-Saxons of the South and East, it lay open, on the other, to the Cumbrians of Strathclyde; while from every point of the compass the menacing Scandinavian pressed on. From Kenneth MacAlpin to David I., Scottish history is a long war of races bent on mutual destruction. Finally, the Scoto-Celt proved his imperial spirit by giving a Kingdom to Scotland, despite the adverse influences that beset him on every hand. Kenneth III. acquired the ancient Kingdom of Strathclyde, and his son, Malcolm II., subjected to his sway the Saxon provinces of the South-East, which comprehended Lothian, Berwickshire, and the lower part of Teviotdale. Thus, after many birth-throes, the ancient realm of Scotia came into being.

No sooner, however, was the new kingdom established than English influence began to be felt, and the conquest, which force of arms could never effect, was not unlikely to be accomplished by more silent, imperceptible, yet no less powerful, influences. Malcolm Canmore had been early attracted by the English Court, where, during the misfortunes of his youth, he had found a friendly refuge. His admiration for England and its people was evinced when, from his warlike incursions to Durham and Northumberland, he carried back with him large numbers of young men and women, whom he settled in various parts of his kingdom. His marriage with

the Saxon Princess Margaret was fraught with many
consequences to the social and religious life of Scotland. The ancient language of the Court, with the
manners and customs of his fathers, were changed
by the unpatriotic King, and conformed to the
English model. Still further to Anglicise his
country, he offered an asylum to those Saxon
refugees who were compelled to leave their native
land during the reign of the persecuting Norman
Conqueror. With Malcolm, the Saxon importation
ceased, and Donald Bane, his brother, who, according
to Celtic law, succeeded him, issued a sentence of
banishment against all foreigners, and an attempt
was made to stem the tide of Southern influence,
and place Celtic culture once more in the ascendant.
This, however, was only temporarily successful.
Donald Bane was driven from the throne after a
short and troubled reign, and the three sons of
Malcolm Canmore, who followed him in succession,
were steady supporters of the new order. It was in
the reign of David I., who occupied the throne from
1124 to 1153, that the most momentous change took
place in the civil policy and social life of Scotland.
David, who had been educated at the Court of
Henry Beauclerc, became inspired by Norman ideas,
and, before his accession to the throne, was advanced
to the dignity of a Norman baron. In the feudal
system, which, for upwards of 100 years, had
operated in England and transformed its institutions, he found an instrument ready to his hand for
remodelling the customs of the Scottish people. He
introduced a powerful Norman baronetage, by means
of whom he planted, on an extended scale, the
principles of feudal tenure, and a ruling idea of his
reign was to suppress Celtic aspirations and institu-

tions, as inconsistent with the new social system and
with loyalty to the crown. Thus did the new feudal
system take root in our Scottish soil, and under its
shadow have flourished those Anglo-Norman institutions which have done so much to mould the
national life.

Having thus endeavoured to indicate the trend of
Scottish history down to the twelfth century, the
period at which Clan Donald history begins to
emerge out of the dim twilight of uncertainty, we
hope to shew how this representative and outstanding family were affected by the new order of Scottish
feudalism. There still remains, however, to be
considered and disposed of, the important question
of the descent of the Clan Donald ; a question which
we have deemed advisable to take up only after all
other preliminary matters pertaining to general
Scottish history, and pertinent to our special theme,
had been, we hope, intelligibly discussed. In our
introductory chapter we drew attention, at some
length, to the various elements that combined to
constitute the Scottish people. To which of the
races that in early times occupied the Highlands and
Islands do the Clan Donald belong ? Taking, for
example, the real founder of the Family of the Isles
in times that are clearly historical—Somerled *Rex
Insularum*—where are we to look for his origin and
descent ? Was he, as his name indicates, of Norse
extraction ? was he of Pictish blood, and thus
descended from the ancient Celtic stock of Caledonia?
did he owe his birth to the Scoto-Irish race of
Dalriada ? or was he of the mysterious Gall-Gael ?
In one sense it is impossible, perhaps, to give a
categorical answer to any of these questions. It is
unlikely that he was purely the offspring of any one

race. Judging by his name, we should pronounce him a Norseman, were it not for other circumstances that point to a different conclusion. He may have received that name through some ancestress, perhaps some "fair-haired"[1] Norwegian mother, who also bequeathed to him the enterprising spirit of the Vikings. That he was of Norse descent in the male line is an hypothesis for which there is not a shred of evidence. The truth is borne in upon us from manifold sources that the spirit and tendency of the house of Somerled, and all the interests of his race, were in direct antagonism to the Norwegian occupation of the West of Scotland. Obviously it does not stand to reason that a Norseman should have made it the main object of his life to overthrow the supremacy of his own race, and erect a Gaelic Kingdom in room of the Norwegian power. The title *Righ Fionnghall*, by which many of the Chiefs of the Clan have been distinguished by the Highland bards and seanachies, is no proof of a Norwegian descent. It would appear that they received this distinction because, after the time of Somerled, the Lords of the Isles ruled over a large extent of territory which in former times had been subject to the Kings of Man, to whom the designation *Righ Fionnghall* had been originally applied.

It remains now to shew to which branch of the Celtic tree the Clan Donald owe their descent. Though the question as to whether the origin of this family is derived from the Picts or Scots is a somewhat subordinate one ; seeing that both these nations were hewn out of the same rock, offshoots of the Goedelic branch of the Celtic tree ; still it is one

---

[1] Hill's Macdonalds of Antrim.

of much importance, and has been earnestly discussed by the best modern authorities. In deciding upon an answer to it, we have to reckon, on the one hand, with the conclusions of Dr Skene, justly regarded as one of the most thorough and painstaking of recent writers upon the history and ethnology of the Gael; and, on the other hand, with the mass of Highland and Irish tradition, the accumulation of many centuries. Gregory, while favouring a Celtic origin, is indefinite in his conclusions, leaving the problem of Celtic *versus* Norse virtually an open question, and consequently, of course, not condescending upon the more special issue of a Pictish *versus* Scoto-Irish descent. In his "Highlanders of Scotland," published in 1837, the work by which Dr Skene first came into notice as a prominent historical writer, he strongly supports the theory of the Pictish descent of the Clan Donald. He maintains that the Gael of Argyll, who afterwards became known as the Gall-Gael, were of the Pictish stock; that the ancestors of the Clan Donald were of the Gall-Gael, and that the Orkneyinga Saga, the traditions of the family, and other sources of historical evidence confirm the same contention. This writer has not, however, been uniformly consistent in the expression of his views in this connection. In the third volume of his "Celtic Scotland," published in 1880, he, no doubt, reminds us in a footnote that he has had no occasion to alter the opinion he held in 1837, but he forgets that in his introduction to the Book of the Dean of Lismore he had, to a large extent, given away his case in the statement that "the spirit and tendency of the whole race was essentially Irish."

Dr Skene, in his advocacy of this view, lays great stress on the following considerations. First of all he quotes at length a letter written in 1543 by a Highland clergyman of the name of John Elder, a Reddshanks, to Henry VIII. of England, in which he emphasises the alleged older tradition that the Macdonalds were, in common with the other Highland Clans, of the "ancient stoke," and denounces in no measured terms the "papistical curside spiritualitie of Scotland," whom he held responsible for what he deemed the later Dalriadic tradition. Furthermore, an argument in support of the same contention is based on a paragraph in a letter written in 1596 by James Macdonald of Dunnyveg to King James VI., which is as follows :— "Most mightie and potent prince recomend us unto your hieness with our service for ever, your grace shall understand that our forbears hath been from time to time your servants unto your own Kingdom of Scotland."[1] From these and other considerations of less weight, Dr Skene has developed an ingenious argument to prove that the Scoto-Irish genealogy of the Clan Donald is an artificial system of no earlier origin than the fourteenth century, concocted by Irish and Highland seanachies, and that the Clan Donald were the principal tribe of the Gall-Gael who inhabited the coastlands of Argyll, and were of the primitive stock of Scotland.

It may at once be admitted that some at least of the main premisses from which Dr Skene deduces these conclusions are substantially correct. It is in the highest degree probable that a large pro-portion of the Highland Clans of the mainland, and

---

[1] The expression "from time to time" meaning here, as in other ancient documents, from time immemorial.

even some of those that are territorially connected
with the Western Isles in modern times, such as the
Macleans and Mackenzies, are remnants of the
ancient system of Northern Pictland. On the other
hand, Dr Skene, in the course of his argument,
makes an assertion which it is impossible to accept.
He maintains that in the eleventh century the
whole Highlands, including Argyll, were inhabited
by the Northern Picts, of whom the Gall-Gael were
an important tribe. Such a statement as this
implies either the extinction of the Scoto-Celtic
race in the Kingdom of Dalriada after 844 A.D., or
a wholesale migration of that stock into the territory
of the Southern Picts. There does not appear to be
historical evidence for any such extraordinary occurrence. A Dalriadic population occupied Argyll for
500 years previous to the reign of Kenneth Mac-
Alpin, and when the union of the Kingdoms took
place, they must have been the preponderating
element in that region. That the race should have
made an exodus out of Dalriada between the ninth
and eleventh centuries is a supposition that makes
excessive demands upon the most vivid historical
imagination.

The proofs adduced in support of these aver-
ments, however much truth they may contain,
cannot be regarded as justifying the conclusions.
The statement that the MacDonalds were indigenous
in Argyll, as shown by the Orkneyinga Sagas, and
that this was the tradition of the Clan, as the letter
of James MacDonald of Dunnyveg illustrates, seem
rather beside the question. From 1596 backwards
to the founding of the Dalriadic Kingdom in the
fifth and sixth centuries, or to the ninth or even the
eleventh century, was a period of time sufficiently

long to constitute a tradition of very respectable antiquity. Besides, the same James MacDonald of Dunnyveg, to whose letter Dr Skene attaches such importance, wrote another letter in 1615 to the Bishop of the Isles, which is capable of the very opposite construction from the theory of a Pictish descent. "My race," Sir James writes, "has been ten hundred years kindly Scottish men under the Kings of Scotland." The "kindliness" may have been dissembled on certain memorable occasions, such as at the battle of Harlaw, but the words are sufficiently suggestive, as indicative of the true descent of the Clan. Touching the epistle of John Elder, we are not disposed to place much reliance upon the letter of a bigoted Highland cleric at any time, much less in 1543, when the Reformation controversy was at red heat. The contents of the letter itself are evidence enough that we are not slandering Mr John Elder. The warmth of his invective and the keenness of his *odium theologicum* against the Church, on which he fastens the blame of what he regards as a false historical conception, do not encourage us to rely upon his testimony as a calm and unbiassed authority.

The conclusions arrived at in our Introductory chapter as to the Gall-Gael are, if tenable, quite subversive of the theory that the Clan Donald belonged to them. There is no evidence that the Gall-Gael were a territorial people or anything more or less than Gaelic pirates, while, as we hope to show, every vestige of Clan Donald history indicates their connection with large territorial, even regal, possessions.

The fact that Suibne, the son of Cineada ri Gall-Gael, is recorded by the Irish Annalists to have died in 1034, and that one of the Clan Donald line of the same name occurs in the genealogies of the Clan, may possibly have helped to lead Dr Skene to adopt what we consider an untenable position. Suibne, the ancestor of Somerled, was the son of Niallgusa; nor does the name Kenneth occur in any of the genealogical lists, a fact that seems conclusive against identifying the one with the other.

We hope now to be able to show from evidence, that seems on the whole convincing, that the Clan Donald are descended from the Dalriadic stock of Argyll. Dean Munro, who flourished like the Red-shanks cleric in the sixteenth century, and was a respected Church dignitary of his day, distinctly favours this conclusion, while the MS. of 1450 and the genealogy of the MacVurichs, whose history as seanachies to this family goes back to Muireadach Albannach in the twelfth century, all afford *prima facie* evidence of the truth of our contention. No doubt we are warned against both Irish and Highland seanachies, and it is necessary that their statements should be duly weighed, especially when questions arise affecting the honour and glory of the family or branch in which they are most specially interested. Yet even Dr Skene admits that, from the battle of Ocha, in 478 A.D., which forms an epoch in Irish history, the Irish Annals may be taken as fairly accurate, though in such details as genealogical links they may not be strictly so. The same is true of the Highland seanachies, especially the Book of Clanranald. Though not perhaps invariably accurate in every date and detail, yet, on the whole, we believe it to be the most honest and reliable of all the ancient authorities on the origin and history of the Clan.

And the argument from these standard authorities is strengthened by the natural inference deducible from the annals of the Clan in historical times. From the very beginning of the Island dynasty founded by Somerled there was a close connection between Ireland and Argyll and the Isles. The establishment of the Gaelic kingdom was largely promoted by Irish aid ; matrimonial alliances with Irish families were frequently formed by the chiefs ; many members of the family acquired settlements in Antrim and Tyrone, and the bards and seanachies of the Isles went for their education to the literary schools of the North of Ireland. These circumstances seem to point all to the same conclusion.

It is necessary for us, however, to go beyond this, and to consider whether the strong probabilities of the case are supported by what we can gather from the history of ancient Dalriada. When the union of Pictavia and Dalriada took place, and the seat of Government in the latter kingdom was transferred from Dunadd to Scone, the shifting of the political centre of gravity from the coast to the interior must have seriously affected the population of Oirthir-Ghael. In circumstances in which society is insufficiently organised for defence when the governing power is withdrawn from the extremities, it is clear that the latter become more open to foreign invasion. In view of this, it is significant that it was in the latter part of the ninth century that the Norwegian invasion began to be felt in the West, in the coastlands of the Gael and the Isles. From the latter half of the ninth century onwards there was a perpetual struggle between the Norsemen and the native population, a struggle in which the people of the Isles soon yielded to the power of

the Norseman; but the Gaels of Argyll continued
bravely to resist the incursions of the foe. Notwithstanding this resistance, the districts both of
Ergadia and Galwallia were largely occupied in the
eleventh century by the Norsemen, for at the battle
of Cluantarf in 1014 there is mention of the Galls or
foreigners of Man, Skye, Lewis, Kintyre, and
Oirthirghael. Further, when Thorfinn, the Earl of
Orkney, conquered the nine rikis in Scotland in 1034,
he included in his possessions Dali or Ergadia and
Gaddeli or Galloway. This being, in brief, the
general history of Argyll or Dalriada up to the
eleventh century, from the reign of Kenneth
MacAlpin, the question arises, how far the traditional
genealogy of the Clan Donald which makes them of
the stock of Dalriada is to be brought into line with
the well-known historical facts to which we have
adverted? In order to do this, we consider it
desirable, for the sake of clearness, to trace from the
earliest times the ancestry of the Clan Donald as we
find it in Irish and Highland genealogies.

The early history of the Clann Cholla—the
designation of our Clan from Donald back to Colla
Uais—penetrates far into the mists of antiquity.
Though, in detail, all that glitters is not gold, yet in
the main the seanachies may, without too much
credulity, be taken as fairly historical. The
genealogists, however, take a still further flight into
the dim past when they connect the Clan with a
celebrated Irish King, *Conn Ceud-Chathach, Con-*
stantinus Centimachus, or Constantine of the Hundred
Fights. Conn, who was *Ard Righ,* or supreme
king, of Ireland, and swayed the sceptre at Tara,
flourished in the second century of our era, and as
his name indicates, was one of the greatest heroes of

antiquity.   The tradition as to this descent has undoubtedly been for ages the living belief of the Clan, and without very strong evidence to the contrary, we are not disposed to surrender it.   At the Battle of Harlaw, MacVurich, the bard, sought to rouse the heroism of the men of the Isles, by stirring up the consciousness of this kingly descent—

> "A Chlanna Chuinn cuimhnichibh
> Cruas an am na h-iorghuill."

And doubtless the same inspiring thought animated the warriors of the Clan Donald on many another bloody field.   Ewen M'Lachlan, the celebrated bard and scholar, in his poem to the Society of true Highlanders, gives to the race of Somerled the same remote and royal lineage :—

> " Before the pomp advanced in kingly grace
> I see the stem of Conn's victorious race,
> Whose sires of old the Western sceptre swayed,
> Which all the Isles and Albion's half obeyed."

The tradition of its descent from Conn has certainly impressed the imagination of the race and inspired many of its singers.   When we come towards the fourth century there appears upon the scene another ancestor of our Clan, hardly less renowned than the famous Conn, Colla Uais, who is also styled *Ard Righ* of Ireland.   Colla's descent from Constantine is a matter on which genealogists are not agreed. The genealogy developed in the MS. of 1450 supplies three or four links which are omitted by the Clanranald seanachie.   Which of the two more nearly approaches accuracy it is, of course, impossible to say.   The fact that there are discrepancies seems, however, to dispose of the theory that the Irish descent of the Clan was an artificial system

concocted by Irish genealogists, encouraged by
th; Scottish ecclesiastics, and adopted by High-
lan l seanachies. Were this the case, we should
have expected, in both cases, an identical and
stereotyped genealogy. The fact that these genealogies, though different in detail, are yet similar in
their main conclusions, is a clear proof that the
Scoto-Celtic origin of the Clan was not artificially
devised to fit in with favourite historical beliefs,
but was a *bona-fide* and actual tradition.

Colla Uais was, according to the MS. of 1450,
eighth; according to MacVurich, fifth, in descent
from Constantine. He was the eldest of three
brothers, each of whom bore the name of Colla—
Colla Uais, Colla Meann, and Colla da Chrich—
their baptismal names being Caireall, Aodh, and
Muredach. The name Colla seems to have been
given them according to an ancient poem, for being
rebellious, and probably means a strong man—

> "Caireall, the first name of Colla Uais;
> Aodh, of Colla Meann of great vigour;
> Muredach, of Colla da Chrich:
> They were imposed on them for rebelling."

According to the genealogists, these brothers were
the sons of Eochaid or Ochaius Dubhlin, King of
Ireland,[1] and their mother was a Scottish princess of
the name of Aileach, a daughter of Ubdaire, King of
Alba. This lady is celebrated in an ancient Irish
poem as "a mild, true woman, modest, blooming,
till the love of the Gael disturbed her, and she
passed with him from the midst of Kintyre to the
land of Uladh." We can gather from the seanachies that, having failed in the attempt to place
Colla Uais on the throne of Ireland, the three

---

[1] Book of Clanranald in "Celticæ Reliquiæ," vol. ii., p. 150.

brothers crossed the Irish Channel for help from their Scottish kindred. Probably through the influence of their mother's relatives, the three Collas were able to muster a considerable force in Scotland, at the head of which they re-crossed the Irish Channel, and with the help of their Irish allies placed Colla Uais on the regal seat at Tàra. Colla Uais, however, reigned only four years, when he was dispossessed by Muredach Tirech, his near relative, who, it appears, had a better claim to the throne. According to Mac Mhuirich, the three Collas after this returned to Scotland, where they obtained extensive settlements; but having afterwards been reconciled to Muredach Tirech, they were invited by him to assist him in the war against the Clan Ruairidh. On the conclusion of the war, the three Collas received extensive possessions in the North of Ireland as the reward of their prowess; but Colla Uais left his share to the other two and returned to Scotland. After a residence of fifteen years in Scotland he went on a visit to Ireland, and died at Tàra of the Kings, A.D. 337.

It seems apparent that although Siol Chuinn thus early established a settlement in Scotland, their headquarters continued in Ireland. For fully a hundred years the region, which was afterwards the Kingdom of Scottish Dalriada, was only a colony of the Scoto-Irish race; as has already been fully narrated.

It was four generations after Colla Uais that the forward movement of the Dalriadic race occurred which eventuated in the new kingdom in the region of Oirthirghael. It is at this point that the Clan Donald line touches that of the Scottish kings, and that their common origin and ancestry appear.

Fergus, the son of Erc, one of the three brothers
who came to Scotland in the fifth century and
founded Scottish Dalriada, was, according to the
MS. of 1450, fourth, and according to the Mac-
Mhuirich genealogy, fifth, in descent from Colla
Uais. MacMhuirich inserts "Maine" between
Fergus and Erc, a variation which, though supported
by some Irish and other authorities, does not seem
to possess much historical probability. The genealogy of the 1450 MS. is, in this respect, supported
by the Albanic Duan.

Fergus Mor, the son of Erc, had two sons,
Domangart and Godfrey. Domangart, the elder
son, succeeded his father, and was the progenitor
of Kenneth MacAlpin and the succeeding line of
Scottish kings. Godfrey, the younger son, was
the progenitor of the line from which the Clan
Donald sprang, and was known in his day as
Toshach of the Isles. It would be absurd to say
that there are no difficulties presented in the
genealogy from Godfrey downwards.[1] Links seem
wanting to fulfil the conditions which the lapse of
so many generations demands. Something like
antediluvian longevity would be needed in several
of the links in order to fill up the centuries. Yet
while this is so, the conclusions suggested by the
main drift of the genealogy seem clear enough. If
links are lacking, those that can be subjected to
historical tests are not found wanting in historical
probability. Gilledomnan and Gillebride, Somerled's
immediate ancestors, can easily be identified, and of
the rest, Imergi, called by MacMhuirich Meargaidh,
is mentioned in the Irish Annals, and is very likely
the Ichmare of the Saxon Chronicle, one of the
three kings who submitted to Canut, the Danish

_____
[1] For genealogies down to Somerled vide Appendix.

King of England, when he invaded Scotland in
1031.

To sum up our discussion of the Clan Donald
descent, the main conclusions which seem deducible
from the field of enquiry are these :—We are satisfied
that the population of Dalriada continued after 844
to be largely Scoto-Irish, and it is highly probable,
apart from any historical knowledge we may possess,
that after the transference of the royal family of
Dalriada to Scone, the chief power in the west
would fall to some family more or less akin to the
line of Kenneth MacAlpin. This is entirely in
accordance with historical analogy, and is countenanced by the authorities so often quoted. It was
undoubtedly in the ninth century that the Clan
Cholla rose into greater consequence in Argyll and
the Isles, until the power of the Norsemen
threatened the Gael with extinction. The Norse
invasion of the West of Scotland had, as we
approach the beginning of the twelfth century,
reduced the fortunes of the Celtic population of
Argyll to a state of great depression. If by the
latter half of the twelfth century the Norwegian
power had been checked, and Gaelic influence
re-established in Argyll and the Isles, it was owing
to the prowess and address of one of the most
celebrated on the long roll of Celtic heroes,
Somerled MacGillebride.

CHAPTER III.

In the 11th century the Irish and Highland
Seanachies throw faint rays of light upon the position and prospects of the Clan Cholla. During
the first half of that century it appears that Gilledomnan, the grandfather of Somerled, was a person
of consequence, and held sway over a considerable
portion of Argyll. That he was a leader of some
note may be inferred from the circumstance of his
daughter having been the wife of Harold, one of
the Kings of Norway. In his time the fortunes of
the family were probably at the lowest ebb. Able
hitherto to hold their own against Scandinavian
assaults, the latter seemed destined to obtain a
permanent supremacy, and Gilledomnan was finally
driven from his territories and took refuge in Ireland, where, after devoting the latter part of his
life to pious duties, he very probably lived till his
death.

Gillebride, the son of Gilledomnan, who had fled with his father to Ireland, now made a vigorous effort to recover the inheritance of his sires. Being among his Irish kindred of the Clan Cholla, in the County of Fermanagh,[1] it was determined to place a force of 400 or 500 men at his disposal to aid him in vindicating his rights. Accompanied by this warrior band, Gillebride landed in Argyll, and made a gallant attempt to dislodge the invader; yet the Norseman had by this time obtained such a firm hold of the country, that Gillebride and his followers were obliged ultimately to retire into the woods and caves of Morvern. From his compulsory seclusion in a cave on the shores of Loch Linnhe, this Gaelic leader came to be known as *Gillebride na h-uaimh*. Gregory, without any authority, save one dark hint from the historian of Sleat, attributes Gillebride's defeat and consequent seclusion to his alleged action after the death of Malcolm Canmore, in supporting the claims of Donald Bane to the throne against the Anglo-Saxon party. This statement does not possess much historical 'probability. It was the aim of Gillebride's life to regain possession of his ancestral domains from the hands of the usurping Norseman; it was against them that all his efforts were directed, and his intervention at any time in the internal quarrels of the Scottish State is in the highest degree unlikely.

From this time Gillebride seems to have made no further effort to regain the territory of his fathers in the region of Oirthirghael. It is therefore clear that a crisis has arrived in the history of the Western Gael, as well as in the fortunes of the Clan

---

[1] The Book of Clanranald in "Reliquiæ Celticæ," vol. II., p. 155. Also see Hugh Macdonald's MS.

Cholla. The Norseman is on the eve, not only of expelling him from the Isles, but of crushing his *prestige* and authority on the mainland as well. It was at this critical moment, when Teutonic ascendancy in the West seemed on the eve of asserting itself finally and triumphantly, that Somerled arose. Gillebride and his cave vanish into the unknown, and his warlike son steps upon the scene of history, to become the terror of the Norseman and the Achilles of his race.

The events of Somerled's life are, like his genealogy, shrouded in the mists of unverifiable tradition. They belong to that borderland of history and legend on which the chronicler can with difficulty find a secure resting-place for the sole of his foot. Yet amid the shifting *debris* of old-world history, there are certain main outlines and facts which have crystallised themselves as genuine and authentic, and afford indications of an impressive and commanding personality issuing out of the dim past, possessing immense force of character, high military talents, great energy and ambition, combined with a large measure of that political sagacity and prudence which constitute a ruler and leader of men.

All we know of the early history of this renowned Gaelic hero is derived exclusively from tradition. Hugh Macdonald, the Sleat historian, who flourished in the latter half of the seventeenth century, embodied that tradition in a MS. history, written in the year 1680, and is responsible for almost every word that has been written since his time upon Somerled's early career. Save when he is tempted to exalt his own branch at the expense of others, he is, though not strictly accurate, still a

fairly reliable exponent of the history and traditions
of his Clan.

When Somerled first comes upon the scene, he is
living with his father in his cave amid the wilds of
Morvern, an unambitious young man, devoted to
fishing and hunting, and as yet apparently without
any intention of thrusting himself forward as a
leader of men. But the exigencies of the time soon
transformed this Celtic Nimrod into a hero. Amid
his devotion to the chase, he must have had many
hours of reflection upon the fallen fortunes of his
family, and unsuspected depths in his nature were
stirred up by the tale of their misfortunes. The
faded glory of the once kingly house, with all
the humiliating conditions that accompanied its
downfall, seized with irresistible force upon his
imagination, and the resolve to build up again its
ruined state became the passion of his life. Often
must he have wished that the day might come when
he could strike a blow for freedom and the right.
That day at length came, and it found Somerled
ready. It seems that about this time a strenuous
effort had been made by the native tribes of Argyll
to free themselves from the Scandinavian yoke.
Their enemies had also prepared themselves to strike
a decisive blow for the final assertion of supremacy.
The galleys of the Norsemen studded the western
sea, and a descent in force upon the shores of Oirthirghael ensued. The result was a terrible onslaught
upon the native tribes that endeavoured to withstand the invading host, and their eventual defeat
ensued. It was observed, however, that one tribe—
the MacInneses—left the field in good order, led by
a young man tall in stature and valiant in fight,
who had performed prodigies of valour that day.

The MacInneses[1] had lost their own leader, but had found one in *Somhairle Mor Mac Ghillebhride.* Some time thereafter this brave sept, loving liberty more than life, resolved once more to make an effort for the achievement of their independence. They assembled to take counsel as to the course they should pursue in so critical an emergency. The *Crann tara* was sent through the land, and soon from far and near the men of Argyll, defeated but not subdued, flocked to the place of rendezvous to the east side of Benmore. A council of war was held, but the unanimity so desirable in the face of a united foe, did not prevail. The leaders of the various tribes respectively strove with one another for the chief command. The camp was in motion like an anthill. All began to draw their weapons, when an aged chief rose in the midst and demanded to be heard, setting forth at great length the dangers to which their dissensions exposed them, and suggesting the appointment to the chief command of one in whom all had implicit confidence. He concluded by recommending the choice of Somerled as one who, from his prowess in the recent conflict, was well fitted for such a post. To this they all agreed, and messengers were at once dispatched to offer him the command. Somerled had some hesitation in accepting the offer on viewing the strength of the opposing force, but he had recourse to a stratagem which served his purpose well. Each man was ordered to kill his cow, and this having been done, and the animals skinned, the Gaels waited the approach of the enemy. Somerled now ordered his little army to march round the eminence on which they lay encamped, which

---

[1] For MacInneses, see Appendix.

having done, he made them all put on the cow
hides to disguise themselves and repeat the movement. He finally ordered his men to reverse the
cowhides, and now, for the third time, to go through
the same movement, thus exhibiting to the enemy
the appearance of a strong force composed of three
divisions. The stratagem had the desired effect.
The enemy, believing that a formidable force was
coming down upon them, fell into utter confusion.
Somerled, taking advantage of the panic, fell upon
the Scandinavian host with great slaughter. The
foe was routed, scattered, and pursued to the north
bank of the Sheill, where they took to their galleys.[1]
Thus did Somerled strike his first successful blow
for the country of his fathers, and started on his
career of warlike triumph. He was not satisfied
with the success of this preliminary skirmish. With
the instinct of the capable man of action, he took
advantage of that turn in the tide of human affairs
which carries those who watch and follow it on to
power and fortune. Somerled followed up his advantage, prosecuted the war still further into the heart
of the enemy's country, and his forces gathering
strength and confidence with continued success, he
was soon able to drive the Norsemen from Oirthirghael to Innse-Gall. His victories were the first
successful rally which, for hundreds of years, had
been made by the Celts of the West of Scotland
against the Norwegian power.

Somerled having thus gained possession of the
mainland domain which belonged to his sires,
assumed the title of Thane or Regulus of Argyll.
A man who had risen thus suddenly to eminence
and power was likely enough, in view of the past, to

---

[1] Hugh Macdonald's MS. New Statistical Account of Morvern.

take advantage of his new position to break still further the sway of the enemies of his race, not only over Oirthirghael but over the Western Isles. It became his settled policy to subdue the Kingdom of Man and the Isles, and whether or not the erection of a Celtic Kingdom upon its ruins was his intention from the beginning of his career, the idea must have gradually shaped itself in his mind, and the progress of events enabled him to carry it into effect. In these circumstances, Olave the Red, King of Man and the Isles, feeling the shocks the Norwegian Power had received at the hands of the Celtic chief, and somewhat uneasy in the possession of the Sudoreys, effected a temporary friendship and a cessation of hostilities by bestowing his daughter upon him in marriage, a compact which probably he would not have cemented so successfully had not the hero of Argyll, from all accounts, been hopelessly in love with the fair Ragnhildis. The story of how he won his bride is told with great minuteness of detail by the historian of Sleat, who makes it appear as if the overtures for her hand were all on the side of Somerled. It was a stratagem, but all is fair in love as in war. Olave lay encamped in Storna Bay, in the neighbourhood of which Somerled also was cruising. The latter, in course of an interview, in which he sought to remain *incognito*, told Olave that he had come from the Thane of Argyll, who promised to accompany him on his expedition if he gave him his daughter in marriage. Olave, recognising the aspirant to his daughter's hand, declined, it is said, the proffered alliance, but expressing his willingness to have Somerled's company on his cruise. A foster-brother of Olave, Maurice Mac-Neill, was a friend of Somerled, and offered to devise means for winning the King's daughter. His offer was accepted. In the night time Maurice scuttled the King's ship. Boring several holes in the bottom, he made pins of the necessary size to stop them when necessity demanded, but meanwhile filled the holes with butter. Next day they set sail, and for a time all went well.

As soon, however, as they came to the stormy point of Ardnamurchan, the action of the waves displaced the greasy packing of the holes in Olave's ship, which immediately began to leak, with imminent danger of sinking and drowning the King and all on board. Olave and his men thereupon called on Somerled, who with his galley followed in their wake, to help them in their extremity. No assistance would be granted unless the King swore that he would give Somerled his daughter in marriage. The oath was taken; Olave was received into Somerled's galley, and Maurice MacNeill fixed the pins he had prepared into the holes, and the King's ship, much to his own astonishment, continued on its way in safety. From that day it is said that the descendants of this Maurice are called MacIntyres[1]—the sons of the wright.

This is Hugh Macdonald's story, and whatever foundation there may be for it, it is hardly credible that the King of Man should have displayed such reluctance in allying his family with a chief of such proved capacity and extending influence as Somerled. The marriage took place in 1140, according to the author of the Chronicles of Man, who refers to it as the cause of the ultimate ruin of the Kingdom of the Isles.

[1] MacIntyre, Gael. Mac-an-t-Saoir.

In the year 1·153-54, the long and peaceful reign of Olave had a sudden and tragic close. He was murdered by his nephews, the sons of Harold, who had been brought up in Dublin, and laid claim to half the Kingdom of Man. The following autumn Godred, the son of Olave, who was in Norway at the time of his father's assassination, set sail for the Isles, was received gladly by the inhabitants as their King, and executed the murderers. Early in his reign he was called to Ireland by the Ostmen of the Kingdom of Dublin, which was at the time a Norwegian principality, to quell disturbances that had arisen, and assume sovereign power. Victory rested on his arms, and he returned to Man flushed with success, and intoxicated with increased dominion. But prosperity turned his head, and his arbitrary and tyrannical exercise of power alienated the loyalty of the Island chiefs. So oppressive and despotic was his rule that many of the principal men of the Isles banded themselves together to resist him.

Thus were events shaping themselves in a way which powerfully affected the interests and inflamed the ambition of Somerled. The Isle of Man was inhabited by a population which was mainly Celtic. The ruling dynasty had, in the person of Godred, incurred extreme unpopularity, and these circumstances seemed more or less favourable to any pretensions which Somerled might advance, connected as he was by marriage with the family which hitherto held sway in the Isles. Thorfin, the son of Ottar, the most powerful of the disaffected barons, was chosen as leader of the contemplated rising, and he made the proposal to Somerled that his son Dugall should be proclaimed King of the Isles.

Somerled readily assented to the proposals of the Islesmen. Dugall, who was only a boy at the time, was carried through the Isles and proclaimed King, while hostages were taken for the loyalty of the Islesmen and their acquiescence in the new *regime.*[1]

This revolution had no sooner been accomplished than a treacherous sychophant of the name of Paul[2]—probably as little in nature as in name, and to whom, doubtless, the smile of the tyrant was as the breath of life—fled to the Isle of Man and informed Godred of the startling events that were happening in the Scottish Isles. Godred, without delay, equipped a considerable fleet, with which he sailed to the Isles with the object of crushing the rebellion. Somerled, having been apprised of the approach of this large armament, collected a fleet of 80 sail, and on the night of Epiphany, 1156 A.D.,[3] a long, obstinate, and sanguinary conflict took place off the north coast of Isla. If we gauge the battle by its results, the advantage lay with the Thane of Argyll. Peace was concluded, and a treaty formed between Godred and Somerled by which the whole of the islands south of the Point of Ardnamurchan, along with Kintyre,[4] came into possession of the latter.

The peace which was thus established proved of short duration. The history of the time tells us little or nothing as to the causes of the second rupture, but within the space of two years after this treaty with Godred, Somerled invaded the

[1] Chronicles of Man Orkneyinga Saga.

[2] Said to have been Paul Balkanson, Norwegian Lord of Skye.

[3] Chronicles of Man.

[4] Since the time of Magnus Barefoot, Kintyre was reckoned one of the Isles

Isle of Man with fifty-three galleys, routed Godred,
and laid the country waste. Godred's power was so
much shattered that he was compelled to fly to
Norway and seek aid from his liege lord against
his victorious brother-in-law. But for a period of
six years, during the life-time of Somerled, Godred
never returned to his usurped dominion, and the
whole kingdom of Man and the Isles lay at the
victor's feet.[1]

This rapid and triumphant revolution in favour
of Gaelic influence on the western shores of Scotland could not be viewed with indifference by the
State, and was the cause of much envy among the
neighbours of the Thane of Argyll. However
unlikely it may be that Somerled's father was
involved in the political complications subsequent
to the death of Malcolm Canmore, it is absolutely
certain that his sympathies, and those of his son,
would be with the Gaelic influence that placed
Donald Bane on the throne, as against the Anglo-
Norman culture which was moulding Scottish
institutions during the reign of Queen Margaret's
sons. Circumstances arose to confirm and increase
any unfriendly feeling already existing between
the house of Somerled and the Crown.

The Province of Moray, inhabited in early times
by the Northern Picts, and long occupying an
independent position as regards the region of
Southern Pictland, was, in the reign of David I.,
attached to the Scottish Crown, and Angus, the
last of the Mormaors, was slain in battle in 1130.[2]
Four years thereafter the rising of Malcolm Macheth and his claim to the Earldom of Moray took
place. This insurrection, with the whole train of

---

[1] Chronicles of Man.   [2] Annals of Ulster and Innisfallen.

relative circumstances, is fraught with such peculiar
interest, and has so direct a bearing upon the life of
Somerled, that it demands more than a passing
reference. Malcolm Macheth first appears in history
as a monk of the Cistercian monastery of Furness,
founded in 1124, under the name of Wymund. He
is said to have possessed qualities of a high order,
calculated to secure advancement and dignity in the
Church. His prospects of preferment appeared
particularly bright. In 1134, Olave, King of Man,
founded and endowed a religious house at Russin, in
affiliation with the monastery of Furness, of which
Yvo was Abbot, and Wymund was placed in charge
of the new establishment. His address was so
winning, and his person so commanding, that he
soon became very popular among the Norsemen, and
they requested him to become their Bishop. In
this their desires were gratified. No sooner was
this step of promotion accomplished than a new and
unexpected development in the career of Wymund
arose. He declared himself to be the son of Angus,
Earl of Moray, who had been slain in 1130, and
that he himself had been deprived of his inheritance
by the Scottish King. The King of Man and
Somerled, whose sister[1] Wymund afterwards
espoused, recognised the validity of his claim, which,
according to the best authorities, appears to have
been well founded. He gave up the monastic name
of Brother Wymund, and assumed his proper Gaelic
name, Malcolm Macheth. He immediately took
steps to vindicate his claim to the Earldom of

[1] Lord Hailes, Vol. I., says :—" Apud Scotiam Somerled et nepotes sui
filii scilicet Malcolmi." It could not have been a daughter of Somerled by
Ragnhildis, whom he married as late as 1140. Possibly, though not probably,
it might have been a daughter of Somerled by a former marriage who was
Malcolm's wife.

Moray. Having assembled a small fleet in the Isle of Man, he sailed to the Western Isles, where he received a friendly reception from Somerled, and from whence he invaded the mainland of Scotland. Shortly after this, the Norwegian Earl of Orkney lent him his powerful support, and gave a strong proof of his faith in the rightfulness of his pretensions by marrying his sister. His connection with two such powerful chiefs enabled him for several years to prosecute his enterprise with a certain measure of success. He maintained an irregular and predatory warfare with David I., at times retiring to his mountain fastnesses, at others taking refuge in his ships when pressed by the royal forces, until at last he was betrayed and taken prisoner while crossing the river Cree in Galloway. David, contrary to the character of saintliness he is said to have possessed, ordered his eyes to be put out, and imprisoned him in the Castle of Roxburgh.[1]

After Malcolm's capture and imprisonment, his sons appear to have sought a refuge with their uncle, the Thane of Argyll, although in their earlier struggles to recover their family rights, he does not seem to have taken a very prominent or active part. His own conflicts with the Norsemen would have occupied all his energies. It appears that some time after his imprisonment in Roxburgh, Malcolm received the royal pardon, and taking up the broken thread of his monastic life he again assumed the cowl; and retired to the monastery of Biland in Yorkshire. The sons of Malcolm Macheth were again in rebellion in 1153 after the accession of Malcolm IV., and there is no doubt that on this occasion they enjoyed the powerful and strenuous

[1] Celtic Scotland, vol. I., pp. 460-64 ; Highlanders of Scotland, vol. II., p. 166.

support of their uncle. Somerled took up arms, however, not merely in support of the Moray family, but as a protest against intrigues among the King's advisers which threatened the subversion of his own influence and position. The war lasted three years, and in course of it Donald, the eldest son of Malcolm Macheth, was taken prisoner at Whithorn, in Galloway, and sent to the Castle of Roxburgh, where his father had been in captivity.[1] Such, however, was the vigour with which Somerled prosecuted the war, that Malcolm IV., considering prudence to be the better part of valour, resolved to come to terms. A treaty was drawn up in which, among other stipulations, it was agreed that Donald should be liberated, and Malcolm Macheth invested with the Earldom of Ross.[2] That Malcolm was advanced to this dignity, although he failed to secure his ancestral position, is proved by letters of protection granted about this time by the King to the monks of Dunfermline, and addressed "Malcolmo Comite de Ros,"[3] &c. The charter, by which Somerled effected such a great deliverance for the family of Macheth, was so important as to mark an epoch in the history of such documents. Thus we have charters by King Malcolm to *Angus de Sandside* and to *Berowaldus Flandrensis*, both " given at Perth in the year of our Lord immediately following the treaty between the King and Somerled."[4]

The peace that was established between the Crown and Somerled in 1157 seems to have lasted about seven years. History is not very clear as to

---

[1] Haile's Annals.

[2] Skene's Historians of Scotland, vol. IV.; Wyntoun, vol. II.

[3] Celtic Scotland, vol. I., pp. 470-71.

[4] Carta . . per Malcolmum regem IV. Dat, apud Pert natali domino proximo post concordiam regis et Somerledi.

J

the causes which led to an outbreak of hostilities in
1164. According to the Chronicles of Man and the
Scottish historians who have professed to record the
transactions of the age, he had formed the ambitious
design of conquering the whole of Scotland. We
confess to attaching very little value to the opinions
of Scottish historians regarding the history of the
Highlands. Ignorance of the language, customs,
and traditions of the people has so tainted their
utterances; racial hatred has likewise so blinded
them to facts, that their deliverances on the difficult
problems of Highland history are in the main quite
unreliable.

That Somerled was inspired by ambition it
would be useless to deny, as otherwise he could
never have carved out so illustrious a career, or laid
the foundation of a great historical dynasty. That
an inordinate desire possessed him to enlarge his
already extensive territories by an attack upon the
Scottish Kingdom, is in the nature of things most
unlikely, and inconsistent with the clear judgment
which seems to have marked his policy even in the
most stormy passages of his warlike life. Here, as
on occasions elsewhere, the historian of Sleat seems
to strike the true historical note. The Scottish King
was anxious to extend his sway over the whole of
Scotland, and showed symptoms of a desire to grasp
the mainland territories of Argyll, Kintyre, and
Lorn.[1] Other reasons also may have operated in
causing Somerled to assume the aggressive against
the King. It is a fair inference from the history of
the time that his action represented a movement on
the part of the Celtic population to resist the policy
of the Crown, which had for its aim to crush the

[1] Hugh Macdonald's MS.

independent princes of Scotland in detail. Malcolm
IV. is said to have invaded both Galloway and
Moray in 1160, and to have introduced large
changes into these regions by the removal of the
native population and the introduction of the
Southerner to occupy their places. That this may
have been true to a limited extent need not be
disputed; but our faith in the statement is not
strengthened when it comes to us on the authority
of John of Fordun. Be this as it may, there is no
doubt as to the proceedings taken by the Crown
against the Celtic chiefs in 1160, and it is in the
highest degree probable that Somerled, by his action
in 1164, sought to make a diversion in their favour
by invading Scotland in force. In addition to
all this, there was the risk to which Somerled's
own interests were exposed. · He had suffered
many provocations from Malcolm and his Min-
isters, and so anticipating danger to his possessions and position from their threatening attitude,
he resolved to take time by the forelock,
and strike a decisive blow in self-defence. As a
protest against the unprincipled greed of Malcolm
the Maiden and the unscrupulous and grasping spirit
of his advisers, Somerled in 1164 gathered a great
host, 15,000 strong, from Ireland, Argyllshire, and
the Isles, and with a fleet of one hundred and sixty-
four galleys, sailed up the Clyde to Greenock, where
he disembarked his force in the bay of St Lawrence.
Thence he marched to Renfrew, where the King's
army lay encamped. The records of the time are not
very trustworthy, but such as they are there are
two important inferences to be drawn from them
which are helpful in arriving at a correct conclusion
as to the events that supervened. In the first

place, it is clear from the statements of the
chroniclers that the King's force was numerically
unfit to cope with the host that Somerled had
brought to the field. In the second place, the
undoubted result of the action was that Somerled
was slain and his army dispersed. Had a battle
been fought it is incredible that the small force
apparently opposed to him would have sufficed to
baffle the tried valour and skilful leadership of
the Thane of Argyll. Hence the ancient chroniclers[1]
call in the special intervention of heaven to account
for the otherwise unaccountable result. On the
whole, we are disposed to accept the traditional
version as that which best fits in with all the known
circumstances of the case. Feeling reluctant to join
issues with the Highland host, and anticipating
defeat in the open field, Malcolm's advisers fell on
the cowardly and ignominious plan of assassinating
the Island leader. To this end they bribed a mis-
creant of the name of Maurice Macneill, a camp
follower, and he being a near relative of Somerled,
the latter had nothing to fear from his presence
in the camp. This individual, coming in the guise
of friendship, was admitted into Somerled's tent,
and finding him off his guard, stabbed him to the
heart.[2] The hero who was unconquered in the field
was not proof against the assassin's knife, and his
large army, on learning the fate of their trusted
leader, melted away like a snow-wreath, betook
themselves to their galleys, and sadly dispersed.

No doubt a different account from this is given
by the Scottish historians. Those who do not

---

[1] Chronicles of Melrose, p. 169 ; Wyntoun, 1164 ; Fordoun, p. 252, in
Skene's Historians of Scotland. See Appendix.

[2] Hugh Macdonald's MS.

attribute the result to the direct intervention of
Providence allege that Malcolm's army not only
defeated, but well-nigh annihilated that of
Somerled. Possibly the retreating host may
have been harassed by the enemy, who hung
upon their rear and cut off some stragglers in
their flight, and this would have lent colour to
the exaggerated tales of slaughter contained in
the records of the age. It is difficult to conceive
how—if Somerled's army, as alleged, was totally
defeated at Renfrew—the territories of the rebel
were neither annexed to the Crown nor awarded
to the hungry Norman courtiers who were yearning
to lay their hands upon them. On the contrary,
Somerled's family suffered no diminution of their
power. Reginald, Dugall, and Angus were all left
in undisturbed possession of their father's extensive
domains. We prefer Hugh Macdonald's tradition
to the exaggerated, inconsistent, and imaginative
declamations of the chroniclers, as bearing far more
of the appearance of sober, historical truth. To the
same authority we are indebted for the statement
that the remains of the Thane of Argyll were taken
at the King's expense to Iona, and buried there
with great pomp and ceremony; but the tradition
of the family has always been that Saddel, where
Somerled had commenced the erection of a monastery
which was afterwards completed by his son Reginald,
was the last resting-place of the great Celtic hero.

The Sleat historian tells us that Somerled was
" a well-tempered man, in body shapely, of a fair
piercing eye, of middle stature and of quick discern-
ment." The reference to his stature contained in
this quotation does not seem to harmonise with
the description stereotyped in Highland tradition,
according to which he is styled *Somhairle Mor*

MacGillebhride. Yet the application of the epithet
Mor may have arisen, not so much from physical size
as from the general idea of greatness, the commanding position of Somerled in the history of his
race, and the description of Hugh Macdonald not
improbably embodies a genuine and authentic
tradition.

RUINS OF SADDEL MONASTERY, THE BURIAL PLACE OF SOMERLED.

Somerled was probably the greatest hero that
his race has produced. It may seem strange that
no Gaelic bard has sung of his exploits, but in his
day and long afterwards, Gaelic singers were more
taken up with the mythical heroes of the *Feinn*
than with the genuine warriors of their native land.
Others of his line may have equalled him in personal
bravery and military prowess; but Somerled was
more than a warrior. He possessed not only the

courage and dash which are associated with the
Celtic character ; he had the organising brain, the
fertile resource, the art not only of winning battles,
but of turning them to account ; that sovereign
faculty of commanding the respect and allegiance of
men which marks the true king, the able man of
Thomas Carlyle's ideal. Without the possession of
this imperial capacity he could never, in the face of
such tremendous odds, have wrested the sovereignty
of the Gael from his hereditary foes, and handed
it to the Clan Cholla, to be their heritage for
hundreds of years. He was the instrument by
which the position, the power, the language of the
Gael were saved from being overwhelmed by
Teutonic influence, and Celtic culture and tradition
received a new lease of life. He founded a family
which played no ignoble part in Scottish history.
If our faith in the principle of heredity is sometimes
shaken by degenerate sons of noble sires, when the
last links of a line of long ago prove unworthy heirs
of a great past, our faith is confirmed in it by the
line of princes that sat upon the Island throne, and
who as a race were stamped with the heroic qualities
which characterised the son of Gillebride. Somerled's life struggle had been with the power of the
Norseman, whose sun in the Isles he saw on the eve
of setting. But he met his tragic fate in conflict
with another and more formidable set of forces.
This was the contest which Somerled bequeathed as
a legacy to his successors. It was theirs to be the
leading spirits in the resistance of the Gaelic race,
language, and social life to the new and advancing
order which was already moulding into an organic
unity the various nationalities of Scotland—the
ever-increasing, ever-extending power of feudal
institutions.

CHAPTER IV.

THE DESCENDANTS OF SOMERLED.—1164-1266.

The Sons of Somerled.—Division of Patrimony.—Strife between
Reginald and Angus.—Death of Angus.—Reginald Succeeds
to his Estates.—Character of Reginald.—Question of
Seniority.—Descendants of Dugall Mac Somerled.—The Sons
of Reginald.—Descent of King Alexander upon Argyll in
1221-2.—Descent in 1249.—Position of Ewin of Lorn.—
Donald of Isla.—Angus Mor.—Scottish Aggression in Isles.—
Roderick of Bute.—Haco's Expedition.—Battle of Largs.—
Cession of Isles.—Position of the Island Lords.

KING MALCOLM IV. of Scotland died in 1165, the
year following Somerled's death at Renfrew, and
was succeeded by his brother, William the Lion.
During the long reign of William (1166-1214) no
further effort seems to have been made to subjugate
Argyll and the Isles. The history of Somerled's
descendants during the century subsequent to his
death is involved in much obscurity. Though the
career of the great Thane is in some respects
shrouded in uncertainty, his personality and enterprise gave such a fresh impulse to Celtic aspirations
in the West that it were strange did we not possess
certain clear historical outlines. When the curtain
that fell upon the tragedy of his life's close rises
again, we are still enveloped in mist, and the
shadows cast upon the background of the historical
stage by his successors are, while less imposing, not
altogether so clearly defined. Somerled left a
Celtic kingdom, partly inherited, but all won by

the sword, extending from the Butt of Lewis to
the most southerly point of Man ; but when the
strong hand of the heroic ruler vanished, Godred,
who for several years had been skulking in Norway,
returned and resumed possession of Man and the
Northern Isles. These latter comprised Lewis and
Harris, Uist and Barra, then known as Innis Fadda,
Skye, Coll,[1] and other lesser Isles.

Besides the three sons of Somerled by Ragnhildis,
it is said that he had other sons. One of these, Gille-
Callum, is supposed to have been slain at Renfrew.[2]
Another son, by a Lowland woman, was named
Gall[3] MacSgillin, said to have been the progenitor of
the Clan Gall of the Glens; while the names of other
two, Gillies[4] and Olave,[5] have also been handed down.
According to the Sleat historian, Somerled's oldest
son bore his own name, and succeeded him as Thane
of Argyll. In this statement he does not appear to
have the support of any other authority, yet it
seems to lend a certain confirmation to references in
the Norwegian Sagas to a second Somerled who
flourished during the early years of the 13th
century.[6] This Somerled is spoken of as a
Sudoreyan King, a cousin of the sons of Dugall
MacSomerled, and was in all probability a grandson
of the great Thane ; but which of Somerled's sons
was his father it is, of course, impossible to say. It
seems probable, on the whole, that descendants of

[1] Gregory is mistaken in including Coll among the possessions of Dugall
MacSomerled. Coll was a seat of the Norwegian Reginald, and in the poem
Baile Suthain Sith Eamhne, in the book of Fermoy, he is referred to as King
of Coll.

[2] Chronicles of Man.

[3] Book of Clanranald in "Reliquiæ Celticæ," vol. II., p. 157.

[4] According to Hugh Macdonald, Gillies had lands in Kintyre.

[5] Hugh Macdonald's MS.

[6] Anecdotes of Olave the Black.

Somerled MacGillebride, other than those by the
daughter of the King of Man, inherited lands in the
district of Oirthirghael, though all traces of their
territorial position have disappeared. The reason
why the light of history fails us utterly regarding
them we shall consider further on.

In the division of the Southern Isles and a
portion of Oirthirghael among the sons of Somerled
and Ragnhildis, the treaty between Somerled and
Godred, in 1155,[1] was carried out in this wise :—
Kintyre [2] and Isla, the patrimony of the Clan Cholla
and the early seat of their power in Scotland, fell to
the share of Reginald; Lorn, Mull, and Jura became
Dugall's; while Bute, with a part of Arran,[3] and
the Rough bounds, extending from Ardnamurchan
to Glenelg, were bequeathed to Angus. The
remaining portion of the North Oirthir, extending
from Glenelg to Lochbroom, passed into the hands
of the Lay Abbot of Applecross.

The possessions thus apportioned among the
three sons of Somerled—won by the might of their
father's sword—were, undoubtedly, held by them
as a free and independent principality. Whether
their immediate descendants after 1222, the year
of King Alexander's descent upon Argyll, owned
the superiority of Scotland for their mainland
possessions, is a question to be considered by-
and-bye. That the sons of Somerled entered into
possession of the Southern Isles, which had been
wrested from Godred, owning allegiance neither to
Scotland nor Norway, is an historical fact beyond all
dispute. This proud sense of independence, which

---

[1] See p. 45.

[2] From the time of Magnus Barefoot, Kintyre was reckoned one of the
Isles.

[3] The rest of Arran belonged to Reginald.

brooked no superior, was perpetuated in the race even after the reality had passed away, and led to the eventual downfall of the family of the Isles—a family characterised by Buchanan as "clarissima et potentissima priscorum Scotorum gens."[1]

The division of the Somerledian possessions does not appear to have given unqualified satisfaction. The partition of Arran especially was fraught with unfortunate results. Where lands are "compassed by the inviolate sea," boundaries are easily preserved, but the line dividing Arran into two equal shares would have been hard to observe without occasional friction and the stern arbitrament of war. Reginald having driven Angus and his sons out of both Bute and Arran, followed them into Garmoran, the northern possession of Angus. There, in the year 1192,[2] a battle was fought, in which Angus was victorious. Eighteen years thereafter (1210), Angus and his three sons were killed by the men of Skye.[3] It does not follow from this that the fatal battle was fought in Skye, for undoubtedly that island, as well as Innis Fadda, were both at that time in the possession of Reginald, the Norwegian King of Man and the Isles. According to the author of the "Historical Account of the Family of MacDonald," published in 1819, Angus and his sons were killed at Moidart, which was a part of their hereditary possessions, probably in the act of repelling an incursion of Norsemen from the Isle of Skye, who still continued to infest the North Oirthir; and this is, no doubt, the correct version of the end of this branch of the house of Somerled.

[1] "The most distinguished and powerful family of the ancient Scots."
[2] Chronicles of Man.   [3] Gregory, p. 17, Annals of Ulster.

Angus' male line having thus become extinct, his possessions passed over to Reginald and his son Roderick. James the son of Angus, however, left a daughter Jane, who married Alexander, eldest son of Walter, the High Stewart of Scotland. This led, in future years, to much trouble as regards the possession of the island of Bute. After the death of Angus and his sons in battle, the mainland and island possessions of the sons of Somerled were divided pretty equally between the families of Reginald and Dugall. The relations between these two branches of the Clan Cholla were never of the most cordial description, and even at that early date a misunderstanding arose as to the ownership of Mull, which lasted over 100 years. The house of Somerled, however, was all powerful in that region; the voice of the Campbell was not yet heard in the land, and the families of Argyll and the Isles were vassals of the Clan Cholla.

Reginald of Isla, according to the Irish historians, seems to have been popular both in Scotland and in Ireland, feared in war but loved in peace. The exigencies of the time often led him to the field of battle, sometimes on the defensive sometimes as the aggressor; yet, as has often been true of the greatest heroes, he loved peace more than war, and we find him acting the part of peacemaker not only among his own people, but also on the other side of the Irish Channel.

It is probably at this stage that we can most conveniently discuss and, so far as possible, dispose of the question as to which of the sons of Somerled was the older, Reginald or Dugall. The seniority of Dugall would not, for reasons that will afterwards appear, constitute the Clan Dugall the senior branch of the house of Somerled, and therefore the question, though one of interest, is not of serious importance.   In those days the feudal law of primogeniture, by which the oldest son succeeds to his father's lands, was not operative in the Isles; lands were gavelled[1] equally among the male members of a family, and in more than one case it is difficult to arrive at definite conclusions when questions as to seniority arise.   It is only inferentially that we can form an opinion as to the point at issue.   The Seanachies give us no assistance.   M'Vurich is silent on the subject, although, in mentioning the sons of Somerled, he names Dugall first.

Hugh Macdonald, adopting what is with him a favourite *role*, bastardises Dugall, evidently with the view of placing beyond doubt or cavil the seniority of the house of Isla.   Historians have followed one another slavishly in making Dugall the oldest of the sons of Somerled.   One reason only can there be for the adoption of such a view.   When the barons of Man and the Isles rose against Godred in 1155,[2] it was Dugall who was carried through the Isles and proclaimed King.   This has been taken as evidence of Dugall's seniority.   It may very well be evidence of the contrary.   Most probably it was because he was the younger son that he was put forward as his mother's heir for the possession of Man and the Isles, while Reginald, as the older son, was regarded as his father's successor in the hereditary domains of Oirthirghael.   We have already stated that primogeniture did not rule in

---

[1] The word "gavel" is an English corruption of the Gaelic word "gabhail," which is still used in the Western Isles in the sense of "holding."

[2] See pp. 44-5

the Isles as regards the inheritance of lands. Yet
the head of the race, whether brother or son to the
last chief, enjoyed certain privileges. Preferably to
others he possessed those lands which had always
been connected with the residence of the head of the
house. Hence, although the territories of Somerled
were divided in somewhat equal portions, it is a
significant fact that the occupancy of the lands of
Kintyre and Isla remained with the descendants of
Reginald. The modern Campbeltown, which was
the cradle of the Scottish monarchy, became in after
times the chief seat of the lords of the Isles in the
peninsula of Kintyre, and went under the name of
Kinloch Kilkerran. It would thus appear that these
lands, which were the seat of the Dalriadic power
and the peculiar patrimony of the Clan Cholla,
became after the days of Kenneth MacAlpin associated with that branch of the Scoto-Irish race which
was represented by Somerled and his descendants.
That Reginald and his posterity held this immemorial
heritage of the Clan Cholla in preference to the line
of Dugall seems to suggest the seniority of the house
of Isla. Still further there is a prominence given in
the records of the time to Reginald and his descendants, which clearly points to their being the chief
inheritors of the name and honours of the house of
Somerled.

Even if it were the case, which in our opinion
it is not, that Dugall MacSomerled was the oldest of
the three sons, that fact would not constitute the
Clan Dugall, necessarily, the senior branch of the
Clan Cholla. There are grave reasons for doubting
whether the Clan Dugall, as represented by the
head of that line for upwards of four hundred years,
are at all descended from Dugall MacSomerled. A

brief glance at the descendants of this Dugall may be helpful in the solution of the question. Dugall, son of Somerled, left three sons, Dugall Scrag, Duncan, and another son named Uspac[1] Hakon, who appears in the Norwegian Sagas. Uspac stood high in the confidence of King Haco, who made him a King in the Sudoreys. It is recorded by the same authority that in 1228-30, when the Norwegian forces came south to Isla Sound, the three brothers, Kings Uspac, Dugall, and Duncan, were already there with a large armament, and it is interesting to find reference to the second Somerled as taking part in the expedition. The Sudoreyan princes invited the Norwegians to a banquet, but the latter having heard of the strong wine drunk at the Celtic *symposia* (does the potent national beverage possess this venerable antiquity ?), and having their suspicions otherwise aroused, declined the proffered hospitality. A night attack was made on the Norsemen, when a considerable number of the Sudoreyans, Somerled among the rest, were killed. Dugall Scrag was taken prisoner and protected by Uspac, who does not appear to have been implicated in the fray. With this incident Dugall Scrag passes out of history.

Shortly after this, Olave King of Man, invaded Bute, then in the possession of the Scots, with a fleet of 80 ships, and besieged the Castle of Rothesay. The Norwegians were eventually successful with a loss of 390 men, and Uspac Hakon, who was among the assailants, was mortally wounded by a stone hurled from the battlements. He survived only till he reached Kintyre, whence his body was borne to Iona.[2]

---

[1] Anecdotes of Olave the Black.   [2] Anecdotes of Olave the Black.

After this, Duncan the son of Dugall MacSomerled was the only member of the family who seems
to have had any territorial position in the Isles;
in fact, so far as history records, he was the sole
representative of the line who left behind him a
traceable posterity. As Duncan de Lorn he
witnessed a charter to the Earl of Athole, and
as Duncan de Ergalita he signs the letter and
oath to the Pope of the nobles of Scotland,
on the treaty of Ponteland, in 1244.[1] Duncan's
son, King Ewin or, as he is designated in the
Sagas, King John, was the son of this Duncan,
and the representative of the family in 1263.
Historians have assumed that King John or Ewin
was the father of Alexander de Ergadia who, with
his son John, was the determined enemy of Bruce
in the war of Scottish independence. Now it is
almost as certain as any historical fact connected
with so remote a period can be, that Ewin of Lorn,
the son of Duncan, left no male issue. It seems
clear that his line terminated with two heiresses,
one of whom married the King of Norway and the
other Alexander of Isla, son of Angus Mor. It is
on record that Alexander of Isla, through his wife
Juliana, possessed lands in the island of Lismore,[2]
which was part of the lordship of Lorn, and that
Edward I. summoned Edward Baliol before him for
preventing them from enjoying possession of these
lands. It is well established that, according to
the feudal and Celtic laws of territorial possession,
females could not inherit lands except on the failure
of heirs male. Only because of such failure do we
find, first Christina, and afterwards Amie Macruairi,
in the line of Roderick, the son of Reginald, inherit-

---

[1] Records of Beauly Priory. [2] Orig. Par.

SEAL OF REGINALD, SON OF SOMERLED.

REGINALDUS REX INSULARUM, DOMINUS DE ERGILE.

1164-1207

REVERSE SIDE OF THE SEAL OF REGINALD.

ing the patrimony of the family. Hence the
succession of Juliana of Lorn to à portion at
least of her father's lands, forbids us to believe that
he left any sons, and strongly suggests the conclusion
that the male descendants of Dugall MacSomerled
terminated with Ewin. Supposing, however, for the
sake of argument, not only that Dugall MacSomerled
was the oldest son, but that Alexander de Ergadia,
who flourished in the time of Bruce, was his direct

KILKERRAN LOCH, KINTYRE.

descendant, this is very far from proving that the
Clan Dugall are the senior branch of the Clan Cholla.
In truth, such a conclusion is impossible in view of
the fact that, in 1388 the line of Alexander de
Ergadia terminated in an heiress, who brought over
the lordship of Lorn to her husband, John Stewart.
It is thus clear to a demonstration that the Clan
Dugall, of whom the family of Dunolly is the leading
branch, cannot, on any supposition, be traced back

in the male line to Dugall, the son of Somerled.
Although we are not writing a history of the Clan
Dugall, it is desirable that their real origin should,
if possible, be pointed out, if for no other purpose
than to give the Clan Donald their true position as
the main branch of the Clan Cholla in the Western
Highlands. An opportunity for looking at the
question in its true bearings will immediately occur.
Meantime our discussion of the question of seniority
as between Reginald and Dugall, the sons of
Somerled, has necessarily led us to anticipate, and
we must now take up the thread of our history
where we dropped it. Reginald, the son of Somerled, died in 1207. This is the date given by
the Book of Clanranald,[1] and is probably correct.
The seal adhibited to his charter to Paisley Abbey
is thus described :—" In the middle of the seal on
one side, a ship filled with men-at-arms ; on the
reverse side, the figure of an armed man on horseback with a sword drawn in his hand."[2] By Fonia,
daughter of the Earl of Moray, Reginald had three
sons—Donald, Roderick, and Dugall. Most authorities mention only two sons, excluding Dugall ; nor
do we find any record of him in the division of his
father's lands. Yet the MS. of 1450,[3] the most
valuable genealogical authority we possess, includes
Dugall among the sons of Reginald ; and not only
so, but traces the descent of the Clan Dugall to him
instead of to the son of Somerled.

As a matter of fact, and in view of all that has
been said, this is the only theory of the descent of
the Clan Dugall that appears on the evidence

[1] Reliquiæ Celticæ, p. 157.

[2] Orig. Par. Scot., vol. I., p. 2.

[3] The Book of Balimote agrees with the 1450 MS. in this respect, while
the Book of Leocan derives the Clan Dugall from Dugall MacSomerled.

possible to adopt; and the value of the testimony of the 1450 MS. on this question is immensely enhanced when we remember, that it was in the years during which the writer of that MS. flourished that the Dunolly family, the undoubted heads of their race, were invested by Stewart of Lorn in the possession of the lands from which they derive their designation, and which they have held down to the present day.[1]

According to the Irish annalists, the sons of Reginald were men of very different temper and calibre from their father. They were found, like him sometimes, among their Irish kinsmen, but never as messengers of peace. The following extract illustrates what manner of men they were :— "Thomas MacUchtry and the sons of Reginald, son of Somerled, came to Doire Chalhuim Chille with 70 ships, and the town was greatly injured by them. O'Domhnaill and they completely destroyed the country."[2]

Donald succeeded his father in the lordship of South Kintyre, Isla, and other island possessions; while Roderick obtained North Kintyre,[3] Bute, and the lands of Garmoran, extending from Ardnamurchan to Glenelg, all of which formed the possessions of Angus MacSomerled; Lochaber passing to the Comyns.

Oirthirghael and the Isles were now divided into a number of little principalities, entirely in the possession of the house of Somerled and of Reginald of Man as feudatory of Norway. The vicinity of such enterprising neighbours could hardly fail to be irksome to the Scottish Kings, and the thirteenth century witnessed a number of efforts on their part

[1] Orig. Par. Scot.   [2] Annals of the Four Masters.
[3] Orig. Par. Scot., vol. II., p. 21.

to bring these regions into subjection. Alexander II.
had no sooner ascended the throne in 1214, than
the old disturbers of the realm, the MacWilliams
and MacHeths, rose again in rebellion, and were
assisted by the potentates of the Isles. In 1221,
after peace had been restored and the royal
influence consolidated, Alexander, fired by resentment against the house of Somerled, made a
descent upon Argyll with the view of carrying out
a long cherished scheme for its conquest. The
elements however were unpropitious ; his fleet was
driven back by a storm, and as winter was coming
on the attempt meanwhile was abandoned. The
following year the King fitted out a fresh expedition.
According to John of Fordun and Wyntoun, who
alone record the enterprise, the latter in doggerel
lines,[1] Alexander, in the course of his campaign, was
successful in conquering and enforcing the allegiance
of the Celtic chiefs of Argyll. Many it is said
submitted, gave hostages and large sums of money
as an earnest of future allegiance ; while others less
able to defend themselves, and dreading the royal
vengeance, abandoned their possessions and fled—
some to Galloway, where they afterwards proved of
service to their kinsmen in that region ; others to
the protection of their more fortunate kindred in the
Isles. What the alleged conquest of Argyll in 1222
actually amounted to, it is really difficult to say, in
the absence of historical testimony more reliable
than that of the chroniclers referred to. That in
some instances the descent of the Scots upon
Argyll resulted in the displacement of the Gaelic
chiefs, is in the nature of things probable enough.
On such an hypothesis we can easily account for the

[1] See Appendix.

disappearance of the descendants of Somerled, other than those by Ragnhildis, from a territorial position in Oirthirghael, a disappearance which would otherwise be somewhat difficult to explain. Whatever results the campaign of 1222 may have had in other respects, it made little or no impression upon the power or position of the Island Princes. As evidence of this we find Alexander II., after wintering in Aberdeen,[1] coming back to the west of Scotland, and using every means diplomatic and otherwise to secure Argyll and the Isles. The Clan Cholla were still a formidable problem in that region. The King had also to reckon with Norway, and he now sent ambassadors to the Court of Haco, empowering them to treat for the purchase of the Isles. Their proposals were treated with scant favour, and from that time down to 1249, matters in Argyll and the Isles continued very much in the same position. In that year Alexander, taking advantage of the death of the Norwegian King of Man and the Isles, collected a large force and proceeded to the Hebrides, declaring "that he would not desist until he had set his standard east on the cliffs of Thurso, and had reduced under himself all the provinces which the Norwegian monarch possessed to the westward of the German Ocean."[2]

The King sailed round Kintyre with his fleet expecting to find Donald of Isla overawed by such a formidable and powerful armament; but it does not appear that the island lord showed any symptoms of submission. The King now made overtures to Ewin of Lorn, whom he sought, unsuccessfully, to win from the Norwegian alliance. Ewin had recently been entrusted by Haco with the administration

---

[1] Wyntoun's Chronicle, Book VII., c. 9.   [2] Saga of Hakon IV.

of affairs connected with the Norwegian possessions
in the Isles. He held the castle of Kiarnaburgh on
the West Coast of Mull and other strongholds in
the name of the King of Norway; and having set
before himself the ambitious design of becoming
master both of Man and the Isles, he was not likely
to take part in Alexander's campaign for a reward
which must, in any case, have fallen short of what
he hoped ultimately to secure. Whether Alexander
in these circumstances would have pursued the
campaign further or to a successful issue it is
difficult to say, for death arrested all his plans in
the small island of Kerrera in the 52nd year of his
age. His army broke up and the campaign closed.
Ewin of Lorn, taking advantage of the lull that
followed the storm, made elaborate preparations
towards the accomplishment of his scheme of taking
possession of Man and the Isles. He invaded Man
and declared himself King; but his reign was short-
lived. He had no sooner taken possession of the
throne than a message was sent to Haco informing
him of the position of affairs. The Norwegian King
invoked the aid of Donald of Isla and his brother
Roderick, and this having been promptly and
effectively given, Ewin, who was obnoxious to
the great majority of the Manxmen, was driven
from the Island, and compelled to take refuge in his
own domains.[1] Donald, by rendering this timely
assistance, secured the friendship of the King of
Norway, and the alliance which was thus cemented
between the family of Isla and the Norwegian Crown
continued without interruption until the close of the
Norwegian occupation of the Isles.

[1] Chronicles of Man; Torfaeus.

King Alexander III. being a minor for many years after his father's death, and Ewin of Lorn having been humbled by his recent defeat, Donald of Isla had little to fear from enemies from without, and during the remainder of his life we hear of him no more as a man of war. That his life had been a stormy one, and not altogether free from the crimes and excesses common in that age, the traditional historian leads us to infer.[1] The same authority informs us that he and his uncle Dugall having discorded, probably about some barren promontory in Mull, the latter was killed by Donald. After this King Alexander sent a messenger to Argyll, Sir William Rollock, to demand of Donald allegiance for his lands. Sir William got decapitation for his pains. Still further, and to fill the cup to the brim, this man of blood and iron put to death Callum Aluinn, the son of Gillies, the son of Somerled, and banished Gillies himself to Ireland, where some of his descendants remain to this day. It is not surprising that these deeds of violence, considered enormities even in an age when might was right, combined with his early depredations in the North of Ireland, should when reflection came have caused qualms of conscience in Donald's breast, which only the unction of the supreme fount of spiritual authority on earth could assuage. To Rome, therefore, the conscience-stricken chief made a pilgrimage.

We trust that in such an emergency the elements were propitious, and that, after a long voyage, when the penitent descendant of Conn arrived in the Eternal City, accompanied by seven priests — a sacred number of a sacred order—he was not left

[1] Hugh Macdonald's MS.

outside by the successor of St Peter longer than the
interests of discipline absolutely demanded. Donald,
having made his confession in the only tongue with
which he was familiar, and this having been made
intelligible to the Holy Father by the learned clerics
from the Isles, received the absolution that he
craved. Having thus obtained the forgiveness of
the Church, it would appear that Donald, in his
future relations with that body, brought forth fruits
worthy of repentance.[1] Like his father and many
of his successors, he enriched the Church with
valuable gifts of land.[2] From this Donald the Clan
takes its name, a fact which indicates his prominence
in the history of his race, and the impression he
created on the age in which he flourished. It is also
observable that in his time, or more probably shortly
after it, fixed patronymics came into existence in
the Highlands, while in the Lowlands the surnames
adopted were generally territorial. The collateral
branches of the house of Somerled after Donald
were more or less independent of one another,
and in order to avoid confusion, such patronymics
as Macruairi, MacDugall, MacAllister, and others
became fixed. After this period, or at anyrate after
the middle of the fourteenth century, there is no
record of a new patronymic springing from the
house of Somerled. The word Donald, which in
Gaelic is *Domhnull*, appears in its oldest form as
Domvall = Dumno Valdos, "a world wielder."[3]

According to the historian of Sleat, Donald died
at Skipness in 1289, but this date is clearly
incorrect, for many years before then his successor
was head and representative of the family. The

[1] What amount of credence is to be attached to this story it is difficult to
say. It does not possess much *ex facie* probability.

[2] Orig. Par. Scot., Chart. of Paisley.

[3] *Vide* Book of Deer.

date of his death is very probably prior to 1249, for before that date we find his son Angus giving a charter for part of his lands in Kintyre.[1] He was buried in that sacred isle in which, after life's fitful fever, many of the Kings of Innse-Gall peacefully repose. By a daughter of Walter, the High Steward of Scotland, he had two sons— Angus, afterwards known as Angus Mor, and Alexander.

During the minority of Alexander III., comparative quietness reigned over Argyll and the Isles. It was different in other parts of Scotland. The kingdom was torn asunder by factions among the nobility, and it was not until 1262, when the young King came of age, that comparative order was restored. Once more the idea of annexing the Isles became the policy of the Crown; and Alexander III., adopting the methods of his father, used every means, both by conciliation and aggression, to bring the Celtic chiefs of the west under his control. He made special efforts to secure the allegiance of Angus Mor of Isla, and seems so far to have succeeded in disarming the opposition of the Island lord.[2] He held his infant son Alexander as hostage,[3] and an instrument was drawn out declaring the instant forfeiture of Angus if he deserted the King's cause. The hollow allegiance proved of short duration.

[1] Orig. Par. Scot., Kilkerran.

[2] Matth. Paris, 770. Antiquarian Transactions, 367-8. Scriptum obligatorium Anegi Dononaldi quod exhaeredetur si forisfecerit contra regem Scotiae.—Sir Joseph Ayloffe's Calendar of Ancient Charters, p. 328. Litera baronum de Ergadia quod fideliter servient regi sub poena exhaeredationis contra Anegum filium Dovenaldi, quod omnes insurgent contra ipsum, si non fecerit voluntatem regis.—Ibid, p. 342.

[3] In the Scottish Chamberlain's Accounts there is the following entry :— " For the expenses of the son of Angus, who was the son of Donald, with his nurse and a waiting woman for two weeks, the King paid 79 shillings and nine pence."

For some time matters had been ripening for a decisive conflict between Scotland and Norway as to the possession of the Isles. We have already seen that, after the death of Angus MacSomerled and his sons in Moidart in 1192, their possessions including Bute, passed to Reginald, and thereafter to his son Roderick. As already pointed out, James the son of Angus MacSomerled left a daughter, who married Alexander, son and heir of Walter Stewart of Scotland, and he in his wife's name claimed the island of Bute. Roderick resisted this aggression with all the force at his command, but he was ultimately dispossessed and outlawed. At the same time, in the North-west of Scotland, events were hastening the inevitable crisis. An assault was made upon the Norwegian Kingdom of Man and the Isles by Ferchar Macintaggart, a son of the Red Priest of Applecross, and the first of the Earls of Ross of that family. He had been knighted by Alexander II. for his services in quelling an insurrection in Moray,[1] and by the same King he was advanced to the dignity of Earl of Ross for services rendered in the suppression of a rising of the men of Galloway.[2] Macintaggart and several of his vassals made a ruthless descent upon Skye. According to the Norse Sagas, they sacked villages, desecrated churches, and in wanton fury raised children on the points of their spears and shook them until they fell to the ground. Scottish aggressiveness had thus, both north and south, displayed such rapacity and violence that the Island Chiefs, having taken counsel together, resolved to solicit the intervention of Norway. From this conference Ewin of

[1] Chronica de Mailros, 117.
[2] Chronica de Mailros, 145. Orig. Par. Scot., vol. II., 486.

Lorn absented himself. Smarting under the remembrance of the treatment formerly dealt out to him by Haco, he seemed disposed to make common cause with Alexander.

Haco, on having been informed of the outrages perpetrated on his vassals in the Northern Isles, resolved upon immediate action. Having equipped a large fleet, he set sail from Herlover on the 7th July, and coming by Shetland and Orkney, he arrived in the Isles about the middle of August. In Skye he was joined by the barons of the North Isles, and, going south by Mull to Kerrera, by Dugall,[1] the son of Roderick. Angus Mor of Isla and Kintyre soon afterwards joined the Norwegian forces, and Allan, the son of Roderick, was also associated with them in the campaign.[2] All the princes of the House of Somerled, with the exception of Ewin of Lorn, appear to have formed an alliance with the Norwegians in this memorable expedition. Roderick of Bute, who had been their envoy to Norway, accompanied the Norsemen on their voyage to the Sudoreys, and during the hostilities that ensued the knowledge of the western seas which his piratical career had enabled him to acquire proved of much service. The losses and indignities which he had suffered at the hands of the Scottish King and his nobles spurred him on to many revengeful deeds.

Divisions of Haco's fleet were sent hither and thither to devastate and plunder on the coasts of Argyll, led principally by Angus Mor, Roderick, and his sons Dugall and Allan. Sailing up Loch Long, and drawing their boats across the isthmus of Tarbat, they came to Loch Lomond, and penetrating to the country of Lennox, on the far side of that

---

[1] Haco's Expedition, 77   [2] Ibid.

famous loch, they laid it waste with fire and sword.
The result of the early part of Haco's expedition was
the re-establishment of the Norwegian authority in
the Northern Isles and the restoration of Bute to
Roderick.[1]

Several overtures for peace passed between Haco
and Alexander, but with no definite result. Delay
was the policy of the Scots, and as the equinoctial
gales were within measurable distance—the summer
being past—time was in their favour. Haco was
far from the base of operations, and the difficulty of
maintaining his grasp of the Isles on the flank of a
growing power like Scotland, demanded sacrifices
more than commensurate with the interests at
stake. One struggle more was, however, to take
place. The battle of Largs was by no means the
decisive conflict which it was described to have been.
The exaggerated accounts of Scottish historians,
whose imaginations leave 25,000 Norsemen dead
on the field, are unworthy of belief. On that
memorable occasion, doubtless, the Scots led by
their valiant King fought with determined courage ;
but the battle on land was indecisive, and were it
not that the elements rose in their fury, driving the
fleet of Haco from the coast and dispersing it,
victory might have rested on the Norwegian arms.
Be this as it may, the battle of Largs did not in any
sense result in the conquest of the Western Isles by
Scotland. The cession of the Isles was accomplished,
not by conquest, but by diplomatic negotiations,
carried to a successful issue in 1266, three
years afterwards. The terms of agreement were
that 4000 merks sterling be paid to Norway,
together with an annual tribute or quit-rent of

---

[1] Haco's Expedition, p. 65.

100 merks sterling, called the Annual of Norway, to be paid in the Church of Saint Magnus in Orkney. The King of Man became a vassal of Alexander, and the parties to the Treaty undertook their respective obligations under a penalty of 10,000 merks, to be exacted by the Pope. Permission was accorded to the Norse inhabitants of the Isles either to emigrate to Norway or, if they preferred it, to remain under the new conditions. It is probable, though history does not record the fact, that many availed themselves of this permission to return to Norway.

From the generous terms which Alexander offered to his opponents in the Isles and on the mainland, it is clear that he did not feel altogether secure in the possession of his new dominions, and thus believed a conciliatory policy to be the safest and best. John of Fordun states that a military force was sent to the Isles against the chiefs who had joined Haco, and that some of them were executed and all reduced. Fortunately for themselves, they were only executed in John of Fordun's imagination. What we find, on the contrary, is that even Roderick, the prime mover of Haco's expedition, continued in possession of all his extensive territories, with the exception of Bute, which he had to resign. If any one deserved hanging, from the Scottish point of view, Roderick was the man. His fate was a very different one. His family became known afterwards as the Macruairis of Garmoran and the North Isles. They were often styled *de Insulis*, as were other cadets of the house of Somerled for centuries thereafter—the main line alone using the designation *de Ile*. Ewin of Lorn, who although hostile to Norway seems to have preserved a judicious neutrality, continued to enjoy his ancestral possessions, while Angus Mor of Isla remained unmolested in his extensive territories.

It is not easy to define with clearness the exact relation of the House of Somerled to Norway and Scotland before and after the years 1263-66. The Southern Isles having been handed down by Somerled as an independent possession, were similarly held by his sons and grandsons. There are certain passages in the Saga on Haco's expedition, which convey the impression that these Southern Isles were re-conveyed to Norway. It is stated that Angus Mor was willing to surrender his lands to Haco, who afterwards, we are told, " bestowed Ila, taken by his troops, on the valiant Angus, the generous distributor of the beauteous ornaments of the hands."[1] It cannot be true that the territories of Angus Mor were both willingly surrendered by him, and at the same time taken from him by force. The series of events leading to the battle of Largs; the mission of Roderick to Norway as the ambassador of the Island chiefs; Haco's response to their representations in the equipment of his great armament, all this forbids the supposition of any hostile movement against the Island Lords. If Haco desired their loyal co-operation, it would have been bad policy to begin with a forcible annexation of their possessions. The association of Haco with the princes of the House of Somerled was neither more nor less than the formation of a league, offensive and defensive, to repel the aggressiveness of the Scottish realm. If Norway ceded the Southern Isles to Scotland in 1266, she gave over what she never possessed since these Isles were wrested from Godred of

[1] The Raven's Ode, p. 57.

Man in 1156.. There is not a scrap of evidence to show that from the days of Somerled down to Bruce's Charter to Angus Og, a period of 150 years, there was any effective acknowledgment of superiority by the princes of the Southern Isles either to Norway or Scotland, if we except Bute alone. It is now evident that a new chapter in the history of the Isles is opening. The feudal system has, theoretically at least, knit into a complete whole the social fabric of the Scottish nation. But, with the people of the Highlands, and particularly with the Lords of the Isles, the superiority of the Crown was but a name, and for hundreds of years there was witnessed a continual struggle on the part of the Celtic system to assert itself against the claims of feudal Scotland. In this struggle the Kings of Innse-Gall were the principal actors. Circumstances at times may have compelled them to accept of charters for their lands and render an insincere allegiance; but the traditions of independence long survived, and are largely accountable for the turbulence and disorder that mark the history of the Scottish Highlands.

CHAPTER V.

BRUCE AND THE CLAN CHOLLA.—1284-1329.

Death of Alexander III., and subsequent Anarchy.—Angus Mor's
Relation to Scottish Parties.—Convention of Estates Settling
Crown.—Angus Mor favours the Bruce Interest.—Death of
Angus Mor.—Division of Territories. — Alexander of Isla
Supports England.—Defeat by Bruce, Captivity, and Death.
—Angus Og joins Bruce.—Bannockburn.—Death of Angus
Og.

ALEXANDER III. lived for twenty-two years after the
battle of Largs.   His death, in 1284, deprived Scotland of one of its wisest rulers, in whose time she
made considerable progress in settled government and
the arts of peace.   His tragic end was the cause of a
series of disasters unparalleled in the darkest period of
Scottish history.   It was felt by the thoughtful
spirits of the time that the land was on the brink of
unprecedented afflictions :—

> When Alexandyr our king was dede
> That Scotland led in lowe and le,
> Away was sons of ale and brede
> Of wyne and wax, of gamyn and gle.
> Oure gold is changed into lede—
> Christ born into virgynyte
> Succour Scotland and remede
> That stodt is in perplexyte.[1]

The death of Alexander's heiress, the Maid of
Norway, on her way to Scotland, in 1290, introduced
still further confusion into the affairs of the realm,

[1] Wyntoun.

FAC-SIMILE OF THE LETTER OF ANGUS OG, LORD OF THE ISLES, TO EDWARD I, 1301.

and Edward I., one of the ablest, as well as most ambitious, of English soldiers and statesmen, sought to bring the distracted country to acknowledge the claim of paramount authority advanced by England since the days of William the Lion, but never actually admitted. The claims of Balliol and Bruce to the crown; the short and humiliating reign of the former; the valiant stand for Scottish independence made by Sir William Wallace; the rise, the struggles, the hardships, the eventual triumph of the younger Bruce, and finally his vindication of his country's freedom, all these followed one another in close and somewhat rapid succession.

The light which the records of the time throw upon the relationship subsisting between the Chief of the Clan Cholla and the other leaders in the political turmoil of that period is somewhat dim and uncertain. It is difficult, therefore, if not impossible, to arrive at a satisfactory conclusion as to the exact position and attitude of the Island Chief amid so many conflicting and tumultuous elements. Reference has already been made to the state of matters in the Highlands and Islands at the time of Haco's expedition, and the allocation of lands that followed on the Scoto-Norse treaty of 1266. The assertion of independence characteristic of the Clan Cholla is borne out by the treatment meted out to Angus Mor of Isla by Alexander III. Angus, as a matter of policy, had espoused the cause of Haco of Norway rather than that of Alexander of Scotland. The formidable armament, headed by Haco, appeared more than a match for the Scottish fleet, and Angus Mor, consulting the interests and independence of his own domains, unhesitatingly threw in his lot with what seemed to be the stronger power. In any case, whether the

G

victory lay with Alexander or Haco, Angus would probably have held his own.

King Alexander, however, notwithstanding the opposition of the Island Chief, does not seem to have interfered effectively with his territorial position. There are indications, doubtless, that towards the end of Alexander's reign Angus appears in relations towards the crown which are distinctly of a hostile nature. Evidence of this is afforded by letters which were addressed to the other barons of Argyll, in 1282, calling upon them to serve the King faithfully against *Angus filius Dovenaldi* under pain of being disinherited.[1] If Angus exhibited on this occasion a spirit of insubordination against the State, he was not solely responsible for the disturbances which arose in Argyll and the Isles in 1482. In these the MacDougalls of Lorn and their allies were largely involved, and the disorder seems to have arisen to such a height as to demand the interference of the Earl of Buchan, who was the Constable of Scotland.[2] Beyond this there is nothing to shew that the Chief of the Clan Cholla was seriously involved in the intrigues of the period, or that he was keenly or aggressively associated with any of the factious elements into which the Scottish nation was then unhappily divided. That Angus Mor was, shortly after this, on friendly terms with King Alexander appears from the circumstance that he was one of the three nobles of Argyll who, in 1284, attended the Convention of Estates convened to settle the succession to the throne, the other two being Alexander MacDugall of Lorn and Allan Macruari of Garmoran.[3] At this meeting Margaret,

---

[1] Act Parl. Scot. Appendix.   [2] Rymer's Fœdera, vol. II., p. 205.
[3] Rymer's Fœdera, p. 760.

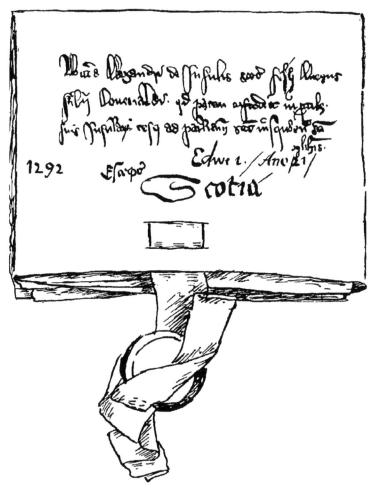

A FAC-SIMILE OF LETTER BY ANGUS MOR, AND ALEX., LORDS OF THE ISLES,
TO EDWARD I.

commonly called the Maid of Norway, grand-
daughter of the King, was declared heiress to the
throne.   It is difficult to account for the presence
at this meeting of such men as Angus Mor and
his kinsmen, whose aims proved afterwards to be
diametrically opposed to those of the King and the
majority of his Parliament.   From what followed in
subsequent years, we are warranted in concluding
that the presence of the descendants of Somerled at
the Convention in 1282 did not arise from sincere
concurrence in the decision arrived at, but from the
desire to conform to the royal summons.   Another
Parliament met at Scone in April, 1286—about two
years after the King's death—at which six guardians
of the realm were appointed.   In this Parliament a
keen discussion took place between the partisans of
Bruce and Balliol regarding the succession to the
throne, which resulted in the formation of a strong
party against the succession of the Maid of Norway.
In September of the same year a meeting of this
party took place at Turnberry, the seat of the
elder Bruce, and among those present were Angus
of Isla and his son, Alexander.   Again, in 1288,
when the Council of the Regency came to be
divided in opinion regarding the succession, the
Chief of Clan Cholla formed a bond of association
with James, High Steward of Scotland, John his
brother, Walter Earl of Menteith, and his two
sons, the Earl of Dunbar, and others who favoured
the claims of Bruce.[1]   There is thus no evidence,
actual or inferred, but rather the opposite, that
Angus Mor ever played a part inimical to the
interests of the family of Bruce, although the
frailties of old age prevented his interposing
actively on their behalf.   The testimony of history

---

[1] Clanranald History, 1819, p. 31.

is clear in favour of the view that he continued
steadfast in his support of the claims of the elder
Bruce, while he was equally consistent in his
opposition to those of Balliol, even after the latter
had been raised to the shadowy honour of king-
ship as the vassal of Edward I.   In 1292 King
John Balliol ordered Alexander of Argyll and his
baillies of Lochaw to summon Sir Angus, the son
of Donald, and others to do him homage within
fifteen days after Easter wheresoever he might be
within Scotland.   Though his citation was repeated
in 1293, Angus Mor of Isla seems to have given no
response either to the one or the other.[1]   He lived
for a part of the last decade of the 13th century ; but
though, with Byron, we "like to be particular in
dates," the exact year of his death cannot easily
be determined.   From the meagre annals of his
time, we can gather that Angus was not behind
his predecessors in those characteristics of courage
and chivalry that always distinguished the chiefs of
Clan Cholla.   He died, according to the Book of
Clanranald, at his seat in Isla, and was buried at
"Columkill, the sacred storehouse of his predecessors, and guardian of their bones."

The extensive territories of Angus Mor were
divided among his sons.   Alexander succeeded him
in Isla and other territories on the mainland of
Argyll ; Angus received the lordship of Kintyre ;
while the lands of Ardnamurchan were bestowed
by King Balliol upon John *Sprangach*,[2] the
youngest of his sons.

Alexander of Isla appears for the first time on
the historical stage with his father at the meeting
already referred to, at Turnberry, to further the
Bruce interest.   In 1291, the next time he comes

[1] Scot. Act. Parl.   [2] Sprangach signifies the "bold."

before us, he is found acting an entirely different character, giving the oath of allegiance to the English King.[1] He had become closely allied by marriage with the family of Lorn, and through them associated with the English interest, and although in his father's lifetime he does not appear to have taken a leading part on either side, now, as the struggle becomes keener, we find him throwing the whole weight of his power and influence into the scale of southern aggression. There were, at an early stage of the conflict, many letters addressed to him from the English Court and in the interests of the English party, and from the rewards which afterwards followed, the services which he rendered to that cause seem to have been very considerable.[2]

Although the House of Isla has at this stage begun to take the part of England in the effort to accomplish the conquest of Scotland, it is only on an inadequate view of the situation that the historian can pronounce its representatives to be lacking in true patriotism. The Scottish claim to the Western Isles was of too recent date to admit of a strong feeling of loyalty to the Crown in that region ; and to accuse the Island princes of that time of a lack of patriotism in the part they played is a pure anachronism, and ignores the political conditions of the time. Besides all this, it must not be forgotten that the sympathies of the Lords of the Isles must have been with the old Celtic system, which was only gradually disappearing before the influence of Teutonic culture; that they regarded

---

[1] Similiter Alexander de Agarithell dominus de Lorun & Alexander de Isles, filius Anegu filii Donevauldi, sacramentum prestiterunt de se fideliter, &c.—Ayloffo's Cal. of Ancient Charters, p. 291.

[2] Fœdera Anglia.

the Norman barons who had supplanted the old
Mormaors not as the real children of the soil, but
as strangers and interlopers in the land, and that
the Crown itself, as the keystone in the arch of
feudalism, must have appeared to them in the
light of a comparatively modern institution, and
lacking in the lustre of a venerable antiquity.
Hence there is nothing that need suprise us in
the fact that, after the death of Angus Mor, his
son and successor, Alexander of Isla, is found
upon the side opposed to Scottish independence.

In the year 1295 we find the English King
summoning King John Balliol before him to answer
for withholding the lands of Lismore from *Alexander
de Insulis et Julianæ uxore sua.*[1] When Edward
received the submission of the Scottish nobility in
1296, we are told that a grant of one hundred
pounds worth of land was given to Alexander of
Isla for services rendered to the English King.[2] We
find still further that Alexander held the office of
Admiral of the Western Isles under the English
Crown, after the ignominious termination of Balliol's
reign, and it appears that the position was not by
any means a sinecure. From letters addressed to
the English King in 1297,[3] it is evident that his
lieutenant, however strenuously he exercised his
commission, found it well nigh an impossible task
to quell the insubordination and turbulence of the
Western chiefs. Among the notables accused of
lawless excesses in regions subject to the authority
of Edward, there is reference to Roderick, the son of
Allan, grandson of Roderick of Bute ; also to Ranald,
another son of Allan, and brother of the said

---

[1] Rotuli Scotiæ, vol. I., p. 21.   [2] Patent Roll 24, Ed. I., 7, 1296, Sep. 12.
[3] Anderson's Historical Documents of Scotland, vol. II., p. 187.

Roderick, as well as to Lachlan MacRuari, probably
a brother of the former two.[1]   The MacRuari family
seem to have inherited a large share of the piratical
tendencies of the ancient Vikings, and we find these
Highland rovers, in 1297, invading and carrying
slaughter and depradations into the islands of
Skye and Lewis, and burning the ships in the
service of the King.   It is against Alexander of
Lorn, however, also known as *de Ergadia*, as
the arch offender, the leader and instigator in these
irregularities, that the King's Admiral makes the
chief complaint ; and this is rather a singular
fact, in view of the strong support which, very
shortly thereafter, was given by Alexander and his
son John to the English interest.   In the previous
year, 1296, Edward had received Alexander's submission, along with that of other Scottish noblemen,
at Elgin, and he seems to have been subjected to a
short term of imprisonment ; but immediately after
his liberation he, along with his accomplices, committed the crimes against the lieges to which the
Lord of the Isles makes reference.   One of his
letters he winds up with a mild reminder of
expenses incurred in the various expeditions conducted that year in the King's service, as well as
to a sum of 500 pounds promised him the previous
year, but not yet paid, showing that the sinews
of war, even in that far past time, were no less a
necessity than they are now.   It is also interesting
to note that, at the end of another letter, in which
he invokes the royal aid in bringing the culprits to
justice, he seeks to be excused for not having his

---

[1] Ranald we take to be here the equivalent of the Latin Rolandus, it and
Lachlan being MacRuari names, and to be met with in the genealogy of the
1450 MS.

own proper seal in his possession, and thus having to adhibit to "these presents" the seal of Juliana, his wife.[1]

From the foregoing circumstances it appears that Alexander de Ile had received ample recognition of his services to the King of England, a recognition which stimulated him to still more zealous efforts in his patron's cause. From 1297 to 1308 we find no further mention of Alexander, though in the interval it is likely enough he did not allow his sword to rust in its sheath. In 1306 Robert Bruce was crowned at Scone, a King without a kingdom, and this was the beginning of a career as interesting as the most thrilling pages in the history of chivalry and romance. The enemies of his house now draw closer to one another, and a strong combination was formed against the heroic King. Alexander of Isla was a powerful and important factor in this combination. So in 1308 we find him fighting against Bruce in the district of Galloway, aided by MacDowall, lord of that region. This district continued obstinately to resist the King's authority and was at the time occupied by English troops. Bruce sent his brother Edward against them, and he prosecuted the campaign with such vigour and success that he soon reduced the country, defeated the combined forces of Sir Roland of Galloway and Alexander of Isla on the banks of the Dee, and compelled the inhabitants to swear allegiance to his brother the King.[2] In the pursuit that followed the dispersion of the Gallowegians and the Islesmen, Edward Bruce took prisoner "The Prince of the Isles."[3] Alexander,

---

[1] Historical Documents of Scotland.   [2] Rymer's Fœdera.
[3] Fordun a Hearne, p. 1005.

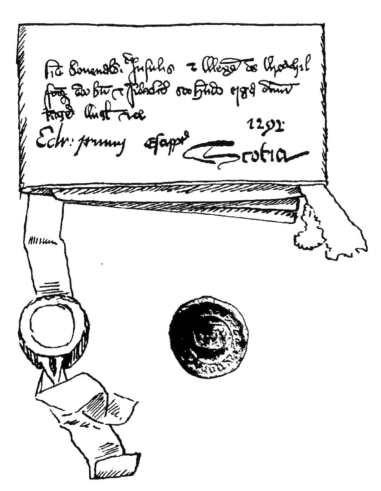

THE ABOVE SEAL OF ALEX. LORD OF THE ISLES IS ATTACHED TO A DOCUMENT
IN THE RECORD OFFICE, LONDON, A FAC-SIMILE OF THE SUPERSCRIPTION
OF WHICH IS HERE GIVEN.

however, very soon escaped from Edward Bruce's custody, and betook himself to the stronghold of Castle Swen, in North Knapdale.[1]   This fortress commanded the entrance to Lochswen, and was regarded as the key to the districts of Knapdale and Glassary.   As such, it was deemed a position of the greatest importance.   In this Castle King Robert Bruce, fresh from his victory over Alexander of Lorn at the Pass of Ben Cruachan, besieged the Lord of the Isles, and Alexander, after defending himself for several days with the utmost determination and bravery, was obliged to surrender to the King.   Bruce sent him forthwith a prisoner to Dundonald Castle in Kintyre, where he is said to have died soon after.   At all events we hear no more of Alexander of Isla in the struggle in which he had taken so prominent a part, and he falls to be buried out of sight amid the ruins of the cause he had so strenuously supported.   The fortunes of war had been unfavourable to him and to his family, and the representation and honours of *Siol Chuinn* pass for ever from their grasp. Alexander left four sons—Reginald, Black John, Angus, and Charles.   These and their progeny, victims of the fate which raised a younger brother to the dignity and honour of their father's house, lost the premier position in the Clan Cholla, though undoubtedly in the light of primogeniture they were the senior family of the line of Somerled.   Whether they preserved any vestige of their ancestral possessions ; whether in the subsequent history of the Clan their descendants left behind them a local

---

[1] In Buchanan's Account of the Campaign in Galloway, he mistakenly refers to Alexander as *Donaldus Insulanus*. The Lords of the Isles are a'l Donald with this historian.

habitation and a name, or whether through the lack
of territorial *prestige* and political influence the
family and name sank into insignificance, is a question
which, meanwhile, must be left unanswered, as it
will more fittingly fall to be dealt with under the
genealogical section of this work.

Angus Og Macdonald succeeded his brother
Alexander, in 1308, both in his lands and in the
chiefship of the Clan.   In tracing his career, we
must again traverse a portion of the ground of
general Scottish history embraced in the period
in which his predecessor flourished.   In 1301 we
find him equally zealous with his brother in his
efforts to hold the Western Isles of Scotland in
subjection to the English Crown, and along with
Hugh Bisset he appears in a capacity somewhat
similar to that which Alexander occupied four years
previously.[1]   In a letter addressed to the English
King, apparently written in October of that year,
he reports that up to the Lord's day immediately
preceding Michaelmas, he and the said Hugh Bisset
had been with the English fleet in the island of
Bute, and that, at the time he wrote, he was
awaiting the royal commands.   Apparently the
loyalty of Alexander of Lorn to the English
interest was still under suspicion.   Angus Og, in
his statement to the King, avoids committing
himself to any opinion, either favourable or adverse,
as to the fidelity of the Lord of Lorn.   He humbly
requests the King, if he believes in Lorn's loyalty,
to order him to assist himself and Bisset in the
reduction of the country ; but, failing such belief,

---

[1] Letter from Engus de Yle to King Edward respecting his proceedings
in the Isles of Scotland.   Rot. Scot. I., 40-41.

to forward written instructions that they may, with Divine help, be able to overcome Lorn and all other enemies of the King throughout the Western Isles. In the same letter the sons of Roderick MacAllan, who seem to have been at the time in the custody of Angus Og, and whose loyalty is guaranteed, are recommended to the royal favour; and it is requested that they be allowed to enter into a pledge and compact of fidelity to King Edward as to their future subjection to his sway.

After this period, until the memorable events of 1306, history does not seem to record with any degree of definiteness the conduct of Angus towards either of the parties that strove for the mastery in Scotland. There is not much reason, however, to doubt that he continued consistently to support the authority of Edward I. But in 1306 there was a marked change. Bruce's coronation at Scone on March 27 of that year was soon followed by the disastrous defeat at Methven, and shortly thereafter by an unsuccessful encounter with John MacDugall of Lorn at Dalry, near the end of Strathfillan. Notwithstanding the magnificent prowess and courage of the King, his followers were obliged to retire in presence of superior numbers. Under the guidance of the Earl of Lennox, whom Bruce, in the course of his subsequent wanderings, met on the shores of Lochlomond; and assisted by Sir Neil Campbell, whom he had sent on in advance, the King reached the district of Kintyre, the country of Angus Og. And here we must pause for a moment to enquire as to the causes of this apparently sudden change of front on the part of

the Lord of Kintyre,[1] and his truly Highland and
hospitable welcome to the royal fugitive. As to
the warmth and friendliness of his reception,
Barbour, the poetic biographer of Bruce, does not
leave us in doubt :—

> And Angus of Ile that tyme was Syr
> And lord and ledar of Kyntyr
> The King rycht weill resawyt he
> And undertook his man to be
> And he and his on mony wyes
> He abandowynt to his service
> And for mair sekyrness gaiff him syne
> His Castle of Donaverdyne.

In estimating the causes of this transference of
allegiance from Edward I. to Bruce, we may regard

Saddell

it as possible, though far from probable, that self
interest may have had some weight. We know
that the relations of Angus with the MacDugalls
of Lorn were not of the friendliest, and that an old
feud as to the possession of Mull had not yet been
set at rest. Had Bruce's star been in the ascendant
in 1306, we might understand that considerations of

---

[1] Though Angus' brother, Alexander, was at this time head of the Clan,
Angus, by disposition of his father, was Lord of Kintyre.

self interest might have weight in determining Angus' action.   But his friendliness to Bruce was first shewn at a time when his fortunes were most depressed and his prospects of success least hopeful ; and to all appearance there was nothing to gain, but everything to lose, by espousing the cause of the newly-crowned King of Scots.   The motives by which Angus Og was actuated at this critical moment in the fortunes of Scotland are not such as have been suggested, but are to be found in less interested and more noble grounds.   Angus Mor, as we have seen, was, in his latter years, a steady supporter of the claims of the elder Bruce, claims which appear to have been abandoned at the fall of Balliol in 1296, when Edward sought to reduce Scotland to the position of an English province. During the ten years that had elapsed since Balliol's deposition, the claims of the family of Bruce were in abeyance.   But now, in 1306, these are once more advanced with most chivalrous daring by the young Earl of Carrick, and Angus Og, adopting the friendly attitude of his father, becomes associated with the stirring events of the war of Scottish independence.[1]

Saddell, in whose castle the Lord of Kintyre first received Bruce, had many associations with the family of the Isles, not the least of these being that the dust of the "mighty Somerled" reposed within the sacred precincts of its monastery.   The Castle of Saddell, at the head of Saddell Bay, is a large, square battlemented tower still in a state of perfect preservation.   It measures 17 yards by 10, and

---

[1] That Angus Og and Bruce had been friends in bygone times seems implied in what Buchanan says, Liber VIII. 30:—"Et cum ne sic quidem sibi tutus a civium perfidia et hostium crudelitate videretur in Æbudas ad veterem quendam amicam transmisit."

is about 50 feet in height. The walls are of great thickness, without buttresses, and a spiral staircase leads through three sets of rooms up to the embattled parapet, whence a commanding view can be obtained of the western sea, as well as the shores of Kintyre and the picturesque isle of Arran. The inevitable dungeon in all its mediæval gloom is still in evidence as a testimony to the power and sway of these Western Island Lords. As Barbour informs us, Angus Og took his royal guest for greater security to the Castle of Dunaverty, another Kintyre stronghold, and residence of the Lords of the Isles. Situated in the parish of South-end, on Dunaverty Bay, five miles east by north of the Mull of Kintyre, it stood on the summit of a peninsula of pyramidal shape, 95 feet high, with a cliff descending perpendicular to the sea. Defended on the land side by a double rampart and ditch, it was, both as to site and construction, a fortress of remarkable strength, and commanded the approach to that part of Scotland where the sea between it and Ireland is narrowest. It was in after times the scene of some remarkable historical events. But there is now hardly a trace of the once almost impregnable walls; only on the everlasting rocks upon which it erstwhile stood do the Atlantic surges still dash and foam as in the days of Angus Og. Even here Bruce did not tarry long. He knew that his asylum in Kintyre could not be long concealed, and in the event of its becoming known prematurely, might expose his friendly host to the ireful vengeance of the English King. Angus now arranged to have Bruce quietly and secretly conveyed to

Rachrin,[1] a small island on the Irish coast inhabited and owned by members of the Clan Donald. Here the King, befriended by Angus Og, found a safe retreat during the following winter. This was the darkest time of Bruce's fortunes, and when the clouds rolled by and prosperity smiled upon the cause, Angus Og shared in the triumphs and rewards which accompanied the glorious day of revived Scottish freedom.

As the spring of 1307 drew nigh, the hopes of Bruce began to rise. The romantic interest that belonged to his career powerfully appealed to the female mind, and Christina of the Isles, the daughter and heiress of Allan MacRuari of Garmoran, was among the first to render important aid.[2] Receiving favourable news from the mainland, the King now began to meditate a descent upon Scotland, and having despatched messengers from his little garrison, he prepared to take his departure. In the beginning of 1307, Angus Og placed a chosen band of Highlanders under the command of Donald, son of Alastair Mor, and these having crossed to Arran, were joined by the King, who meanwhile had taken the decisive step of quitting Rachrin Isle.[3] From that day Angus Og of Isla, and with him the MacRuaris of Garmoran, were closely associated with Bruce in the task of vindicating the independence of Scotland. In his descent upon Carrick, where he "wan," if not his father's hall, at anyrate his father's territory, the Islesmen

---

[1] "On the south-west frae the promontory of Kintyre, upon the coast of Ireland, be four myle to land, layes an iyle callit Rachlaine, pertaining to Ireland, and possessit thir money zeires by Clan Donald of Kintyre, four myles longe and twa myle braid, guid land, inhabit and manurit."--Munro, 1549.

[2] Fordun.

[3] Clanranald History, 1819.

bore an honourable part. . The only cloud that darkened the political outlook in 1307 was the defeat and capture of the King's brothers, Thomas and Alexander, in Galloway by Roland MacDowall, lord of that region. It is recorded that Angus Og took part in that engagement, but escaped the disaster that overtook his friends.[1] Next year, as has already been narrated, this reverse was amply avenged. Not only so, but in 1308 the King wreaked signal vengeance upon the Mac-Dougalls of Lorn, the most implacable and determined of his foes. Marching towards Argyllshire, he totally defeated the Lords of Lorn, both father and son, took the Castle of Dunstaffnage, and laid the country waste. Alexander of Lorn was taken prisoner, and permitted to depart with a safe-conduct to England, where he is said to have died soon after in poverty.[2]

On Angus Og becoming the head of the Clan Donald, after the defeat and discomfiture of his brother Alexander, already referred to, he was able to cast the whole influence of his tribe upon the patriotic side of the struggle. And so, when at last the King's toils and perils were crowned with victory on the field of Bannockburn, Angus Og and his Islesmen, variously estimated at from 5000 to 10,000 men, were an indispensable factor in determining the fortunes of the day. The incidents of that ever memorable field are well-known to readers of Scottish history, and need not here be detailed, save so far as they relate to Macdonald of the Isles and his followers. These formed a corps of the rear or reserve

---

[1] Clanranald History, 1819. [2] Buchanan, Liber VIII., 34.

ANGUS OG AT BANNOCKBURN.-1314.

division, and was under the King's own immediate command :—

> " Sir Angus of the Isles and Bute alswae
> And of the plain lands he had mae
> Of armed men, a noble rout,
> In battle stalward was and stout.
> He said the rear guard he wad maw
> And even before him should gae
> The vanguard, and on either hand
> The other battle should be gangand,
> Behind ane side a little space ;
> And the King that behind him was
> Should see where there was maist maister
> And there relieve them with his banner."[1]

It was not until the critical moment arrived that the men of the Isles were summoned to the fray. The impetuous Celtic phalanx, like the stag hound held by the leash, burned to rush upon the foe; but their native ardour must needs be restrained until the King's experienced eye saw that their action should prove of most effect. Despite the enormous disparity of numbers, the chivalry of England was beginning to fall into most perilous confusion before Bruce's skilful dispositions and the stubborn courage of his army. It was then the King resolved to bring up his reserves. He directed Angus of Isla to march the Islesmen to the assistance of Edward Bruce, who was engaged with the enemy on the right, and addressed him in the memorable words which to this day illustrate the arms of the Clanranald Chiefs—" My hope is constant in thee." The stirring lines of Scott in "The Lord of the Isles" worthily interpret the spirit of that great and epoch-making scene :—

---

[1] Barbour's Bruce.

7

> " One effort more and Scotland's free !
> Lord of the Isles, my trust in thee
>   Is firm as Ailsa rock ;
> Rush on with Highland sword and targe,
> I with my Carrick spearmen charge ;
>   Now forward to the shock !"

Angus Og and his men exhibited the traditional valour of their race on that eventful day. Like the headlong rush of their native torrents as they dash and foam over rock and precipice, with the shrill note of the martial pipe rousing them to the onset, and with the wild ringing slogan of the hills echoing to the sky, the brave Islesmen swept on to meet the southern foe :—

> " At once the spears were forward thrown,
> Against the sun the broadswords shone ;
> The pibroch lent its maddening tone,
> And loud King Robert's voice was known—
> Carrick, press on ! they fail, they fail !
> Press on, brave sons of Innisgail,
>   The foe is fainting fast !"

The attack of the Highlanders and the men of Carrick at that critical moment settled the fortunes of the day, and the victory lay with the "fourth battle." The great army of 100,000 fled before the prudent valour of the Bruce and the determined bravery of the Scots, and Bannockburn was won.

As a reward for the undoubted services rendered by MacDonald of the Isles and his Clan at Bannockburn, they always thereafter had allotted to them, at the express desire of the King, the honourable distinction of a place in the right wing of the royal army. Bruce, however, did not confine his patronage to sentimental favours of this kind. Out of gratitude for the yeoman service rendered by the Island chief

in the momentous struggle, he bestowed upon Angus
extensive possessions in addition to those which he
already enjoyed.   Besides Isla and Kintyre, the
islands of Mull, Jura, Coll and Tiree, and the
districts of Glencoe and Morvern, fell to his lot.
Lorn was bestowed upon Roderick, son of Allan
Macruari, who, not being considered feudally legitimate, received from his sister Christina, his father's
legal heiress, a large share in her inheritance in
Garmoran and the North Isles.[1] Lochaber, which
had for a long time been in the possession of the
Comyns — the determined foes of Bruce — was
forfeited, and divided between Angus of Isla and
Roderick of Garmoran; but the latter having,
about 1325, entered into a treasonable league
against the Crown—probably the Soulis conspiracy—
was afterwards deprived of that territory, and it
was bestowed upon Angus Og.   Bruce was no doubt
well aware of the impolicy and danger to the authority of the Crown involved in the bestowal of such wide
possessions upon a subject, for although the loyalty
of Angus Og himself was undoubted, his successors
might not prove so friendly to the Scottish State.
Indeed, one of the weighty counsels which King
Robert left behind him for the guidance of the
kingdom in future times, was not to let the lordship of the Hebridean Isles be in the hands of any
one man.[2]   Still the services of the Lord of the
Isles were too great to be overlooked, and the only
condition made to neutralise the power which thus
accrued to him was the erection of Tarbert Castle,
in Kintyre, to be occupied as a royal stronghold.

---

[1] Skene's Highlanders of Scotland, vol. II., p. 56.

[2] Ne quenquam unum Hebridarum insularum dominum facerent.
Buchanan, Lib. VIII., 57.

Angus Og married a daughter of Guy or Con-
buidh O'Cathan or O'Kane, one of the greatest
barons of Ulster, Lord of Limvady, and Master of
the whole County of Derry.[1] The O'Cathans were
originally a branch of the Cinel Eoghain, descended
from Neil of the nine hostages, King of Ireland.
The Lord of the Isles obtained a unique dowry
with his bride, whose name, according to the most
generally accepted traditions, was Margaret,[2] but
according to another, less known but more correct
account, was said to be Ann, Aine, or Agnes.[3] The
lady's portion took the form of 140 men out of
every surname in O'Cathan's territory, and the
descendants of those who left representatives are
known to this day in the Highlands as "tochradh
nighean a' Chathanaich"—"The dowry of O'Cathan's
daughter." The importation of so many stalwart
Irishmen shows that the Highlands were somewhat
sparsely peopled, and that there were no apprehensions of a congested population in the days of
Angus Og. It was still very much the time when
might was right—when there prevailed :—

> "The good old way, the simple plan,
>   That he should take who has the power,
>   And he should keep who can,"

and when property could only be held by the strong
hand of him who could muster the biggest force of
armed retainers. In these circumstances, the arrival
of this "tail" of youths from the Emerald Isle, to
help the security of the lady's new domains, was
by no means an unwelcome occurrence. The names
of some of these immigrants have come down by

---

[1] Hugh Macdonald's MS. ; 1700 MS.
[2] Hugh Macdonald's M.S.
[3] 1700 MS. Hill's Macdonalds of Antrim, p. 17. Rot. Scot., vol. 1., p. 534.

tradition. Two families, the Munroes, so called because they came from the innermost Roe water in the County of Derry, their name being originally O'Millans, and the Roses of Kilravock,[1] rose to territorial distinction in the North Highlands. The other names preserved by Hugh Macdonald are the Fearns, Dingwalls, Beatons, Macphersons, Bulikes of Caithness, while the MS. of 1700

FINLAGGAN.

mentions, in addition to the foregoing, Dunbar, Maclinen, and the MacGilleglasses.

Angus Og's loyalty to Bruce never faltered. It stands in marked contrast to the policy of the succeeding Lords of the Isles. Loyalty to Scottish nationality was, however, a plant of slow growth, even among the great baronial families of the South.

---

[1] The historian of the Kilravock family does not dispute, but, on the contrary, admits that the family came directly from Ireland, though he maintains that England was the nursery of the race, whence they may have emigrated to Ireland. *Vide* Kilravock Charters.

These were, in blood and social ideas, as much Anglo-Norman as Scottish, and swayed from one side to the other in the time of conflict just as self-interest suggested. The case of the Lords of the Isles was similar, and, if Angus Og was a notable exception to his line, it was because in following the impulses of friendship for the great and chivalrous deliverer of Scotland, he departed from what was in reality the traditional policy of the Kings of Innse-Gall. Angus Og died shortly after his illustrious patron (whose death occurred in 1329) in his Castle of Finlaggan in Isla, and was buried in the tomb of his ancestors in Iona. On his tombstone are his arms—a ship with hoisted sails, a standard, four lions, and a tree—and the following inscription :—" Hic jacet corpus Angusii filii Domini Angusii MacDomhnill de Ila."

SEAL OF ANGUS MOR OF ISLA
1248-94.

Legend.

Sᴿ ENGUS DE YLE FILII DOMNALDI.

TOMBSTONE OF ANGUS OG OF ISLA
LORD OF THE ISLES, OB. 1330.

Inscription.

Hic jacet corpus Angusii filii Domini
Angusii Mac Domhnill de Ila.

CHAPTER VI.

THE GOOD JOHN OF ISLA.—1330-1386.

John of Isla.—His relation to Scottish Parties.—Treaty with
Balliol.—Forfeiture.—Forfeiture of Reginald Macruari.—Par-
don and Reinstatement.—Assassination of Reginald Mac-
ruari.—John and the Lands of Garmoran, &c.—John at the
Battle of Poictiers.—His Captivity.—Ransom.—Connection
with the National Party.—Second Marriage.—Constable of
Edinburgh Castle. – High Steward of Scotland.—Rebellion.—
Treaty of Inverness.—Lordship of the Isles.—John's
Eminence.—Death.—Controversial Questions.—The Two
Marriages.

JOHN OF ISLA's succession to the extensive territories
left by his father was almost contemporaneous
with the accession of David II., then a mere child,
to the Scottish throne. The woes that tend to
accompany a long minority, and in which Scottish
history largely abounds, were for a few years
mitigated by the firm and sagacious regency of
Randolph, Earl of Moray ; but when his strong hand
was removed from the helm of State, Scotland was
again plunged into anarchy and confusion. Disaster
fell upon the Scottish arms at Dupplin ; the power
of the executive was shattered ; English influence
began to make itself felt once more, and Edward
Balliol was crowned at Scone in 1332, and soon afterwards did homage as the vassal of Edward III. The
cause of Scottish independence, though thus betrayed,
was not by any means crushed ; the spirits of
Wallace and Bruce still ruled the people " from their
urns." For nine years the patriotic barons, backed

by the national sentiment animating the great mass
of the peasantry and middle class, were successful in
maintaining the independence and integrity of the
realm, in the face of domestic disloyalty fomented
by the ambitious English monarch.

The early years of John of Isla's occupancy of the
Island throne were passed during this transition
from the comparatively settled order of Bruce's reign
to the confusions of that which followed, and the
history of the lordship of the Isles during, as well as
subsequent to, that period derives its colouring from
the varying vicissitudes of general Scottish history.
John was undoubtedly one of the most distinguished
of his distinguished line. The circumstances of his
time were not such as to shed the halo of martial
glory on his name. He did not, like his father or
son, engage in a great or epoch-making battle.[1] He
did not share in the glory of a great field like
Bannockburn, nor did he play the chief part in an
heroic struggle like Harlaw. But peace has its
victories no less than war, and John's long life
illustrated the exercise of far-sighted and, on the
whole, successful diplomacy. He was animated all
along by the dominant idea of his family, the
maintenance of the honour of his house, and of the
integrity of his ancestral domains. Loyalty to the
Scottish crown was a question of expediency rather
than of principle with the descendant of a line of
chiefs who regarded themselves as hereditary kings
of the Scottish Gael, as well as lords of Innse-Gall.
Viewed in this light, John's conduct amid the stormy
drama of Scottish politics during the fourteenth
century is intelligible enough. Seeking to exercise
independent sway within the Celtic sphere, he

---

[1] Unless we except Poictiers, of which hereafter.

AROS CASTLE, MULL.

clearly saw that English influence in Scotland, with
its natural correlative a weak Scottish executive,
would serve his purpose best.   This undoubtedly
was his chief motive in espousing the cause of Baliol.
But his attitude of hostility to the patriotic party
was still further strengthened by a difference with
the Regent regarding certain of the lands which he
had inherited from his father.   Randolph's successor
refused to confirm him in these possessions, with the
result that when Balliol assumed the crown the Lord
of the Isles became associated with his party as that
which would the more likely establish him in his
just and lawful rights.   Hence it came to pass that
on the 12th September, 1335, John entered into a
treaty of alliance with Edward Balliol, in which he
was put into possession of the lands inherited from
his father, and others.   This treaty, which was concluded at Perth, was on the 6th October of the
following year ratified by Edward III. at Auckland,
Balliol acknowledging the English King as his
superior and Lord Paramount.   Edward's confirmation of the treaty to which Balliol and John
of Isla were parties contains the tenour of the
compact, and as it throws an interesting light
upon our subject, the substance of it may be quoted
here :—

"The King to whom, &c.   We have examined certain letters of
indenture drawn up between the magnificent prince Lord Edward
King of Scotland, our illustrious and most dear cousin, and John
of the Isles, in the following terms :—In this indenture, made at
the town of Perth on Tuesday, 12th December, 1335, between the
most excellent prince Lord Edward, by the grace of God the
illustrious King of Scots, on the one part, and John of the Isles on
the other part, it is certified that the said Lord the King has
granted, in so far as in him lay, to the foresaid John for good

and praiseworthy service rendered to himself, and in future to be rendered by him and his heirs,

> The Island of Ysle (Isla)
> The land of Kentyre (Kintyre)
> The land of Knappedoll (Knapdale)
> The Island of Githe (Gigha)
> Half the Island of Dure (Jura)
> The Island of Golwonche (Colonsay)
> The Island of Mulle
> The Island of Sky
> The Island of Lewethy (Lewis)
> The land of Kenalbadon and Ardinton (Morvern and Ardnamurchan)

to be held by the same John and his heirs and assignees. The same Lord the King has also granted to the same John the wardship of Lochaber until the attainment to man's estate of the son and heir of Lord David of Strathbolgy the last Earl of Athol. And for these foresaid concessions the foresaid John of the Isles binds himself and his heirs to be leal and faithful men to the said Lord the King and his heirs for ever, and he binds himself and his heirs to pursue all his foes and rebels whatsoever, on what days, in what places and ways he may be able to do so. And in security for the faithful performance of all these promises the oath shall be given by the said John on the holy eucharist, the cup of the altar, and the missal. Likewise the said John wishes and grants that if the foresaid Lord the King should desire to have from him a hostage or hostages for greater security, that a cousin or cousins of his own under age, very nearly related to him, may be delivered over to the said Lord the King when a suitable time has come, seeing that the said John has as yet neither son nor heir lawfully begotten of his own body. Besides, the foresaid Lord the King wishes and grants that at whatever time he may have an heir of his own body legitimately begotten the office of godfather to his heir may be granted to the foresaid John.

"But we accept, ratify, approve, and confirm the whole and each of the contents of the foresaid letters for ourselves and our heirs so far as in us lies, as the foresaid letters more fully testify."[1]

It is evident that John himself was present, and paid his respects to King Edward when these important negotiations were taking place. The

---

[1] Rotuli Scotiæ, vol. I., p. 463.

Scottish records of the time indicate that on the
very day on which John's League with Balliol was
confirmed by the English monarch he received a safe
conduct from that potentate.   Intimation was made
to all sheriffs, bailies, and other faithful subjects
that John and his retinue, servants, and equipage,
whether staying with the King, on their way to see
him, or on their return home, were under his special
protection and care.[1]   In all this we have evidence
of the value placed by Balliol and his suzerain
upon the power and resources of the Island Lord,
and his adhesion to the anti-Scottish party.   This
alliance with Edward III. continued for several
years, gathering rather than losing strength, and in
the records of 1337 we find frequent traces of
friendly intercourse between the English monarch
and the Lord of the Isles.   On 3rd December of
that year John received a safe conduct couched in
still more forcible language than that of 1335, and
the most extreme pains and penalties are threatened
against such as would cause injury or molestation to
himself or his followers when coming, staying, or
departing from the royal presence.   This is followed
on the day immediately succeeding by a commission
to the Earl of Salisbury to enter into a league with
the Lord of the Isles.   On the same day a letter is
sent by Edward to John by the hands of this same
plenipotentiary, abounding in the friendliest, the
most honeyed phrases—*epistola blandiloqua* it is
styled.   He calls him his dearest friend, and offers
him the best safeguards in his power, whether he
comes with 60 or 80 or 100 attendants with the view
of drawing closer the bonds of amity and concord
between them.[2]   The relations between the English

---

[1] Rotuli Scotiæ, vol. I., p. 464.   [2] Ibidem, p. 516.

King and John, of which we have evidence in these transactions, seem to have lasted until a fresh crisis arose in the position of Scottish parties. Edward, recognising the power and capacity of the Island lord, seems to have done all he could to stimulate his discontent, secure his friendship, and establish his connection with the party of Balliol.

After a few years' struggle, the patriotic party was successful in vindicating the independence of Scotland, and the Steward, the nephew of David Bruce, having been appointed Regent, and finding his uncle's cause in the ascendant, arranged for his return from France to assume his father's sceptre in 1341. Owing to the attitude of John of Isla during the troublous times of David Bruce's minority, it might naturally be expected that the vengeance of the King would, on the overthrow of his enemies and his accession to the throne, be directed against him. As a matter of fact, in or about 1343, John was nominally forfeited in the lands of Gigha, Isla, Jura, and Colonsay, all of which were granted by the King to Angus Macian of Ardnamurchan,[1] a kinsman of his own, and the head of a house that was yet to play a not unimportant part in the history of the Highlands. Reginald Macruari joined with John of Isla in offering a stout and effective resistance to the royal decree. His possessions seem also to have been involved in the confiscations of the time, although the Macruari tenure at that particular period is not altogether clear. The Island Chiefs were not, however, strong believers in the efficacy of parchments, and seem to have felt none the worse of their irregular relations to the crown. It was not long ere the

---

[1] Charter in Haddington's Collection.

exigencies of the Scottish State wrought in favour
of the Island interests. David Bruce, taking
advantage of the absence of Edward III. in France,
resolved to invade England in 1346. Wishing to
bring the whole military force of his kingdom into
action, and with the view of conciliating all whose
hostility might be feared, he pardoned both John
of Isla and his kinsman, Reginald Macruari. The
whirligig of time had brought about its revenges,
and David Bruce repeated the work of Balliol. In
1343—before the invasion of England, and the
very year of his forfeiture—he confirmed John
in the lands of Durdoman (Duror), Glenchomyr
(Glenco), Morimare (Morvern), Geday (Gigha),
Ardinton (Ardnamurchan), Golwonche (Colonsay),
Mulle, Kernoburgh, and Iselborgh Castles, with
the lands pertaining to them; Tirayd (Tiree), Yle
(Isla), Dure (Jura), Scarba, Lewis, and Lochaber.[1]
It will be seen from this that Kintyre, Knapdale
(South), and Skye, which formed part of Balliol's
grant in 1335, are excepted, these lands having
reverted to their former owners. To Ranald Mac-
ruari[2] there were granted the Isles of Uist, Barra,
Eigg, and Rum, and the lordship of Garmoran,
which included the districts of Moydart, Arisaig,
Morar, and Knoydart—all of which formed the
ancient patrimony of the Macruari family.[3]

On the eve of David Bruce's invasion of England,
there occurred a tragedy which resulted in a considerable enlargement of the power and possessions
of the House of Isla. Reginald Macruari met
with a violent death. The Scottish barons hav-

[1] Robertson's Index, p. 48-1.

[2] This Ranald is referred to as "Ranald the White" in the genealogy of
the 1450 MS.

[3] Robertson's Index, p. 48-3.

ing been convoked to meet at Perth, Reginald, obeying the summons, and accompanied by a considerable body of men, took up his quarters in the monastery of Elcho, a few miles from the ancient capital. Reginald held the lands of Kintail from the Earl of Ross, the instrument being thus defined :—" Carta Regnaldi filii Roderici de terris de Kintale in Ergadia Boreali data per Dominum Ross." [1] The Charter of confirmation for the same lands is thus described :—" Carta ejusdem Regis confirmans cartam consessam per Wilhelmum Comitem de Ross filium et heredem quondam Hugonis Comitis de Ross Reginalde filio Roderici de Insulis decem davatorum terre de Kennetale in Ergadia Boaeali data apud castrum dicti Comitis de Urcharde, 4th Julii an Dom 1342, testibus (names of witnesses), Carta Regis est fine data." [2]

Mr William Mackay, in his admirable History of Urquhart and Glenmoriston, makes reference to the circumstances in which this charter was bestowed. At that time Glen-Urquhart Castle was in the keeping of Sir Robert Lauder of Quarrelwood, on behalf of the Scottish Crown. Mr Mackay says :—

" Within the old walls of his Castle, Sir Robert Lauder entertained right royally. Among the guests who were met together there on 4th July, 1342, were William, Earl of Ross; Reginald, son of Roderick of the Isles; the Bishop of Moray, the Bishop Ross, Sir James de Kerdale, Sir William de Mowbray, Sir Thomas de Lichtoun, Canon of Moray; John de Barclay, Adam de Urquhart, John Yong de Dingwall, 'and many others, clergymen

[1] The Charter of Reginald, son of Roderick, for the lands of Kintail, in North Argyll, given by the Earl of Ross. Robertson's Index, p. 48-2.

[2] The Charter of the same King, confirming the Charter granted by William, Earl of Ross, son and heir of the late Hugh, Earl of Ross, to Reginald, son of Roderick of the Isles, for the ten davochlands of Kintail, in North Argyll, given at the said Earl's Castle of Urquhart on the 4th of July, 1342 A.D. The King's Charter is given at the end.

and laymen'—a goodly company truly. These all witnessed a charter by the Earl to Reginald of the lands of Kintail, as a reward for his services."[1]

A bitter feud as to the tenure of these lands seems to have arisen between the superior and vassal, and the opportunity of wreaking vengeance upon his foe seemed to the Earl too favourable to be lost. In the middle of the night he broke into the monastery, surprised the occupants, treacherously and sacrilegiously slew Reginald and seven of his men within the holy building, and immediately thereafter betook himself to his northern fastnesses. It was considered a bad omen by many at the time that King David's campaign should have been immediately preceded by so fell a deed.[2]

The foregoing incident materially affected the fortunes of John of Isla. In 1337, or shortly thereafter, he had married his third cousin, Euphemia Macruari, sister of the slaughtered chief. In terms of the Royal gift to her brother, Reginald, she succeeded to the estates, and brought them over to her husband in 1344. Although John's right emerged through his marriage, he had also, as a male heir not remotely akin, a feasible right to the inheritance. In this way he had a double claim to Garmoran and the Northern Isles. The Scottish Government, however, did not regard the matter in this light. They considered John already too powerful a subject for the safety of the realm, and rightly feared that the vast territories to which he now laid claim threatened a revival of the ancient kingdom of the Isles. Consequently, they refused to acknowledge John as the rightful heir of the Macruaris, or to give him legal investiture in

[1] P. 35.

[2] For Wyntoun on Ranald Macruari's death, see Appendix.

their possessions. Whatever ostensible reason the Government may have advanced for their action— and these we shall afterwards consider—the motives which really animated them were concern for the safety of the State. It is not surprising that the proud Chief of the Clan Donald was indignant at the attitude of the Government, and felt disposed again to espouse the fortunes of the Balliol party. In 1346, the year of Reginald Macruari's assassination, the fortunes of that faction seemed once more in the ascendant. King David Bruce's invasion of England opened with disaster. At the battle of Neville's Cross the Scottish army was defeated with great slaughter, and the King taken a prisoner to England. Yet although it might well seem that a fatal blow had been struck at Scotland's independence, and Balliol's position been re-established by England's success, neither of these results ensued. Balliol obtained not even the semblance of kingly authority ; and the Scottish nobility were successful in placing the Steward, the next heir to the throne, in the regency of the kingdom. In 1351, Edward III., whose attention was largely taken up with his French wars, concluded a truce with Scotland, which he renewed from time to time, as he entertained prospects of replenishing the coffers of the State by a large ransom for the royal captive.

In the circumstances to which we have just referred, the friction which was caused between John of Isla and the Government in connection with the estates of Garmoran does not seem to have led the Island Chief into aggressive hostility. From all that we can learn, during the eleven years of David's captivity in England, John was left in undisturbed possession, not only of the lands con-

firmed to him by the royal authority, but also of
the Macruari territories, his right to which was still
unacknowledged.   Certain of the lands which were
granted by David Bruce to John in 1343, namely,
the lands of Duror, Jura, and Mull, and the fortresses of Kerneburgh and Iselburgh, of which
John had received the custody, had been held by
John of Lorne as the vassal of John of Isla.   The
privilege of holding these fortressees had been
accompanied by certain conditions.   One of these
was that until John of Lorne delivered the Castle
of Kerneburgh to John of Isla he should give
him three hostages, namely, a lawful son of Lachlan
MacAlexander, a lawful son of Ywar MacLulli, and a
lawful son of John MacMolmari, or of another good
man of his clan ; and another was that John of
Lorne should never give the keeping of the castle of
Kerneburgh to any of the Clan Fynwyne (Mackinnon), who, at that time, seem to have had a
settlement in Mull.   These, with the exception of
the three unciates of Tereyd (Tiree), next to Coll,
were all resigned to John of Isla, it being stipulated
that the Steward of the three unciates should not
make a domestic establishment (domesticatum) or
a dwelling (habitaculum) on those lands without
leave obtained from the superior.   The Island of
Coll was retained by John of Lorne, and, in the
deed recording the transaction, was confirmed to
himself and his heirs for ever.   These negotiations
took place in 1354, and in the record of the proceedings we find John of Isla described by the title
"Lord of the Isles."

It may be true, as Gregory says, that there is no
previous record of this particular chief of the Clan
Cholla being called *Dominus Insularum* in the

8

annals of that age. It is, however, a most
unwarrantable inference to draw from that fact, as
the same historian does, that the title " Lord of the
Isles" was a new one in the history of the family.
This particular question we propose to touch upon
more fully in a subsequent chapter.

Shortly after this time an incident occurred in
John's career which shows that English influence
had lost its hold upon him, and that in his public
conduct he had allowed himself to be drawn into
the full tide of Scottish policy. In 1354-5, just as a
treaty for the ransom of David Bruce was on the
eve of being ratified, the Scots nobility were persuaded by the potent argument of forty thousand
moutons of French gold to break the truce with
England.[1] This was followed by a series of hostilities
both in Scotland and France, in both which lands
the able and ambitious Edward III. still sought to
obtain supreme dominion. In 1356, the Black
Prince having penetrated far into the interior of
France, the French King assembled an army vastly
superior in numbers, and determined to cut off his
retreat. A number of Scottish chiefs and nobles
accompanied him to the field, and, among others,
John of Isla,[2] with a powerful body of Highlanders.
With all his numerical advantages, the French King
was unable to prevail against the valour of the
English army. In the famous battle of Poictiers,
fought on the 19th September, 1356, the Scots
contingent sustained great losses, and the Lord of
the Isles was taken prisoner. From that date to
16th December of the following year, he was in

[1] Scott's History of Scotland, vol. I, p. 201.

[2] On the 31st of the preceding March, Edward III. sought to bring
John of Isla over to his interest, and a commission for treating with him was
executed ; but this commission was rendered nugatory by John's refusal to
treat. Rymer's Fœdera.

captivity, the greater part of the time in England. Once more John obtains from the English King a safe conduct for his return to his Island home, but it is notable that the terms of the document are less endearing than of old.   Sheriffs and bailies and other faithful ones, however, are told that the Lord of the Isles, who was a prisoner of the Prince of Wales his dear son, was in the King's safe conduct going to Scotland, accompanied by four knights, with the view of providing the means necessary for his ransom.[1]

Two years after this we find John of Isla taking a prominent part in promoting the treaty for the liberation and ransom of David II., and thus still further indicating his abandonment of the English alliance and his assumption of a friendly attitude towards the Crown.   It was stipulated in this treaty that, for the more sure payment of the ransom of 100,000 marks, twenty hostages were to be sent to England, and that three of the following seven were always to be of the said twenty, viz.:—the Steward of Scotland, the Earls of March, Marr, Ross, and Sutherland, the Lord Douglas and Thomas de Murray ; that in the meantime, during the whole period of the ten years over which the payments were spread, an inviolable truce should subsist, in which truce were to be included *Monsieur Edward de Balliol* and *Johan des Isles*.[2]

Soon after the return of David Bruce to the Scottish throne, a complete revolution took place in the mutual relations of political parties.   The party adhering to the King was wont to be regarded as patriotic and national, that of Balliol

---

[1] Rotuli Scotiæ, vol. I., p. 817.   [2] Robertson's Index, 107-19.

being favourable to English influence. But now
David Bruce began to show symptoms that his
long residence in England had enervated his
patriotism. He betokened a willingness to admit
English influence into the affairs of the realm,
and even to promote the nomination of an
English successor to the throne of Scotland. The
consequence was that the Balliol faction became
the party of the court, while the national party,
with the Steward at its head, found themselves
in the cool shades of opposition. Yet although
the Lord of the Isles found himself, for the first
time, in a position in which antagonism to the
Government was consistent with adherence to the
party of Scottish independence ; and although his
connection with this party was further cemented
by his marriage with Lady Margaret, daughter of
the Steward, yet we do not find that he assumed a
strenuous attitude in opposition to the policy of the
King. The date of this marriage, in the absence of
definite information, it is difficult to state with
exactness, but it must have taken place about, and
certainly not much later than, David Bruce's return
from captivity.

We do not purpose at this stage to discuss the
merits of this union, the circumstances of which the
history of the time has left, to a large extent, in
obscurity. The voice of tradition is unanimous as
to the fact that, in order to carry out the marriage,
the Lord of the Isles divorced or abandoned his first
wife, Amy Macruari. In this he had the support
and advice not only of the Steward, but—according
to Hugh Macdonald, the Sleat historian—of his
council, and, pre-eminently, MacInnes of Ardgour.
The same authority—who, by the way, describes

Amy as "a good and virtuous gentlewoman"—
throws an interesting side-light upon the pride of
the great Highland Chief, who would not perform
the unwonted act of obeisance—uncovering his head
in the royal presence on the occasion of his marriage
—but ingeniously evaded the courtesy by not wearing
a head-dress at all. MacInnes's untoward intervention in the domestic affairs of the family of Isla
was neither forgotten nor forgiven by Amy or her

RUINS OF BORVE CASTLE, BENBECULA.

sons. It is alleged that a commission was given to
Donald, son of Lauchlan MacLean, to slay MacInnes
with his five sons, and this having been done, he
obtained possession of Ardgour, which his posterity
still enjoy. Amy is said to have lived for a number
of years after her separation from John of Isla, and
to have built Castle Tirrim in Moidart, and Borve
Castle in Benbecula, as well as places of worship, of
which notice shall be taken hereafter.[1]

[1] Hugh Macdonald's MS..

Although John's connection with the family of
the Steward would naturally, as we have seen,
lead him to espouse the policy of his party, yet
his past conduct, both in war and diplomacy,
in recent years, continued to secure for him the
favour of the Crown.   He enjoyed certain high
offices of State, his tenure of which does not
seem to have hitherto attracted the attention of the
historian.   Such was the confidence that seems to
have been reposed in him, that, in or shortly before
1360, he was appointed Constable of Edinburgh
Castle, a responsible and exalted military position,
which reflected much credit upon the character and
ability of the Chief of the Clan Donald.[1]   This, however, was not the only function which John, during
these years of loyalty, discharged under the Scottish
Crown.   It is, indeed, a singular circumstance that,
in 1364, we find him acting in the highest office
which it was possible for a Scottish subject to occupy,
viz., that of Senescall, or High Steward of the King's
Household,[2] an office which had for generations
come down by hereditary descent as the possession
of a family nearly akin to the throne.   The history
of the time leaves little doubt as to the reasons for
which, at the period under consideration, John of
Isla, rather than the hereditary holder of the
position, is found discharging the functions of High
Steward of Scotland.   Robert, the High Steward,
had, by various Acts of Settlement passed by the
Estates of Scotland, been called to the Crown as
next heir to his uncle David Bruce, in default of the
latter leaving heirs of his body.   Queen Joanna died
childless in 1363, and early in the following year

---

[1] Rotuli Scacarii Regum Scotorum, vol. II., pp. 50-78.
[2] Ibidem, pp. 129, 134, 140, 173.

the King, having contracted a violent fancy for a beautiful young woman named Margaret Logie—of comparatively humble origin—insisted, contrary to the advice of his Court, on bestowing his hand upon her in marriage. This unequal alliance caused an open rupture between David and his kinsman the Steward, whose reversion of the Crown would certainly be disappointed if the fair Margaret should bear a son. Such was the discord that arose out of this episode and the angry feelings to which it gave rise, that the Steward and his son, the Wolf of Badenoch, were thrown into prison, where they seem to have been detained for several years. The royal resentment does not seem, however, to have extended to the Steward's son-in-law, John of Isla, for undoubtedly he exercised the functions of Seneschall during a part, at least, of his father-in-law's imprisonment, a fact which seems to indicate that he must have been a special favourite with the King, and kept himself free from the contending factions of the time.

Two years after John of Isla first comes before us as Steward of Scotland, he appears as a royal envoy to Flanders to transact some business for the King.[1] Again the history of the age helps us to determine the nature of the negotiations in which the Lord of the Isles was engaged during his visit to Flanders. The payment of the King's ransom was one of the chief obstacles in the way of a lasting peace between the two kingdoms, and to secure the regular payment of the first instalment the Scottish Parliament had made great sacrifices. It was ordained that the wool of the Kingdom, apparently its most productive export at that time, should be sold to the King at a

[1] Rotuli Scacarii Regum Scotorum, vol. II., p. 261.

low rate, and it was afterwards disposed of under the King's instructions to merchants in Flanders, where textile industries seem at that early time to have flourished, and the surplus produced over prime cost was applied in discharge of the royal ransom. John of Isla, in virtue of his office as Senescall, had the management of the royal revenues, and his voyage to Flanders in 1366, accompanied by John Mercer, who was probably better versed than the Lord of the Isles in the price of wool, was no doubt undertaken with the view of negotiating with the Flanders merchants as to the value to be placed upon the precious commodity which was to yield a King's ransom.

The burdensome exactions which were thus necessary for completing the ransom of the King were felt to be a heavy impost by a country naturally poor and lately impoverished by a series of desolating wars. In the Highlands especially the taxation was found to be oppressive, and John of Isla, so recently a high official under the Scottish Crown, is found, along with other northern barons, refusing to pay the national taxation or attend a meeting of the Estates of the realm.[1]

Some years before this outbreak of disaffection, as already stated, the King had thrown the Steward into prison for his opposition to the royal policy, but now finding himself unable to cope with the forces of disorder, he gave him his freedom, in the belief that he would lend his influence successfully to the vindication of the authority of the Crown. The Steward undertook a task dictated alike by policy and patriotism. His son-in-law, John of Isla, was the most difficult to reduce to subjection. There was peace, however,

[1] Acts of Scottish Parliament, vol. XII., p. 503, June 12, 1368.

between Scotland and England; John of Isla had no foreign ally to whom to turn, and so David Bruce was able to bring all his resources to bear upon the Island potentate. At last, after years of open and successful defiance, the Steward prevailed upon the haughty and turbulent chief to meet the King at Inverness, when the following instrument of allegiance was finally drawn up in 1369 :—

"To all who may see the present letters :—John de Yle, Lord of the Isles, wishes salvation in the Saviour of all. Since my most serene prince and master, the revered lord David, by the Grace of God, illustrious King of Scots, has been stirred up against my person because of certain faults committed by me, for which reason, coming humbly to the presence of my said lord, at the Town of Inverness, on the 15th day of the month of November, in the year of grace 1369, in the presence of the prelates, and of very many of the nobles of his kingdom, I offered and submitted myself to the pleasure and favour of my said master, by suppliantly entreating for favour and for the remission of my late faults, and since my said lord, at the instance of his council, has graciously admitted me to his goodwill and favour, granting besides that I may remain in (all) my possessions whatsoever and not be removed, except according to the process and demand of law : Let it be clearly patent to you all, by the tenor of these presents, that I, John de Yle, foresaid, promise and covenant, in good faith, that I shall give and make reparation to all good men of this kingdom whatsover, for such injuries, losses, and troubles as have been wrought by me, my sons, or others whose names are more fully set forth in the royal letters of remission granted to me, and to whomsoever of the kingdom as are faithful I shall thus far make the satisfaction concluded for, and I shall justly note purchased lands and superiorities, and I shall govern them according to my ability ; I shall promptly cause my sons and my subjects, and others my adherents, to be in peaceable subjection, and that due justice shall be done to our lord the King, and to the laws and customs of his kingdom, and that they shall be obedient to, and shall appear before the justiciars, sheriffs, coroners, and other royal servants in each sheriffdom, even better and more obediently than in the time of Robert of good memory, the predecessor of my lord the King, and as the inhabitants of the said lands and superiorities have been accustomed to do. They shall answer, both promptly and dutifully, to the royal servants what is imposed regarding contributions and other burdens and services due, and also for the time past, and in the event that within the said lands or superiorities any person or persons shall offend against the King, or one or more of his faithful servants, and if he or they shall despise to obey the law, or if he or they shall be unwilling to obey in the premises, and in any one of the premises, I shall immediately, entirely laying aside stratagem and deceit, pursue that person or those persons as enemies, and as rebels of the King and kingdom, with all my ability, until he or they shall be expelled from the limits of the lands and superiorities, or I shall make him or them obey the common law : And for performing, implementing, and faithfully observing these things, all and each, I personally have taken the oath in presence of the foresaid prelates and nobles, and besides I have given and surrendered the under-written hostages, viz., Donald, my son, begotten of the daughter of the Lord Seneschal of Scotland, Angus, son of my late son John, and one Donald, another and natural son of mine, whom, because at the time of the completion of this present deed I have not at present ready and prepared, I shall cause them to go into, or to be given up at the Castle of Dumbarton, at the feast of our Lord's birth now next to come, if I shall be able otherwise on this side, or at the feast of the Purification of the Blessed Virgin (or Candlemas, 2d February) next following thereafter, under pain of the breach of the oath given, and under pain of the loss of all things which, with regard to the lord our King, I shall be liable to lose, in whatever manner. And for securing the entrance of these hostages as promised, I have found my Lord Seneschal of Scotland, Earl of Strathern, security, whose seal for the purpose of the present security, and also for the greater evidence of the matter is appended, along with my own proper seal, to these presents in testimony of the premises. Acted and given, year, day, and place foresaid."

Two years after the Treaty of Inverness was ratified, David II. died and Robert II. ascended the throne.[1] Owing to his close connection by marriage with the reigning family, the subsequent relations of the Lord of the Isles to the Court were of a

[1] In the list of names of persons who took oath of homage and fealty to Robert II. on the day after coronation is that of Johannes de Lyle.

friendly nature, and before his father-in-law was long upon the throne he was confirmed in possession of a domain which might well be called princely. It may be stated, generally, that the greater part of the territories that first belonged in their integrity to Somerled, but were afterwards divided among the houses of Isla, Bute, and Lorne, were now consolidated under one powerful family. One of the first acts of King Robert II., on assuming royal sway, was to confirm his "beloved son, John of Isla," in the 300 merklands, once the property of Allan, the son of Roderick, namely, the lands of Moidart, Arisaig, Morar, Knoydart, being in the lordship of Garmoran; also the Islands of Uist, Barra, Rum and Eigg, and Harris, being part of Lewis. This deed was executed at Scone, during the session of Parliament, on the 9th March, 1371-2. According to Skene and others who have followed him as an authority incapable of erring, this was the first time John of Isla had received feudal investiture of the patrimony of the Macruaris. As a matter of fact, however, we find that on 4th July, 1363—the time of John's enjoyment of high court favour and office—David II. bestows upon him a Charter of Confirmation under the Great Seal for all lands possessed by him, by whomsoever these had been granted, a deed intended to make good all previous gifts granted by Balliol or by David, or inherited through his first wife.[1] In the same year there is a grant of these lands made by John to his son Reginald, born of the first marriage, with the addition that the castles of Benbecula and Island Tirrim, and also the lands of Sunart, Letter-lochletter, Ardgour, Hawlaste, and sixty merklands in Lochaber, namely, Kilmald[2] and

---

[1] Register of the Great Seal.   [2] Probably Kilmallie.

Locharkaig, are also included.[1] This grant is accompanied by a royal confirmation. It is remarkable that neither John's first wife, through whom he received the lands, nor her brother Reginald, from whom she inherited them, receive any notice in the charter. This gift was further confirmed by Robert III. in 1392.[2] One point only calls for remark in the disposition of lands provided for in this instrument; but it is of great importance, in view of future discussions, namely, that these lands of Garmoran and the North Isles and others were to be held by Reginald and his heirs from John and his heirs. Some years later, in 1376, the Lord of the Isles received three charters for the remainder of his lands, in which Colonsay, Lochaber, Kintyre, and Knapdale, and other lands not previously disposed of, were granted by the King to himself, "John del Ile," and his heirs by his wife Margaret, the daughter of the King. The territories of John of Isla were, in this manner, divided into two large divisions or lordships—the first, in the order of time, being the lordship of Garmoran and the Northern Isles, possessed by Reginald as the vassal of John and of John's feudal heirs—the other being the lordship of the Isles proper, with John himself as crown vassal, with a special destination of the lands in question in favour of the second family.

Some idea of the extent of this territory may be gained by enumerating the different districts in the following order :—

MAINLAND TERRITORIES.

The Lordship of Lochaber, including Kilmallie and Kilmonivaig.
The Lordship of Garmoran, including Moydart, Arisaig, Morar, and Knoydart.
Also Morvern, Knapdale, Duror, Kintyre, and Glenco.

---

[1] For Charters see Appendix.   [2] Orig. Par. Scot.

It is obvious that the Lord of the Isles must have possessed conspicuous ability, force of character and prudence, to have been able so to build up the power and prestige of his race. The circumstances of the time, no doubt, were favourable to the aggrandisement of the Family of Isla. The successive transformations in Scottish politics; the continual struggle against English domination, and the frequent weakness of the executive power, rendered the formation of a semi-independent principality possible of achievement. But although the conditions were auspicious in view of that end, only a man of great foresight and commanding personality could have seized the golden opportunity for promoting the fortunes of his house. That he became a man of the first consequence in Scottish public life—although his loyalty was not above suspicion—has already been fully set forth, but it may be added in proof of this that, when the abortive Treaty of Newcastle for David's liberation was formulated in 1354, John of Isla was one of the four barons named as securities for its observance, the others being the Steward of Scotland, the Lord of Douglas, and Thomas of Moray.

After 1372 there is little left to record regarding John of Isla or his fortunes, until his death in 1386. Here, as elsewhere, the dulness of the annals betokened the happiness born of prosperity. The Lord of the Isles breathed his last in the Castle of Ardthornish at an advanced age, and his dust was laid in the Church of Oran, in Hy, where

the ashes of his father, Angus Og, reposed. His
obsequies were observed with great pomp and
splendour by the Churchmen of the Isles, among
whom he was known as the "Good John of
Isla," on account of a munificence to their order,
in which he more than vied with the pious liberality
of his fathers.

From Photo. by   Messrs O. W. Wilson & Co., Aberdeen.
RUINED KEEP OF ARDTHORNISH CASTLE.

We have purposely refrained from disturbing the
continuity of our narrative by dwelling upon certain
controversial episodes in John's career which have
an important bearing upon the future history of
his family. These questions are in themselves so
important that there is an obvious advantage in
dealing with them in the closing part of the present chapter, where they can be treated with some
measure of thoroughness rather than touched upon
as mere passing details.

The two marriages of John of Isla open up far-
reaching questions of genealogical interest, which it

is not our purpose in this volume to go into with detailed exhaustiveness. We cannot, however, avoid disposing, if possible, of one question upon which future genealogical discussions must hinge, and that is the regularity, or the opposite, of John's union with Euphemia Macruari, the heiress of Garmoran.

Undoubtedly there has been a tradition which seems to have acquired a certain amount of weight, that this was one of those irregular unions known as handfasting which seem to have prevailed to some extent among the ancient Highlanders, and which, though recognised in the law of Celtic succession, were irregular in the eye of the feudal law. We are not, of course, surprised to find the historian of Sleat, Hugh Macdonald, stating, not that John married, but that he lived for ten years[1] with the mother of the first family, seeing that this seanachie is always ready to cast doubts upon the legitimacy of heads of branches of the clan whose claims to seniority might otherwise be preferred to those of the Chiefs of Sleat. We also place little reliance upon the conclusions of an *ex parte* document compiled in the same interest, in which—very unnecessarily for proof of the main contention— the legality of the marriage in question is scornfully put out of court.[2] It is, however, somewhat surprising to find the Clanranald historian make an admission so damaging to the legitimacy of the line from which the Clanranald Chiefs were descended as that John of Isla "did not marry the mother of these men (his sons by Euphemia Macruari) from the altar."[3] It is equally strange that the MS. of

[1] Collectanea de rebus Albanicis.
[2] Abstract view of the claims to the representation of the Lords of the Isles and Earls of Ross.
[3] Reliquiæ Celticæ, vol. II., p. 159.

1700, written also in the Clanranald interest, should, while maintaining the legality of the marriage, do so with reasons so feeble and inconclusive.[1]

How such a misconception of the true facts of the case should have arisen can only be accounted for in one way. The Scottish Government, when refusing to acknowledge John's right to the lands of Ranald Macruari, supported the refusal by the allegation that his marriage with Amy was irregular, and could not be reconciled with the principles of feudal tenure. This contention, however unfounded, and though a mere pretext for curbing a powerful subject, was quite sufficient, coming as it did from such high quarters, to impress the popular mind and create a tradition which appears to have received a considerable amount of credit.

That John's marriage with Amy was a perfectly legal and regular union is a fact amply attested. That a lady in Amy's position, belonging to a noble Highland family, should have contracted an irregular alliance of the nature suggested is in the highest degree improbable. But apart from this consideration, which is not without its own weight, two undoubted facts may be adduced in proof. First of all, there is a dispensation granted by Pope Benedict XII. to John and Amy permitting them to enter the state of matrimony. According to the canon law of the Church of Rome, which was then very rigid, the parties, as third cousins, were within the forbidden degrees of consanguinity, and this barrier to their union could only be removed by the grace of the Church's earthly head. And it may be stated, in passing, that this very dispensation,

[1] See Appendix,

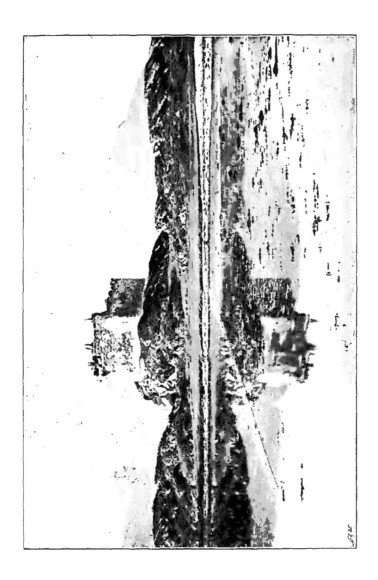

implying as it did some sort of irregularity, may have been one ground upon which the Government based their declinature to confirm John in the Macruari lands, and thus propagated the tradition to which we have referred.

But there is more than this. In the Treaty of Inverness the Lord of the Isles, in enumerating the hostages pledged for the performance of his sworn allegiance, draws a distinction between his " late son John and one Donald, another and natural son of mine."[1] This John was the eldest son of Amy, and is spoken of in the same terms as Donald his son by the daughter of the Steward of Scotland. There seems, therefore, no ground for doubting—and in this the standard authorities are at one—that the first marriage of John of Isla was a perfectly valid and legal union. In point of fact, John's marriage with the daughter of the Steward is exposed to far more objections, both from a legal and moral point of view, than his first marriage. Assuming, as the evidence compels us to do, that the first marriage was regular, and there being nothing to shew that Amy was guilty of any conduct unbecoming a true and faithful wife, the competency of a divorce and the power to contract a second marriage in her lifetime is subject to very grave doubts. This aspect of the question, however, we are not disposed, at present, to discuss. Looking at the transaction in the most favourable point of view, the alliance with the daughter of the future King of Scotland was animated by motives of worldly policy rather than of lofty principle, was a cruel slight upon a pure and honourable lady, and is an indelible stain upon the domestic life of " The Good John of Isla."

[1] See p. 122.

9

CHAPTER VII.

DONALD OF HARLAW.

The Succession of Donald to the Lordship of the Isles.—Reginald and the Crown Charter of 1373.—The position of Godfrey.—John Mor Tainistear and Alasdair Carrach.—Donald's policy.—Celtic supremacy.—Alliance with England.—Richard II. at Finlaggan in Isla.—Rebellion of Alasdair Carrach.—The Earldom of Ross.—The Lord of the Isles invades the Earldom.—Defeat of Angus Dubh Mackay at Dingwall.—Donald takes possession of Inverness.—March to Aberdeen.—The Battle of Harlaw.—Defeat of Mar and his Lowlanders.—Donald retires to the Isles.—The Regent Albany with an army invades Ross, and takes possession of the Earldom.—Albany's Campaigns in Argyle.—John of Fordoun's Treaty of Portgilp.—The Rebellion of John Mor.—Character and death of the Hero of Harlaw.

DONALD, the eldest son of the second marriage of John of Isla, succeeded his father as Lord of the Isles, to the exclusion of the eldest surviving son of the first marriage. This was not the first instance in the genealogy of the Clan Cholla in which the line of succession was diverted from the eldest son. We have seen how the sons of Alexander, the eldest son of Angus Mor, were excluded from the succession, owing to the determined opposition of their father to the interests of Bruce. It must also be borne in mind that the line of succession in the family of the Isles, like that of every other Highland family, was sometimes regulated more by the Celtic law of tanistry than by the feudal law of primogeniture. The title of Lord of the Isles—an assertion of

independence—was itself a Celtic dignity, assumed
by the heads of this family, and not conferred by the
Scottish monarch. It had not been assumed for the
first time by John, as affirmed by Gregory and
echoed by others, who call that chief the first Lord
of the Isles. On the contrary, we find in charters
granted by several heads of the family before the
time of John the dignity of Lord of the Isles
assumed and, in several State documents, acknowledged.[1] Somerled himself, the modern founder of
the family, is referred to again and again as both
Dominus and *Rex Insularum*, and Reginald his
son, as well as Donald his grandson, are referred to
as Lords of *Innsegall*, or of the Isles. Gregory
affirms that John, on his marriage with the Macruari heiress, and adding her patrimony to his already
extensive territories, assumed the title of Lord of
the Isles. But Somerled, the ancestor of John,
possessed a much wider and more extensive territory, both in the Isles and on the mainland, than
any of his successors. It seems, therefore, clear
that if John assumed this title for the extent of his
possessions he could not have been the first to do so
in the family of the Isles. In a very ancient MS.
quoted by the Seanachies, Gillebride, the father of
Somerled, is referred to as *Righ Eilein Sidir*, or
King of the Isles; while another progenitor of the
family is styled Toiseach of the Isles. Even as far
back as the 8th century, we find reference in an
old Scots Chronicle to the " Chief of the Isles," and
it was only towards the middle or end of the 12th
century, when feudal institutions had been for some
time established in the country, and Latin Christianity had taken root in the soil, that the title of

[1] See Chartulary of Paisley. Register of Great Seal, January 1st, 1507.

Dominus Insularum first appears on the page of history.

But the designation which the family of the Isles seems to have preferred to all others was *de Ile*, or of Isla, to which successive chiefs, from Reginald, the son of Somerled, to John, the last Lord, clung with the fondness of a first love. We might infer from this alone, even if there were not other and stronger indications pointing in the same direction, that from the very beginning of the history of Clan Cholla as a family in Argyle, green, grassy Isla, the Queen of the Hebrides, was the home of the race.

We are far from affirming that the old Celtic law of tanistry alone, or even principally, operated in the accession of Donald to the lordship of the Isles and chiefship of the Clan Donald. While no doubt it must have been an important factor in disarming opposition amongst a people thoroughly Celtic and, to a large extent, influenced by Celtic laws and usages, there were other and more powerful elements that conspired to place Donald, and not Reginald, in the position of head of his father's house. The first family of John of Isla had been already thrown in the shade by his splendid alliance with the family of the High Steward of Scotland through his marriage with the Lady Margaret, daughter of the now reigning King, if not also by the degradation of their mother, Amy Macruari, the unrighteously divorced wife of the Island Lord. Reginald himself, the surviving eldest son of the first marriage, surrendered his rights indifferently, without making any claim to the honours of his house, and, according to MacVuirich, in direct opposition to the wishes of the men of the Isles. John, the eldest son of the first marriage, is referred to in the Treaty of 1369 as then dead, while his son Angus, given as a hostage on that occasion for the future good behaviour of his grandfather, did not survive that potentate, and left no issue. According to the MS. of 1450, than which there is no higher authority on this matter, Reginald was the second son of the first marriage of John of Isla, and, failing the issue of the first son, his father's feudal heir. The authority of the MS. of 1450 is supported by others, among whom Mac-Vuirich, who, though he makes no mention of John, places the name of Reginald before that of Godfrey. Reginald had already, in the year 1373, received a Crown Charter of the lands of Garmoran and the North Isles, all of which were included in the old Macruari territory ; but the same charter added also the lands of Swynort, Letter-Lochletter, Ardgowar, Hawleste, and 60 marklands in Lochaber, namely, Lochkymald and Locharkage. In this Charter of 1373, Reginald is to hold his lands of John of Isla, and his heirs. Who was John of Isla's feudal heir ? Not Angus, the son of John, who, as already stated, had died without issue. It could not have been Reginald, now the eldest surviving son of John of Isla, for Reginald could not be his own vassal. The next heir after Reginald is Godfrey, but he lay no claim to the lordship of the Isles, and from what we know of his character, if his father's heir, he was not the man to stand tamely aside and allow Donald take possession of the lordship. Besides, the Charter of 1373 is itself the best evidence that Godfrey could not have been his father's heir. It seems amply clear that the policy of John of Isla in securing the Charter of 1373 for Reginald was to bribe him out of the succession. If Godfrey had been the eldest son, it is difficult to see how he could have been so

utterly ignored by his father. Neither in the
Charter of 1376, which conveys the lands of
Colonsay and others to the sons of the second
marriage, nor in Reginald's Charter of 1373 is there
mention made of Godfrey, or any disposition made
in his favour. The subsequent history of the lordship of the Isles shows very clearly who the heirs
were referred to in the Charter of 1373. Reginald,
though the eldest surviving son, became Donald's
vassal, as the descendants of Reginald continued to
be the vassals of the future lords of the Isles.
Donald, however, undoubtedly became, whether by
a feudal or Celtic law, the superior of all his brothers,
and his succession as Donald *de Ile* leaves no doubt
as to the meaning of the Charter of 1373.

But Donald, besides being backed by the powerful influence of the King, his grandfather, and being
in the advantageous position of eldest son of the
family then in possession, appeared in every other
way, as events afterwards proved, to have been fitter
to rule over the vast territories of the family than
Reginald. John of Isla himself took care to disarm
opposition by making Donald in the Crown Charter
of 1373 the feudal superior of Reginald. In all
the circumstances, therefore, and in view of the
unambitious character which we must ascribe to
Reginald, the latter acted wisely in accepting the
situation, and offering no opposition to the succession
of his brother. Accordingly, as we find from the
Book of Clanranald, Reginald, as High Steward of
the Isles, gave over all the rights and privileges of
the lordship of the Isles to Donald at Kildonan, in
Eigg, and he was nominated Macdonald, and Donald
of Isla, in presence of the principal men of the Isles.[1]

---

[1] Book of Clanranald in Reliq. Celt., p. 161.

Donald had now become not only the feudal
superior of his brothers, but also, by the consent of
the men of the Isles, the chief of the Clan Donald—
another instance of the practical operation of the
unwritten Celtic law which permitted the deposition
of one chief, as well as the election of another who
might not be the direct feudal heir.

Whatever opposition there may have been to
Donald's succession, it appears, by his firm yet
generous rule, to have gradually ceased ; and the
vassals of the Isles had never been so strongly
cemented together, nor at any period in the history
of the lordship of the Isles do we find the followers
of the Macdonald standard stronger in their attachment to their chief than we now find them. This
fact is sufficient proof of Donald's administrative
powers, no less than of his wise and just rule in an
age and at a time in the history of the country when
the strongest often failed. He conciliated his
brothers by the generous terms meted out to them
in the division of the lands of the extensive territories of which he was the superior. He confirmed
Reginald in the lands of Garmoran, the North Isles,
and others, after the death of his father, John of
Isla. The position and attitude of Godfrey, the
third son of Amy Macruari, does not appear,
however, to be very clear, either at this juncture
or during his subsequent history. We may infer
from the Charter of 1373, by which Uist, with the
Castle of Benbecula and other lands, are conferred
on Reginald, that North Uist had been the portion
allotted by John to his son Godfrey, and that he
possessed it during the lifetime of his father. The
same *Insula de Wyst*, mentioned in the Charter of
1373, is confirmed to Ranald MacAllan in the

year 1498, and all the lands specified in that charter
as being in *Wyst* are in South Uist. In a charter
conveying the Trinity Church of Carinish, with the
lands of Carinish and Illeray in North Uist to the
Monastery and Convent of St John the Evangelist in
Inchaffray, Godfrey styles himself *Godfridus de
Insulis Dominus de Wyst.* But he dates his charter
apud castrum nostrum de Ellantyrum, the principal
residence of the Clanranald. According to the Book
of Clanranald, Reginald died in 1386, and Godfrey's
Charter is dated 7th July, 1389. It appears, therefore, that on the death of Reginald, Godfrey possessed
himself of Garmoran and other lands granted to the
former, and that he was allowed to keep possession,
notwithstanding a confirmation, in the year 1392 by
Robert III., of the Castle of Ellantirrim, the lands
of Garmoran and others, to Reginald's heirs.[1]
Whether Godfrey was encouraged or in any way
assisted by Donald in this enterprise we have no
means of knowing; but it is evident that he could
not have kept possession long if Donald had chosen
to oppose his pretensions, and in view of all the
circumstances we are warranted in concluding that
Godfrey made out a plausible claim, as a descendant
of the Macruaries, to the lands of which he possessed
himself. The sons of Reginald were likely enough
to have assumed a defensive attitude, and resisted
the aggressive pretensions of Godfrey to the utmost;.
but it is difficult to say, in the absence of any
positive evidence, with what immediate result, even
though supported, as they were, by the Crown
Charter of 1373. It appears to be abundantly
clear that, in the lifetime of Godfrey at least, the
principal lands in the Macruari territory were not
possessed by the sons of Reginald.

[1] Register of the Great Seal.

SHIELD OF THE LORD OF THE ISLES.

The sons of the second marriage of John of Isla were amply provided for out of the family inheritance. Donald himself, besides the superiority of the whole Macdonald territory included in the lordship of the Isles, possessed directly the lands of Colonsay and others not included in the grants bestowed on the younger sons. John Mor Tainistear, the second son, received a grant of 120 marklands in Kintyre and 60 marklands in Isla. He became the founder of the family styled of Dunnyveg and the Glens, the latter of which he acquired through his marriage with Margery Bisset, the daughter and heiress of MacEoin Bisset, Lord of the Antrim Glens. It will be observed that only certain lands in Isla were granted to John Mor, whose residence there was the Castle of Dun-Naomhaig, while Finlaggan Castle, in the same island, was the residence of Donald, his brother, the Lord of the Isles. As matter of fact, the family of John Mor never did possess the whole of the island of Isla, either before or after the forfeiture of the lordship of the Isles, and they never arrogated to themselves the designation *de Ile*, or of Isla, which was the peculiar and exclusive designation of the head of the house of Macdonald, and ceased with John, the last Lord of the Isles, who died in 1498.

The next son of the second marriage of John of Isla was, according to the MS. of 1450—which is always safe to follow—Angus, who having died young without issue, there is nothing recorded of him but the bare name. The fourth son was Alasdair, afterwards known as Alasdair Carrach, progenitor of the Macdonalds of Keppoch. On him were bestowed lands in Mull, and also the lands of Lochaber, preferring these, according to the Sleat historian, to the lands of Troternish, in Skye, of which he had his choice.

Besides these, there appears also to have been another son of the second marriage of John of Isla, named Hugh, hitherto ignored by the historians of the family. Robert the Steward of Scotland, before he succeeded to the throne, granted, as Lord of Athol, a charter of the whole thanage of Glentilt to Eugenius, Thane of Glentilt, and brother of Reginald of the Isles.[1] From the fact that the lands were conferred by the Steward, we naturally conclude that Hugh was of the second family of the Lord of the Isles, and, therefore, the Steward's own grandson. In 1382, a safe conduct, dated at Westminster on the 21st of October, is granted to Hugh of the Isles by Richard II., and an escort of six horsemen accompany him to the English borders.[2] In the same year we find the following entry in the Scottish Exchequer Rolls :—" Et Hugoni de Insulis, de dono regis, ut patet per literam suam de precepto sub secreto, ostensam super compotem sub periculo computantis iijli."[3] Again in the year 1403 we have :—" Et domino quondam Hugoni de Insulis, de dono regis, prout pater per literas suas de recepto de anno hujus compoti ostensas super compotum vli."[4] Skene asserts that the family descended from Hugh became McIntoshes from one of them whose name was Finlay Toiseach, Thane of Glentilt. This is highly probable, for we have never been able to identify any of the descendants of Hugh under the name of Macdonald, and from the fact that the heads of the family were styled Thanes

[1] Skene's Celtic Scotland, vol. III., p. 272. Atholl Charter Chest.
[2] Rotuli Scotiæ, vol. II., p. 45.
[3] Exchequer Rolls, vol. III., p. 92. [4] Ibid., vol. III., p. 576.

or Toiseachs, there is every reason to suppose that in time they became McIntoshes.

Though the lands of the lordship of the Isles were thus divided between the sons of the two marriages of John of Isla, the superiority of the whole still remained in Donald, now the acknowledged chief of the Clan Donald, and we are not by any means disposed to agree with Skene and others in saying that this division of the lands of the lordship weakened the power of the Clan Donald, and finally brought about the downfall of the lordship itself. The real cause of the downfall of the lordship of the Isles must be sought elsewhere, and may be summed up briefly in the struggle of Saxon against Celt—a struggle which could only result finally, as we find it did, in a fight so unequal, in the triumph of the stronger over the weaker forces. Instead of weakening the power of the Lord of the Isles, the division of the heritage of the family seems very materially to have increased it. If the intention of the Charter of 1373 was partly to cripple the resources, influence, and organic unity of the Island family, that policy certainly did not succeed, for the cadets of the family themselves, no less than the other vassals of the lordship of the Isles, continued to adhere loyally to the Macdonald standard until the final attempt to set up the Celtic supremacy in the Isles failed in the rebellion of Donald Dubh.

The first mention we have of Donald, Lord of the Isles, in any record, is in the year 1369, when, according to the Treaty of Inverness, he was given as a hostage to the king for the future good behaviour of his father, John of Isla. Donald would then have been about ten years of age, if we are

right in assuming that the second marriage of John
of Isla took place in the year 1358. His compulsory
residence in the Castle of Dumbarton could not in
the nature of things have tended to make him loyal
to the Scottish throne. The policy of the Scottish
State in detaining Donald, and the other sons of the
Lord of the Isles, though the means of bringing
about a temporary cessation of hostilities in the
Isles, proved ultimately an unwise and short-sighted
policy. Donald is no sooner set at liberty than he
assumes a defensive attitude, and he seems determined to wreak vengeance on his former jailers.
He at once assumed the *role* of an independent
prince. He owed no loyalty to the Scottish State;
on the contrary he looked upon the Kings of
Scotland as interlopers within the Island territory.
The Celt and the Saxon had little in common, and
Donald was intensely Celtic. The two races, in all
their aims and characteristics, in language and in
sentiment, were as wide apart as the poles.
Donald's policy clearly was to set up a Celtic
supremacy in the West, independent of all interference from the Saxon importation in the South.

It is from this purely Celtic point of view that
his conduct and that of his house must be judged,
and viewing it in this light it may well be justified.
Loyalty to the Scottish State in these circumstances
could hardly be expected, and could not consistently
be observed by the Island Lord. A princely inheritance had been handed down to him through
successive generations of men inspired by the same
motives and actuated by the same feeling of hostility
towards the enemies of their race, and Donald must
now consider how best to preserve it.

The strained political relations between England and Scotland favoured negotiation with the former country, and accordingly the Island Lord and his brothers are found visiting the English Court frequently during the years from 1378 to 1408. In the year 1378 a safe conduct is granted 'by Richard II. to Donald, " filio Johannis de Insulis, clerico," on his return from the University of Oxford, where he had been educated for the Church.[1] This Donald is referred to in the treaty concluded between David II. and John, Lord of the Isles, in 1369, and is given on that occasion as a hostage for the future good behaviour of his father.[2] In 1382, Hugh of the Isles, as we have seen, visits England, probably as ambassador from the Isles, and is honoured on his return with an escort of six horsemen.[3] In 1388, the Lord of the Isles and his brothers, Godfrey and John Mor, visit the English Court and are received as independent Celtic princes, while at the same time they enter into a league with Richard II., to which John, Bishop of the Isles, is a party.[4]

In the year 1400, a safe conduct, dated at Westminster on February 5th, is granted to John of the Isles and Donald his brother with an escort of 80 horsemen.[5] From the language in which this document is couched, it seems the brothers were

---

[1] Rotuli Scotiæ, vol. II., p. 11.

[2] *Vide* Treaty of Inverness, p. 121.

[3] "Salvus Conductus pro Hugone of the Oute Isles." Westminster, Oct. 21, 1382.—Rotuli Scotiæ, vol. II., p. 45.

[4] " Episcopo Sodorensi datur potestas tractandi de confederationibus cum filiis Johannis, nuper domini Insularum."—Rotuli Scotiæ, vol. II., p. 94.

[5] "Rex universis et singulis admirallis, etc., salutem Sciatis quod cum nobilis vir Johannes de Insulis Dominus Dunwage et de Glynns et Donaldus fratur ejus, etc."—Rotuli Scotiæ in Turri Londonensi, vol. II., 155.

received at the English Court with much distinction
and ceremony.   In July of the same year we find
the two brothers again visiting England and
entering into a defensive league with Henry IV.[1]
In the years 1405 and 1408, Donald and John
repeat these visits, and renew their alliance with the
English monarch.[2]   Thus the exigencies of political
warfare forced the Island family to seek the friendly
alliance of England against an aggressive Scottish
neighbour, and English statesmen were not slow to
take advantage of so favourable an opportunity to
advance the English policy towards Scotland.   The
conduct of the Island Lord may appear on the face
of it unpatriotic, but in reality it was not so, though,
as it ultimately proved, it was an unwise and short-
sighted policy.   It was a consistent and open
declaration of the policy of his house, and an
assertion of the ancient Celtic independence of his
family.   Meantime it served to disarm opposition on
the part of the Scottish State, and secured the
independence of the Island Lord for a time, though
ultimately it helped to bring about the downfall of
his family.

A peculiar incident in the romantic exile of
Richard II. of England is an indication of the
friendly alliance between the family of the Isles
and the English Court at the period under review.
The revolution that placed Henry of Lancaster on
the throne of England drove Richard II., as a State
prisoner, to Pontefract Castle.   Shortly afterwards
the news spread abroad that Richard was dead, but,
in reality, and there is no reason to doubt the
accuracy of the story, he had escaped from his

[1] Rymer's Foedera, vol. VIII., p. 146.   [2] Ibidem, pp. 418, 527.

jailers and, in the disguise of a beggar, found his way to Finlaggan Castle in Isla, the seat of the Lord of the Isles. Here he was recognised by Margery Bisset, the wife of John Mor Tainistear, brother of the Lord of the Isles. This lady, who had recently been married to John Mor, had seen the unfortunate royal exile in her native Ireland, and immediately recognised him though in such humble disguise.[1] Donald received the deposed monarch kindly, and hospitably entertained him, until a safe asylum had been secured for him at the court of the Scottish King.

The differences between Donald of Isla and his royal relatives, though at first not very easily defined, seem to have had the effect of causing a domestic quarrel between them. Donald and his brothers, John Mor and Alasdair Carrach, were accused of want of filial affection towards their mother, the King's sister. What grounds there were for this serious charge against the brothers it is difficult to say, for none were specified, though we may easily conjecture that the brunt of their

[1] " Bot in the Out-Ilys of Scotland than
There was a travelland a pure man ;
A Lordis dochter of Ireland,
Of the Bissatis there dwelland,
Wes weddyt with a gentleman—
The Lord of the Ilys bruither than,
In Ireland before quhan schee had bene,
And the King Richard thar had sene ;
Quhen in the Islys schee saw this man
Schee let that she weel kend hym than,
Till her maistere soon schee past
And thar till hym all sae fast
That hee wes the King of Yngland
That she before saw in Irland,
When hee wes tharin before,
As schee drew than to memore."—WYNTOUNE,

offending was their Celtic tendencies generally, and particularly their independent attitude towards the Scottish State. In these circumstances, and amid such surroundings, the King enjoined the Earl of Fife to protect his sister, the Lady of the Isles. This interference was very naturally resented by Donald and his brothers, and it so exasperated them that they immediately raised the standard of rebellion. Though Donald had made no formal claim to the Earldom of Ross at this early stage in the chequered history of that much contested possession, we may well believe that he followed closely the course of events, and that he was by no means a disinterested spectator. On the death of the notorious Wolf of Badenoch in 1394, the Castle and lands of Urquhart, which formed part of the extensive Earldom of Ross, and which were held by the Wolf in right of his wife, the Countess of Ross, became the scene of much confusion and strife. Alasdair Carrach, aided and abetted by his brother, the Lord of the Isles, threw himself into the conflict and took possession of the Castle and lands of Urquhart. His tenure was a short-lived one. The details of this rebellion have not been preserved, but it had one result at least in the imprisonment of Alexander Carrach, who seems to have rendered himself more conspicuous than the other brothers, and thus sustained the character which so well became him in after years. The imprisonment of Alexander was little better than a farce, which, having been played out, in the course of the following year he was released. Donald, who had been his kindly jailer, had, however, to appear before Parliament to answer for his prisoner, which having done, the feigned royal anger was assuaged.[1]

When Donald of Isla again appears on the historical stage it is as chief actor in the drama of the year 1411. He does not appear to have taken any prominent part in the politics of the years immediately following the death of King Robert III., nor do we find him opposing, or acquiescing in, the appointment of the Duke of Albany as Regent of the Kingdom, though we may conjecture from after events that he did not look upon it with favour. The remote situation of the island lordship, the assertion of independence on the part of Donald himself, together with the entire want of sympathy with southern aims, explains the disappearance of a nobleman of the Island Lord's rank from the Scottish politics of this period. It is only when the interests of his own family and race are at stake that the Island Chief steps boldly upon the stage and plays a prominent part. The rumoured resignation of her rights by Euphemia Lesley, the daughter and heiress of Alexander Lesley, Earl of Ross, is the cause of his now re-appearing from his temporary retirement. The Earldom of Ross was too great a prize to be lightly passed over by the Island Lord, and he eagerly watches his opportunity to lay hold on it. In extent the earldom comprised the old district of Ross, Cromarty, and that portion of ancient Argyle extending westwards from Glenelg to Lochbroom, including the coast lands of Kintail, Lochalsh, Lochcarron, Applecross, and Gairloch.

---

[1] Acts of the Parl. of Scotland, Vol. I., p. 503. April 22, 1398—" Preterea ordinatum est quod si offeratur tractatus ut submissio ex parte rebellancium quod non recipiatur nisi in forma que sequitur viz. quod dominus insularum et fratres sui Johannes et Alexander et consilarii eorum principales, etc., etc."

It extended inland as far east as Urquhart, and included the parish of Kilmorack, now in the county of Inverness. In addition to the foregoing the Earls of Ross were superiors of lands of which the following are the more important :—In the County of Aberdeen, the lands of Auchterless and King Edward; in the County of Inverness, the lands of Innermerky in the lordship of Badenoch; in the County of Nairn, the lands of Balmakayth, Both, Banchre, Rate, Kynowdie, Kinsteary, Kilravock, Easter Geddes, Dumnaglass, and Cawdor.

This large territory, or at all events Ross proper, had formerly been under the sway of Celtic maor-mors, and for centuries had suffered from the incursions of both Norse and Dane.[1] At this time the Scandinavian element largely preponderated over the original Pictish inhabitants, but the two had gradually become amalgamated into one people, and the Celtic spirit, which had survived the shock of centuries of Teutonic oppression, seems still to have pervaded the great body of the population. The introduction of feudal laws and institutions in the South affected, almost simultaneously, the old order of things in the North. The Celtic maormor gave place to the Norman baron. The last maormor of Ross of whom we have any record was Macbeth, who became King of Scotland in 1040, and was murdered in the year 1056.[2] The first Earl of Ross of whom there is any notice was Gillanders, of the Celtic family of Obeolan, who were hereditary lay abbots of Applecross ; but whether he assumed the dignity or had it conferred upon him, he is at all

[1] Annals of Tigernach. Nennius (Irish Version), pp. lxxvii., lxxix.
[2] Reg. Prior S. Andre, p. 114. Chron. de Mailros, pp. 47-51. Innes's Critical Essay, pp. 791, 803.

events referred to as Earl in the year 1160.[1] The next
Earl of Ross appears to have been Malcolm MacHeth,
who held the earldom only for a very brief period.[2]
In 1161, William the Lion created Florence, Count
of Holland, Earl of Ross, on his marriage with that
King's sister.[3] In or about the year 1212, Alexander II. created Ferchard Macintagart, of the
Obeolan family of Applecross, Earl of Ross, for
services rendered to the King. He was succeeded
by his son William as second Earl of the new
creation. William was succeeded by his son William
as third Earl. The third Earl was succeeded by
his son Hugh as fourth Earl. Earl Hugh, who
was killed in the battle of Halidon Hill, was
succeeded by his son William as fifth Earl.
Earl William, on the death of his brother Hugh,
his heir, resigned the earldom, but David II.
renewed a grant of it to him and his heirs
male, with remainder to Sir Walter Lesley and
his wife, the Earl's daughter. Thus the line of
succession was diverted from heirs male exclusively
to heirs general, and accordingly on the death of
the fifth Earl in 1372, his daughter succeeded him
as Countess of Ross. Sir Walter Lesley having
died in 1382, his widow, Euphemia, Countess of
Ross, married Alexander Stewart, Earl of Buchan,
to whom the King, at the desire of Euphemia,
confirmed a grant of the earldom, and he afterwards appears in record as Earl of Ross, to the
exclusion of Alexander Lesley, Euphemia's son.
Alexander Lesley, however, ultimately succeeded to
the Earldom in the year 1398, and dying in 1402,
his only daughter, who bore the family name of

---

[1] Wyntoune.   [2] Register of Dunfermline, p. 25.
[3] Palg. Illust., vol. I., pp. 20, 21.

Euphemia, became Countess of Ross. The mother
of the Countess of Ross was the Lady Isabella
Stewart, daughter of Robert, Duke of Albany, the
regent of the kingdom, and her aunt was Margaret
Lesley, daughter of Sir Walter Lesley and the
Countess Euphemia of Ross. The Lady Margaret
Lesley was the wife of Donald, Lord of the Isles,
and therefore the nearest living relative in the line
of succession to the Earldom of Ross after the
Countess Euphemia.

In the event of Euphemia's death or resignation,
it is obvious that we have abundant materials for a
fierce domestic quarrel, and on account of the
position of the parties, the elements of a stirring
historical drama. The principal actors in the events
that followed were all nearly related by blood to one
another, as well as kindred to the Scottish throne.
Chief in position was Albany, who for many years
held, as Regent, the supreme power in the State.
Devoid of the warlike qualities which his brothers
possessed, in fact a man of suspected courage in the
field, he was intellectually head and shoulders above
all the other sons of Robert II. But his talents,
which undoubtedly were lofty, were prostituted
to dark and selfish intrigue. It is no unfounded
suspicion that he condoned, if he did not actually
compass, the murder of the Duke of Rothesay, his
nephew, and heir apparent to the throne; and if
he did not allow his other nephew James to be
captured by the English, he offered no protest
against his long imprisonment. Of determined
resolution and unflinching purpose, he never amid
the various and conflicting currents of State policy
lost sight of his own ends, nor did he scruple to
sweep out of his path whoever stood in the way of

the execution of his designs. Had he been a single-hearted Scottish patriot, animated by zeal for the national welfare, and the safety of the State, his policy in keeping the family of the Isles out of the succession to the Earldom of Ross would, from a national standpoint, have been worthy of all praise. If the addition of Garmoran and the North Isles to the House of Isla in the reign of David II. constituted a source of danger to Scottish supremacy, the further addition of the Earldom of Ross to the already extensive Island domains, would make the Island Lord a still more formidable antagonist. But there were interests dearer to Albany than the Scottish weal. His own interests came first, the aggrandisement of his family came second in the order of importance, and the interests of Scotland came last. But it suited his personal and family ambition to put on this occasion the last first, and thus, under cover of patriotism, play the game which through his far-sighted policy he had so elaborately planned. The course pursued reveals the hand of a master in diplomatic arts. Euphemia Lesley, the heiress of Ross, was sickly, some say deformed, and not likely to live long.[1] If she died without making a special destination of·her possessions and honours, these would in the natural course of things devolve on Lady Margaret of the Isles. This was a consummation by all means, fair or foul, to be prevented, and hence the cunningly devised plot. The heiress of so much worldly wealth and

---

[1] " Alexander Lesley, Earl of Ross, married Euphame, and had issue a crookbacked daughter, Euphame "—Rothes MSS. in the Adv. Lib., p. 99. " Alexander Lesley, after the death of his father, succeeded in the Earldom Ross. He married Lady Euphame, &c., and by her had issue a daughter Euphame 'yat was crouchbacked'"—MS. History of the Earls of Ross in Advocates' Library, Iac. v. 6-17, p. 327.

honour is found to have interests that are not of
this world. She is found to have a call from heaven
to devote herself to the exclusive exercise of piety.
She must be secluded from all earthly interests, and
resign for ever every worldly ambition. Above all,
she must not directly or indirectly be brought under
the influence of the Lord of the Isles and his lady.
Euphemia at length betakes herself to a convent,
and the cool and wary schemer that wielded the
helm of State was biding the time when she came of
legal age to resign her rights into his hands. If she
died before then, he probably had another card to
play, but meantime she was secure against all
machinations but his own.

Donald was no match for Albany in this game of
political *finesse*. Whatever were his faults, or those
of his race, they never fought with the weapons of
duplicity or intrigue, though often their victims.
The Lord of the Isles, therefore, had recourse to the
argument which was best understood in the brave
days of old. In addition to the conquest of Ross, it
is said that Donald had other designs, but it is
difficult to conceive what these could have been.
The wild and extensive scheme which historians
have alleged Donald to have conceived of making
himself master of all Scotland is too utterly
incredible, and may be dismissed at once as
unworthy of any consideration. The conflict, moreover, was not one between Celt and Saxon as such,
nor was the struggle one for the supremacy of the
one race over the other. Unquestionably the
occasion of unfurling the Macdonald banner at this
time was the conduct of Albany, in relation to the
disputed succession to the Earldom of Ross, and
Donald had no higher ambition than to make himself master of that extensive territory.

According to the Sleat historian, Donald told the Governor that he would either lose all or gain the earldom to which he had such a good title. He maintained that Euphemia, the heiress to the earldom, having become the bride of heaven, and given up the world, might be regarded as legally dead, and Lady Margaret of the Isles became *ipso facto* her successor.[1] The contention seemed a sound enough one, according to the canons of equity, and our sympathies are naturally with Donald, who, with chivalrous daring, was prepared to fight with his strong right arm for what he deemed his own, rather than with the wily Regent, who pulled the wires of State, and had the resources of a kingdom at his back.

The heather was soon aflame, and the fiery cross blazed through the Isles, as well as through those mainland regions in which the Macdonald power was predominant. The whole Clan, with its vassals, rallied to the fight. From many a glen, and strath, and isle, the Gaelic warriors hastened to the rendezvous, where the ancient banner of the Kings of Innsegall was unfurled to its native breeze. The Macleans and Mackinnons, the hardy Clans of Mull, the Clan Chattan from lone Lochaber, and the Macleods from the rugged hills of Harris and Lewis, obeyed the call to arms.

On the point of Ardthornish, in Morvern, commanding the water-way which washes the shores of ancient Oirthirghael, stood a residence and stronghold of the Macdonalds,

> " Which on her frowning steep
> Twixt cloud and ocean hung."

[1] Euphame "rendered herself religious among the nuns of North Berwick in Haddingtonshire"—MS. Hist. of the Earls of Ross, &c.

Only the walls of its keep are still erect, towering high above the rocky promontory like a sentinel grim and hoary keeping watch and ward, where of old, in the days of its glory, it

> " Overlooked dark Mull thy mighty sound,
>   Where thwarting tides with mingled roar
>   Part thy swarth hills from Morvern's shore." [1]

From its commanding position, Ardthornish was well adapted as a vantage ground for defence or attack, by land or sea, and there could be no better rendezvous for the assembling of the host that was to invade the Earldom of Ross.

> " 'N uair dh' éireas Clann Domhnuill
>   Na leomhainn tha garg
>   Na beo-bheithir, mhòr-leathunn
>   Chonnspunnach, gharbh,
>   Luchd sheasamh na còrach
>   Do 'n ordugh Lamh-dhearg,
>   Mo dhoigh gu 'm bu ghòrach
>   Dhaibh tòiseachadh oirbh." [2]

> " When the valiant Clan Dònuill,
>   The lions in might,
>   Like thunder bolts gleaming,
>   With blades flashing bright,
>   Brave sons of the Red Hand,
>   Declare for the right,
>   Then woe to the foeman
>   That meets them in fight."

It was a little after midsummer when Macdonald and his fleet arrived on the West Coast of Ross-shire, and the army disembarked at Strome. Marching through the great glens of Ross they soon reached the vicinity of Dingwall. But the conquest of Ross was not to be unopposed. The county of Caithness, as might be expected from its position,

---

[1] The Lord of the Isles.   [2] Iain Dubh Mac Iain-Ic Ailein.

was from an early period subject to Norse influence, and in the course of time came to be occupied by a population largely Norse in composition. It formed part of the possessions of the great Norwegian Jarls of Orkney from the beginning of the 10th down to the end of the 12th century. The district of Strathnaver, however, which formed the western portion of the ancient county of Caithness, differed from the rest of that region not only by reason of its wild and mountainous surface, but also in being the abode of a people who, amid the racial changes that took place in that time, retained their Celtic blood and speech largely unaffected by Norwegian admixture. The most powerful clan that occupied this portion of Caithness at the beginning of the 15th century was the Clan Mackay. It is said that at that time Angus Dubh Mackay could bring into the field 4000 fighting men. The news of Donald's march through Wester Ross having penetrated to far Strathnaver, Angus Dubh Mackay determined to oppose the progress and clip the wings of the Hebridean eagle. He hastily gathered his forces, said to have been 2500 strong, and marching to Dingwall, arrived just as the Islesmen were seen approaching. He immediately assumed the offensive, but failed to stem the tide of the advancing force. A fierce engagement took place, in which the men of Caithness, though they fought with the bravery and firmness characteristic of the Mackay clan, were routed. Rory Galld, brother of the chief, and many others were slain, whilst Angus Dubh himself was taken prisoner. Macdonald of the Isles having taken possession of the Castle of Dingwall and garrisoned it, resumed his march, and proceeded to Inverness by Beauly. At the latter

place he halted, and diverting his line of march he
proceeded to Castle Downie and administered a
well-merited chastisement to the Laird of Lovat
and his Frasers, who had the temerity to oppose
the Island Lord's pretensions to the Earldom of
Ross. Having at length arrived at Inverness, he
planted his standard in the Highland Capital, and
summoned all the fighting men of Ross, and of the
North generally, to his banner. The summons met
with a wide response from the purely Celtic regions
of Scotland, and many, emboldened by the success
that already attended the Island Chief's efforts,
took up arms to support his cause.

According to a MS. history of the Mackenzies,
quoted in the Macdonald Collections, "Murdoch
Nichoil Mackenzie was the only chief in the North
Highlands who refused assistance to Macdonald
when he fought against the Governor's forces at
Harlaw. He was taken prisoner by the Earl of
Ross at Dingwall."[1] The Chief of the Mackenzies
was at this time of so little consequence that it
was hardly worth while keeping him in "durance
vile" during the absence of the Island Chief at
Harlaw. But he was not the only chief in the
North who opposed Macdonald's invasion of Ross.
A much more powerful individual, in the person of
the Chief of the Frasers, had not only endeavoured
to check Donald's progress through the Earldom,
but afterwards fought against him at Harlaw.

No sooner had Donald mustered the full force
of his followers than he launched on what was
apparently a fresh enterprise. Instead of standing
on the defensive and guarding what he had gained,
he again assumed the aggressive. It has by some

---

[1] Macdonald Collections, p. 1248.

been conjectured that, in addition to the invasion
of Ross, there was another and more ambitious
plan of campaign in which Donald expected to
form a junction with his English allies.   If this
was so, and we can only speculate, England's own
difficulties in France proved Scotland's friends in
need, and if Donald cherished any expectations of
southern aid, he was doomed to disappointment.
Donald, though in possession of the Earldom of
Ross, well knew that he was not to be left long
undisturbed in the enjoyment of his recent acquisition, and, taking time by the forelock, he resolved
to push his way eastwards in the expectation of
swelling his ranks as he proceeded, and thus pre-
senting such a formidable and imposing appearance
as to strike terror into the heart of the opposing
host.   Besides, Donald, in the course of his quarrel
with the Regent, threatened to burn the town of
Aberdeen, and to put that threat into execution
was, at least, one motive for the intended invasion
of the granite city.   The partial or total burning
of the town of Inverness, in which the famous
oak bridge over the Ness perished, though valiantly
defended by a stalwart townsman of the name of
Cumine, and the ravages committed by the Island
host as they traversed the counties of Moray and
Aberdeen ought, without any hesitation, to be taken
with a very large grain of salt.   That Donald used
the weapons at his disposal to advantage may well
be believed—those weapons that at that time were
inseparable from and incidental to the fortunes of
war; but the fire and sword with which he
devastated any portion of the large district of
country through which he passed were not used
wantonly or merely in quest of plunder, though

that was always acceptable and needful for the support of his army, but largely because he had not received the accession to his ranks which he anticipated and demanded.

Three weeks of July of the year 1411 had elapsed when the Highland army, which cannot be estimated at less than 10,000 strong, quitted Inverness. The Island Lord himself commanded the main body, which was composed of the Isles-men, including the Macleods of Lewis and Harris under their chiefs. The right wing was commanded by Hector Maclean of Duart, commonly known as *Eachunn Ruadh nan Cath*, while the left was under the command of The Mackintosh. John Mor Tainistear of Dunnyveg led the reserve. When the news arrived in Aberdeen that Donald and his host were on their way to consign the town to the flames, the panic may well be conceived. The terror which the approach of the Highlanders struck into the popular mind has been reflected in the ballad poetry of the country. Scott, in "The Antiquary," seems to have caught the spirit of the time, and the following lines, written, of course, from the Lowland point of view, show that Donald was not to have it all his own way on his memorable march towards Harlaw :—

> "Now haud your tongue, both wife and carle,
>   And listen, great and sma',
>   And I will sing of Glenallan's Earl
>   That fought on the red Harlaw.
>
> "The coronachs cried on Benachie,
>   And doun the Don and a',
>   And Hieland an' Lawland may mournfu' be
>   For the sair field of Harlaw.
>
> "They saddled a hundred milk white steeds,
>   They hae bridled a hundred black,
>   With a chafron of steel on each horse's head, ﹍
>   And a good knight upon his back.

" They hadna ridden a mile, a mile,
    A mile, but barely ten,
    When Donald came bauking down the brae
    Wi' twenty thousand men.

" Their tartans they were waving wide,
    Their glaives were glancing clear,
    Their pibrochs rung frae side to side,
    Would deafen ye to hear.

" The great Earl in his stirrups stood
    That Highland host to see :
    Now here a knight that's stout and good
    May prove a jeopardie :

" What wouldst thou do, my squire so gay
    That rides beside my reyne,
    Were ye Glenallan's Earl the day,
    And I were Roland Cheyne ?

" To turn the rein were sin and shame,
    To fight were wondrous peril,
    What would ye do now, Roland Cheyne,
    Were ye Glenallan's Earl ?

" Were I Glenallan's Earl this tide,
    And ye were Roland Cheyne,
    The spur should be in my horse's side
    And the bridle upon his mane.

" If they hae twenty thousand blades,
    And we twice ten times ten,
    Yet they hae but their tartan plaids,
    And we are mail-clad men.

" My horse shall ride through ranks sae rude,
    As through the moorland fern,
    Then ne'er let the gentle Norman blude
    Grow cauld for Highland kerne."

The chief magnate of the regions of Garioch and
Strathbogie through which Donald and his host
advanced was Alexander Stewart, Earl of Mar, the
Glenallan's Earl of Scott's ballad, and it is a remark-

able fact that as the quarrel had been from the
outset between kinsfolk, Donald's career was destined
to be interrupted by a first cousin of his own.   The
career of this nobleman is an interesting chapter
in the annals of that wild and romantic age, a
blending together of the lawlessness and chivalry so
characteristic of the time.   In early life he had been
the leader of a band of freebooters from the wilds
of Badenoch, with which his father, the notorious
Wolf, known as *Alasdair Mòr Mac an Righ*, was
so much associated.   By means of his banditti, he
eventually raised himself to the Earldom of Mar.
Having surprised Sir Robert Drummond of Stobhill
in his castle, and probably hastened his end, this
freebooter shortly afterwards took captive Sir
Robert's widow, who was Countess of Mar in her
own right, in her Castle of Kildrummie, and forced
her to give him her hand in marriage.   Subsequent
events seem to show that the lady was not unfor-
giving in her resentment at the conduct of this
"braw wooer," although his first advances were none
of the gentlest.   When afterwards he appeared
before the castle gates, placing its contents, adjuncts,
keys, and title-deeds, at her disposal, she not only
received him as her husband, but conveyed to him
the earldom with all its wealth and dignities.   On
her death, the Earl, inspired by the knight-errantry
of the time, visited foreign lands in quest of adventures.   Having taken part in the Continental wars
of the period, and sown his political wild oats, he
returned to Scotland, and now we find him the
chosen leader of the knights and burgesses of Aberdeen in their preparations to resist the advance of
the men of the Isles.

The battle of Harlaw has been described as a critical conflict between the opposing forces of civil order and barbarism. Donald has been pictured as the leader of plundering bands ; Mar as the representative of civilised virtue. In view of the facts of the case, we can hardly accept of this rough and ready classification. The feuds of the Lowland barons, the fire and sword, and rapine, which they often carried, not only into England, but into each other's domains, are quite as much opposed to the laws that regulate civilised communities as the *creachs* of their Highland neighbours. This fact has too often been calmly overlooked by the writers of Scottish history. No doubt there are very marked differences between the forces that met on the field of Harlaw. The distinctions between Celtic and feudal Scotland were there brought out into bold relief. Whether the one was a higher type of culture than the other ; whether the men-at-arms who fought in a panoply of mail, with spear and battle axe, and metal shield, were more refined specimens of the human race than the plaided and kilted warriors who fought with claymore, and were protected by their wooden shields, may be a matter of opinion ; but the one type is not further removed than the other from the civilisation of to-day.

When the news of Macdonald's march through Moray went abroad, the gentlemen of Aberdeenshire, with their armed retainers, assembled under the leadership of the Earl of Mar. Mail-clad mounted knights, armed to the teeth after the manner of Norman chivalry, the number of which is not easily determined, but generally estimated at a little more than a thousand men, rode off to meet the foe. Inferior in numbers to the forces of the Isles, the disadvantage was heavily discounted by the completeness of their equipment and their strong defensive armour. Mar advanced by Inverury, and came in sight of the Highland army at the village of Harlaw, some ten miles from the county town of Aberdeen, whither had flocked to his standard the gentlemen of Aberdeen, Angus, and the Mearns. The Ogilvies, the Lindsays, the Carnegies, the Lesleys, the Lyons, the Irvings, the Gordons, the Abercrombies, the Arbuthnots, the Bannermans, the Leiths, the Douglases, the Barclays, the Mowats, the Duguids, the Fotheringhams, the Frasers, and the Burnets—all were there in stern defence of hearth and home. Mar himself commanded the main body of his small force, while Sir Alexander Ogilvie, Sheriff of Angus, and Sir James Scrymgeour, Constable of Dundee, led the vanguard.

Donald's army, consisting chiefly of the Macleans, the Mackintoshes, the Camerons, the Mackinnons, the Macleods, and all the vassals of the lordship of the Isles, was drawn up in imitation of the old Pictish mode, in the cuneiform order of battle.[1] Donald himself commanded the main body, with the Macleods of Lewis and Harris as his lieutenants; while the right and left respectively were under the command of Hector Roy Maclean of Duart and Mackintosh. John Mor Tainistear stood at the head of the reserve. The courage of the men of the Isles was roused to the most patriotic fervour by the stirring appeal of MacVuirich, the Tyrtaeus of the campaign, to remember the ancient valour of the race of Conn—

---

[1] Logan's Scottish Gael., Ed. 1876, Vol. I., p. 155.

BATTLE OF HARLAW 1411.

"A chlanna Chuinn, cuimhnichibh,
Cruas an am na h-iorghuill." [1]
"Sons of Conn remember
Hardihood in time of strife."

The Highlanders, armed with broadswords, bows and axes, and wooden shields, rushing forward with furious onset and shouting the slogan of their clan, were received by the Lowlanders with steadiness and valour. Sir James Scrymgeour, Constable of Dundee, and Sir Alexander Ogilvie, Sheriff of Angus, who with a band of knights occupied the van of the Lowland army, endeavoured to cut their way through the Highland columns that were bearing down upon them like a flood, but they were soon overwhelmed and slain. In other parts of the field, the contest raged with fury. The brave Mar with his knights fought on with desperate courage till the Lowland army was reduced to a skeleton; but it was only after the long summer day had faded away at last, and the dark curtain of night enfolded the blood-stained field, that the exhausted combatants sheathed their blades. The Lowland army was annihilated, and the flower of the chivalry of Angus and the Mearns lay dead upon the field :—

"There was not sin' King Kenneth's days,
Sic strange, intestine, cruel strife
In Scotlande seen, as ilka man says—
Where monie likelie lost their life ;
Whilk made divorce 'tween man and wife,
And monie children fatherless.
And monie a ane will mourn for aye,
The brime battle of the Harlaw."

[1] Prosnachadh-catha, le Lachlainn Mòr Mac Mhuirich Albanaich, do Dhomhnull a Ile, Righ Innsegall, latha Cath Ghariach. This extraordinary poem is given in full in the Collection of the Stewarts only, and it was printed for the first time in Ronald Macdonald's Collection in 1776; where only a few lines are given.

11

To the east of Scotland, Harlaw was a miniature
Flodden, and the wail of a hundred years later over
that bloody field, "that the flowers of the forest
were a' wede away," would not have been inappro-
priate here.   On Mar's side, according to the
Lowland chroniclers, 500 were killed and many
wounded.   Among the men of note who fell were
Sir Alexander Ogilvie, Sheriff of Angus, Sir Thomas
Murray, Sir James Scrymgeour, Sir Alexander
Irvine of Drum, Sir Robert Maule of Panmure,
Sir William Abernethy of Salton, Sir Alexander
Straiton of Lauriston, Sir Robert Davidson, Provost
of Aberdeen, James Lovel, Alexander Stirling, and
Lesley of Balquhain, with his six sons.

On Donald's side 900 are said to have fallen,
among whom were Gilpatrick MacRory of the
Obeolan family, and Lachlan Macmillan, who, with
Norman and Torquil Macleod, were the first at the
head of their men to charge the Lowland host.[1]
Besides these, according to Hugh Macdonald, "two
or three gentlemen of the name of Munroe were
slain, together with the son of Macquarry of Ulva,
and two gentlemen of the name of Cameron."[2]   The
brave Hector Roy Maclean of Duart and Irvine of
Drum fought hand to hand until they both fell
together.

Trustworthy records of this famous fight there
are none.   Lowland historian and ballad composer,
as well as Highland seanachie, described what they
believed must and should have happened.   Certain
main facts, however, we are assured of.   That both
sides fought with valour and determination, and
that Scotland alone was capable of being the nursing

MacVuirich in Reliquiæ Celticæ, p. 213.
[2] Hugh Macdonald in Collectanea de Rebus Albanicis, p. 301.

mother of such heroes, may well kindle the pride of
Lowlander and Highlander alike. Yet the field of
Harlaw, in proportion to the number engaged there,
was one of the greatest reverses that ever befell the
Scots. To say in the face of such a calamitous
reverse that the Lowland army was victorious at
Harlaw, as some historians have alleged, is to be
blind to the most obvious facts. It is admitted on
all hands that Macdonald's army could not have
been under 10,000 strong. Of these, according to
the Lowland estimate, 900 lay dead on the field,
and granting that as many more lay wounded,
Donald's force when the fight ceased numbered at
least 8000 strong, ready to renew the contest with
the returning day. The Earl of Mar himself lay
covered with wounds on the field. Five hundred of
his small force lay dead around him, while the
remainder of his army lay mostly wounded, and
unable to renew the fight. These are facts, if the
Scottish historians are to be believed, but the conclusions they arrive at are not obvious, and cannot
in reason be justified. That Macdonald of the Isles
at the head of 8000 clansmen, or even half that
number, retreated in dismay before a wounded leader
lying prostrate on the field of battle surrounded by
a mere handful of men, most of whom were crippled
with wounds, cannot easily be believed by any
unprejudiced person. If Donald ever expected
English help, he now realised that he must do
without it, and knowing well that all Lowland
Scotland was arrayed against him, he judged it the
wisest policy to betake himself to his Island fastnesses. There is every reason to believe that this
was his main motive in not pursuing his campaign
further against the Duke of Albany, while at the

same time the Island Lord must have experienced the same difficulty which confronted Montrose, Dundee, and Prince Charles, in after times, of keeping a Highland army gathered from widely scattered districts for any length of time together in the field.

The Scottish historians, ignoring all such considerations, and blinded by race prejudice, have inferred from the retreat that followed what they call a drawn battle the defeat of Macdonald at Harlaw. Very different accounts of the famous engagement are given both by the Highland and Irish historians. Hugh Macdonald, MacVurich, and many others, refer in no vague terms to the complete overthrow of the Lowland army ; while the Highland bards, who are never inspired by defeat, celebrate the victory of the men of -the Isles in their loftiest strains. The Irish Annals are no less emphatic, as may be seen, among others, from the Annals of Loch Cé :—" A great victory by Macdhomhaill of Alba over the foreigners of Alba ; and MacGilla-Eoin of Macdonald's was slain in the counter wounding of that victory."[1]

The battle of Harlaw was fought on the 26th of June, 1411, and resulted, as we have seen, in well nigh the total annihilation of the Lowland army.

On the news of the crushing defeat at Harlaw reaching the ears of the Regent Albany, he made an unusual display of military spirit and activity. He resolved without delay on an invasion of the Earldom of Ross, and putting himself at the head of a sufficiently strong force, he advanced to Dingwall, took possession of the castle, and established, without any opposition, his authority through Ross.

[1] Annals of Loch Cé, by W. M. Hennessy, 1411. Vol. II., p. 137.

Donald and his clansmen had retired to their Island strongholds. Within his own domains, the Island chief was impregnable, for his naval force was superior to the whole Scottish fleet at that time. He must, however, defend his mainland territories, and here the Regent, who determined to crush his power and humble the Island Lord, had his opportunity. In the following year, smarting from the humiliation and defeat at Harlaw, Albany resumed hostilities, proceeded at the head of an army to Argyle, and attacked Donald where alone he could do so with any chance of success. The records of the period are very obscure as to the fortunes and reverses alike of the Regent's campaign against the hero of Harlaw; but subsequent events indicate very clearly that Donald held his own, and that Albany was baffled in the effort to humble him.

The story of the treaty with the Governor at Polgilb, now Lochgilp, where we find Donald coming forward humbly, laying down his assumed independence, consenting to become a vassal of the Scottish crown (which he was already—at least nominally), and delivering hostages for his future good behaviour, is given on the authority of that unreliable choronicler, John of Fordun, and as he is corroborated by no authority whatever, but, on the contrary, flatly contradicted by subsequent events, we refuse to receive it as anything but the purest fable. Such a treaty would undoubtedly have been looked upon as an event of national importance, yet the national records are dumb regarding it. No contemporary chronicler, Highland or Lowland—if we omit John himself—records this successful termination of a rebellion so formidable as to have shaken the Scottish State to its very

centre. Both in the Chamberlain and Exchequer
Rolls we find references made to the campaign of
Albany against the Lord of the Isles in Argyle, but
not the remotest reference is made to the alleged
treaty of Polgilb. What we find is the complaint
made that the Governor had not been recouped
for conveying an army to Polgilb against the
Lord of the Isles, and for his expedition to Ross
against the Caterans for the tranquillity of the
realm.[1] If the Lord of the Isles, as John of
Fordoun would have us believe, had surrendered
at Polgilb and given hostages, the tone of the
Scottish Chamberlain would have been more triumphant, and direct reference would have been
made to such an important event. Donald well
knew he could not take possession of the Earldom
of Ross against all Scotland, and that he had
resolved to make no further attempt in that
direction his retreat from Harlaw clearly proves.
His position in the Isles was too strong to be
successfully attacked. Why, therefore, should he
surrender at Polgilb? The fiction may be placed
side by side with that other fable of the defeat,
death, and burial of Donald at Harlaw, where his
tomb is pointed out to this day!

Albany undoubtedly took possession of the Earldom of Ross, and prevented the Lord of the Isles
from pushing his claim to that important inheritance;
but Donald held undisputed sway to the day of his
death within his own island principality. In no
sense can Donald be said to have enjoyed the
Earldom of Ross, save during those weeks when he

---

[1] "Neque pro expensis suis factis cum transitu exercitus semel apud
Polgilb contra dominum Insularum, et una alia vice apud Rosse, pro pacifi-
cacione regni contra Ketherauos,"—Exchequer Rolls, vol. IV., p. 213; vol.
IV., p. 239. The Chamberlain Rolls, 14.

invaded and occupied the district by force of arms. He never was, and never could have been *de jure*, Earl of Ross. The Regent carried his point. In 1415, Euphemia resigned the earldom in favour of her grandfather, who thereafter conferred it on his son, John Stewart, Earl of Buchan.

The next time the Lord of the Isles emerges from his retirement is in a domestic quarrel with his brother, John Mor Tainistear, a quarrel which seems to have assumed a formidable appearance from the array of neighbouring clans that appear on either side. The cause of the quarrel seems to have arisen from differences over some lands in Kintyre, claimed by John Mor as his share of his father's patrimony. The real instigator was the Abbot Mackinnon, who, from his position as a churchman, was a man of considerable influence in Argyle, and with whose family John Mor's own relationship was none of the purest, if the historian of Sleat is to be believed. Maclean and Macleod of Harris espoused the cause of John Mor, while Donald was supported by Macleod of Lewis, the Mackintoshes, and other vassals of the Isles. The issue was not for a moment doubtful. John Mor was defeated, and, passing into Galloway, where Donald pursued him, he found his way to Ireland, and took refuge in the Antrim glens. He and his brother Donald, however, were shortly thereafter reconciled.[1]

The hero of Harlaw now passes finally from the public gaze, and, joining one of the religious orders, he finds solace for his declining years in the exercise of quiet religious duties. The main features of his character have already passed under review. He stands before us, if not the greatest in a long line of

[1] Hugh Macdonald in Collectanea de Rebus Albanicis, p. 303.

distinguished chiefs of his family, a powerful and impressive personality, a leader who sustained the best traditions of the Clan Cholla, and who kept untarnished, in peace and war, in the senate and in the field, the name and fame of Macdonald. By far the most powerful nobleman in the realm, both from the extent of his immense territories and the influence he exercised over his many vassals in the Isles and on the mainland, Donald also possessed the qualities of a statesman. He entered into repeated alliances with England. In the year 1389, among the allies of that country, consisting of several foreign princes and others, we find the name of Donald, Lord of the Isles, and commissions at different times are issued by the English Kings to treat with the Island Chief on the footing of an independent prince. Some authorities affirm that the Lord of the Isles died in France in the year 1427, but these go on the assumption that Donald was Earl of Ross. The Earl of Ross who died in France in that year, having been killed at the battle of Verneuil, was John Stewart, Earl of Buchan, on whom the Earldom of Ross was conferred on the resignation of Euphemia Lesley, in 1415. We have already assumed that the second marriage of John, Lord of the Isles, took place about the year 1358, and that he, the eldest son of that marriage, mentioned in the treaty of 1369, must have been ten years of age when in that year he was given as a hostage to David II. The year of Donald's death is somewhat uncertain, though 1423 seems approximately correct. If this is so, he must have attained to the age of 64 when he died. He breathed his last at his Castle of Ardthornish in Morven, and was buried with befitting pomp and solemnity in the tomb of his ancestors at Iona.

CHAPTER VIII.

ALEXANDER DE ILE, EARL OF ROSS.—1425-1449.

Alexander's Accession to the Lordship.—James I. returns.—
Earldom of Ross in the Crown.—James I. visits Inverness.—
Convention.—State of Highlands.—Murder of John Mor.—
Dispute about Garmoran.—Murder of Alexander MacGorrie.—
Imprisonment of Lord of Isles.—His Liberation.—His Revolt.
—Surrender at Holyrood.—Captivity in Tantallon, Inver-
lochy.—Release of Alexander.—Murder of James I.—Alex-
ander receives the Earldom.—Appointed Justiciar.—Favours
to Mackintosh.—Death of Alexander.—His Character.

ALEXANDER of Isla, Donald's eldest son, succeeded
on his father's death to the dignities and possessions
of his house. Donald's heroic effort to secure the
Earldom of Ross as the lawful inheritance of his
wife did not meet with complete success, and
although the Sleat historian strives to make it
appear otherwise, the testimony of all the most
undoubted authorities is at issue with him. The
Earldom, which, after Euphemia's resignation, was
bestowed by the Regent upon his son, the Earl of
Buchan, fell vacant again in 1424, upon the fall of
that nobleman at the fateful battle of Verneuil, and
thereupon reverted to the Crown. Indeed, many
years were to elapse before the rightful heir of the
Earldom was to be invested with the position for
which so much blood had been shed on the memorable field of Harlaw.

In 1424, an event fraught with much importance
to general Scottish history took place. On the

death of Robert, Duke of Albany, in 1420, he was succeeded in the Regency of the Kingdom by his son Murdoch. A man of feeble capacity for rule, he proved utterly unable to control the turbulent spirits of the time, and the government of the country gradually subsided into utter anarchy. At last, in despair at the political chaos for which his own sons were so largely responsible, Murdoch entered, with some degree of earnestness, into the negotiations for the young King's ransom, with the final result that James was released from captivity in England, and restored to his ancestral throne.

It has been alleged by historians, notably by Gregory, that one of the earliest acts of James' reign was to restore the Earldom of Ross to the heiress of line, the mother of Alexander, Lord of the Isles. In proof of this, reference is made to what is certainly recorded, that in 1426 Alexander, Lord of the Isles and Master of Ross, was one of the "assiers" that condemned the Regent, his two sons, and the Earl of Lennox to death.[1] It is also on record that, in 1427, Alexander of Yle, Lord of the Isles, in a charter dated at the island of Saint Finlaggan in Yle, and also in another charter bestowing a grant of the lands of Barra and of Boisdale in South Uist on his "alumpnus and armiger," Gilleownan, one of the family of Macneill, calls himself Master of Ross.[2] From these references, it has not unnaturally been inferred that the mother of Alexander, "Lady Mary of the Yles and of Rosse," had been invested by the Crown with her hereditary rights and honours, and that the Lord of the Isles had been duly acknowledged as heir apparent to the Earldom of Ross. Yet the historical references in question prove

[1] Balfour's Annals of Scotland.   [2] Orig. Par. Scot.

nothing beyond the fact that Alexander styled himself Master of Ross, and that he received the title as a matter of courtesy.   Nothing can be clearer, as we shall hereafter show, than the tenure by the Crown of the powers and privileges of the Earldom at a much later date than 1426.   Still, Lady Mary of the Isles had every right in law and equity to the Earldom, so long as she lived, with reversion to her heir, and the continued assumption of its rights and functions by the Crown was rightly considered an illegal usurpation. Hence, despite the action of the King, the Lord of the Isles and his mother seem to have laid claim, at anyrate to the titles of the Earldom, during the reign of James I.   Whether the more substantial interests involved accrued to them, in whole or in part, is a question that we purpose considering at a later stage.

Alexander's position on the jury, before which so many of the Scottish nobles were arraigned for treason in 1426, appears to suggest a certain measure of royal favour.   It was not long, however, before his relations to the Crown underwent a complete revolution.   The storm-cloud had been gathering in the Highlands, was assuming darker and more ominous hues, and was soon to burst in fury, bringing disaster and desolation in its train.   James had devoted the first two years of his reign to the reduction of the lawlessness which had so widely prevailed in the southern regions of his kingdom, and already a measure of tranquillity had ensued. Now, in 1427, he turned his attention to the Highlands, which, during the late corrupt administration, had lapsed into a state of virtual independence.   The bonds of sovereignty had been dissolved, and every

man did that which was good in his own eyes.
James I. was undoubtedly one of the ablest statesmen that ever occupied the throne of Scotland. The
main lines of his policy, which he handed on to his
successor, were absolutely indispensable for the
general welfare of the realm. The keynote of that
policy was to curb the dangerous and increasing
power of the nobility, and it is evident that the
vindication of the sovereign authority as supreme in
the State was, in those days, the only guarantee for
the maintenance of law, order, and individual liberty
among all classes of the people. The struggle of the
Crown with those great nobles, who in their
own districts exercised power that was well nigh
unlimited, is the explanation of much of the civil
discord that prevailed in Scotland during the
fifteenth century. While the policy of James I.
was thus in its main design well conceived, yet it
is plain that, in applying his remedies to the
diseases of the body politic, he displayed a harshness,
as well as impatience, which sometimes defeated the
ends he had in view, and proved, eventually, the
cause of his tragic fate. Hence it was that his
palliatives, instead of soothing at all times the
unhealthy social organism, sometimes produced an
unwholesome and dangerous irritation. The effects
of a long period of misrule were not to be cured in a
day. The Herculean task of cleansing the political
Augean stables was one that demanded the exercise
of patience as well as energy.

After the battle of Harlaw, the Castle of Inverness, which, from its position, lay peculiarly exposed
to hostile operations, had been fortified and recon-
structed on a larger scale than before under the
supervision of the Earl of Mar. In 1427 it played

an important part in the royal policy of Reform. In this the third year of his reign, James marched to Inverness at the head of a formidable army, and accompanied by the leading Lowland barons. There he convened a Parliament, and summoned the Crown vassals and others to be present. The citation met with a large response. From the far north came Angus Dubh Mackay, who in 1411 unsuccessfully opposed Donald of the Isles at Dingwall, but who was the most powerful chief in the Celtic region of Caithness, and a leader of 4000 men. Kenneth Mor Mackenzie, a leader of 2000 men, with his son-in-law, John Ross, William Leslie, Angus de Moravia, and Matheson, leaders of 2000 men, likewise responded to the call. From Argyllshire came John Macarthur of the family of Campbell, the leader of 1000 men, and James Campbell, to the place of rendezvous. The principal leaders of the Clan Donald, Alexander Lord of the Isles, and Alexander MacGorrie of Garmoran, obedient to the King's citation,[1] came also to this convention, which was destined to leave its mark upon the general history of the Highlands, but especially upon the annals of the Family of the Isles.

There is much obscurity, it is needless to say, resting upon the history of these years, and the influences that determined the conduct of the King in the events that followed the Parliament of Inverness are far from being easy to gauge. Some clues, however, we do possess which seem to lead us to a certain extent through the labyrinth of confusion, anarchy, and treachery which are characteristic of the time, and explain the political convulsion into which the Western Highlands were plunged. The

[1] Fordun.

first and most important of the causes productive of
this state of matters was the murder of John Mor
Tainistear, the founder of the family of Dunnyveg
and the Glens, whom even Buchanan, that sweeping
denunciator of the Highland Chiefs, speaks of as a
man illustrious among his own countrymen.[1] John
Mor's death was the tragic culmination of a series of
intrigues promoted by the courtiers of King James,
and apparently winked at by royalty itself. The
hungry Scottish barons who shaped "the whisper of
the throne" were jealous, many of them, of the
power and independence of the Lords of the Isles,
and, instigated by their counsels, James resolved to
curb and break the power of Alexander, who doubtless by this time was manifesting a very natural
impatience at his mother's prolonged exclusion from
the earldom of Ross. He further resolved to take
John Mor into his confidence, with the view of
investing him with the territories of which he
decided to deprive the Lord of the Isles, ostensibly
on the ground that John, being Alexander's uncle,
was more nearly akin, by blood, to the Crown.[2] The
Lord of Dunnyveg did not entertain the proposals
favourably, and an individual of the name of James
Campbell is said to have received a commission from
the King to arrest him under cover of a friendly
interview. Whatever the powers granted under
this commission, whether Campbell received instructions to perpetrate the bloody deed that followed
or not, certain is it that John Mor was the victim
of the blackest and most abominable treachery. He
received a message from the King's delegate to meet
him in peaceful guise at Ard Dubh point in Isla, for
the purpose of communicating the royal pleasure.

[1] Rerum Scoticorum Historia, Liber X. cap. XXX.
[2] Collectanea de Rebus Albanicis,

John Mor came to the place of meeting attended by
a slender retinue, and in the course of the interview
was attacked, overpowered, and slain.[1]   It was a
shameful and most villainous deed, and it is to be
feared that the King's hands were not altogether
innocent of the blood that had been shed.   Subsequent events do not clear him of the suspicion
of treacherous conduct, and there is strong reason
to believe that, while the King's orders were vague
and undefined, his commissioner only too well
understood the spirit and purpose of his instructions.   In Campbell he found a willing instrument
ready to his hand, and it is to be noted that now
for the first time there fell athwart the path of
the Family of the Isles the shadow of that ill-
omened house which was to be its evil genius in
time to come.

The murder of the Lord of Dunnyveg caused
deep resentment among many powerful Scottish
families, and the King's policy was not so generally
popular that he could afford to incur the odium
which it undoubtedly entailed.   Especially throughout the Highlands were feelings of the deepest
resentment, accompanied by a desire for vengeance,
aroused, and the confusions of the time became
worse confounded by the spirit of antagonism to the
throne, which the dark suspicions that fell upon the
King, evoked.   The King protested that he had not
planned the murder, and had the assassin tried for
his life, while Campbell continued to assert that,
though not possessed of written instructions, he had
the royal authority for what took place.   These
were among the leading circumstances which, on
account of the turmoil they created in the High-

[1] Hugh Macdonald's MS. Balfour's Annals, Vol. I., p. 157.

lands, led to James' march to Inverness, and his summoning a convention of the Highland chiefs.

This, however, was not all. John Macarthur, another scion of the House of Campbell, had taken the opportunity afforded by the unsettled condition of the country to advance a claim to a portion of the lands of Garmoran and the North Isles. His pretensions to these territories were based upon a charter by Christina, daughter of Allan MacRuari, to Arthur, son of Sir Arthur Campbell, Knight, early in the fourteenth century.[1] Christina, being her father's heir, was acting within her legal rights in this disposition of the lands in question; but what her reasons were for putting them past her brother Roderick, who, though not feudally legitimate, she made her heir for the rest of her property, is a question which, at this time of day, it is impossible to answer. Whatever validity such an instrument may have possessed, whether it received the necessary royal confirmation or not, it is clear that several conveyances of the lands in question had taken place since the days of Christina, and that any claim founded upon her charter must have been of the most shadowy and baseless description. The occupier of Garmoran in 1427 was Alexander MacGorrie, according to Skene, and Gregory, the son, but more probably the grandson, of Godfrey, son of John of Isla.[2] The Clan Gorrie had, apparently, still the ascendancy over the progeny of Reginald, and, whether by right or by

[1] Arthuro Campbell filio Domini Arthuris militis de terra de Muddeward Ariseg et Morderer et insulis de Egg et Rumme et pertenari.

[2] According to Buchanan and others, his surname was MacReury, the patronymic of Amy, John of Isla's first wife. According to Fordun, he was MacGorrie, this latter patronymic having been used for several generations as a surname by Godfrey's descendants. There is no Alexander, son of Godfrey, in any of the genealogies.

the strong hand, were in possession of Garmoran and
the Castle of Ellantirrim, which had been seized by
Godfrey in 1389.   Alexander, the representative of
the family in the year of the Inverness Convention,
was a leader of 2000 men, and would be very
unlikely tamely to submit to any aggressive action
which the Macarthur claimant might be disposed to
take.   Attempts at possession on the one hand and
vigorous resistance on the other would, during the
late discredited administration, lead to a state of
continued disorder in the regions of North Argyll.
All this must have been aggravated by the feud which
undoubtedly existed between the Clan Ranald and
the Clan Godfrey as to the occupancy of the vast
region conferred upon and confirmed to Reginald
and his descendants in 1373.   In view of the foregoing circumstances, of which the scant annals of the
time give us but intermittent glimpses, there were
rich possibilities of feud and bloodshed, and it is
certain that the social system of the Highlands
presented a scene of wild and chronic dispeace
demanding the serious attention of the Crown.

The events that took place in connection with the
King's visit to Inverness cannot very well be estimated apart from more complete information than is
at the historian's disposal.   Yet, so far as we can see,
the proceedings that were conducted under the royal
authority are incapable of justification upon any code
of ethics.   They bring out the character of James I. in
an aspect of meanness and deceit unbecoming in any
one, but particularly so in a King, and leave a dark
and ineffaceable stain upon the history of his reign.
These Highland chiefs came as they were summoned
to a free and open convention of the nobles of the
north, trusting to the faith and honour of his

Majesty.   As the event shows, the confidence was misplaced.   On their arrival at Inverness, they were all immediately apprehended.   Some were led to prison, each being immured in a separate apartment, while others became the victims of a judicial butchery which has few parallels in Scottish history.   The King is said to have chuckled at the success of his most unkingly manœuvre, and to have given vent to his satisfaction in a Latin couplet *ex tempore*, which Scott thus freely translates :—

> " To donjon tower let the rude troop be driven,
>   For death they merit by the cross of heaven."[1]

James Campbell justly expiated his crime, but the slaughter of Alexander MacGorrie of Garmoran,[2] along with others, seems, in the absence of any evidence of guilt, and without the vestige of a trial, a monstrous exercise of royal power.

The foregoing incidents must have powerfully affected the relations of the Lord of the Isles to the Crown.   The murder of his uncle, John Mor, Lord of Dunnyveg, and of his cousin, Alexander of Garmoran, must have created the deepest indignation in the breast of the Island Lord, and would have aggravated his previous discontent and displeasure at his own continued deprivation of the Earldom of Ross. History does not clearly record his share in the troublous times prior to the convention of Inverness; but, judging from Alexander's character and subsequent conduct, it is safe to say that his attitude would not have been passive.   Little is definitely known beyond the fact that the Lord of the Isles

---

[1] This couplet, according to Fordun, ran :—

> " Ad turrem fortem ducamus caute cohortem
>   Per Christi sortem meruerunt hi quia mortem."

[2] Balfour's Annals of Scotland.

and his mother, the titular Countess of Ross, were among the Highland potentates or, as Burton would style them, the " beasts of prey," whom the King entrapped and incarcerated at Inverness.

One of the Scottish chroniclers tells us that Alexander, Lord of the Isles, was the " fomentor and foster father" of the northern rebellion, while "Angus Duffe, Kenneth Moire, John Robe, Alexander Mackmurkine, and Alexander Macrorey," are characterised as " his gray hondes."[1] Whether the relation of Alexander of Isla to the Highland chiefs whose names are quoted was of a nature to justify the canine simile, there is not sufficient evidence to show ; but it is clear that the Royal policy towards the Highlands at this juncture was not of a nature to mitigate the widespread disorder that had reigned for so long a period.

James I. is not without his defenders in the bloody and treacherous policy of 1427.   Burton, whose calmness at once deserts him when he treads the heather, justifies the King in the somewhat savage remark " that there was no more notion of keeping faith with the Irishry, whether of Ireland or Scotland, than with the beast of prey lured to its trap."   A sentiment of this nature cannot be seriously regarded save as a melancholy instance of Lowland prejudice and racial rancour.   The perusal of such remarks is irritating to the Celtic mind, but as an illustration of the falsehood of extremes we can afford to pass them by.

The Lord of the Isles was not detained in custody at this time for more than a couple of months.   He had to accompany the King from Inverness to Perth, where, on the 1st March, 1427,

---

[1] Balfour's Annals of Scotland, vol. I., p. 157.

in presence of the whole estates of the realm, he is
said to have received a royal admonition as regards
his past delinquencies, but on promise of amendment
was restored to favour and set at liberty. It is
also said that his mother was retained as a hostage
for his loyalty in the island of Inchcolm, in the
Firth of Forth.[1]

It was not to be expected that, after the extraordinary events of 1427, matters were to settle
down in the Highlands, as if neither cruelty nor
treachery had been enacted in the name of justice.
The King found that his methods of dealing with
a proud and independent people were not conducive
to the promotion of peace, and the embers of disaffection which he had sought to remove were
fanned into the hot flame of rebellion. It was
hardly to be expected also that the Lord of the
Isles should immediately forget the treatment to
which he himself had been subjected, or the ruthless
slaughter of his relatives, which had recently taken
place. Events proved that his countrymen and
vassals sympathised with him. No sooner did he
return to his island territories than the standard
of revolt was at once unfurled. Collecting 10,000
men from the Isles and from the earldom of Ross,
he invaded the mainland of Scotland in 1429. The
district of Lochaber, the country of Alastair Carrach,
seems to have been the headquarters of the Lords
of the Isles—at any rate of Alexander and his
successor—when engaged in warlike operations
on the mainland. With Lochaber as the basis
of his movements, Alexander marched to Inverness—a town which on all such occasions received
the unwelcome attentions of the fierce warriors from

[1] Balfour's Annals of Scotland, pp. 157-8.

the West.   Alexander, after the manner of his
father, consigned Inverness to the flames, wasted
the crown lands in its neighbourhood, and thus
avenged, to some extent, the indignity he had
suffered, and the oppressive deeds that had been
perpetrated two years previously within its walls.[1]

The Lord of the Isles found, however, that he
had measured himself against a King who, whatever
had been the blunders and faults of his administration, was prompt and vigorous in action as he was
on many occasions wise and prudent in counsel.
Thus it was that, having failed to storm the Castle
of Inverness, and having retired into Lochaber,
Alexander soon found himself pursued by the
King's army.   The circumstances were of a nature
to render defeat inevitable.   Even before retiring
from the siege of Inverness it was found that the
rapid approach of the royal army was followed by
disaffection among the Camerons and Mackintoshes,
the two most powerful vassals of the Isles.   In
Lochaber the situation became desperate when the
disaffected clans deserted and ranged themselves
under the royal standard.   After this the King's
vigorous attack was impossible to resist successfully,
and the Lord of the Isles was constrained to sue
for peace.   The King insisted on an unconditional
surrender, but Alexander was not, at the outset,
disposed to accede to terms so extreme.

The character and sequence of the events that
followed are far from clear.   According to Buchanan,[2]
Alexander retired to the Isles, and meditated flight
to the north of Ireland, where Donald Balloch, son

---

[1] Testimony to this is borne by the Exchequer Rolls, vol. IV., p. 416, as
follows :—" pro combustione dicti burgi per Dominum Insularum reoellem
domini regis £58 8s."

[2] Lib. X., 32. Rerum Scoticarum Historia.

of John Mor Tainistear, and now head of the
Family of Dunnyveg, possessed extensive sway
and influence. While there is nothing inherently
improbable in this account, it does not seem to fit in
with the facts that are generally accepted. It is
difficult to see how, if Alexander had retired to the
Isles, the ignominy that followed need have occurred.
The pursuit by the King's troops became so hot that
Alexander was driven south, step by step, to the
very headquarters of the enemy's power. The
sequel, as told in works of history, was a humiliating
episode. The proud representative of the Kings of
Innse-Gall must have been in terrible straits, indeed,
ere he placed himself in a position not only abject
but grotesque. On Easter Sunday the King and
his Court were assembled in the Church at Holyrood to celebrate the sacred festival. Before the
high altar, it is said that Alexander presented
himself in attire so scanty that the congregation
was deeply impressed. The authorities are so conflicting as to be untrustworthy. According to one
writer he appeared in a white shirt and drawers,[1]
according to another he came with a rope about
his neck.[2] We are inclined to think that
Alexander, even in the hour of his extremity,
would still have worn the garb of his country, a
garb unfamiliar to the minions of the Court, and
hence, quite possibly, the tradition may have
obtained currency that he appeared before the King
in his shirt. On bended knee, holding his bonnet in
one hand and the point of his sword in the other,
he made his submission. On the intercession of
the Queen, the proffered sword was accepted, and
Alexander's life was spared, but he was committed

[1] Fordun.   [2] Balfour's Annals of Scotland, pp. 147-8.

a prisoner to Tantallon Castle, under the custody of William Douglas, Earl of Angus. His mother, who was blamed for instigating him to rebellion, was still a prisoner at Inchcolm.

The Clan Donald bitterly resented the humiliation to which the Lord of the Isles was now, a second time and in aggravated form, subjected. It was resolved by the foremost leaders of the Clan to strike a blow for honour and for vengeance. The whole strength of the Clan was mustered under Donald Balloch, Lord of Dunnyveg, who, though still a youth,[1] was a redoubtable champion, the most distinguished warrior of his race. His career was destined to be stormy, but those writers who express horror at the violence of some of his acts should have remembered that, according to the code of honour of his day, the filial duty devolved upon him of wreaking vengeance upon the Scottish State, which he rightly held accountable for the murder of his father by the hand of treacherous hirelings.

The Royal army lay encamped in Lochaber, under the leadership of the Earls of Mar and Caithness. These noblemen were the King's lieutenants in that region, whose function it was to extinguish any sparks of disaffection to the Crown that might still be lingering in the north. It was once more the destiny of Mar to meet the Clan Donald in deadly combat, and another Donald, nephew to him whose prowess he felt at Harlaw, was now to prove himself a foeman worthy of his steel. It is strange that Mar should have under-estimated the warlike qualities of his opponents; though it is possible enough that the recent discomfiture of the men of the Isles in Lochaber may have bred undue con-

[1] Collectanea de Rebus Albanicis, p. 309.

fidence.   Relying on the superior armour and
discipline of his host, he sat calmly in his tent
playing cards with Mackintosh, who still acted the
part of a disloyal vassal.[1]

Meanwhile, the fighting men of the Clan Donald,
under their brave leader, were drawing nigh.   From
their imprisoned chief in Tantallon Castle a message
had come to all faithful friends and clansmen to face
the foe bravely, whatever the consequences might be
to himself, and now, burning with the memory of
wrongs sustained, and inspired by devotion to the
head of their house, they longed to meet the enemy in
the field.   From far and near, wherever the Lord of the
Isles held sway, the loyal vassals and their followers
mustered under the ancient banner.   The fiery cross
flew from glen to glen, from isle to isle, nor did it
fly in vain.   The lines of Sir Walter Scott—though
composed to the air of a Cameron piobroch, whose
Donald Dubh was not Donald Balloch, but the chief
of the Clan Cameron—are so spirited and rousing
that they well be quoted here.   Sir Walter's
"Piobroch of Donuil Dubh" was undoubtedly intended
to glorify Donald Balloch and his host :—

> " Piobroch of Donald Dhu,
>   Piobroch of Dònuil,
>   Wake thy wild voice anew,
>   Summon Clan Conuil.
>   Come away, come away,
>   Hark to the summons !
>   Come in your war array,
>   Gentles and commons.

> " Come from deep glen
>   And from mountain so rocky,
>   The war pipe and pennon
>   Are at Inverlochy.

[1] Hugh Macdonald's MS.

BATTLE OF INVERLOCHY—1431.

Come every hill plaid and
True heart that wears one,
Come every steel blade and
Strong hand that bears one."

The MacIans of Ardnamurchan, MacAllans of
Moydert, the followers of Ranald Bane, brother of
Donald Balloch—these, with the rest of the Clan
Donald, the Macleans, MacDuffies, and Macgees,
sailed in their galleys to Inverskippnish, two miles
distant from the Royal forces at Inverlochy.

The scene of the ensuing conflict was the country
of Alastair Carrach, uncle to the Lord of the Isles,
who, by the disposition of his father, had received
Lochaber as his inheritance.   It is said that about
this time there was a proposal on the part of the
Crown to deprive the Macdonalds of their rights in
Lochaber and to bestow the same upon the Earl of
Mar,[1] but there seems no evidence to shew that such
a transference ever took place.   If, however, Alastair
Carrach considered his patrimony to be in danger,
his interest in the approaching battle must have
been much intensified.   With two hundred and
twenty archers he marched to the aid of Donald
Balloch's forces, and took up his position on the hills
above Inverlochy.

The Earl of Mar found that a far more serious
game than he had been playing was now on hand,
and that the men of the Isles, of whose approach
he was warned, were rapidly bearing down upon
his encampment.   At last the critical moment
arrived when the Highland host came into conflict
with their Southern foes.   The issue was not long
doubtful.   The wild onset of the Islesmen, who
carried death upon the blades of their claymores

---

[1] Hugh Macdonald's MS.

and Lochaber axes, plunged the Earl's army into confusion, while the galling fire of Alastair Carrach's archers, whose successive volleys from the heights seemed to darken the air, still further carried destruction into the ranks of the enemy. The result was the complete discomfiture and utter rout of the King's army, accompanied by great slaughter. The Earl of Caithness, sixteen of his personal retinue, a number of Lowland knights and barons, with hundreds of the rank and file were left dead upon the field. The Earl of Mar was wounded in the thigh by an arrow, and, accompanied by one attendant, had to take refuge in the hills. Hugh Macdonald, the historian of Sleat, narrates certain adventures which befell the Earl of Mar subsequent to his reverse at Inverlochy. In his wanderings among the mountains, during this not least interesting episode in his eventful career, he and his servant are said to have fallen in with women who were tending cattle. Having obtained from these a little barley meal, the wanderers mixed it with water in the heel of the Earl's shoe—no other vessel being available—and the pangs of hunger were, for the time being, appeased. Despite the simplicity of the meal and the strange utensil in which it was prepared, to the Earl it was the sweetest morsel he ever tasted, while in remembrance of the occasion he is said to have composed the Gaelic stanza :—

> " 'S maith an còcaire 'n t-acras
> 'S mairg a ni tailceas air a' bhiadh
> Fuarag eorn a sail mo bhroige
> Biadh a b' fhearr a fhuair mi riamh." [1]

[1] The following is a free translation :—

> " The pangs of hunger are a skilful cook,
> Woe to the man who scorns the humblest brew,
> The sweetest fare of which I ere partook
> Was barley meal and water in my shoe."

But the Earl's adventures were not quite over. Fleeing through Badenoch in disguise, and hard pressed by the pursuers, he was sheltered in a hut among the hills by an Irishman named O'Birrin, and hospitably though rudely entertained. The Earl told his host, who was ignorant of the stranger's rank, that if he ever was in need he was to go to Kildrummie Castle, and there ask for Alexander Stewart, when he would hear something to his advantage. In the course of time, O'Birrin arrived at the Castle, and found, to his great astonishment, that it was the life of the Earl of Mar which he had, in all probability, saved. The Earl desired him to bring his wife and son to Kildrummie, but this the Irishman declined to do, as his wife was too old to leave her native district. After some days, O'Birrin was sent on his way rejoicing in 60 milch cows, and with an invitation to his son to come and settle at Kildrummie. The son came and acquired a freehold from the Earl, which was occupied by his descendants for many generations.[1] Such stories as these well illustrate the conditions of life in those old unsettled times. The latter in particular, showing as it does a generous appreciation of bygone kindness, not too common in the world, casts a pleasing light upon the character of Mar, and happily relieves a story of strife and vengeance.

After the battle of Inverlochy, the first but not the last fought by the Clan Donald in that region, Donald Balloch, having routed the chivalry of Scotland, and ravaged the country of the Camerons and Mackintoshes in revenge for their desertion of the Lord of the Isles in the unfortunate hostilities in Lochaber, returned with much booty to the Isles,

[1] Hugh Macdonald's MS.

and thence took ship to his Irish territories. The
feelings of the defeated Camerons were poetically
immortalised in the well-known piobroch of Donald
Dubh, to which reference has already been made.
The words[1] to which the music is wedded lament
the discomfiture of the Clan Chattan and Clan
Cameron, and both words and music abound in
mournful cadences and wailing repetitions. The
following lines, not a translation but an enlargement, so to speak, of the original words of the
piobroch, are supposed to convey the sense of defeat
and humiliation on the part of Alexander of Isla's
disloyal vassals :—

> Piobroch of Donald Dubh,
> Piobroch of Dònuil,
> Sad are thy notes and few,
> Piobroch of Dònuil.
> Proud is Clan Donald's note,
> Gaily their banners float
> O'er castle, tower, and moat
>   At Inverlochy.
>
> Routed we are to-day,
> Spearman and bowman,
> Victory in the fray
> Gone to the foeman ;
> Lost many a hero's life,
> Sad many a widowed wife,
> Triumph in battle's strife
> Rests with Clan Dònuil.
>
> Mighty Clan Chattan's fled,
> Famous in story,
> Gone from the battle red,
> Vanquished and gory.
> Where is Clan Vurich's host ?
> Great is Clan Donald's boast,
> Long shall the field we've lost
> Heighten their glory.

---

[1] The version here referred to is the original Gaelic by some unknown
author.

The news of the revolt and of the battle of Inverlochy filled King James with wrath and consternation, believing, as he did, that the turbulence of the Highland chiefs had been effectually quelled at Inverness and Lochaber. He accordingly took measures to put down the disturbers of the peace with a strong hand. He got Parliament to impose a land tax to defray the expenses of the new campaign which he felt it necessary to undertake against the Highlanders. He soon made his appearance at Dunstaffnage Castle, in the neighbourhood of Oban, with the view of proceeding to the Isles and visiting with condign punishment Donald Balloch and his coadjutors. The statements of Scottish historians regarding the events that followed are exceedingly unreliable and to be received with great caution. It is averred that all those who had taken part in the insurrection, except Donald Balloch, came to James at Dunstaffnage and made their submission, while 300 of them were hanged or beheaded, and that, as the conclusion of the whole matter, the head of the Lord of Dunnyveg was sent from Ireland as a present from Odo, Prince of Connaught, to the King.[1] The amount of truth in this version of what took place may be tested by the accuracy of the reference to the arch offender, Donald Balloch himself. Long ere the King's arrival at Dunstaffnage the hero of Inverlochy was safe beyond pursuit. Through his mother, Marjory Bisset, he had inherited the territory of the Glens in Antrim, a region to this day associated with the family of Dunnyveg, and there he found a secure retreat from the anger of the Scottish King. The

[1] Chronicle of the Earls of Ross, pp. 11-12.

Scottish Court, however, was misled into the belief that Donald Balloch was no more. Word was sent by James to Hugh Buy O'Neill, an Irish chief of Ulster, with whom he had been for some time previous associated in a friendly league against England, with the request that he should capture Donald Balloch and send him to Scotland alive or dead. O'Neill was desirous of retaining the King's friendship, while he was reluctant to take hostile action against the powerful Lord of Antrim. With a humour, grimmer and more ghastly than is usually met with in the Emerald Isle, a human head, dissevered from the body, was somehow got hold of, and sent to James as the head of Donald Balloch. The deception served its purpose, for it was the decided belief for many a day among the Scottish nobles, and Scottish historians have gravely placed it on record, that the Lord of Dunnyveg and the Glens had actually been put to death, and the Scottish King laid the flattering unction to his soul that the most formidable warrior of the Clan Donald must now, perforce, cease from troubling. That Donald Balloch did not lose his head through the agency of O'Neill, but that he lost his heart irretrievably through O'Neill's daughter, is abundantly attested by a matrimonial alliance which was soon afterwards cemented between the families. Lowland historians, as already stated, and among the rest Buchanan,[1] were taken in by the pretended decapitation ; but many years after the first two Jameses had been gathered to their fathers, Donald Balloch was once more making a mighty stir on the stormy scene of Scottish civil war.

The battle of Inverlochy was fought in the early weeks of 1431, by which time the Lord of the Isles

[1] Liber X., chap. 36.

had been pining a prisoner in Tantallon Castle for a
space of well-nigh three years.   But now the time
was rapidly approaching when he was to be set at
liberty.   At first sight it seems somewhat remarkable that a King who had proved himself so inexor-
able to offenders against his authority should have
displayed such leniency to the Lord of the Isles,
when others had been made to endure the last
penalty of the law.   His conduct in this particular
instance towards a subject who had been more than
once guilty of rebellion, was not characteristic of
his policy or methods.   It is hardly to be accounted
for by Alexander's kinship to the throne, as the
blood of many of the King's relatives had already
flowed upon the scaffold.   The reasons, however,
may not be far to seek   It is probable that by this
time the King had discovered the impolicy of harsh
measures, and that at a time when murmurs of discontent were beginning to be heard in other quarters,
the more prudent course was to put an end, if
possible, to the quarrel with the Lord of the Isles.
The supposed death of Donald Balloch had also, to
the King's fancy, removed the most formidable dis-
turber of the peace, and a favourable opportunity
alone was awanting to open the gates of Tantallon
Castle and set the prisoner free.   Such an opportunity soon arose.   In October, 1431, the heir to the
Scottish Crown—afterwards James II.—was born,
and it is said that during the public rejoicing connected with this auspicious event, an amnesty was
granted to a number of political delinquents, and,
among others, to Alexander, Lord of the Isles, who
was restored to his freedom, dignities, and possessions.[1]

[1] MS. History of the Mackintoshes.

If the early years of Alexander's public life were
crowded with troublous events, after 1431 his career
was peaceful and prosperous, his life being spent in
the enjoyment of the honours, and the discharge of
the duties of his high position.   It has been the
prevailing belief among historians that at the date
of Alexander's liberation from Tantallon, he not
only received restitution of his ancestral rights as
Lord of the Isles, but likewise full investiture of the
Earldom of Ross.   Of this latter, however, there
does not seem to be anything like adequate or
satisfactory proof.   The evidence seems all the
other way.   It is unquestionable that the functions
of the Earldom of Ross lay in the Crown as late as
1430.   No doubt at that time Alexander, Lord of
the Isles, lay a prisoner at Tantallon, which might
be adduced as a reason for the Crown possessing
the Earldom, seeing that the possessions and
dignities of the family had been forfeited.   The
contrary will appear from consideration of the
following facts:—On the 11th April, 1430, there
was an enquiry made at Nairn, in presence of
Donald, Thane of Cawdor, regarding the tenure
of the lands of Kilravock and Easter Geddes, an
enquiry rendered necessary by the destruction of
the ancient writs in the burning of Elgin Cathedral
in 1390.   In the record of that inquisition, it is
stated with the utmost clearness, that the lands in
question were held from the Crown in ward for the
Earl of Ross, who had not received the Crown
confirmation as such since the death of the last
Earl of Ross in France six years previously.[1]   Still
stronger testimony to the same effect is borne by a
Crown charter of James I. to Donald, Thane of

[1] The Family of Rose of Kilravock, pp. 127-128.

INVERLOCHY CASTLE.

Cawdor, on 4th September, 1430, which opens
with the words, "James, by the grace of God King
of Scots and Earl of Ross."[1] Nor is this all. It
appears from the evidence of contemporary records
from 1431 down to 1435 that payments of £10,
£24, and £34 were made out of the Royal Treasury
to the Countess of Ross as "Dowager Lady of the
Isles." Two inferences may be drawn from these
references without straining the probabilities of the
case. In the first place, it may reasonably be supposed that the King, who drew the revenues of the
Earldom, acknowledged by these payments a certain
moral right to them on the part of the Lady of the
Isles, and, in the second place, her designation in
these accounts, not as Countess of Ross, but as
Dowager Lady of the Isles, seems an undoubted
proof that, as late as 1435, James continued to
withhold his formal recognition of her title to the
Earldom.[2]

There is, in fact, the best reason to believe that
the Lord of the Isles did not enter into possession of
the Earldom of Ross during the life-time of James
I., and however good and equitable his claim to the
privileges of that high position, no effective right
could accrue to him without the acknowledgment of
the supreme fountain of property, as well as honour,
in the realm. James I. was assassinated on the 21st
February, 1437, and the first charter proceeding
from Alexander, in his capacity as Earl of Ross, is
dated September of the same year. This seems
to suggest that in the interval the Regents acting
for the young King had given the Lord of the Isles

<hr />

[1] Jacobus Die gratia rex Scotorum ac Comes Rossiæ.—The Thanes of
Cawdor, p. 11.

[2] Exchequer Rolls, vol. IV., 541.

investiture of the Earldom, which the late King so
long continued to withhold. During the half-dozen
years that intervened between Alexander's restoration and the death of James, the chronicles of the
age have little to say about the Lord of the Isles,
and although we may naturally suppose that he
would have occupied an attitude of opposition to
the Court, it is evident that he stood apart from
the conspiracy by which the dark deed of murder
was plotted and perpetrated. A period of quiet
had come to Alexander after the tempestuous
episodes of his earlier years, and down to the
close of his life he and his vassals enjoyed the
happiness of the nation whose annals are dull.

James II. was only a child of six at his father's
death. Either by the will of the late King, or by
the ordinance of a Parliament called at Edinburgh
the year after his death, two Regents, Sir William
Crichton and Sir Alexander Livingstone of Cal-
lendar, were given the supreme power in the State,
and they, in the exercise of their functions, appointed
Archibald Earl of Douglas Lieutenant-General of
Scotland. It is probable that the friendship between
the Lord of the Isles and the Douglas family, which
afterwards assumed a form dangerous to the State,
led to the advancement of Alexander to the high
position which he occupied, not only as Earl of Ross,
but as Warden, or Justiciar, or High Sheriff of the
whole region north of the Forth, an office which we
find him exercising in 1438, the year following the
death of James I.[1] The tenure of an office so
important implied the confidence of the Crown, and
we find in 1438, and on occasions afterwards, that
John Bullok, Bishop of Ross, was Alexander's

---

[1] *Vide* Charter in Family of Innes.

delegate to the Council of Regency, when he
wished to consult the supreme authority as to his
judicial duties in the North.[1]   During the long
minority of James II., the name of Alexander of
Isla appears frequently in the records of the north,
and there is every reason to believe that the confidence reposed by the State in his distinguished
abilities and force of character was amply justified
in the performance of his judicial duties.   The office
of Justiciar gave him command of the town of
Inverness, where many of his Courts were held,
and there is something surely of the irony of history
in contemplating the turbulent rebel, the fierce
incendiary of 1427, now appearing in the Capital of
the Highlands representing in his own person the
supreme majesty of the law.   It may well be
believed that the feelings of the Invernessians would
be of a somewhat mingled nature on Alexander's
appearance amongst them in this unwonted guise.
There is no evidence, however, that the Earl of Ross
exercised the duties of his office in any unjust or
oppressive manner.   An exception to this may
possibly be the case of Donald Dubh, the Chief of
the Clan Cameron.   It will be remembered that
this chief and his clan, though vassals of the Lord
of the Isles, treacherously deserted him during the
hostilities of 1427, and went over to the King's side.
This desertion by the Clan Cameron, as well as by
the Clan Chattan, proved disastrous to Alexander,
and was the direct cause of his discomfiture and
humiliating surrender.   The Lord of the Isles would
have been more than human did the memory of his
betrayal not rankle in his breast.   According to the

[1] Book of Douglas, vol. I., p. 440 ; Exchequer Rolls, vol. V., p. 33.

code of honour of the time, to forget and forgive so grave an injury without due reprisals would have been regarded as pusillanimous and cowardly. And now Nemesis has come. The Scottish Government has put in Alexander's hands a powerful weapon of revenge by giving him authority over the persons and property of the lieges in the north, and in this case he is not slow to exercise it. Donald Dubh was dispossessed of his lands in Lochaber, and forced to take refuge in Ireland.

The Clan Maclean, also vassals of the Isles, were already in possession of extensive lands, and were rapidly rising in importance as a territorial family. A number of years previous to the dispossession of the Clan Cameron, a scion of the House of Maclean, John Garve, a son of Lachlan Maclean of Duart, had received from Alexander of Isla a grant of the lands and barony of Coll, and now he obtains the further grant from him of the forfeited lands of Donald Dubh. It is rather singular that the Mackintoshes, who were equally disloyal to Alexander in 1427, escaped the outpourings of the Island potentate's wrath. No doubt, in the latter case, there were relationships by marriage, though such alliances between Highland families were not always effective in averting feuds and bloodshed. In any case, the Mackintoshes made up the peace with Alexander, and remained on the same terms of vassalage as before. The favour shewn to the Clan Chattan by Alexander was indeed excessive, for it was at the expense of a branch of his own family, the House of Keppoch. The family of Alastair Carrach was forfeited in 1431 for their action in the rising of Donald Balloch ; but it does not appear that the Lord of the

Isles, on his own restoration to his liberty and possessions, made any attempt to reinstate them in their lands. Instead of that, we find him, in 1443, not only confirming Mackintosh in the lands he formerly possessed, but also giving him a grant of the patrimonial lands of the Keppochs. This unjust and unfriendly action was strenuously and successfully resisted by the Lords of Lochaber, who refused to bow to the majesty of parchment, and for hundreds of years there is witnessed the singular spectacle of a clan, in actual possession of their ancestral acres, holding them without a scrap of title, without any instrument of tenure, save their good sharp broadswords and the strength of their right arms. Alexander still heaps favours upon the Chief of the Clan Chattan, for we find him in 1447 granting him the bailliary of all Lochaber in perpetual fee and heritage. This was a most important as well as lucrative appointment, and was of a nature to lead to still greater sway and influence.

There seems little reason to doubt the statement of Scottish historians that Alexander, despite his apparent loyalty and the confidence reposed in him by the Council of State during his latter years, was drawn into that league with the Douglas family which, in after years, descending as an heritage to his successor, proved at last the ruin of his House. We find the Lord of the Isles and Douglas having an interview in Bute in 1438, and although the purpose of the meeting was not disclosed, it not improbably had reference to the treasonable compact which, though not finally concluded at that time, was in serious and earnest contemplation.[1] It was

---

[1] The Douglas Book, vol. I., p. 440.

in March 7, 1445, that the three Earls—Crawford, Douglas, and Ross—subscribed and sealed the offensive and defensive league which, for the parties concerned, bore such disastrous fruits.[1]

Not much more that is noteworthy remains to be recorded of the latter years of Alexander de Ile. According to the Chronicle of the Earls of Ross[2] he died at his Castle of Dingwall, and was buried in the Chanonry of Ross on the 8th May, 1449. His mortal remains were not conveyed to their kindred dust in Hy, within whose chapel of Oran the Lords of the Isles for many a generation found their last resting place. Alone of all the heads of his race he lies beneath the shadow of that once noble fane[3]— desecrated and converted into a stone quarry by that stout defender of the faith, Oliver Cromwell —but from the desolation and wreckage of the time not a vestige has survived to mark the place of sepulture of the great Earl of Ross.

From all that we can gather, Alexander was little past his prime when he died. But his youth of trouble and hardship may well have sown the seeds of premature decay and hastened the length-ening of the shadow. Despite some humiliating episodes of his younger days, he worthily upheld the name and honour of his line. The testimony borne by the ancient record of his race bears out the view that while he was valiant in the field he was kindly and generous towards his dependants, and that he ruled his vast territories, in his latter years, with tranquil and beneficent sway.[4] If his early career was turbulent and warlike, his latter

[1] Balfour's Annals of Scotland, vol. I., p. 173.

[2] pp. 10-11.   [3] Fortrose Cathedral.   [4] Ibid.

life was full of peace and dignity, and he handed down unimpaired to his successor the great and ancient heritage of his fathers.

SIGILLUM ALEXANDRI DE YLE DOMINI INSULARUM ET ROSSIE.

CHAPTER IX

JOHN DE ILE, EARL OF ROSS.

John de Ile, Earl of Ross and Lord of the Isles.—The Earl a
Minor when he succeeded.—Minority of James II.—League
between the Earls of Ross, Crawford, and Douglas.—The
Earl of Ross in Rebellion.—Murder of the Earl of Douglas.—
The Earl of Ross and his Ross-shire Neighbours.—Raids on
Orkney by the Islemen.—Meeting of Douglas and Macdonald
at Dunstaffnage.—Invasion of the King's Lands by Donald
Balloch.—Raid of Lismore.—Discomfiture of Bishop Lauder.
—The Lady of the Isles Escapes from the Highlands.—John
receives favours from the King.—He is appointed one of the
Wardens of the Marches.—The Earl of Ross at the Siege of
Roxburgh.—Treaty of Ardthornish.

ON the death of Alexander of Isla, Earl of Ross, in
1449, his son John succeeded him both in his island
and mainland territories. The period was a comparatively quiet and prosperous one in the history
of the family of Macdonald. Alexander, after many
struggles and vicissitudes, had succeeded at length
in uniting to the Lordship of the Isles the mainland
inheritance of his mother, and thus both in extent
of territory and influence he had elevated himself to
a pinnacle of power unequalled even by the Lord of
Douglas in the South. The policy of Alexander seems
to have been dictated by the wise and firm resolution not to involve himself again in an open quarrel
with the Scottish State. Though his sympathies
lay entirely with Crawford and Douglas, having,
as stated in the last chapter, entered into a

league with them, he played no active part in
the civil commotions in which these noblemen
were such able actors.   Far removed from the
base of operations, he remained an interested
spectator of a kingdom torn asunder by factions
and transformed into a stage on which the actors
played each for his own hand.   This wise and
prudent policy evidently did not commend itself to
Alexander's son and successor, John.   The state of
matters in the Highlands at the death of Alexander
favoured the continuation of a defensive rather than
an aggressive policy.   The state of matters in the
South was very different.   The kingdom was still in
the throes of a long minority, and suffering from the
woes pronounced upon the nation whose king is a
child.   The assassination of James I., whose wise, if
sometimes harsh, rule had done so much to restore
order and tranquillity throughout his kingdom, was
contemplated with   secret   satisfaction   by those
turbulent noblemen whose excessive power the King
had so successfully curbed.   Now that his powerful
personality is removed, and the reins of State are
placed in other hands, we can readily conceive how
those ambitious and powerful barons, on whose
feudal privileges the King had encroached, would
seize the opportunity with which fortune favoured
them and devote their energy towards the restoration of lost power and prestige.   The moving spirits
in the struggle for place and power were the
Douglases, the Livingstons, and the Crichtons, the
great object governing the policy of each being the
destruction of the other, while the great body of the
lieges groaned under the cruellest oppression.

While Lowland Scotland was thus distracted by
petty feuds and tumults, the Highland portion of
the kingdom seems to have enjoyed comparative

peace and prosperity. This is true in an especial
manner of the extensive domain over which John,
Lord of the Isles, held sway, and it was mainly
owing to the wise policy of his father, Alexander.
There was no call for an aggressive policy on the
part of John in the circumstances in which he found
himself on his accession to the honours and dignities
of his house. By taking part in the quarrels of his
Southern neighbours, he had everything to lose, and
it is difficult to see what, under the most favourable
circumstances, he could have ultimately gained by
pursuing a course so unwise and unpatriotic. He
was already in possession of a vast territory, and
surrounded by loyal vassals and cadets of his house.
But John was a minor at the time of his father's
death, and this, no doubt, largely accounts for the
rash policy which he pursued on the very threshold
of his career. From an entry in the Chamberlain
Rolls, it would appear that that official charges himself with the rents of the lands of the barony of
Kynedward for two years, that barony being in
ward through the death of Alexander, Earl of Ross.[1]
This means that John was either a minor or had not
at this time received confirmation of the lands of
the barony of Kynedward But an entry in the
Exchequer Rolls of the year 1456 leaves no doubt
as to the age of the Earl of Ross when he succeeded
to that dignity. In this entry reference is made to
the barony of Kynedward as having been in ward
for three years, during which the Earl of Ross was
a minor.[2] John was, therefore, eighteen years of

---

[1] Chamberlain Rolls, vol. III., p. 527.

[2] "Et non onerat se de firmis terrarum baronie de Kynedward, que
fuerunt in manibus domini regis in warda per spacium trium annorum, que
extendunt se ad quingentas marcas per annum et ultra, cum tenandiis
ejusdem, ante saisinam datam Johanni Comiti Rossie, quia ex gracia domini
regis in minore etate constitutus intravit in eisdem," &c., &c.—Exchequer
Rolls, vol. VI., p. 158. Vide Ibidem, vol. V., p. 393.

age when he succeeded his father in 1449. But
though thus still of tender years, he would not have
lacked for counsel at so critical a moment in his
career as head of the House of Macdonald. The
veteran Donald Balloch, Lord of Dunnyveg and the
Antrim Glens, was the principal Councillor of the
Island Lord, as well as Captain of the Clan Donald,
and there were other cadets of the family who had
attained to considerable power and influence in the
Highlands and Islands. These were the Clanranald
branch, the Macdonalds of Ardnamurchan, the Macdonalds of Glencoe, and the Macdonalds of Keppoch.
Surrounded by these, as well as by the other vassals
of the family, whether at Dingwall or at Ardthornish,
John had little to fear from his foes inside or outside
the Highland boundary.

Both at Dingwall and at Ardthornish, the Earl
of Ross held Court on a scale approaching that of a
sovereign prince. From several charters granted by
him, we find the names of his councillors and the
offices held by them in the government of the Isles.
Donald Balloch comes before us as president of the
Council, while Maclean of Ardgour and Munro of
Fowlis were Treasurer of the Household and
Chamberlain respectively : other offices were held
by Maclean of Dowart, Macneill of Barra, Macdonald of Largie, and others of the vassals of the
Isles. One of the first charters granted by John on
his becoming Earl of Ross was that to the Master
of Sutherland of the lands of Easter Kindeace for
his homage and faithful service, and among the
witnesses are the names of several members of the
Island Council. The Earl of Ross, however, did not
confine himself to the affairs of his own principality.
It would have been well if he had. He had barely

succeeded to his patrimony when we find him in league with the Earls of Douglas and Crawford. These noblemen had raised the standard of revolt in the Lowlands, and had set all law and order at defiance. Both were selfish, cruel, and ambitious, and being possessed of great power and influence, their rebellious attitude was a constant menace, and a source of danger, to the Scottish State. Their extensive estates gave them the command of a powerful army of military vassals, but this only stimulated their ambition to grasp at still greater power, and they seem to have set before themselves no less a task than the dismemberment of the kingdom. A mutual oath was entered into between them, "that each of them should be aiding and assisting against all the world, to the friends and confederates of one another."[1] Into this dangerous league the young Earl of Ross threw himself, prompted, no doubt, by the vain ambition of acquiring yet greater power and adding to his already far too extensive domains. Only a momentary lull, and the heather is ablaze. It is not in the north alone the standard of revolt is raised, the whole kingdom is thrown into a turmoil of rebellion. The confederate lords are acting in concert. The signal is given, and the dogs of war are let loose. The Earl of Ross, who had married the daughter of Sir James Livingston, the King acting in the interesting capacity of matchmaker, was no doubt somewhat disappointed at not receiving the tocher, with the promise of which His Majesty had clinched the matrimonial bargain. But the disgrace and attainder of Livingston intervening was the cause, no doubt, why the royal promise was not imple-

[1] Buchanan, vol. II., p. 239, Ed. 1821.

mented.   Neither the nonpayment of the tocher,
however, nor the disgrace of Sir James, was the
prime motive for the conduct of the Earl of Ross
in the present revolt against the King's authority.
It was, as we have seen, part of a great scheme,
into which John had entered with the insurgent
lords of Douglas and Crawford, and from which he
hoped to gain a much greater prize than Elizabeth
Livingston's dowry.

The Island Lord summoned his vassals to his
standard, and from island and mainland they rally
to the fray.   The details of this formidable rebellion
have not been recorded, but the great outlines of
the transaction remain.   John, at the head of a
large body of his vassals, marched to Inverness,
and without much opposition took the Castle,
which having strongly garrisoned, he proceeded to
Urquhart.   He claimed the lands of Urquhart as
part of the Earldom of Ross, which lands, with the
Castle, had formerly been in the possession of his
family.   The stronghold of Urquhart, which was
almost impregnable in its great size and strength,
was now held for the King.   The Island Lord at
once attacked it, and after a short but stout resistance on the part of the garrison, John became
master of the situation.   His father-in-law, Livingston, who on hearing of the commotion in the
North had escaped from the King's custody, was
made governor of Urquhart Castle by John.
Intoxicated with the success which attended him
at Urquhart and Inverness, he marched southwards
through Moray, and taking the Castle of Ruthven,
another royal stronghold, he committed it to the
flames.   The King, who had evidently not yet
discovered the treasonable league between Douglas,

Crawford, and Macdonald, devoted all his energy and resources to the Southern portion of his kingdom. At all events, no immediate step was taken to punish the island rebel, and that potentate remains defiantly in possession of his recent conquests. James II., who had just come of age, was not by any means wanting in administrative capacity or military ardour. Both were very soon put to the test. The Southern portion of his kingdom, torn and distracted by the feuds of the Lowland barons, had become a fertile region of all confusion and rapine. It required the possession of a steady judgment and a firm hand to restore order and good government, and the energy of the young monarch was taxed to the utmost in the attempt to accomplish this desirable result. The King's whole attention, therefore, being meanwhile devoted to his unruly subjects in the South, the Earl of Ross and his clansmen enjoy the benefit of complete immunity from the royal vengeance. But the tide of affairs, after a brief interval, took a sudden turn, and the Island Lord appears in a new light. The treasonable league between Macdonald, Douglas, and Crawford, very probably recently renewed, was at length discovered by the King, and he at once realised the powerful combination arrayed against him.

Meanwhile an event happened which changed the King's plans, and helped to break up the league between the confederate lords in an unexpected manner. The Earl of Douglas, on his return to Scotland, and at the instigation of the English Court, put himself without delay in communication with Macdonald and Crawford, and in order to carry out the elaborate scheme against the Scottish State,

Douglas opened the campaign by summoning his vassals and retainers to his standard. One only, it would appear, disobeyed the call, and, asserting his independence, refused to join in the insurrection. This bold vassal, whose name was Maclellan, was closely allied by blood to Sir Patrick Gray, a courtier of high standing in the King's household. Douglas, highly incensed at the conduct of his retainer, ordered his arrest and imprisonment at Douglas Castle. On the news of the imprisonment of Maclellan reaching the Court, the King at once despatched a messenger demanding the release of the prisoner. Divining the purport of the royal messenger's visit, and knowing well that his presence betokened no good omen, Douglas gave orders privately to have Maclellan beheaded. This defiant conduct on the part of Douglas, so utterly regardless of the King's authority, roused the indignation of James, who would have taken immediate steps to bring him to justice if he had not dreaded his power. Meantime the King, suppressing his indignation, prudently determined to have a secret conference with Douglas in the Castle of Stirling, ostensibly with the purpose of making a better citizen of the haughty baron. James gave his assurance under the Great Seal for the personal safety of the Earl. Relying on the Royal assurance, Douglas sped to Stirling, where the King and Court then resided, and presented himself before His Majesty. The King remonstrated with him for his treasonable proceedings, and especially for the league he had entered into with Macdonald and Crawford. The proud Lord of Douglas listened with impatience to the reproaches of his Sovereign, and, at length, defied James, whereupon the King, losing all control of his temper, drew his dagger and stabbed the rebel lord. The courtiers present rushed to the scene, and in a few moments the unfortunate nobleman succumbed to their vengeance. It is impossible to justify the conduct of the King. Whether premeditated or in a fit of temper, no justification can be pleaded for an act committed in direct violation of his solemn promise to protect the person of his victim. There can be but little sympathy, on the other hand, for the murdered nobleman, whose own hands were not free from blood, and whose career throughout was marked by the most cruel and tyrannical actions.

Thus the first blow was aimed at the Macdonald, Crawford, and Douglas league, but it did not prove effective. The leading spirit of the cabal was removed only to make room for another Douglas, whose chief aim was to perpetuate the policy of his house towards the Scottish State. The aspect of affairs in the Highlands present a very favourable contrast to the state of matters in Lowland Scotland. It would be difficult to conceive a picture darker in its outlines than that drawn by the hand of a well-known historian of this period in the history of Scotland south of the Forth. The history of the Highlands may be searched in vain for a parallel, often as that history has been perverted to suit the prejudices of the Lowland mind. The cold-blooded murders, the selfish schemes to gratify family ambition, the cruel oppression and tyranny, which stain the whole social fabric, are on a scale unequalled by the darkest period in the history of Celtic Scotland. The governing principle in such a state of society invariably is to keep and acquire as much as

DEID·SCHAW·TO·THE·END

The Lorde of the Illes

possible whether by fair means or foul. Judged
from this point of view, the present attitude of
the Island Lord may well be justified.

The temporary discomfiture of the Douglas party,
and the strong measures taken by the King and his
advisers to put down the rebellion of Crawford, were
not without their effect on the Earl of Ross. The
King appointed the Earl of Huntly, a nobleman of
great courage and ability, lieutenant-general of the
kingdom, and granted him a commission to proceed
against the rebel Earls of Crawford and Ross. Huntly
devoted his attention, in the first place, to Crawford,
whom he defeated in a pitched battle near the town
of Brechin. Though not personally present in this
engagement, the Earl of Ross sent a contingent of
clansmen to the assistance of the Earl of Crawford.
Huntly's plan of campaign was to attack the rebel
lords one after the other, and defeat them in turn.
Macdonald, who still held his own in the North,
realising his danger, began to make elaborate
preparations to resist the threatened invasion of
the King's lieutenant. The formidable defence
made by the Earl of Ross struck terror into the
heart of the invading host, and Huntly, who had
penetrated as far as Moray, retired in dismay. No
further attempt was made, at least meanwhile, to
subdue the Northern potentate. The Earl of
Huntly's services were required elsewhere, and
the Douglasses seem to have taken up the whole
attention of the King. In any case, the Earl of
Ross still continued to hold the castles of Inverness
and Urquhart, and suffered no diminution of his
power in the North. Though in league with
Crawford and Douglas, he cannot be said to have
taken an active part with them in the recent revolt

14

against the Scottish Government. He prudently remained at home, and allowed his confederates to fight for their own hand. The King was too busy elsewhere to attack him in the North, and the Island Lord was a formidable problem at any time.

Though free from Southern interference, the Earl of Ross was not without his troubles at home. Ever since the Macdonald family settled in Ross-shire, the neighbouring clans, and even some of the vassals of the Earldom, looked with a jealous eye on their growing power and influence. Chief among these were the Mackenzies, at this time of no great account as a clan, the Mackays, and the Suther-lands. Sir Robert Gordon, in his "Earldom of Sutherland," gives accounts of the clan battles, or skirmishes, that took place about this time in the North. He records how the Earl of Ross, accompanied by a force of between 500 and 600 clansmen, had the presumption to invade Sutherland and encamp near the Castle of Skibo. Macdonald's object in invading Sutherland seems to have been to harry the country, injure the inhabitants, and carry off as much spoil as circumstances would permit. John, Earl of Sutherland, however, being far above soiling his own hands in a petty quarrel between his vassals and Macdonald of the Isles, sent a Neill Murray (the descent of Neill still remains an open question) with a company of the brave men of Sutherland to give battle to the invading Macdonald host. The issue was not for a moment uncertain. The Macdonalds, after a sharp conflict, were put to flight, and they beat a hasty retreat to Ross without spoil. Though for the time repulsed, the Macdonalds were not quite annihilated, and recuperating

their exhausted energies, they made another
incursion into Sutherland in the hope of repairing
the loss they sustained at the hands of Neill Murray
at Skibo. Penetrating into Strathnaver, they were
met on the sands of Strathfleet by Robert Sutherland, brother of the Earl of Sutherland, at the head
of " some men assembled in all haste." Here the
Macdonalds were again defeated, which was to be
expected, and believing discretion to be the better
part of valour, they never again invaded the
territory of the great Earl John of Sutherland. Sir
Robert Gordon is, of course, writing up the Earls of
Sutherland, and, in the process, he considers it to
be his duty by way of contrast to write down all
who oppose themselves to his family gods. From
the well-known character of his book, it is not
necessary to enter here into any detailed criticism
of its value historically. His clan stories and genealogies, so persistently repeated by others, should
be received with due caution, and, if in any way
associated with the family of Sutherland, for what
they are worth, which, in our opinion, is very little.
Sir Robert Gordon was a family *seanachie*, and his book
is marked by the blemishes that generally taint such
works and render them often practically valueless as
guides to historical research. It is amusing to read
the glowing accounts given by this historian of the
prowess in the field, the eloquence in council, and
the domestic virtues of his Earls of Sutherland, most
of which unfortunately are contradicted by the stern
facts of history. The independence of Scotland
would have been delayed, it is hard to say how
long, if the prowess of the Earl of Sutherland had
not secured it for ever on the bloody field of
Bannockburn. An Earl of Sutherland was never

wanting when the welfare of the realm was at stake, and this country will never know all it owes to that great family of which Sir Robert Gordon was so faithful a chronicler.

There is no doubt some slight foundation for Sir Robert Gordon's stories of the clan feuds of this period. Macdonald of Lochalsh, Hugh of Sleat, and Roderick MacAllan of Clanranald, were always ready, when not engaged against the Saxon, to pounce upon their Celtic neighbours. The Munroes, the Rosses, the Mackenzies, the Frasers, and others, were quite as ready to give them a warm welcome. Nothing is more likely to have happened than a series of plundering raids by Roderick of Clanranald and the other leaders of the clan into Sutherland, and we can imagine without much effort the consternation of the natives at the approach of these plundering bands. We confess to finding it somewhat difficult to imagine any such scenes of slaughter as are alleged, in Sir Robert Gordon's pages, to have been witnessed at Skibo and on the sands of Strathfleet. *Creachs*, however, were common to both Highlands and Lowlands; but so far as the annals of the time furnish us with any hints, this period was, on the whole, an uncommonly quiet and prosperous one in the history of the Clan Cholla. The quiet periods in the history of the Highlands and Islands, consisting of those intervals, generally short, during which the Lords of the Isles and their vassals maintained friendly relationships with the Scottish Government were, however, only relatively tranquil. It was seldom the House of Isla was free from those domestic feuds which bulk so largely in the traditions of the country. The seanachies, embodying these

traditions in their manuscripts, give us vivid,
if sometimes exaggerated, pictures of the marauding
and piratical expeditions engaged in by the restless
spirits of those times. The stories told by some of the
seanachies, when brought under the light of authentic
history, are found in many instances to be wonder-
fully reliable. Both MacVuirich and Hugh Macdonald refer to a raid on the Orkney Islands by
the young men of the Isles, led by Hugh Macdonald
of Sleat, brother of John, Earl of Ross.[1] Authentic
records of the time not only confirm this raid but
refer to a series of other raids on Orkney, and other
Norse possessions, by the men of the Isles. In a
manifesto by the bailies of Kirkwall and community
of Orkney the complaint is made that the Orkneys
were habitually overrun by bands of Islesmen sent
thither by the Earl of Ross, designed as "*ab antiquo
inimicus capitalis.*" These invasions were of yearly
occurrence during the reign of James II. The
Islanders, according to the manifesto, plundered,
burned, and ravaged the country, and carried off
cattle and whatever else they could lay their hands
on.[2] In a letter by William Tulloch, Bishop of
Orkney, dated 28th June, 1461, the same complaint
is made against the men of the Isles, and the Bishop
alludes to the efforts which he was then making to
come to an arrangement with the Earl of Ross to
put a stop to these marauding expeditions.[3] What
success attended these laudable efforts on the part
of the good Bishop history does not record. The
Earl of Ross and his Islesmen are soon required

[1] Hugh Macdonald in Collectanea de Rebus Albanicis, p. 306; MacVuirich
in Reliq. Celt., p. 213.

[2] Diplomatarium Norwegicum X., 606.

[3] Ibidem, 599.

elsewhere, and little time is left for raids, naval or other, in the North.

The Earl of Douglas, who had long kept the Lowlands in a perfect turmoil of civil war, was finally defeated by the King's forces at Arkinholme, in Annandale. Disappointed of expected English aid, and having been declared traitor to the Scottish State, Douglas, as a last resort, betook himself to Argyleshire, where, in the Castle of Dunstaffnage, he was received by Donald Balloch Macdonald, who may not inappropriately be called the lieutenant-general of the Isles.[1] Here the Earl of Ross, who had come from the North, and Douglas met in solemn conference to decide what steps should be taken in the present emergency. The result of their deliberations was soon apparent. Both, with equal sincerity, vowed vengeance on the royal party. Douglas having persuaded the Island Lord, apparently without much difficulty, to espouse his cause, and thus set the ball a-rolling, hastened across the border into England, where he was cordially received by the Duke of York. Macdonald immediately prepared for an invasion of the King's lands, and summoning his clansmen and vassals, he soon gathered to his standard a force 5000 strong. The command of this force he bestowed on the veteran Donald Balloch, whose prowess in many a field had been the admiration alike of friend and foe. A fleet of 100 galleys was equipped for the expedition, and Donald, directing his course towards the mainland, proceeded to Inverkip, where he landed his force. There appears to have been no opposition offered to this formidable armament, and Donald was allowed, not only to land unmolested,

[1] Lives of the Douglases, p. 203. Origines Par. Scotiæ Appendix, p. 826.

but on penetrating into the country he carried fire
and sword everywhere he went with impunity.
From Inverkip he directed his course towards the
island of Arran, which, with the Cumbraes and
Bute, he invaded in turn, burning and plundering
wherever he went. Donald's object primarily, however, was not plunder but revenge, and this he now
gratified to the full. After besieging the Castle of
Brodick and burning it to the ground, he next
attacked the Castle of Rothesay, which having
taken, he made himself master of Bute. According
to the Auchinleck Chronicle, he carried away
immense spoil from this and the adjacent islands
and mainland, including a hundred bolls of meal, a
hundred bolls of malt, a hundred marts and a
hundred marks of silver, five hundred horses, ten
thousand oxen and kine, and more than a thousand
sheep and goats. The loss in lives and property
does not appear to have been very great in pro-
portion to the strength of the invading forces. If
we are to believe the chronicler, there were slain
only " of good men fifteen, of women two or three,
and of children three or four."[1] It would appear
from this that Donald's object was not so much to
punish the natives as the superiors of the lands
which he had invaded, and according, therefore, to
the standard of the time, the Island leader, tempering
his revenge with mercy, behaved in the circumstances in a manner worthy of some commendation.
Donald's conduct, however, in the episode which
followed, and with which his naval raid was concluded, is deserving of the severest condemnation.
Lauder, the Bishop of Lismore, a Lowlander, had
evidently through over-zeal in the exercise of his

[1] Auchinleck Chronicle.

sacred calling made himself obnoxious to the men of
Argyle.   Instead of going cautiously to work, and
making himself acquainted with the mode of living
of the people, with the oversight of whom he had
been entrusted, he exercised discipline with a strong
hand, and sought to bring the inhabitants into
conformity with the ways and manners of the South.
This he found by no means an easy task.   The
people, of whose language and manners the bishop
was utterly ignorant, stubbornly resisted his reforms,
and were driven by his high-handed policy to commit outrages on his person and ravage and plunder
the sacred edifices of his diocese.   The bishop had
besides, as one of the King's Privy Council, affixed
his seal to the instrument of forfeiture against the
Earl of Douglas, and this only added another to his
already many offences against the Lord of Dunnyveg.
Donald now had his opportunity of punishing the
obnoxious prelate, and without delay he proceeded
to Lismore, where the bishop resided, and besieged
him in his sanctuary.   After ravaging the island
with fire and sword, he put to death the principal
adherents of the bishop, in all likelihood natives of
the Lowlands, while the prelate himself escaped
with his life by taking refuge in the Cathedral
Church of his diocese.   Without wishing to condone
the conduct of the Island leader in any way, it may
be permissible to say that this prelate, by his short-
sighted and unwise policy, had himself done much
to provoke this and other outrages on his sacred
calling and jurisdiction.   That, however, does not
warrant the outrages committed on this or on
former occasions on the Bishop of Argyle, and
Donald Balloch nowhere comes before us in a worse
light than in his expedition to Lismore.

No immediate action seems to have been taken
by the King to punish the rebel Lord of Dunnyveg,
or his chief, the Earl of Ross, in the recent treasonable proceedings.   In Argyle and the Isles it would
have been vain to attack them.   The Scottish navy
at this time was not fit to cope with the strong
maritime power of the Isles, and this probably was
the principal reason why the King thought it
prudent not to hazard an expedition to Argyle.
In any case there is no record of the pains and
penalties which should have fallen on the devoted
head of the sacrilegious spoiler of the sacred Island
of Lismore.   One incident may be recorded which
throws light on the turmoil into which the Douglas-
Macdonald league had thrown the Highlands and
Islands.   Feeling no longer safe in these regions,
John of Isla's consort, the Lady Elizabeth Livingston, escaped with all haste from the country, and,
finding her way to Court, threw herself on the
protection of the King.   According to one of the
Scottish historians, this lady married the Island
Lord with the laudable view of toning down his
rugged disposition and making him a loyal Scottish
subject.   In this, it would appear, the Lady
Elizabeth utterly failed, and her return to Court at
the present juncture is a clear indication of the
policy of the Earl of Ross towards the executive
government, as it also makes only too apparent the
wide gulf that separated racially the North from the
South.   The King received the Countess of Ross
with much cordiality, and a suitable maintenance
having been assigned her, she appears to have
remained at Court during the remainder of her life.

The Earl of Ross, weakened by the defeat of the
Douglas party, finally sent messengers to the King

offering to repair the wrongs he had committed on
his majesty's lieges, and promised in anticipation of
the royal clemency being extended to him to atone
with good deeds in the future for his rebellious
conduct in the past. The Earl well knew that his
wisest policy in the present state of affairs was to
make his peace with the King. He could not very
long stand out in his present attitude and expect
much success to attend his efforts in opposition to
the Scottish Government. But he appears to be
perfectly sincere in his desire to be reconciled to the
King, and there is reason to believe that in this
loyal attitude he would have remained, if evil
counsel, to which he had been at all times
susceptible, had not prevailed. The King at first
was not disposed to treat with John on any terms,
but finally, by a judicious union of firmness and
lenity, and dreading another insurrection in the
Highlands, his Majesty granted the Northern
potentate a period of probation during which he was
to shew the sincerity of his penitence. Meanwhile the King summoned a meeting of Parliament
to consider the affairs of his realm. Whether the
Earl of Ross was present at this meeting, or was
represented, does not appear very clear, but it seems
that much attention was devoted to the Highlands
and Islands, and that many good and salutary
laws were passed for the welfare and peace of the
realm generally. The Earl of Ross, it would appear,
is now on his good behaviour, for, according to the
good Bishop Lesley, the King in this Parliament
" maid sic moyennis with the principallis captanis of
the Ilis and hielands that the same wes als peacable
as ony parte of the Lawlandis, and obedient as weill
in paying of all dewties of thair landis to the King,

als redy to sarve in wearis with greit cumpanyis."[1] " The principallis capitanis of the Ilis," including no doubt the hero of the recent naval raid, had from all appearance been suddenly converted, but like most sudden conversions, there do not appear to have followed any results of a permanent kind.

Notwithstanding the friendly relations in which the Earl of Ross now stood to the Crown, the King, in a Parliament held at Edinburgh in 1455, deprived him of both the castles of Inverness and Urquhart.[2] Next year, however, the Castle of Urquhart, together with the lands of Urquhart and Glenmöriston, were granted to John at an annual rent of £100.[3] To these were added at the same time the lands of Abertarff and Stratherrick,[4] and to still further confirm the loyalty of the Island Lord, the King conferred upon him the lands of Grennane in Ayrshire.[5]

What conspicuous services were rendered to the State by the Earl of Ross after his sudden conversion history does not record, but his behaviour seems to have been such as to warrant us in believing in the sincerity of his repentance. The King himself must have received some proof of his loyalty, for in the year 1457 His Majesty appointed John one of the Wardens of the

[1] Historie of Scotland by John Lesley, Bishop of Ross, p. 27.

[2] " Thir ar ye lordschippis ande castellis annext to ye croune. . . . . Item ye hous of Innurness and Urcharde and ye lordschippis of thame and ye lordschippe of Abernethy with ye wattles maylis Iuunerness togidder with ye baronyis of Urcharde glenorquhane boniche bonochare annache Edderdaill callyt Ardmanache peety brachly Stratherne with ye pertinentis."—Acta Parliamentorum Jacobi II., vol. II., p. 42.

[3] Exchequer Rolls, vol. V., p. 217.

[4] " Et allocate eidem de firmis terrarum de Abertarf et Strathardock de termino hujus compoti, concessarum dicto comiti Rossie apud Invernys per dominum nostrum regem."—Exchequer Rolls, vol. V., p. 222.

[5] Ibidem, vol. VI., 236.

Marches, an office of great importance and responsibility.[1]   No doubt the King's policy was to
attach John to his person and Government.   In
bestowing upon him this office of trust under his
Government, the King evinced his desire to cure
the northern potentate of his rebellious tendencies,
and wean him from the influence of those factions
which had been so baneful in the past.   As a
further proof of his confidence, the King appointed
John with other noblemen to conclude a truce with
England.[2]

The history of the Highlands during the next
few years, so far as the Earl of Ross is concerned,
is almost a blank.   The only reference to him in his
official capacity which we have been able to find is
in a document preserved in the Kilravock Charter
Chest, and which bears that the Earl granted Rose
of Kilravock permission to " big ande upmak a toure
of fens."   The document, which is written in the
vernacular of the 15th century, is in the following
terms :—

" Johne of Yle, Erle of Ross ande Lord of the Ilis, to all ande
sundry to qubais knawlage thir our present letteris sall come ;
Greeting : Witte us to have gevyn ande grantit and be thir present letteris gevis ande grantis, our full power ande licence till
our luffid cosing, man ande tennand, Huchone de Roos, baron of
Kylravok, to fund, big, ande upmak a toure of fens, with barmkin
ande bataling, wpon quhat place of strynth him best likis, within
the barony of Kylravok, without ony contradictionn or demavnd,
questionn, or any obiection to put in contrar of him or his ayris,
be vs or our ayris, for the said toure ande barmkyn making, with
the bataling, now or in tyme to cum : In witness hereof, ve haf
gert our sele to ther letteris be affixt at Inuernys, the achtend day
of Februar, the yer of Godd a thousand four hundretd sixte yer."

[1] Rymer XI., 397.   [2] Ibidem, 397.

The time soon arrived when the Earl of Ross,
emerging from his temporary obscurity, acts a part
very different from that which he was accustomed
to play on the stage of Scottish history.   In
the year 1460, James II. entered on his campaign
against England.   The truce between the two
countries to which, as we have seen, John, Earl of
Ross, was a party had not lasted long.   The King
opened his campaign by attacking the Castle of
Roxburgh, an important frontier stronghold, then,
and for long prior to this time, in the possession of
the English.   Here he was joined by the Earl of
Ross at the head of 3000 clansmen, "all armed in
the Highland fashion, with habergeons, bows and
axes, and promised to the King, if he pleased to pass
any further in the bounds of England, that he and
his company should pass a large mile afore the rest
of the host, and take upon them the first press and
dint of the battle."[1]   The Island Lord was received
with great cordiality by the King, who commanded
him, as a mark of distinction, to remain near his
person, while his clansmen meanwhile set themselves
to the congenial task of harrying the English borders.
The unfortunate and melancholy death of the King
from the bursting of a cannon at the very com-
mencement of the siege of Roxburgh virtually
brought the campaign against England to an end,
and the Earl of Ross had no opportunity of proving
his own fidelity, or the courage and bravery of his
clansmen.   The untimely death of the King in the
flower of his youth and at the very beginning of his
vigorous manhood exposed the country once more to
the dangers attendant on a long minority.   James,
during his comparatively short reign, had proved

---

[1] Lindsay's History of Scotland.

himself a wise and judicious ruler. Of this we have ample evidence in the success which attended his efforts in destroying the overgrown power of the house of Douglas, and attaching to his interests such men as the Earl of Ross.

Shortly after the death of the King, on the 23rd of February, 1461, a Parliament was held at Edinburgh to consider the affairs of the realm, when the Queen-mother was appointed regent during the minority of her son, the heir to the throne, then only in his seventh year. This Parliament, which was largely attended by all the estates of the realm, was also attended by John, Earl of Ross, and many other Highland chiefs. Though no detailed record of it remains, we can gather from the main outlines of the proceedings the elements of civil commotion in the near future. Parliament had no sooner dissolved than an insurrection broke out in Argyleshire, the fertile region of dissensions. The cause of the commotion was a quarrel between Allan Macdougall, of the house of Lorn, and his brother, John Ciar Macdougall. Allan, who was a nephew of Donald Balloch Macdonald, lay claim to certain lands in the possession of John Ciar. This claim the latter resisted, but he was overpowered by Allan, and imprisoned by him in a dungeon on the island of Kerrera. This was the signal for a rising on the part of the friends on both sides, and a bloody conflict ensued. Allan was defeated, but as a result of the commotion, the whole Western Highlands were thrown into the wildest confusion.[1] In the southern portion of the kingdom the aspect of affairs presents no brighter prospect for the future

[1] Buchanan, vol. II., 279. Auchinleck Chronicle, 58.

prosperity of the country. The welfare of the nation is sacrificed to the private ambition of factious nobles.

The Earl of Ross, whose loyalty, as we have seen, was so conspicuous during the latter portion of the reign of the late King, now that that strong personality is removed from the helm of state, allows himself once more to become the victim of the Douglas faction. By a judicious combination of firmness and moderation, the King had disarmed the enmity of the Island Lord, and had James not been cut off so prematurely, there is every reason to believe that John would have continued loyal to the Scottish throne. The death of the King, however, soon plunged the Scottish State into the difficulties that are always inseparable from a minority. It will be remembered that the last Earl of Douglas had been forfeited in all his estates, and was now undergoing his sentence of banishment at the Court of Edward IV. Douglas had, in the days of his prosperity, maintained friendly intercourse with the family of York, and now that Edward IV. seemed in a fair way to crush the House of Lancaster, Douglas would fain hope that the power and influence of England might be directed towards the restoration of his lost territories and position in Scotland. Meantime the banished Earl watched with deepest interest the passing phases of political feeling between the English and Scottish crowns, and he left no means unused to win his old ally, the Earl of Ross, from the friendly relation in which he now stood towards the Government of the northern kingdom. As had often happened in the past, the difficulties which England had to

deal with at home and in France had hitherto
proved a barrier against active interposition in the
affairs of Scotland, and the Wars of the Roses had
particularly absorbed all the energies of the House
of York.   In the year to which we have come,
however, the two events already referred to, the
accession of Edward IV. to the English throne
and the death of James II. of Scotland, seemed
to shed a gleam of hope on the broken fortunes
of the exiled Earl.   Edward lent his countenance
to the Douglas scheme all the more readily because
the Scottish Court had afforded an asylum to his
opponent, Henry of Lancaster, whose defeat at
Taunton had driven him to Scotland, while it
placed Edward on the English throne.   Various
schemes were devised in Scotland for the restoration of the exiled English monarch, all of which
proved futile.   To counteract these and divert the
Scottish rulers from their object and neutralise
their efforts, Edward lent a willing hand to Douglas
in his desperate scheme.   The King of Scotland was
a child, and past experience had taught that a
Scottish regency, accompanied as it often was by
faction and conspiracy, would afford scope for the
execution of such a scheme as Douglas might devise
for his restoration to the honours which he had
forfeited.

The time had evidently come when the old league
with the Macdonald Family might be revived in a
bolder spirit and with more ample scope.   In these
circumstances we are not surprised to find that a
few weeks after the King's death the first overtures
are made to the Earl of Ross for the formation of
an offensive and defensive league with England.

That the English Government was the first to move
in the matter is evidenced by the fact that the writ
empowering the Commissioners from England to
treat with the Lord of the Isles was issued on the
22nd of June, 1461, while the ambassadors from the
Isles were not formally commissioned until the 19th
October following.   The English Commissioners to
the Isles were the banished Earl of Douglas, his
brother, John Douglas of Balveny, Sir William
Wells, Dr John Kingscote, and John Stanley.
The following is the text of the writ appointing
the English Commissioners :—

" AMBASSIATORES ASSIGNANTUR AD TRACTANDUM CUM COMITE
ROSIAE.

Rex omnibus ad quos &c. salutem. Sciatis quod nos de fidelitate
et provida circumspectione
carissimi consanguinei nostri Jacobi Comitis Douglas ac
dilectorum et fidelium nostrorum   Willelmi Welles militis et
Johannis Kyngescote legum
doctoris necnon
dilectorum nobis   Johannis Douglas et
Johannis Stanley.
Plenius confidentes assignavimus et constituimus ipsos comitem
Willelmum Johannem Johannem et Johannem ambassiatores
commissarios sive nuncios nostros speciales ad conveniendum cum
carissimo consanguineo nostro Johanne comite de Rosse ac
dilecto et fidele nostro   Donaldo Ballagh
seu eorum ambassiatoribus commissariis sive nunciis sufficientem
potestatem ab eisdem consanguines nostro Comite de Rosse et
Donaldo in ea parte habitentibus.   Necnon ad tractandum et
comicandum cum eisdem de et super cunctis materiis et negotiis
nos et ipsos consanguineum nostrum comitem de Rosse tangentibus
sive concernentibus ac de et in materiis et negotiis predictis
precedendis appunctuandis concordandis et concludendis.
Ceteraque omnia et singula in premissis et eorum dependentiis
debita et requisita concedenda facienda eb expedienda. Promittentes bona fide et verbo regio in hiis scriptis quod omnia et
singula que in premissis vel circa ea per ambassiatores commissarios

15

sive nuncios predictos appunctuata concordata et conclusa fuerint
rata grata firma habevimus pro perpetuo. In cujus &c.

T. R. Apud Westminstrem xxij die Junii. Per ipsam regem."[1]

For consideration of the proposals about to be
submitted to the English envoys, the Lord of the
Isles with his council, a body that existed in
connection with the family from the earliest times,
met and deliberated in the Castle of Ardthornish,
which, in the time of John, Earl of Ross, was the
meeting place on important and State occasions.
The Douglasses and the other Commissioners of
Edward seem to have come all the way to
Ardthornish to lay their proposals before John
and his privy council. What the conclusion
arrived at, after mature and solemn deliberation,
was, we are not informed. In any case, it was
necessary that the tentative compact must be
considered and ratified in the great English
capital itself. To represent the interests of

---

[1] AMBASSADORS ARE APPOINTED TO TREAT WITH THE EARL OF ROSS.

The King to all to whom, &c., salvation. Know ye that we, trusting
very fully in the faithfulness and prudence of our dearest cousin James Earl
of Douglas and of our dear and faithful William Welles, Knight, and John
Kyngescote, Doctor of Laws, also of our dear John Douglas and John Stanley,
have nominated and appointed these same, the Earl, William, John, John and
John our special ambassadors, commissioners or messengers, for meeting with
our dearest cousin John Earl of Ross and our dear and faithful Donald Balloch
or their ambassadors, commissioners, or messengers having sufficient power
from our same cousins the Earl of Ross and Donald Balloch—on that part.
Also for treating and communicating with these same concerning and with
regard to all matters and affairs touching and concerning ourselves and our
cousin Earl of Ross and with regard to what is contained in the matters
and affairs aforesaid that have to be proceeded with, determined, agreed upon
and concluded. And other matters all and each which ought to and must
needs be granted, carried out and arranged as in the premisses and their
conclusions. Promising in good faith and by our royal word in these
documents that all and each of the items in or bearing upon the premisses
that shall have been appointed agreed upon and concluded by the foresaid
ambassadors, commissioners or messengers we shall hold settled agreeable to
us and fixed for ever. In testimony of which, &c.

T. R. At Westminster 22nd day of June.   By the King himself.

the Macdonald Family at Westminster, two
Commissioners were appointed.   Ranald Bane
of the Isles, son of John Mor Tainistear, and
founder of the family of Largie, and Duncan,
Archdean of the Isles, were appointed to meet
the English Commissioners ; and it was no ordinary
sign of confidence that they were entrusted with
such important and delicate negotiations.   The
English Commissioners appointed to meet the
Commissioners of the Isles at Westminster were
Lawrence, Bishop of Durham, the Earl of Worcester,
the Prior of St John's, Lord Wenlock, and Robert
Stillington, Keeper of the King's Seal.   The treaty
that was concluded in the name of the English
King and the Earl of Ross, with the Earl of
Douglas as the moving spirit of the plot, was
bold and sweeping in its provisions.   It was
undoubtedly treasonable to the Scottish State,
but the whole history of the family of the Isles,
and in a measure, of that of Douglas, was a
continued protest against the supremacy of the
Crown.   From the terms of the treaty, it would
appear that the object in view was nothing less
than the complete conquest of Scotland by the
Earls of Ross and Douglas, assisted by the English
King.   The Earl of Ross, Donald Balloch, and
John, his son and heir, agreed to become vassals
of England, and with their followers to assist
Edward IV. in his wars in Ireland and elsewhere.
For these services, and as the reward of their
vassalage, the Earl of Ross was to be paid a
salary of £200 sterling annually in time of war,
and in time of peace, 100 merks ; Donald Balloch
and his son John were to be paid salaries respectively of £40 and £20 in time of war, and in time

of peace half these sums. In the event of the
conquest of Scotland by the Earls of Ross and
Douglas, the portion of the kingdom north of the
Forth was to be divided equally between the Earls
and Donald Balloch. Douglas was to be restored
to his estates in the south. On the division of the
north being completed, the salaries payable to the
Macdonalds were to cease.[1] In case of a truce with
the Scottish monarch, the Earl of Ross, Donald
Balloch, and John his son, were to be included in
it.[2] This extraordinary treaty is so important in
its relationship to the Family of the Isles that we
give it here in full :—

[3] "FOEDUS INTER EDWARDUM REGEM ANGLIAE ET JOHANNEM
COMITEM ROSSIAE ET DOMINUM INSULARUM, DE SUB-
JUGANDO SCOTIAM, ET EAM PARTIENDO INTER DICTUM
COMITEM ET COMITEM DOUGLAS ; CUM CONFIRMATIONE
REGIS EDWARDI.

Rex omnibus ad quos &c. salutem. Notum facimus quod
vidimus et intelleximus quedam appunctuamenta concordata
conclusa et finaliter determinata inter commissarios nostros ac
ambassiatores commissarios et nuncios carissimorum consanguineorum nostrorum.

Johannes de Isle comitis Rossie et domini Insularum.
Donaldi Balagh et
Johannes de Isle filii et heredis ejusdam Donaldi
sub eo qui sequitur tenore verborum.[4]

[1] Rymer's Foedera, vol. XI., 483-87. Rotuli Scotiæ, vol. II., 407.
[2] Hector Boece's History of Scotland, App. 393.
[3] Rotuli Scotiæ in Turri Londinensi, vol. II., pp. 405-7.

[4] LEAGUE BETWEEN EDWARD KING OF ENGLAND AND JOHN EARL OF
ROSS AND LORD OF THE ISLES CONCERNING THE CONQUEST OF
SCOTLAND AND THE DIVISION THEREOF BETWEEN THE SAID EARL
OF ROSS AND THE EARL OF DOUGLAS ; WITH THE CONFIRMATION
OF KING EDWARD.

The King to all to whom, &c., salvation. We make it known that we have
seen and understood that certain matters have been agreed upon, concluded
and finally determined between our commissioners and the ambassadors,
commissioners and messengers of our dearest cousins John of Isla Earl of Ross
and Lord of the Isles and Donald Balloch and John of Isla son and heir of the
same Donald who follows after him in the order of the names.

We

    Laurence bishop of Duresme

    John erle of Worcestre

    Robert Botill' priour of Seint Johns of Jerusalem in
        Englonde

    John lord Wenlok   and

    Maister Robert Stillyngton keper of the kynges
        prive seal

deputees and comissaries to the most high and mighty prynce
Kynge Edward the Fourth kynge of Englonde and of Fraunce
and lorde of Irlande

    and

        Reynold of the Isles   and

        Duncan archediaken of the Isles

ambassiatours comissaries or messagers of the full honorable lorde
John de Isle erle of Rosse and lorde of the Oute Isles to all thos
that this presente writyng endented shall see or here gretyng.
Be it knowen that we the seid deputees commissaries and ambassatours by vertu of power committed unto us whereof the tenures
ben expressed and wreten under after longe and diverse tretes and
communications hadd betwix us upon the maters that folwen by
vertu of the seid power have appoynted accorded concluded and
finally determined in maner and fourme as folweth FURST it is
appointed accorded concluded and finally determined betwyx us
that the seid John de Isle erle of Rosse Donald Balagh and John
of Isles son and heire apparaunt to the seid Donald with all there
subgettez men people and inhabitantes of the seid erldom of Rosse
and Isles aboveseid shall at feste of Whittesontide next commyng
become and be legemen and subjettes unto the seid most high
and Christen prince Kynge Edward the Fourthe his heires and
successours kynges of Englond of the high and mighty prince
Leonell sonne to Kynge Edward the Thridde lynially descendyng
and be sworne and do homage unto hym or to such as he shall
comitte power unto you at the seid fest of Whittesontide or after
And in semble wyse the heires of the seid John th' erle Donald and
John shall be and remaigne for ever subjettis and liegemen unto
the seid Kynge Edward, his heires and successours kynges of
Englonde as it is aboveseid yevinge unto his highnesse and his
seid heires and successours as well the seid John th' erle Donald
and John as theire heires and successours and eche of them verrey
and trewe obeysaunce in obeinge his and there commaundementes

and do all thyng that a trewe and feithfull subjette oweth to doo
and bere to his soveryane and lige lord and as hit accordeth to his
ligeaunce ITEM the seid John th' erle Donald and John and eche
of them shall be alwaye redy after the seid feste of Whittesontide
upon convenable and resounable warnyng and commaundement
yeven unto them by the seid most myghty prynce Edward kynge
of Englonde his heires and successours kynges of Englonde of the
seid Leonell in fourme aboveseid descendyng or be eny other on
his or their behalfes havyng power therto to do diligente and
effectuall service with and to all them uttermest myght and power
in suche werres as the seid most high and myghty prynce his
heires and successours kynges of England as is above seid shall
move or arreise or to moved or arreised in Scotlande or ayenste
the Scottes in Irlande or ayenst the kynges ennemyes or rebelles
there and in the same werres remaigne and continue with all ther
aide myght and power in such wyse as they or eny of them shall
have in commaundement by the seid high and myghty prince his
heires and successours and as longe as it shall please hym or them
ITEM the seid John erle of· Rosse shall from the seid feste of
Whittesontyde next comyng yerely duryng his lyf have and take
for fees and wages in tyme of peas of the seid most high and
Christen prince C merc sterlyng of Englysh money and in tyme of
werre as longe as he shall entende with his myght and power in
the said werres in maner and fourme aboveseid he shall have
wages of CCli sterlyng of Englysh money yerely and after the rate
of the tyme that he shall be occupied in the seid werres   ITEM
the seid Donald shall from the seid feste of Whittesontide have
and take duryng his lyf yerly in tyme of peas for his fees and
wages XXli sterlyng of Englysh money and when he shall be
occupied and intende to the werre with his myght and power and
in maner and fourme aboveseide he shall have and take for his
wages yerly XLli sterlynges of Englysh money or for the rate of
the tyme of werre   ITEM the seid John soun and heire apparant
of the said Donald shall have and take yerely from the seid fest
for his fees and wages in the tyme of peas Xli sterlynges of
Englysh money and for tyme of werre and his intendyng therto
in manere and fourme aboveseid he shall have for his fees and
wages yerely XXli sterlynges of Englysh money or after the rate
of the tyme that he shall be occupied in the werre   And the seid
John th' erle Donald and John and eche of them shall have gode
and sufficaunt paiment of the seid fees and wages as well for tyme

of peas as of werre accordyng to thees articules and appoyntementes
ITEM it is appointed concluded accorded and finally determined
that if it so be that hereafter the seid reaume of Scotlande or
the more part therof be conquered subdued and brough to the
obeissaunce of the seid most high and Christen prince and
his heirs or successours of the seid Leonell in fourme
aboveseide discendyng be th' assistence helpe and aide of
the seid John erle of Rosse and Donald and of James erle
of Douglas then the seid fees and wages for the tyme of peas
cessyng the same erles and Donald shall have by the graunte of
the same most Christen prince all the possessions of the seid
reaume beyonde Scottyshe See they to be departed egally betwix
them eche of them his heires and successours to holde his parte
of the seid most Cristen prince his heires and successours for
evermore in right of his croune of Englonde by homage and
feaute to be done therefore   ITEM if so be that by th'aide and
assistence of the seid James erle of Douglas the seid reaume of
Scoctlande be conquered and subdued as above then he shall have
enjoye and inherite all his owne possessions landes and inheri-
taunce on this syde the seid Scottyshe See that is to saye betwix
the seid Scottyshe See and Englonde suche he hath rejoiced and
be possessed of before this there to holde them of the seid most
high and Cristen his heires and successours as is aboveseid for
evermore in right of the coroune of Englande as well the said erl
of Douglas as his heires and successours by homage and feaute to
be done therefore   ITEM it is appointed accordett concluded and
finally determined that if it so be the seid most high and myghty
prince the kynge after the seid fest of Whittesontide and afore
the conquest of the reaume of Scottelande take any trewes or
abstinaunce of werre with the kynge of Scottes then the seid erle
of Rosse Donald and John and all their men tenantes officers and
servantes and lordships landes tenementes and possessions whereof
the same erle of Ross Donald and John or eny of them be nowe
possessed within Scottland and the seid erldom of Rosse and also
the isle of Arran shall be comprised within the seid trewes or
abstinaunce of werre olesse then the said erle of Rosse signifie
unto the high and myghty prince the kynge before Whittesontide
next comyng that he woll in nowe wyse be comprised therein
ITEM it is appointed accorded conclused and finally determyned
that the seid John erle of Rosse Donald and John shall accepte
approve ratifie and conferme all these presente articles appoynte-

mentes accordes conclusions and determinations and thereunto
geve thaire aggrement and assent and in writyng under there
seeles of armes sende and delyvere it to the seid most Cristen
kynge or his chaunceler of Englande afore the furst day of Juyll
next comynge receyvynge att that tyme semblable tres of ratification of the seid appoyntementes to be made undre the grete
scall of the seid most high and myghty prynce   All these thinges
in maner and fourme aboveseid we the seid commissiaries and
ambassatours have appointed accorded concluded and finally
determined and that they shall be trewly observed and kepte we
permitte by vertue of our severall powars and commissions yeven
and made unto us whereof the tenures worde by worde ben such
as folwen.

> Edwardus dei gratia Rex Angliae et Franciae et
> dominus Hibernie omnibus ad quos presentes
> litere pervenerint salutem.

Sciatis quod nos de fidelitatibus et providis circumspectionibus
    Venerabilis prioris   Laurentii Episcopi Dunolm' ac
    Carissimi consaunguinei nostri Johannis comitis Wygorn
Necnon dilectorum et fidelum nostrorum Roberti Botill' prioris
Sancti Johannis Jerusalem in Anglia
                    Johannis Wenlok
de Wenlok militis et Magistri Roberti Stillyngton legum doctoris
custodis privati sigilli nostri
plenius confidentes assignavimus et constituimus ipsos episcopum
comitem priorem Johannem et Robertam ambassiatores commissariis sive nunciis sufficientem potestatem sub eo consanguineo
nostro comite Rossie in ea parte habitentibus necnon ad tractandum
et communicandum cum eisdem de et super cunctis materiis et
negotiis nos et dictum consanguineum nostrum comitem Rossie
tangentibus sive concernentibus ac de in materiis predictis precedendis appunctuandis concordandis concludendis determinandis
et finiendis ac appunctuamenta concordata conclusa determinata
et finita per eosdem vice et nomine nostris in scriptis redigenda
seu redigi facienda ac etiam sigillanda.   Ceteraque omnia et
singula in premissis et eorum dependentiis debita ut requisita
concidenda et facienda et expedienda.   Promittentes bona fide et
verbo regio quod omnia et singula que in premissis vel circa ea
per ambassiatores commissarios sive nuncios nostros predictos
quatuor vel tres eorum appunctuata concordata conclusa determinata et finita fuerint rata grata firma stabiliter habebimus pro

Anno 1 Regis Edwardi Quarti membr. 26.

perpetuo. In cujus re testimonium has literas nostras fieri fecimus patentes.

T. Me ipso apud Westminstrem octavo die
Februarii anno regni nostri primo. Bagot.[1]

Johannes de Yle comes Rossiae dominus Insularum omnibus ad quos presentes litere pervenerint salutem. Sciatis quod nos de fidelitate et provida circumspectione consanguineorum nostrorum

Ronaldi de Insulis et

Duncani Archedeaconi Insularum

Plenius confidentes assignavimus et constituimus ipsos Ranaldum et Duncanum ambassiatores commissarios sive nuncios nostros speciales ad conveniendum cum excellentissimo principe Edwardo dei gratia rege Angliae et Franciae et domino Hibernie seu ejus ambassiatoribus commissariis sive nunciis sufficientem potestatem sub eodem excellentissimo principe Edwardo dei gratia rege Angliae et Franciae et domino Hibernie in ea parte habitentibus. Necnon ad tractandum et communicandum cum eisdem de et super cunctis materiis et negotiis nos et dictum excellentissimum principem tangentibus sive concernentibus ac de et in materiis

---

[1] EDWARD BY THE GRACE OF GOD KING OF ENGLAND AND FRANCE AND LORD OF IRELAND TO ALL TO WHOM THESE PRESENT LETTERS SHALL HAVE COME—SALVATION.

Know ye that we being fully confident of the faithfulness and prudence of the venerable prior Laurence Bishop of Durham, and our dearest cousin John Earl of Worcester, also of our dear and faithful Robert Botill, prior of St John Jerusalem in England, John Wenlok of Wenlok, Knight, and Master Robert Stillyngton, doctor, Keeper of our privy seal—have nominated and appointed these, the Bishop, Earl, prior John and Robert ambassadors, there being also commissioners or messengers possessing full power under our cousin Earl of Ross on that part, for treating and communicating with these same concerning and regarding all matters and affairs touching and relating to us and our said cousin the Earl of Ross and regarding the matters aforesaid to be proceeded with, appointed, agreed upon, concluded, determined, and ended, and that the points agreed upon, concluded, determined, and ended by these same, in turn and by name must be entered among our writs or must be drawn out and sealed, to be so entered. And the other matters, all and each in the premisses and their conclusions must as required be finished, carried out, and arranged. Promising in good faith and by our royal word that all and each of the matters in the premisses or bearing upon these as shall have been agreed upon, concluded, determined, and ended, whether by our ambassadors, commissioners, or messengers aforesaid, or by four or three of them, we shall hold as settled agreeable to us and firmly fixed for ever. In testimony of which we have caused these our letters patent to be written.

Testified by myself at Westminster, the eighth day of February, in the first year of our reign. Bagot.

predictis precedendis et appunctuandis concordandis concludendis determinandis et finiendis ac appunctuata concordata conclusa determinata et finita per eosdem vice et nomine nostris in scriptis redigendis seu redigi facere ac etiam sigillandis. Ceteraque omnia et singula in premissis et eorum dependentiis debita et requisita considenda facienda et expedienda. Promittentes bona fide et christianitate qua astricti deo in hiis scriptis quod omnia et singula que in premissis vel circa ea per ambassiatores commissarios sive nuncios predictos vel unam eorum appunctuata concordata conclusa determinata et finita fuerint rata grata firma et stabilia habebimus pro perpetuo. In cujus re testimonium has literas nostras fieri fecimus patentes.

Ex castello nostro Ardthornis decimo nono
die mensis Octobris anno Domini millesimo
quadringentesimo sexagesimo primo.[1]

In whittenesse whereof to that on' partie of these indentures delyvered and remaignyng towardes the deputees and commissaries of the seid high and myghty prynce Kynge Edward we

---

[1] John of Isla Earl of Ross Lord of the Isles, to all to whom the present letters may come—salvation. Know ye that we, fully trusting in the faithfulness and prudence of our cousins,

Ronald of the Isles and
Duncan Archdeacon of the Isles,

have nominated and appointed these same Ranald and Duncan our special ambassadors, commissioners or messengers, to meet with the most excellent prince Edward by the grace of God King of England and France and Lord of Ireland, or his ambassadors, commissioners or messengers, having full power under the same most excellent prince Edward by the grace of God King of England and France and Lord of Ireland—on that part. Also for treating and communicating with these same concerning and with reference to all matters and affairs touching or relating to us and the said most excellent prince and concerning the matters aforesaid to be proceeded with and appointed, agreed upon, concluded, determined and ended—the matters appointed, agreed to, concluded, determined and ended by these same in turn and by name having to be entered among our writs or drawn out and sealed that they may be thus entered. And the rest all and each ought as required in the premisses and their conclusions to be finished, carried through and arranged. Promising in good faith and by the Christianity by which we are bound to God in these documents that all and each of the matters in the premisses or bearing upon them, appointed, agreed to, concluded, determined, and ended by the foresaid ambassadors, commissioners or messengers aforesaid or by one of them, we shall hold settled, agreeable to us, fixed and fast for ever. In testimony of which we have caused these letters patent to be written.

At our Castle of Ardthornish, the nineteenth day of the month of October, the year of our Lord one thousand four hundred and sixty one,

the seid Raynald and Duncan ambassitours and commissaries of
the seid erle Rossie have putte our seales and signe manuelles.

Writen att London' the xiij dey of Februer
the yere of the birth of our Lorde
MCCCCLXII and the furst year of
the reigne of the high and myghty
prince Kynge Eward the Fourth above
rehersed.

Nos vero eadem appunctuamenta concordata conclusa et finaliter
determinata ac omnia et singula in eisdem contenta et specificata
rata et grata habentes eadem acceptamus approbamus ratificamus
et confirmamus eisdemque nostrum assensum primiter et con-
censum damus et adhibemus et in eisdem vigore robore et virtute
remanere et haberi volumus ac si per nos appunctuata concordata
conclusa et finaliter de terminata fuissent necnon ea omnia et
singula ad omnem juris effectum qui exinde poterit tenore presentium innovamus.   Promittentes bona fide et verbo regio nos
dicta appunctuamenta concordata et conclusa et finaliter determinata omnia et singula in eisdem contenta quatinus nos
concernant pro parte nostra impleturos et observaturos imperpetuum.   In cujns &c.

T. R.   Apud Westminstrem xvij die martii.

Per breve de prevato sigillo et
de data predicta auctoritate &c." [1]

Such was the Treaty of Ardthornish, a diplomatic
instrument most daring in its conception and big
with the fate of the Island Family.   Considering the
commanding position John already occupied, it is

---

[1] But we, holding these same points agreed to, concluded and finally determined, as well as all and each of the matters contained and specified in them,
accept, approve, ratify and confirm them, and we give and adhibit our assent
and consent in chief, and wish them to remain and be held in these same in
their strength, force, and validity, as if they had been appointed, agreed upon,
concluded, and finally determined by ourselves ; also, we renew all and each
of these things with the full effect of law which shall henceforth exist in the
tenor of these letters.   Promising in good faith and by our royal word that
for our part we shall fulfil and observe the said points agreed upon and concluded and finally determined in all and each of their contents so far as they
may concern us, for ever.   In testimony of which, &c.

Royal certification—At Westminster, 17th day of March.

In brief from the private seal and
On the date aforesaid by authority, &c.

strange he should have allowed himself to be entangled in a scheme so wild and perilous. He was already by far the most powerful noble in Scotland, with a vast territory and almost regal sway. But he seems to have been ambitious of acquiring still greater power and *prestige*. The bribe held out to him proved a strong temptation, and undoubtedly influenced his conduct in the step he took; yet the scheme was so wild that we are amazed at the eagerness with which he entered into it, and at his simplicity in allowing himself to be blindly led into so hollow an alliance. It is plain that the scheme did not emanate from the brain of the Earl of Ross. On this, as on critical occasions before, John was under the controlling influence of wills stronger and more persistent than his own. It was the scheme of a bold and desperate man who was playing a hazardous game for tremendous odds. For the provisions of the Treaty of Ardthornish we are indebted mainly to the banished and forfeited Earl of Douglas. But there was another party to the contract who must not be overlooked. Donald Balloch was thoroughly imbued with the Celtic spirit, keen, restless, and eager, the determined foe from his early years of the Scottish State, and still in his declining years burning for dangerous and exciting adventures. From these and other circumstances we may well believe that his voice would have been loud for the league embodied in the Treaty of Ardthornish.

This remarkable compact between the Lord of the Isles and the English King, with the Earl of Douglas as the moving spirit of the plot, implied the adoption of military measures to carry its provisions into effect. The events that followed

almost immediately after the ratification of the
Treaty seem to suggest an understanding between
the parties that no time was to be lost in taking the
contemplated action.   On the side of the Earl of
Ross proceedings were taken with almost precipitate
haste.   The two foremost Clan Donald warriors of
the day were placed at the head of the vassals of
Ross and the Isles.   First in command was Angus
Og, son of the Lord of the Isles, who now for the
first time makes his appearance upon the arena of
war, but who had already, though scarcely more
than a boy, begun to show indications of the daunt-
less courage, the unconquerable spirit which future
years were more vividly to disclose.   Second in
command was Donald Balloch, the hero of Inverlochy, a fight the memory of which was beginning
to grow dim in the minds of the generation that
witnessed it.

The Lord of Dunnyveg and the Glens of Antrim
had only once unsheathed his sword since he over-
threw the Earl of Mar in Lochaber, but he was still,
though past his prime, well nigh as formidable an
antagonist as of old, always to be found where the
hurricane of battle was brewing, now, as of yore, the
harbinger of strife, the stormy petrel of Clan Donald
warfare.   Angus Og, destined to play the leading
part in the decline and fall of the Lordship of the
Isles, was a natural son of the Earl of Ross.   The
historian of Sleat, whether inadvertently or of set
purpose, would make it appear otherwise, and says
that Angus Og was the issue of a marriage with a
daughter of the Earl of Angus.[1]   There is no
evidence that such a marriage ever took place, and
John had no male issue by his wife, Elizabeth
Livingston.   The question is placed beyond dis-

---

[1] Hugh Macdonald in Collectanea de Rebus Albanicis, p. 315.

pute by a charter which was afterwards given to
John in confirmation of his possessions, and in which
it was provided that, failing legitimate heirs male,
the title and estates were to descend to his natural
son Angus.[1] The mother of Angus is said to have
been a daughter of Macphee of Colonsay, so that the
heir of the Lordship of the Isles was of gentle if not
legal origin.

The army of the Isles, under the leadership of
Angus Og and Donald Balloch, marched to Inverness, once more the theatre of warlike operations.
Taking possession of the town and castle, the latter
one of the royal strongholds in the north, they at
once, in the name of the Earl of Ross, assumed
royal powers over the northern counties, commanded
the inhabitants and all the Government officers to
obey Angus Og under pain of death, and to pay to
him, as his father's lieutenant, the taxes that were
exigible by the Crown. In this way did the Earl
of Ross attempt to carry into immediate and forcible
execution the provisions of the Treaty of Ardthornish.
It is hardly credible that John would have taken a
step so daring and extreme did he not expect that
the English portion of the Treaty would have been
carried out at the same time by the dispatch of a
strong body of auxiliaries to form a junction with
the Highland army. There is evidence that an
English invasion of Scotland was contemplated at
the time, and that apprehensions of its imminence
prevailed in the Eastern Counties. Especially in
the town of Aberdeen the Provost and inhabitants
were warned to keep their town, sure intelligence
having been received that an English fleet was on

---

[1] Reg. Mag. Sig. VII., No. 335. Acts of Parl., vol. II., p. 189-90. Haddington Collections, vol. I., p. 336.

the way to destroy not only Aberdeen but other
towns upon the coast.[1] Had Edward IV. been able
to support the action of the Earl of Ross in the
North by throwing an army across the border in aid
of the Earl of Douglas, it is quite possible that the
State might have fallen, and Scotland have lost the
independence for which she had made such heroic
struggles. Fortunately for the Kingdom of Scotland, this was not to be. The Wars of the Roses
were still raging in the sister country, and the
resistance of the heroic Margaret of Anjou to the
pretensions of the House of York absorbed the
energies of the reigning power. Edward IV. was
unable to dispatch the expeditionary force to the
assistance of the Highland insurgents, the scheme
for the division of Scotland, after the manner prescribed in the Treaty of Ardthornish, came to naught,
and the rebellion finally collapsed.

What actually followed the campaign of Angus
Og and Donald Balloch, whether they were called
to account and subdued by force of arms, or whether
matters were allowed to adjust themselves without any active measures being undertaken by the
State, are questions upon which the annals of
the age do not throw much light. It seems clear,
however, that, whether through want of will or
power, no decisive steps were taken to award to
the Earl of Ross any punishment commensurate with
his disloyalty. It must be remembered, however,
that the full measure of the treason was very far
from being known. The invasion of the northern
counties, with the seizure of Inverness, and whatever
hostilities accompanied the proclamation of sover-

---

[1] Buchanan, Lib. XII., c. 19. Note (3).

eignty, must have come to the knowledge of the Government; but the serious aspect of the whole affair, the negotiations embodied in the Treaty of Ardthornish, still remained a secret buried out of sight in the archives of the English Crown at Westminster. It needed but a favourable opportunity for that explosive document to bring dismay and consternation to the minds of those involved.

CHAPTER X.

DECLINE AND FALL OF THE HOUSE OF ISLA.—1462-1498.

Events following Ardthornish Treaty.—Its Discovery.—Cause of
Discovery. — Indictment. — Summons. — Forfeiture.—Expedi-
tions against John.—He Submits.—Resignation.—Partial
Re-instatement and New Honour.—Charter of 1476.—
Sentiment in Isles.—Angus Og.—His Attitude.—Rebellion in
Knapdale. — Invasion of Ross.—Feud with Mackenzie.—
Lagabraad.—Bloody Bay.—Abduction of Donald Dubh.---
Raid of Athole.—The Probable Facts.—Angus' Reconciliation
to his Father.—Assassination of Angus Og.—Alexander of
Lochalsh.—Invasion of Ross.—Battle of Park.—John's Final
Forfeiture and Death.

THE Earl of Ross does not appear to have suffered
either in dignity or estate after the rebellion of
1463. For at least twelve years after that maddest
of engagements, the Treaty of Ardthornish, he
pursued the even tenor of his way with little or no
molestation from the Scottish State. That John
maintained his position intact is evidenced by Crown
confirmations of grants of land bestowed upon his
brothers Celestine and Hugh. These twelve years,
from 1463 to 1475, are years of well-nigh unbroken
darkness so far as the Lordship of the Isles and the
Earldom of Ross are concerned. The rebellion of
1463, short-lived though it was, and comparatively
little as we know of its details, left abundant seeds
of future trouble. There is undoubted reason to
believe that John was summoned to appear before
the Parliament of 1463 to answer for his conduct
under pain of forfeiture, but despite the threatened

1ɔ

penalties, the Earl of Ross, whose love for these conventions seems never to have been strong, did not put in an appearance.[1] Whether it was that his command of the Scots tongue was limited, and he did not care to mix with the Southern nobles for that reason, or whether he ignored the jurisdiction of that august body, we know not, but certain it is that on almost all occasions he was represented at the Scottish Parliament by procurators, his proxy in 1467 having been his armour-bearer, William, Thane of Cawdor. Owing to John's non-compearance at the Parliament of 1463, his case was postponed, and the Parliament adjourned to meet in the city of Aberdeen on the Feast of St John the Baptist the same year.[2] Of neither of these Parliaments have any records survived, but subsequent proceedings clearly show that John still elected to remain in his Castle of Dingwall rather than respond to the summons of the High Court of the realm. That same year there is evidence that efforts were not awanting to bring the rebel to task, though these do not appear to have been conducted with much earnestness or resolution. Several Royal Commissioners, including the Earl of Argyle and Lords Montgomery and Kennedy, and Treasurer Guthrie, came North to lay the royal commands before the Earl of Ross, for it is on record that expenses amounting to £12 10s 4d were allowed them for two days' sojourn at Perth on their way to Dingwall Castle.[3] Definite knowledge of the result of this mission we do not possess. The probability is that John was neither punished nor forgiven, but was left, like Mahomet's coffin, in a condition of suspense as to his standing with the Crown, and this leaving

[1] Asloan MS., 23-60.　　[2] Ibid.　　[3] Exchequer Rolls *ad tempus.*

of the matter undecided explains why, in after years,
the Government was enabled to go back upon the
delinquencies of 1463. Although the Treaty of
Ardthornish was still a secret, the Government
seems to have had sufficient evidence that John had
been guilty of treason against the Crown by the
assumption of royal prerogatives in the North, and
the appropriation of taxes and revenues pertaining
to the Crown alone. He and his brother Celestine
were justly accused of having retained the Crown
lands in 1462-3, as well as £542 5s 7d of the farms
of Petty, Leffare, Bonnach, Ardmannach, the vacant
See of Moray, &c., wrongfully and without the
King's warrant.[1] It was probably no easy task for
the Earl of Ross to prevent disturbances breaking
out between the restless Islesmen by whom he was
surrounded and the occupants of the lands adjacent
to his territories. We find, in 1465, reckoning
made of the wasting and burning of the lands of
Kingeleye, Bordeland, Drumdelcho, Buchrubyn,
Drumboye, Turdarroch, and Monachty, to the extent
of £31,[2] for all of which the Earl of Ross and
his followers were held responsible. Quarrels were
likewise breaking out occasionally betwixt the Earl
of Ross and his neighbours in the East of Scotland.
Thus, in 1473, and in the month of August, there is
strife between himself and Alexander of Setoun
regarding the lands of Kinmundy, in Aberdeenshire,
so much so that the matter evokes the royal displeasure, and an Act of Parliament is procured to
provide for the punishment of the culprits, though
we are not enlightened as to the nature of the
penalty administered.[3] A feud also arose with the

---

[1] Exchequer Rolls, vol. VI., p. 356.   [2] Ibid., p. 357.
[3] Acta Auditorum.

Earl of Huntly in 1474, and this also was the theme of remonstrance by the King, who, in the month of March, sent letters to both Earls "for stanching of the slachteris and herschippes committit betwixt theer folkis."[1]

Whatever may have been John's relations to the Scottish Crown, on the one hand, or to his neighbours in the North and West, on the other, his intercourse with his own dependants seems to have been of the friendliest and most peaceful character. So true is this that beyond the granting of charters to some, and the confirmation of grants to others, the records of the period have almost nothing to say as to the relations between the superior and his vassals of the Earldom of Ross, while in the Lordship of the Isles, since the last outbreak of Donald Balloch, a wonderful and unwonted calm seems to have reigned from 1462 to 1475. All this is an indication that whatever may have been the foreign relations—if we may use the term—of the Earl of Ross and Lord of the Isles, there seems to have been harmony and concord between his subjects and himself.

At last the ominous quiet is broken, and all at once there is a great convulsion and upheaval. The Treaty of Ardthornish is exhumed, dug out of the oblivion to which for twelve years it had been consigned, and in which, no doubt, its perpetrators prayed that it might for ever rest, and the rash and daring instrument, which aimed at the destruction of a great State, is thrust upon the notice of an astounded and indignant nation. The Scottish Government felt that the ship of State had been sailing among hidden yet dangerous rocks, and that

[1] Treasurer's Accounts, vol. I., 48.

serious disaster had by no means been a remote contingency, and it was determined to take resolute and immediate action against the only party to the compact on whom the hands of the Executive could be laid. The Earl of Douglas was an outlaw beyond Scottish jurisdiction; Donald Balloch was secure from danger amid the Antrim glens; and so the Earl of Ross, perhaps the least culpable of the contracting parties, becomes the victim and scapegoat of the conspiracy.

Highland historians do not afford us much assistance in tracing the causes which led to the disclosure of this treaty, a disclosure which was, to all appearance, a gross breach of faith on the part of the Power in whose archives the document must have been preserved. Yet the causes that led to the revelation of the secret may be estimated with tolerable accuracy, if not with absolute certainty. In 1474 Edward IV. was contemplating the invasion of France, and, in the circumstances, he deemed it his wisest policy to secure his frontiers at home by a treaty of friendship with the Northern Kingdom. A treaty was consequently drawn up, the main provision of which appears to have been, that a contract of marriage should be entered into between the Prince of Scotland, son of James III., and Cecilia, daughter of the English King, the subjects of this interesting arrangement having attained respectively to the mature ages of two and four years. Into the details of this international compact, which never came to anything, it is beside our present purpose to enter. We refer to it because it indicates new and friendly relations between the two countries, and because it would be impossible for Edward IV., under the conditions that had arisen, to continue the promises of support to the Earl of Douglas, or abide by a treaty which was a standing menace to the quiet and integrity of the sister land. There was nothing therefore more natural than that in the course of friendly negotiations between the two kingdoms, in 1474, the Treaty of Ardthornish should have issued out of its obscurity, and become the signal for hostile proceedings against the Earl.

After the discovery of the Treaty, the Government seems to have lost little time in calling John of Isla to account for his twelve-year-old treason, and an elaborate process was instituted against him in the latter months of 1475. On the 20th November of that year, Parliament met, and an indictment containing a formidable record of his political offences was drawn up. In the forefront of the crimes of which he is accused stands the Treaty of Ardthornish, but other charges of treasonable conduct are likewise included in the document. The various letters of safe conduct to English subjects passing to and fro between the two countries, the rebellion of 1463 and the imperative commands issued then to the King's lieges to obey his bastard son Angus on pain of death; the campaign of Donald Balloch, his siege of Rothesay Castle, and his depredations in Bute and Arran, with the slaughter of many of the King's subjects, events of a much earlier date than the Treaty of Ardthornish; in fact, the whole sum of John's offences from the beginning are all narrated with greater or less fulness. John himself, hereditary Sheriff of Inverness, being under the ban of the law, Alexander Dunbar of Westfield, Knight, Arthur Forbes, and the King's herald, are conjointly and severally appointed Sheriffs of Inverness, by special royal warrant for the legal execution of the summons. These emissaries of the law are commanded to present the summons personally to John, Earl of Ross, in presence of witnesses, and it is enjoined that this be done at his Castle of Dingwall, but the prudent proviso is inserted, *if access thereto should with safety be obtained.* Failing this safe delivery of the citation at the Castle, it was provided that it should be made by public proclamation at the cross and market place of Inverness, while it bore that the Earl of Ross must appear in presence of the King at Edinburgh, at the next Parliament to be held there on the 1st December following. It is noticeable that, while the Parliament which authorised the summons met on the 20th November, 1475, the document was issued under the great seal at Edinburgh, on the last day of the previous September. It is evident that Parliament was simply called together to endorse what the royal prerogative had already enacted.[1]

The next step in the process was the execution of the royal summons, and this also took place before the meeting of Parliament on 20th November. The copy of the execution of citation being drawn out, not as usual in Latin, but in the Scots tongue of the day, may here be quoted *verbatim*, though very much a repetition of what has gone before :—

"The xvj day of Octobere zeire of oure Lorde J^m iiii^c lxxv zeres I Unicorne pursewant and Sheriff of Innuerness in thus part specially constitut be our souerain lord the King be these his letteres past to the Castell of Dingwail in Roisse and askit entrance to the presens of Johne Erle of Rosse and lorde of Ilis the quhilk I couth no get and than incontinent at the zetts of samyn Castell I summond warnit and chargit peremptorly the said John erle of Rosse to compear personaly befor our souerain lord the King in his burgh of Edinburgh in his next pliament thar

<hr>

[1] Acts of the Scottish Parliament, vol. II., p. 108.

to be holdin the first day of the moneth of december next to cu
with continuation of days to ansuer til our said souerain lorde
hienes in his said parliament upon the tresonable comonyng with
our souerain lordes ennemys of yngland and for the tresonable
liges and baudes mad be him with Edvarde King of Yngland and
Inglysmen And for the tresonable comonyng with the tratour Sre
James of Douglas sumtyme erle of douglas And for the tresonable
help council fauore and supple gevin be him to the sayme
tratour And for the tresonable gevin of save conductes to our
souerain lordes ennymys of yngland And for the tresonable
usurpacione of ouere souerain lordes autorite in makin of his
bastard sone a lieutennand to him within ouere souerain lordes
Realme, and comittand powere to Justify to the dede oure
souerain lordes lieges that ware in obedientis to him And for the
tresonable connocacione of ouere souerain lordes lieges and
sezeing of his castel of Roithissay in bute and birning slaing
wasting and distrueying of oure souerain lordes lieges and
landes of the Ile of bute efter the forme contenit in letteres And
also to ansuere upone al uder crymys offensis transgressionis and
tresonable dedes comittit and done be the said Johne erle of
Rosse tresonably againe ouere souerain lorde and his Realme and
til al ponctis and articulis contenit in thes letteres and efter the
forme of the samyn And this execucione I maid befoir thir witnes
donalde waitsone m^{c}beth Thome donaldsone wil adamsone Johne
of paryss and diuersis utheris And attour the samyn day befoir
the samyne witnes I summond the said Johne to compere as
said is in al forme and effect aboue writtyne And also the samyn
day at the markat corsse of Inuernes I summonde be opin
proclamacione the said Johne erle of Roysse in forme and effect
aboue writtyne to ansuere till the punctis and al articulis contenyt
in this summondes as said Is befor thir witnes Johne leffare henry
finlaw bailzeis of the said burgh Johne of dunbare Archibald
brothy and diuersis utheris In wittness of this my execucione I
have affixit my sele to this my Indorsyng day zeire and place
befor writtin

" Et sic est finis executionis" [1]

Two other similar instruments containing weari-
some repetitions of the summons and, to the non-legal
mind, abounding in superfluities follow after the
foregoing, the sum and substance of the enormous

[1] Acts of the Scottish Parliament, vol. II., p. 109.

mass of verbiage being that John is cited to appear
at Edinburgh before a Parliament to be held on the
1st of December, 1475.   In due course the Convention of the Estates of Scotland met, and full
certification was given that the Earl of Ross had
been lawfully cited at the cross and market place
both of Dingwall and Inverness.   John not com-
pearing, Andrew, Lord of Avondale, Chancellor of
Scotland, by command of the King, charged him in
presence of the assembled nobles with the high
crimes and misdemeanours already fully detailed;
upon which it became the unanimous finding of
Parliament that his guilt was established.   Finally,
judgment was given by the mouth of John Dempster,
Judge for the time being of the Court of Parliament,
that for the treason proven against him, John, Earl
of Ross and Lord of the Isles, had forfeited his life
as well as his dignities, offices, and possessions,
which latter were thereby alienated not only from
himself, but also from his heirs forever, and attached
to and appropriated by the Crown.[1]

These drastic proceedings of the Scottish Parliament, were immediately followed by formidable
preparations, to wring from the attainted noble by
force what he would not voluntarily concede.   Colin,
Earl of Argyle, already scenting from afar the broad
acres of the Island lordship, willingly adopted the
role of public policeman, and accepted with alacrity
of a commission to execute the decree of forfeiture
which had recently been pronounced.[2]   It does not
appear, however, that Argyle was entrusted with
the reduction of the Earl of Ross to submission, for
in the following May a strong expeditionary force
was raised and divided into land and naval sections,

---

[1] Acts of Scottish Parliament, vol. II., p. 111.   [2] Argyle writs.

under the command of the Earls of Athole and
Crawford respectively, for the invasion of John's
extensive territories.[1]   As it turned out, forcible
measures ceased to be necessary when, on the advice
of Athole, the King's uncle, John at last agreed to
make a voluntary submission and throw himself
upon the royal mercy.   Once more Parliament met,
and on 1st July, 1476, John appeared before it with
all the semblance of humility and contrition.   On
the intercession of the Queen and the express
consent of the nobles, John was there and then
pardoned and restored to all the honours and possessions he had forfeited.   Apparently this investiture
was only a form for enabling him to denude himself
of a large portion of his inherited estate.   The same
day on which he was re-instated he made a voluntary
resignation of the Earldom of Ross and Sheriffdom
of Inverness and Nairn, with all their pertinents,
castles, and fortalices to the King.   He did so, the
record says, of his own pure and free accord; but
we may well believe that this renunciation was the
condition of his being restored to favour.   On the
same day the King confirmed to Elizabeth, Countess
of Ross, all the grants of lands within the Earldom
formerly made to her by the Crown, as not being
included in the foregoing renunciation.[2]   John,
having made these concessions, received in recognition of his obedience a new distinction.   He still
remained John de Ile, and retained the ancient
heritage of his house with the old historic dignity,
the Lordship of the Isles, which no Scottish monarch
had bestowed and, from the Celtic standpoint, none
could take away; but the ancient honour, with all

---

[1] Chronicle of the Earls of Ross, pp. 15, 16.
[2] Acts of the Scottish Parliament, vol. II., p. 113.

the proud memories it enshrined, was now combined
with the gaudy tinsel of a brand new, spick and span
title of Baron Banrent and Peer of Parliament.

It soon appeared that the King and Government
were not completely satisfied with the reduction
which had thus been made in the power and
possessions of the Chief of Clan Donald.   On the
26th of July, the same month that witnessed his
surrender, resignation, and partial reinvestiture, he
received a formal charter[1] for all the territories
which it was resolved by the Government he should
be permitted to retain.   This charter contains evidence that John was deprived of territories other
than those he gave up in his resignation of 1st
July, namely, the lands of Kintyre and Knapdale,
with which exception all the other estates which
belonged to him in the Lordship of the Isles
were allowed to remain in his possession.   The
historian of Sleat connects the loss of these
lands with certain dealings which John had with
Colin, Earl of Argyle, and while the details of his
story do not seem very probable, there is every
likelihood that that wily and unscrupulous nobleman
and courtier may have had something to do with
that unfortunate occurrence.   This charter of 1476
contained other important provisions connected with
the transmission of the still important possessions
and honours of the House of Isla.   John had no
legitimate male issue, but the family succession was
secured to his natural son Angus, and failing him,
to his natural son John and their heirs after them,
failing legitimate issue of their father's body.

It is thus plain that the situation, however
disastrous, was not without its compensations, and

[1] Reg. Mag. Sig. VIII., No. 132.

that John issued out of the terrible ordeal in which
the Treaty of Ardthornish placed him, with as little
loss of outward estate as could possibly have been
expected in the circumstances.   Others not more
guilty had lost life and property.   The comparatively
fortunate result may be attributed, less to his own
sagacity and force of character, than to the leniency
of the Crown, and contemporary records are pretty
clear in showing that, in the eyes of the King, blood
was thicker than water, and that John's kinship to
the royal line of Scotland had much to do with the
large measure of clemency that was displayed.
Had John been a stronger man than he was, with
the political calibre of his namesake " the good," or
had he possessed the lofty qualities of his father
and grandfather, he might either have avoided the
pitfalls that lay in his path, or made a better fight
for the interests at stake when the hour of trial
came.   But John, even discounting the forces he
had to contend with, was the weakest potentate of
his line, and there must be something after all in
the verdict of Hugh Macdonald, that he was a
" meek, modest man. . . . more fit to be a
churchman than to rule irregular tribes of people."
Taking all these things into consideration, the
position in which John found himself after the convulsion of 1475-6 was still not unworthy of the
traditions of his house ; and the family of Isla,
though the glory of their territorial position was
much bedimmed, still occupied one of the highest
places among the nobles of the land.   It also
appeared as if an era of peace and friendship with
the Crown was beginning to dawn upon the House
of Macdonald when, not long after the reconstruction
of John's estate, his son Angus married a daughter

of that eminent Scottish courtier, Colin, Earl of
Argyle.   That instead of a time of peace, a period of
almost unprecedented turmoil and conflict was at
hand, events were soon to show.

The scant records of the time distinctly prove
that the large sacrifice of his status and possessions,
which the head of the Clan Donald had been compelled to make, proved exceedingly unpopular among
those chieftains and vassals who were directly
descended from the family of the Isles.   The exalted
station of the head of the House of Somerled shed a
reflected lustre, not only on the chiefs of the various
branches, such as the Clanranalds, the Sleats, the
Keppochs, and others, but upon every individual
who bore the name, and in whose veins ran the
blood of Macdonald, and who exulted in the *prestige*
and renown of his chiefs.   For many ages the Lords
of the Isles had represented the ancient Celtic spirit
and social life in Scotland, which outside their
influence had been rapidly disappearing, and despite
the paramount and growing power of the Scottish
national system, these potentates had continued to
maintain, and even to enlarge, their territories.
Hence the idea was bound to prevail and gather
force, that the Lord of the Isles, in surrendering
great interests without affording his devoted vassals
the chance of striking a blow in defence, had failed
to keep untarnished the name and honour of his
clan.   The historian of Sleat has recorded that a
chief cause of John's unpopularity, during the days
of his undiminished greatness, among his Clan
Donald vassals, lay in his improvident grants of
land to the chiefs of other clans who were vassals of
the Isles, such as the Macleans, Macleods, Macneills,
and others.   All these, however, occupied extensive

tracts of territory in feu from John's predecessors, and it does not appear from the evidence of history that John was in this respect so much more lavish than his sires, or that he to a large extent impoverished the heritage of his Family. In the eyes of those who sighed over the fading glory of his House, the *gravamen* of his offence consisted in his not only parting with the Earldom of Ross, which was, after all, but a recent possession of the Island Family, but what was perhaps more galling to the *amour propre* of the Clan, his tamely giving up the patrimonial lands of Kintyre and Knapdale, the heritage of the Clan Cholla from far distant times. This was undoubtedly the universal and deeply seated sentiment of his Clan—a sentiment not only in itself excusable, but springing from a just self-respect, and burning as it did with a fiery glow in the bosom of many a valiant clansman, it needed only a leader or head to give it fitting and powerful expression.

It is equally intelligible that the other vassals should have regarded the crisis from a somewhat different point of view. The clans other than Clan Donald, who held their lands from John, had greatly increased in power and dignity under the kindly sway of the Lords of the Isles. The loss of sway by their superior did not, however, imply their decadence. On the contrary, the greatness of the Family of the Isles overshadowed their attempts at self-assertion, and the signs of a new order of things, in which they might rival the historic house in property and influence, were naturally not unwelcome. Thus there came to be a parting of the ways between those clans that held their territories, less on account of ties of kinship, and more by the bonds of feudal tenure, and those other tribes who regarded the Lord of the Isles, not merely as the superior of their lands, but as the acknowledged head of their race. No doubt these other clans, forming as they did a component part of the Island lordship, were still deeply interested in the preservation of the Celtic system which that lordship represented, and, as a matter of fact, we find them in after years fighting strenuously for its restoration. Yet at this particular crisis these clans were undoubtedly less zealous for the maintenance of the honour and glory of the House of Isla than the Clan Donald itself, and that most probably for the reasons that have been assigned. Hence we find them adhering to the Lord of the Isles in his attitude of concession and submission, while the Clan Donald, eager for the maintenance of the ancient power of the Family, sympathised with a policy of greater boldness and less compromise, while they found in Angus Og, the son and heir of John, the hero and exponent of their aspirations.

We are far from giving an unqualified assent to the verdict of previous writers who have dwelt upon the career and character of Angus. All modern historians who have discussed the theme, from Gregory[1]—who says that the violence of his temper bordered on insanity—down to the latest historian of the Clan, have limned his portrait with brushes dipped in darkest hues. To say the least of it, the materials for the formation of any such judgment are of the scantiest. That Angus behaved with brutal violence to his father, is a statement that has been accepted upon the sole authority of the historian of Sleat, who has circulated not a few myths in

[1] Highlands and Islands, p. 54.

connection with the Clan of which he writes. The tradition of filial impiety he has embodied in the strange tale, that Angus Og in his family residence at Finlaggan drove his father out of seven sleeping apartments successively, at last compelling him to take shelter under cover of an old boat for the night, and that next morning, on returning to the house, the old man uttered maledictions against his son.[1] A legend such as this, in which, like all legend, there may be a germ of truth, would need strong confirmatory evidence to make it credible in all its improbable details, and may very well have been propagated by the vassals of the Isles other than Clan Donald, who supported the yielding policy of John, and were antagonistic to the stronger attitude of his son. That in the circumstances which led Angus in public matters to oppose his father, regrettable scenes may have occurred, angry words been spoken, and stormy interviews taken place by which the two became estranged, may freely be admitted. That Angus was hot tempered and even violent, in an age when the Pagan virtues of courage and determination were more esteemed than the Christian graces of patience and self-restraint, especially in a fierce and warlike community, need not be denied; but that his fiery temper partook of the insanity and unreasoning fury which historians one after another have described, there is really no evidence to prove. It is not surprising that the circumstances of his family and race, and the depressed condition into which they had fallen under his father's reign, proved vexing to a proud and resolute spirit, and if it is borne in mind that his efforts were all along directed towards the re-

[1] Collectanea de Rebus Albanicis.

building of the ruined fabric of the family state, his conduct will appear intelligible, and from his particular standpoint worthy of praise.

Whatever estimate may have been formed of Angus Og by the outside world—and, no doubt, he proved himself a terror to his foes—he was certainly a great favourite with those of his name and lineage. Not only did they esteem his heroism and regard him as the restorer of their pristine greatness, but they loved him for his own sake. He possessed the popular manners and generous impulses of his race. He was open-handed and liberal with his means, and while he was brave as a lion on the field of battle, he followed with zest those sports and recreations with which even the most warlike beguiled the tedium of peace. He was a keen lover of the chase, and his unbounded hospitality in the banquetting hall was affectionately remembered in after times. He also seems to have possessed the same pleasing aspect and luxuriant flowing locks which were characteristic of his scriptural prototype—the rebellious son of David.[1] Such was unquestionably the verdict of his contemporary clansmen, and their devotion was evinced by the unanimous support accorded him in all his undertakings. Such could hardly have been the case had Angus Og been the deep dyed villain whom certain historians have portrayed.

There is very great uncertainty as to the sequence of events during the years that followed the forfeiture and partial restoration of John, Lord of the Isles. Down to the fall of the Lordship of the Isles, chronological difficulties abound. There is evidence, however, that from 1476 onward, Angus Og, sup-

---

[1] Poem by John of Knoydart in the Dean of Lismore's book.

ported by the general sentiment of the Clan, resisted what with some reason was considered his father's pusillanimous surrender. Undoubtedly the beginning of the long series of troubles, which filled the remaining years of the history of the Lordship of the Isles, was associated with John's deprivation of the lands of Knapdale and Kintyre. Castle Swin, in North Knapdale, long ago the scene of Alexander of Isla's discomfiture by Bruce, and destined in a future century to play a part in the annals of the Clan, was from 1476 to 1478 the scene of operations evidently carried on for the restoration of the surrounding territory to the family from which, in the opinion of its vassals, it had been unrighteously diverted. Whether the Lord of the Isles had been art and part in the rebellious proceedings or not, he was held responsible for what was done, and the following summons issued to him in 1478 contains an account of the hostilities which called for the attention of the Government :—

"Parliament held in Edinburgh 6th day of April, 1478.

"The seventh day of the moneth of Aprile the secund day of the said Parliament Johnne lord of the Ilis lauchfully personali and peremptourli summond to the said day to ansuer to owre souerain lorde the King in his said parliament for his tresonable assistence counsale fauoures help and supportacioune geveing to his Rebellis and tratoures being In the Castell of castelsone[1] And for art and part of the tresonable stuffing of the said Castell with men vitalis and Armis for weire And for the tresonable art and part of the holding of the said Castell contrare to the Kinges maieste. And for his manifest Rebellioun agane the King oure souerain lord making weire apoune his lieges Attoure his forbidding And for supportacioune and Resetting of the Kingis Rebellis donald gorme and Neile Makneile and thair complices the quhilkes dali Invades the Kinges lieges and distrois his landes. And for uther tresouns transgressionis and Rebelliouns again oure said

[1] Castle Swin.

souerain lordes maieste wro^t and committit. The said lord being
oft tymes callit and not comperit the summonds being lauchfull
tyme of day biding thereafter Ouer souerain lord with the
avise of the thre estatis continewis the said cause and accioun of
summondis maid uppoune the said Johnne of Islis to the secund
day of the moneth of Juin nixt to cum with continuacioune of
dais to his parliament to be haldin at his burgh of Edinburgh
And to begyn the first day of this moneth of Juin forsaid w^t
continuatione of dais.

   "In the sammyn forme strinth and effect as it now is." [1]

The opinion has been advanced that a second
forfeiture ensued as a consequence of the rebellion
which the foregoing citation records, and that,
similar to the first, it was soon followed by John's
second reinstatement in his property. The evidence
for this belief is contained in a charter of 16th
December, 1478, containing very nearly the same
provisions as that of 1476. Had not the forfeiture
taken place a second time, it is supposed that this
re-grant would have been unnecessary, both charters
having been given under the hand of James III.,
and neither requiring confirmation save in such circumstances as we have described. It is not clear,
however, that any such forfeiture and restoration
took place in 1478, or that the charter of that year
contains proof of such. As the tenor of that document shows, there is simply a confirmation by the
King, now having attained his majority, of the
grant made by him, as a minor, to John, Lord of
the Isles, in 1476. In other respects, both charters
are in identical terms. Similar provision is again
made for continuing the family succession through
Angus Og, and as John, the second son of the Lord
of the Isles, is not mentioned in the deed, we
conclude that he died in the interval. It seems

---

[1] Acts of Scottish Parliament, vol. XII., p. 115.

probable that John satisfied the Government that the irregularities complained of had been perpetrated, if not without his knowledge, at anyrate contrary to his wishes, and that he was successful in procuring pardon for his son, Angus Og, who was now beginning to display decided symptoms of unwillingness to accept of the situation created by the misfortunes of his father.

From 1478 to 1481 a fair condition of tranquillity seems to have prevailed in the Highlands and Islands generally. The Government seem to have been so convinced of the loyalty of John of Isla, that in the latter year large tracts of land in Kintyre, formerly in his possession, were now re-conveyed by royal charter for his life-time, as an acknowledgment of faithful service. It may be of interest to some of our readers if the places designated in this charter are here detailed. They are as follows :—

"The 12 merklands of Killewnane, the 6 merklands of Owgill, Auchnaslesok, Achencork and Kenochane, the 9 merklands of the two Knokrenochis, Glenmorele, Altnabay, Baduff, et Areskeauch ; the 5 merklands of the two Tereferguse and Largbane ; the 3 merklands of Kynethane and Hening ; the 6 merklands of the two Knokantis and Calybole ; the 5 merklands of Lossit and Glenhawindee ; the 4 merklands of Balleygrogane and Cragok ; the 8 merklands of Catadill, Gertmane, Gartloskin, Bredclaide, and Keppragane ; the 2 merklands of Ballenbraide ; the 4 merklands of Kilsolane ; the 2 merklands of Achnaclaich ; the 2 merklands of Teridonyll ; the 1 merkland of Lagnacreig ; the 1 merkland of Kerowsoyre ; the 1 merkland of Gartloskin ; the 3 merklands of Glenraskill ; the 2 merklands of Glenvey ; the 4 merklands of Browneregyn, Drumtyrenoch, Dalsmerill, Lagnadaise, and Enyncokaloch ; with the half of the 1 merklands of Kildallok and Lonochane ; the half of the 2 merkland of Ellerich and Arronarroch ; the 13 merklands of Cralekill, Macharanys, Darbrekane and Clagkeile ; claimed by Maknele, lying in the lordship of Kintyre and sheriffship of Tarbert :—And also he granted to the said John for the whole term of his life the lands underwritten, viz.:—the 12 merklands of Arymore; the 21 merklands of Owragag, Achtydownegall, Scottomyl, Drummalaycht, Downskeig, the Lowb, Lemnamwk, Gartwaich; the 31 merklands of Barmore, Garalane, Achnafey, Strondowr, Glenmolane, Glenraole, Largbanan, Barnellane, Kowildrinoch, Glannafeoch, Ardpatrick, Ardmenys, Largnahouschine, Forleyngloch, Crevyr, and Drumnamwkloch; the 4 merklands of Kilmolowok; the 2 merklands of Drumdresok; the 4 merklands of Schengart; the 4 merklands of the two Bargawregane; the 2 merklands of Clachbrek; the 4 merklands of Barloukyrt; the 1 merkland of Altbeith; the 1 merkland of Cragkeith; the 27 merklands of Achetymelane, Dowynynultoch, Renochane, Kilcamok, Gartnagrauch, and Ormsay claimel by Maklane and Maknele and lying in the lordship of Knapdale and sheriffdoms of Tarbert."[1]

No sooner, however, did matters seem to be settling down than we find Angus Og and his clansmen once more launching the thunderbolts of war. For the events of the period at which we have now arrived, and embracing a long term of years, we have little to guide us beyond the unreliable, conflicting, and exaggerated accounts which have been handed down to us by family historians, and we are like mariners on an unknown sea, the chart for which is blurred and dim, and the compass disturbed by the neighbourhood of magnetic influences. Out of these materials it seems hopeless to construct a clear, consistent, or intelligible narrative. In one MS. history of the Mackenzies, Angus Og is made to fight a battle which took place after his death; while his uncle Celestine, who died in 1473, is killed at the battle of Park in 1491. The battle of Lagabraad, in which the Mackenzies were defeated by Angus Og, has failed to find a record in the chronicles of that family, while the battle of Park, in which the Macdonalds were

[1] Reg. Mag. Sig., vol. II, 1485.

worsted, is honoured with particular and detailed notice. Such being the character of the records with which we have to deal, it is obvious that great caution has to be observed in separating fact from fiction.

On the whole, there is no reason to doubt that the invasion of Ross by Angus Og took place in 1481, nor is there any improbability in the story that it sprung out of one of those family feuds with which the history of the Highlands so largely abounds, though doubtless other and deeper motives may have been at work. On the forfeiture of the Earldom of Ross in 1475, the Mackenzies, who had previously been vassals of Macdonald, became vassals of the Crown, and as such, began to assume a certain measure of territorial dignity and importance. About that time, or shortly thereafter, Kenneth Mackenzie, son and heir to Alexander Mackenzie of Kintail, or as he was known in his day, *Alastair Ionraic*,[1] married Lady Margaret of the Isles, daughter of John of Isla, and half-sister to Angus Og. The lady is said to have been blind of an eye, and her value as an eligible bride was thereby greatly diminished in the matrimonial market. Yet there is no doubt that Kenneth Mackenzie, or, as he afterwards came to be known, *Coinneach a Bhlair*,[2] without any disparagement to his dignity, was considered to have made a brilliant match in marrying a daughter of the House of Isla, even with so serious a facial disfigurement as the loss of one of her eyes. Their married life was neither long nor happy, and it is clear that Kenneth's conception of conjugal fidelity was in no wise in advance of the practical ethics of his day. The

---

[1] Meaning Alexander the upright.   [2] Kenneth of the Battle, meaning Park.

story goes that Angus Og was in the North, living in the castle of Balconie, in the parish of Kiltearn, a house which, with the surrounding lands, appears to have been left in possession of the Countess of Ross after the forfeiture of the earldom, and thus continued a residence of the Macdonald Family in that region.   Angus, true to his reputation for hospitality, gave a feast to the old vassals and retainers of his family, no doubt with the object of ingratiating himself with them, in view of possible designs in the future.   Balconie Castle was undergoing repairs, and the guests were insufficiently provided with sleeping accommodation.   Macdonald was compelled, in consequence of this deficiency, to arrange some of the outhouses as sleeping apartments for his friends.   Maclean of Duart, Macdonald's chamberlain, offered to accommodate the redoubtable Kenneth in the kiln, deeming that, as a friend of the family, such a liberty might be taken.   Kenneth, with the irascibility bred of an undue sense of self-importance, considered his dignity grossly insulted by the bare suggestion of such an idea, and fetching a blow with all the might of his fist, struck Maclean in the ear and felled him to the ground.   The savage and gratuitous assault was felt to be a blow no less aimed at their chief than at his vassal, and the Clan Donald blood rising, weapons began to be handled. Kenneth and his retinue, deeming it the more prudent course to eschew the festivities, immediately took to their heels.   Finding a number of boats on the shore below the house, they sank all but one, in which they crossed to the Black Isle, thus for the time being baffling all pursuit.   Next day Kenneth found his way to Kinellan, and was immediately followed by a threatening message from Angus Og,

commanding himself and his father and household to
quit the place within twenty-four hours, giving the
Lady Margaret liberty to move in a more leisurely
manner, as best suited her convenience. Kenneth
was of course highly incensed on receiving such a
message, and returned an indignant answer, but
meanwhile commenced his reprisals by the cowardly
device of wreaking vengeance upon his unoffending
wife. The method of his revenge has done service
in tales of later times, but there is reason to believe
that *Coinneach a Bhlair* deserves all the discredit
of being the original inventor of the cruel insult.
He sent his wife home to Balconie riding on a one-
eyed horse, attended by a one-eyed servant, followed
by a one-eyed dog. Soon thereafter he took, with
no ceremony, a lady of the family of Lovat to wife,
showing the free and easy manner in which the
nuptial knot was sometimes tied and loosened in
these olden days.

The proud scion of the family of Isla could ill
brook the additional insult so savage and deliberate
in its conception. The grotesqueness of the
monocular retinue evinced a cruelty and malice
which could be interpreted in no other light than a
wanton and deliberate insult not only to Lady
Margaret but her whole kith and kin. Angus Og
was determined to be avenged upon Mackenzie ; but
it soon appeared that the private feud was but the
pretext for more extensive designs, the invasion and
forcible acquisition of the whole Earldom of Ross.
With this in view, Angus collected a large force in
the Isles, as well as in those regions of the mainland
where the Macdonald influence was still predominant. The Keppochs, Glengarrys, and many
other clansmen from the Isles rallied to his standard,

and with a formidable force he set out for Ross.
The Government, by this time realising that they
were face to face with a rebellion of some magnitude,
commissioned the Earl of Athole to march against
and subdue the Islesmen.   That nobleman, putting
himself at the head of the Northern Clans, including
the Mackenzies, Mackays, Brodies, Frasers, and
Rosses, took the field against the Western host.
The two armies met at a place called Lagabraad,
and a sanguinary battle was fought, which resulted
in the triumph of Angus Og and the utter rout of
his opponents.   There were slain of Athole's army
517 men, the chief of the Mackays was taken
prisoner, while Athole and Mackenzie narrowly
escaped with their lives.[1]   So far as we can gather
amid so much uncertainty as to the actual sequence
of events, this battle was fought about 1483.   It
proved that Angus Og, as a brave and accomplished
warrior, was second to none of his race, and that if
he had received the possessions of his house intact
he would have died sooner than surrender them.

Soon after Lagabraad, the Government gave
instructions to the Earls of Huntly and Crawford
to lead a new expedition against this formidable and
enterprising rebel ; but it is not clear whether they
took hostile action or did so with complete success.
We are equally in the dark as to the result of
Angus' victory in Ross, or whether he was able to
maintain his hold upon any part of that extensive
region.   The next time light falls upon this obscure
period we find Angus in the Isles when the Earls of
Argyll and Athole have brought about an interview
between himself and his father for the purpose, it is
said, of effecting a reconciliation.   Well might father

[1] Collectanea de Rebus Albanicis.

and son, like the Trojans of old, fear the Greeks
when they came with gifts, and it is not strange
though under such auspices meek-eyed peace would
not descend. The old lord was dominated by the
party of the Court, Angus commanded the steadfast
devotion of the Clan, and with a record of
triumphant success behind him he was not likely to
yield to the representations of the Government
without the retrocession of some at least of the
rights that had been surrendered. It would appear
that the Lord of the Isles had been consistently
loyal in his subjection to the Crown since 1476, and
that the disturbances that took place subsequently,
were regarded as being caused by his warlike son.

When the curtain next rises upon the *dramatis
personæ* in the Isles, Angus is on the eve of the
battle of Bloody Bay. Once more the Earls of
Argyll and Athole undertook to subdue the un-
daunted rebel, and prepared an expedition for the
purpose. The lords and chief men of the Isles,
those favouring a policy of concession and those
that supported the attitude of Angus, sailed in their
galleys up the Sound of Mull, and ranged along the
opposite side of that beauteous waterway—one of
the fairest scenes of which the Western Highlands
can boast—prepared for the internecine warfare.
The combination against Angus Og had been
organised by the two nobles whose names appear
so prominently in the annals of those years; but
when the day of battle came they seem to have
kept at a safe distance. Thus it came to pass
that in this fight of saddest omen, the most noted
naval battle in the Isles since the days of Somerled,
in which the ancient Lordship of the Isles was being
rent in twain, the Lord of the Isles was left in

command of the force which was to engage the
warriors of his race and name under the leadership
of his own son. The battle fought in the neighbourhood of Tobermory was fiercely. contested and
sanguinary. Little is known of the details of this
memorable engagement beyond what has been
preserved by the historian of Sleat. Angus Og's
galleys were drawn up on the north side of
Ardnamurchan, and detained by stress of weather
for a space of five weeks. At the end of that time
the laird of Ardgour was observed sailing up the
Sound, and he, on observing Angus Og and his
fleet, at once displayed his colours. Donald Gallach,
son of Hugh of Sleat, and Ranald Bane, son of Allan
MacRuari, chief of Moidart, were in the company
of Angus Og, and they steered towards Maclean's
galley. This was the signal for the opposing force
coming to the assistance of Ardgour, conspicuous
among the rest being William Macleod of Harris.
Ranald Bane grappled Macleod's galley, while one
of Ranald's company, Edwin Mor O'Brian by name,
put an oar in the stern-post between the helm and
the ship, which immediately became unmanageable,
and was captured with all on board. Macleod was
mortally wounded, and died shortly afterwards at
Dunvegan. Maclean of Ardgour, who was taken
prisoner, had a narrow escape for his life. Angus
Og is said to have suggested hanging, and this
would probably have been his end were it not
that the Laird of Moidart, with a touch of humour,
interceded for him on the ground that, if Maclean's
life was taken, he himself would have no one to
bicker with. This view seems to have commended
itself to the leader, and on Ardgour taking the oath
of fealty he was spared, presumably to save Clan-

ranald from too monotonous a life.[1] Here we are
afforded but a glimpse of an incident in this famous
sea fight, the result of which was the discomfiture
of Angus Og's opponents and his own secure establishment as the Captain of the Clan Donald. So
far as we can calculate without accurate data, the
Battle of Bloody Bay was fought in 1484.[2]

Fateful events followed each other in rapid
succession during these later years of the Lordship
of the Isles, and very shortly after this victory of
Angus Og, an incident occurred which aggravated
the enmity between the opposing parties, and
became a fruitful cause of trouble for many years
to come. It is not to be forgotten that the agents
in provoking this outburst of renewed bitterness
were the two noblemen who, a few short months
before, are alleged to have done their utmost to
bury the hatchet of strife. Angus Og, as has
already been stated, was married to a daughter
of Colin, Earl of Argyle, probably about 1480, and
at the time of the battle of Bloody Bay this lady,
and an infant son Donald, were living in the family
residence at Finlaggan. The Earl of Athole, with
the connivance and assistance of Argyle, who
furnished him with boats, crossed secretly to Isla,
stole the infant son of Angus, and delivered him
to Argyle, who immediately sent him under careful
guardianship to the Castle of Inchconnel in Lochow.
The reasons for this shameful abduction do not
appear to us very far to seek. We do not wish to
bestow unmerited censure even upon the inveterate
enemy of the House of Isla, but facts, however
repulsive, must be stated unreservedly. Even the

[1] Collectanea de Rebus Albanicis.

[2] According to a History of the Clan Maclean, by "Seanachie," the Lord
of the Isles was taken prisoner by his son at this battle—p. 24.

most strenuous apologists of the House of Argyle can hardly get the facts of history to prove that they were either unselfish or unrewarded in their vaunted support of Scottish nationality, or that their conduct amid the turmoil of Highland politics was noble or disinterested.   The abduction of Donald Dubh was an act of unspeakable meanness, and was instigated by the basest motives.   So long as there was an heir to the Lordship of the Isles, so long was there a likelihood at least, of the Macdonalds retaining the family inheritance, and so long must there be a postponement of the family of Argyle entering into possession of their estates. To prevent, if possible, the Macdonald succession, Argyle gets hold of the heir presumptive, with the view of retaining him a perpetual prisoner.   Still further to prevent the succession of his grandson, he concocted and got the Government to believe the story of Donald's illegitimacy—a pure fabrication to promote his sinister ends.   If Donald Dubh was really illegitimate, that fact would of itself suffice to prevent his succession to the honours and possessions of the Clan Donald, and, in the circumstances, the Government would be most unlikely to grant a charter of legitimation in his favour.   Hence, if the story had been true, the measure of consigning Donald to perpetual captivity, would have been altogether unnecessary.   It was because of Donald's legal birth, and his undoubted right to succeed his father, that the dastardly device was adopted of stealing the unoffending and ill-starred child, and making him virtually a prisoner for life.   Our aspersions on the conduct of Argyle in connection with this particular event are warranted by the testimony of history.   How, indeed, can we contemplate without indignation the character of a man who,

to further his own schemes of policy, not only
consigned an innocent grandchild to a living death,
but cast an unfounded suspicion on the fair fame
of his own daughter?

It is not by any means surprising that this
abduction, in which Athole was the catspaw of the
crafty Argyle, caused the deepest resentment in the
breast of Angus Og, and no sooner did it come to
his knowledge than he took immediate steps to
execute vengeance on the actual perpetrator of the
deed. Collecting a band of warriors in the Isles,
Angus sailed with a fleet of galleys up to Inverlochy,
a landing-place which, from its position in the far
interior, was well adapted for a descent upon any
part of the North of Scotland. The Highland host,
disembarking in this historic scene, marched through
the great mountain passes of Lochaber and Badenoch
until at last, swooping down upon the lowlands of
Perthshire, they passed into the region of Athole.
Tidings having reached Blair of the rapid approach
of the Islesmen, and time not availing for the organi-
zation of defence, the Earl and Countess of Athole,
with a number of dependants and retainers, and a
large quantity of valuable effects, took refuge in the
sanctuary of the Church of St Bridget's. There
is great uncertainty as to the events that followed.
The facts of history have in this connection been so
twisted and misplaced, and the religious preconcep-
tions of the narrators have so obscured the issue,
that it is well nigh impossible to extricate the real
occurrences from the mythological haze in which
they are enveloped. The consequence is, that modern
Scottish historians have presented us with a blend
of legend and fact which does great credit to their
imagination and eloquence, but very little to their

critical acumen.   The historian of Sleat, who at no
time is the apologist of Angus, flatly denies the
story of the burning of St Bridget's, and it is, no
doubt, to be placed in the same category of fabulous
traditions as other conflagrations with which the
family historians of the North of Scotland have
credited the Clan Donald.   The same authority
remarks, with truth, that the Lords of the Isles
were generous benefactors, and not the destroyers
of churches, and this is more than can be said of
some of the historical houses that rose upon the
ruins of their fallen state.   Certain facts connected
with the raid of Athole seem beyond dispute.   That
Angus and his followers invaded the sanctity of St
Bridget's; that they took captive within that shrine
the Earl and Countess of Athole, in revenge for the
abduction of Donald, Angus' infant son, and that
probably a quantity of valuable booty at the same
time was seized; that Angus took the high-born
captives with him, by way of Inverlochy, to Isla, as
hostages for the restoration of his son; that the
hurricanes of the wild western sea may have engulfed
some of the treasure-laden galleys on their home-
ward voyage; that the leader and his captains in
after times went back on a pilgrimage, probably
directed by Mother Church, to seek the divine
mercy at the shrine which, in their wrath, they had
desecrated but not destroyed, doing so with all the
outward symbols of contrition which the piety of
the age prescribed; and that the Earl and Countess
of Athole were unconditionally set free from their
captivity in Isla after the expiry of a year—all this
appears to be fairly well authenticated.   But the
exaggerations and improbabilities that have gathered
round the facts in the pages of the credulous chroni-

cler—that Angus and his men burnt churches wholesale in the course of their march through Athole;
that they tried three times to fire the Church of St
Bridget's, which at first miraculously resisted the
devouring element; that when they launched out
into the open sea they were seized with such judicial
frenzy that they were unable to steer their ships,
which consequently were driven by the tempest on
a rock-bound coast and wrecked—all this belongs to
the large mass of fable with which the history of the
period so much abounds. The act of sacrilege and the
subsequent act of penitence are both characteristic of
the time. The atonement so humbly offered by
these fierce warriors from the Isles is a gleam of light
athwart the dark tale of vengeance. It shows how,
even amid the violence of war and rapine, the sense
of responsibility was but asleep, needing but the
shock of some convulsion or catastrophe to rouse it
into active being. The Raid of Athole took place
about the year 1485.

Little is known of the subsequent career of
Angus Og, until the tragic close which seems to
have taken place some five years later. So far as the
government of the Isles was concerned, his position
was unquestioned, and had his life been prolonged,
the vigour and determination of his character would
not improbably have done much to restore the
ancient power of his family. A pleasing feature in
these latter years lay in his reconciliation with his
father. Angus Og seems never to have abandoned
his scheme for the conquest of Ross, and it was
probably with the view of reducing to subjection
the old vassals of the Earldom, and particularly of
chastising the Mackenzies, that he took his last

A TOVT POVER

LORD OF ye ILLIS

fatal journey to the North.   Angus halted at Inverness, where, as was his wont, he gave hospitable entertainment to his friends and allies in that region.   The story is told by the historian of Sleat with his usual amplitude of detail, and bears upon the face of it the mark of truth.

The heir of the Lewis had been recently a minor under the tutelage of Rory Black Macleod, whose daughter was married to the Laird of Moydart. Rory the Black coveted the succession, and refusing to acknowledge the true heir to the Lewis, assumed the lordship himself.   His schemes, however, were thwarted by Angus Og, who displaced Rory. from the position he usurped, and put the rightful heir in possession, acting in the matter as the representative of his father, of whom the Macleods were vassals. The Lady of Moydart, Rory the Black's daughter, moved by hatred of Angus for thus vindicating a righteous cause, compassed his death.   There was a harper of County Monaghan, named Art O'Carby, who was either in Macdonald's retinue or a frequenter of his establishment.   This Irish Orpheus conceived a violent passion for the daughter of Mackenzie of Kintail, who was at feud with Angus Og, and it would appear that the Lady of Moydart put Mackenzie up to the scheme of promising his daughter in marriage to O'Carby if he did away with the heir of the Isles.   He made the harper swear never to disclose the secret of who instigated the deed.   The Irishman undertook to carry out the dark conspiracy, and in token of his villainous intention was wont, when in convivial mood, to repeat doggerel verses of his own composition, of which the following is a couplet :—

18

" T' anam do Dhia a mharcaich an eich bhall-bhric
   Gu bheil t' anam au cunnart ma tha puinnsean an Gallfit."

"Rider of the dappled steed, thy soul to God commend,
   If there is poison in my blade, thy life right soon shall end."

One night after Angus had retired to rest, the harper entered his apartment, and perceiving he was asleep, killed him by cutting his throat. O'Carby was apprehended, but never confessed who his tempter was, or what inducement was held out as a reward for the murderous act. Jewels found upon him which formerly belonged to Mackenzie and the lady of Moydart proclaimed their complicity in the crime. The harper, according to the cruel fashion of the time, was torn asunder, limb from limb, by wild horses.[1]

Thus fell Angus Og, and although the Sleat historian tells us that his father's curse visited him, his theory of retribution hardly fits in to the facts of his own narrative. Angus fell a victim, as better men have done before him, to the malignant spite of an unscrupulous and designing woman, and that not for any deed of cruelty or oppression, but for upholding the cause of justice in the succession to the Lordship of Lewis. With Angus vanished the best hopes of the Clan Donald for the restoration of their proud pre-eminence, and there is surely pathos in the thought that, as the Founder of the Family in historic times had his warlike career cut short by treachery, so now three hundred years later the last direct representative of the line save one, also died by the assassin's knife. Our estimate of his character and the date at which we have placed his death, are both confirmed by the Irish Annals of Loch Ce, in which at the year 1490 the tragedy is

---

[1] Hugh Macdonald in Collectanea de Rebus Albanicis, p. 319.

thus referred to :—" MacDhomhnaill of Alba, *i.e.*, the best man in Erin or in Alba of his time, was unfortunately slain by an Irish harper, *i.e.*, Diarmaid Cairbrech, in his own chamber."[1]

At the period to which we have now come, it may well be said that, although many bright pages of the story of the House of Somerled still remain to be written, yet its heroic age as the dominant power in the Western Isles of Scotland is beginning to pass away. After the death of Angus, the Clan Donald were never afterwards united under a leader so able, or in whom they reposed such confidence. From 1476 down to his death his father's headship of the house was nominal; for it was round Angus that the kindred clans rallied at every juncture that arose. On his death, John again became the effective ruler in the Isles, and there was still a possibility, had he possessed an imperial spirit, of the Lordship of the Isles being maintained. Not long after Angus' death, John, though still far short of extreme old age, ceased to take an active part in the government of his territories, which he seems to have surrendered to his nephew, Alexander, son of Celestine of Lochalsh. Alexander acted ostensibly in the interests of Donald Dubh, who, though still in prison, was undoubtedly heir apparent to John ; but as there was little hope of his ever being released, Lochalsh doubtless contemplated, with few misgivings, his own succession to the Lordship of the Isles. At the same time it is clear, from subsequent events, that notwithstanding Donald's continued captivity, the Islesmen were

[1] The name of the assassin given in the above authority differs from that given by Hugh Macdonald, which is "Art" (not Diarmaid) " O'Cairbre." Hugh Macdonald in Coll. de Rebus Alb., p. 318.

unanimous in regarding him as his grandfather's rightful heir.

It had often been the fate of the last Earl of Ross to be under the influence of wills more imperious and resolute than his own, though, strangely enough, he offered a stubborn resistance to the aims and policy of his son. It was so now in his declining years. He who had so strenuously resisted the resolute stand made by Angus against the encroachments upon the family estates, now abandoned every attempt to curb the turbulence of his nephew, Alexander of Lochalsh. Whether he approved of the rising of 1491, or whether he made unavailing protestations against it, we are unable to say. All we know is that Alexander seems, without any delay, to have taken up the schme for the invasion of Ross, which was interrupted by the death of Angus Og. Owing to his territorial position in Wester Ross, Alexander naturally possessed great influence in that region. The extensive lands of Lochbroom, Lochcarron, and Lochalsh were his, and he doubtless expected that the other vassals of the earldom, always of course excepting the Mackenzies, would attend the summons to his banner. In this he was to a large extent disappointed. Still his following was a formidable one. The whole power of the island and mainland Macdonalds, along with the other vassals of the lordship, and the Clan Cameron, who were vassals of Alexander for the lands of Locheil, formed no inconsiderable array, and with all these resources at his back, he might hope, with some prospect of success, to win back the inheritance which his uncle had lost. Indeed, he possessed far greater resources than Angus Og was ever able to command, in view of the divided state of the Lord-

ship of the Isles in his time.   We have no reason to
doubt the personal bravery and prowess of Alexander, but he seems to have lacked that inexplicable
power of organising forces and leading them to
victory which is born with a man, and constitutes
the true commander.   Alexander and his army,
taking the time-honoured highway, marched through
Lochaber into Badenoch, where they were joined by
the Clan Chattan, under the command of Farquhar
Mackintosh, captain of the Clan.   Arriving at Inverness, which he stormed and garrisoned, and where
he was joined by Hugh Rose, younger of Kilravock,
the only vassal of the Earldom that seconded his
undertaking, Alexander next directed his march
towards Ross.   Invading the Black Isle, he and his
host penetrated to its extremest limit, plundering
the lands of Sir Alexander Urquhart, Sheriff of
Cromarty.   Authorities are agreed that at this stage
Lochalsh divided his forces into two sections, one
detachment having been sent home with the spoil,
while the other marched to Strathconan to ravage
and lay waste the Mackenzie lands.   Like almost all
the chronicles of this age bearing upon the history
of the Highlands, the annals of this campaign
abound in absurd inaccuracies and exaggerations.
When we find a mythical Celestine[1] performing deeds
of valour, and meeting with a hero's death ; Angus
Og or his father[2] taken prisoner, but soon thereafter
magnanimously released by *Coinneach a Bhlair* ;
Alastair Ionraic, who died in 1488, giving his
benediction to his son before going to battle ; a
supernatural being of diminutive stature appearing

[1] For this and the most of the other fictions, the apocryphal MS. history
of the Mackenzies, belonging to the Cromartie Family, is responsible.

[2] It is difficult in some parts to make out whether John of Isla or his son
Angus is meant.

and vanishing mysteriously, and in the interval doing great havoc among the invaders,[1]—when we find 'all this taking place at the Battle of Park in 1491, we are warned that the stories of the Northern chronicles of the time must be accepted with great reserve. In these circumstances, we do not attach the slightest credence to the legend of Contin Parish Church being set on fire by Alexander of Lochalsh and his men on their march from Strathconan. Neither do we believe that *Alastair Ionraic*, having departed this life three years previously, could have congratulated his people—as he is said to have done —that now this sacrilegious act had enlisted Omnipotence on the side of the Mackenzies. The whole bombastic and inflated Mackenzie history of *Blar na Pairc* is correct only in this one particular, namely, that the Macdonalds were worsted, and had to retire from Ross.

So far as we can gather, the sober facts of history in this connection are clear enough. Alexander and his men arrived at Park late in the evening after harrying and laying waste the lands of Strathconan. Wearied with the day's labours, they slumbered on the field, and apparently committed the fatal oversight of keeping neither watch nor ward. Meanwhile Kenneth of Kintail, who was by all accounts a brave warrior, had assembled his available strength, and now under the silence of night, while the Islesmen were asleep, bore down upon their encampment.[2] The Macdonalds were taken completely by surprise, and there ensued one of those panics which sometimes, like an electric shock, have been known to pass through bands of armed men. Their confusion became hopeless and inextricable, and was

[1] New Statistical Account of Fodderty, p. 255.
[2] Hugh Macdonald in Coll. de Reb. Alb., p. 321.

aggravated by the boggy nature of the ground
which lay between them and the river Conon, but
with which their enemies were well acquainted.
There is no reason to question the tradition that,
while many were put to the sword, a considerable
number were drowned in the Conon, towards which
they were driven by their triumphant foes. Such
was the Battle of Park, an illustration of the
advantage possessed by an enemy, resolute and
wary, taking an encampment by surprise. The
result was the retirement of Alexander of Lochalsh
from Ross, and his abandonment for the time being
of all attempts to accomplish its conquest. It has
been held by some that Park was fought in 1488,
but the evidence is all in favour of the later date.
Angus Og was alive in 1488, and it is not likely
that he would have played a subordinate part in
such a campaign, or that Alexander would have
borne the prominent part he did had Park been
fought in the lifetime of John of Isla's son. We
find also that in 1492 Sir Alexander Urquhart
obtained restitution on behalf of himself and others
for the spoil carried away by the Islanders, and it
is very unlikely that a claim of such magnitude
would have lain dormant from 1488.[1] Hence there
seems little doubt that the Battle of Park was
fought in 1491.

The invasion of Ross, undertaken undoubtedly
with the view of gaining forcible possession of the
Earldom, which was since 1476 vested in the Crown,
could not fail to be regarded as an insurrection
against the State, and, as such, calling for the

[1] The spoil amounted to 600 cows and oxen, 80 horses, 1000 sheep, 200
swine, 500 bolls victual—plenishing £300 in value, and £300 of the mails of
the Sheriff's lands.

severest measures. Whether John of the Isles
approved of his nephew's rebellion or not, it appeared
to the authorities that the time had come for depriv-
ing him finally of every vestige of power he possessed.
If he aided and abetted in the proceedings of 1491,
he would appear to the Government in the light of
a hopeless rebel, into whom the experience of forty
years failed to instil the lessons of loyalty. If he
disapproved of but failed to prevent the disorderly
proceedings in Ross, his deprivation would seem
equally called for, on the ground of his utter inability
to exercise authority in the regions or over the
vassals subject to his sway. It was on one or other
of these grounds that in May, 1493, John was
forfeited in all his estates and titles, and this
measure was formally implemented by himself in
1494, when he made a voluntary surrender of
them all.[1]

Thus fell the Lordship of the Isles, and with it
the dynasty which for hundreds of years had continued to represent, in a position of virtual independence, the ancient Celtic system of Scotland.
The natural result of such a catastrophe was that
for a long term of years the region that had been
ruled by these Celtic princes was subject to prolonged outbursts of anarchy and disorder. There
arose a *vacuum* in the social system which the
authority of the Scottish State, anti-Celtic as it had
increasingly become, failed adequately to fill up.
Social order depends as much upon sympathy with
the governing Power as upon force, and the amal-
gamation of the Celtic and Saxon elements of
Scottish society must inevitably prove a long
process. Still further, while the feudal position of

[1] There seems to be no public record of this final forfeiture.

the Lordship of the Isles was one that Parliament could abolish, the Highlanders regarded it, not as a feudal, but as a Celtic dignity, older than, and independent of, the Scottish State—a dignity which no individual could surrender, and no King or State could destroy. Thus it was that for two generations after John's forfeiture Highland politics swayed between efforts on the part of the Crown to reduce the Clans to subjection, on the one hand, and spasmodic movements by the Clans, on the other, to restore the Celtic order which they loved, by rallying to the banner of one scion of the Family of the Isles after another, each of whom laid claim, with more or less appearance of justice, to the ancient honours of his house.

Events of consequence transpired between John's political demise in 1494 and his death in 1498, but these will more appropriately fall to be considered in a succeeding chapter. At this stage we can most fittingly record the few facts that are known regarding the declining years of the last of the Earls of Ross and Lords of the Isles. What we do know of the fallen potentate during his latter days gives us a sad picture of departed greatness. He, the descendant of kings, lived as a pensioner upon the bounty of James IV. down to the day of his death, having his clothes and shoes and pocket money doled out to him like a pauper. The general belief has been, and historians have consistently followed one another in stating, that after his forfeiture John lived and died an inmate of the Monastery of Paisley, an institution that had in former years enjoyed the munificent patronage of the House of Isla. The records of the period tell a somewhat different tale.[1] The monastery doubtless

---

[1] High Treasurer's Accounts.

was his home, but he sometimes left it, paying visits, among other places, to his old dominions in Lochaber and the Isles. At last we find him falling sick at Dundee, where he dies in an obscure lodging-house, and the sum due to his landlady and the expenses of his "furthbringing" are charged to the Scottish Treasury.[1] All this is quite consistent with the tradition that his remains were buried at his own request in the tomb of his ancestor, Robert II., in the ancient Abbey of Paisley,[2] whither they must have been conveyed all the way from Dundee. Here closes the record of a "strange eventful history"—and as we part with this last of the line of Somerled, who swayed the sceptre of the Gael in the ancient Kingdom of the Isles, we conclude with the legend which seems more descriptive than any other of so much glory and so great a fall, *Sic transit gloria mundi*.[3]

[1] "Item (Feb. 5, 1498), to Pate Sinclair, to send to Dunde to pay for Johnue of Islis furthbringing and berying, and to lones his gere," *i.e.*, to settle with his landlady.—The High Treasurer's Accounts.

[2] Hugh Macdonald in Coll. de Reb. Alb., p. 317.

[3] Successive historians have spoken of John in his latter years as the "aged" Lord of the Isles ; but as he was only 18 when he succeeded his father in 1449, he could only have been 67 at his death.

CHAPTER XI.

THE CLAN DONALD UNDER JAMES IV.—1493-1519.

State of the Highlands after the Forfeiture of the Lord of the
Isles.—James IV. visits the Highlands, and holds Court at
Dunstaffnage.—Several Highland Chiefs submit to the King.
—The King at Tarbert in Kintyre.—Left Garrisons at
Tarbert and Dunaverty.—Revolt of the Clan Iain Mhoir.—
The King at Mingarry receives Submission of many of the
Highland Chiefs.—Legislation for the Isles.—Rebellion of
Alexander of Lochalsh.—The King grants Charters at his
new Castle of Kilkerran, in Kintyre.—The King revokes
Charters formerly granted by him to the Highland Chiefs.—
Rebellion of Donald Dubh.—Legislation for the Highlands.—
Appointment of Sheriffs. —The position of the different
Branches of the Clan Donald.— The Highlanders at Flodden.
—First Rebellion of Sir Donald of Lochalsh.—Second Rebellion
of Sir Donald of Lochalsh.—His Death.

THE fall of the Lordship of the Isles, consequent on
the forfeiture of John, resulted, as might have been
expected, in much disorder and bloodshed.   The
Celtic system, which had flourished for centuries
under the suzerainty of the Scottish State, was
deeply rooted in the Highlands and Islands, and
was not easily supplanted by the desperate policy of
destroying " the wicked blood of the Isles" pursued
by the King and his advisers.   The Celtic system,
on the whole, had worked well, and suited the genius
of the people.   This will become apparent if we draw
a parallel between the state of the Highlands during
the period of the Lordship of the Isles and that
which followed down to the abolition of the Herit-

able Jurisdictions. No doubt the downfall of the Lordship of the Isles and the final overthrow of the Celtic system were brought about entirely by the restlessness of and the short-sighted policy pursued by the Island Lords themselves, and considering the chequered history of each successive head of the family, we only wonder how the present catastrophe has been averted so long. If John, the last Lord of the Isles, had pursued a more prudent line of policy towards the Scottish State, the Celtic system would undoubtedly have lasted longer, and its gradual merging into feudal Scotland would have averted much of the bloodshed and turmoil of the next hundred years.

James IV. set himself to solve the difficult and formidable problem before him with much energy and perseverance. His policy at first, though firm, was conciliatory. He resolved on visiting the Highlands, making himself acquainted with the vassals of the Isles, and with the real state of matters in the altered circumstances consequent on the forfeiture of the Island Lord. On the 18th of August, 1493, we find him at Dunstaffnage, where he held Court, and received the homage of several Highland chiefs, and, among others, of John of Dunnyveg, John Cathanach his son, John MacIan of Ardnamurchan, and Alexander of Lochalsh.[1] In October of the same year he visited the North Highlands, very probably not on State business, but on one of those frequent pilgrimages which he took to the shrine of St Duthus in Tain.[2] James was so desirous of conciliating the

---

[1] At "Dunstaffynch," the King, on the 18th of August, 1493, confirms John Ogilvy in the barony of Fingask.—Reg. Mag. Sig., vol. II., No. 2171.

[2] On the 25th of October, 1493, the King grants a charter, at the Castle of Dingwall. Gregory is mistaken in saying that the King held Court at Mingarry on that date.—Vide Reg. Mag. Sig., vol. II., 2181.

Clan Donald vassals that he knighted John of Dunnyveg, the son of Donald Balloch, and Alexander of Lochalsh, and confirmed them in their lands.[1] The honour conferred on Alexander of Lochalsh and the leniency shown to him are all the more remarkable on account of his recent rebellion against the King's authority. It would appear that he, and not Donald Dubh, notwithstanding the charter of 1476, which makes Angus Og heir to the Lordship of the Isles, is of all the Macdonald chieftains the one looked upon as having the best claim to the forfeited Island honours, and the most likely to push that claim. It was, no doubt, with this in view that the King, wishing to attach Alexander to his interest, conferred upon him the honour of knighthood. The favour bestowed on the son of Donald Balloch was no less remarkable, in view of the treasonable conduct of both father and son in connection with the Treaty of Ardthornish. The other Clan Donald vassals, consisting of Allan of Moydart, John of Sleat, John Abrachson of Glencoe, and Alister MacIan of Glengarry, had not yet acknowledged the new order of things. The only chieftain of the Clan Donald who made any show of loyalty was MacIan of Ardnamurchan, whose allegiance and services at this time and afterwards were amply requited at the expense of the other clansmen.

Notwithstanding the King's conciliatory measures, the Islanders seem slow to accept them. The King was perhaps too precipitate in his legislation for the Highlands. We have no reason to suspect his sincerity, but his zeal was without knowledge. The Scottish Kings had not hitherto troubled themselves much with the personal oversight of their Celtic

[1] Treasurer's Accounts, 1494.

subjects. A wide gulf separated Highlander and Lowlander, both socially and racially, and it was not to be bridged over by a few flying visits by King James to Kintyre and Mingarry. These visits lacked the sympathy in dealing with the situation which would have cemented the Highland chiefs to the Scottish throne. The policy of legislating for the Highlands from the Lowland point of view was pursued, and as subsequent events show, it proved futile, if not indeed disastrous. The Highland problem was one the solution of which seemed entirely beyond the capacity of the Lowland mind. Though, as we have seen, a few of the vassals of the Lordship of the Isles had made a show of allegiance at Dunstaffnage, many others still remained unsubmissive. Their conduct rendered it necessary for the King to again visit the Highlands. At the head of a strong military force he pushed his way westwards as far as Kintyre.[1] The Castle of Tarbert was erected, as we have already seen, by Robert Bruce to check the power of the Island Lords. Here the King, with the view of strengthening the defences of the important peninsula of Kintyre, left a strong garrison. He also took possession, apparently without any opposition, of the Castle of Dunaverty, a stronghold of the Macdonalds, in South Kintyre, which, situated on the top of a tremendous precipice, nature, assisted by art, rendered impregnable. Having made Dunaverty secure, as he thought, against any possible assault, the King returned South by sea. What success attended his visit to the Highlands in the way of receiving the submission of those chiefs who had hitherto held aloof we have no means

[1] Treasurer's Accounts for 1494.

of knowing, though it would appear from after
events that the success of his expedition in this
respect fell far short of his expectations. He had
already so far conciliated the Clan Iain Mhoir by
confirming them in at least the principal lands
which they held under the Lords of the Isles, that
opposition on their part was not looked for. The
King, however, had taken the precaution in case of
revolt to place the district of Kintyre under military surveillance.   By this bold stroke of policy he
expected to overawe the men of Argyle, but he soon
found out his mistake.   Though the district of
Kintyre was resigned by John, Lord of the Isles, in
1476, many of the same lands were afterwards
restored to him in 1481, and whether the lands
possessed by the Clan Iain Mhoir were in any way
affected either by the forfeiture of 1476, or the
restoration of 1481, there seems every reason to
believe that the family were in possession of almost
the whole lordship of Kintyre in 1494. It was
not, therefore, we think, the loss of their lands in
Kintyre, as suggested by Gregory, that roused this
family into opposition to the King's policy ; it was
rather the presence of a military force in their midst
that the proud spirited Lords of Dunnyveg could
not brook. The King had barely gone on board the
ship that was to carry him back to Dumbarton,
when Sir John of Dunnyveg, assisted by his son,
John Cathanach, besieged Dunaverty.   After a
stout resistance on the part of the Lowlanders, Sir
John and the men of Kintyre took possession of the
Castle, and hanged the King's governor over the
precipitous rock on which that stronghold stood.
The King, who from the deck of his ship witnessed
this horrible deed, vowed vengeance, as might have

been expected, on the Lord of Dunnyveg, who by and by was made to pay the penalty of his daring.

It may be as well at this stage to refer to the confusion which seems to exist with reference to the family of Dunnyveg and the part played by the different members of that family in the history of this time. It has generally been believed that the rebel who defied the King in Kintyre was John Cathanach, while his father, John, the son of Donald Balloch, has been entirely dropped out of the history of the family. No doubt John Cathanach played a conspicuous part in the history of those stirring times. He had been fostered with the O'Cathans, his mother's kin, in Ireland, where love to the Saxon was not, we may be sure, one of the graces with which his young mind was imbued. In any case, John's character was intensely Celtic, and he bore no love to his Saxon neighbours. Some have asserted that John, the father of John Cathanach, died before his own father, Donald Balloch. We find Donald Balloch witnessing at Isla a charter of John, Lord of the Isles, on the 20th of August, 1476, and as we hear no more of him, and being a very old man, he probably died shortly after that event.[1] At all events, as we shall soon see, his son John, and his grandson, John Cathanach, perished together for the part they took in the affair of Dunaverty. That the John who was knighted by the King shortly before this time was not John Cathanach, but his father, is proved beyond any manner of doubt by the royal charter of lands in Isla granted to John MacIan of Ardnamurchan for apprehending "Johannes de Insulis de Glennys

<hr>

[1] Reg. Mag. Sig., vol. II., No. 1277.

militis, Johannes Caynoch, ejus filii, et complicum
suorum."[1]   The King, immediately on his return
South, sent a messenger to Kintyre to summon Sir
John of the Isles for treason, which no doubt refers
to his conduct at Dunaverty.[2]   Sir John ignored
the summons, but the King employed other and
more effective means of apprehending the rebel.
MacIan of Ardnamurchan, as we have seen, is
already in high favour with his sovereign.   There
had been a dispute between him and Sir John of
Dunnyveg over the lands of Suanart, and therefore
no love was lost between the clansmen.   MacIan
had besides married a daughter of the Earl of
Argyle, and through this matrimonial alliance had
become a tool in the hands of that crafty nobleman,
which he was not slow to use against the Clan
Donald.   Instigated by Argyle, MacIan treacherously apprehended at Finlaggan, in Isla, in the end
of the year 1494, " Sir John of the Isles and Glens,
John Cathanach his son, and their accomplices,"
and brought them to Edinburgh, where, after being
convicted of high treason, they were all hanged on
the Boroughmuir, and their bodies were buried in
the Church of St Francis, then called the New
Church.[3]   The exact date of the execution of Sir
John of Dunnyveg, and his son John Cathanach, is
not given by any authority, but it may be taken for
granted that it took place shortly after they were
apprehended, and, therefore, about the beginning of

[1] Argyll Charter Chest.   The Charter is dated 29th March, 1499, and is
given in full in " The Book of Islay," pp. 28-30.

[2] In the Treasurer's Accounts for the year 1494, the sum of £6 13s 4d is
charged as having been paid to a messenger " to passe to summond Sir John
of the Ilis of treasone in Kintyre and the expensis of the witnes."—Pitcairn,
vol. I., p. 116.

[3] MacVuirich in Reliq. Celt., p. 163.

19

the year 1495. According to Gregory, four sons of John Cathanach were executed with their father on the Boroughmuir, but the references he gives are the Charter of 1499, already quoted, MacVuirich, and Hugh Macdonald. In the charter there is no reference to any son of John Cathanach, while MacVuirich has it that three sons of John Cathanach were executed, namely, John Mor, John Og, and Donald Balloch.[1] Hugh Macdonald, in his MS., printed in the Collectanea de Rebus Albanicis, says that " Alexander of Kintyre and his two sons, one of whom was called John Cathanach, were by the King's orders hanged at the Borrowmuir, near Edinburgh, because after the resignation of John of the Isles they neither would take their rights from the King nor deliver up to him those lands which Macdonald had in Isla and Kintyre."[2] In the portion of his manuscript still unpublished, Hugh Macdonald, referring to John Cathanach, says that at the instigation of Argyle and Glencairn, Mac-Ian of Ardnamurchan apprehended him and his two sons, John Galld and John Gallach, and brought them to Edinburgh. Thus we see how Hugh Macdonald contradicts himself as well as MacVuirich, while Gregory, so persistently and slavishly copied by all who have come after him, misquotes both Hugh Macdonald and MacVuirich, as well as the Charter of 1499. In that charter it is stated very clearly that MacIan of Ardnamurchan is rewarded for apprehending " John of the Isles and Glens, Knight, John Cathanach, his son, and their accomplices." We have no hesitation in accepting the authority of the charter and refusing to accept

[1] MacVuirich in Reliq. Celt., p. 163.
[2] Hugh Macdonald in Coll. de Rebus Alb., p. 324.

statements so confusing and contradictory as those of Hugh Macdonald and MacVuirich.

All the sons of John Cathanach, as well as Alexander and Angus Ileach, would have found refuge from the Royal vengeance and the persecution of MacIan in the Antrim Glens. According to MacVuirich, MacIan destroyed nearly the whole race of John Mor. He pursued Alexander, the son of John Cathanach, to the Glens of Antrim, which evidently at that time were thickly wooded, for MacIan expended much wealth in making axes to cut down the trees, so that the Lord of the Glens and his followers would have no hiding place within their own territory.[1] MacIan, however, notwithstanding all the gold and silver spent by him on instruments of destruction, did not succeed in driving Alexander, the son of John Cathanach, out of the Antrim Glens. Though banished from Scotland, the Clan Iain Mhoir held considerable sway in Ireland, and were able to check the progress of the English invaders through Northern Ulster. It is almost certain that none of them ventured to return to Scotland during the lifetime of James IV.

After the episode of Dunaverty, the King paid several visits to the Highlands in close succession. Many of the chiefs still held out, but James was determined to bring them to subjection. Besides the Castles of Tarbert and Dunaverty, which he had already garrisoned, he also placed strong garrisons in Mingarry, and Cairnburgh,[2] in Mull, and having secured these, which were the most important defences in Argyleshire, he set about making preparations for a military expedition on a large scale.

---

[1] MacVuirich in Reliq. Celt., p. 165.
[2] Treasurer's Accounts for the year 1494.

About midsummer, 1495, he left Glasgow at the
head of a strong force, and marched to Dumbarton.[1]
At Dumbarton he embarked his troops, and proceeded by the Mull of Kintyre to Mingarry, in
Ardnamurchan, where he held Court.[2] Awed by
the presence of so formidable an armament in the
Western seas, many of the chiefs hastened to Mingarry and paid homage to the King, among whom
were Allan of Clanranald, John of Sleat, and Donald
of Keppoch.   MacIan had already shewn much zeal
in the King's service, and had recently been rewarded
by a grant of lands in Isla.[3] Thus all the Macdonald
vassals within the Lordship of the Isles, with the
exception of Macdonald of Glencoe and the banished
Macdonald of Dunnyveg, submitted to the King,
and the aspect of affairs augured well for the future
government of the Southern Highlands at least.

The King went back to Edinburgh quite elated
at the success of his efforts, and to ensure the success
of his policy he called a meeting of his Council, and
submitted to them measures for the better government of the Isles. The Council passed an Act which,
in the present unsettled state of the Islands, if
carried out, could hardly fail to be productive of
good fruit. This Act provided that every chief must
be answerable for the serving of summonses and
other writs against his own clansmen, under the
penalty of being himself liable to the party bringing
the action.[4] As a result of these proceedings, several
chiefs appeared before the Council in Edinburgh,

[1] Treasurer's Accounts for the year 1495.
[2] " At Meware in Ardmurquhane the King granted a charter on the 18th
May, 1495, to Sir William Stirling of Ker."—Reg. of Great Seal, vol. II., No.
2253.
[3] Reg. of Great Seal, 14th June, 1494, vol. II., No. 2216.
[4] Acta Dom. Con. VIII., folio 39.

among whom were MacIan of Ardnamurchan, Clanranald, and Keppoch, and bound themselves by a
bond of £500 each to refrain from injuring one
another.[1] What effect this Act had on those whom
it concerned, we know not, but it manifests, at all
events, the earnest desire of the King to bring about
peace and good government in the Isles.

The state of matters in the North Highlands did
not render it necessary for the King to devote so
much attention to that region. We find him indeed
often visiting the North during those years, but
always in a very different capacity from that in
which we find him in Argyleshire. The great object
of the King's visits was the shrine of St Duthus in
Tain, which, in James's eyes at least, had a peculiar
sanctity. His father had endowed the Church of
St Duthus, and the King almost yearly went to
Tain to worship at the sacred shrine. Interesting
glimpses may be gathered from the Treasurer's
Accounts of the King's visits to Ross-shire. On one
occasion we find him at Dingwall, after his devotions
in Tain, evidently bent on devoting his time more
to the pursuit of pleasure than to the exercises
of piety. The Treasurer charges to the Scottish
Exchequer the sum of ten shillings and sixpence given to the King "for playing at the
cartis," while one shilling and sixpence is paid to
the "maddins" that sang before His Majesty. The
neighbouring magnates send presents to the King.
Lord Lovat sends "ane hert and ane ram," the
Bishop of Ross "ane selch and oysteris," while
another sends "ane flacat of aqua vite." Twenty
years have now elapsed since the Lord of the Isles
resigned the Earldom of Ross, but the vassals of the

[1] Acta Dominorum Concilii, VIII., fol. 39.

Earldom were not in any way affected by the final forfeiture of that nobleman and the fall of the Island Lordship. With very few exceptions, the vassals of Ross never were very sincere in their attachment to the Lords of the Isles, while, on the contrary, the vassals of the Isles had always been loyal, and when therefore the Lordship of the Isles came to an end through the forfeiture of John in 1493, the result was open rebellion on the part of the Islesmen against the Scottish State. We have seen that Alexander of Lochalsh was not among the Macdonald chieftains who paid homage to the King at Mingarry Mackenzie of Kintail, a vassal of Ross, and Mackintosh, one of the vassals of the Isles, were at this time thrown into prison in Edinburgh. Mackenzie, though nearly related by marriage to the Island family, was very probably convicted for the excesses committed by him after the Lochalsh rebellion of 1491, and not for any help he had given, or was likely to give, to the rebels of the Isles. His family, on the contrary, had all along opposed the Lords of the Isles in Rossshire. The case of Mackintosh was entirely different. Besides his close blood relationship to the Lords of the Isles, his family had been greatly enriched by them with grants of lands in Lochaber. It is likely enough, therefore, that his imprisonment at this time was the result of his opposition to the new order of things both in Ross and in the Isles. Though the northern portion of the Highlands was thus meanwhile in a comparatively quiet state, it was not destined to remain so for any length of time. Alexander of Lochalsh, notwithstanding the favours bestowed upon him by the King, ventured once more into the arena of rebellion. His motives in raising again the flag of revolt are not far to seek. His former

rebellion undoubtedly brought about the final forfeiture of the Lord of the Isles, and he perhaps
thought the present a favourable opportunity to
strike a blow for the restoration of the family
honours in his own person. The King had of late
paid little attention to Highland politics, his
Majesty's time being absorbed by English intrigue,
and that foreign impostor, Perkin Warbeck. It is
not at all likely that Lochalsh had the Earldom of
Ross in view, though, according to Hugh Macdonald,
he put forward a claim as tutor for Donald Dubh.
It appears that the King himself looked upon Alexander as the nearest heir to the forfeited Lord of the
Isles, for he received a promise from His Majesty
that the tenants of the Lordship would have security
in their holdings.[1] It is hardly conceivable that with
so small a following Lochalsh could have had the
presumption to attempt the restoration of the Island
Lordship in his own person. This, however, and
nothing less, was the goal which he had set before
himself, and he no doubt expected that the vassals
would all in time join his standard. He opened his
campaign by making a descent on his Ross-shire
neighbours, in revenge for his defeat at Park. After
ravaging several districts with fire and sword, he
was at length met at Drumchatt by the Munroes
and Mackenzies, and, according to the historian of
the Sutherland Family, was there defeated with
great slaughter.[2] Alexander now betook himself to
the Isles, and went south as far as Colonsay, with
the view, according to Hugh Macdonald, of raising
more men to recover his lands in Ross,[3] but more
probably with the object of creating a rebellion for

---

[1] *Vide* Charter to Ranald MacAllan of Clanranald in Register of Great
Seal, vol. II., No. 2438.

[2] Gordon's Family of Sutherland, p. 77.

[3] Hugh Macdonald, in Coll. de Rebus Alb., p. 321.

the purpose of recovering the Island Lordship. In this, however, he was not successful. The strong defensive measures taken by the King had had their effect on the Islesmen, and they were not prepared, however much they wished it, to join in an insurrection against the Scottish Government. Alexander of Lochalsh had barely time to mature his plans, whatever these may have been, for he perished by the hands of the assassin, at Orinsay, very soon after his arrival at Colonsay. The foul deed was perpetrated by his own kinsman, MacIan of Ardnamurchan, either to please the King, or Argyle, or both. According to the seanachies of Sleat and Clanranald, MacIan had as his accomplice on this occasion Alexander, the son of John Cathanach,[1] but that hero, as we have seen, took refuge in Ireland after the execution of his father and grandfather in 1495, and as he did not venture to set foot on Scottish soil again for many years after the murder of Alexander of Lochalsh, he cannot have been guilty of the serious crime alleged against him.

The King after a short interval again devoted his attention to the South Highlands. Not regarding the two fortresses of. Tarbert and Dunaverty as affording sufficient protection to his lieges in Kintyre, he built another stronghold at Kilkerran. In the summer of 1498 he visited Kintyre, and held court at Kilkerran, where several chiefs came to meet him and renew their allegiance. Here the King granted several charters, the first of which is dated on the 30th of June, while the last is dated on the 5th of August, which indicates a long stay on this occasion at his new Castle of Kilkerran.[2]

---

[1] H. Macdonald, in Coll. de Rebus Alb., p. 321. MacVuirich, in Reliq. Celt., p. 165.

[2] Register of the Great Seal, vol. II., pp. 515-18.

Part of that time at least was devoted to the settling of disputes between the Clanranald and Clan Uisdean on the one hand, and the Clan Uisdean and the Macleods of Dunvegan on the other. On the 3rd of August the King granted a charter of lands in Uist to Ranald MacAllan for services rendered by him in time of peace, and again on the 5th of the same month other lands in Uist, Eigg, and Arisaig are granted to him.[1] In the latter charter the King confirms to Ranald the lands resigned in his favour by John, the son and heir of Hugh of Sleat. The Clanranald family, however, never obtained possession of the lands in Skye and North Uist, formerly held by Hugh of Sleat. The King also on the 5th of August granted a charter of lands in Benbecula in Uist, in Moror, and in Arisaig, to Angus Reochson MacRanald, all of which formerly belonged to Hugh of Sleat.[2] At the same time the lands of Troternish, with the bailliary of that district, were granted to Torquil Macleod of Lewis and his heirs by Catherine, daughter of Archibald, Earl of Argyle.[3] Here it is evident we have material for family feuds for many a long year to come.

The King had no sooner returned from his long sojourn in Kintyre than he revoked the charters recently granted by him, as well as all others which he had formerly granted to the vassals of the Isles. What induced him to change his policy so suddenly, in view of its apparent success, is not at first sight easily understood. We are not long, however, left in any doubt as to the real cause of this sudden turn in the

[1] Reg. Mag. Sig., vol. II., No. 2437 and 2438.
[2] Ibidem, No. 2349.   [3] Ibidem, No. 1424.

tide of affairs. The King early next year visits
Kintyre to initiate his new policy. He grants a
commission of lieutenandry to Archibald, Earl of
Argyle, over the whole Lordship of the Isles, and
appoints him Keeper of the Castle of Tarbert and
Bailie of Knapdale. He also gave the Earl a commission to let on lease for three years the whole
Lordship of the Isles, except Kintyre and Isla.[1]
Thus it is only too evident who had induced the
King to change his plans in regard to the Government of the Isles. The crafty Argyle succeeded in
persuading the evidently too impressionable James
that he had acted far too leniently towards the men
of the Isles, and that a less conciliatory policy would
in the long run prove the wisest. The King's
conduct in breaking faith with the Islanders and
yielding to the evil counsel of the wily schemer
cannot be too severely condemned. It was conduct
altogether unworthy of a King, and such as to make
us suspect the genuineness of his motives in every
previous effort made by him to legislate for the
Islands. Argyle succeeded in attaining the object
of his ambition, but not, as we shall soon see, in
making the Islanders more law abiding, or more
loyal to the throne. His administration had, on
the contrary, the very opposite effect. It seems
that the King, no doubt at the instigation of
Argyle, had resolved to expel the Macdonald landholders from their possessions, as well as other
vassals who were supposed to be favourable to the
claims of Donald Dubh, and others, to the Lordship of
the Isles. As long as any claimant to the forfeited
Island honours remained there was danger of an insurrection in the Islands, and the King had evidently

[1] Register of the Privy Seal, Book I., folio 3 ; also fol. 108, 122.

come to the conclusion that the only cure for these
disaffected Islanders was expulsion from their
possessions.   This proved, however, a difficult task,
but James was determined to give effect to his new
scheme.   To strengthen his government in the
Highlands, he began to parcel out the lands of the
Lordship of the Isles among his own favourites.
To John MacIan of Ardnamurchan, presumably
"for his good and faithful service done and to be
done" to the King, and "for the taking, trans-
porting, and handing over to him of the rebels, John
of the Isles and Glens, John Cathanach, his son,
and their accomplices," a charter was granted of
many lands in Isla and Jura.[1]   To Stewart of Appin
the King granted a charter of the lands of Glencoe
and Duror;[2] while Lord Gordon, the eldest son of
Huntly, received a charter of many lands in
Lochaber.[3]   The first step taken in the process of
expelling the vassals of the Isles was to summon
them before the Lords of Council for not having
charters for their lands, but, as might have
been expected, none appeared in response to the
summons, and decree accordingly was pronounced
against them.[4]   This was the signal for rebellion.
Donald Dubh, who had been kept in custody ever
since he was a child, was looked upon by the
Islanders as the heir to the Lordship of the Isles.
It was also well known to the Government, though
for political reasons it was not acknowledged, that
Donald was the lawful son of Angus Og, who, by
an Act of Parliament in 1476, was declared heir
to his father, John, Lord of the Isles.

[1] "The Book of Islay," pp. 28-30.
[2] Register of the Privy Seal, Book I., fol. 99.
[3] Register of the Great Seal, vol. II., No. 2259.
[4] Acta Dom. Con. XI., folio 13.

The Islanders were now compelled by the harsh measures adopted against them to take steps to defend their territories, and they naturally turned to Donald Dubh as their legitimate leader. Means were taken secretly to effect Donald's escape from Inchconnel, where he was kept a close prisoner by his maternal grandfather, the Earl of Argyle. This was accomplished, evidently without much difficulty, by the men of Glencoe, who, by what MacVuirich calls "a fenian exploit," broke into his dungeon and released the heir of Innsegall.[1] Donald had no sooner been set free than he betook himself to the Isles. He was loyally received by the vassals, and was forthwith proclaimed Lord of the Isles. Torquil Macleod of Lewis, who was one of the most powerful of the vassals of the Isles, was the first to join the standard of the newly proclaimed Island Lord, and being closely related to him by marriage, he took Donald meanwhile under his protection in his Castle of Stornoway. The Macdonald standard was now once more set up in the Isles, and the old vassals, with very few exceptions, made haste to join it. The Macleans, the Camerons, the Mackinnons, the Macleods, the Macneills, the Macquarries, and others, were all ready to strike a blow for the fatherland and the heir of the House of Isla. The rebellion very soon assumed a formidable appearance, and the Islanders, being determined to restore the old Celtic order of things, sought the assistance of both England and Ireland. This we learn from the proceedings of the Parliament which met in 1503, but there is no evidence of the assistance sought having ever been rendered, and it may have been, after all, nothing more than mere suspicion on the part of the Scottish

[1] MacVuirich, in Reliq. Celt., p. 168.

Government.[1] What defences the Islanders made
against a Lowland invasion, or whether they waited
to be attacked in the Isles, we have no means of
knowing, for very meagre details of this insurrection
have been preserved. It is very probable, however,
that the Islanders were themselves the aggressors,
and that they did not wait to be attacked. As
evidence of this, we learn from the proceedings
of the Parliament which met in 1505 that the
Islanders, under Donald Dubh, invaded the mainland in 1503 and advanced to Badenoch, which they
wasted with fire and sword.[2] At the same meeting
of Parliament a letter was read from John Ogilvy,
Deputy Sheriff of Inverness, setting forth that he
had been unable to apprehend Torquil Macleod,
summoned for assistance given to " Donald Yla
bastard sone of umquhile Anguss of ye Ilis alsua
bastard sone of umquhile Johne lord of ye Ilis," and
for insurrection, and taking part in invading the
King's lieges in " maner of batell." It appears from
Ogilvy's letter that Donald Dubh was proclaimed
not only Lord but King of the Isles, and that his
ambition was to set up a Celtic Kingdom altogether
independent of Saxon Scotland.[3] The letter also
refers to the depredations committed by the Islanders
on the King's lieges on the mainland, and it would
appear from the whole tone of it that the rebels had
ravaged the country to a considerable extent before
their progress was stopped by the Royal forces.

The King, who was fully aware of the movements
of the Islanders, recognised the magnitude of the
revolt against his authority, and without delay took
the strongest measures to quell the rebellion. He

---

[1] Acts of the Parliament of Scotland, vol. II., p. 240.
[2] Ibidem, p. 263.   [3] Ibidem, 263-4.

now probably saw the folly of his harsh proceedings in the Isles and the policy inspired by Argyle. A meeting of Parliament was summoned to consider the situation in the Highlands, and elaborate preparations were made to bring the unruly inhabitants into subjection. Torquil Macleod of Lewis, the leader of the vassals in the Isles, was declared rebel, and all his lands in the Isles and on the Mainland were forfeited to the Crown.[1] Efforts were made at the same time to win over the other Island leaders, but in vain. In these circumstances, the King fell back on his original policy of expelling "the broken men," or, in other words, all the rebellious vassals of the Isles and their adherents. For the carrying out of this measure, commissions were given to the Earl of Huntly, Lord Lovat, and Munro of Fowlis, but no success attended their efforts, whatever these may have been, and the tide of rebellion still rolled on with great fury. At length the Government adopted still stronger measures. It was resolved to proceed against the rebels both by sea and land, and an effort was made once more to secure the services of some of the rebel chiefs by offering them large bribes, with the alternative of the pains and penalties of treason. Lachlan Maclean of Dowart had been already forfeited and declared traitor for "maintaining, fortifying, and supplying of Donald, bastard and unlauchtfull sone of Anguss of the Ylis, bastard son to umquhile Johne of the Ilis."[2] Ewen Allanson of Lochiel had also been declared traitor for intercepting the King's letters, and the "withhaldin of his messingers and berars of ye said letrez in presone."[3] The Government ordered

---

[1] Acta Dominorum Concilii, Book XII., p. 123.
[2] Acts of Parl., vol. II., p. 247.   [3] Ibidem, p. 248,

letters to be sent to MacIan, Maclean of Lochbuy,
Macleod of Dunvegan, Ranald Allanson of Clanranald, MacNeill of Barra, Mackinnon, Macquarrie,
and Torquil Macleod, informing them of the forfeiture
of Lachlan Maclean of Dowart and Ewin Allanson
of Lochiel for usurping the King's authority and
offering them, if they should assist in bringing these
rebels to justice, grants of half their forfeited lands ;
while in the event of their refusing to give this
assistance, they shall be " reputt art and part takars
with thaim and be accusit and followit on tresonne."[1]
The Earl of Huntly undertook to deliver the letters
of Ranald Allanson and Mackinnon, Argyle those of
MacIan and Maclean of Lochbuy, while to the Bishop
of Ross was entrusted the hazardous task of
delivering the letter of Torquil Macleod of Lewis.[2]
It is somewhat surprising to find the name of
Torquil Macleod, so recently declared traitor,
amongst those to whom overtures were made on
this occasion by Government.   His name was
included probably on the suggestion of his father-in-
law, the Earl of Argyle, with the view, even at this
late hour, of winning him over to the side of law
and order.   Of the fate of the Government missives
the annals of the time have nothing to say, but it is
certain that no heed was paid to them by the rebel
chiefs.

These overtures having entirely failed in their
object, the Government prepared for an invasion of
the Highlands and Islands on the most elaborate
scale.   One division of the royal forces, commanded
by the Earls of Marshall and Argyle, was sent to

[1] Acts of the Parliament of Scotland, vol. II., p. 248.
[2] Ibidem,

invade the Islands from the South by Dumbarton, while another division under the command of the Earl of Huntly, with the Earl of Crawford and Lord Lovat, went North. The Castles of Strome and Ellandonan were the most important places of defence on the West Coast of Ross-shire. Huntly undertook to reduce these, and to supply, or raise, men, to keep them, which was " rycht necessar for the danting of the Isles," on condition that the King should furnish a ship and artillery for the purpose.[1] What success attended the efforts of Huntly to reduce the Islesmen we know not, but it is evident the artillery necessary for the storming of Ellandonan and Strome were not forthcoming, and that without such aid it was vain to attack them. The Castles of Kintyre had been in possession of the King since 1493, but as the rebellion centred more in the North than in the South Isles, these were for the present practically valueless as places of defence. No details of the movements of either division of the royal army have been preserved. We can, however, infer that little success attended their efforts to suppress the rebellion in the Isles. We can well understand the difficulties in the way of the invading forces owing to the inaccessibility of the Islands and their natural defences, but these were all in favour of the rebels, who might have held out much longer if only unanimity had prevailed in their counsels. They lacked the perseverance and stolid patience of their opponents, and as success did not attend them in their first rush for the attainment of their object, they began to give way to despair.

[1] Acts of the Parl. of Scotland, vol. II., p. 240-249.

The King himself now headed a new expedition to the Isles, but he had got only as far as Dumbarton when an insurrection in the southern division of his realm compelled him to return. A naval force, however, under Sir Andrew Wood and Robert Barton, was despatched to the Isles, while a land force was sent under the Earl of Arran. Huntly renewed operations in the North evidently with greater success than had formerly attended his efforts in that region.[1] Wood and Barton directing their course to the West Coast of Argyleshire, and the Island of Mull, reduced the Castle of Cairnburgh and otherwise overawed the inhabitants. The flame of rebellion in the Isles was thus being gradually extinguished, and some of the disaffected chiefs were already beginning to show signs of surrender. Macleod of Dunvegan, who had recently joined the King's party, and MacIan of Ardnamurchan, sent messengers to Court informing the King of the state of matters in the Isles, and assuring him at the same time of their readiness to assist him to the utmost of their power to put down the insurrection. In response to these representations, James, with characteristic energy, at once set about collecting an army, at the head of which he marched into Argyleshire. John Barton was sent with a fleet to the Isles. Whether any resistance was at first offered on the part of the Island Chiefs does not appear, but before the King returned South they all, with one notable exception, came forward and gave in their submission. The rebellion was now suppressed, and the King generously extended a free pardon to the rebels, all except Torquil Macleod

[1] Treasurer's Accounts for 1505.

20

of Lewis. The public records furnish us with only the broad outlines of this rebellion, and only vague hints are given as to the conduct of the leading spirits in the movement. The only reference to the part played by Donald Dubh and his followers is that to which we have already alluded, and beyond this invasion of the district of Badenoch by the Islanders, we have not the slightest hint as to the manner in which they conducted the war against the Saxon. It is evident, however, from the repeated attacks made by the Lowland forces, and the failure of one expedition after another, that the Islanders gave a good account of themselves in the fight. The unfortunate Donald Dubh, who had been partly at least the cause of so much turmoil during these years, and who had made so gallant a fight for his rights, is again made a prisoner. One of the charges made against Torquil Macleod in 1506 is his refusal to deliver up Donald Dubh to the King. He, however, finally surrendered him to Lachlan Maclean of Dowart, now on his good behaviour, and he in turn gave up the fugitive to the King. The King sent Donald a prisoner to the Castle of Edinburgh.

Torquil Macleod still held out, fearing, no doubt with good reason, that, if he submitted, the pardon which had been extended to the other rebels would be withheld from him. After being summoned to appear before Parliament and refusing to attend, he was again declared traitor, and his lands were forfeited. His lands on the mainland, consisting of the extensive districts of Coigach and Assynt, were given in life-rent to Mackay of Strathnaver, for his good services and assistance in putting down the rebellion.[1]   The Earl of Huntly was sent with a force against Torquil, and, proceeding to Lewis, he besieged and took the Castle of Stornoway.   Torquil, however, managed to make good his escape, and was never, so far as we know, brought to task for his share in the rebellion of Donald Dubh.   We learn from a spirited poem by the family bard, MacCalman, the high estimation in which this Lord of Lewis was held by his clansmen and followers :—

> " Many his gifts which we might praise,
> Torquil of the famous race ;
> His are a hero's strength and vigour,
> Which he brings into the fight.
> I say of him, and say in truth,
> Since I have come so well to know him,
> That never was there of his age
> Better King who ruled in Lewis.
>
> .   .   .   .
>
> Not braver of his age was Cuchullin,
> Not hardier was he than Torquil." [2]

In 1508, Andrew, Bishop of Caithness, Ranald Allanson of Clanranald, and Alexander Macleod of Dunvegan were commissioned by the King to let for five years, to sufficient tenants, the lands of Lewis, and of Waternish, in Skye, which were forfeited by Torquil Macleod of Lewis.[3]   When the extensive estates of the Siol Torquil, consisting of Lewis, and the district of Waternish, in the Lordship of the Isles, Coigach, in the Earldom of Ross, and Assynt, in the Earldom of Sutherland, were restored to the family, in 1511, the rebel Torquil was probably dead, for, if living, he would not have

---

[1] " Rex,—pro bono servitio in resistatione et invasione rebellium suorum, —concessit Odoni Makky in Strathnavern, pro tempore ejus vite,—terras de Assent et Ladachchogich, &c., quequidem regi pertinebant ratione forisfacture super Torquellum Makcloid olim de Lewis," &c.—Reg. Mag. Sig., vol. II., 3202.

[2] The Book of the Dean of Lismore, p. 146.

[3] Reg. Sec. Sig., vol. III., fol. 166.

allowed his brother, Malcolm, take possession without striking a blow for his rights.[1] Now that the last spark of rebellion had been extinguished, comparative peace and order prevailed throughout the Islands, and it does not appear that the King's threat of expelling the " broken men" had been carried out, at least to any appreciable extent. A very different policy seems to have been pursued. In the Parliament which met in 1503 an important Act was passed bearing on the Highlands and Islands, and which could hardly fail to have in time a salutary effect on these regions. This Act reformed the administration of justice, which hitherto in the Highlands had been under the jurisdiction of the old sheriffdoms. In the preamble a complaint is made in the strongest terms of the lawlessness and disorder that prevailed in the Highlands, and especially in the Isles. The new sheriffs appointed under the Act were to hold courts at Tarbert in Kintyre for the Southern Isles, and at Dingwall and Inverness for the North.[2] The Earl of Argyle was appointed to the office of King's Lieutenant in the Southern Isles, while to the Earl of Huntly was committed the administration of justice in the North.

This legislation and the policy pursued generally towards the Highlands were, for a time at least, productive of good results. The King now paid special attention to the Highland portion of his kingdom, and he seems to have been successful at last in attaching the Islesmen to his interest. He had made himself acquainted with the real condition of affairs in the Highlands by his frequent visits, and through personal contact with the chiefs he had been

[1] Reg. Mag. Sig., vol. II., No. 3578.   [2] Acts of Parliament, vol. II., p. 241.

able ultimately to restore order and peace among
them. We cannot praise too highly the King's
conduct for the conciliatory manner in which he
acted towards the Islanders after the rebellion of
Donald Dubh, and it says much for his sagacity as a
ruler that he had been able, in so short a time, to
bring about changes so beneficial in circumstances so
difficult. There is every evidence that to the end of
his reign he retained great popularity with all classes
of his Highland subjects.

The light which the history of that time throws
on the position of the different chieftains of the
Clan Donald and their relationship to the Crown
waxes somewhat dim after the suppression of
the rebellion. The King, as we have seen,
revoked in the year 1498 all the charters which
he had formerly granted to the vassals of the
Isles. It appears that during the remainder of
his reign he made no further grants of lands to
the Macdonald chieftains, with the exception of
MacIan of Ardnamurchan and Ranald Allanson of
Clanranald. The other chieftains were allowed to
keep possession of their lands without any title.
MacIan, largely no doubt influenced by the Earl
of Argyle, had all along remained firm in his adherence to the King's cause, and he now reaped the
reward of his loyalty in large grants of lands which
the King bestowed upon him in Isla, Kintyre, and
elsewhere. In 1494, James granted him, for his
willing obedience and good service, a charter of
lands in Isla and Morvern—forfeited by the Lord
of the Isles—with the office of Bailie of the lands
of Isla, which MacIan had formerly held of John,
Lord of the Isles.[1] In 1499 the King makes a

[1] Register of the Great Seal, vol. II., No. 2216.

further grant of lands in Isla and Jura to MacIan, extending in all to 200 marklands.[1] In 1505, "for the good, faithful, and willing service done to him by his dear John Makkane of Ardnamurchane," the King confirms him in all the lands formerly granted to him in Isla and Jura, and in the lower part of Ardnamurchan and Suanart, with the Castles of Mingarry and Dunnyveg, and the office of bailliary formerly conferred upon him.[2] Again, in 1506, the same lands are confirmed to him.[3] MacIan was therefore at this time the most influential and powerful chieftain of the Clan Donald.

Of all the families of the house of Somerled, the Macdonalds of Dunnyveg and the Glens fared worst. Their history is somewhat obscure during this period. The survivors of 1495, escaping from the vengeance which overtook Sir John and his son, John Cathanach, in that year, took refuge in their own territory and amongst their relatives in the Antrim Glens. Hugh Macdonald, in the un-published portion of his manuscript, referring probably to the period after King James's death at Flodden, tells how MacIan of Ardnamurchan sent his two sons, at the head of a body of men, from Isla to the Glens of Antrim to capture Alexander, the son of John Cathanach. Alexander was at Glensheich with 140 men when the MacIans and the men of Isla landed. He at once attacked the invaders, and after a sanguinary encounter, the Isla men were worsted and most of them slain, among the latter being MacIan's two sons. During the engagement the Smith of Isla, followed by 50 men, deserted the MacIans and joined the banner of the

[1] Argyle Charters.

[2] Reg. Mag. Sig., vol. 11., No. 2895.   [3] Ibidem, vol. 11., No. 3001.

Lord of the Glens.   Alexander, with his men, took the enemy's boats and crossed over to Isla. MacNiven, the Constable of Dunnyveg, gave him possession of that stronghold, and informed him that MacIan was on Island Lochgorm, which Alexander forthwith besieged, and MacIan was compelled to surrender.   Before doing so, however, and agreeing to surrender his lands in Isla to Alexander, the latter implemented the bargain by faithfully promising to marry MacIan's daughter.[1] Alexander of Dunnyveg appears to have taken no part in the rebellion of Donald Dubh, and it is certain that from 1495 to the death of King James in 1513 he held no lands in Scotland.

Less perhaps is known of the history of the family of Hugh of Sleat at this period than of any of the families of Macdonald.   John of Sleat, the eldest son of Hugh, for some unknown reason passed over his estates to the family of Clanranald, and ignored the claims of his brothers.   This seems altogether strange in view of the differences which had lasted now for some time between the two families over lands in Benbecula, for which Hugh of Sleat held a charter.   It would appear, for some reason or another, that John had quarrelled with his brothers, and took these steps to exclude them from the succession.   But though the conveyance of the lands of Hugh of Sleat to the Clanranald was ratified by a charter of confirmation from the King in 1498, to which we have already referred, it is certain that the Clan Uisdean kept possession of their lands both in Skye and in North Uist, though they had no legal title.   John of Sleat himself died at the very beginning of the sixteenth century, and he therefore

---

[1] Hugh Macdonald's MS.

could not have taken any part personally in the
rebellion of Donald Dubh.   Donald Gallach, however, the second son of Hugh of Sleat, who became
head of the family on the death of John, played a
prominent part in the insular insurrection; but his
career was cut short, according to the tradition of
the country, by the hand of his brother, Gilleasbuig
Dubh.   From a "Respitt" granted by the King to
Gilleasbuig, and dated at Edinburgh in 1508, it
would appear that, though accused of other crimes,
the murder of Donald Gallach was not specially laid
to his charge.   On the contrary, what we find is a
"Respitt to Archibald Auchonsoune of the Ilys and
XXVIII. utheris (because of thair grit lawbouris
deligence and gude and thankfull service done be
his hienes in the perserving and taking of Auchane
Duncane Dowsone, Sorle his sone, and Donald Mule
Makalester, his rebellis, and being at the horne;
and for the bringing and delivering of thaim to
be maid to his gude grace (or to quham he ordanis
thame to be deliverit be his writingis) for the
slauchter of unquhile Donald Hutchonsoune other-
wayis called Gauldlauche, bruder to the said
Archibald.   And for all otheris Slauchteris, Here-
schippis, Birningis, Reffis, Murtheris, &c., before
the date of his Respitt; for the space of 19
yeris.   Providing alwayis that gif his said Rebellis
beis not brocht, &c., his Respitt to be of none avail,
&c. (Subscript per dominum Regem apud Edinburgh)."[1]   The persons charged here with the murder
of Donald Gallach are Auchane Duncane Dowsone,
Sorle his sone, and Donald Mule Makalester, evidently Gilleasbuig Dubh's former accomplices.   There
need be no doubt, however, notwithstanding the

---

[1] Pitcairn's Criminal Trials, vol. I., p. 105.

attempt to shield him on the part of the Government, that Gilleasbuig was guilty, not only of the murder of Donald Gallach, but also of the murder of Donald Herrach, in North Uist. These two alone stood between him and the accomplishment of the ambitious scheme which he had conceived of possessing himself of the family inheritance. In this he succeeded, but he soon made himself so obnoxious to the adherents of the family that they compelled him to surrender his newly acquired dignity. Gilleasbuig had to reckon, not only with the Clan Uisdean, but also with the Clanranald ; for, as we have seen, the King had confirmed to them the lands surrendered by John of Sleat, both in Skye and in North Uist. Thus, hemmed in on all sides, Gilleasbuig abandoned himself to a wild and lawless career, and in a short time he and his piratical band became the terror of the Western Isles. According to Hugh Macdonald, Gilleasbuig was expelled from the North Isles by Ranald Bane MacAllan of Clanranald, and having taken refuge in the South Isles, he was joined by Ronald Mor and Alester Bearnach MacAlister, with whom he remained for three years. With these as his lieutenants, Gilleasbuig, at the head of his band, plundered all the ships that passed through the Southern seas.[1] By whatever means, he, however succeeded in again taking possession of a portion of the territories of Clan Uisdean, and, turning King's evidence, he was pardoned by Government for his past crimes and misdemeanours. In 1510, at a Justiciary Court held at Inverness, precept of remission is issued to Gilleasbuig Dubh, Bailie of Troternish, and others, John MacGillemartin and sixty-three others, for common

[1] Hugh Macdonald.

oppression of the lieges, and for resetting, supplying, and intercommuning with the King's rebels, and also for fire raising.[1] Shortly after this Gilleasbuig is confirmed in the office of Bailie of Troternish, which he had assumed, by a Privy Council missive, and the tenants of Troternish are enjoined not to disturb him in the possession of that extensive district.[2] Thus Gilleasbuig Dubh became at least *de facto* head and leader of the Clan Uisdean, and he continued to occupy that position during the remainder of his life. His tenure of his usurped position was, however, a short-lived one, for we find that, on the 10th of March, 1517, the King gave to Lachlan Maclean of Dowart the 4 marklands of Scalpa, in the Lordship of the Isles, pertaining to His Majesty through the decease of Archibald, bastard son of Hugh of Sleat, without legitimate heirs.[3] According to Hugh Macdonald, Gilleasbuig Dubh was murdered while out shooting on Ben Lee, in North Uist, by his nephews, Donald Gruamach Macdonald Gallaich and Ranald Macdonald Herraich.

The position of the Clanranald at this period is somewhat obscured by the contradictory statements of historians in regard to their attitude towards the Scottish Government. At one time we find them in high favour with the King, but on the change of policy by James in 1498, they undoubtedly, like the other Islanders, broke out into open revolt against his authority. There are indications of their having been shortly after this received into royal favour, but these are not clear enough to warrant us in concluding that they had not rallied round the

[1] Inveruessiana, by Mr Fraser-Mackintosh, p. 193.
[2] Reg. Sec. Sig. IV., fol. 70.   [3] Reg. Mag. Sig., vol. III., No. 134.

standard of Donald Dubh.   There appears to be
little doubt that they supported to the last the
pretensions of that unfortunate man.   On the
suppression of the rebellion, however, we find them
again in favour at Court.   The King, on the 23rd
of August, granted at Stirling to Ranald Allanson,
of Island Begram, while his father was still alive,
the lands of Sleat in Skye, with the Castle of
Dunskaich, the lands of Illeray, Paible, Paiblisgarry,
Balranald, Hougarry, Watna, Scolpeg, Griminish,
Vallay, Walis, Islandgarvay, Orinsay, Talmartin,
Sand, Boreray, and Garrymore, all in North Uist,
and Lordship of the Isles.[1]   Very soon after this the
Clanranald Chief, Allan MacRuarie, was according
to Gregory, brought before the King at Blair-Athole
and executed for some undefinable crime.   Gregory
gives as his authority the Book of Clanranald, but
MacVuirich makes no reference to the crime, trial,
or execution, of Allan MacRuarie, though, if the
traditions of the Clan are to be believed, that
"demon of the Gael and fierce ravager of Church
and Cross" richly deserved capital punishment.[2]
We infer from MacVuirich, on the contrary, that
Allan was well received by the King, and that
having obtained a confirmation of his lands by the
hand of his Majesty, he died at Blair-Athole in
1509.[3]   The same story is repeated in almost every
detail of Allan's son and successor, Ranald, who
having gone to pay homage to the King at Perth,
died there in 1514.[4]

Little or nothing is known of the history of the
Macdonalds of Glencoe at this time, though we may

[1] Reg. Mag. Sig., vol. II., No. 2873.

[2] *Vide* poem by Finlay, the red-haired bard, on Allan MacRuarie in " The Book of the Dean of Lismore," p. 143.

[3] MacVuirich in Reliq. Celticæ, p. 169.

[4] Ibidem, p. 169.

conclude from their act in liberating Donald Dubh from Inchconnel that they played a prominent part in the troubles that followed.

The Macdonalds of Keppoch shared alike the fortunes and the reverses of the other branches of Clan Donald. They followed the banner of Donald Dubh with the other clansmen, and did so probably with less compunction on the score of consequences than any of the clans, for the gallant Keppochs were among the few who acted independently of Royal Charters. They were occupied later on with domestic differences which fall to be dealt with more appropriately in our next rather than in this volume.

The Chief of Lochalsh, who was a minor at the time of his father's death, was too young to take any part in the recent insurrection. It seems that the King, on one of his visits to the Highlands, persuaded the sons of Alexander of Lochalsh to accompany him to Edinburgh, no doubt with the view of teaching them, among other things, loyalty to the Scottish throne. They remained at Court for several years, and many references are made to "Donald of the Ilis, the King's hensboy," in the Treasurer's Accounts of that time. Several items appear in these Accounts of payments for Donald, in passing to and from the Isles, and for clothes and other necessaries, and also for Ronald of the Isles, who no doubt was another son of Alexander of Lochalsh.[1] Donald, who, for his residence in the Lowlands was called by the Highlanders "Donald Gallda," became a great favourite with the King, who, it is said, knighted him on Flodden field.

[1] Treasurer's Accounts, 1508-13. Acta Dominorum Concilii, Book 24, p. 186.

The King, besides, gave him possession of his father's lands of Lochalsh.

We find no reference made to the family of Glengarry at this time in the history of the Clan Donald, though we may be sure they had an active share in the attempt of the Islanders to set up the Celtic supremacy once more in the Isles. They afterwards became a powerful family on succeeding by marriage to the lands of the Macdonalds of Lochalsh.

We have thus endeavoured to trace briefly the history of the different branches of the Family of Macdonald subsequent to the fall of the Lordship of the Isles, and the changes brought about by that event in their attitude towards the Scottish State. With one exception, they had all united in the attempt to set up again the Celtic *regime* in the Isles, and though during the lull that followed the storm they appear to acquiesce in the new order of things, they are far, as we shall soon see, from being satisfied with it. To Argyle had been entrusted the government of the South Isles, with a plenitude of power dangerous in less unscrupulous hands. To Huntly was committed the government of the North, with equal power over the King's lieges in that region. The men to whom the government of the Highlands and Islands was thus committed were both grasping and unprincipled noblemen, whose chief aim was to enrich themselves at the expense of the old vassals of the Isles. In these circumstances, peace could not be expected to reign long in these regions. The King himself did not now visit the Highlands so frequently, being engaged elsewhere, and in those transactions which proved finally so disastrous to the country and to himself. To the dark field of Flodden James was followed by many of the hardy clans of the North, including the Macdonalds. Here they fought with the courage and bravery characteristic of the sons of the mountains, and suffered so severely at the hands of the English pikemen as to have been well nigh annihilated. Some historians have attributed to the Highlanders a large share in bringing about the defeat of the Scottish army at Flodden. Eager to engage in a hand-to-hand fight, so characteristic of Highland warfare, they broke their ranks and threw themselves with great violence on the foe. Notwithstanding this irregularity on the part of the Highlanders, the defeat of the Scottish army was brought about mainly by the wrong-headedness of the King himself, who paid the penalty of his obstinacy with his life. On the morning after the battle, the body of the gallant James was found among the thickest of the slain. The character of the King in the administration of the affairs of his kingdom deserves, in many respects, our admiration. Great activity and earnestness, combined with much patience and moderation, characterised most of his efforts to restore order and good government throughout his kingdom, and it is safe to say that none of his predecessors had been altogether so successful in the government of the Highlands and Islands.[1] The King's death had the effect of bringing disorder and confusion into every department of the State. The removal of so strong a personality from the chief place in the counsels of the nation had an immediate and injurious effect on the condition of his Highland subjects.

[1] In the Register of the Great Seal and Treasurer's Accounts for the years 1488-1513, we have ample evidence of the King's administrative powers and indomitable energy.

· The surviving Highlanders had no sooner returned from Flodden than the standard of rebellion was again raised, and Sir Donald of Lochalsh was proclaimed Lord of the Isles. It is not necessary at this stage to enter with any minuteness into the claims of Sir Donald Gallda to the Lordship of the Isles. Donald Dubh still remains a prisoner in Edinburgh Castle, but even after him there were others who might put forward claims at least as good as those of Sir Donald of Lochalsh. Sir Donald himself, it is said, affirmed that he claimed the Lordship of the Isles for Donald Dubh. At a meeting of Islesmen, held at Kyleakin, Alexander of Dunnyveg, according to Hugh Macdonald, proposed Donald Gruamach of Sleat for the Lordship of the Isles.[1] It seems to us that at this time it was not a question with the Islanders who had the best claims among the competitors to the Island Lordship. What they desired above all was a change in the government of the Isles, and they were, therefore, prepared to rally round any leader likely to bring about this result. This explains the readiness with which they joined the standard of Sir Donald of Lochalsh. The Macleods of Lewis and Harris, Maclean of Dowart, Alexander of Dunnyveg, Chisholm of Comer, and Alexander MacIan of Glengarry now rally round the newly proclaimed Lord of the Isles. Sir Donald, at the head of a considerable force, and assisted by Alexander of Glengarry and Chisholm of Comer, opened his campaign by invading the lands of John Grant of Freuchy, in Urquhart, which he laid waste with fire and sword. Having next directed his attention to the Castle of Urquhart, he besieged it and expelled the garrison. According to Mr William

---

[1] Hugh Macdonald, in Collectanea de Rebus Albanicis, p. 322.

Mackay, in his " Urquhart and Glenmoriston," the spoil that fell to Sir Donald was rich and varied, and consisted of household furniture and victuals, of the value in all of more than £100 ; while the booty from the different lands consisted of 300 cattle and 1000 sheep, 740 bolls of bear and 1080 bolls of oats.[1] Sir Donald kept possession of the Castle and lands of Urquhart until he made his peace with the Regent Albany, in 1515, and although Grant of Freuchy obtained a decree against him for " Tua Thousand pund with the mair," it appears the debt was never recovered.

The rebellion proceeded apace, and raged with great fury in the Islands. Maclean of Dowart seized the royal Castle of Cairnburgh in Mull, and Macleod of Harris seized the Castle of Dunskaich in Skye, which they held for the new Lord of the Isles. Alarmed at the formidable appearance which the insurrection now assumed, the Regent Albany took immediate steps to crush it. The Earl of Argyle was commissioned by the Council to take proceedings against Lachlan Maclean of Dowart and others in the South Isles. Munro of Fowlis and Mackenzie of Kintail were employed to harass Sir Donald in the North ; while Lochiel and Mackintosh were appointed guardians of Lochaber. The Council besides caused letters to be written to the chiefs whose lands lay along the mainland coast urging them to resist the landing of the Islesmen. All these measures seemed to have no appreciable effect in quelling the rebellion. MacIan of Ardnamurchan, who had still retained his old loyalty, was commissioned to treat with the less rebellious section of the insurgent Islesmen, promis-

---

[1] " Urquhart and Glenmoriston," p. 85.

ing on behalf of the Regent pardon for past transgressions, and offering favours to such as should shew themselves willing to submit. It would appear that MacIan's interposition had the desired effect on several of the Islesmen. Argyle also had succeeded in persuading the Macleans and others in the South Isles to submit to the Regent. On September 6th, 1515, John, Duke of Albany, Regent of the Kingdom, granted to Lachlan Maclean of Dowart and Alexander Macleod of Dunvegan, their servants, landed men, gentlemen, and yeomen, a remission for all past crimes, and in particular for besieging and taking the Castles of Cairnburgh and Dunskaich, and holding them against his authority, and for assisting Sir Donald of Lochalsh and his accomplices, the remission to last till January, 1516.[1] The arch rebel, Sir Donald of Lochalsh, himself and Albany were shortly thereafter reconciled. So we have, on the 23rd August, 1515, "Ane Respit maid be avise of the Governour to Donald of the Ilis of Lochalsh Kynt and with him uther thre scoir of persons, his kynnsmen, freindis, or servandis, for all maner of actionis, and crimes, bigane to cumand repare to Edinburgh or ony uther place within the realms to commune with the said governour and do thair eirrandes and return agane; for the space of IX dayis next to cum after the date hereof."[2] Disputes between MacIan of Ardnamurchan and Sir Donald having been submitted to neutral parties for adjustment, the last spark of rebellion was extinguished. The aspect of affairs now seemed to augur well for the peace of the Isles. The Government had been most lenient with the rebels,

---

[1] Orig. Par. Scot., p. 323.   [2] Pitcairn's Criminal Trials, vol. I., p. 533.

and with none more so than with the leader himself, who, as we shall see presently, least of all deserved the pardon that had been extended to him.

It is difficult to account for the conduct of Sir Donald. Evidently he was not satisfied with the award of the arbiters in the dispute between him and MacIan of Ardnamurchan, and the old feud between them was revived. At all events, the restless chief of Lochalsh again began to show signs of disaffection, and the quarrel between him and MacIan was made a pretext for hostilities in the Northern Highlands. Besides, a favourable opportunity to strike another blow for the Lordship of the Isles had now come in the rebellion of Lord Home, with whom Sir Donald appears to have been in league for English assistance.[1] Any pretext seemed to serve the Knight of Lochalsh in raising the standard of revolt, and every fresh opportunity was taken to gain the object of his ambition, which seems to have been nothing less or more than the restoration of the Lordship of the Isles in his own person. He succeeded in gaining the adherence of some of the Island chiefs by making them believe that he had been appointed by Government Lieutenant of the Isles. His object, in the first instance, was to punish MacIan of Ardnamurchan for, among other things, the murder of Alexander of Lochalsh at Orinsay. He invaded MacIan's lands accordingly, took possession of the Castle of Mingarry, which he razed to the ground, and wasted the district with fire and sword. His principal supporters, Lachlan

---

[1] "Remission to Alexander Mackloid of Dunvegane, and all his kinsmen, friends, and servants, &c., for their assistance and supply given to Donald of the Isles of Lochalsh Knight at the time of his being with Alexander Lord Hume in his treasonable deeds ; and for all other crimes, offences, and actions whatsoever without any exception."—Pitcairn, vol. I., p. 534.

Maclean of Dowart and Alexander Macleod of Dunvegan, now understood the real motive that actuated Sir Donald's conduct, which had become so violent that they resolved to apprehend him and hand him over to the Government. He, however, succeeded in making good his escape; but his two brothers, who seem to have been art and part with him in his recent violent proceedings, were captured by Maclean of Dowart and taken to Edinburgh, where, after trial before the Council, they paid the extreme penalty of the law.

Alexander Macleod of Dunvegan, and the Macleans of Dowart and Lochbuy, who had been led by the pretensions of the Knight of Lochalsh to join in his rebellion, now hastened to give in their submission to the Regent and Council, and offered their services against Sir Donald. They sent separate petitions to the Council, in which they asked a free pardon for past offences, and especially for assisting Sir Donald of Lochalsh in his recent treasonable doings, which was granted on the 12th of March, 1517.[1] The petitioners further demanded grants of lands in Mull, Tiree, and Skye,[2] as the price of the services to be rendered by them to the Government. These lands, with few exceptions, the Council agreed to give them possession of, and as proof of their earnest desire to aid the Regent against the rebels, Macleod and the Macleans demanded the forfeiture of Sir Donald Gallda as the first step towards the restoration of peace in the Isles. Lachlan Cattanach

[1] Reg. Secreti Sigilli, vol. V., folio 101.

[2] Alexander Macleod was continued as Crown tenant of the extensive district of Troternish, in Skye. Lachlan Cattanach demanded "the hundreth merk landis in the Ile of Tery and utheris landis in the Mule." "As to the landis of Mul and utheris landis that the said Lauchlane had of befoir of the Kingis grace now desirit in few ferm be him."—Acta Dom. Con., vol. XXIX. fol. 130.

demanded a remission for himself, "kynnsmen, servandis, frendis, and partakars, that is, Donald Makalane, Gillonan Maknele of Barry, Nele Makynnon of Mesnes, Downsleif Makcura of Ulway, and Lauchlan MacEwin of Ardgour, for all crimes be past." After specifying the lands which he desired the Regent and Council to give him possession of, and the conditions on which these were to be held, the petitioner recommends the " justifying (execution) of Donaldis twa brethir and forfactour aganis the said Donald ;" but there is no desire expressed in regard to the " destroying of the wicked blood of the Isles," with which Gregory credits Lachlan Cattanach.[1] The Earl of Argyle at the same time petitioned the Council, craving a commission of lieutenandry over the Isles, " for the honour of the realm and the common-weal in time to come," which was granted.[2] The Council further gave him full power to grant remission for past offences, and restore their lands to such of the Island Chiefs as should deliver hostages, or find other security for the payment of Crown dues, " because the men of the Isles are fickle of mind, and set but little value upon their oaths and written obligations." From this immunity, however, " Sir Donald of the Ilis his brethir and Clan and Clan-donale" were excluded. The Earl, whose commission was limited to three years, was instructed by the Council to " persew Donald of the Ilis and expell him out of the Ilis and hald him thairout, and sege his hous incontinent and do at his utter pouer," but no success seems to have attended his efforts in this direction.

[1] The petition of Lachlan Cattanach Maclean is given in full from the Acts of the Lords of Council, vol. XXIX., fol. 130, in Mr J. P. Maclean's History of the Clan Maclean, pp. 68, 69.

[2] Acta Dominorum Concilii, vol. XXIX., fol. 210.

The Knight of Lochalsh had meanwhile taken refuge in the Isles, and notwithstanding the determined opposition of his recent allies, he still seems to have had a considerable following. He was evidently not satisfied with the punishment he had already been able to inflict on his enemy, MacIan of Ardnamurchan. MacIan had made himself obnoxious not only to his own clan, but also to all those who still remained faithful to the Family of the Isles. It was against him, therefore, that Sir Donald in the first place directed his energies, and he resolved to make every effort to crush him. Besides the murder of his father, Sir Alexander, which he had not sufficiently avenged on MacIan, that chieftain was also one of the most powerful among those who opposed Sir Donald's pretensions to the Lordship of the Isles. During the interval in his operations which followed the siege of Mingarry, Sir Donald, it would appear, had put himself under the protection of Macleod of Lewis, and assisted by that chief, Macleod of Raasay, and Alexander of Dunnyveg, now that a favourable opportunity had come, he opened his campaign afresh in the district of Ardnamurchan. After several skirmishes, Sir Donald and MacIan met in bloody conflict at a place called Craiganairgid, in Morven. MacIan and his followers were defeated with great slaughter, while MacIan himself, and his two sons, Angus and John Suanartach, were found among the slain.[1] Sir Donald, after this victory, was again proclaimed Lord of the Isles, and many of the Islanders flocked to his standard. The Regent and Council at once took measures to put down the rebellion, which seemed now to have assumed a more formidable appearance

---

[1] Hugh Macdonald in Collectanea de Rebus Albanicis, p. 324.

than ever, and proposals were made to have the rebel of Lochalsh forfeited for his treason. While these preparations were going on, the restless Sir Donald of Lochalsh died, according to MacVuirich, at Cairnburgh, in Mull, and with him the male line of Celestine became extinct.[1] The character of Sir Donald Gallda stands out before us in the sketch of his brief career given in this chapter as that of a bold and resolute clansman, who possessed in an unenviable degree the restless ambition and self-assertion characteristic of the chiefs of Clan Cholla. His residence at the Scottish Court, and the favours bestowed upon him by the King, only made this scion of the House of Isla more determined than ever to restore and maintain the ancient prestige of his house against the enemies of his race. Now that through his death the Lochalsh confederacy was dissolved, the Council did not feel called upon to take any harsh proceedings against the rebels, and for some years to come the Isles are free from the presence of a claimant to the honours and dignities of the House of Macdonald.

[1] According to Hugh Macdonald, Sir Donald of Lochalsh died on the Island of Teinlipeil, in Tiree.

CHAPTER XII.

THE CLAN DONALD UNDER JAMES V.—1519-1545.

SIR DONALD GALLDA of Lochalsh, who died in 1519,
left no son, and this house, so closely allied by kin
to the Lords of the Isles, came to an end in the male
line, although the family claims to the Earldom of
Ross—or at least to the representation of that forfeited honour—were perpetuated by the marriage of
Sir Donald's daughter with one of the Glengarry
chiefs. Although one source from which aspirants
to the old honours of the Family of the Isles might
arise was forever closed, yet time was to show that
strenuous efforts would not be wanting for the

establishment, not only of the Lordship of the Isles,
but of the Earldom of Ross as well.

For a number of years after the death of Sir
Donald Gallda, the most striking feature in the
history of the Western Isles of Scotland is the
rapid and widespread advance of the power and
influence of the House of Campbell. The principal
heads of that House, Colin Campbell, Earl of
Argyle, and his brothers, Sir John Campbell of
Calder and Archibald Campbell of Skipness, were
exercising all the astuteness and political craft so
characteristic of the family, with the view of con-
solidating their influence in those regions, North
and South, in which the Lords of the Isles had once
borne almost sovereign sway. In 1517 Argyle had
received a Royal Commission as Lieutenant of the
Isles, and this office involved the possession of
immense authority in a quarter where the power of
the central Government had been exercised in a
spasmodic and intermittent fashion. Bonds of manrent and maintenance were particularly rife at this
period within the Lordship of the Isles, showing
that, with the passing away of the old order, society
in that region being insufficiently protected by the
Crown, sought to save itself during the transition
to greater security and a more settled state of
things. In these bonds of manrent, both in the
North and South Highlands, the Argyle Family was
in a preponderance of instances the superior. The
Earl of Argyle received a bond of manrent from
Alexander Makranald of Glengarry and North
Morar, and his brothers were equally indefatigable
in establishing by similar means the power and
position of their House.[1] In 1521,[2] Donald

---

[1] Gregory, p. 126.   [2] Thanes of Cawdor ad tempus.

Gruamach, son of Donald Gallach of Dunskaith, in
Skye, and head of the Clan Uisdean, gave a bond
of manrent to Sir John Campbell of Cawdor.   In
1520, Dugall Makranald of Ellantirrim gives a bond
of service to the Knight of Cawdor,[1] while in the same
year his successor in the command of the Clanranald,
Alexander McAllan, with his hand at the pen, signs
a similar instrument, undertaking the same kind of
engagement.[2]   In the same year Alexander of
Dunnyveg signs a bond of manrent, gossipry, and
service also to Sir John Campbell of Cawdor.[3]   It is
thus evident that the House of Argyle was using
every means that lay to its hand for assuming the
functions and filling the position left vacant by the
forfeiture of the Island Lordship, while the cadet
families of the fallen House of Isla were in a measure
compelled to cultivate the favour and goodwill of
these politic and ambitious chiefs.   It was a time of
triumph for the Clan Campbell, whose star was now
steadily in the ascendant, while the Clan Donald,
with the loss of their ruling family, had fallen upon
evil times and evil tongues, " with danger and with
darkness compassed round."

In order to review with clearness the progress of
events from 1520 to 1528, it may be desirable, in
the meantime, to pass on to the latter year, in the
course of which an incident occurred which exercised
a far-reaching influence upon contemporary events,
and in the light of which the past, as well as the
future, becomes clearer to the historian's gaze.
Previous to 1528, James V., who was but a child
of two when his father fell at Flodden, had been
virtually a prisoner in the hands of the Earl of
Angus, who acted in the capacity of Regent.   In

---

[1] Thanes of Cawdor *ad tempus.*   [2] Ibid.   [3] Ibid.

that year, however, James, having attained to the
age of seventeen, succeeded in effecting his escape,
and having selected a new set of Councillors, the
policy of the executive underwent a remarkable
change—a change, in some respects, fraught with
injurious effects to the peace and prosperity of the
Isles.   During the King's subjection to the power
of Angus, various grants of land had been bestowed
upon different individuals, no doubt for the purpose
of attaching them to the party of the Regent.   The
Government that came into power on the King's
recovery of his freedom reversed the policy of
their predecessors.   They took the view that
by the prodigality with which these grants had
been bestowed the revenues of the crown were
dilapidated and the royal estate impoverished.
Hence all gifts of land bestowed during the King's
minority, and while he was unable to give his
consent, were pronounced null and void, and it
was announced that no further grants should be
made without the sanction of the King's Council
and of the Earl of Argyle, the King's Lieutenant
in the Isles.[1]   This change of policy, this breach
of national faith, as it may with justice be called,
was the immediate cause of much discontent among
the Hebrideans.   If, in some instances, the reversal
was equitable, the general character of the proceedings was such as to discredit the public honour
and impair the confidence of the lieges in the
stability and continuity of the national righteousness.   In the Isle of Skye, the transference of the
district of Troternish, part of the patrimony of
the Clan Uisdean, to the Siol Tormoid branch of
the Clan Macleod, was the prolific source of strife

[1] Collectanea de Rebus Albanicis, p. 155.

and bloodshed.   In the minority of James V.,
Macleod had received a lease as crown tenant of
the lands in question, as well as of those of Sleat
and North Uist, all of which, since the charter of
1449, were the undisputed possessions of Hugh,
son of Alexander, Earl of Ross, and his descendants.   By this charter—granted by John, Earl of
Ross, and confirmed by the Crown in 1495—the
Clan Uisdean were rightly determined to abide,
and although John, Hugh's son, had, in 1498,
resigned the patrimony of his family in favour of
the Chief of Castle Tirrim, the latter does not
seem to have taken actual possession, and it is not
strange, although the Sleat Family regarded that
transaction, as well as the Regent Angus' later
grant to Macleod, as a usurpation of their just
and lawful rights.   Under the leadership of Donald
Gruamach, and with the aid of Torquil Macleod of
Lewis, half-brother to that chief, the Clan Uisdean
were successful in expelling the Dunvegan Chief
and his clan from Troternish, and by the same
forcible means prevented their taking possession
of the lands of North Uist and Sleat.   Donald
Gruamach, on the other hand, rendered powerful
aid to John MacTorquil in seizing the barony of
Lewis, of which his father had been forfeited in
1506, but which, with the assistance of his vassals,
he was able to hold during the remainder of his
life.[1]

The grant of Troternish, Sleat, and North Uist
to Macleod of Dunvegan was, with other similar
gifts bestowed in the minority of James V., revoked;
but as these lands did not revert, at anyrate by
legal process, to their hereditary owners, the Clan

[1] Gregory, p. 131.

Uisdean, the islands continued to be the scene of strife and discontent. The Family of Sleat were evidently regarded by the Government as the lineal representatives of the House of Isla, and the policy of repression, so consistently adopted towards them after the forfeiture of John, probably arose from the suspicion that, if allowed to flourish and hold territorial possessions, they might perchance at some future time endeavour to revive the ancient principality of the Isles. We thus see the evils of the transition from the ancient order of the Lordship of the Isles to the control and authority of the Crown at their worst in the Isle of Skye, and the net result of the confusions of the period as regards the family most nearly akin to the House of Isla is found to be, that the powerful influence of the State is employed to withhold from them their patrimonial rights, and, after the manner of their kinsmen of Keppoch, they are compelled to hold their lands by the most ancient of all instruments of tenure, their strong arms and trusty claymores.

The troubles which in the North followed the disappearance of the ancient government of the Isles are also paralleled in the South Isles. The Chief of Clan Iain Mhoir early in the sixteenth century was Alexander, son of John Cathanach, a man who seems to have inherited a considerable share of the force of character and resolute independence characteristic of his sires, and was destined to play no inconsiderable part in the Highland politics of the reign of James V. By far the greater portion of his influence and possessions lay in the Routes and Glens of Antrim, where he and others of his line often found a welcome haven when hard pressed by the Scottish Power. Yet we may be sure that in his case, as in that of

other members of his family, the tendrils of affection
clung tenaciously to the island home with which
so many proud memories were associated, and he
strove in the midst of many difficulties, which he
eventually overcame, to retain an interest in its soil.
In 1528, we find Alexander of Dunnyveg in rebellion
against the Crown.   That he and his tribe received
grants of Crown lands in Isla and elsewhere during
the minority of James V., in addition to the 60
merklands which were the patrimony of the Family
of Dunnyveg, seems sufficiently well attested.   That
portion of Isla and of the other islands, which had
been the immediate and direct property of the
Lords of the Isles, became, after the forfeiture in
1493, the legal property of the Crown, though we
do not find that these were actually appropriated
for many years thereafter.   Indeed, at the period in
question, 1528, many of these lands were in the
possession of the Earl of Argyle and his brother, the
Thane of Cawdor, but upon what conditions we
are not able to say.   It is clear that the House
of Argyle had the disposal of these lands in 1520,
for in a band of gossipry and manrent between
the Thane of Cawdor and Alexander of Dunnyveg,
the Thane engages that, for certain services he exacts
from the former, he will give him a grant of 45
merklands in Isla, with the 15 merklands of Jura
and the lands of Colonsay, the same to run for a
period of five years.[1]   The indenture was made at
Glenan in the Taraf, the 7th May, 1520.   It seems
that the bond of gossipry and manrent did not last
to the end of the five years during which it was to
run, and so far as can be judged from contemporary
records, the Thane of Cawdor was to blame for the

[1] Thanes of Cawdor.

breach of peace and amity which caused the premature dissolution of the agreement, for on the 15th
December, 1524, there is a remission to the Thane of
Cawdor for having wasted the lands of Colonsay,[1]
and there seems to be no indication that there was
any aggression or violence on the part of the lord of
Dunnyveg to provoke the Thane to such serious
reprisals. This was the beginning of strained relations between Alexander and the House of Argyle,
and subsequent events would have served to intensify
the hostility. Whether or not the lease of Colonsay
was renewed at the expiry of five years, it seems
that it remained in the Family of Dunnyveg, notwithstanding the policy of revoking grants which
the new Administration adopted in 1528. When it
is borne in mind that after this date the Earl of
Argyle used all his powerful influence to procure the
revocation of all grants from 1513, the year of the
King's accession, up to the time he took the reins
of Government into his own hands, it is in the
highest degree probable that Alexander's quarrel
with the new order, and his resistance to the policy
of the Government, would have originated in some
attempted breach of public faith involved in the
revocation of a grant of land, probably the island of
Colonsay, as already indicated.

When Alexander of Dunnyveg is found in 1528
in arms against the Crown, or, to put it more
correctly, against the Campbell direction of the
policy of the State, he is receiving the hearty and
powerful support of the Clan Maclean. This Clan,
which had grown in numbers and in property under
the generous sway of the Clan Donald chiefs, had
for a long time been on terms of cordial friendship

---

[1] Thanes of Caw'or, 1524.

with the Clan Iain Mhoir, and might not unnaturally
be expected to support them in the time of need.
But at this particular juncture the Macleans had a
feud of their own with the Campbells, upon whom,
if a favourable opportunity arose, they were determined to wreak the most signal vengeance.
Lauchlan Cattanach, the Chief of Maclean, was one
of the darkest and most repulsive characters in the
whole history of the Isles. The great majority of
the Highland Chiefs, though turbulent and restless,
were seldom lacking in a certain chivalrous generosity and honour measured by the canons of their
day. Lauchlan Cattanach was a notable exception
to this rule. He was selfish and treacherous, as
well as lacking in personal courage, and it needed
all the loyalty of the Clan to his position as
hereditary Chief to reconcile them to his rule, or
even to refrain from deposing him from the headship
of his race. There is no one indeed who has drawn
his portrait in darker colours than the partial
historian of his clan.[1] Lauchlan had taken to wife
the Lady Elizabeth Campbell, daughter of Archibald,
second Earl of Argyle. We are not astonished to
find that their tempers proved incompatible, and
that, especially when no children blessed their union,
the relations of the ill-matched pair proved unhappy
in the extreme. For the romantic story which forms
the basis of "The Family Legend," as well as of
Thomas Campbell's ballad of "Glenara," we are
indebted to the authority already referred to. It
was alleged, but altogether on insufficient grounds,
that the Lady of Maclean had conspired to take her
husband's life by poison. The real cause for his
desire to do away with his wife was, as future

---

[1] The History of the Clan Maclean, by a Seannachie, pp. 25-31.

events were to prove, that he conceived a violent passion for the daughter of one of his vassals, Maclean of Treshnish. Thus it was that the Lady of Dowart was one evening invited to take an excursion on the water in a galley manned by some of the myrmidons of the Chief, who were cognisant of the dark secret. The unsuspecting lady agreed to the proposal, but on reaching a solitary rock two miles to the east of Dowart Castle, and in the direction of Lismore, and which was only uncovered at half-tide, she was left there to be drowned by the advancing waters. The scene of the intended murder is still known as *Creag-na-Baintighearn*—the Lady's Rock. Fortunately the plot was disclosed by a remorseful conspirator, and before the fatality could occur, a boat was launched by some of the Chief's bodyguard, who, rowing rapidly to the scene of the outrage, found the victim seated on the rock, with the sea already beginning to break over her, and conveyed her to Lorn, where she was safely landed, and whence she soon found her way to Inverary, the residence of her brother the Earl of Argyle. This incident was supposed to have originated the feud between the Macleans and the Argyle Family, although, undoubtedly, it was aggravated by the policy of the Government regarding the Maclean possessions in the Isles. Vengeance soon overtook the would-be murderer. Some time in 1523[1] Lauchlan Cattanach was staying over night somewhere in the neighbourhood of Edinburgh. John Campbell, Thane of Cawdor, his brother-in-law, having become cognisant of his whereabouts, broke into his apartment under cover of night, accompanied by a number of his followers,

---

[1] Diurnal of Occurrents in Scotland.

FAC-SIMILE OF SIGNATURE OF JOHN CARSWELL, AFTERWARDS BISHOP OF THE ISLES, AND OF ARCHD. MACGILLIVRAY, VICAR OF KILLEAN,

AS NOTARIES SIGNING THE COMMISSION BY DONALD DUBH AND COUNCIL TO THE PLENIPOTENTIARIES TO TREAT WITH HENRY VIII.

and surprised and assassinated him in bed, and what added aggravation to the bloody deed was, that the Chief of Maclean was at the time travelling under a safe conduct from the Government, of which the worthy Thane was regarded as a strenuous supporter. On the 15th December following, we find the Thane exerting his influence successfully with the Government to obtain a remission for the deed, he and his accomplices undertaking to make such amends to the friends of the slaughtered Chief, as might prove satisfactory to the authorities.   Though Lauchlan Cattanach was very far removed from being an ideal character, or beloved chief, he was still the head of the Clan Maclean, and the fatal blow was felt as a deadly insult by every member of the tribe.[1]

The foregoing episode in the history of the Dowart Family has been narrated here for two reasons. First of all it shows that, notwithstanding the wariness and political talent of the Family that had so largely supplanted the House of Isla, the feeling against them in the Western Isles, instead of becoming favourable, was becoming more accentuated in its bitterness, acquiring, in fact, a volume and intensity which might in time prove fatal to their supremacy.   The incident has also been referred to for the purpose of showing that the Lord of Dunnyveg was not likely to be isolated in any stand he might propose to take against the selfish and aggressive policy of the Argyles.

It was only after several years had elapsed since the murder of Lauchlan Cattanach, by Campbell of Cawdor, that a favourable opportunity arose for vengeance.   In 1529 the Clan Donald South and the Macleans united their forces against the common

---

[1] Thanes of Cawdor *ad tempus*.   Letter from Donald Dubh's Council.

foe, The combined clans burst with fire and sword
into the regions of Rosneath, Lennox, and Craignish,
the records of the time accusing the invaders of
having plundered and slain many of the inhabitants
of these districts.[1] The Clanranald-bane of Largie,
a Kintyre branch of the Clan Donald South, were,
conjointly with the Macdonalds of Dunnyveg,
involved in this invasion. The Chief of the Campbells and his vassals[2] were of course resentful of this
attack upon their territories, and we find them with
little delay having their revenge, not on this
occasion upon the Macdonalds, but upon the
Macleans, whose lands they specially selected for
invasion and attack. In the same year—1529—
they invaded Morvern and the islands of Tiree and
Coll, burning and slaying and destroying wherever
they went. For this Campbell raid there was a
remission by Government on March 17th, 1532, to
Archibald, Earl of Argyle, and eighty-two others,
the King and his Council having dispensed with the
General Act on condition of the Earl satisfying the
kin of Donald Ballo McAuchin, Donald Crum
McCownane, and Farquhar McSevir, and others
having lawful claims.[3] It is evident that on this
occasion the *MacCailein Mor* did not act in his
public capacity as the King's lieutenant of the Isles,
or punish the rebellious and disloyal lieges in the
name of his royal master. We look in vain for that
lofty national spirit which their modern apologists
claim for the House of Argyle, and find instead
thereof the old-fashioned method characteristic of
the age and country.

In this same year Sir John Campbell, Thane of
Cawdor, on behalf of his brother Colin, Earl of

---

[1] Reg. Priv. Seal IX., fol. 18.   [2] Ibid.
[3] Pitcairn's Criminal Trials, vol. II., *ad tempus.*

Argyle, Lieutenant of the Isles and the adjacent bounds, made certain proposals to the Government for the suppression of the King's rebels. The righteous soul of this single-hearted patriot and supporter of law and order, the assassin of Lauchlan Cattanach, who had wasted and ravaged the island of Colonsay, and whose nephew, Archibald, the heir to the Earldom, had the same year invaded and pillaged the country of Maclean, is greatly exercised at the terrible dispeace prevailing in the Scottish Isles. Though he himself had called up the spirits of anarchy from the "vasty deep," he stands astonished and aghast at the result. He is seized with great searching of heart as to the best methods of producing social tranquillity, and yearns to sacrifice himself upon the altar of Scottish nationality by offering to bring these disturbed regions in subjection to the Crown. Inspired by such a patriotic resolve, this scion of the House of Argyle made certain proposals to the King, which were undoubtedly of a thorough and adequate nature. He suggested that the house-holders of Dumbartonshire and Renfrew-shire, and of the bailiaries of Carrick, Kyle, and Cunningham, should be ordered to assemble at Lochranza, in Arran, with victuals for twenty days, to meet the Earl of Argyle and assist him in his efforts to reduce the Isles to order.[1] It soon appeared, however, that whatever confidence the King and his Council may once have reposed in the public spirit and disinterestedness of the Argyle Family, they were now beginning to regard with suspicion their professions of zeal for the service of the country. As a matter of fact,

[1] Gregory, p. 132.

jealousy of the rapid rise and increasing power of
the Chiefs of Inverary animated the breasts of
many members of the Council, and the tendency
towards self advancement, which sometimes became
visible through the vail of vaunted patriotism,
was gradually being unfolded to the vision of
the young King. It was also felt on all hands
that the lieutenancy of the Western Highlands
and Islands, in itself a position of commanding
influence, was in danger of becoming hereditary
in the Family of Argyle, as public offices in these
days had a distinct tendency to become ; and, still
further, that if the Lordship of the Isles had
proved dangerous to the well-being of the State
in the past, this new office of Lieutenant, for the
very reason that in form it was constitutional and
responsible, might be fraught with greater peril
to the commonwealth if its powers were wielded
in the interests of one aggressive and ambitious
House. Hence, when the policy of Sir John
Campbell was, in the first instance, unfavourably
viewed by those in power, there was witnessed the
faint beginning of a rift in the lute, which, by
and bye, might assume larger and more dangerous
proportions, and those who cast the horoscope of
the future might well and safely predict that the
sun of Argyle, which had long been unclouded,
was soon to suffer a temporary eclipse.

The first step resolved on by the King indicated
that a wiser and a more discriminating policy was
now to be adopted towards the Western Isles than
that which had hitherto prevailed. It was decided
that, instead of endeavouring to pacify the Isles by
aggressive military operations, a Herald or Pursuiv-
ant should be entrusted with a mission to treat

with the Western Chiefs, with special reference to Alexander of Dunnyveg.[1] This Herald, whose name was Robert Hart, was despatched on 3rd August, 1529, and the following is the Resolution of the Lords of Council in accordance with which he was sent upon his mission :—·

"Anent the articulis and desiris proponit and gevin in be Sir Johnne of Calder, Knight, in name and behalff of Colyne Erle of Ergile for suppleing of him in the resisting and persute of the Kingis rebellis inhabitantis the Ilis makand insurrectionis aganes oure Soverane Lord and his auctoritie quhilk may returne to displeasour of the hale cuntre nixt adjacent to the bordouris of the Ilis, without provisioun and gude ordonre be put thairin dew tyme, and for remeid thairof, it is divisit, concludit, and ordanit as efter followis,—

"Item it is thocht expedient be the saidis Lordis that thar be ane officiar of armis that is of wisdom and discretioun send to McKynmont and his complices . . . . The said officiar of armis to have this discretioun, in the first to charge the said Allestar and his complices to desist and ceis fra all convocatioun or gaddering for the invasioun of our Soverane Lordis leiges, bot he reddely ansuer and obey to our Soverane Lord and his Lieutenant under the payne of tresone. . . . . Item the said officiar sall have commissioun and power of the Kingis Graice to commone with the said Allestar upoun gud wais and gif the said Allestar plesis to cum to the Kingis Graice to gif him assuirance to pas and repas with aue certane nomer he beand content to gif plegis of Lawland men for keping of gud renle and till obey the King and pay him his malis and dewiteis of sic landis as his Graice sall gif to the said Allestar."

In due time Robert Hart returned from his mission in the Isles ; but whether it was that the Chiefs were obdurate, or that Argyle was then, as afterwards, acting a double part, his report upon the attitude of Alexander of Dunnyveg towards the Crown was in the highest degree unsatisfactory. Whatever influences operated against the submission

[1] Acts of Lords of Council, XL., fol. 80.

of the Islanders, the assertion of the authority of
the King seemed so far productive of little good.
The Council thereupon decided upon taking more
stringent action ; but it is evident from surviving
records that they were resolved to exercise due
caution and deliberation.   Argyle's offer for the
reduction of the South Isles to order was accepted,
while similar proposals by the Earl of Murray for the
pacification of the North Isles were likewise ordered
to be carried into effect.   The Lieutenant of the
Isles was to direct special attention to Alexander
of Dunnyveg, the most powerful and outstanding of
the Island Chiefs, who apparently took the leading
stand against the proceedings of the Government.
The following is an extract from the Decree of the
Lords of Council upon the failure of Robert Hart's
mission :—

"Anent the articulis send to Alester Canoch with Robert Hart
pursevant, and the respons of the saidis articulis schawin be the
said Robert to the Lordis of Counsale, and thai, beand avisit
thairwith at lenth, has concludit and thocht expedient that the
Erle of Ergile, Lieutenent of the Ilis and boundis adjacent thairto
sall pas forthwart into the Ilis and to persew the said Alester and
all utheris inobedient liegis to the Kingis Hienes taking of thair
houses and strenthis and for punyssing of trespassoris, ordouring
of the boundis of the Ilis and putting of tha pairtis to pece and
rest, and to subject thame to the Kingis obedience and lawis of
the realme efter the forme and tenour of the commissioun direct
to him thairupoun."

The Decree of the Lords of Council contained full
provision for accomplishing the ends shadowed forth
in the foregoing extract.   A roll of the tenants of
the Isles was placed in Argyle's hands, with a
citation that they should all come into the King's
presence in order " to commune with His Majesty
upon good rule in the Isles."   All were inhibited

from rendering any assistance to the rebels, or
calling the King's lieges together for offensive purposes, under pain of death. The fighting men of
Perth and Forfar, and of the South of Scotland
generally, were summoned to meet the King at Ayr,
with provisions for forty days, to accompany him on
his expedition to the Isles. The men of Carrick,
Kyle, Cunningham, Renfrew, Dumbartonshire, Bal-
quhidder, Braidalbane, Rannoch, Apuadill, Athole,
Menteith, Bute and Arran were charged to join the
King's Lieutenant at such places as he should
appoint, and to continue with him in the service for
a month. The burghs of Ayr, Irvine, Glasgow,
Renfrew, and Dumbarton were to send boats for
victualling his army, all of which were to be paid for
out of the Royal revenues. Protection was offered
to the Islesmen, in case they should fear to trust
themselves to the tender mercy of the Lowlanders,
and especially of the Campbells, and this protection
was to endure for thirty days, an additional period
being allowed them for returning home.[1] Not only
so, but the King promised to take hostages from the
Earl of Argyle for further security of the Island
Chiefs, Duncan Campbell of Glenurchy, Archibald
Campbell of Auchinbreck, Archibald Campbell of
Skipnish, and Duncan Campbell of Llangerig being
proposed as a list out of which any two might be
selected for confinement in Edinburgh Castle until
the Islanders were safely back to their sea-girt
fastnesses.[2]

While the commission given to Argyle to pass
into the Isles was intended to be put in action
without delay, it does not appear that the materials
for its execution were placed immediately in his

[1] Acts of Lords of Council, XLI., fol. 77.   [2] Ibid., fol. 79.

hands. The King and his Council seemed still to entertain some hopes of a peaceful solution of the Island problem. Orders were given to provide the Lieutenant of the Isles with a cannon, two falconets, and three barrels of gunpowder, with other conveniences for his expedition; but it was agreed to delay the calling out of the levies until it was seen how Argyle sped in his mission, and "becaus the harvest occurs now and uther greit impedimentis."[1] It is also very certain that suspicions regarding Argyle's good faith were growing apace. In addition to all this, an indefinite postponement of the expedition was caused by the illness of the Earl of Argyle, and his death in 1530, and although his son Archibald succeeded him in all his offices and honours, the circumstances were unfavourable to immediate and decisive action.

It was not until the early months of 1531 that Archibald, the new Earl of Argyle, along with the Earl of Murray, went upon their mission for the reduction of the Hebrides. The former nobleman, previous to his departure, gave abundant proof to the King and Council that he possessed the energy and ambition, with probably no small share of the unscrupulous character, of his predecessors. He gave an undertaking that he would carry out his commission with the most unsparing thoroughness. He would insist upon the inhabitants taking their lands in lease from the King, and upon the regular and punctual payment of the Crown rents into the royal treasury; and, if opposition were offered, he undertook to destroy the recusants root and branch, and to bring the Isles eventually to a condition of peace and order. He, at the same time, requested

---

[1] Acts of Lords of Council, XLI., fol. 80.

FAC-SIMILE OF DONALD DUBH'S LETTER TO HENRY VIII., 1545.

that the commission of Lieutenandry which his
father had possessed should be bestowed upon him,
and that he should at all times be consulted by the
Council of State as to any steps that might be
deemed necessary to take in dealing with the
Western Isles.[1] After having submitted these
proposals—not unduly modest in their tone—the
new Earl of Argyle, armed with the royal commission, proceeded on his way.

The events that followed will be better understood when it is borne in mind that the missions
both of the Earls of Argyle and Murray, the former
in the South and the latter in the North Isles, were
conducted under the immediate and vigilant supervision of the King. It was resolved that James
should proceed in person against the rebels on the
1st June, 1531, and from that moment there
emerges a new and happier relationship between the
Islesmen and the Crown.

The Macdonald Chiefs, like the other vassals of
the Isles, were during the early part of summer of
this year repeatedly cited to the royal presence.
On the 28th April, Parliament met in Edinburgh,
and John Cathanachson, Donald Gruamach, John
Moydartach, Alexander MacIan of Ardnamurchan—
who seems to have grown weary of being an under-
study of Argyle — Alister of Glengarry, Donald
McAllister McRanaldbane of Largie, were all summoned, and not appearing, the citation was renewed
till 26th May.[2] We are particularly informed that
the first-named in the foregoing list, Alexander of
Dunnyveg, or John Cathanachson, as he was sometimes called, received a respite under the privy seal

---

[1] Acts of the Lords of Council, XLII., fol. 186.
[2] Acts of Scottish Parliament, vol. II., p. 333.

for himself and his household, men and servants, to
the number of thirty persons, to come to the King's
presence and return again to the Isles in safety.
After the expiry of some weeks, the royal summons
is responded to. On former occasions the proceedings for the pacification of the Islesmen were
under the immediate direction of those whose
interest, and consequently whose wishes had lain,
not in the tranquillity of the Isles, but in such
chronic disaffection and dispeace as would prove the
ruin of the Western Chiefs, and the consequent
advancement of the House of Argyle. The Lord
of Dunnyveg, recognising that the King was disposed to deal with the Hebridean chiefs on
honourable and generous terms, resolved to make
his submission. On the 7th June he came to
Stirling, and on certain conditions received the
royal pardon. The Act of Council recording the
negotiations is in the following terms :—

"It is the Kingis Graice mynd, with avise of the Lordis of his
Counsale, that Alexander John Canochsoun, becaus he hes cumin
to our said Soverane Lord and offerit his service in his maist
huimle maner like as in certane articulis gevin in be him to the
lordis of Counsale thairupoun is contenit, and refferit him hale in
the Kingis will. Thairfor it plesis his Hienes to give to the said
Alexander the proffetis of the landis contenit in his privie sele
gevin to him of befoir be his Hienes be the avise of the Duke of
Albany his tutour for the tyme, insofar as pertenis to the Kingis
Grace in propirte within the boundis of Kintyr or ony pairtis of
the Ilis during the Kingis will, and for his gude service to be done
to his Hienes in eschewing of trouble and in quietation of the
Kingis lieges and heirschip of the cuntrie, and for the helping of
our soverane Lordis Chalmerlanys to be maid be his Grace for
inbringing of our said Soverane Lordis malis, proffettis and
dewiteis of the Ilis and Kyntyr as he sal be requirit, and als to
solist and caus at his power all the heidsmen and clannys of the
Ilis and Kintyr and to cum to the Kingis obedience and gude
reule of the cuntre and for sur payment of the malis and proffetis

of his landis in the Ilis and Kyntyr intromettit with be thame ;
provydant that the said Alexander sall put to fredome all
prisoneris that he hes pertenand to the Erle of Ergile and utheris
and sall on no wis assist (or) fortifie John McClane of
in assegeing of his hous nor hereing of his landis, but sall stop the
same at his utter power, and sall fortify and kepe the Kirkmen in
thair fredome and privilegis, and caus thame to be ausuerrit of
thair landis malis fermis and dewiteis thairof."

In the foregoing conditions of pardon, acknowledgment is made of Alexander's powerful influence
among the Islesmen, which he is called upon to
exercise for the promotion of law and order, and in
proof of this we find that on the same day, not only
the cadets of the House of Isla but other vassals of
the Isles follow the example of the Lord of Dunnyveg, and on making their submission to the King
are immediately received into royal favour. Thus it
came about that while the Earls of Argyle and
Murray were cruising among the Western Isles,
probably doing more to stir up disaffection than to
create loyalty, the rebellion came to an end through
the direct intervention of the King. By a combination of firmness and generosity, and by personal
intercourse with the Islesmen, James brought about
in a few days a condition which years of Argyle's
lieutenandry had only served to render more remote.
Had James' life been spared for even a few years
longer than the date of his sad demise, and had he
and his successors continued to apply to the problem
of the Isles the same wise and patient policy, the
future history of that region could have been
delineated in brighter and more glowing hues.

The tranquillity of the Isles and the submission
and pardon of the Chiefs were far from being a
pleasing spectacle to the Earl of Argyle, who found
a very unexpected state of matters awaiting him on

his return from his Hebridean tour. The turn of
affairs was so thoroughly satisfactory from a public
point of view that Othello's occupation was meanwhile gone. Finding that the remission granted to
the Islesmen by the King had placed them completely
beyond his power, he did all he could to exasperate
and annoy them and to kindle anew the expiring
flame of disloyalty. The raids of 1529 into the
territories of Argyle are once more raked up against
the Macdonalds and Macleans, although these had
been wiped away by the pardon of 7th June, 1531.
The noble Earl, besides, seems to have forgotten his
own invasion and wasting of the lands of Morvern
and others in that same year, or, if he remembered
these things, he acted as if on the principle that—

> " That in the captain's but a choleric word
> Which in the soldier is flat blasphemy."

The immediate result of the Earl's proceedings in
this matter was, that Alexander of Dunnyveg and
himself both received a remission for the violent
conduct of which they had been guilty in 1529,
although, in the case of the latter, the necessity for such a remission does not in the circumstances seem clear.[1] The action of the Earl in
these matters, however, proved eventually disastrous
to himself. Alexander of Dunnyveg unhesitatingly
appeared in response to the summons issued to him
at the instigation of his grace of Argyle ; but when
the day appointed arrived, the accuser found it convenient to cultivate the privacy of Inverary Castle.
Indeed, the tables were completely turned upon this
magnate, who, with the cadets of his house, had
evidently come to regard the Western Isles as their

[1] Pitcairn's Criminal Trials *ad tempus.*

own special preserve. His accusations were met by a statement from the Lord of Dunnyveg, in which he not only vindicates triumphantly his own position since his restoration to Royal favour, but puts the King's Lieutenant completely in the wrong. The statement has such an important bearing upon the Clan Donald history of the period that we shall quote it here in full :—

"STATEMENT BY ALEXANDER OF DUNNYVEG ANENT CERTAIN
    COMPLAINTS PREFERRED AGAINST HIM BY THE EARL OF
    ARGYLE.

"In presence of the Lords of Council compeared Alexander John Cathanachson, and gave in the articles underwritten, and desired the same to be put in the books of Council ; of the which the tenor follows :—My Lords of Council, unto your Lordships huimlie menis and schawis I, your servitor Alexander John Cathanachson; that quhar lately Archd. Earl of Argyle of verray prover malice and envy gave in ane bill of complaint of me to your Lordships, all.ging that I had done divers and sundry great faults to him and his friends, which is not of veritie ; for the which your Lordships commanded me by ane maiser to remain in this town to answer to his complaints. And I have remained here continually these 13 days last by past daily to answer to his said bill ; and because he perfectly knows that his narration is not nor may not be proved of veritie, he absents himself and bydis away and will not come to follow the same. And since so is that that his narration is all wrong and feynyeit made upon me without any fault of very malice as said is as manifestly appears, because he will not come to pursue and verify the same, I answer to the points of his bill in this wise—In the first, I understand that no person has jurisdiction of the Lordship of the Isles but my master the King's grace alanerly. And insafer as his highness gave command and power to my sympilnes at my first incoming to his grace at Stirling, I have obeyed and done his highness's commands in all points and fulfilled the tenor of all his acts made in Stirling in every point as I was commanded. And gif it please his grace to command me to give his malis and duties of his lands and Lordship of the Isles to any person, the same shall be done thankfully after my power. And in sa fer as the said Earl alleged that I did wrong in intromitting and uptaking of the malis and dewities of the Isles, he failyeit thairin, because I did nothing in that behalf but as I was commanded by the King's grace, my master.

"Further, my Lords, I at your Lordships' command has remained in this town thir days last by past ready to answer to the said Earl in anything he had to lay to my charge to my great cost and expense. He as I am informed is past in the Isles with all the folks that he may get and with all the men that the Earl of Murray may cause pass with him for heirschip and destruction of the King's lands of the Isles and for slaughter of his poor lieges dwelling therein; which as I trust is done without his grace's advice, license, authority or consent. And if so be the whole fault is made to his highness considering both the land and the men and the inhabitants thereof are his own; and well it is to be presumed that his grace would give no command to destroy his own men and lands. And if the King's grace my sovereign Lord and Master will give power or command to me or any other gentleman of the Isles to come to his highness to pass in England in oisting or any other part in the mainland within this realm, I shall make good we shall bring more good fighting men to do his grace honour, pleasure, and service than the said Earl shall do.

"And, if the said Earl will contempne the King's grace's authority his highness giving command to me and his poor lieges of the Isles, we shall cause compel the said Earl to dwell in any other part of Scotland nor Argyle, where the King's grace may get resoun of him.

"And further, there is no person in the Isles that has offended to the said Earl or any others in the Lowlands but I shall cause him to come to the King's grace to underly his laws and to please his highness and the party be ressoun, suchlike as other Lowland men does, the brokynes and heirschip of the Isles being considered made by the said Earls father, the Knight of Calder, and Gillespy Bane his brother.

"And mairattour, what the King's grace and your Lordship will command me to do for his highness honour and weal of his realm the same shall be done with all diligence of my power without my dissimulation.

"And further, my Lords, I have fulfilled your lordships' command and bidden aye in this town and kept the day that your Lordships assigned to me to answer to the said Earl's complaint and that he came not to follow the same, that ye will advertise the King's grace thereof, and of my answer to his complaint, and give command to the Clerk of Council to subscribe the copy of my answer here present to be sent to the King's grace for information to his highness of the veritie.   And your answer humbly I beseech."

The statement just quoted was certainly not lacking in boldness and self-confidence, and its honesty and candour, and the unshrinking desire it manifests that the whole issue should be strictly investigated, contrasts most favourably with the evasive conduct of Argyle.   The undertaking to compel his Grace of Inverary to retire into a more remote place of residence affords refreshing evidence of a desire on the part of the Lord of Dunnyveg to come to close quarters with the enemy of his House.   The King seems to have been deeply struck by Alexander's indictment, and with characteristic sense of justice caused a minute enquiry to be made into its leading allegations, as well as into the whole question of the Argyle policy in the Isles, which the statement directly impugned.   The result was a repetition of the story of Haman and Mordecai; a case of the biter bit.   Argyle sank in the pit he made for others, in the net which he hid was his own foot taken.   Alexander of Dunnyveg was triumphantly vindicated.   It was clearly brought out that the policy of the Argyle Family in the Isles had been animated by motives of private interest rather than by zeal for the peace and welfare of His Majesty's lieges in that part of his dominions, and that they were largely to blame for fomenting much of the turbulence and disaffection which had arisen within recent years. Still further it was brought out that Argyle's intromissions with the Crown rentals were not so advantageous to the royal revenues as with strictly honest accounting they should have been.   The

Earl was thrown into prison, and although his liberation soon followed, he was discredited and disgraced, while the public offices he filled were all taken from him, and some of them bestowed upon the Lord of Dunnyveg, who continued, during the reign of James V., to receive numerous marks of royal favour. From the Clan Donald point of view, the pleasing, but in those days the unwonted, spectacle is witnessed of the head of a great branch of the Family of the Isles high in confidence of the Crown, while the Chief of the Clan Campbell has to retire into obscurity and disrepute.

RUINS OF KNOCK CASTLE, SLEAT.

From 1532 down to 1538 the history of the Western Isles appears to have been quiet and uneventful; at anyrate the surviving records of the age have little to say regarding the history of the Macdonald Family, a clear vindication of the methods of governing the Highlands adopted by James V. and his advisers. The problem of the

Hebridean clans, especially, proved not hopelessly insoluble when approached in a spirit of generosity and firmness ; while, looked at through Argyle spectacles, and treated in the tortuous methods of Argyle policy, it was a standing menace to the peace of Scotland.   In 1539, however, the Isle of Skye and the western border of Ross-shire became the scene of a fresh attempt to restore the lordship of the Isles and, to all appearance, also the Earldom of Ross.

It was the universal belief in the Western Isles, and there seems little reason to doubt that the feeling was well founded, that the real heir to the Lordship of the Isles was the unfortunate Donald Dubh, who since 1506 pined in solitary confinement as a State prisoner in Edinburgh Castle.   His claims to the Earldom of Ross were by no means so clear.   The Charter of 1476, in which Angus Og and his issue were legitimised, was granted after the forfeiture of the Earldom of Ross, and the succession of John's descendants was legalised only so far as the Lordship of the Isles was concerned.   Hence, although Donald Dubh was, undoubtedly, the lineal heir to the Lordship of the Isles, it could not be contended with the same degree of confidence that he represented any hereditary right to the Earldom of Ross—all the more because this dignity had come into the Family of the Isles not as a Celtic but as a feudal honour. In any case, seeing that Donald Dubh was apparently a prisoner for life, there was only one family akin to the main stem of the House of Macdonald that could lay just claim to represent the combined dignities of both Earldom and Lordship.   Now that the Family of Lochalsh had become

23

extinct in the male line, the succession to the who.e
honours of the House of Isla—as regards descent—
appeared to devolve upon the Family of Sleat.
Without prejudging any genealogical questions that
must present themselves hereafter for solution, this
certainly was the view taken by the vassals of the
Isles in 1539, when the Chief of the Clan Uisdean
once more unfurled the ancient banner and determined to lay claim to and take possession of the
time-honoured heritage of his sires.

There is nothing, we think, more remarkable in
the history of the years between 1493, when the
Lordship of the Isles was forfeited, and the final
effort made for its revival about the middle of the
sixteenth century, than the almost unanimous
support, despite of all opposing forces, that claimants
to the ancient honour received at the hands of the
chiefs and clans of the West. Not only were these
insurrections countenanced by cadet families of the
Isles, but other vassals than those of the Clan
Donald rallied to the support of aspirants to the
Lordship. It was the same tendency which in later
centuries and on a larger scale was displayed by the
Celtic inhabitants of Scotland, in the strenuous
effort to restore the fallen Stuart dynasty to the
British throne. The Highland Clans had not as yet
begun to feel at ease under the yoke of a Government becoming more and more out of sympathy
with Celtic culture and sentiment, and with the
conservatism characteristic of the race, they
cherished the hope that the good old times might
be restored when they lived under the sway of
native lords, who kept up the institutions and
language of the Gael as these were nowhere else
maintained. They did not follow the Lordship of

the Isles as the swallow follows summer, with
chivalrous devotion they clung to it after the
winter of its misfortune had set in. The system
once was theirs, and—

> "Once though lost
> Leaves a faint image of possession still."

Thus do we account for the fact that Donald Gorme
of Sleat, in his plot to lay hold of the Lordship of
the Isles and Earldom of Ross, was supported by a
majority of the Highland Chiefs, and particularly
by the Macleods of Lewis, to whom his family had
long been united in bonds of blood and friendship.

It is evident that at this particular stage the
Macleods of Dunvegan had, despite the opposition of
the Clan Uisdean, obtained a footing in the region
of Troternish, for Donald Gorme's first move in the
new campaign was to invade that district and lay it
waste. He then turned his attention to the mainland of Ross, and, with fifty galleys and their
complement of fighting men, set sail for the shores
of Kenlochewe. The Barony of Ellandonan was at
that time in the possession of John Mackenzie, 9th
Baron of Kintail, who was at the time away in the
south, but who was well known to be adverse to the
pretensions advanced by the Chief of Sleat, as well
as to have aided Macleod of Dunvegan in his designs
upon the Barony of Troternish.

> " M'Donald has chosen the best of his power ;
> On the green plains of Slate were his warriors arrayed ;
> Every warrior came before midnight an hour,
> With the sword in his hand and the belt on his plaid.
>
> .   .   .   .
>
> " At the first of the dawn, when the boats reached the shore,
> The sharp ridge of Skooroora with dark mist was crown'd,
> And the rays that broke thro' it seemed spotted with gore
> As M'Donald's bold currach first struck on the ground.

" Of all the assailants that sprung on the coast,
      One of stature and aspect superior was seen ;
  Whatever a lord or a chieftain could boast,
      Of valour undaunted, appeared in his mien.
      .   .   .   .

" 'Twas the Lord of the Isles whom the Chamberlain saw,
      While a trusty long bow on his bosom reclined,
  Of stiff yew it was made, which few sinews could draw :
      Its arrows flew straight, and as swift as the wind.

" With a just aim he drew—the shaft pierced the bold chief ;
      Indignant he started, nor heeding the smart,
  While his clan pour'd around him, in clamorous grief,
      From the wound tore away the deep rivetted dart.

" The red stream flow'd fast, and his cheek became white ;
      His knees, with a tremor unknown to him, shook ;
  And his once piercing eyes scarce directed his sight,
      As he turned towards Skye his last lingering look."[1]

The foregoing lines seem to embody an authentic
tradition regarding the invasion of Ross and siege of
Ellandonan by the Chief of Clan Uisdean.   Here, as
elsewhere, the traditional historian of the Mackenzies
presents to us as sober fact a most luxuriant growth
of legend, expecting us calmly to endorse a narrative of almost miraculous incidents.   Only three
men, we are gravely informed, were in occupation of
Ellandonan Castle when it was besieged by the men
of the Isles, and we are asked to credit the astound-
ing statement that these three warriors, the governor,
the watchman, and an individual abounding in
patronymics—Duncan MacGillechriost MacFhionn-
laidh MacRath—successfully opposed fifty boat loads
of chosen warriors of the Clan Donald north.   We
can gather this grain of truth from amid the
mountain of chaff, that on arriving at the stronghold of Ellandonan, Donald Gorme, at the head of

---

[1] Scott's Border Minstrelsy.

his men, came perilously within bowshot of the walls, when Duncan, the man of surnames, fired an arrow with unerring skill, and struck the Chief of Sleat in the leg. The wound would not have proved fatal were it not that Macdonald, failing to perceive that the arrow was barbed, plucked it impatiently out of the wound, thus causing a severance of the main artery, and hemorrhage, which his attendants knew not how to staunch. The dying Chief was removed to a sand bank on the shore, where a temporary hut was erected for his protection, and the place is still pointed out as *Larach Tigh Mhacdhomhnuill*, because it was there that the gallant Donald Gorme lay while the crimson tide of life gradually ebbed away. Then, when he had breathed his last, the same tradition tells us that his clansmen lovingly laid his body in its last resting-place, at Ardelve, on the opposite shore of Loch Loung.

That the followers of the Chief whose career terminated thus fatally and prematurely did not retire in dismay before a garrison of three, is attested by the authentic records of the age. Under the leadership of Archibald the Clerk, the death of Donald Gorme was amply avenged by his clansmen. The Castle of Ellandonan was burned, as were also Mackenzie's fleet of galleys, while the country around Kenlochew was harried and laid waste.

The rebellion of Donald Gorme, which, but for the death of the leader, might have assumed formidable proportions, afforded ample proof to the Government, if such indeed were required, that there still existed a widespread desire among the Western clans to bring back the Lordship of the Isles. For this reason James V., who seems to

have understood the Highland character better
than any of his race, resolved to make an imposing
progress through the Western Isles, with the view
of impressing upon the chiefs the power and majesty
of the Crown. For this purpose a fleet of twelve
ships was equipped with artillery and various other
accoutrements of war. Six of these were set apart
for the special use of the King, his retinue, and
soldiers ; while, as evidence of his intention to take
a prolonged cruise, three were loaded with provisions, the remaining three having been appropriated
for Cardinal Beaton, the Earl of Huntly, and the
Earl of Arran respectively. After visiting Orkney
and Caithness, the royal fleet doubled Cape Wrath,
and visited a number of the Hebridean Isles. Among
other regions, the King touched at the district of
Troternish, in Skye, lately the scene of invasion
and attack by the deceased head of the Clan
Uisdean. The fleet dropped anchor at Portree—in
former times known by the name of Loch Challuim
Chille, or Saint Columba's Loch—and there is little
reason to doubt the tradition that it received its
more modern name of Port-an-Righ owing to its
association with this royal visit to the Isle of Skye.
Here James interviewed the famous John Moydartach and Archibald the Clerk, Captain of the
Clan Uisdean (his grand-nephew Donald Gormeson
being but a child), and also Alexander of Glengarry.
The first of these, the redoubtable Captain of the
Clanranald, was, with Macleod of Dunvegan and
others, compelled to accompany the King on his
southward voyage ; but the head of the Family of
Sleat seems to have preserved his freedom, and it is
on record that, in the following year, 1541, he and
the principal men of his clan obtained the royal

pardon for the excesses and "heirschippes" of
Donald Gorme's campaign in 1539.

From Skye, the King directed his course to the
South Highlands, calling at Kintail in the passing
by, and having among others taken on board his
ship James Macdonald of Dunnyveg, the son of
Alexander John Cathanachson, memorable in the
annals of his race for his triumph over Argyle, he
sailed up the Firth of Clyde and landed at Dumbarton. According to Bishop Lesly, the King
proceeded homewards by land, while the ships
containing the captive Chiefs, whom he had kept
as hostages for order and good government, were
sent back by the West and North of Scotland,
until they arrived at Edinburgh, in whose Castle
they were immured. History is not definite as to
the *personel* of these imprisoned potentates, but it
is certain that John Moydartach and Macleod of
Dunvegan were of the number, while it is highly
probable that Macleod of Lewis, Alexander Macdonald of Glengarry, and Maclean of Dowart were
likewise their companions in affliction. It is not
likely that James Macdonald of Dunnyveg, who had
been educated at Court under the royal supervision,
and who appears to have been a favourite with the
King, suffered even a short imprisonment. Several
of the Chiefs were liberated after a brief captivity
on their giving hostages for their good behaviour,
while some of the most dangerous to the peace
of the Highlands, including John Moydartach,
were kept in durance. As a consequence of this
summer cruise among the Isles, it is said that peace
and quietness prevailed among the lieges in districts
hitherto perturbed, and that the Crown rents were
promptly and regularly paid.

Although the Lord of the Isles had been forfeited in 1493, the Lordship of the Isles was not then nor long after, by any formal Act of the Legislature, attached to the Crown. In 1540, however, certain measures were enacted by Parliament for increasing the royal revenues, and among other means it was resolved to annex the lands and Lordship of the Isles, North and South, with the two Kintyres, and the Castles pertaining thereto, and their pertinents.[1] In consequence of these enactments, we find a royal garrison this same year occupying the Castle of Dunnyveg, with Alexander Stewart as the King's Captain in charge, as also the Castle of Dunaverty in Kintyre, both of which were the property of the *Clann Iain Mhoir*. This procedure, although it might be regarded as the natural sequel to the Act of Forfeiture, was a decisive step so far as the principality of the Isles was concerned. The forfeiture of 1493, followed by John's resignation in the following year, does not stand on record among the Parliamentary enactments of the time, and their terms are merely a matter of conjecture. Judging, however, by this Act of 1540, John's forfeiture did not extend beyond his own possessions, and the Lordship of the Isles still continued a separate superiority, and it does not seem very clear how far its revenues were levied, or if so, to what purpose they were applied. Now, however, the Crown becomes the superior of the lands and Lordship of the Isles, and it is a question whether this decided step on the part of James V. was calculated to promote the peace of that region, especially in view of the events that darkened the years that almost immediately followed the appropriation.

[1] Acts of Parliament of Scotland, vol. II., 1540.

In 1542 events occurred fraught with disastrous results to Scotland. James V. was at war with Henry VIII., and in the course of the campaign of that year incidents took place most discreditable to the loyalty and patriotism of the Scottish barons. We are not called upon in such a work as this, written for readers of all shades of Christian belief, to discuss the merits of the religious controversy which was then raging. We can, however, without offending ecclesiastical susceptibilities, estimate its political effects at the period at which we have arrived ; and it is safe to say that the influence of Henry VIII. with the leaders of the Reformation movement in Scotland was the main cause of the disaffection of the barons to the King, who still continued to support the Church of Rome.   In addition to all this, it had been the policy of James V. in recent years, as it had been the traditional policy of the Stewart dynasty for generations, to lessen the power of the nobles and increase the perogatives of the Crown. The discontent arising from these causes came to a height in 1542. First of all, at Fala Muir, the barons flatly refused to lead their men to battle, and shortly afterwards, at Solway Moss, a still more indelible disgrace befell the Scottish arms. A body of 10,000 men, under Lord Maxwell and the Earls of Cassilis and Glencairn, entered England, and on being attacked by 1400 English, the whole Scottish army took to flight, while nearly 1000 rank and file, and 200 lords, esquires, and noblemen fell as prisoners into the enemy's hands. The leaders were corrupt and the men mutinous, and for the reasons already suggested they entered with no heart or energy into the conflict. Many instances are on record of men having been cited to the royal army against this raid of Solway, and receiving remissions for their failure to attend. We find on January 21, 1542, that a remission is granted to Donald MacAlister of Largie, John, his son and heir apparent, Ranald Boy, Archibald and John Makranaldvane, with twenty-four others, and Alexander McAlister of Loupe and two others, for treasonable abiding from the raid of Solway. How far, if at all, the other branches of the Clan Donald were involved in the same default, we find nothing in contemporary records to indicate.[1] The King felt so keenly the national disgrace involved in the flight of his army at Solway, as well as the ominous political complications by which he was on all hands beset, that he became a prey to the deepest despondency, and finally to despair. His proud spirit never rallied from the humiliation, and the fever of the mind so consumed his physical frame that in a few weeks he died from the saddest, the most tragic of all complaints—the pain which no anodyne can soothe and no physician heal—a broken heart. He was the victim of a powerful set of political forces which were beyond the control of any individual, however gifted, either to oppose or direct ; but he had given promise of great administrative power, and, humanly speaking, the wellbeing of the Highlands, and the interests of the Clan whose story we are telling, and towards which he acted with great wisdom and consideration, were prejudicially affected by his death, in the rich summer of his years.

The first notable event in the history of the Clan Donald after the death of James V. was the escape of Donald Dubh from Edinburgh Castle in 1543.

[1] Pitcairn's Criminal Trials, vol. II., ad tempus.

How his deliverance was effected, whether the men
of Glencoe or other clansmen practised any further
" Fenian exploits" for the liberation of the heir of
the House of Isla, we have no materials for judging.
He himself, in the course of a correspondence with
Henry VIII. two years afterwards, acknowledged his
indebtedness for his freedom more to the good grace
of God than to the Scottish Government.[1]   It
is obvious that, owing to the political conditions of
the time, the Government's hold upon the Celtic
region had grown lax and feeble ; the Isles particularly were ripe for insurrection, and we may be
sure that no pains would be spared, no device left
untried, to effect the release of the captive who,
more than any other, had an hereditary right to the
homage of the ancient vassals of the Isles.

It will assist us to understand the influences that
moulded Clan Donald history at this period if we
give a brief glance at the relations between parties
in Scotland.   The Reformation was the most
important factor in the political conditions both of
England and Scotland at the time of Donald Dubh's
escape.   Among the large masses as well as the
middle classes of the population religious feelings
were deeply moved, and religious motives largely
operated ; but among the nobility the controversy
assumed, in a great degree, a political complexion,
and dominated, to a marked extent, the relations of
political parties.   As an inevitable consequence, two
factions arose out of the turmoil of the time ; on the
one hand, the Catholic party, headed by Cardinal
Beaton, wedded to the old order and opposed to the
policy of Henry VIII., the leader of the reformed
movement in England, and, on the other, the Pro-

[1] Document in State Paper Office.

testant party, under the leadership of the Earl of
Arran, favouring the attitude of the English monarch,
and encouraging his interference in the affairs of the
Scottish State.

Whatever estimate may be formed of the private
character of Cardinal Beaton, a question that we are
not called upon to discuss here, he was undoubtedly
a man of great political talent, and his maintenance
of a national and independent policy for Scotland is,
from a patriotic standpoint, worthy of commendation.
A determined foe of the Reformation, he was a
devoted upholder of the Roman See, as well as of
the alliance with France, all of which implied enmity
to England and hostility to Henry VIII., the political
head and mainspring of the Protestant cause in that
country.   Beaton had failed in his design upon the
Regency, but down to the day of his death he
exercised the largest measure of influence in the still
powerful party with which he was so closely allied.
The Earl of Arran, who, on account of his close
relationship to the Throne, was appointed Regent,
had embraced the principles of the Reformation,
but neither his political nor religious convictions
were sufficiently steadfast or profound, to cause him
to take a resolute or consistent attitude, in his
handling of the reins of his exalted office.

The interference of Henry VIII. in the affairs of
Scotland took the form of an attempt to negotiate a
marriage between the Prince of Wales and the
infant Queen of Scots.   Facilities for promoting this
match lay to his hand in the return of the Earl of
Angus and the exiled Douglasses, as well as of
numerous prisoners of rank taken at the disgraceful
raid of Solway in 1542, all of whom were strictly
enjoined by Henry to use their endeavours for the

furtherance of his pet scheme.   This scheme, had it
only aimed at a union honourable to both countries,
need not have been regarded with any suspicion,
even on the ground of patriotism ; but when other
designs were entertained subversive of the national
liberties, such as the surrender of the fortresses and
the acknowledgment of Henry's paramount authority,
those Scottish nobles who promised their support
were guilty of the most ignominious treachery.
Cardinal Beaton was, of course, the most prominent
in his opposition to the designs of the English King,
and left no means untried to thwart them.   Among
other means, he got Matthew, Earl of Lennox, to
return from abroad, and he being nearly related to
the Royal Family, Beaton proposed him for the
Regency in opposition to Arran, and thus wrought
upon the Regent's fears.

Whatever, in other circumstances, might have
happened, the Scottish factions were soon thrown
into each others' arms by the violent and precipitate
temper of the English King.   The disclosure of his
ulterior designs so alarmed statesmen of all parties,
that something like a rupture of diplomatic relations ensued, and the treaty for the marriage was
abandoned.   The coalition thus entered into by
Cardinal Beaton and the Regent soon produced
its natural results.   The Cardinal, who had prevailed upon the Earl of Lennox to come to Scotland
by holding out to him high prospects of political
advancement, now grew cold in his attentions when
he had no further ends for him to serve, and we are
not surprised to find this nobleman taking umbrage
at the treatment, espousing the cause of the party
opposed to the Cardinal, and becoming a strenuous
supporter of English influence in Scottish affairs.

Lennox had gone the length of securing the assistance of the French King for the prosecution of the
war with England, now regarded as inevitable, and
a French fleet actually arrived in the Firth of Clyde
laden with military stores and a sum of 10,000
crowns, to be distributed among the Cardinal's
friends.　The French Ambassador, not knowing
that the Earl of Lennox had recently changed his
political connection, allowed himself and the Earl
of Glencairn, a staunch upholder of the English
interest, to help themselves to the gold which he
had in his custody, and it was only after the
mistake could no longer be repaired that he
discovered how adroitly the two noblemen had
circumvented him.

It was at this juncture, when the Scottish body
politic was rent by conflicting interests, passions,
and intrigues, and English influence was actively
interposing in Scottish affairs, that Donald Dubh
once more made his *debut* upon the stormy theatre
of war.　At the time of his escape from Inchconnel,
forty years before, he had been proclaimed Lord of
the Isles with all the traditional rites and cere-
monies ; but now he lays claim to the Earldom of
Ross as well, and, as soon as circumstances permit,
addresses himself to the task of dislodging the Earls
of Argyle and Huntly from the possessions which
belonged to his ancestors, the former in the South
Highlands, the latter in the region of Lochaber.
Both these noblemen have received praise from
writers of history for their loyalty to the throne
during the confusion and political corruption of
these troublous times.　It must, however, be
remembered that the interests of both were intim-
ately bound up with the maintenance of the

established order, and that with Argyle especially,
threatened as he was with eviction, bag and
baggage, from the Lordship of the Isles, antagonism
to England—the ally of his foe—and consequent
support of the Scottish cause, was the only possible
line of action for the preservation of his estates.

When Donald Dubh found himself at large, he
realised the necessity of proceeding with caution
and deliberation. The most powerful of the Highland chiefs were still prisoners in the Castle of
Edinburgh, from which he had just escaped, and,
consequently, the Western Clans were bereft of
the hereditary leaders, without whose presence the
movement could not possibly gather its full and
legitimate force. In these circumstances a truce
was arranged with the Earl of Argyle to last till
May-day of that year; but although on the expiry
of the *induciae* both sides were engaged in hostilities,
these did not, at the outset, assume very formidable
proportions. At last an event occurred which
immediately and powerfully affected the position
and prospects of the new Lord of the Isles. The
Regent Arran, a man of indolent and facile disposition, did—on the suggestion of the Earl of
Glencairn—liberate the Highland chiefs, who had
been imprisoned since 1540 as hostages for the
peace of their districts. The object of Glencairn
clearly was to create such discord and civil strife
in Scotland as would absorb the energies of loyal
nobles and weaken the forces available for resisting
the designs of the English King. The conduct of
the Regent, assuming, as we may, that he was
sincere in his maintenance of the national integrity,
was little better than midsummer madness. He
took bonds from the liberated chiefs " that they

should not make any stir or breach in their country but at such time as he should appoint them," and, no doubt, they were delighted to obtain their freedom upon terms so easy ; but bonds imposed under such conditions were soon found to be value-less. It appears from Donald Dubh's correspondence with Henry VIII. that the Regent made overtures to him also to secure his submission and allegiance upon favourable terms ;[1] but in this also he was unsuccessful, and very shortly after the Chieftains of the Isles had shaken the dust of Edinburgh from their feet, Celtic Scotland was once more in the throes of a revolution.

The liberation of the Chiefs was soon followed by overt action on the part of the Lord of the Isles. He took the field with 1800 men, and, invading the terri-tories of Argyle, he plundered the country and put many of the vassals to the sword. In this, Donald had the unanimous support of the vassals of the Isles, with the single exception of James Macdonald of Dunnyveg, who withheld his personal co-operation. If Argyle in the South Highlands was sore beset by the Western Clans, the Earl of Huntly, as Lieutenant of the North and owner of extensive territories there, had similar difficulties to contend with. The follow-ing extract from the Council records of the Burgh of Aberdeen illustrates the feeling of insecurity that existed in the North, and the preparations for resistance that were being made against the antici-pated invasion from England, as well as expected incursions by Donald and his Islesmen :—

"January 26th, 1544.—The sayd day the hayll tooun beying varnit to this day be thair hand bell passand throcht all the rewis and stretis of this said toun be the berar therof on the quhilk he maid fayth in iugment and in speciale be the officiaris of the said

---

[1] Documents in State Paper Office.

burghe on the quhilks inlikwyise thai maid fayth in ingment and comperand for the maist part representand the haill body of the townn thar was presentit to thame the quenis grace lettres afor written ; ane one the sowme of four hundredth lib. xiiij lib. vjs. viid. of taxt, for furnesing of ane thousand horse to remain with the locumtenant on the bordouris, for resisting of our auld enemies of Ingland during the space of thre moneths, and als thair was presentit in ingment two writingis of the Erle of Huntlie locum-tenant generale of the North of Scotland be the sernandis upoun the said townn in fear of weir, with all necessaris as efferit, with twenty days vitelling to pas with the said locumtenent for resisting of Donald Ilis quhilk with his complices is cumand, as is allegit upoun the quenis landis of Ross for inuasion thairof and con-quesing of the same."

In the very midst of Donald Dubh's rebellion the Northern Highlands were plunged into still greater disorder by a feud that sprung up between John Moydartach of Clanranald and the Frasers of Lovat, and which resulted in the sanguinary battle of Kinloch Lochy, known in the Highlands as *Blar Leine,* and fought on the 15th July, 1545. The details of this tragic field will fall to be narrated in a subsequent volume. We refer to it at this stage to show that John Moydartach, by engaging Huntly and Lord Lovat, the partisans of the Crown, was fighting, not only for his own hand, but in the interests of the Lord of the Isles as well. In the meantime, the relations between Henry VIII. and the Scottish Government grew, if possible, more bitter. The English King sent an expedition, under the command of the Earl of Lennox, which did much havoc in the West Highlands. Arran was attacked and plundered, and the Castle of Brodick reduced to ashes, while the Island of Bute, with its Castle of Rothesay, was reduced. After an ineffectual attempt to take Dunbarton Castle, Lennox returned to Eng-land. On the 13th of August, 1545, the Scottish

24

Lords addressed a letter from Melrose to Henry
VIII., in which they advised an invasion of Scotland
in force, and that an expedition for that purpose
should be organised, under command of the Earl of
Hertford. Preparations were already in progress
for an invasion by land, as well as a naval descent
upon the West Coast, and, in the course of these,
negotiations were opened with Donald Dubh, who
was now at the head of the whole military strength
of the Isles. Alliances with England were nothing
new in the history of the House of Isla, and Donald,
true to his family traditions, and smarting under his
imprisonment of half a century, disclaimed allegiance
to Scotland, and, with the Earl of Lennox as inter-
mediary, entered into a treaty with the English
King. In the month of June, it is evident that the
communications passing between the English interest
and the Lord of the Isles had come under the notice
of the Scottish Government, and a Proclamation was
issued by the Regent Arran and his Council against
"Donald alleging himself of the Isles and other
Highlandmen his partakers." Donald and his accomplices were charged with invasions upon the Queen's
lieges, both in the Isles and in the Mainland,
assisted by the King of England, with whom
they were leagued, shewing that they purposed
bringing these under obedience to that Sovereign.
The Proclamation called upon them to desist from
such treasonable and rebellious conduct, failing
which they were threatened with serious pains
and penalties. It is thus apparent that before
we have any record of a formal league between
Donald Dubh and Henry VIII., the Scottish
Government regarded the alliance as practically
complete, and Henry's expedition to the West under

Lennox as in aid of the efforts of the Lord of the
Isles for the recovery of his patrimony.   This Proclamation failed, of course, to produce the desired
result, and processes of treason were commenced and
carried through as expeditiously as was compatible
with Parliamentary procedure.   So far as we can
ascertain, the first extant record of the league with
England bears the date of 23rd July, 1545, and is
contained in the " Commission from the Lord of the
Isles of Scotland to treat with the King of England,"
the tenour whereof follows :—

" Be it kend till all men be ye put wryt We Donald Lord of
ye Ilis and Erll of Roiss with adviss and consent of our barronis
and counsaill of ye Ilis that is to say Hector Maclane Lord of
Doward Jhonn Macallister Capitane of Clanranald Lord MacLeod
of Lewiss Alex^r MacLeod of Dunbeggane Murdoch Maclane of
Lochbouy Angus Maconill brudir german to James Maconill Allan
Maclane of Torloske brudir german to ye Lord Maclane Archibald
Maconill Capitane of Clan Hustein Alex^r Mackane of Ardnamurchan Jhonn Maclain of Coll gilliganan MacNeill of barray
Mackiynnan of Straquhordill Johnn Macquore of Ulwy Jhonn
Maclane of Ardgor Alex^r rannoldson of Glengarrie Angus ronaldson
of Cnoeddart Donald Maclane of Kengarloch, to have maid
constitud and ordauit and be yir our presentis makis constitutis
and ordanis giffand our full power express bidding and command
to honorable personis and our kynnsmen yat is to say Rore
Makallester elect to ye bishoppe of the Isles in Scotland and doyn
of Moruairin and Mr Patrik Maclain brudir german to ye said
Lord m^c lain bailze of ycomkill and iustice clerk of ye South Ilis
cointlie and sevralie our ald and indorsetit Comissionaris, We
beand bodely swarne to stand ferme and stable at all and haill ye
saidis Comissionaris promittis or does in our name and behalve
We neer to own in ye contrar of ye samyn and We admit ye sadis
Comissionaris to bind and to lowss to follow and defend to tyn
and wyn to end and compleit as such awin proper persins war
presentis in all materis as will be commandit yame be Mathew erll
of Lennox and secund persoun of ye realm of Scotland endowdit
and in speciall testifying our Landis instantlie be maid to aue
most nobill and potent prince Harye ye acht be ye grace of god

King of ingland france and ireland yir forsadis Comissionaris
haiffand our full power to acit and to end in all udir our
affairis concerning ye Kingis maieste of ingland france and
ireland and ye said erll of Lennox as ye said erll will comand.
Comanding yir our sadis Comissiouaris and for better sccuorite of
yis present we ye said Donald has affixit our proper seill wit our
hand at ye pen becaus we can not writ and has causit ye baronis
aboun writtin becaus thai co^d not writ to cause ane notar to
subscribe for yame w^t yair hand at ye pen w^t yair bodely auttie
neir to cum in ye contrar of ye samyn And als we have giffin
Commissioun to our saidis Comissiounaris to mak ye selis of yir
our baronis aboun wtin gif neid be or requirit ye qlk ye saidis
baronis has swarne afore ane notar publick to stand and abyd at
ye saidis selis[1] selit be saidis Comissionaris and nere to cum in ye
contrar of ye sam and has selit our proper seill and signet w^t ye
saidis Comissionaris for ye completing and ending of all besynes
comandit or requirit be ye said erll of Lennox In witness heirof
we have yir pret Comissioun afoir patrik Colquhoun of pemwul
Walter macfarlan of Ardlys Sr archibald m^cgillivray Vicar of
Killane Mr Jhonn Carswell notaris publick requirit to ye samyn
w^t witness."[2]

The foregoing document, drawn up in the island
of Eigg—or Ellancarne as it is designated in the
conclusion of the deed—contains the names of all
the Island vassals, with the exception already
referred to, and even the Lord of Dunnyveg was
efficiently represented by his brother Angus, who,
no doubt, was accompanied by a contingent of
fighting men from his native Isla. The deliberations which find expression in this remarkable
paper seem to have been conducted with a unity and
cohesiveness of purpose not always characteristic of
the policy of the Western Chiefs. Even MacIan of
Ardnamurchan—who, in former days, was wont to
play into the hands of the House of Argyle, acting
the part of jackal to the lion of Inverary—now falls

---

[1] "Seal" in this connection evidently means "signature."
[2] Extracted from Correspondence in State Paper Office.

in line with the rest of the Clan Donald chiefs. The leading motive of the movement was undoubtedly the attachment of the Islesmen to the historic family which had so long borne sway in the Western Highlands, and though the attitude of the Chiefs would not have been weakened by the vision of English gold held up to them by the emissaries of Henry, the history of the Highland people is very far from justifying the suspicion that mercenary motives played more than a very subordinate part in the support now accorded to the last representative of the House of Isla.

From the Isle of Eigg, a favourite rendezvous with the men of the Isles, the scene changes to the North of Ireland. There, about a week later, we find the Island Lord with all his barons, an army of 4000 men, and 180 galleys. The meeting place of the Council of the Isles was the chapter house of the Monastery of Greyfriars at Knockfergus, and there were also present Patrick Colquhoun and Walter Macfarlane, Commissioners of the Earl of Lennox[1]; also Walter Cluddy Constable, Henry Wyld Mayor, Patrick Macgelloquhowill and Nicolas Wild Bailies, of the same town. It is also interesting to note the presence of John Carswell, who afterwards rose to eminence as the first Protestant Bishop of the Isles, and whose edition of the prayer-book in the vernacular is one of the treasures of Gaelic literature. He signs and indorses, in the capacity of Notary Public, several of the more important documents written in the course of this unique correspondence with the English Govern-

---

[1] Agreement of Lord of the Isles and other Chieftains and Commissioners of Lennox, in State Paper Office.

ment. The Islesmen pledge anew their allegiance to the English monarch, and promise to do all in their power to promote the scheme which Henry still hoped to carry into effect, the marriage of the Prince of Wales and the infant Princess of Scotland. This is but a preliminary to other instruments of agreement and concord which are formulated upon the same days. In a letter of 6th August, from Donald to the Privy Council of Henry VIII., we have for the first time an intimation of the monetary assistance offered to him for his services, as well as to aid him in the recovery of his rights. This aid consisted of a gift of 1000 crowns, sent by the Privy Council by the hands of Patrick Colquhoun, who, in the interval since the meeting of Council at Eigg, has found time to be the bearer of English treasure to the Island Lord. This is accompanied by the promise of an annual pension of 2000 crowns for life, conditioned, of course, by the continuance of his allegiance—*ad vitam aut culpam.* The Commissioners from the Lord of the Isles have not yet, however, gone on their important errand to lay their master's commands before the King and Council of England. A series of Articles,[1] to be placed in the hands of the Island Deputies in support of their Commission, was drawn up on the 5th August; but it would appear that, on the arrival of the Earl of Lennox on the scene of Council, other Articles, similar in number and substance, but containing much additional matter, were substituted in their room, and as these shed an interesting light upon the transactions of the period, we propose to quote them here as fully and accurately as we can.

[1] Documents in State Paper Office.

" Item first, that quhare we desyrit in our artikills to your
Lordshipis bewrtt afore my lord therlle of Lenox coming (second
ppersoun of the realme of Scotland), his Lordship to be send in
Scotland w^t ane arme for settin fast of the Kingis enemys of
Scotland. In the nixt artikill quhar our Lord and Maister t' erll
of Ross and lord of the Ilis promittis that his Lordship shall
distroye the tane half of Scotland or than mak theyme to cum to
the Kingis maiesties obedience and to my Lord t' Erlle of Lenox
his hienes subject. The third artikill quhar the said erll of ross
our Maister   him becom the Kingis grace subject bodelye
sworne wyt the lord Maclane and the rest of the barronis of the
Ilis . and desyris the Kingis grace w^t awise of your Lordships his
good counsall to mak no aggreance with Scotland, and in speciall
w^t the erllis huntlie and argyll, wy^{t}out the said erll of ross, the
lord Maclane Captain of Clanranald wy^t the rest of the barronis of
the Ilis, the quhilkis ar becom the Kingis grace subjectis be
includit therin the fourt artikill quhar it specifyith of the Kingis
maiesteis most noble gudness and your Lordships his most honorable counsall hath written w^t patrick colquhoun seruaud to our
good lord t' erlle of Lenox to gif the said erll of ross ane yeirlie
pension of two thousand crownis for service doyne and to be doyne
of the quhilk sum his Lordship hath rasawit be the said patrick
Colquhoun xiiii. hundreth crownis w^t uderis presentis send be
t' erlle of Lennox as his discharge at more lenth beareth, of the
qlk yeirlie pension the said erlle of ross desyris sich suirness of
his hienes as sal be requirit rasonable be us his Commissionaris,
and his most noble hienes and your good Lordships thinkis
expedient, w^t his grace mainteinyng and defending the said erll of
ross injoeing and bruiking all heretages and possessionis that his
forbearis erlles of ross and Lordis of the Ilis bruikit of befoir.
The fift artikill and last of all beareth that quhar the said erll of
ross promittis to serve the Kingis maiestie and my lord t' erlle of
Lennox w^t the number of viii. thousand men, four thousand men
of the same now instanllie is come in the Kingis maiesteis boundis
of Ireland, the uther four thousand is keepand thair awin boundis
agains the erlles huntlie and argyill, the quhilk stayis the saidis
erllis to remane in thair awin boundis, and may not supplie nor
defend the bordoris of Scotland in contrarie the Kingis maiesteis
arme the said erll of ross desyris to have wagis to three thousand
of the said eytht thousand the uther five thousand to serve the

Kingis maiestie in favour of my lord t' erlle of Lennox not takand wagis and this my lordis the said erll of Ross the lord maclane and the rest of the barronies of the Ilis to becom the Kingis grace is subjectis as said is, in the fauor causing and your affectioun had in the said erlle of Lennox and in especialle be suir knowledge of the gudness that the Kingis most noble maiestie hath doyn and dalie dois to the said erll of Lennox.

" Item after the comying of the said erll of Lennox we hearand his Lordship's mynd concernynge the Kingis graces affaires with presents in or Lord and maistiris name the said erlle of ross and Lord of the Ilis, of my lord of Lennox wt the Kingis grace is arme pass uppon Dunbertan or uppon any uther the weast ptis of Scotland we sall mak the number of vi. thousand men wyth their galays and vesshells conforme to the said number to forme the Kingis graces and my lord errle of Lennox, and yf his Lordship pass uppon the erllis huntlie or Argyill we shall mak the holle number of viii. thousand, for yf we laif or awin boundis, It most needis that we laif sum men keepand theym, and those at remains at hoyme dois the Kingis grace als good service in defending agains the erllis huntlie and Argyill as they do that comynd furt.

" Item secondlie my lordis we exhort your Lordships to remembr and consider quhat honorable and faithful service we pinit to do the Kingis maiesties in or Liffis and honor and quhath our maister t' erll of ross hath refusit all offeris offerit unto his Lordship be the guvernor and Lordis of Scotland and in cause of our good lord t' erlle of Lennox is become the Kingis graces subject. And now lastlie hath made slachtir burnying of and herschipps upon the Scottis men takand the pursute of all Scotland upon him. This my Lordis because it is the Kingis graces and your Lordships let not the said erll of ross be dethroynit be the holle realme of Scotland, for if his boundis be destroyit, he may not mak the Kingis maiestie so good service as he may quhil his cuntrie is sawf, and considder quhat the Kingis maiestie lyekith to spend in his grace and my lord of Lennox affairis and that our Maistir and Lord is defended agains the Scottis men, wt the grace of god It shall redound in much more value to his maiesties is proffitt honor and obedience, the qlkand his grace walden have of Scotland If it shal be socht and win be the weast parts and Ilis in suiretie.

" Item thirdly becaus we have hard and considerit quhow that the Kingis maiestie and my lord t' erlle of Lennox hath beyne defraudit be the Lordis of Scotland, the quhilk schuld caus the

Kinge graces and your good Lords of the counsall to be the more warr with all the nation of Scottis, this for their frauds, and in speciall wyt we that is callit the wyld Ilis of Scotland, for the cans my Lordis we besech your Lordships to have no sich conseit in us, as we belieff suirlie your Lordships wisdom will not quharfor your Lardships sall consider we have beyne auld enemies to the realme of Scotland, and quhen they had peasthe with the Kingis hienes, they hanged hedit prisoned and destroied many of our Kyn friendis and forbears as testefyit be our Maistir terlle of ross now the Kingis grace subject the quhilk hes lyin in preson afoir he was borne of his modir, and nocht releissit wit thair will bot now laitle by the grace of God. In likewise the lord Maclane is fadir was cruillie murdessit onder traist in his bed in the town of edinbruighe be Sr John Cambell of Calder brudir to terlle of Argyill. The Captain of Clanranald the last yeir ago in his defence slew the Lord Lowett his sone and air, his thre brothir with xiii. score of men and many uther cruel slachter, burnying and herschep that hath betuix us and the sadis Scottis the qlk was lang to wrythe, for the qlk causis we are not able to agre w^t the sadis Scottismen, and now most of all can thai knaw that we ar becom the Kingis grace subjectis the hatrand wilbe the grittar betwixt us and them yan it was afoir, and

"Item fourtlie and last of all your Lordship to considder that sen we have no uther refuge bot onlie his most noble hienes and o^r good lord t' erlle of Lennox, the q^{lk} lord and we hath no help bot of his gracious hienes. And for the tyme is most convenient now betwix and Christmas to perseue Scotland, and that we are not best holdin w^t wittalis, and most able to do theym grittast skayth in cornis cattell goodis and biggynis to assay the said erll of Lennox and o^r maistir t' erll of ross be the Kingis grace is supple And or his hienes spend anything that may do his Maistir hurt it shalbe persewit gif our Maistir and Lord performe as we promist in his name, and It is now convenient to go to warr nor if continow longer becaus off my Lord terlle of Lennox he is not sett furtly and our Lord and maistir suppleit now instantlie, our enemy wilbe the more bawld uppoun us, and mak their vaunt that our Maister t' erlle of ross is service Is not acceptil be ye Kinge hienes, and in lyke manner the frenchmen will say that they hold the Kingis grace in sich besynes that his maiestie may not supple o^r Maistir nor persew his gracis rychtis of Scotland for feir of theym, and this we pray your Lordship to inform the Kingis hienes of the sam, that the precious and convenient tyme be no lost ye q^{lk} onis lost is unretrevable and on o^r Lyffis your Lordshippis had neir as good tyme as now.

"Finale my Lordis to concluid we pray your good Lordshopps to have us excusit of our lang wryttand and barbarous discourse to consider o^r mynd and not the wryttand that our mind is not to persuaed your Lordshipps w^t wordis, or to be desyras of the Kingis grace is money bot It shalbe onderstand be our good Lord t' erll of Lennox and theym that gois in his company as pleses the Kingis maiestie and your good Lord that quhar we desyre one crowin of his hienes we shall spend thre in his grace is service w^t the grace of God prayand Christ Jesu to have ye Kingis maiestie in keeping and yor Lordshipps, w^t aught as your Lordshipps thinkis expedient."

The foregoing lengthy statement exhibits a considerable amount of astuteness both in its conception and its terms, and the programme laid down, had it been pushed with vigour and determination, might have proved disastrous to the freedom of Scotland. The policy of keeping Argyle and Huntly engaged in the defence of their own territory, by maintaining an army in the Isles, and thus preventing their taking part in the general defence of the kingdom; the appeal to Henry's pride not to delay the invasion of Scotland lest the French should say that the war against their country absorbed the whole of his resources; all this displayed some diplomatic ability, while the closing paragraphs give vent to feelings of bitterness engendered by the memory of past oppression.

The letter of Donald Dubh to Henry VIII. concludes the more important portion of this correspondence on the part of the Lord of the Isles. It has never hitherto been published, and a document so remarkable both as to form and substance well deserves reproduction in the annals of the Clan. The tenour of this epistle is as follows :—

"To your most illustrious highness, most invincible King, from our inmost heart we offer most humble submission. We accept truly both the letter and the magnificent gift of your highness, rejoicing not so much in the gift itself as that your highness has deigned to look upon our low estate, and receive us into favour ; and this by suggestion of our singular friend, the Earl of Lennox, the true and undoubted Governor of Scotland, with whom we are ready even to the last day of our life, either in war or in peace to live, yea, if it should be necessary to meet death. We have come therefore most potent prince to your Majesty's country of Ireland attended by 4000 soldiers in that place (and also wherever your highness shall wish) according to the wish and desire of the foresaid Earl to offer most diligent service ; on which account our Commissioners and dear friends the bearers of these presents we have good to send to your most magnificent excellency of whom one is elected to the dignity of the bishopric of the Isles, the other, a brother of laird MacLane of Dowart, bailie of Icolumkill and chief Justiciar of the Isles ; to whom equally as to ourselves we wish faith to be given. And how great is the joy I feel, reflecting in my mind how your most Christian Majesty, imitating the example of Christ (who chose not the great and the rich but the poor and fishers to be disciples and Apostles), hath not disdained to stoop yourself to our humble con-dition although from our mother's womb we were bound in the yoke and servitude of our enemies, and to this very time overwhelmed with the filth of the prison and with intolerable fetters most cruelly bound. But lest by excessive and rude talk I cause any weari-ness to your magnificence, one thing is most certain that we by our Earl Lennox (who ought to govern Scotland) will as long as we live be most obedient and submissive to your most Christian Majesty, whom may Jesus Christ vouchsafe to preserve in pro-sperity of soul and body. At Knockfergus the fifth day of August 1545.

"To your most invincible highness the most obedient and humble Donald Earl of Ross and Lord of the Isles of Scotland, etc."

From the correspondence thus quoted at some length, we learn that certain definite proposals were made to Henry VIII. by Donald Dubh and his Council, proposals which had been clearly elicited by previous overtures on the part of the English King. The main drift of the message borne by the Commissioners was to the effect that the territories claimed by Donald Dubh were to be held of Henry VIII. as liege Lord, and that Donald was to assist in the invasion and conquest of Scotland with 8000 men, 3000 of whom were to be in the King's pay, while the rest were to be maintained at Donald's own charges. For these services the Lord of the Isles was to receive an annual pension of 2000 crowns, in addition to a gift of 1000 crowns already given him as a token of goodwill and as an earnest of future favours. The first payment included, along with 1000 crowns, 300 crowns additional, which must have been either an instalment of the annual pension voted by the English Privy Council, or a sum to account for the maintenance of the host. Armed with the fullest instructions, the two plenipotentiaries of the Lord of the Isles set sail for England.

The scene of diplomacy next shifts to the King's Manor of Oatlands, where Henry VIII. receives the Deputies of Donald Dubh on 4th September of that year. The primary result of the negotiations conducted there was an agreement arrived at between the English King and the Commissioners on the basis of the Island Lord's proposals. The agreement is in the following terms :—

" To all men to quhome theiss presentis sall cum be It known that quhair our Lord Donald of the Ilis and erll of ross has direckit us Lord Macallister eloct of the Ilis and deyn of Morverin and Maister patrick Maclano brudir german to Lord Maclane bailzie of ycomkil and justice clerk of the South Ilis as his commissionaris to the most noble hieast and victorius prence Henry be the grace of god King of Ingland France and Ireland supreme head

of the fayth and of the Churchis of ingland and Ireland supreme
hed not onlie to present a wrytting of en othe maid to his
Maiestie be the said erll of ross as in the letters thereof maid
selit and delyeverit is contenit bot also has giffen us authorite to
promiss and bynd the said erll and others adhering to him to
observe and keip sich covenants and conditions as sal be be us
aggreit their unto We theirfore the said Commissionaris considering the grit gudness speciall favour and benignite of the Kingis
said maiestie speciallie that it plesis the same to grant unto the
said erll a yeirlye pension of two thousand crownis as appearis by
his hienes lettres patentis made of the same and that furthermore
his maiestie is content so to accepit the said orll and uther to him
adhering unto his protection as if ony aggrement be maid wythin
the realme of Scotland to comprehend the same Comissionaris doo
promiss for in the behalf of the said erll that they sall trewlie and
faythfullie serve his maiestie to their powaris and to the anoyances
of the governor and his partakers in the realme of Scotland we
shall not entre any practiss of agrement wyth t' erllis of huntlie or
Argyill or any of the realme of Scotland or other in their name or
otherwise to the Kingis maiesti's prejudice, but always persist and
continow the Kinge maiestis trew ffrinds and subject wythout
doing any act to the contrarye And uthers the Kingis maiestie
sendis at this present th' erll of Lennox and his company th' erlle
of Osmond and Osserey of Ireland with a number of men to invade
the realm of Scotland and besides general annoyance to be doon in
burnying herwing and spoiling as they have opportunitie contre
so farre as Stirling iff they may see the enterprise faisable   The
said Comissionaris promiss that the said erll an others to him
adhering shall furnishe presentlie in the said enterprise to goo
under the rule and leading of the said erll of Lennox VIII
thousand men so long as the said erll of Lennox shall remayn in
the countrey of the erlle of Argyill and for the tyme the said erll
of Lennox shall be in any other parte of Scotland the said erll of
ross and others shall furnishe only VI thousand and tother II
thousand to be employed otherwise at home in the noyaunce of
the said erll of Argilis country in the meane season   In which
case the kingis maiestie is content uppon such service doon to
allowe unto the said erll and others besides the number furnished
at the kingis maiesti's charge out of Ireland wage for three
thousand of their said men for the space of two monthis after such
rate as highnes is accustomed to pay to his own.

"In witnes hereof we have subscribed these presentis with our own hande and sette the seal of the said erll our Master delyward by him unto us for that purpose at the Kingis manor of Otland ye fourt daye of September ye yeyr of God anno fourtie fyef yeyrs."

The Commissioners from the Lord of the Isles, in addition to the foregoing agreement, bore with them a letter direct from Henry in answer to that which Donald had sent to the English King a month previously. This letter is in the following terms :—

"Right trusty and right well beloved Cousyn we grete you well and late you wite that we have recyved your letters and wid of your submission to our service and allegeannce made by our welbeloved the Bishop elect of thyles and the lord Maclane's brother which we have taken in verrye good and thankfull parte And we have harde the credence which they had to declaire unto us on your behaulf and having communed thereupon with our right trusty and right welbeloved Cousin therlle of Lennox and the rest of our counsall we have made such an honorable answar to the same as you shall have good cause in reason to be contented likeas presently our said consin of Lennox at his coming hither and the said bishop and the lord Maclane's brother will signify unto you shall proyve by such writinge as they bringe with them Praying you good Cousin to proceed like a noble man to the revenge of such dishonoures as your enemyes and ours to have doon both to you and to us and to retrieve the same as moch as you can and you shall well prove that you have given yourself to

the servyce of such a Prynce as will consider your welldoing
herein and the good service which you shall minister unto us in
this behalf has the same shall redound to your own benefit and
comeditie Given under our signet at o^r manor of Oteland the
nyth daye of September the xxxviith yere of our Reign."

A letter in precisely similar terms was addressed
by Henry to Hector Maclean of Dowart, whose
name appears at the beginning of the list of Island
barons, and who seems to have taken a leading part
in all the negotiations connected with Donald Dubh's
rebellion and his treaty with the English Government. He seems to have naturally stepped into his
hereditary position as Seneschall or Steward of the
Isles, and his well-known ability in war and council
qualified him to be Donald's chief adviser during his
brief and troubled rule. The Commissioners of the
Lord of the Isles, Roderick MacAlister, Dean of
Morvern, and Patrick Maclean, Justiciar of the
South Isles, having carried out to the letter the
instructions wherewith they had been charged,
returned to Knockfergus. It was understood that
the Earl of Lennox was to lead an expedition against
the West of Scotland, assisted by the Lord of the
Isles, with eight thousand men. It was stipulated,
in terms of the agreement already quoted, that so
long as Lennox remained in the country of Argyle,
the forces of Donald were to aid him in undiminished
strength, but on his proceeding to any other part of
Scotland, he should be accompanied by six thousand
men. It was also arranged that the Earl of Ormond
should levy two thousand " kerns and gallowglasses"
to assist Lennox in his campaign, while the Irish
Privy Council made all necessary preparations to
equip this force for military duty.

Matters were thus maturing rapidly for an invasion of Scotland in force, and vexed as that country

was at the time by civil and religious discord, it is hard to say what the result might have been had not circumstances intervened to postpone decisive action. At this particular moment the Earl of Hertford was preparing to invade Scotland, and for some reason which history does not record, Lennox, along with other Scottish nobles in the English interest, was summoned to his camp. Lennox, who seems all along to have displayed a lack of promptitude and resolution, lingered among his English friends, and his procrastination proved fatal to the projected descent upon the West of Scotland. Donald Dubh and his Council had all along pressed upon their English allies the necessity of immediate action if success was to crown their efforts, but now the golden opportunity was lost, and the Lord of the Isles, after waiting for Lennox till his own patience and that of his followers was exhausted, and becoming concerned about his own interests in Scotland, returned thither with his army. Shortly thereafter discord and contention, the inevitable percursors of failure, began to appear among the barons of the Island Council. The distribution of the gold given by Henry VIII. for the payment of a section of the Highland army awakened murmurings and discontent. Hector Maclean, Lord of Dowart, had been entrusted with the disbursement of the funds, but whether the distribution was not impartially conducted, or some other unrecorded causes operated, it is clear that the treasure-laden Argosy, which, according to M'Vurich,[1] came from England to the Sound of Mull, had a demoralising effect upon the unity and loyalty of Donald Dubh's following, and

---

[1] Reliquiæ Celticæ, vol. II., p. 167.

his once formidable array became a dissolving scene
of anarchy, and melted away like a snow wreath in
thaw.

When the Earl of Lennox arrived in Ireland he
found, not only that the armament on which he so
much relied had quitted Knockfergus for the Isles,
but that on arriving at its native shores it had been
dispersed, resolved into its constituent elements.
He, however, determined to avail himself of the
force that was being organised by the Earl of
Ormond, under instructions of the Irish Privy
Council, for the invasion of Scotland, and pending
the completion of the preparations, he despatched
Patrick Colquhoun with a few vessels to the Isles,
with the view of ascertaining whether Donald Dubh
remained loyal to Henry, and if an army could still
be raised to help in the projected invasion. On the
17th November Lennox sailed from Dublin with a
considerable and well-equipped fleet and 2000 Irish
soldiers, with the Earl of Ormond in command.
Meanwhile the Castle of Dunbarton, one of the main
objects of the intended attack, had been delivered
into the hands of the Regent, and the Earls of
Lennox and Ormond, on learning this, as well as
becoming fully aware of the hopeless disorganisation
among the barons of the Isles, seem to have
abandoned aggressive action in the West. The
records[1] from which we derive much of our knowledge of Scottish history in this age break off
abruptly in October, 1545, and we are left in comparative ignorance of many of the events that
followed. According to MacVurich, Donald Dubh
accompanied the Earl of Lennox back to Ireland,
with the view of raising a new force for the pursuit

[1] State papers.

25

of his cause in the Scottish Isles ; but we gather
from the same authority that on his way to Dublin
he died at Drogheda of a fever of five nights.   Mac-
Vurich says that he left neither son nor daughter,
but according to the documents in the State Paper
Office, already quoted at such length, in his dying
moments he bequeathed his affection to the English
King, to whom also he commended the care of his
natural son.[1]   Thus died Donald Dubh, after a
gallant though unsuccessful struggle to recover and
maintain the power and possessions of his fathers.
He cannot justly be blamed for disloyalty to Scotland and trafficking with her foes ; for if Scotland
was his mother country, she acted from his infancy
as a cruel and relentless stepmother, to whom he
owed neither gratitude nor affection, but who had
robbed him of his patrimony, cradled him in a prison,
and placed the stigma of illegitimacy on his name.
Loyalty among those of his time who owed more
than he did to their country, was scarce as roses in
December, and it was not to be expected in one who,
like the last of the House of Isla, had been the
victim of half-a-century of wrong.   Donald Dubh
must have inherited much of the intrepidity of his
father when his ardour was not quite crushed by
fifty years of confinement.   Instead of suffering his
spirit to be broken, his courage survived the squalor
and the fetters, the lion though caged was a lion
still, and as soon as he trod his native heather, he
shows the imperial spirit of his race by taking the
place which by rights was his at the head of the
vassals of the Isles.   The Earl of Lennox paid every
mark of respect to the memory of the departed
chief, and his obsequies were celebrated with a

[1] Gregory's History *ad tempus.*

magnificence acceptable to the minds of his Island vassals.

We have it on the authority of Tytler[1] that Donald Dubh, having left no legitimate heir of his body, nominated as his successor to the Lordship of the Isles James Macdonald of Dunnyveg, and that, notwithstanding the fact that he alone, among the Highland chiefs, refrained from following his banner. That his brother Angus, however, appears among the barons of the Isles who constituted the court of the late Lord seems to indicate that the Chief of Clann Iain Mhoir may have been at heart, if not ostensibly, in sympathy with the movement. The Chief of Sleat. was a minor, and in the unsettled condition of affairs, if the Lordship of the Isles had any chance of being maintained upon the old footing it must be represented by a capable and mature head. Failing a descendant of Donald of Harlaw to succeed Donald Dubh, the representation naturally devolved upon the head of the family of John Mor Tainistear.

The Earl of Lennox, who still contemplated the conquest of Scotland, sent messengers to the Isles with intimation of Donald's death, as well as his nomination of his successor, and shortly thereafter James Macdonald of Dunnyveg was elected by the clansmen to assume the vacant honour. We find, however, that while the cadet families of Macdonald favoured his pretensions, the majority of the other vassals—including such powerful chiefs as Maclean, Macleod of Lewis, Macleod of Harris, along with the Macneills, Mackinnons, and Macquarries—were opposed to the election.[2] A reaction had set in against the English alliance, and the Highland Chiefs, beginning to anticipate the probable failure

[1] Vol. V., p. 406.   [2] Gregory *ad tempus*.

of English designs in Scotland, were endeavouring to make their peace with the Regent Arran.

Meanwhile the messengers of Lennox returned to Dublin bearing letters from James Macdonald of Dunnyveg, "which now declareth himself Lord of the Isles by the consent of the nobility of the Insulans as the bearers affirm," to the Privy Council of Ireland. On their arrival at the Irish capital on the 10th February, 1546, a plenipotentiary from the Lord of Dunnyveg, who accompanied the messengers to Ireland, was dispatched at the request of the new Lord to deliver an important letter to the King of England. This letter was in due course delivered, and as it represents the last flickering flame of Celtic sovereignty in the Isles, its precise terms may here be quoted :—

"Att Arnamurchan, the 24th day of Januar, the yeir of God ane thowsand fyef hundyr 46 yeir

"We James McConaill of Dunnewaik and ye glinnis, and aperand aeyr of ye Yllis grantis us to sene speciall letter deretik fra your Lordschip to owr knyis men and alyas thchyng the effecte and forme of yair promyssis to ye Kyng of Ynlandis Majeste to fortyfe and suple our noble cusyng Mathew Erle of Lennox. Quairfoir we exort and prais your Lordschip, my Lord Deput of Yrland, with ye weill awyissit Consall of Duplyn, to schaw in owr behalf and exprem to ye Kingis Majeste, that we are reddy, eftir our extrem power, our Kinyesman and alya namely our cusyng Alan McKlayn of Gyga, Clanronald, Clanechanroun, Clancayn, and our awin sowrname, bayth north and sowth, to tak ane pairt with ye said Erll of Lenox, or ony oder qwhat sumever, ye Kingis Majeste plaissis, to have antyrize or constitut be his grace, in Scotland ; leilly and trewly the foirsaid Kingis Majeste sendand pairt of power to us, in company with ye said Erll of Lenox in ane honest army to ye Yll of Sanday, besyd Kintyer, at Sanct Patrikis day next to cowm, or yairby, athowe ye said maist excellent Prence giffand to us his Majestes raward and sikar, band conformand and equivalent his Gracis band maid to our cheyf maister Donald Lord Yllis, whom God asolzeit, ye quhilk deid in his Graceis serwece

yis beand acceptibill promist and admittit, we require twa or thre
schyppis to be send to us to ye abowen expremit place, with yois
berar Hector Donaldsone, beand ane pylayt to ye sammyn, 20
dayes or ye army cowmes, that we might be fornest and gadderit
agayns ye comyng of ye said army ; to quhawm plais your Lordschip geif firm credence in our behalf. And for kepying and
obserwyng of yir presente promittes, desyring siklyke formaly to
be send to us with ye said schippis, we haif affixit our proper seill
to the samyng, with our subscription manuall, the day, zeir, and
place abown expremit.

"JAMES McCONIL of Dunnewaik and Glennis."

The overtures of the Lord of Dunnyveg did not,
so far as we can gather, meet with any response
from the English King or his Council. The reasons
for this oversight, so inconsistent with Henry's
policy in the past, are to be found in contemporary
history. For one thing, the Earl of Lennox, who the
previous year had by his delay on the English
borders led to the failure of Donald Dubh's rebellion
now by undue haste rendered abortive the proposals
of the new Lord of the Isles. Without waiting for
the return of his own envoy from the Isles bearing
communications from James Macdonald of Dunnyveg, he had, with the Earl of Ormond, led an
expedition to the Western Isles, which eventually
succeeded in nothing, because it had attempted
nothing beyond a naval demonstration ; and now
when the messengers from Macdonald arrived at
Dublin, the absence of Lennox, who was the mainspring of Henry's designs and the chief instrument
of his policy in Scotland, proved disastrous to the
new undertaking. On the other hand, Henry VIII.,
deeply engrossed in the intrigues with the Scottish
nobles that led to the murder of Cardinal Beaton,
found his hands too full to permit attention to the
particular detail of his policy which affected the

Isles of Scotland. It was not, we suppose, that he underestimated the importance of this particular card in the diplomatic game which he was playing, but he seems to have put off consideration of it to a more convenient season. By the time he was prepared to take it up again, the Lord of Dunnyveg had abandoned his claim. Having met with no active co-operation from England in vindicating the position to which he was elected, he took no overt action, subsided once more into the attitude of a loyal subject, and was restored to favour with the Scottish Regent. This was the final episode in the eventful history of the Island Lordship, and with it passed away the last vestige of hope among the Clan Donald vassals that the ancient principality, which had withstood the political storms of ages, might yet be restored.

CHAPTER XIII.

SOCIAL HISTORY.

Structure of Celtic Society.—The Council of St Finlaggan.—
Accounts of Proclamation of Lords of the Isles.—An Inde-
pendent Mortuath.—Tanistry.—The Toshach.—The Judge.
—Officials.—Relation to the Land.—The Tribe-lands.—
Demesne and Church Lands.—Law of Gavel.—The Nobility
and Commonalty.—Mackintosh Charter.—Herezeld Blodwite.
—Ward and Relief.—Marriage Law.—Hand-fasting.—State
and Wealth of Island Princes.

THE Lordship of the Isles, as must appear to our
readers, was the most considerable survival in
Scotland of the old Celtic system which in earlier
ages so widely prevailed. It was on account of the
truly Celtic character and spirit of the heads of the
House of Isla and their maintenance of the traditions
of the Gael, that the distinctively Celtic elements of
society throughout the Western Highlands clung so
tenaciously to the order of things represented in the
institutions of the Island Lordship. We have seen
that the history of this principality was to a large
extent a conflict between the two sets of social
forces represented by the words Celt and Saxon.
In the course of our narrative it was felt to conduce
to clearness if we dealt separately and with greater
minuteness with those characteristics of Gaelic
society embedded in the systems that prevailed
under the Clan Donald chiefs. We therefore
propose in this chapter to glance, not exhaustively
or with great or original research, at the structure

of Celtic social polity and at the conditions of social life, as both these are connected directly or indirectly with the history of the Lordship of the Isles. It can hardly be expected that, in a country where Celticism and Teutonism co-existed so long during ages of which the social history is very obscure, we should be able to find the former flourishing in a condition unaffected by the predominant influence of the latter. As a matter of fact, much of our knowledge regarding the ancient Celtic polity of Scotland is arrived at by inference and deduction, aided by what is known of other Celtic lands such as Ireland and Wales, rather than from actually ascertained facts. The evidence is to a large extent circumstantial rather than direct. Our enquiries must be begun, continued, and ended amid circumstances largely conditioned by feudal influences, and in the midst of these we can obtain but occasional and dim conceptions of Celtic polity in its pristine integrity.

Feudalism had gained a thorough ascendancy in Scotland in the twelfth century, when the Clan Cholla emerge out of the obscurity in which the Norse occupation had placed them, and although Somerled and his descendants strenuously opposed its encroachments upon their own domains, that system was gradually becoming the most powerful influence in the political life of the country. In one respect, viz., their relation to the Crown, Celticism and feudalism produced similar results. If the great feudal baron, the lord of wide acres, who through his ownership of the soil wielded supreme power over his vassals, often acted as an independent prince, the great Highland chief, who, as head of his tribe, possessed their undying homage, was equally disposed to assert his independence; and at some critical periods both proved equally dangerous to the authority, and even the existence, of the State.

In considering the structure of Celtic society, we may naturally expect that the growth and development of the system should proceed according to the analogy of all organic progress. In nature we find organisms adapting themselves to their environment, and·the functions which their surroundings compel them to discharge inevitably lead to the development of special organs. The complex organism of society is no exception to the rule, and it will be found that the peculiarities of Gaelic society owe their special form and character to the exigencies of its history. In early times, and before the growth of those great and manifold industries which have arisen in modern times, and are not directly connected with pastoral or agricultural pursuits, society was solely dependant upon the primary products of the soil. Hence, as might be expected, the organisation of ancient society, with its gradation of ranks and differentia-tion of functions and offices, was conditioned by its relation to the occupancy of land. As of other branches of the great Aryan Family, this is true of the two kindred branches of that family, the Celt and the Teuton. Much of the philosophy of their social development is found in their respective methods of occupying and possessing land. While there are certain resemblances, as might be expected, between the land system of the Celt and of the Teuton, we find also wide and deeply-seated distinc-tions. There are two leading types of land tenure to be met with in the ancient history of nations, one or other of which is characteristic of all European

nations—indeed, it may almost be said of all nations
—one of which may be described as feudal and the
other as tribal. According to the former of these,
the land was the absolute property of the overlord,
who exacted from the occupiers military service, or
such commutation thereof as he might accept,
while, according to the latter, the land was
the property of the community or tribe, whose
patriarchal head or chief exercised superiority over
it in name and on behalf of the tribe. Variations of
each of these types no doubt are observable, owing
to the mingling of races and the consequent modification of culture and institutions which now and
then occurred during the progress of so many ages ;
but the systems stand out clear and distinct in their
main character and outlines. It seems fairly well
proved by the learned researches of the best
authorities that the land system of Teutonic nations
was feudal, and that of Celtic nations tribal and
patriarchal. The vassal of the feudal baron owed
allegiance to him, not as the head of his race, but as
the superior of the land he occupied ; while the
Celtic vassals owed allegiance to their chief, not
primarily as the lord from whom they derived the
right to till the soil or pasture their flocks, but as
the head of the race to which they owed their origin.
This tribal tenure, with its various characteristics,
became in historic times subject to many modifica-
tions, through its contact with the feudal system,
but its main features are not difficult to perceive ;
and it is interesting to observe this common property in land surviving in the township system which
prevails to some extent in the crofting areas of the
Western Isles.[1] A modern writer, one of the most

[1] Skene's Celtic Scotland, vol. III., p. 378, et seq.

learned of our Scottish historians, seeks to minimise
the distinctions between the social polity of the
Teuton and the Celt.[1] He does not admit that the
definition of "patriarchal" at all applies to the latter
as distinguished from the former, and he maintains
that the land tenure of the Celt is not based upon the
principles of the community, in which all share alike,
but upon those of the kingdom, with its various
gradations both of property and rank. While it is
possible unduly to accentuate the differences between
the two phases of polity, it is equally so to ignore
those differences. The principles of the kingdom are
no doubt traceable in the structure of Celtic society,
but this does not imply that the relation of the community to the land was ought else than tribal, and
this we hope, in some measure, to indicate in the
course of the present chapter.

The Lordship of the Isles having survived as a
form of Celtic polity for hundreds of years after the
dissolution of the great tribes or Mortuaths of Scotland, affords us at some points an interesting light
upon the social life of the Gael in ancient times.
Hugh Macdonald, the Seanachie of Sleat, has conferred a boon upon the students of Highland history
if for naught else for the record he has left of the
crowning of the Lord of the Isles, as well as of the
Council of Finlaggan, with its gradations of social
rank.[2] The proclamation of the Kings of Innse-Gall
was a ceremony of much display and pomp, as well as
affording evidence of the poetic symbolism characteristic of the people. The Bishops of Argyle and the
Isles, on account of their territorial connection with
these Island magnates, gave the benediction of the

[1] Robertson's Scotland under her Early Kings, vol. II., p. 197, et seq.
[2] Collect. de Reb. Alb., p. 296-97.

Church to the function, while the Chieftains of all the families and a ruler of the Isles were also present on the occasion. The newly proclaimed King stood on a square stone seven or eight feet long, with a foot-mark cut in it, and this gave symbolic expression to the duty of walking uprightly and in the footsteps of his predecessors, while his installation into his dignities and possessions was also in this fashion set forth. He was clothed in a white habit as a sign of innocence and integrity of heart, and that he would be a light to his people and maintain the true religion. The white apparel did afterwards belong to the poet by right, probably, though the seanachie does not say so, that it might inspire him to sing of the heroes of the past. Then he was to receive a white rod in his hand, the whiteness indicating that though he had power to rule it was not to be with tyranny and partiality, but with discretion and sincerity. Then there was given to him his fore-fathers' sword, signifying that his duty was to protect and defend his people from the incursions of their enemies in peace or war, as the customs and obliga-tions of their predecessors were. The ceremony being over, mass was said after the blessing of the Bishop and seven priests, the whole people pouring forth their prayers for the success and prosperity of their newly created Lord. When they were dis-missed the Lord of the Isles feasted them for a week thereafter, and gave liberally to the monks, poets, bards, and musicians.

The foregoing description is in almost all its details identical with Martin's account of the cere-monial prevalent early in the eighteenth century in connection with the entrance of a new chieftain upon the Government of his clan. The Lordship of

the Isles had fallen about two hundred years previous
to this time, yet the custom of his day is carefully
modelled upon the time-honoured ceremony of the
crowning of the Lords of the Isles; and Martin
having been by birth and upbringing a Skyeman
and a native of Troternish, it is highly probable that
he refers to the inauguration of the barons of Sleat
into the Chiefship of Clan Uisdein. The only variation is that the young chieftain stood upon a
pyramid of stones while his friends and followers
stood round about him in a circle, his elevation
signifying his authority over them, and their
standing below their subjection to him, also that
immediately after the proclamation of the chief, the
chief Druid (or Orator) stood close to the pyramid
and performed a rhetorical panegyric setting forth
the ancient pedigree, valour, and liberality of the
family as incentives to the young chieftain and fit
for his imitation. Hugh Macdonald indicates the
presence of the bard at the older ceremonial, though
he says nothing about the metrical effusion in which
the event must always have been celebrated. The
office of the bard had also been closely associated
with the coronation of the Celtic Kings of Scotland,
and even after the days of David I., when a feudal
monarchy was firmly established on the throne, the
Celtic ceremonial continued in use after the feudal
observances were concluded, and the bard recited
the royal genealogy in Gaelic to show that the
Kings ruled over the realm of Scotland by the right
of long descent, and as the representatives of the
line of Alban's Kings.[1] The coronation stone seems
to have been a common feature of these Celtic
celebrations, and in the stone on St Finlaggan Isle

[1] Robertson's Scotland under the Early Kings, vol. II., p. 54.

we have something similar to the *lia fail*, or stone of destiny, still to be seen beneath the coronation chair at Westminster, a survival of the immemorial custom among ancient peoples of marking, by monuments of stone, events which they desired to keep in perpetual remembrance. That the ceremony thus described by the authorities quoted was based upon ancient Irish usage seems to be beyond question, and there is evidence that the custom survived in Ireland as late as the sixteenth century, and probably existed there up to a later day. Edmund Spenser, author of the "Fairy Queen," who spent many years in that country as secretary to Lord Grey of Wilton, gives an account of the installation of a chief among the Irish, which by reason of its confirmation of the statements of Highland authorities is deserving of literal quotation :— "They use to place him that shall be their Captain upon a stone always reserved to that purpose, and placed commonly upon a hill. In some of which I have seen formed and engraven a foot ; whereon he, standing, receives an oath to preserve all their ancient former customs inviolate ; and to deliver up the succession peaceably to his Tanist ; and then hath a wand delivered to him by some whose proper office that is, after which, descending from the stone, he turneth himself round thrice forwards and thrice backwards."[1] Hugh Macdonald does not inform us where the coronation of the Lords of the Isles actually took place, but the inference to be drawn from his description is that *Eilean na Comhairle*, the Island of Council, was the scene of that ceremonial. There would be no reason to doubt such a conclusion were it not that the only other reference

[1] View of Ireland, by Edmund Spenser.

to the Proclamation of the Lord of the Isles locates
the crowning of Donald of Harlaw at Kildonan, in
the Island of Eigg. While this was undoubtedly
the case, we think it still the more probable view
that the islet on Loch St Finlaggan, with its table
of stone, and its place of judgment, close by the
larger isle, on which stood the chapel and palace of
the kings, must have been the scene of the historic
rite, and that the proclamation of Donald as Lord
of the Isles at Kildonan must have arisen out of
conditions which at this time of day it is difficult to
estimate. It seems, however, that the Isle of Eigg
must have been regarded as a suitable place of
gathering for the vassals of the Isles, for we find the
Council of Donald Dubh assembled there in 1545,
when they appointed Commissioners to treat with
Henry VIII. It is to be noted that the place of
sepulture for the wives and children of the Lords of
the Isles was on the larger isle on Loch Finlaggan,
while the Island potentates themselves were always
borne in solemn state to the sacred Isle of Hy.

The supplementary passage to that in which the
historian of Sleat records the proclamation of the
Lords of the Isles, and in which he describes the
constitution of the Council of Finlaggan, is also
worthy of consideration in any review of the social
history of the Island Lordship. The constitution
or government of the Isles, he says, was thus :—
" MacDonald had his Council at Island Finlaggan in
Isla to the number of 16, namely, four thanes, four
armins, that is to say, four lords or sub-thanes, four
bastards (i.e.) squires or men of competent estates,
who could not come up with Armins or Thanes, that
is freeholders or men that had the land in factory as
Magee of the Rinds of Isla, MacNicoll in Portree in

Skye, and MacEachren MacKay and MacGillivray in Mull. There was a table of stone where this Council sat in the Isle of Finlaggan ; the whole table with the stone on which MacDonald sat were carried away by Argyle with the bells that were at Icolmkill. Moreover, there was a judge in every Isle for the discussion of all controversies who had lands from MacDonald for their trouble and likewise the 11th part of every action decided. But there might still be an appeal to the Council of the Isles. MacFinnon was obliged to see weights and measures adjusted, and MacDuffie or Macphee of Colonsay kept the Records of the Isles."

We have here a complete and self-contained system of Gaelic polity representing in outline the action of a free and autonomous principality. The question naturally arises, whence does it come ? and before entering with any minuteness into the condition of things adumbrated by the Seanachie, it may be desirable to point out the historical relation of the Lordship of the Isles to the rest of Celtic Scotland. On this point it will be unnecessary to dwell at length, inasmuch as certain aspects of it were dealt with in an early chapter. Historians are agreed that Scotland, during the period of the Picts or ancient Caledonians, was divided into seven provinces, all owning the supremacy of one *Ardrigh*, or high King, while each of the provinces was under the government of a king of less dignity and power than the supreme head, called *Oirrigh*, but who within his own dominions exercised something ʿapproaching absolute power. Two of the leading authorities are somewhat at issue as to one at least of the leading features of Celtic polity in the great provinces or Mortuaths. Dr Skene maintains that

these petty kingdoms under their Mormaors endured
as part of the national Celtic system, until it gave
way in the eleventh and twelfth centuries before the
establishment of a feudal monarchy, and that these
Mormaors were their hereditary rulers.[1] Dr J.
Stewart, on the other hand, upholds the view that the
seven provinces of Celtic Scotland disappeared with
the Union of Dalriada and Pictavia in the ninth
century; that this fusion of the two kingdoms
resulted in a large increase of the power and
possessions of the supreme King, owing to the
annexation of considerable portions of the tribe-
lands to the crown, and that the Mormaors were
not the hereditary kings or provincial orrighs, but
stewards appointed by the crown and answerable
for the crown dues. In most cases the hereditary
rulers stepped into the fiscal office. We are disposed
to adopt the views of Dr Stewart on this matter as
that best borne out by the ascertained facts of
history. It is, on the whole, the more feasible view
that the seven divisions disappeared as hereditary
principalities or kingdoms after the Pictish monarchy
was replaced by the Scoto-Irish dynasty of Kenneth
MacAlpin, and that Southern Scotland became one
state with an undivided rule. It also seems well
established that it is only after this period of national
consolidation that there is any record of the title
Mormaor being used, that being the time *ex hypothesi*
that these provincial officers came into existence;
while in Galloway and Lothian, which were not
united with Scotia until after the period of
Mormaors, such a name never appears. On the
whole there seems no sufficient evidence of any
trace either in Gaelic history, poetry, or tradition

[1] Skene's Celtic Scotland, vol. III. The Book of Deer, preface, pp. 78, 79.

26

of the term Maor or Mormaor as applied to the chief or king either of a province or tribe, certainly not to any of the hereditary rulers of Argyle and the Isles, which Dr Skene reckons as one of the seven ancient provinces of Alban. The term *Maor*, whether *Mor* or otherwise, always means an officer acting under some superior authority for the administration of law, or the collection of rates or dues, or some other civil or ecclesiastical purpose. Dr Skene emphasises the significance of a passage in the Book of Deer in which the names of the seven Mormaors of Buchan appear as flourishing during the five centuries between the foundation of the Celtic monastery in the time of Columba and the reign of David I., and this he regards as a confirmation of his view. It must be borne in mind, however, that the historical entries in the Book of Deer were written in the eleventh century, three hundred years after the Mormaors, according to our view, had superseded the Orrighs or provincial Kings, and the name had long become the traditional title of these ancient *reguli*, and as a part of the social system were only passing away. It was very natural, therefore, for the writer to describe the ancient hereditary rulers of Buchan in the terms most intelligible in his own time.

In what relation did the Lords of the Isles and the community, of which they were the heads, stand to the general system of Celtic Scotland? Dr Skene's theory that the *reguli* of Argyle, Somerled and his predecessors, were the representatives of the Mormaors of Oirthirghael, and that the tribe over which they reigned formed one of the seven great communities of ancient Pictdom, would no doubt fit in symmetrically with his main historical induction.

We have not, however, disputed the general trend of Gaelic and Irish tradition, that the line of Somerled was a branch of the Scoto-Irish race, owning allegiance to the Kings of Dalriada during the separate existence of that dominion, but after the ninth century becoming the chief Dalriadic family in Oirthirghael and Innse-Gall. This question has been already discussed by us, but we wish, in this connection, to lay stress upon the fact that the branch of the Clan Cholla, represented by the tribe of Somerled, rose into eminence after the disappearance of the seven provinces that constituted the national system of Scotland, and that, therefore, their position was absolutely unique. Hence it was that the Lordship of the Isles never formed part of the old system of Caledonia, and that these kings of the Western Gael were for ages independent princes, owning no allegiance to Celtic or Saxon potentate.

Before proceeding further in our review of the political elements embraced in the Lordship of the Isles, it is desirable that we should at this stage touch briefly and in a general way upon some of the features of the tribal organisation of the Celt, after which we shall enquire how far these features are to be met with in the history of the Island Lordship. The social unit was the *Tuath* or *Cineol*, while several *Tuaths* constituted a *Mortuath* each with its King, while in Scotland the seven *Mortuaths* were, as already stated, subject to the one *Ardrigh*. The structure of society in Ireland was very much after the same type, save that instead of seven provinces there were but five, each of which was called a *coigeamh* or fifth, while these provinces, well known in Highland legendary lore as *Coig Choigeamh na h-Eirinn*, were all subject to one *Ardrigh*, who swayed the sceptre in Tara. The Kingdom of Dalriada in Scotland embraced too small a territory to constitute so large a social organism. It never attained to more than the dimensions of a *mortuath*, consisting of three tribes or Cineol, viz., Cineol Lorn, Cineol Gabhran, Cineol Eoghainn, though it always had its independent kings. Again, within the *Tuath* there arose the *fine* or sept, a miniature of the larger polity, in which its features were reproduced ; in fact, throughout the tribal organisation of the Celt, from the congeries of Cineols which formed the Kingdom, down to the *fine* or sept, a unity of type and idea prevailed. The head of a tribe, or of the series of tribes constituting a *mortuath*, occupied that position in virtue of his descent from the founder of the race, whether mythical or historical.

While, however, the headship of a race always remained in one particular family—so long as a male representative of a race existed capable of succeeding, the succession did not descend from father to son in the more primitive stages of Celtic culture. It proceeded according to the law of Tanistry, a principle which, in view of the causes that produced it, was a fundamental element of Celtic society. In accordance therewith, brothers succeeded preferably to sons ; and this for two reasons. The root idea of the system lay in the connection of the tribe with its founder, and the Chief or King held his position as head of the race on account of his comparative nearness of kin to the founder. But the brother was a step or generation nearer the founder than the son, and for this reason his claim to succeed was considered stronger. There was, however,

another, and for practical purposes a stronger reason
than sentiment for the operation of this law of
succession. As distinguished from feudalism, with
its well-nigh absolute property in land, and its
absolute claim upon the service of the vassals, the
patriarchal system was largely limited by the will
and interests of the tribe. The chief was the father
of his people, but his paternity must be exercised
for the good of the entire family, and whether this
ideal was actually fulfilled or not in individual
instances, it was the principle upon which the Celtic
system was based. He was the superior of the land
for the people, and in all other respects was supposed
to rule in a manner productive of the greatest
happiness of the greatest number. It was, no
doubt, from this fusion of the interests of the Chief
and his clan, and the absence of anything like an
iron despotism ; from this enlargement of the
family idea centred in the head and realised more
or less by all the members, that sprang that devoted
attachment to the person of the Chief which characterised the Highlanders as a race. Now, in this
law of succession by Tanistry, matters were ordered
in the interests of the community. Self-preservation
is an elementary law of nature in society as well as
in the individual, and here we meet with an application of the law by which society developes its life
according to the exigencies of its environment. The
welfare of a tribe and its retention of its possessions
largely depended upon its having a chief of mature
years and tried valour, capable of administering its
internal affairs in time of peace and of leading its
hosts to battle when threatened by the foe. Thus
it came to pass that in order to obviate the possibility of having a minor as chief, it became a settled

law of Celtic polity that during the lifetime of every chief, a brother or the nearest male representative of the family was installed into the position of Tanist, who, upon the chiefship becoming vacant, immediately and indisputably stepped into the vacant place. The feudal law of primogeniture may have controlled, and of course largely did control, the later phases of Celtic life in Scotland ; but the law of Tanistry was undoubtedly the old law of succession, and amid the din of controversy which sometimes assails our ears as to the chiefship of Highland clans, it seems to be often overlooked that primogeniture cannot be regarded as the sole or even the main principle to guide the settlement of the question.

We have ample evidence of the existence of the law of Tanistry in the succession of the Celtic Kings of Scotland disclosed in the Albanic Duan, and it is interesting to notice that in the controversy between the elder Bruce and Balliol for the Crown, the former bears testimony to the existence in former times of this tanistic law. Bruce's third pleading was, "that the manner of succession to the Kingdom of Scotland in former times made for his claim, for that the brother as being nearest in degree (*ratione proximitatis in gradu*) was wont to be preferred to the son of the deceased King. Thus when Kenneth M'Alpin died, his brother Donald was preferred to his son Constantine ; thus when Constantine died, his brother Edh was preferred to his son Donald, and thus the brother of Malcolm III. reigned after him to the exclusion of the son of Malcolm III."[1] As, however, the succession always remained in the same family, it very generally came back again, by

[1] Skene's Highlanders of Scotland, vol. I., p. 160.

the operation of the same law, to the surviving son
of the chief who had formerly been passed over. Dr
Skene quotes a curious passage from an old chronicle,
which sheds an interesting light upon the same
question.[1] It informs us that there was an ancient law
by which "in case that the children of the deceissand
suld not have passit the aige of fourteen zeirs, that
he of the blude wha was nerrest beand worthie and
capable suld be elected to reign during his lyffe,
without prejudice of the richteous heretouris whan
they atteinit the parfite age." We learn from this
writer that a considerable modification had taken
place in the law of succession in his time. The
tanist in this case occupied the position of regent,
and only when the son of the chief was a minor did
he assume the reigns of government. It thus
appears that in course of time the sentiment which
confined the succession to the generation next of kin
to the founder was beginning to lose its force, and
that the practical question alone was considered, how
to secure a capable head for the tribe. It is noteworthy that the early age of fourteen years was not
considered too young for a son to succeed to the
headship of a clan. While the choice of Tanist
usually fell upon the oldest brother of the last chief,
circumstances were always considered, and in the
case of age or physical incapacity or any kind of
unworthiness, the clan or tribe was supposed to
possess a residuum of power, by which, in cases of
emergency, it made its own selection. In virtue of
this ultimate authority, cases have been known, in
comparatively modern times, in which power was
exercised for the deposition of chiefs who proved
unworthy of their position, and whose sway was

[1] The Highlanders of Scotland, vol. I., p. 161.

intolerable to the vassals. Instances entirely
analogous are to be met with in the history of the
British dynasty, which, although hereditary in its
occupancy of the throne, has yet, in the person of
individual monarchs, been removed from the position
by the common and irresistible sentiment of the
community.

The Tanist was thus a recognised functionary in
the political system of the ancient Celt, and by
reason of his position as the heir apparent of the
chief he was specially provided for out of his estate.
It was the immemorial custom that a third part
of the chief's income should be set apart for him—
trian Tighearnais—the third part of a lordship the
old Highlanders used to call it. Tanistry thus arose
out of the necessity that the tribe should have a
capable man of mature, or, at any rate, of competent
age at its head. As the military head of his race—
that being, of course, the most important aspect
of his position—the chief was denominated the
Toshach, a word obviously corresponding with the
Gaelic word for *first*, viz., *toiseach*, which in turn is
derived from *tus*, signifying beginning.[1] In the
course of time the tendency of society is to become
more complex, and for its officials to increase in
number. Hence the function of Toshach came to be
separated from the chief and became the hereditary
position of the oldest cadet family of the tribe.
Under the peculiar system of *gavel*, which falls to
be considered later on, the family longest separated
from the main stem, and, consequently, whose
property was least subject to division, possessed
its territories in the greatest integrity, and became
the most outstanding in influence and estate next

[1] The Welsh equivalent of Toshach is Twysog.

to that of the chief himself. Hence it was the most fitted to produce a leader or lieutenant-general for the tribe, to go before its fighting men when the day of danger dawned. The same necessity that resulted in the appointment of a tanist or successor to the chief, also when offices became more widely differentiated, produced the military captain or Toshach.

That the designation of Toshach was also interchangeable with the Saxon title Thane seems to be made clear by Dr Skene's researches into the system of thanages elucidated in his edition of Fordun's Scotichronicon.[1] There seems little or no reason to doubt that the ancient thanages, of which numerous traces remained in the South and West of Scotland in the reigns of Malcolm Canmore's sons, were the survival, under a Saxon designation, of the ancient Tuaths or tribe-lands which existed under the old polity of Celtic Scotland, but which were attached to the crown. With the reigns of Malcolm Canmore and his successors Saxon culture was beginning to impress Scottish institutions, and while the tribe or *Tuath* retained many of its Celtic characteristics, these, until we examine the social texture, are apt to be concealed from us under the disguise of Saxon terminology. Thus it was that the Mormaor, the successor of the King or Righ Mortuath, the head of each of the sevenfold divisions of Scotland, was replaced by the Earl or *Comes*, and the *Righ Tuath* or King of the smaller tribe came to be designated Thane or Maor. An interesting proof of the identity of the old thanages with the Gaelic Tuaths, and of Thane with Toshach, is given by Dr Skene in his larger

---

[1] The Historians of Scotland, vol. IV., 441-460.

and later work on Celtic Scotland. When the
Earl of Ross was forfeited in 1475, the lands of
William Thane of Cawdor, who was a vassal of
the Earldom, were erected into a new thanage
with the privileges of a barony ; certain lands in
the parish of Urquhart, in the Black Isle, detached
from the old thanage, were incorporated in the new,
and these lands are to this day designated locally
and by the Gaelic people *Fearann na Toiseachd*,
i.e., Ferintosh, the land of the thanage, evidence of
the ancient tribal organisation over which the *Righ
Tuath* or *Toshach* or Thane in ancient times held
sway. The title more generally applied within
historical times to a chief or laird, and corresponding
with Thane or Toshach, was *Tighearn*, which conveyed the idea of lordship, and of which the Welsh
equivalent is *Teyrn*, both evidently cognate with
the Greek *Turannos*. The word *Tighearn* must
have been originally applied to the highest royal
dignitary, and this is indicated by the application
universal among the Gael of the same term to the
Supreme Being. Though we find the same designation used with regard to chiefs in a state of
vassalage, this is only an instance of the retention
of a name after it has ceased to be strictly applicable.

So far, then, we have glanced at the two higher
grades of Celtic society, the *Righ Mortuath*, who
became the Mormaor, and was still further feudalised into the Comes or Earl, who had his lands
in capite from the King, and the *Righ Tuath*, who
was also the Toshach, and became feudalised into
Maor or Thane, responsible for the rents and
revenues of a thanage. The character of a patriarchal chief has thus been subject to a certain course

of development. He is not only the father of his tribe, but its military leader, and under feudal influences becomes an official with fiscal duties and responsibilities to discharge. The exigencies of society have also compelled a devolution of functions. The military leadership devolves upon the oldest cadet, who becomes the official Toshach, but we find that the Toshach has civil duties to perform as well, that to his hands are committed the responsibility for the fiscal administration of the Crown lands within the chief's domains.

Another important function which originally rested in the chief was that of judge. In this, as in other respects, the patriarch of the tribe was the fountain of authority, and was known of old in Wales and Ireland as the Brennin or Brehon. Here also, both among the Cymric and Gaelic Celts, there seems to have been a separation of the judicial from the military and other functions of the chief, and a devolution of the same upon functionaries specially set apart. The Welsh Cynghellwr, the Manx Deempster, and the Toshachdeorach of Gaelic Scotland, bear testimony to this fact.

Having thus briefly indicated the first degree of rank in the polity of a Celtic tribe, with some of the functions and offices connected therewith, we have arrived at a stage at which we can more conveniently discuss the relation of the Chief to the occupancy of the land, as well as the rights pertaining to his tribe. As already stated, the land belonged to the community, but the Chief exercised a certain superiority or lordship over it, not in his individual and private capacity, but as head and in name of the tribe. In the earlier stages of Celtic society, private property in land did not exist, even on the part of the patriarchal head. Individual property was confined to what in modern parlance is known as personal or moveable estate, such as cattle, sheep, goods and chattels. Private property in land was an innovation on primitive Celtic culture—the Chief having in olden times only the same right of pasturage and of the allotment of agricultural land awarded in the annual division. The land was owned by the Chief and his kindred in common, and all within the limit of three generations from the head of the race had a claim upon the family inheritance. As each generation passed away, or upon the death of the head of the house, a fresh division of the Orba, or inheritance, took place, those entitled to a share being designated *Aeloden* among the Welsh, and *Flaith*, or nobles, among the Gaelic Celts. This division took place upon the principle of *gavel*, a law not confined to Celtic races, but more tenaciously adhered to by them than by their Saxon neighbours. The division of land among the nearest kindred of the Chief had the effect of modifying the practical operation of a common property in land, and promoted the growth of an aristocracy or privileged caste, who became in time privileged owners of the soil. The Orba, or inheritance land, did not exhaust the property of the tribe; for, in addition thereto, there was the tribe-land proper, occupied by the *Ind-fine*, the commonalty, who, though of the same race as the Chief and his immediate kindred, were yet beyond the degrees of consanguinity that constituted a claim upon the special property of the kindred. This was the *duchas*, or immemorial right of the clan, free from taxation, which, under the early feudal Kings of Scotland, became attached to the Crown. This, according to Dr Skene, and he has excellent grounds for the opinion, constituted the Saxon thanages. The tribe lands were partly agricultural and partly pastoral, the latter being grazed according to the number of cattle possessed by each, and the former being subject to periodical division, when, owing to the death of former occupants and the emergence of new claimants, a redistribution became necessary.

Along with the *Saor-chlann*, the free members of tribe, who held their untaxed *duchas* land in virtue of a real or supposed consanguinity with the royal race, there usually existed the *daor-chlann*, or, as they have also been termed, the native men, or Laetic population. These consisted of tribes or septs who had lost their rights through conquest, and became subject to the conquering clan, or took refuge in some neighbouring territory. In the former case, having lost their freeborn rights, whether of *Duchas* or Orba, owing to the subjugation of the Chief through whom all their privileges flowed, they became virtually bondmen, subject to any servitude or taxation imposed upon them, their only surviving privilege consisting of the inborn right to remain upon the land. These usually obtained land from the *Flaith*, or nobles, and in Ireland were termed *Fuidhir*. They constituted the bands known in Irish history as Galloglach,[1] or Galloglasses, who followed the chiefs to war. They were not only subject to compulsory military service, but also to taxation in kind, particularly the *calpe*, a word signifying a horse or cow, the exaction being usually paid in this special form. Members of the clan were not supposed to pay this tribute. From

---

[1] Probably meaning stranger servants—from *Gall* = stranger, and *oylach*, in its secondary sense, a servant man.

the relation of these broken clans or stranger septs to the dominant races arose those peculiar conventions known as bonds of manrent, in which, for services rendered by the subject parties to the superiors, the latter undertook their protection within their jurisdiction.

We have seen how the division of the Orba, or inheritance lands, upon the succession of a new Chief, was always kept within the limits of three generations. Consequently, although in each instance the fourth in descent was not included in the distribution of the ancestral property, yet he not improbably might fare better than had he been so included. He inherited his father's allotment as a separate and fixed inheritance, not subject to the periodical subdivision which rendered the tenure of Celtic nobles so fluctuating and uncertain. From the ranks of the nobles, therefore, there sprang, and was continually recruited, a class of landholders inferior to the *Flaith*, but still of gentle birth, called among the Irish Gaels *Saertach* or *Brugaidh*,[1] among the Scottish Gael *Ogtiern*, signifying primarily a young lord, but coming secondarily to mean an inferior grade of lord. This class was the ancient representative of the modern tacksman, both being kinsmen of the Chief, and both at times converting their tack into a chartered freehold when feudal land tenure came into operation. It is also intelligible that as the ranks of the *Ogtierns* were continually swelled by descendants of the nobility, so members of this inferior grade of *Flaith* supplied the ranks of the commonalty with fresh blood when the periodical division of the agricultural lands came about.

---

[1] *Brugaidh* was originally the member of an Irish clan who possessed a *Brugh*, or homestead with a holding.

In addition to the lands already specified—the inheritance and tribe lands proper—there was a third class of lands, which may be described as official. There being little or no money in these early times, land and its products constituted the wealth of society, and those for whom the *Tuath* found it necessary to provide were endowed with an interest in the soil. Thus the Chief and Tanist had to be maintained in a manner suited to their lofty station, and for this purpose, along with the residence of the hereditary head of the race, there was set apart the tribe demesne-lands for the support of the royal dignity. The same rule applied to the judges and bards, for whom special provision was made out of the tribe lands; and when Christianity obtained a footing in the country, and churches with their religious establishments were planted here and there under the protection of the great Celtic Chiefs, donations out of the inheritance lands were bestowed for the maintenance of the Christian community. An interesting quotation from the Brehon laws indicates the view taken of the institutions of the Celt in those far off times :—" It is no *Tuath* without three noble privileged persons, *Eclais* or Church, *Flath* or Chief, and *file* or poet." The judge is not mentioned in this quotation, but possibly the function of judging may still have been vested in the *Ard Flath* when the saying was first uttered. The Church lands possessed many privileges, and, on account of their sacred destination, were regarded as conferring a right of sanctuary to all who were fortunate enough to obtain a refuge within their consecrated borders. On the principle of the cities of refuge of Old Testament times, even should the avenger of blood be in pursuit of his foe,

once the latter planted his feet within the holy
domain, the hand of violence at once was stayed.
On some notorious occasions sanctuaries have been
outraged, but in those ages of blood and vengeance
the deterrent power of the *Comraich*[1] must have
exercised a salutary influence.

Having thus, with as much brevity as is consistent with clearness, endeavoured to point out
some of the leading features of Celtic polity, it
remains for us to shew under this branch of our subject how far the relations of the Lords of the Isles to
the community over which they ruled, illustrate the
leading phases of that polity. Taking up the various
topics in the order in which they have already been
discussed, we enquire first of all what traces, if any,
of the Celtic law of Tanistry are to be met with in
Clan Donald history up to the middle of the
sixteenth century. To this enquiry we think it may
be confidently answered that, in the first place, in
the succession of Angus Og to his brother Alexander,
the principle of Tanistry entered as a dominating
influence. It may certainly be said with truth that
Alexander's opposition to Bruce was a determining
factor in the case, inasmuch as it shut out himself
and his posterity from the possession of the territories which belonged to him by hereditary right,
but could not be enjoyed without the royal favour.
On the other hand, succession to the chiefship of a
clan was quite a different matter from lordship over
lands, and was governed by totally different principles. If succession to lands was now affected by
feudalism, succession to a chiefship was still, and
long after, a question upon which the voice of the
clan, which was a potent element in the law of

[1] Comraich = protection, *vide* Macbain's Etymological Dictionary, p. 284.

tanistry, made itself effectually heard. The succession of Angus Og to the exclusion of the son of Alexander could hardly have been accomplished so quietly, and without any apparent dissent, were it not that the succession of one brother to another appealed to the traditional sentiments of the race. We may be sure that the question was well weighed by the Council of Finlaggan, and that the assumption of the sceptre of the Clan Cholla by Angus Og, only took place after due and earnest consideration on the part of the officials of the Clan.

The operation of the same law is to be seen in the succession of Donald of Harlaw, preferably to his brother Reginald, the son of John of Isla by the first marriage. Here also there were causes determining the issue, other than the law of tanistry. The whole train of events was set in motion by the influence of Robert II. to divert the honours of the House of Isla to the family of his own daughter. It is clear that Reginald, the oldest surviving son of Amie Macruari, was the lawful son, and by the law of primogeniture the heir of John of Isla. It is equally clear that Reginald abandoned his position as the heir of his father, both to the chiefship and the estates, by two acts which are indubitably vouched. In the first place, he resigned his rights as the heir of his father's lordship by accepting of a charter for a portion of the lands of that lordship, and however princely in extent the domain thus accruing to him certainly was, the charter in question transferred him from the position of the prospective Lord of the Isles to that of a vassal of the Isles. And in the second place, he deprived himself of the Chiefship of the Clan, and made himself a vassal Celtically as well as feudally, by handing over the sceptre of

27

Innse-Gall to Donald at Kildonan. The ceremony
that took place there was a purely Celtic function,
and not in any sense a feudal investiture, and it
seems unquestionably to prove that as, according to
a root idea of tanistry, Celtic succession was hereditary
in the family, while it was elective in the individual,
Donald, on the resignation by his brother Reginald
of his reversion to the Chiefship, became, with the
approval of the Clan, Donald of Isla, Lord of the
Isles, and head of the Family of Macdonald.

John Mor, second son of John of Isla by his
second marriage, was called, as is well known, the
Tainistear of Macdonald. The principle of the title
and the functions exercised by him in that capacity,
must have been in accordance with the restricted
application of the law set forth in the ancient
Chronicle quoted by Dr Skene. It could not have
meant that there was any provision for his succeeding, on the death of his brother Donald, if Donald
left heirs male of his own body, for the feudal law of
primogeniture was now too strong to permit of such
an eventuality. There must, however, have been
some publicly acknowledged position given to John
Mor as the Tainistear, though no specific record of the
fact seems to have survived. Such an appointment
may have been made to meet certain contingencies
that were by no means impossible or improbable.
During the latter days of Donald of Harlaw, his
son Alexander was in reality the only individual
standing between the House of Dunnyveg and the
succession, for Angus, the only other son of Donald,
had entered the Church, and was therefore ineligible
for the position. This fact, coupled with Alexander's
youth, was to all appearance the reason, and a
sufficient reason it was, why the name of the founder

of the House of Dunnyveg should have come down
to us as John Mor Tainistear.   Other instances
of the operation of this Celtic law arose, but these
belonged to a period rather later than that under
consideration.   Those already cited are sufficient to
indicate traces of a principle which in early times
must have been a dominant feature in the political
life of the Clan Cholla.

Of the office of Toshach, or military leader, as
distinct from the hereditary Chief, we find traces in
the history of our clan.   We have the authority of
Dr Skene in his earliest work for believing that such
an office existed, and was recognised, as vested in
the oldest cadet of the clan ; but although this
would be in entire accordance with the history and
genius of the Celt, we have come across no direct
proof of the fact.   Whether this be so or not, we
find that, practically, the military leader was at times
some one else than the Chief.   Whether Godfrey
Mac Fergus, Toshach of the Isles, who flourished in
the eighth century, was the chief of his race, or,
according to Dr Skene's view, the military leader
only, and the senior cadet of his tribe, we are unable
to say.   We find, however, a practical application
of the principle, if not of the name, in the events of
the time of Alexander, Earl of Ross, and his son
John.   Donald Balloch was the son of John Mor,
the Tainistear of the Isles, and although that
title was not applied to Donald, so far as we
are aware, he probably filled the position, as he
certainly exercised the functions of the kindred
office of Toshach, or Captain of the hosts of Clan
Donald, in the time of both these chiefs.   From
1431 down to 1463, Donald Balloch was the leader
of the Clan Donald hosts in battle, and remembering

that he was the head of the leading cadet family of the House into which the honours of the line had passed, his position is so far a confirmation of the view that has been referred to. In more recent times the Highlanders seem to have recognised a distinction between the military and patriarchal head, though neither bard nor seanachie makes use of the designation Toshach. The term most closely akin is "Captain," which the Gaelic people seem very readily to have appropriated to signify the same idea. We find it in some instances made use of when doubt existed as to the individual so named being actually the chief of the clan. John Moydartach and his father, Alastair Mac Allan, were each styled Captain of the Clan Ranald, its fighting as distinguished from its patriarchal head, the latter being a position which their opponents rightly or wrongly— we cannot pause to enquire at present which—were not disposed to allow them. Only once or twice do we find this title of "Captain" applied to any individual of the Family of Sleat. In 1545, Archibald the Clerk, who was head of the Clan Uisdean during the minority of his grand-nephew, styled himself, and was described in public records, as "Captain" of the Clan Uisdean. John Lom, the Lochaber bard, in his poem to the first Sir James Macdonald of Sleat, concludes his first verse with the words—

"Slaint do Chaiptein Clann Domhnuill," &c.

In this latter case, the title of Captain is applied to the actual Chief, but this evidently in his capacity of military head of his people. On the whole, we are disposed to think that as "Captain" was applied to the leader of the tribe in war, as distinguished from the hereditary Chief, so its ancient synonym (Toshach) would have been the title among the Clan Cholla given to the official lieutenant-general, when he was separate and distinct from the *Ceann Cinnidh*. Like all ancient Celtic offices, it was hereditary, and, according to Dr Skene, vested in the family of greatest power and influence next to that from which the Chief was chosen.

We have touched upon the judicial functions resting in the Chief, or *Ceann Cinnidh*, and in the more advanced stages of Gaelic society devolving upon hereditary officials specially endowed with lands for their support. Previous to the days of Somerled, the Norwegians had a Sheriff of the Isles, but under the House of Isla, as Hugh Macdonald, the Sleat Seanachie, affirms, there was a judge in every isle for the discussion of all controversies, who had lands from Macdonald for their trouble, and also the eleventh part of every action decided, but from whose judgment there was an appeal to the Council of Finlaggan, whose decision was absolutely final.[1] The judges of the Isles, who might be the local barons or special officials, often held their courts on the summit of a rising ground, and were usually helped in their decisions by local or provincial councils. A hill in Skye, at Duntulm, an ancient residence of the Chiefs of Sleat, is called *Cnoc na h-eiric*,[2] or the hill of ransom, so called because the settlement of causes was determined— save in instances of capital punishment—by the administration of fines. Among questions that came up for settlement, a frequent one was the arrangement of boundaries, and the method sometimes adopted for preserving a record of these matters

[1] Collectanea de Rebus Albanicis, p. 297.   [2] Pennant, vol. II., p. 304.

partook of the quaintness spiced with cruelty characteristic of a primitive time. When the marches had been fixed, several boys received a sound thrashing on the spot, and thus it was provided that, if no record was kept on sheepskin, there would be those among the rising generation who bore the impress of the transaction upon their own skins, and thus from whose minds the memory of the day's proceedings would never fade away.

We have already seen that the ancient name for the judge under a tribe was "Toshachdeora," which signifies derivatively "the chief man of law," the name of his office being Toshachdeorachd. The existence of the designation in records connected with particular districts in comparatively modern times affords an interesting testimony to the existence of the tribal organisation there in days long gone by. We find a reference to this office in regions within the Lordship of the Isles, and once at least apparently existing side by side with the feudal office of bailie. In 1455, John, Earl of Ross, and Lord of the Isles, confirms to Neill McNeill a grant made by his father to Torquil McNeill, constable of the Castle of Swyffin, the father of Neill, of the office called Toshachdeora of the lands of Knapdale.[1] In 1456, the same John, Earl of Ross, grants to his esquire Somerled, son of John, son of Somerled, for life, and to his eldest son for five years after his death, a . davach of his lands of Gleneves, with the office commonly called Toshachdeora, of all his lands of Lochaber, and he seems to have derived from it the name of Toche or Tosach, as in 1553 or 1554 the same lands of Gleneves are granted to his grandson, here called Donald Mac-

[1] Orig. Par. Scot., vol. II., p. 61.

Allaster Mic Toche.   It is somewhat singular that, notwithstanding the maintenance of this Celtic office by the Lord of the Isles, a feudal bailiary co-existed with it, for in 1447, Alexander, Earl of Ross, granted to the Mackintosh a charter of the bailiary of the lands of Lochaber, an office which became hereditary in that family.   In what relation the bailie and the Toshachdeora stood to one another; whether the former alone exercised an effective magistracy, and the latter was only an honorary appointment, a sinecure valuable to the holder because of the lands connected with it as the survival of a past order; or whether the holder of the office acted as an officer under the bailie, we cannot exactly say.   It is highly probable that, at the time of which we have these scanty notices, the office was fast decaying, and was of service only in providing a snug provision for favourites of the Island Lords.

We have seen that, originally, succession to the headship of a tribe or clan, was not according to the feudal law of primogeniture, but by the Celtic law of tanistry.   We also find that the transmission of lands was not dominated by primogeniture, but by the Celtic law of *gavel*, by which a father in disposing of his territories divided them equally among his sons.   The circumstances of these far past times rendered such proceedings necessary and even desirable. There did not then exist those manifold outlets for the industry and energy of sons which render society now-a-days less dependent than formerly upon the soil.   When sons grew to man's estate, and possessed families of their own, the only possible provision for them was to settle them upon the land, nor was the necessity so much to be deplored at a time when the

population, as a whole, was sparse, and the power
and security of a tribe depended so largely upon the
numbers that could be mustered when the day of
battle came. The gavelling of lands was a distinct
feature of the social history of the Lords of the Isles.
Somerled divided the greater part of his immense
territory in equal portions between his sons, Reginald,
Dugall, and Angus, while the other sons seem to
have obtained smaller grants upon the mainland.
Reginald similarly divided his lands among his sons,
Donald, Roderick, and Dugall. Donald divided his
lands between Angus Mor and Alexander, while
Angus Mor acted similarly to his three sons, Alexander, Angus Og, and John Sprangach. The
tendency towards a gradual attenuation of the
ancestral domains was arrested in the case of the
"Good John," for he, being the only legitimate son
of Angus Og, inherited, not only the lands gavelled
by Angus Mor to his father, but also those forfeited
by his uncle, Alexander, Lord of the Isles, along
with others that accrued through the forfeiture of
the Comyns, Macdougalls, and others. His estates
were still further enlarged by his first wife, Amie
Macruari, bringing over to him the patrimony of the
branch of the House of Somerled of which she was
the sole legitimate surviving heir. No sooner has
this remarkable consolidation of territory taken
place than the law of gavel again steps in, and a
new division of the estates of the House of Isla takes
place. John divides his lands by charter and otherwise among his seven sons, thus keeping up, amid
feudal forms, the old succession to lands by the law
of gavel.

As already stated, the Chief's direct possession
or occupancy of land seems to have originally

extended little beyond the demesne or manor lands, which were attached to his principal residence. Thus we find that, of the immense territories governed by the Lords of the Isles, a comparatively small portion was in their actual occupation. The great bulk of its area was held of them in vassalage by cadets of their own House and by other Western clans. Over the lands held of them in vassalage they seem to have maintained sovereign and undisputed sway. Although charters confirming the ownership of land seem to have been in existence even in the days of Somerled, not until the days of Angus Og, one hundred and fifty years later, did the Lords of the Isles give any real acknowledgment of superiority, either to Norway or Scotland. On the other hand, they exercised their lordly or kingly rights by bestowing lands by verbal gift, as well as by feudal charters. Verbal gifts of land were, of course, the ancient method of conveyance, and accompanied, as these always were, by appropriate symbols of investiture, such as sword, helmet, horn, or cup of the lord, sometimes spur, bow and arrow, the act was regarded as solemnly conferring real and inalienable rights. An interesting verbal grant has survived, made by Donald, either the progenitor of the clan or the hero of Harlaw, in which, sitting upon Dundonald, he grants the lands of Kilmahumaig, in Kintyre, to Mackay for ever :—

> " Mise Domhnull Mac Dhomhnuill
> Am shuidh air Dun Domhnuill
> Toirt coir do Mhac Aigh air Kilmahumaig
> S gu la brath'ch mar sin."

From a very early period, from Reginald, the son of Somerled, downwards, the Lords of the Isles, if they did not receive, granted lands by charter to the Church and individuals ; and, at intervals, as long as the Lordship lasted. The earlier charters, those of the twelfth and thirteenth centuries, are couched in mediæval Latin, and it is a peculiar feature of these that they are never dated, neither the year of the Lord nor of the reigning sovereign given to indicate the period. In some Scottish records of the age, such an entry as we find in the Book of Innes Charter, *Post con-cordiam cum Somerledo*, helps us to specify a certain year ; but the dates of the charters granted by the earlier Lords of the Isles can only be a matter of conjecture. It is only about the middle of the fifteenth century that we find a charter of the Lords of the Isles written in the vernacular Scotch of the day, showing that the spoken language of the people was beginning to supersede Latin for documentary purposes. Judging, however, from the verbal charter already quoted, as well as from the still more interesting charter of 1408, by Donald of Harlaw, many of the Macdonald grants, both verbal and written, must have been expressed in the language of the Gael. On a strip of goatskin the Lord of the Isles conveys certain lands on the Rhinns of Isla to " Brian Bicare Magaodh," on con-dition that he would supply his house annually with seven—probably fat—kine. The Magaodhs seem to have emigrated to the North of Ireland, having lost their property after the fall of the House of Isla, and a few years ago this unique charter was found in the possession of one Magee, resident in County Antrim, a descendant of the original grantee. Magee was persuaded that the Register House in Edinburgh was, on the whole, more likely to preserve the terms of this ancient charter than the peat-bank in which, for safe custody, it was deposited until the family estates in some good time coming are restored. In the Register House, therefore, it is now kept, an interesting testimony to the Gaelic spirit and sentiment of the great Highland Lord who braved the might of Scotland.

Hugh Macdonald, the Sleat Seanachie, informs us that among the functionaries of the Island Lordship there was a Recorder, or, as we might term him, a Secretary of State of the Isles, an hereditary office belonging to the MacDuffies of Colonsay. We do not suppose that the keeping of the Island records meant that the MacDuffie of the day was of necessity the actual scribe. The clergy, both of Ross and the Isles, sometimes performed the part of notaries public for the lords of these regions. Not only so, but we find Thomas of Dingwall, sub-deacon of the Diocese of Ross, acting as Chamberlain for the Earldom in 1468, a fact that need not surprise us when we remember that the education needed for the management of revenues, keeping of accounts, and other estate business was almost confined to the clergy in those days. The Betons, who were hereditary physicians to the Family of Isla, sometimes acted as clerks, and it was by one of them that the Gaelic Charter of 1408 was written. The Records of the Isles, ever since Iona became the centre of learning and religion, have been subject to an unhappy fate. The repeated and savage inroads of the Danes destroyed what must have undoubtedly been a valuable collection of MSS., and the fall of the Lordship of the Isles in 1493, with the turmoil that ensued for upwards of half a century, resulted in the loss of the Records of that principality, which would probably, had they survived, have

shed a flood of light upon certain problems connected with Highland history which, with our
present information, seem well-nigh insoluble.

The dignity of the Lord of the Isles was
maintained by the mensal lands set apart for him,
and by the tribute paid him by his vassals. But
there were also old forms of Celtic taxation which
the Chief enjoyed, and which, according to certain
interesting evidence, prevailed within the Lordship of the Isles, either appropriated by Macdonald
himself, or conveyed along with lands to his vassals.
The charter by Alexander, Earl of Ross, in which he
grants the Lordship of Lochaber to the Mackintosh
in 1443, sheds an interesting light upon the rights
and privileges of the Lords of the Isles and those
who held lands of them by feudal tenure. Taking
the latter part of the deed in question first, as
bearing more directly upon the rights of the superior,
we find the conditions of grant to be *servitium
Wardi et Relevii*, the service of wardship and relief
on the part of the vassal. The right of wardship
was one of the feudal casualties which usually
belonged either to the King or to the highest rank
of lay and ecclesiastical magnates. It consisted of
the guardianship of a fief during the non-age of the
heir apparent, and this meant nothing less than the
actual possession of the estates by the tutor during
his tenure of office. These wardships appear to have
frequently been sold or granted to the nearest male
relative, and have proved stumbling blocks to
modern antiquarians, who have at times in their
genealogical researches failed to remember the
operations of this feudal principle. In this manner
David of Huntingdon enjoyed the Earldom of
Lennox, Alan Durward that of Athol, and Earl

Malcolm of Angus that of Caithness, during the
minority of the heirs.[1] It will be remembered that,
in the treaty between England Balliol, and John of
Isla, in 1335, by which various lands were bestowed
upon the Lord of the Isles, not the fee simple, but
the wardship of Lochaber, "until the attainment
to man's estate of the son and heir of Lord David
of Strathbolgy, the last Earl of Athole," was bestowed
upon the Lord of the Isles.[2] It was not until 1343
that Lochaber, owing to the death of the heir referred
to, was actually conveyed to John of Isla by charter.
Now, a little over 200 years later, the Earl of Ross,
in granting the same lands to the Mackintosh,
retains the reversion of the wardship, his interest in
the lands being precisely that enjoyed by his grandfather under Edward Balliol. The wardship by
itself, however, might prove a barren honour if, as
was possible, the heir on all occasions succeeded
when he was of full age ; so there accompanied the
wardship a fine or tax called "Relief," exacted from
every heir on succeeding to his patrimony.

Looking further into the contents of the same
charter, we find enumerated among the perquisites
of the vassal for the Lordship of Lochaber three
items which lend some interest to the social history
of the day, namely, *Blude-wetis, herezaldis, mulierum
merchetis*. Each of these in turn demands some
attention. The word *Blude-wetis* is a Latinized
form of the ancient *blodwite*, also known among the
Saxons as *Wergild*, and among the Gael as *Èirig*.[3]
It signified the compensation payable by any who
had committed homicide to the kindred of the

---

[1] Scotland under her Early Kings, vol. II., p. 129.

[2] Vide p. 106 of this vol.

[3] *Èirig*, supposed to be derived from *fear*, a man, and *reic*, to sell, thus
meaning a man's value in money or kind.

deceased. The custom was very ancient, and seems to have been known, though divinely disallowed in the case of wilful homicide, at the time when the Mosaic code was being formulated.[1] It was not incumbent upon the friends to accept a compensation for their kinsman's slaughter, as the stern desire for vengeance could not always be set at rest by any means save the blood of the offender. When the fine was accepted, the amount was determined by the rank of the deceased, and the ancient codes detailing the *Cro* or liability of persons according to the rank of the slain, have been among the chief sources of our knowledge of social grades among Teutonic and Celtic nations. The early principle by which the immediate kindred of the deceased were regarded as alone interested in the blood feud seems to have become modified with time. Homicide or murder was looked at as a crime against the community or state as well as against the individual, and part of. the blood money came to be a public due paid into the coffers of the King, the official head of the nation. This reference to the custom in the Mackintosh charter is the only evidence we have hitherto come across as to the existence of the *blodwite* within the Lordship of the Isles, at anyrate so late as the middle of the fifteenth century.

We have already referred to the *calpe*, an impost paid by the " native men" for the benefit of living under the protection of a conquering Chief. This is doubtless synonymous with the *herezeldis* of the Charter, for a tax somewhat similar to the calpe, entitled " heregild," prevailed in the Saxon districts of Scotland certainly as late as the fifteenth and sixteenth centuries.[2] It is notable that a curious

[1] Numb. xxxv. 31-32.   [2] Sir David Lindsay's " Three Estates."

variation of this tax of calpe existed until last
century in North Uist, said to have been introduced by a son of Godfrey, lord of that Island. On
the death of any of the tenants, the best horse in
the widow's stable was appropriated for the behoof
of the landlord, and this horse, for what reason
it is difficult to say, was called the *each ursainn.*[1]
Singular to say, while the Celtic law of *calpe* was
abolished by the Legislature in the seventeenth
century, this tax lingered in North Uist for upwards
of one hundred years thereafter.

Once more reverting to the Mackintosh Charter
of 1443, we find a tax which has given rise to a
good deal of speculation, namely, that designated
Mulierum Mercheta, and which consisted, at anyrate in later days, of a tax payment by a vassal to
his lord upon the marriage of his daughter. In
connection with this particular point, and arising out
of it, we think it desirable to enter briefly into the
wider question of the marriage laws that existed of
old in Celtic Scotland. Roman writers, from Julius
Cæsar downwards, have stated, one after the other,
that a system of community of wives prevailed
among the ancient Caledonians. There are undoubtedly indications in what has survived of the
history of pre-Christian ages that the relations
between the sexes were, as might be expected, looser
and less regulated among the ancient Celts of Scotland than they have been within the Christian
period. Sons were regarded as belonging to their
mothers' rather than to their fathers' tribes, while it
was through females that the succession to family
honours, and particularly to the supreme dynasty of

---

[1] By a process quite intelligible to a Gaelic speaker, *ursainn* may be a
corruption of " herezild."

Pictland, was regulated. The succession of Kenneth M'Alpin to the throne of united Alban was brought about through his being the grandson of Ungusia, wife of a Pictish King. Social laws and customs long survive the causes that produce them, and this succession through a female probably indicates the existence of a state of society at a vastly remoter time, when the parentage of the mother was the only certain guarantee as to a particular line of descent.

Whether the custom known in Gaelic history as "hand-fasting" was that which suggested to Cæsar and other Roman writers this somewhat revolting idea of "polyandria," or whether hand-fasting may be a modification or development of the social condition described, it is difficult to say. If hand-fasting did not amount to a community of wives, it certainly meant that a woman could possibly enter into conjugal relations with several living men within the limits of a few years. The contract sometimes took place in this wise. An agreement was entered into between two chiefs, that the heir of the one should live for twelve months and a day with the daughter of the other. The contract provided further that, in the event of the lady, within that period, becoming a mother, the marriage became good in law, even without the *imprimatur* of the Church, but if there was no appearance of issue, the contract was dissolved, and each was allowed to marry or hand-fast with another. The survival of a custom so abhorrent to the Church, and inconsistent with feudal law, long after the introduction of Christianity and Saxon culture, is only to be accounted for by its being congenial to the Celtic system. The form of Gaelic society was of such a nature that the welfare of the community depended greatly upon the birth of heirs to carry on the ancestral line, and this fact was sufficient to perpetuate for ages a system of men taking wives unto themselves on approbation. The Highlanders regarded the issue of such marriages as perfectly legitimate, and absolutely distinct from bastardy. Instances of the issue of hand-fasted parents being regarded as legitimate could easily be quoted. John Maclean, fourth laird of Ardgour, hand-fasted with a daughter of Macian of Ardnamurchan, taking this lady, according to the seanachie of the clan, "upon the prospect of marriage if she pleased him. At the expiration of two years (the period of her noviciate), he sent her home to her father, but his offspring by her were reputed lawful children, because their mother was taken upon a prospect of marriage."[1] Another case in point was when the issue of a hand-fast marriage claimed the Earldom of Sutherland in the sixteenth century "as one lawfullie descended from his father, Earle John the third, because, as he alleged, his mother was hand-fasted and fianced to his father." As shewing the strength of his claim, Sir Adam Gordon, who had married Earl John's heiress, bought it off by the payment of a sum of money.

The opinion has been advanced that the union of John of Isla with Amie Macruari was a hand-fast marriage, and this has been adduced as accounting for the surrender by Reginald of the sceptre of the Isles to Donald, the eldest son of the second marriage at Kildonan. We have already given our decision, whatever be its worth, against this view.[2] Only a word or two need be said in supplement. The authority of MacVurich and the Dispensation

<hr />

[1] The Clan Maclean, by a Seanachie, p. 265.   [2] *Vide* pp. 128-9

of 1337 are the main grounds set forth in proof of the feudal illegitimacy of Amie's sons. The accuracy of the Clanranald Seanachie, when he tells the story of these years, is by no means unimpeachable, and his deliverances display an amount of historical incoherence which is a little perplexing to the reader. He propounds an absurd theory as to the parentage of the Princess Margaret; he says that Reginald's abdication in favour of Donald was against the wishes of the men of the Isles, and almost in the same breath makes the statement, diametrically opposed, that it was with their consent, while he seems entirely ignorant of the Papal Dispensation which, for whatever reason it was obtained, rendered John's marriage absolutely legal, and his eldest son his feudal heir.[1] Neither priest nor altar could make this surer than the authority of the Church's earthly head. Clearly MacVurich's views upon the subject were created by the fact which he could not account for, except by illegitimacy, that John's eldest son did not succeed his father. But why did the " Good John" get this Papal Dispensation? In the circumstances of his third cousinship to his wife, it was absolutely necessary. In the fourth Council of the Lateran, the question of the forbidden degrees of consanguinity, which had been a burning one in the Church for ages, was taken up. There was a relaxation of the stringency of former times which forbade marriage between sixth cousins(!), while now it was restricted to fourth cousinship.[2] Amie Macruari being John's third cousin, the marriage could not possibly take place without the high authority of Rome. Then there was obtained, not a legitimation of offspring as was

[1] Reliquiæ Celticæ, p. 159.   [2] Conc. Lat. IV., Act. 50.

bestowed upon *Coinneach a' Bhlair*, the Chief of Kintail, in 1491, but a licence, or Dispensation, which permitted the celebration of a union which would otherwise by canon law have been irregular.

We must now pass from this subject of hand-fasting to the special aspect of the ancient marriage laws suggested by the third item quoted from the Mackintosh Charter of 1443. It seems necessary to discriminate between the law of *Maritagium*, which meant the right of bestowing the hand of an heiress in marriage, and the *mulierum mercheta*, or maiden fee, which was a tax imposed upon a vassal on the occasion of his daughter's marriage.[1] This maritage, like the rights of Ward and Relief, represented at times a considerable pecuniary interest, and it was sometimes bestowed in charters by Kings and great Crown vassals, and sometimes sold. In the sixteenth century we find James Macdonald of Dunnyveg and the Earl of Argyle eagerly contending for the wardship and marriage of Mary Macleod, the heiress of Dunvegan, which the Queen Regent had compelled the Earl of Huntly to relinquish. The *mulierum mercheta*, or marriage tax, paid by a vassal to his lord, has been made the basis of purely fanciful and long-exploded theories. According to Hector Boece, the law of *jus primæ noctis* was devised and introduced by a profligate King Evenus, who reigned in Scotland shortly before the Christian era, and it was in force until the time of Malcolm Canmore, who commuted it into a fine. Modern writers have striven with great ingenuity to prove that it prevailed not only in Scotland, but also in England, France, and other continental countries as a recognised right of the

---

[1] Scotland under her Early Kings, vol. II., p. 129.

overlord in the dark ages of feudalism. After all, this theory has been founded upon a mistaken interpretation of old feudal phraseology, into which imaginative writers have read a meaning which it never bore.[1] As a matter of fact, it was from the very earliest times of which we possess any record nothing else than a marriage tax, though, of course, there is room for differences of opinion as to the causes of its origin. According to one view it arose in this wise. Only freemen who were possessed of property could enter into the stipulations necessary for contracting a marriage. Among the servile classes marriage could not exist ; they were looked upon as cattle or stock, having lost their rights of kindred, or *duchas*, and possessing no privileges except the pleasure of their masters. But there were also dependent freemen, such as the military followers among the Germanic nations, and the *amasach* of Gaelic races, who, having surrendered their birthright of land for knightly service under their lord or chief, could neither marry nor give in marriage without his permission, this permission being granted on payment of a sum of money. Another view of the origin of this impost is that it was paid by a tenant or vassal to the Chief as a recompense for the loss of the bride's services when she transferred her allegiance to another lord, services to which the Chief, *jure sanguinis*, was entitled. Both theories are feasible, and while we do not presume to decide between them, it is evident that in either case the *mulierum mercheta* was a marriage tax, originating among feudal peoples, but, with other Teutonic customs, finding its way at an early period into the social culture of the Celt.

[1] Scotland under her Early Kings, vol. II., p. 307.

Before closing this chapter, it will be desirable to give a short survey of the dignity, sway, and wealth of the family whose story we have tried to tell. As we have seen, the chiefs of Clan Cholla became independent rulers within Dalriada after Kenneth McAlpin had moved eastward to become King of the new realm of Scotia. Somerled, after he had vindicated his rights, assumed like his forbears the title King of the Isles, and was to all intents and purposes an independent prince. This sense of independence he transmitted to a long line of successors, and, although at times compelled by the force of circumstances to profess allegiance to the Scottish Kings, no amount either of force or conciliation could make them long adhere to a submissive attitude. Reginald, son of Somerled, styled himself Lord of Argyle and King of the Isles, a two-fold designation which seemed to indicate that the relation of his dynasty to the Isles was of an older and more independent character than their relation to Argyle. Reginald was also the first of the family known as *De Ile*, though the Isles must have been the home of the race several centuries before his day. This title of *De Ile* was the oldest territorial designation of his family, and always stood first and foremost in the order of their honours and dignities. It was confined to the heads of the race, and while cadets of Macdonald might designate themselves *De Insulis*, or assume any other title they chose, they never presumed to adopt that of *De Ile*. It is from this fact, mainly, that we conclude the seniority of the Clan Donald line over all other branches descended from Reginald MacSomerled. Reginald was himself *De Ile*, as were his ancestors probably for many

generations, and while other junior families branched
off, that of *De Ile,* from Donald down to the last
John, were undoubtedly the heads of the Clan
Cholla. While they had this territorial title, they
were also known by others. Both in Ireland and
Scotland they were frequently designated *Righ
Innsegall*—Kings of the Isles—and in the beginning
of the fifteenth century we find McVurich the bard
addressing his " Brosnacha Catha" to Donald of
Isla, King of *Innse-gall.* Both in Ireland and
Scotland the heads of the Clan Donald were called
Ardflath Innse Gall. On the other hand it is
undoubtedly the case that the Celtic or patriarchal
title of the heads of the family, down from the time
of the first Donald *De Ile,* was *Macdhomhnuill.*
There is only one signed charter from any of the
heads of the House of Isla, namely, the Gaelic
Charter by Donald of Harlaw, in 1408, and in this
deed he styles himself without any territorial
addition, simply as Macdonald. The Chiefs of Isla
were all Macdonald, from the time of Angus Mor
down to Donald Gallda, and Donald Dubh, who
were both proclaimed " Macdonald" in their unsuccessful efforts to revive the fallen principality of the
Isles. In the arming of the last Lord of the Isles,
McVurich speaks of John as "Macdonald," the noble
son of Alexander, the heroic King of Fingall, and a
poem by a contemporary bard, quoted by the same
seannachie, begins with the words, " True is my
praise of Macdonald." In Ireland, also, from very
early times, the heads of the race were known by
the same Celtic title. In the Annals of Loch Ce,
1411, we read of a " great victory of the Macdonalds
of Alba," and in the Annals of Ulster we find that
"in the year of Christ 1490, Angus, son of Mac-

donald of Scotland, who was called the young lord, was murdered by his Irish harper Dermod O'Cairbre, and at Inverness he was slain." It seems necessary to dwell with some emphasis on this fact, inasmuch as Gregory, and others who have followed him, *longo intervallo*, have persisted in maintaining that Macdonald is a comparatively modern surname adopted by the Barons of Sleat and the Lords of Dunnyveg, from one or more noted chiefs who bore the name of Donald.

We find in those heraldic emblems, which can with certainty be regarded as belonging to the Lords of the Isles, evidence of their premier position among the western clans of Scotland. Amid all the variations which the taste and fancy of later ages have introduced into the Macdonald arms, there are two features that stand out prominently as belonging unquestionably to the Family of Isla, and these are the galley and the eagle. We find the galley as far back as the time of Reginald MacSomerled, and the galley with an eagle against the mast we find in the seal of John, last Lord of the Isles, after he was forfeited in the Earldom of Ross in 1476. The galley is intended to convey the idea of the sovereignty of these Celtic Lords over the western seas, and the eagle symbolizes, under another form, the royal superiority of the Macdonald Chiefs. No doubt other western clans have the galley in their armorial bearings, but these in every case have borrowed the emblem from the arms of the house of which in previous ages they had been feudatories and vassals.

All the information we can obtain suggests the possession of great power and wealth by these Island Lords. Somerled seems to have had the command of immense maritime resources, for from the time that he conquered Godred down to his last struggle with the Scottish Crown the number of galleys that accompanied him to sea varied from 60 to 160. Angus Og led 10,000 Highlanders to the field of Bannockburn, and Donald commanded no less a force at the battle of Harlaw. From the large numbers which at various times these Lords of the Isles were able to assemble on the day of battle, we conclude that the population of the Western Highlands must have been larger than is usually supposed. Nothing of the nature of a standing army seems to have existed beyond the *luchd tighe*, body guard, or garrison, who kept ward on Isle Finlaggan, where the Macdonald Lords held court. The remains of their dwellings are still to be seen. "The *luchd tighe* attended the chief at home and abroad. They were well trained in managing the sword and target, in wrestling, swimming, jumping, dancing, shooting with bows and arrows, and were stout seamen."[1] The *luchd tighe* were composed of the strongest and most active young men in the best families in the Isles, and were called *Ceatharnaich*, from their great strength and feats of daring. They were known in the Lowlands, where their forays were rich and frequent, as "Kernes" or "Caterans." The military strength of the lordship was not, however, to be measured by the *luchd tighe*. The vassals of the Isles, not only those of the same blood and lineage, but others who held lands of the House of Isla by feudal tenure, were bound to provide a certain number of men when the fiery cross went round. While the Stewart Kings, with all the encouragement they gave to the cultivation of

[1] Martin, p. 103.

archery, were never able to bring a band of efficient bowmen to the field, the Islesmen were expert archers, and when fighting in the Royal army were always placed in a position in which their superiority in this respect would have the best effect. Remains of the butts of Imiriconart, in Isla, where the archers of Macdonald practised their art, survived as late as the time of Pennant.

While the Lords of the Isles thus encouraged the cultivation of warlike courage and skill, we are not to suppose that the arts of peace were neglected according to the standards of their day. The numbers, extent, and solidity of the castles, fortifications, and religious houses, whose ruins are scattered over the Western Highlands and Islands, show that encouragement of a distinct kind must have been given to the crafts of masonry, carpentry, and others, while they at the same time suggest the expenditure of great wealth. No doubt some of this wealth would have been derived from the tribute paid by the vassals, which must have amounted to a considerable sum, measured by the conditions of these olden times. There are also other ways of accounting for the well-filled coffers of the Macdonald Chiefs. They were acquainted, through their seafaring habits, with the navigation of foreign seas, and made many descents upon the maritime countries of Western Europe, carrying with them to the Islands golden vases, silks, armour, money, &c. An art which the seafaring habits of the Kings of Innse-Gall must have greatly promoted was that of shipbuilding. In this particular craft, doubtless, the Norwegians would have promoted their instruction, but the Western Gaels must very early have become skilled in an art so necessary in an insular region like the Lordship of the Isles. It is also extremely probable that timber grew more plentifully in the Hebrides then than in modern times, a supposition which is supported by the numerous roots of trees which now and then are exposed to view in the extensive bog-lands of Lewis and Uist. In 1249, Hugh de Chatillon, one of the richest and most powerful of French barons, consented to accompany Louis IX. of France to the crusades, and the ship that was to carry him was built in the Highlands, a fact to be seriously considered by those who would fasten the stigma of barbarity upon the Scottish Gael of bygone ages.

Various other proofs of the wealth of these Island Lords might be adduced, but one significant proof will suffice. Reginald MacSomerled did in 1196 purchase the whole of Caithness from William the Lion, an exception being made of the yearly revenue due to the Sovereign, which the Lord of the Isles did not acquire.[1] That the chronicler does not, in recording this transaction, confuse Reginald of the Isles with him of the same name who became King of Man, is clear, from the fact that the Lords of the Isles for many ages thereafter continued to possess lands in Caithness, for we find both Donald of Harlaw and John, last Earl of Ross, giving charters of land in that county during the fifteenth century.[2]

A certain amount of trade must have been encouraged by the Lords of the Isles, and frequent intercourse with Ireland on the one hand, and Norway on the other, led to the exchange of commodities which were useful to both. An official

---

[1] Venit ergo Reginaldus filius Somerlett rex de Mannia et Insularum ad regem Scotiæ et emit ab eo Cathanesiam.—Chron. of Man, by Johnstone, p. 58.

[2] *Vide* Appendix.

mentioned by Hugh Macdonald as exercising an important function under the Lords of the Isles was the Chief of Macfingon, who looked after the adjustment of weights and measures, a fact which shows, not only that encouragement was given to trading, but also that they recognised the abomination of a false balance and the righteousness that exalteth a people. The stately and even royal Court kept by these potentates involved the distribution of wealth around them whether they held their court in Isla, Ardtornish, or Dingwall, and it is on record that after the Earldom of Ross was forfeited and Dingwall Castle had to be abandoned, that burgh for a long time languished and decayed through the withdrawal of the business which the presence of the Island Chiefs and their numerous retainers created. The trade of the Islands would probably consist of the staple commodities produced in those regions, and by means of which the rents and tiends would to some extent have been paid, such as wool, cloth, flax, linen, fish, butter, eggs, and corn. It is interesting to note that, when the Earl of Douglas visited the Earl of Ross at Knapdale in 1453, the former brought presents of wine, silken cloths, and silver, while the Highland Chief in return gave mantles and Highland plaids.[1] We find in some of the older accounts that the spinning of wool and flax and the manufacture of cloth were industries practised in the Hebrides from a very remote period. The cultivation of the arts and sciences has with every appearance of probability been ascribed to the influence of the Gaelic clergy who were established over the Western Isles prior to the arrival of the

[1] The Book of Douglas, vol. I., pp. 485-86. Scott's History of Scotland, vol. I., p. 307.

Norwegians, as well as to numbers of Britons flying thither from the ravages of the Saxons, who bore with them the remains of Roman culture and of the arts of life. At anyrate, it is a fact that an Icelandic Skald, describing an elegant dress for a hero of the seventh century, says—" Enn Sudreyskar spunnu," which is, being interpreted, " Sudreyans spun the web."[1] This manufacture of cloth from home-grown wool and flax was an art universally cultivated and always preserved under the sway of the Lords of the Isles. It is evident that whatever trade existed in the Isles and with foreign countries must have been conducted by the medium of barter or exchange. Money as an instrument of commerce must have been scarce in these ages, down from the time of Angus Mor, "the generous dispenser of rings," to his latest successor in the sovereignty of the Isles.[2]

Considering the character of the ages in which they flourished, it is not difficult to see that the influence of the Lords of the Isles was exercised for the good of the lands which owned their sway, and the terrible state of anarchy and darkness which for generations supervened the fall of their Lordship is alone sufficient to prove the fact. To the Kings and State of Scotland they were turbulent and dangerous, because they never forgot the ancient traditions of independence, but to their own vassals and subjects they were kindly, generous, and just, abounding in hospitality, and profuse in charitable deeds. Had this not been the case, it is hardly possible to conceive that the High-

[1] Lodbrokar Quida (Johnstone's Edition, 1782), p. 103. Macpherson's Geographical Collections.

[2] Haco's Expedition (Johnstone's Edition, 1782), p. 57.

landers should have rallied to so many forlorn
hopes to re-establish the fallen dynasty. In their
proud independence, they were to the Highland
people the representatives of what was best in
Gaelic history, who never owned a superior, either
Celt or Saxon. Only the king of terrors himself
could lay Macdonald low; such was the feeling of
the devoted subject who engraved the brief but
expressive legend on his tomb, *Macdonald fato
hic.*

CHAPTER XIV.

THE CHURCH AND EDUCATION.

The Celtic Church.—Its Character.—Its Decay.—Rise of Latin
Church.—Diocese of Isles.—Somerled in Man.—S. Machutus.
—Saddell.—Its Foundation and Endowment.—Tayinloan.—
Abbey of Iona Built and Religous Orders Established by
Reginald.—Connection with Paisley.—The Good John and his
Wife as Church Patrons.—Oransay Priory.—Trinity Chapel,
Carinish.—Grimsay Oratory.—Sons of John of Isla and the
Church.—Howmore.—Earls of Ross.—Education.—Art.

THE connection of the Lords of the Isles with the
Church of their time, illustrated as it was by
many gifts and endowments in lands, church
buildings, and other effects, was sufficiently notable
to call for special treatment in a chapter devoted
to itself. It was in the eleventh century, that
which witnessed the fallen fortunes of the Clan
Cholla at the lowest ebb, that the Celtic Church
began to be supplanted by the Latin form of
Christianity which had been introduced into Scotland mainly through the agency of Margaret, the
saintly Queen of Malcolm Canmore. The Celtic
Church in Scotland, as an organised institution,
partook largely of the character of the social
system in the midst of which it was situated. In
type it was monastic, and in the scope of its
operation tribal, that is to say, on the Celtic
inhabitants of Scotland being Christianised, the
Church formed a part of the social system of the
Tuath or tribe, under whose protection it was

planted. The Church and the polity of the Celt mutually acted and reacted. The Church influenced and promoted the progress of the community in civilisation and morality. It elevated the relationship between the sexes, regulating and imparting a sacred significance to marriage, with the result that, instead of the old system of descent in Caledonia through a female, a system arising out of a primitive state of society and a loose relation between the sexes, Christianity placed the father at the head of the family, and created the system of hereditary descent. As the Church in this way raised the tone of Celtic society, the latter in its turn imparted a colouring and tendency to ecclesiastical life. Both in Scotland and Ireland the Church system was grafted on the patriarchal form of society, and nearness of blood to the founder of the tribe to a large extent regulated succession to ecclesiastical dignities and possessions. This, of course, might be looked for when the Church was under the protection of the tribe, and owed to the liberality of its head all its secular possessions, he consequently retaining in his own hands a large share of the Church's patronage. We often find that, although originally the Abbots were distinct from the Clan, in the course of time the lay and ecclesiastical lines are merged into one, and finally the holder of the Abbatial lands is found to be a lay official. The tribe lands, as already seen, were first occupied in common, and out of the Orba or inheritance lands of the *Ardflath* and nobles, termon lands were set apart for the maintenance of the Church. It thus came about that the system of hereditary possession to the headship of a tribe was impressed upon the organisation of the Church. As a matter of fact, we find this hereditary principle extending far into the history of the mediæval or Roman Church in the Lay Abbots of Apercrosan or Applecross, who for ages were heads of the powerful Celtic monastery that held the greater part of the North *Oirthir*, and of whom were the sept of the MacTaggarts. This encroachment of the secular element upon the life of the Church largely contributed to its decay, and the introduction of a secular order of clergy in the seventh and eighth centuries, combined with the destruction of the monasteries by Danish invasions, still further hastened its downfall. It was, however, the policy of Queen Margaret and her sons, but particularly of David I., that had the largest share in modifying the outward form of the Christian Church in Scotland. The Celtic Church had, as stated, been monastic and missionary. From centres where its institutions had been planted it worked for the evangelisation of the people without establishing itself as a territorial system covering the whole land. Its jurisdiction was thus confined to its religious houses, and the functions of its Bishops did not extend beyond the monasteries. As distinguished from this, David I. introduced a parochial system, the foundation of that which still prevails in Scotland, and he established a diocesan episcopacy over the parochial clergy, each diocese embracing a large number of parishes. He also introduced the monastic orders of the Roman Church, hardly if at all known in this country before his day.

The Celtic Church, with its Culdees, the clerical residue of the old order, soon fell into disrepute before the more novel, comprehensive and aggressive system of the Latin Church. The change from the one system to the other was marked by a great advance in church architecture, the transition being more advanced in this respect than in any other.

The primitive church architecture of St Columba's day, consisting of church or oratory and the detached cells or huts of the brotherhood, all made of wattles, had long ago been exchanged for stone buildings. Of these older Celtic stone remains, small rectangular church and beehive-shaped cells, such as are to be seen in *Eilean Naomh*, few traces are to be found in Scotland; but there is enough to shew the tremendous stride that was made within a limited period to the church architecture of mediæval times. The transition to the cruciform plan, as well as from the round to the pointed arch, and afterwards from the simple Gothic to the late ornate style, and from that afterwards to the perpendicular, were certainly remarkable enough. Yet in other details the change was, if possible, still greater and more sudden. Especially is this to be noted in the quality and style of the masonry. The old Celtic churches, even the best of them, were built of rough field stones, occasionally touched with a hammer, and cemented with shell mortar, apparently poured hot among the stones, this being also the style adopted in the older castles of the Highland nobility. It may have been a method rude and ungraceful from an æsthetic point of view, but it certainly was calculated to withstand the ravages of time and the warfare of the elements. Very different was the style of masonry applied to the new and fairer type of Gothic buildings that came into vogue in the twelfth century in Scotland. It consisted in the use of quarried freestone, regularly hewn and dressed, and laid in regular courses with well-prepared mortar, resulting in those beautiful remains, alas! too rare, which testify to the artistic

29

genius, as well as technical capacity, of the generations that gave them birth.

Having thus very briefly sketched the change
from the Celtic to the Latin form of Christianity in
Scotland, it will be desirable to give a brief account,
from the ecclesiastical point of view, of the region in
which the influence of the Island Lords was mainly
exercised. The territories in which these magnates
of Innse-Gall, from Somerled downwards, exercised
authority for a longer or shorter period, lay in
three dioceses—the Isles, Lismore, and Ross. The
ecclesiastical history of the first of these districts,
like its secular history, abounds in interesting
and eventful episodes, owing, in the first place,
to its being the scene of the introduction of
Christianity into Scotland by Columba and his
followers, and, in the second place, to their
being so much exposed to the devastating incursions of Scandinavian pirates. While the Diocese
of the Isles was the last of all the Scottish
Sees to arrive at full Cathedral *status*—this only
having taken place in 1506—its history as an abbey
goes back to a remoter period than any of the other
twelve. The eighth and ninth centuries witnessed
the decay of the influence exercised by the religious
establishment of Iona over the Christian Churches
of the mainland of Alban. In the first place, its
resistance to the ordinances of the Roman Church as
regards the burning questions of Easter and the
tonsure led the Churches of Pictland to throw off
the authority of that which was the mother of them
all. Further, the awful peril to which Iona and its
community were exposed from the attacks of the
savage Danes, particularly in the ninth century,
rendered it difficult to secure the services of

Churchmen who would occupy a post which, if it was one of honour, was also one of danger. The causes that led to the decay of the authority of Iona over the Churches of Alban were likewise instrumental in producing similar results in its relation to the Irish monasteries. About the beginning of the ninth century the monastery of Kells was built; the relics of St Columba were deposited there, and the primacy of the Irish religious houses, which had from the days of the Saint belonged to the Isle of his affections, now passed away from it for ever. Although various attempts were made to restore something of its former glory by bringing back the relics of its Saint, Iona never during the existence of the Celtic Church, which it had fostered into life and usefulness, recovered its former power and sway. When Kenneth McAlpin resolved to re-establish the Columban Church in Southern Pictdom, he built a church at Dunkeld, which he made the *annoid* or mother church over the Columbans in Scotland. From that period the Western Isles continued largely under Scandinavian sway, now under the Kingdom of Dublin, now under the Earls of Orkney, though once at least they relapsed into the hands of Celtic rulers. In 1072 the Isles passed for little less than a generation into the hands of Malcolm Canmore. The ecclesiastical position of Iona and the Isles during these troubled centuries is a little difficult to define. According to some accounts, a bishopric of the Isles—apart from Man—was founded in 838 A.D., but this is entirely out of keeping with the facts that the stream of history has borne down to our day.[1] It may, however, be gathered that though

---

[1] Matthew Paris.

the Norsemen and their Kings in Man and the Isles are supposed to have adopted Christianity at the beginning of the eleventh century, the Church of Iona seems to have benefitted little or nothing by their patronage, for the monastery built of stone in 818, and attacked and partially demolished by the Danes in 986, seems to have remained in a ruined state until 1074, when it was restored, rebuilt, and furnished with monks and an endowment by Queen Margaret, the wife of Malcolm Canmore. During a great part of that time it had hardly any connection with Scottish Christianity, and had frequently to fall back for support upon the Irish monasteries. About 1098, the Western Isles fell into the hands of Magnus Barefoot, when Sodor and Man were united into one diocese, and made suffragan to Drontheim in Norway. Thus for the first time did Iona and the Isles, hitherto monastic in their church government, with the Abbot at the head of the ecclesiastical district, become merged in the system of Diocesan episcopacy soon to dominate the religious life of the country. For nearly three hundred years after this, Iona and the Isles were ecclesiastically connected with Man ; but from the middle of the twelfth century their history was bound up with the Lords of the Isles, all of whom proved munificent patrons of the Church within their own domains. In 1154, the Southern Isles were wrested by Somerled from the grasp of Godred of Man, and it is notable that while he and his successors strenuously resisted the inroads of Scottish feudalism, their attitude towards the mediæval Church, which embodied the religious aspect of the same national movement, was widely different. From the very beginning they adopted the policy of the Scottish

Kings, which was to encourage and foster within their own domains the Latin form of Christianity, which was rapidly absorbing and supplanting the old Celtic Church.

Somerled, the founder of the Family of the Isles within historical times, becomes, before the close of his stormy career, a generous patron and benefactor of the Church. A semi-fabulous incident connected with one of his campaigns in Man has been reserved for this portion of our work, as it has, not without reason, been cited as suggesting a cause for, or indicating a tendency towards, the special form of Christian liberality characteristic of his age. The monks of Rushin who chronicled Somerled's doings in the Isle of Man tell us that after he had finally crushed his brother-in-law, Godred, in 1157, and expelled him thence to Norway, he wasted the island and retired with his troops to the town of Ramsa. The Church of St Manghold, known of old as Machutus, stands three miles from the modern town of Ramsey. This was the scene of the incident referred to in the life of the great Chief of Clan Cholla, which has received detailed narration combined with much mystic embellishment. The story, which is, of course, couched in Monkish Latin, is as follows:—At the same time when Somerled was in Man, in the Port called Ramse, it was told his army how the Church of St Machutus was crammed full with great store of money, for this place, by reason of the reverence paid to the most holy confessor Machutus, was a safe place of refuge for those who fled from any kind of danger. But a certain leader, more powerful than the rest, named Gilcolm, made suggestions to Somerled about the foresaid money, and declared that it would in no wise prejudice the peace of S. Machutus to carry off the animals grazing outside the enclosure of the cemetery to supply the army with food. But Somerled began with a refusal, saying he could by no means allow the peace of S. Machutus to be violated. On the other hand, Gilcolm insisted with urgent entreaties, praying that he and his son might be allowed to go to the place, and the guilt should be altogether on himself. Somerled, though unwilling, gave permission, and said—"Let the matter be between thee and S. Machutus, I and my army are innocent; we want no share of your booty." Upon this Gilcolm rejoiced; went off to his people, and summoning three sons and all his dependents, commanded them to be ready that night so that at the first break of dawn they might be on the watch to make a rush on S. Machutus' Church, two miles distant. Meanwhile a rumour reached the church of the enemy's approach, which raised such universal fear that many fled from the church and hid themselves in the caves of the rocks. The rest, with incessant cries, continued all night calling upon God for pardon through the mercies of S. Machutus. The weaker sex, with dishevelled hair, ran wailing to and fro around the walls of the church, shouting with loud cries, " Where art thou now, O Machutus ? Where are thy miracles once wrought in this place ? Wilt thou forsake us now for our sins ? If not for our sakes, for the honour of thy name, help us in this our misfortune." Moved by their prayers, as we believe, S. Machutus, having compassion on their miseries, rescued them from immediate danger, and condemned their enemy to a terrible death ; for as soon as the aforesaid Gilcolm had laid him down in his tent to sleep, S. Machutus appeared to him, robed in a white raiment and a pastoral staff in his hand. Standing before his bed, the saint addressed him in these words, " What is it, Gilcolm, between thee and me ? In what way have I done evil to thee or thine that thou art now planning to rob my shrine ?" To this Gilcolm replied, " Who art thou ?" Said the saint, " I am Machutus, the servant of Christ, whose church thou art purposing to contaminate, but this thou shalt not accomplish." Having said this, he raised up the staff (baculum), which he held in his hand, and pierced him to the heart. The wretched man gave a dreadful shriek which startled everybody in their tents, and at another thrust from the saint he shrieked again, and again at a third thrust. Then, indeed, his son and all his army, disturbed by his cries, ran to him to know what had happened. But he, hardly able to speak, said with a groan, " S. Machute has been here, and has thrice stabbed me with his staff. But haste, speed to his church, and bring hither his staff and the priests and clerks, that they may intercede for me with S. Machute, if peradventure he will be lenient to me for the things I plotted against him." These injunctions were quickly obeyed, and the clerics were entreated by his followers, who told them all that had happened, to bring with them the saint's staff, and come and visit their lord, who now appeared to be in extremes. Hearing these things, the priests and the rest of the multitude rejoiced with a great joy, and sent off certain of the clergy with the staff, one of whom, when they reached his presence, and saw that he was now almost lifeless, for he had lost his speech a short time before, uttered this curse :—" May S. Machute, who has begun to punish thee, no cease till he has brought thee to destruction, so that others seeing and hearing (these things) may learn to show more reverence for holy places." After speaking these words, the clergy returned home, and after their departure a huge swarm of flies (great and loathsome) began to buzz about his face and mouth, that neither he nor his servants could drive them away—thus in the most intense agony he died. At his death such terror seized Somerled and his army that they set sail from that port, and in extreme haste departed to their own country.[1]

Such is the semi-mythical account of an incident which, with little doubt, rests upon a basis of genuine history. The soul of the Celtic warrior seems to have been deeply impressed by the threatened sacrilege and the retribution that ensued, and whatever may have been the true links in the chain of historical events, the conjecture is by no means improbable that Somerled's intention to found and endow a church may have sprung from, or at anyrate would have been greatly strengthened by, his experiences at the shrine of Saint Machutus. It is undoubtedly the case that, from Somerled's time down to the fall of the Lordship of the Isles, the Church in Scotland had no more generous friends or patrons than the heads of the House of Isla. This patronage of the Church by the Lords of the Isles was not exercised, as we might expect, for the maintenance of what survived, and was ready to perish, of the old Celtic establishments, but rather to promote, as has already been remarked, the more aggressive order of Latin Christianity. In 1164, shortly before his death, we find the influence of Somerled exercised in con-

[1] Chronicle of Man A.D. 1158, but more correctly 1156.

nection with the monastery of Iona, by that time in a state of decay. The last of the Abbots of Iona of whom any record survives died in the last year of the eleventh century, and for over fifty years thereafter all contemporary records are dumb regarding this ancient nursery of Scottish Christianity.[1] This is to be accounted for, not merely by the decay of the Culdee Church, but to the fact that the Norwegian Kings of the Isles, though professing Christianity, do not appear to have been nursing fathers of the Church, at anyrate within the Scottish portion of their domains. It was after Somerled had become virtually King of the Sudoreys that we find a movement taking place for the reorganisation of this community of Iona. We find that in 1164 the chiefs of the Family of Iona, acting on the advice of Somerled and the men of Argyle and the Isles, invited Flaithbertach O'Brolchan, Abbot of Derry, to become Abbot of Iona,[2] but for some unrecorded reason their proposal was vetoed by the King of Ireland and the chiefs of the Cinel Eoghain. The authorities who have recorded this episode throw an interesting light upon the constitution of the establishment of Icolumkill during this period of decay. There was the "Sacartmor," or great priest ; the "Ferleighinn," or lector ; the "Diseartach," or head of the Disert, for the reception of pilgrims and the head of the Cele De, or Culdees. The efforts to revive the Celtic establishment in Iona failed as it did elsewhere, and the system soon gave way to the newer and more energetic orders of the Church of Rome, and this reconstruction of Church life, at anyrate as regards its outward form and material support, was to owe its existence in

[1] Skene's Celtic Scotland, vol. II., p. 413.
[2] Annals of Ulster. Chronicle of the Picts and Scots.

St Columba's Isle to the patronage of the Clan Cholla.

The oldest religious foundation connected with the Family of the Isles—at anyrate within the historical period—is the Abbey of Saddell, and a brief sketch of its origin and early history must be given before we pass on to the more widely known and still beautiful Church of St Mary's in Icolumkill. Tradition is not unanimous as to whether Saddell Monastery was founded by Somerled or his son Reginald, while Hugh Macdonald, the Seanachie of Sleat, ascribes its origin to Donald, the son of Reginald and the founder of the Clan. It is highly probable that so extensive a building would have been the work of several generations of the Lords of the Isles, and that while Somerled founded and endowed it and its erection was begun in his life-time, his son and grandson enriched it with further gifts, and it was completed only in Donald's time. That it owes its original foundation to Somerled is confirmed by the almost universal tradition that his remains were interred within the Abbey,[1] while

---

[1] "Sandallum, Saundle ; al. Sandalium, Saundalium de Stagdalo, Saundell, Sandal, Sandael, Sanadale, Sadael, Sadale, Saldal, Sagadal, Sadagal, Sagadul, de Sagada, Sagadach de Ulconia v. de Ulcone, v. de Vasconia, Sagadoch.

"Sandallium in Cathyra et diocesi Dunkeldensi (pup. Cathanensi) in Scotia situm, Somerledus (Soirle Mackilvrid, alias Sourle MacLerdy, filius Gilbride) insularum Scoticarum dominus, quem Marianus Brockie 'piratam et latronem famosissimum' vocat, a. 1164 devictus et interfectus, condere coepisse et Reginaldus filius circa annum 1220 absolvisse leguntur (A.R.E.E.M.S.C.N.L.La) 1219 ; v. 1216, M.Pa, 1163 ; Birch I. inter a. 1160 et 1200 ; Brockie, 1256 ; v. I., I.C., Bo Ve, St. Matrem Russinium (de linea clara Vallis) extitisse arbitramur, aliis Furnessium vel Mellifontem exhibenti-bus ; Demsterus Thomae Abbatis mentionem facit, a. 1257 florentis, quem 'ita se gessisse asserit, ut neque doctiorem neque moribus sanctiorem aetas illa tulerit.'" (Maur 1216, X. 1. Iong VIII. 17. N. 20, ej Origg. Donschou ; Arnott, D. Mariana Brockie ib. Theiner Hib., 608. Chalmers I., 683. Spottiswood ap Keith, 421. Demster II., 592. Fordun II., 538.) Extract, page 224, No. DLXXXI., "Originum Cisterciensium," Tomus I.—P. Leopold Iananscheck.

one authority places the completion of the building as late as 1256—after the death of Donald de Ile and the succession of his son Angus Mor. The Church of Saddell was cruciform in structure, with the orientation and pointed arch characteristic of Gothic buildings; but, except in the windows, we miss the dressed sandstone which marked the full advance from the Celtic to the Gothic age. The

PART OF THE RUINS OF SADDELL MONASTERY.

Monastery lies in an exact position towards the four cardinal points. Its dimensions were at one time imposing, though little now survives beyond a mass of featureless confusion. Part of the gable of the transept and the aperture for a window alone survive; but vandalism here, as elsewhere, has done its unhallowed work, and the finished stonework of the window has almost all been removed. The cruciform minster was 136 feet long from east to west, by 24 feet broad, while the transepts from north to south measured 78 feet by 24. The conventual buildings were on the south ; the dormitory was 58 feet long, and there are traces of the study room. The cloister girth was 58 feet square. Within the arched recess in the south wall of the choir, Somerled's tomb is pointed out. The sculpture represents him as wearing a high pointed head-piece, a tippet of mail hanging over the neck and shoulders, and the body clad down to the knees with a skirt or *jupon* scored with lines to represent the folds. The right hand is raised up to the shoulder, while the left clasps a two-handed sword. The inscription on the corner of the slab has been worn away by the elements, and has for ages been indecipherable.

There are few more charming spots anywhere than the delightful glen where, 700 years ago, this venerable house of prayer was reared to the glory of God. From the beautiful beach of whitest sand, close to which the residence of the genial laird of Glensaddell[1] stands, the stranger wends his way through an avenue of immemorial trees, and when at last the eye rests upon the scant remains of what was once a structure of no small magnitude, one's piety glows with quite as much warmth (if with less sonorous expression) as did that of the learned Doctor who felt so much overcome among the ruins of Iona. Down the glen runs *Allt nam Manach*, or

---

[1] J. Macleod, Esq. of Kintarbert and Saddell, to whose courtesy and kindness the authors were much indebted during a flying visit to the historic region. Mr Macleod, who is an authority on the antiquities of Argyllshire, has recently restored and made habitable the ancient castle, in which Angus Og entertained the Bruce.

the monks' burn, and on the further bank there is a well, scooped out of a rectangular block of dressed freestone, almost concealed by long grass and coronals of fern, and bearing a Latin cross carved on its front. Into this basin the crystal water, deliciously cool even in midsummer, continually trickles from the rock, as it did in those far off days when the matins and vespers of the holy men rose to the morning and evening sky.

The Abbey of Saddell, which was in the Diocese of Dunkeld, was founded for monks of the Cistercian or Bernardine order, instituted in 1098 by Robert, Abbot of Molesne, in the Diocese of Langres, in Burgundy. Their designation of Cistercian originated where their chief house and first monastery were situated, and the alternative title, Bernardines, was in honour of Bernard, a Burgundian, who was sometime afterwards elected Abbot of Clairvaux. The brethren of the Cistercian order wore a black cowl and scapular, the rest of their dress being white, and from this came their common designation of white or gray friars to distinguish them from the Benedictines, who were clad altogether in black. This institution was well endowed by Reginald, who gave the monks the lands of Glen Saddell and the 12 marks of Baltebean, in the lordship of Kintyre, and the 20 merklands of Cesken, in the Isle of Arran. Dempster[1] refers to Thomas, an abbot of this monastery who flourished in 1257, as one who was unsurpassed in his age for piety and learning, and it was he, in all probability, who, six years later (1263), the year of Haco's famous expedition, placed the monastery of Greyfriars under the protection of the Norwegian King, a

[1] Vol. II., p. 592.

protection which he received from him in writing.[1]
The same authority informs us that this Thomas
Sandalius wrote several books, which were kept in
the library of St Andrews, but these, if they
existed, have long since disappeared.[2] Friar Simon,
Haco's chaplain, who died at Gigha during the same
expedition, was carried to Kintyre, and received
sepulture within the church of the Greyfriars.[3]
Tayinloan, in the parish of Killean, is said to have
been a cell or chapel of Saddell, but there are no
traces whatever in the spot so called of the existence
of any ecclesiastical building, and it is almost certain
that the reference to Tayinloan is, in this connection,
a mistake.   Saddell and Killean were originally one
parish, and the old Church of St John's (Killean),
the remains of which are in the cemetery at Largie,
must have been really the cell of Saddell referred to,
though, owing to its proximity to Tayinloan, it has
gone under that name.   This view, we think, is
conclusive, when it is borne in mind that, before
the year 1251, early in the history of the Abbey,
Roderick, the son of Reginald, gave for the service
of the Church of St John (Killean) five penny-
lands.[4]   Among the sculptured stones in the
Largie burying ground — north transept of old
Killean Church—is one bearing the figure of an
ecclesiastic in full canonicals.   Whether it rests
over the remains of Friar Simon, Haco's chaplain, to whose obsequies the Greyfriars paid
much honour, spreading a fringed pall over his
grave and calling him a saint, or whether the
dust of Abbot Thomas lies beneath it, has, with
good reason, been conjectured; but the existence

---

[1] Haco's Expedition, pp. 52-53.   [2] Keith's Catalogue, p. 258.
[3] Ibidem.   [4] Reg. Mag. Sig. Liber XIV., No. 389.

of the sculptured stone seems to us to mark out the old Church of Killean as probably the last resting place of the Vicars to whom, under Saddell monastery, the spiritual oversight of that region pertained. To the Church of Killean probably smaller cells were attached.[1]

The most important of the churches that owed either their origin or resuscitation to the Lords of the Isles was the Abbey Church of Iona. About 1072, Queen Margaret had restored the monastery and revived its establishment, but by the latter half of the twelfth century these had again fallen into ruin and decay. Reginald MacSomerled, whom M'Vurich describes as "the most distinguished of the Galls, that is, the Norwegians, and of the Gaels for prosperity, sway of generosity, and feats of arms," resolved to repair the waste places of the sacred island and restore its church and monastery to more than their pristine glory. According to the same authority, "three monasteries were formed by him—a monastery of black monks in I, or Iona, in honour of God and Saint Columchille; a monastery of black nuns in the same place; and a monastery of gray friars at Sagadul, or Sadelle, in Kintyre," which latter we have already described. A column on the south-east, under the tower of St Mary's, bears the inscription—"Donaldus O'Brolchan fecit hoc opus." This "Donaldus" was prior of Derry, and a relative of Flaherty O'Brolchan, bishop and Abbot of Derry, and although there is no distinct record on the subject, "Donaldus" must have been prior of Iona during the period these buildings were erected. As he died in 1203, the

---

[1] For notes on the Cell of (sic) Tayinloan we are indebted to the Rev. D. J. Macdonald, minister of Killean and Kilchenzie.

Church and Monastery of Iona must have been completed before that date, and this is further placed beyond doubt by the deed of confirmation of the Benedictine Monastery, which is still in the Vatican, and bears the date of 9th December, 1203.[1] The Tyronensis Order of Benedictine Monks, founded by Benedict, an Italian monk of the fifth and sixth centuries, and called black monks from the colour of their habits, was planted in the Monastery of Iona by Reginald of the Isles. He also established there, in connection with it, an order of Benedictine nuns, over whose convent his sister Beatrice was the first prioress; differing in this respect from the policy of the great Columkill himself, of whom tradition says that he would suffer none of the softer sex to set foot upon Iona, and to whom the somewhat acrid saying is ascribed—

> " Far am bi bo bi bean
> 'S far am bi bean bi mallachadh."

> (Where there is a cow there is a woman,
> And where there is a woman there is mischief).

Early this century the inscription on the monumental slab over the remains of the first Prioress was legible to this extent—" Behag Nyn Shorle Ilvrid Priorissa," that is, "Beatrice daughter of Somerled Prioress." There is a tradition that the same pious lady built Trinity Temple, Carinish, the ruins of which are still standing in a state of comparative preservation.[2] The historian of Sleat, on the other hand, ascribes its construction to another lady—also a descendant of Somerled— Amie Macruari, famous in her day for works of piety and charity, and whose memory is still fragrant

[1] Skene's Celtic Scotland, vol. II., p. 416.
[2] McVurich in Reliquiæ Celticæ, vol. II., p. 157.

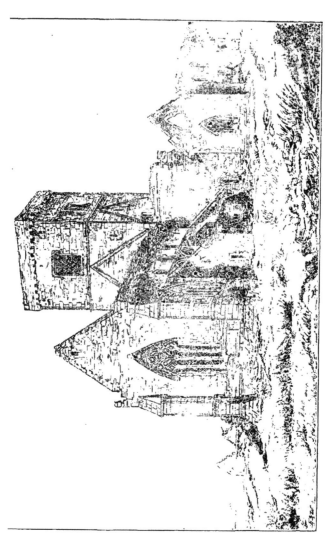

NORTH-EAST VIEW OF THE ABBEY CHURCH, IONA.

among the people of the North Isles. Trinity
Temple is probably not the architectural product of
any one age. There are traces of a foundation older
than the days of Somerled, going back to the time
of the Celtic Church, shown by indications of one at
least of those bee-hive cells characteristic of that
early phase of church architecture. It is also to be
noted that Christina (daughter of Allan Macruari
and aunt of Amie), who flourished about the end of
the thirteenth and beginning of the fourteenth
century, gave a grant of the chapel and lands of
Carinish to the Monastery of Inchaffray, from which
we infer that the Temple or Church in question is
older than Amie, the wife of the "good" John of
Isla. Hence the probable correctness of the
McVurich tradition that Trinity Church was built
by the daughter of Somerled on a site formerly
occupied by a Culdee establishment, though we may
likewise adopt the tradition of Hugh Macdonald to
the extent that, in later times, Amie Macruari did,
as we shall see, repair and possibly enlarge the
building. The Church of St Mary's, in Iona,
measured 160 ft. × 24, and 70 feet across the transepts, while its central tower, which still survives,
is 70 feet in height. The high altar was of marble
6 ft. × 4, but not a fragment now remains. Cockney
tourists have gradually extracted it chip by chip,
and Pennant not only is unashamed but rather
makes merry over the fact that he himself was a
unit in the noble army of Vandals ![1]

The connection of the Lords of the Isles with the
Abbey of Paisley, with which they had no territorial
bond, was maintained from the days of Somerled

[1] Vol. II., p. 253.

down to the fall of the House of Isla, a period of
300 years. We can only conjecture as to the
original cause of this connection ; but we can hardly
be mistaken in the view that the death of Somerled
and of a number of his men in the region of West
Renfrewshire would have led his son to give grants
to the Monastery of Paisley to secure the offices of
the Church for the souls of the fallen heroes.
Before 1200, Reginald became a monk of Paisley,
and granted to the monastery eight cows and two
pennies for one year, and one penny in perpetuity
from every house on his territory from which smoke
issued, and his peace and protection whithersoever
the monks should go, enjoining his dependants and
heirs in no way to injure them, and swearing by
St Columba to inflict on the former the punishment
of death, and that the latter should have his male-
diction if they disobeyed his injunction. His wife
Fonia, who was a sister of the convent, granted to
the monks the tithe of all her goods, whether in her
own possession or sent for sale by land or sea.[1]
After the year 1210, Donald, the son of Reginald,
who also had joined the brotherhood of Paisley, and
whose wife became a sister of the convent, confirmed
his father's grants both of the eight cows and of the
smoke tax, for his salvation and that of his wife.[2]
Before 1295, Angus Mor, son of Donald, after the
example of his father and grandfather, gave donations to the same institution as a friend and brother
of the order. The annual smoke tax is continued in
the same terms, while the eight cows are commuted
for a half merk of silver for each of the houses whence
smoke issues, and half a merk also from his own
mansion, the donor giving also his peace and friend-

---

[1] Reg. of Paisley, p. 125.   [2] Ibid.

ship.[1] Also he grants them the right of fishing if they should desire it in any waters upon his territories. Still further, for the salvation of his Lord and King Alexander II., and his son, Alexander III., also for his own and his heirs' he devoted to God and St James and Mirinus of the Monastery of Paisley and the monks there serving God and to serve God for ever, the Church of St Kiaran, in his lands of Kintyre, with all its pertinents. This was confirmed by his son Alexander. We do not find any further grants or confirmations on the part of the Lords of the Isles until the time of the last Earl of Ross, whom we observe on the 21st May, 1455, bestowing on the Abbey and Convent of Paisley, for the honour and glory of God, and of the Virgin Mary and Saint Mirinus, and of all the Saints, the Rectories of the Churches of St Kerran, Colmanell in Kintyre, and Knapdale, in the diocese of Argyle, given by his predecessors to them, for their and his salvation.[2] We thus see that from the very beginning of the Island dynasty, reckoning from the time of Somerled, down to its direct close, this remarkable connection with Paisley Abbey is maintained, and what is still more strange, three in succession of these powerful and warlike Lords, Reginald, Donald, and Angus Mor, and last of all the line, John, Earl of Ross, quitting the stormy scene of battle, and entering the quiet and peaceful haven of monastic life.

Having thus indicated, briefly, the relations of the Island Lords to the Monastery of Paisley, we may take up the thread of our narrative as regards their patronage of the Church within their own domains. The first of the Lords of the Isles, after the time of Reginald MacSomerled, who stands forth

[1] Reg. of Paisley, p. 127.   [2] Ibid, 156.

as a conspicuous ecclesiastical patron, is John, the
son of Angus Og of Isla. During the wars of
Scottish independence, which went on without much
intermission from the death of Angus Mor, about
1295, on to 1314, society was too much unsettled to
admit of that devotion of the community to the
affairs of its higher life, which needs a measure of
tranquillity to call it forth, and even during the
remainder of the reign of Bruce, the energies of that
King and his supporters were directed to the consolidation of the national power, which had received
such rude shocks at the hands of foreign aggression
and domestic treachery. Consequently, we can
understand that ecclesiastical buildings would, in
many cases, have fallen into a state of disrepair, and
the interests of the Church been in a measure overlooked. Probably for this reason there is no record
that Angus Og of Isla was able to devote such
attention as his predecessors to the promotion of the
Church's material welfare within his domains. If
this was the case with regard to Angus Og, his son
and successor amply atoned for it. Whatever may
have been his own proclivities in this connection,
his marriage with Amie Macruari, a lady of great
piety and benevolence, would have helped any bias
he possessed towards promoting the interests of the
Church, and to her is due no small share of the
credit which won for this eminent Chief the gratitude and affection of the Island clergy. The grants
of land he bestowed upon the Church, and the
liberality with which he defrayed the cost of new
erections, as well as the repair of former desolations,
many of which have doubtless escaped the record of
the historian, all this certainly entitled him to the
respect of the churchmen of the Isles, and gained for

him, not undeservedly, the name by which he is best
known in history, " the good John of Isla."

In the island of Finlaggan, on which stood the
palace of the *De Ile* family, there was also a small
chapel, which, owing to the troublous times of John's
predecessor, had become roofless and dilapidated.
This, with the chapels on Isle Eorsag and of Isle
Suibne (in Loch Sween), was roofed and made habitable by authority of the Lord of the Isles, while
he also made provision whereby they should be
appointed " with all their appropriate instruments
for order and mass for the service of God, for the
better upholding of the monks and priests this lord
kept in his company."[1] He also made gifts, probably
of land, to the monks of Iona, and we find him
granting to the monks of Saddell two merklands,
called Lesenmarg, in the district of Kintyre. The
most considerable, however, of all his gifts to the
Church in the Hebrides was the erection of the
Priory of Oransay, the remains of which, with the
exception of Iona, are the most interesting in the
Western Isles. St Columba and his disciple Oran
are said by tradition to have settled in Colonsay and
Oransay before they finally determined to take up
their abode in Hy.   Be this as it may, there appear
to have been in both islands religious establishments
under the Columban Church, but all traces of the
buildings must have disappeared centuries ago. It
is probably on the sites of the older churches that
the newer ones were built. There is a strong probability that the Church of Colonsay, which was
an Abbey, was built by the good John, though
Father Hay says in his *Scotia Sacra* that the name
of the founder had been lost through the mistake of

---

[1] Reliquiæ Celticæ, vol. II., pp. 159-161.

transcribers, or the ignorance or negligence of librarians. It was built at a place still known as Kilouran, but the stones were long ago carted away for the construction of a farm house. The canons were of Holyrood. While there is some obscurity as to the origin of Kilouran, there is none as regards the Priory of Oransay, for none other does Mac-Vurich refer to when he says that John, Lord of the Isles, erected the monastery of the holy cross (Holyrood) a long time before his death.[1] It is said to have been built as a cell of Holyrood, but tradition says that Kilouran, or the Abbey of Colonsay, was the Church on which Oransay Priory was dependant; and while the Augustinian order of canons regular might have been originally brought from Holyrood, the verdict of tradition is very probably correct. Transitional Early English in style, its roofless church measures 77⅔ feet in length and 18 feet in width, and has a fine three-light Gothic E. window. It retains a very peculiar cloister girth forming a square of 40 feet without and 28⅔ feet within. In Pennant's time[2] (1772) the cloister had on one side a round arcading of five members, or small arches; while two other sides facing each other showed seven low triangular head arches with plain square columns. The adjoining buildings are ruined; but a handsome cross remains, 12 feet high by 1½ feet broad and 7 inches thick, while the mutilated fragments of another cross lie near. The church contains a number of curious effigies. One of these is in a side chapel beneath an arch, and is of an abbot of the MacDuffie family (who, according to Hugh Macdonald, were Recorders of the Isles), holding two fingers erect in the attitude of benediction.

---

[1] Reliquiæ Celticæ, vol. II., pp. 160-1.　　[2] Vol. II., p. 236.

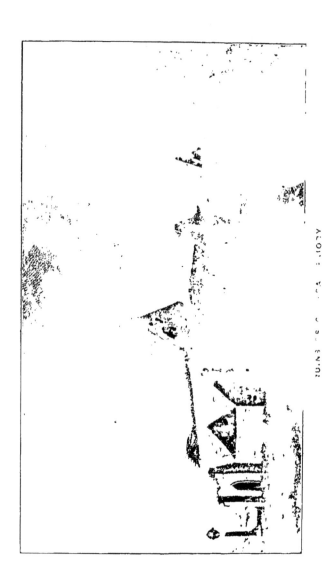

We have already referred to the MacVurich tradition that Trinity Chapel, Carinish, N. Uist, was built by Beatrice, the daughter of Somerled. It is equally probable that owing to the ravages of time it had become dilapidated, and its repair and probable enlargement by Amie Macruari so far justifies Hugh Macdonald's tradition that it was built by her. This ruin stands on a commanding elevation at the southern extremity of the island of North Uist, in early times the property of the Macruari family. Though the area covered by its site is not extensive, the height of the walls and the size of the east window indicate a foundation of some importance. The apertures are partly pointed and partly round in their heads, but although the main building stands east and west there is no trace of a cruciform construction, a fact which seems to indicate that in its chief outlines it must have existed before the Gothic type of structure came into vogue in the Islands; and thus it may be a genuine relic of the architecture of the Celtic Church. On the south there has been a side building, used now as a separate burying ground, and on the north-east there is communication by a round-headed doorway and a short waggon-vaulted passage with a small chapel lighted by a small square topped window in each end. Trinity Temple and its church lands were famous in olden times as a place of sanctuary or girth, a refuge from the avenger of blood. When the waters separating N. Uist from Benbecula ebb twice in the twenty-four hours, there remains a ford or stream which bounds the southern extremity of the Church or *termon* lands still called "sruthan na Comraich," a name which bears, and for ages to come will continue to bear, interesting testimony to a phase of Celtic Church life which has long since passed away.

The rebuilding or repair of Trinity Temple was but one among many pious deeds wrought by Amie. She also built the Parish Church of St Columba, in Benbecula, and the little oratory in the island of Grimsay; while her husband, the good John, mortified eight merklands in N. Uist and two farms in Benbecula to the Church in that region. While these cases of her pious interest in religion remain on record, she probably did much that is unrecorded to strengthen and support the ecclesiastical organisation in the Isles.

The sons of John of Isla, both of the first and second marriage, seem to have followed in their father's footsteps. Donald of Harlaw, who succeeded as Lord of the Isles, was, according to MacVurich, "an entertainer of clerics and priests and monks; gave lands to the monastery of Iona, and every immunity which the monastery of Iona had from his ancestors before him." He made a covering of gold and silver for the relic of the hand of St Columba. He is also said to have presented vessels of gold and silver to Icolmkill for the monastery, and, like several of his ancestors, and like his grandson long after him, he at last retired from the world and joined the brotherhood of the order of that monastery.

Godfrey, the second son of John of Isla by Amie, became, on the death of his father, Lord of Uist, and we find him in his castle of Ellantirrim, on the 7th July, 1389, confirming a grant by his grand-aunt, Christina, daughter of Allan Macruari, of the Church of the Holy Trinity in Uist and the whole land of Carinish, and four pennylands in Ilara

RUINED GABLE OF ST MARY'S CHURCH, HOWMORE, SOUTH UIST.

RUINED GABLE OF ST. COLUMBA'S CHURCH, HOWMORE, SOUTH UIST.

between Husabost (Kirkibost) and Kennerach to
the monastery and convent of John the evangelist
at Inchaffrey. Ranald, the eldest son of John of
Isla, who resigned in favour of his brother Donald,
received a princely heritage by charter from his
father, and that he realised the responsibilities
attached to the possession of such wide territories is
confirmed by the testimony of MacVurich, who
speaks of him as "a man of augmenting churches
and monasteries. . . . He bestowed an Unciata
of land in Uist on the monastery of Iona forever
in honour of God and of Columba." Other churches
and religious houses—of which the remains are still
extant, or existed until recent times in Uist, and of
the foundation or erection of which no record remains
—may probably be traced either to the Macruaris of
the North Isles, or Ranald, the founder of the Clanranald family, or his descendants. On a farm in
Benbecula, now called Nunton, there were last
century the ruins of a nunnery; but when the
mansion and office houses were built for Clanranald,
about 150 years ago, the old nunnery was not
considered an unsuitable quarry, and not a vestige
of the walls remain. About two miles or so north
of Nunton, and at Balivanich, the remains of a
monastery are still to be seen on a small islet in
a lake. The parish of Howmore, or *Skeirhough*
as it appears in ancient records, now the main
portion of the modern parish of S. Uist, contains
in the neighbourhood of the present church ecclesiastical remains of some antiquity. Two ruined
gables—one of St Mary's and the other of St
Columba's Church—are still pointed out, with
several smaller chapels or oratories; but although
situated in the midst of a Roman Catholic com-

munity, it is singular that hardly a hint of tradition survives regarding the history of these pre-Reformation buildings. They probably belong to the fourteenth or fifteenth centuries, having been erected not by any of the Lords of the Isles, whose connection with Uist was never very direct, but either in the latter days of the Macruari sway or early in the history of the Clanranald chiefs.

Under the sway of the two last Lords of the Isles recognised by the Crown, who were also Earls of Ross, we find a continuance of the same policy towards the Church which had so long and without interruption been pursued by the Chiefs of Clan Cholla. At a date so uncertain that it can only be referred to as before 1449, we find Alexander, Lord of the Isles, granting to the monks of Sagadull (Saddell) the island of "Sanct Barre" (now called Davaar island), and also the two merklands called Cragvan, in Gigha, with their pertinents. The gifts of these Lords were not confined to their island territories. In the Earldom of Ross and Sheriffdom of Inverness they apparently adopted the same course. On the 4th September, 1437, Alexander de Ile, Earl of Ross, made the following donation to the Prior and Friars of Inverness :—

"To all the faithful to whose knowledge the present letters shall come, Alexander de Ile, Earl of Ross and Lord of the Isles ; Greeting eternal in the Lord ; Know that we for the salvation of our soul and for the salvation of the souls of our fathers, ancestors, and successors have given, granted, and by this present writ confirmed to the religious men, the prior and friars of the Dominican Preachers of Inverness, twenty shillings of annual rent, of the usual money of the Kingdom of Scotland, to be paid annually at two terms of the year, viz., of Pentecost and St Martins, by equal portions of our land and ferry of Easter. Kessock, with the pertinents in pure and perpetual charity as freely as any annual rent is given and granted to any other religious men in the Kingdom of Scotland. In testimony of which matter we have caused our seal to be appended at Inverness, the 4th day of the month of September, in the year of the Lord 1437. These, with many others, being witnesses, viz., Torquil McLoyde, Lord of Leyvhous (Lewis), George Munro of Foulis, Alexander McCullach, and Lord Blanc."

By the Roll of Rents, Feus, and Maills it appears that the above annual of twenty shillings is still payable by the Estate of Redcastle for the lands of Kessock, having been transferred at the Reformation to the Burgh of Inverness, and forming part of its revenues to this day.[1] There is also a grant by the same Earl of Ross, not apparently to the Church but personally to the parish clergyman of Kiltearn, made 23rd March, 1439.

"Be it maid kend till all men be thir present letters US Alexander the Earl of Ross and Justiciar to our Soveraue Lord the King fra the north part of the water of Forth till haf giffyn to Walter of Urchard our cousin parson of Kilteyrn all the right of the lands of Finlay and Rosan within the burgh of Cromathy and his ousgang of Newaty notagane standand that the foresaid Walter is sister dochter wes ayr to the foresaid lands We gif that as of free gift to the said Walter as throw vertue of our office and throw power at 'langs til our lege lord the King, the fee as giffyn throw our gift, the Frank tenement remanand with the foresaid Walter quhilke be parte of the same at lyes upon the foresaid land as the Indenter party proports maid tharupon. And we the forsaid Alexander Earl of Ross warrands to the said Walter his ayrs and his assigneys the foresaid lands and at no man be so hardy to make grife molestation to the said Walter in the said lands onder the panes of lywis lands and guds at they may tyne agains the King and us giffyn onder our greit seil at Balkny the xxiii. day of March the zeir of our Lord m° iiii^v xxxix."

Before the year 1475, John, Lord of the Isles, and Angus, his son, granted to the Abbey of Sagadull the lands of Knockantebeg and 12 unciate of

---

[1] Invernessiana (by Charles Fraser-Mackintosh, Esq.), p. 109.

land called Kellipull,[1] while in 1492, the year before
his final forfeiture, we find the same potentate as
patron of the Church of Kilberry in Knapdale
granting to Robert, Bishop of Argyle, his rights as
such, upon which it was united to the Bishoprick as
a mensal Church. Owing to the loss of the writs of
the See of the Isles, we cannot pretend to give
anything like a complete account of the Church
built or the lands mortified to the service of religion
by the Lords of the Isles. The Pre-Reformation
Church of Morvern, known as Kilcholumchill, was a

From Photo by   *Messrs M'Isaac & Riddle, Oban.*
WINDOW OF ST COLUMBA'S CHURCH, MORVERN.

deanery, and it derives interest from the fact that
Roderick M'Allister, called by M'Vurich "Parson
Rory," and a brother of the famous John Moydart-
ach, the incumbent in 1545, was one of the Plenipo-
tentiaries of Donald Dubh in his negotiations with
Henry VIII. The fine window alone remains in

[1] Reg. Mag. Sig. Lib. XIV., No. 408.

outline of what must once have been a handsome
Gothic structure. It stands in the neighbourhood
of Ardthornish Castle, and it is not unnatural to
suppose that it owed its origin to the Lord of the
Isles. A tall Celtic cross stands in the immediate
vicinity.

From Photo by   *Messrs M'Isaac & Riddic, Oban.*

CELTIC CROSS AT MORVERN.

In thus concluding our review of the numerous
and costly gifts by " the clan who never vexed the
Church," we cannot but be struck by the thought
that amid all their generosity to religious establishments throughout their domains and elsewhere, they
never, from the days of Somerled downwards, ceased
their benefactions to the Abbey of Saddell. Amid
all changes of time and fortune they always turned
to it as the chief claimant upon their wealth, the
earliest and most beloved home of their faith.

Having thus considered the relation of the Lords
of the Isles to the Church as an outward organisation, we may now devote a very brief space to a

consideration of the Church under their sway as an educative agency in the life of the people. It is well known that learning as well as religion was for many centuries in the hands of churchmen. Owing to the long connection of the Columban Church with Ireland, it was inevitable that the standard of written Irish should have been introduced by the Columban monks into Scotland. Irish Gaelic thus became to a large extent the language of the Church, the monastery, and the school. The literary connection between Ireland and Iona was thus for ages very pronounced, and was only interrupted in the eighth century, when the Scandinavian invasions, among other causes, reduced that Celtic shrine to a state of ruin and decay. The connection thus broken was again renewed in the eleventh century, after the Norseman had embraced Christianity and a settled government was established in the Isles ; but especially when the Scoto-Irish race of Somerled became, in the twelfth century, the ruling family in the Western Highlands. The revival of Gaelic culture in these regions through the *De Ile* Family, and, to some extent, also through the MacDugalls of Lorn, is exemplified by the fact that almost all the known Scottish MSS. are to be traced to the seats of learning in Iona, Saddell, Ardchattan, Lismore, and Kilmun. The government which the Lords of the Isles thus maintained for three hundred years in the West rendered possible and easy not only the cultivation of Gaelic as a spoken, but also to a large extent as a literary, language. This of course could only be done through the countenance and fostering care of the religious houses in the North of Ireland, which, in times of peace and security, were nursing mothers to Iona and other monasteries in the

Western Highlands. Although Latin had always been the language of literature, of sacred learning, and of business, the study of Gaelic as a literary language must have been largely encouraged by the Church in the more purely Celtic regions from the days of St Columba. Hence, under the shelter of the Church, itself the earliest home of letters, as well as of the arts and sciences, there arose Gaelic literary schools in Ireland which embraced the West Highlands in the sphere of their operations. In illustration of this, we find the Annals of the Four Masters, in 1448, recording the death of Teague O'Coffey, " chief preceptor of the poets of Erin and Alban." Of these schools, the bards and seanachies of Ireland were the heads, and it was quite a usual course for the family bards and chroniclers of the Isles, as in the case of the Mac-Vurichs, to resort to those bardic colleges to receive instruction in the accomplishments and *technique* of their art, sometimes, no doubt, in defiance of the truth contained in the adage, " Poeta nascitur non fit." On this account the Gaelic of the Book of Clanranald abounds in Irishisms which clearly differentiate it from the common Scottish Gaelic, as well as from the dialect that came gradually into written use after the fall of the Lordship of the Isles severed the connection with Ireland.

Dr Skene, whose researches into the organisation of the Celtic Church both in its heyday and fall are most exhaustive and full of interest, tells us that among the functionaries of that Church, as late as the thirteenth century, was the *ferleiginn*, lector or man of learning, whose duties seem to have been purely educative as distinguished from the more sacred or religious phases of ecclesiastical life.[1] The work of the *ferleiginn* consisted in teaching the arts of reading, writing, and other necessary accomplishments to those who were undergoing a course of instruction to fit them for the service of the Church, and doubtless also in imparting knowledge to members of the higher classes who sometimes, if not universally, were sent to acquire the elements of knowledge in the monastic institutions both of Ireland and Scotland. The range and extent of the learning conveyed in these monasteries may perhaps seem narrow if judged by the standard of to-day, but so far as it went it must have been sufficiently thorough. In one of the polite arts we, of this age, can certainly not hope to equal them. The finer types of MS. which have survived from the time of the Columban Church downwards for many centuries—of which the Books of Kells and Deer, the Lindisfare Gospels, and other beautifully written documents of the fourteenth and fifteenth centuries are specimens—bear abundant testimony that in the art of penmanship, as well as of decorative skill, nothing can be produced to-day equal in beauty of execution to these monuments of past ages. It would appear that while the *ferleiginn* was a survival of Celtic Christianity, the function of education must have been carried on by the Latin Church probably by means of an official of similar standing, though the name itself may have disappeared. The close connection between the Lords of the Isles and the Church down to the end of the dynasty suggests the probability that, although learning was often regarded as a monkish accomplishment by men

[1] Celtic Scotland, vol. II., pp. 447-48.

RUINS OF TRINITY TEMPLE, CARINISH, N. UIST.

whose true business was to fight, yet they may not have been, and probably were not, altogether illiterate. These Lords almost invariably appended seals instead of signatures to such surviving documents as they had to attest, and this renders the question difficult to answer—had they any literary education? The sole signature we possess of a Lord of the Isles—that of Donald of Harlaw to the Gaelic charter of 1408—seems to throw some light upon the subject. The large bold characters, quite worthy in that respect of the King of Innse-Gall, are clearly the work of one who was versed in the art of writing. It is surely not an unwarrantable inference that, whatever his forbears may have been educationally, his son and grandson would have received no less advantages in this respect than he did. Judging, indeed, by Hugh Macdonald's tradition, which in this matter may be trustworthy enough, the last John would appear to have been endowed with more education than was prevalent at the time, except among the professional classes. A change for the worse, however, seems to have taken place educationally in the Western Isles in the first half of the sixteenth century. By the year 1545, there is disclosed a literary dearth betokening a previous famine intense and prolonged. It is not only that we find Donald Dubh, the aspirant to the Island honours, signing with his " hand at the pen," as might be expected from his life-long imprisonment, but every one of the 18 barons of his Council, the principal chiefs in the Isles, from Sir Hector Maclean, his Chamberlain, downwards, having their signs manual to the Commission in favour of the plenipotentiaries, adhibited by a notary public. This in itself is a clear proof that, educationally, the hands

31

of the clock of history had gone back hundreds of
years. As a further sign that education was
stagnant, and particularly that the standard of Irish
Gaelic had disappeared from the Western Highlands,
we have the Book of Dean McGregor of Lismore,
written in phonetic Gaelic, in 1512, a knowledge of
the standard Irish having been, from the circumstances of his time, denied him. These facts, of
course, are not difficult to account for. The
transition from the dominance of the Roman
Catholic Church to the new order of the Reformed
Religion, revolutionary in its nature, and accompanied by the fall or decay of the monasteries, must
for the time being have proved unfavourable to
educational progress. More directly affecting the
Western Isles, however, was the fall of the House
of Isla in 1493. Hitherto the central bond of social
order and authority in the West, in the Church,
education, and secular life; with the fall of that
House the connection with the literary schools of
Ireland ceased, the patronage of learning in the Isles
passed away, and the principality became for upwards
of a generation the scene of feuds and struggles, of
chronic strife and disorder, which proved entirely
subversive of a condition of things in which such a
matter as education could for a moment be considered.

We have already referred to the beautiful embellishment of some of the rarer types of MSS., but
this is by no means the only proof that the ancient
Celt excelled in artistic work. The sculptured
remains in church and cemetery clearly indicate
their superiority in other forms of decorative art.
In the architecture of. such remains as· Iona and
Oronsay, in the crosses and gravestones to be met

with in Isla and other Hebridean isles, there is often
shown an elaborate ornamentation evincing a high
degree of artistic skill.   In these sculptured stones
we come across many illustrations of a poetic
symbolism peculiarly Celtic.   The shears cutting
the thread of life, borrowed from classic myth ; the
trefoil and triangle, emblems of eternity or of the
Trinity ; the struggle with wild beasts, indicating
man's subjugation of the brute powers of nature, all
illustrate the same characteristic.   Common among
the *tableaux* we meet with are hunting scenes ; dogs
in pursuit of deer, suggestive of men's favourite pursuits in time of peace ; low relieved by warriors and
ladies, vested ecclesiastics, archers and harpers,
galleys, griffins and armed horsemen.   No doubt the
original home whence these arts of architecture, sculpture, and others were imported into the Highlands
was Ireland ; but the connection between it and the
Western Isles was for centuries so close that in all
the essential features of their intellectual life they
were the same.   If the master craftsmen came first
from Ireland, they doubtless found apt and willing
pupils among their kinsmen of the Scottish Isles.
This alone would furnish proof, if proof were needed,
that during the middle ages the Gaelic races of
Scotland were not, as some writers would have us
believe, sunk in the depths of barbaric ignorance.

APPENDICES.

CARTA REGINALDI FILII SUMERLEDI DOMINI INCHEGAL DE
UNO DENARIO EX QUALIBET DOMO IN TERRA SUA DE
QUIBUS EXIT FUMUS. C. 1180.

Sciant omnes tam presentes quam futuri quod ego Reginaldus
filius Sumerled dominus de Inchegal factus sum frater, et uxor
mea Fonia soror in capitulo domus de Passelet et in toto ordine
Cluniacensi et ego verus frater et bonus amicus predictis monachis
fratribus meis de Passelet imperpetuum mansurus, cum heredibus
meis et hominibus meis, testimonio sigilli mei concessi eis me
daturum sibi pro salute mea et uxoris mee et heredum meorum
et hominum in hoc anno octo boves et duos denarios ex qualibet
domo unde fumus exit, et post hunc annum singulis annis unum
denarium ex qualibet domo totius terra mee unde fumus exit dabo
illis et post me heredes mei dabunt, aut maledictionem meam
habebunt nisi promptissime dederint Preterea uxor mea Fonia
concessit eis se daturam illis in elemosinam decimam omnium
rerum que sibi Deus dederit, scilicet tam ex ipsis que apud se
retinere voluerit quam ex illis que per terram vel per mare ad
vedendum imperpetuum miserit. Et quia ego et heredes mei
participes sumus et imperpetuum erimus omnium bonorum que in
domo de Passelet in todo ordine fiunt vel imperpetuum fient, tam
in orationibus quam in ceteris divine servitutis obsequiis, dedi eis
et concessi et hoc presenti scripto auctoritate sigilli mei roborato
confirmavi, firmam pacem meam et omnium heredum meorum et
hominum, cum manutenemento bone fraternitatis, ubicunque ipsi
vel homines eorum fuerunt aut venerint, in terra vel in mari,
supplicans amicis meis et precipieno omnibus hominibus meis et
ubicunque invenerint predictas monachos fratres meos aut eorum
homines ipsos manuteneant et in suis auxilientur negotiis, scientes
pro certo quod per Sanctum Columbam si aliquis heredum meorum
eis malefecerit, maledictionem meam habebit, vel si quid mali

forte ab hominibus meis, vel ab aliis de quibus esos vindicare potero, sibi vel suis factum fuerit, mortis pena punientur. Hiis testibus Ameleo filio Gillecolmi, Gillecolmo filio Gilmihel, Mauricio capellano meo, et multis aliis ibi tunc presentibus.

CARTA DOVENALDI FILII REGINALDI SUMERLED, DE UNO DENARIO EXPIENDO EX QUALIBET DOMO IN TERRA SUA UNDE EXIT FUMUS. C. 1210.

Sciant omnes tam presentes quam futuri quod ego Dovenaldus filius Reginaldi filii Somerled dominus de Inchegal factus sum frater et uxor mea, soror in capitulo domus de Passelet et in toto ordine Cluniacensi; et ego verus frater et bonus amicus predictis monachis fratribus meis de Passelet imperpetuum mansurus cum heredibus meis et hominibus meis quibus fraternitatem predicte domus et participationem et omnium beneficiorum totius ordinis Cluniacensis, a jam dictis monachis adquisivi concessi eis me daturum sibi, testimonio sigilli mei octo vaccas pro salute mea et uxoris mee [et de qualibet domo] unde pro ipsis denariis octo vaccas. Et quia ego et heredes mei et homines mei participes sumus et imperpetuum erimus omnium sicut, tam in orationibus quam in ceteris divine servitutis obsequiis dedi eis et concessi, et hoc presenti scripto auctoritate sigilli mei roborato confirmavi firmam pacem meam et omnium heredum meorum et hominum meorum cum manutenemento bone fraternitatis ubicunque ipsi vel homines eorum fuerint aut venerint in terra vel in mari Supplicans amicus meis et precipiens omnibus hominibus meis ut ubicunque invenerint predictos monachos fratres mea et eorum homines ipsos manuteneant et in suis auxilientur negotiis scientes pro certo quod per Sanctum Columbam si quid mali forte ab hominibus meis vel ab aliis de quibus eos vindicare potero sibi vel suis factum fuerit, morti pena punientur. Et notandum quod ubicunque ego vel heredes mei aut aliqui ex hominibus meis mortui fuerimus, in terra vel in mari, predicti monachi orabunt pro nobis imperpetuum ut salvi simus, et per totum ordinem Cluniacensem orationis pro nobis fieri facient. Hiis testibus Ameleo filio Gillecolmi, Gillicolmo filio Gilmihel, Mauricio capellano meo et multis aliis, ex propriis hominibus meis.

CARTA DE DIMIDIE MARCE, ET UNIIS DENARII ANNUATIM DE SINGULIS DOMIBUS DE QUIBUS EXIT FUMUS IN TERRA ANGUSII FILII DOVENALDI. 1253.

Sciant omnes tam presentes quam futuri quod ego Angus filius Dovenaldi verus frater et amicus domus de Passelet ad exemplum avi mei et patris mei, dedi, concessi, et hac presenti carta mea confirmavi Deo et monasterio de Passelet et monachis ibidem Deo servientibus in puram et perpetuam elemosinam dimidiam marcam argenti de domo mea propria et heredum meorum annuatim et de singulis domibus per omnes terras meas de quibus fumus exit unum denarium singulis annis imperpetuum. Dedi, etiam et concessi dictis monachis et hominibus suis firmam pacem meam et heredum et hominum meorum cum manutenemento bone fraterni-tatis, ubicunque fuerint aut venerint per potestatem nostram in terra vel in mari, Supplicans amicis meis, et precipiens omnibus meis super meam plenariam forisfacturam, ut ubicunque invenerint predictos monachos fratres meos et eorum homines ipsos manu-teneant et in suis auxilientur negotiis. Et si dicti monachi vel eorum litteras Abbatis vel conventus diferentes ad partes nostras causa piscandi aliquando venire voluerint dedi et concessi eisdem licentiam et facultatem piscandi ubique in potestate mea et heredum meorum congruentibus piscature et piscatoribus. In cujus rei testimonium presenti scripto sigillum meum apposui. Hiis testibus Alexandro fratre meo. Ferchardo de Buit Duncano fratre sua Throfino, Gilberto filio Samuelis Petro clerico Henrico Russel Thomas justore Wilelmodi Stragrif, Laurentio clerico et multis aliis.

Chartulary of Paisley.

COPIA DONATIONIS ET ETIAM CONFIRMATIONIS ECCLESIE SANCTI QUERANI IN KENTYIR. 1283.

Venerabili patri in Christo domino Laurencio Dei Gratia Ergadiensi episcopo ceterisque Christi fidelibus ad quorum aspectum presens scriptum pervenerit Jacobus senescallus Scotie dominus Robertus thesaurarius ecclesie Glasguensis Magister Thomas Nicholai subdecanus ejusdem loci et Magister Alexandri Kenedi canonicus ejusdem ecclesie, salutem in Domino sempi-ternam. Quia pat pecatum est mendacio consentire et veritati Testimonium subtrahere, in falsitas prevaleat veritati vel iniquitas prejudicet equitate inversitati vestro presentibus significamus nos inspexisse cartam domini Engus filii Dovenaldi super (ecclesie)

Chartulary of Paisley.

Sancti Querani in Kentyir necnon et confirmationes venerabilium patrum dominorum, Alani et Laurenti Ergadiensium episcoporum super eadem ecclesia religiosi viris Abbati et conventiu de Passelet concessas et roborates non rasas, non abolitas non laniatas nec ni aliquia parte vitiatas, in hec verba. OMNIBUS Christi fidelibus tam presentibus quam futuris Engus filius Dovenaldi eternam in Domino salutem. Sciates me intuitu pietatis et pro salute domini mei Alexandri illustris regis Scotie et pro salute Alexandri filii ejus, et pro salute mea propria et heredum meorum, dedisse concessisse et hac carta mea confirmasse Deo et Sancto Jacobo et Sancto Mirino monasterii de Passelet et monachis ibidem Deo servientibus et imperpetuum servituris ecclesiam Sancti Querani in Serra mea (que) Kentyir appelatur Tenendam el habendam in liberam, puram et perpetuam elemosinam cum omnibus justus pertinentiis suis ita libere et quiete sicut aliquia ecclesia tenetur et possidetut liberius et quietus in regno Scotie ex donatione comitis vel barones habentis jus patronatus in ecclesiis. Hic Testibus Alano de Nef milite, Ferchar filio Nigilli de Buyd Dovenaldo clerico de Kildufbenin, Gilhis Macduntith, Kennauth Macgilruth, Gilleshop nuntio, et aliis.

DONATIO ECCLESIA SANCTI QUERANI IN KENTYIR PER ALEXANDRUM DE HYLE. C. 1295.

of Omnibus Christi fidelibus presens scriptum visuris vel audituris Alexander de Hyle filius et here domini Engusii filii Dovenaldi domini de Hyle, salutem in Domino sempiternam. Noverit universita vestra me inspexisse et palpasse cartam domini patris mei, non rasam, non abolitam nec maliquia parte sui vatiatam vel reprehensibilem, in hec verba OMNIBUS Christe fidelibus tam presentibus quam futuris Engus filius Dovenaldi eternem salutem Sciatis me intuita pietatis et pro salute domini mei Alexandri illustris regis Scotie, *et cetera omnia de verbo ad verbum ut prescribitur usque illuc*, habenti jus patronatus in ecclesiis Hanc siquidem donationem, concessionem, et confirmationem ratam et firmam habere volens imperpetuum, eam sigillo meo duxi roborandam ; et nichilominus ex habundant ut omnis materia controversie tollatur de cetero, predictis monachis pronominatam ecclesiam sicut scriptum est in omnibus do, concedo et presenti scripto meo confirmo Et ne ceca depereat oblivione aliquo tempore quod per me pia devotione gestum est et recognitum, presens scriptum sigillo meo una cum sigillo domini Laurencii Dei gratia Ergadiensis episcopi, et domini Roberti Brus' comitis de Carric gratia Majoris testimonii roborari procuravi. Hiis testibus domino Patricio Dei gratia abbote monasterii de Crosragal domino Roberto Brus' comite de Carric Roberto filio ejusdem et herede domino Roberto Anglico milite, domino Marico vicario de Aran Patricia clerico de Kentyir domino Nicholao Monacho de Crosragal et aliis.

SAFE CONDUCT TO ANGUS MACDONALD, LORD OF THE ISLES, AND ALEXANDER HIS SON. 1292.

Consimiles litteras de conductu habet Anegus filius Dovenaldi Patent Roll. et Alexander filius ejus, pro se, hominibus et mercatoribus suis in Hibernia, cum clausulis prædictis duraturas quamdiu regi placuerit, ut supra.

Teste rege, apud Berewyke super Twedam, xj. die Julii.

LITTERA ALEXANDRI DE INSULIS SCOTIÆ, FILII ANEGUS FILII DOVENALDI EJUSDEM CUM PRIORE TENORIS, QUOD PACEM CUSTODIET IN PARTIBUS SUIS INSULARUM, USQUE AD PARLIAMENTUM SCOTIÆ IN QUINDENA SANCTI MICHAELIS. 1292.

A Touz ceaus qi eelte lettre veront ou orront, Alisaundre des Record Office, London. Isles fuiz Anegus fuiz Douenald. Saluz en Dieu. Sachez nous le jour de la Feste de la Translation Seint Thomas le Martin, lan de grace millyme deu sentyme nonauntyme secund, a Berwick sur Twede en la presence nostre Seignour, mon Sire Edward par le grace Deu Roy du Engleterre, e soverein Seignur du Reaume d'Escoce, par celte presente lettre avoir grantes e sur seintes Evangeles avoir juree e a nostre pouer se restent sauveroms gareeroms e meintendroms la pees du Reaume d'Escoce, e especiaument la pees des Ylles e des terres forreines dever noz parties.

E. qe toutz contents, debatz e demaundes des terres, e de tenementz, chauteaus, e de tote mainere des trespas, mutz ou a movoir entre nous, e Alisaundre Eragaithel seigneur de Lorne et · John son cyne fiz, cesserount, e en quieto reposerount entre cy e le parlement, establi a Berewyk par devant nostre Seignour le Roy a la quinzeme apres la Sein Michel prochein avenyr, e durant le dyt parlement. En quel il lyst a nous feure nos pleintes devaunt le devauntdit nos Seignur le Roy, e son counseil. Selom les leys e les usages du Reaume d' Escoce ; enfint qe les pleintes de une part e de autre, soient adonges en meisme l' estat, qil furent le jour qe celte lettre fust fete.

E. qe nous endementiqs ne froms procuroms estre fet mal, ne damoge a les avaunt dix Alisaunder de Eregaithel et son fiz ne la soens voloms ensement, e grauntoms qe nous ne rescetteroms en nule maniere, ne Sustendroms nul mesfesour, ne nul autre, qe Justicer ne se voille par la commune ley de la terre ; e nomement Roulaunde le fuiz Alcyn, o Dunckan le fuiz Dugald si il ne voillent estre obeisaunt al avauntdit nostri Seignour le Roy e venir a sa pees. E si il seent trouey desobeisauntz nous grauntoms e promettoms qe nous o tot nostre pouet, en aide a Sire Johan Comyn e a Sire James Seneschal d' Escoce, deuz de Gardeins du Reaume leveroms, e eyderoms, e les pursuiroms en totes manieres qe meismes ceaus Gardeins ordonerount o purverunt, jesqes a tant qil soient prix on cint le Reaume voide ; mes que alowe nous feit ceo, qe nous froms outre nostre deu servise.

E. leaument promettoms qe nos, en totes chose, qe touchent la pees, e la garde du Reaume d' Escoce, e des avaunditz Ylles e terres forreines, as avaunt dits Gardeins serront entendauntz, responauntz o obeisauntz.

E. si il oveigne qe nous encountra nul des articles, avaunt nomez denz le tens avavndyt, sesoms ou veignoms, e de ceo Sesoms ateynt ; nous nous obligeoms par cette lettre a nostre Seignur le Roy avauntdit a perte de vie e de membre, de terre e de tenement, e de touz nos biens a sa volunte ; e qe encountre ceo nule ley, ne coustume, valoir nous puisse. En tesmoigne de cestes choses a cette presente lettre nous avoms mis nos seals.

Don. a Berewyk sur Twede, le jour de la Feste de la Translation Seint Thomas le Martir, lan du Regne nostre Seignur le Roy avauntdit vyntyme

(sub sigillo proprio)

CITATIO REGIS SCOTIÆ AD RESPONDENDAM ALEXANDRO DE INSULA ET JULIANÆ UXORI SUÆ—1294.

Scotiæ.   Rex et superior dominus regni Scotiæ dilecto et fideli suo Johanni eadem gratia regi Scottorum illustri salutem. Querulam Alexandri de Insula et Juliane uxoris sue recipimus · continentem quo cum ipsi in cura nostra coram vobis terram partem terre de

Lysmor cum pertinentibus que est in manu vestra ut dicitur ut jus suum de hereditate ipsius Juliane sibi reddi pettivissent et cum magna instantia vobis pluries supplicassent quod eis inde in curia vestra justitiam fieri facietis vos id eis facere denegastis et in justitia eis super hoc exhibenda totaliter defuistis propter quod iidem Alexander et Juliana nobis ut superiori domino regni Scotiæ cum instantia supplicarunt ut eis super hoc in vestri justitiam fieri faciamus Nos igitur qui sumus et esse debemus singulis de potestate et dominio nostro in exhibenda justitia debitores adjornamus vos quod sitis coram nobis in Crastino Animarum ubicunque tunc fuimus in Anglia prefatis Alexandro et Juliane super premissis responsuri et ulterius futuri et recepturi quod cura nostra consideraverit in hac parte.   Et habeatis ibi hoc breve

 Tempus ut supra   Et fuit clausa

  Et mandatum est vicecomitatu Northumbrie &c. ut in similibus.

REX EDWARDUS CONSTITUIT ALEXANDRUM DE INSULA BALLIVUM SUUM AD CAPIENDUM KENTYR IN MANUM SUAM. 1296.

Rex omnibus ad quos &c. salutem Sciatis quod constituimus Rotuli Scotiæ. dilectum nobis Alexandrum de Insula ballivum nostrum ad capiendum in manum nostram terram de Kentyr cum pertinentibus que prius capi debuerat in manum nostram per defaltam quam Johannes de Balliolo nuper Rex Scotie fecit in cura nostra coram nobis in Crastino Animarum proximo preterito versus Malculmum le fix Lengleys de Scotia qui terram illam in eadem cura coram nobis tanquam superiore domino regni Scotie petiit versus prefatum regem ut jus et hereditatem suam et que ad manam nostram jam devenit tanquam escaeta nostra per forisfecturam ejusdem regis et etiam per redditionem quam nobis fecit de homagio suo quod nobis prius fecerat de eodem regno et ad terram illam cum pertinentibus custodiendam quamdiu nobis placuerit ita quod nobis inde respondeat ad mandatum nostrum.   In cujus &c.

T. R. apud Berewyk super Twedam XV. die Aprilis.

GRANT BY EDWARD I. OF ENGLAND TO ALEXANDER OF THE ISLES. 1296.

Pro Alexandro de Insula. Patent Roll.

Rex omnibus ad quos, *etc.*, salutem.

 Sciatis quod pro bono servitio quod dilectus nobis Alexander de Insula nobis hactenus impendit et impendet in futurum, concessimus ei centum libratas terrae et redditus de primis custodiis quas ad manus nostras accidere contigerit citra mare Scotiae per quinquennium a tempore quo hujusmodi custodia sibi per praeceptum nostrum fuerit liberata.   In cujus, *etc.*

Teste rege apud Berewicke super Twedam, xij de Septembris.

Et mandatum et Petro de Donewyco, escaetori regis citra mare Scotiae, quod praefato Alexandro de hujusmodi custodiis centum libratas terrae et redditus habere faciat, juxta formam concessionis praedictae.   Test, ut supra.

DE MALEFACTORIBUS IN ERGADIA ET ROS ARRESTANDIS.   1297.

Rotuli Scotiæ.   Rex universis et singulis fidelibus suis terrarum de Ergardia et Ros salutem—

Mandamus vobis quod dilecto et fideli nostro Alexandro de Insulis intendentes respondentes consulentes sitis et auxiliantes ad quosdam malefactores et pacis nostre perturbatores qui per divisa loca in partibus illis vagantur et discurrunt homicidia depredationes incendia et alia dampna diversa contra pacem nostram perpetrantes et de die in diem perpetrare non desistentes arrestandos et in persona nostra salvo custodiendos donec aliud inde precepimus quotiens ex parte nostra a prefato Alexandro super hoc fueritis premuniti In cujus &c. usque ad festum Sancti Michelis proximo futuro duratur nisi aliud interim inde duximus ordinandum.

T. R. apud Buffast ix die Aprilis.

STATEMENT BY ALEXANDER DE YLE, LORD OF THE ISLES, IN WHICH HE VINDICATES HIS CONDUCT.   1297.

Record Office, London.   Memorandum quod iste est processus . . . anno M.C.C. nonogesimo septimo, videlicet, quod cum Laclan Magrogri fecisset hom . . . utum, dictus L. ad insulas rediens, dominicas domini regis terras sibi usurpavit . . . ricum prædæ totaliter devastavit.   Super quibus homines insulani Alexandro de Yle nuncios miserunt . . . negotiis, et dictus Alexander misso exercitu securitatem recepit a præfato Rodrico et ab hominibus dicti . . . compentete quod starent regis voluntati et mandatis. Postmodum vero prædictus Lachlan, unico filio . . . nec ulla permissione retenta præfatas insulas domini regis invaserunt, ac in eisdem insulis . . . incendia et deprædationes atrociter perpetrarunt, et irruentes ex improviso super quosdam ex hominibus dicti Alexandri ipsos galeis et bonis suis spoliaverunt. Quo facto, insulani iterato ad Alexandrum destinaverunt nuncios, petentes quod dictus dominus Alexander personaliter cum suo exercitu ante dominicum in Ramis Palmarum versus insulas access . . . et dictum Lohlan, in primis cum ita esset obsessus quod resistere non posset, ad voluntatem domini regis recepit permissionem ut . . . filium suum regi daret in obsidem, et quod castrum suum redderet ad regis voluntatem. Ipso vero L. sic constituto . . . prædictus Rodricus frater suus cum potentia dicti L. et suggestione, ut dicitur, quosdam de hominibus dicti Alexandri . . . ad quandam insulam divertere hostiliter invasit, et ex eis circiter triginta interfecit; quo facto, Alexander cum tota potentia sua prædictum Rodricum per terram et mare prosecutus est, ita quoad vi compulsus se reddidit, et in vinculis tanquam priso tenetur.

Dictus vero Lochlanus filium suum Alexandrum reddidit in obsidem, et etiam castrum, et quia continebatur in littera domini regis quod Alexander de Yle salvo custodiret præfatos malefactores, donec aliud a rege reciperet in mandatis, dispositis insulis regis meliori modo quo poterit, et pace reddita huspandis et mulieribus (qui prius non audebant pro timore dictorum malefactorum extra castrorum refugia commorari), duxit secum dictum Lochlan donec per ballivos regios esset consultus quid de tali homine foret agendum. Sed dictus L., relicto filio in obside et fratre suo in carcere, relictis etiam galeis suis clam et furtive recessit, et (ut creditur quantumcunque poterit), homines et terras regis molestabit.

Dictus vero Alexander, praemissis fratribus suis cum exercitu ad dictum L. prosequendum, et ad terras suas in manu regis Sesyandum, personaliter cum expeditione cito sequendum. . . . sit dictus Alexander ubi dictus L. receptabitur, nisi in terris domini Alexandri de Ergadia, cujus filiam . . . vel in terris domini Johannis Cumyn de Lochabor, quia homines dictæ terræ dicto L. et Duncano filio domini Alexandri de Ergadia contra pacem domini regis jurati fuerant et uniti quod juxta castrum Johannis Cumin in Lochabar duæ magnæ galeæ fuerant, quibus in insulis non fuerunt majores. . . . dictæ terræ renuerunt tradere Alexandro d' Eyl, juxta tenorem litteræ domini regis, sed potius Duncanum filium Alexandri de Ergadia, qui adhuc fidelitatem domino regi non fecerat, in capitaneum recoperunt, ac

˙ dibtas galeas festinanter ad mare praeparaverunt, ac homines hinc inde in regno se regi objecerunt. Dictus Alexander, misso navali exercitu, dictas galeas sibi petiit reddi ex parte regis, tanquam constituto capitaneo per litteras regis de Ergadia et de Ross ; sed homines existentes in præfato castro simpliciter galeas reddere renuerunt, et homines Alexandri de Yle petentes naves cum sagattis et carellis vulneraverunt, nec aliquam fidem voluerunt facere quod dictæ galæ contra regem non venirent. Et quia homines dicti Alexandri propter pugnam imminentem de castro non poterant galeas salvas educere, vel ad mare trahere, ipsas in eodem loco combusserunt, ne terris et fidelibus regis forent periculum et descrimen. Dictus etiam Alexander de Yle, audito quod Senescallus Scotiæ contra dominum regem insurrexit, quoddam castrum cum baronia, nomine Glasrog, quæ prædictus Senescallus tenuit, in manu regis sesiavit et adhuc detinet, paratus ad alias terras procedere ad domini regis commodum et mandatum, et de terris quas occupat nomine regis secundum ordinationem suam et ballivorum suorum in omnibus parere.

Dictus Vero Alexander de Yle supplicat domino Johanni de Benestede quod ista ostendat domino regi cum effectu, et quod super istis dominus rex voluntatem suam dicto Alexandro celeriter transmittat, et quod etiam supplicat domino regi de expensis dicti Alexandri in expeditionibus ejusdem anni et quod nichil recepit de quingentis libris [?] quas dominus rex anno præterito sibi concessit, nec a balliva sua adhuc super eisdem aliquam sufficientem habet responsionem. Super hiis et omnibus aliis petit regis voluntatem.

LETTER FROM ANGUS OG OF ISLA, LORD OF THE ISLES, TO EDWARD I. RESPECTING HIS PROCEEDINGS IN THE ISLES. 1301.

Record Office, London.

Nobilissimo viro ac excellentissimo, domino Eduardo Dei gratia regi Angliæ, domino Hibernæ, suus Enegus de Yle, humilis et fidelis, salutem quam sibi.

Vestra sciat nobilitas quod Ego fui in comitatu domini Hugoni Bisseth et cum classe vestra quamdiu fuit in insula de Buth, videlicet, usque diem Dominicam proximo ante festum Michaelis ultimo præteritum, et adhuc sum, expectans mandatum vestrum.

Quare vestram nobilitatem exoro umiliter et requiro, quatinus quod si creditis quod Alexander de Ergadia sit in pace vestra et protectione mandetis dicto Alexandro ut sit ausilians et consulens domino Hugoni Bisseth et Engusio mihi de Yle, et omnibus hominibus vestris ut mediante sua potentia et vestra inimicos vestros possimus destrucre et vires inimicorum ad nichilum redigere. Et si creditis quod non est in pace vestra, miltatis ad nos consilium vestrum litteratorie, ut possimus, Deo adjuvante, ipsum ac alios vestros inimicos per insulas destruere.

Cacterum vestram dominationem humiliter exoro pro filiis Rodrici, qui in potentia nostra sunt, 'in hiis annis,' et fuerunt contra omnes vestros adversarios et nostros ; quatinus si placet velitis concedere eis nativum feodum colere, ut vobis scrviant humiliter et fideliter, prout regi debeant obedire.

CHARTER BY ROBERT I. TO RODERICK, THE SON OF ALLAN.
C. 1320.

Robertus &c. Confirmasse Roderico filio Alani dilecto et fideli et servitio suo davatam terre cum dimidia de Modworth cum advocatione ecclesie ejusdem loci : Tres davatas terræ de Knod-worachc—dimidiam davatum de Dyrliaks viz. quinque denariatas : terræ de Gedwall et quinque denariatas de Glenbrescall et Bethey ; Sex davatas terræ de Egis et de Rum cum advocatione ecclesie ejusdem et aliis pertinentiis : Sex davatas et tria quarteria terræ in parochia de Kilphedder blisten ; Insulam de Barray cum pertinentiis ; et Insulam de Harris cum pertinentiis : Quasquidem terras Christina de Mar filia quondam Alani filii Roderici per fustum et baculum nobis sursum reddidit ; Tenendas et habendas prædicto Roderico et heredibus suis masculis de corpore suo legitime procreatis de nobis et heredibus nostris in feodo et hereditate &c. Faciendo servitium unius navis viginti et sex remorum cum hominibus et victualibus pertinentibus et eando in exercitu nostro cum opus habuerimus et super hoc fuerint rationaliter summoniti. Voluimus tamen et ordinamus quod si dictus Rodericus heredem masculum non habeat quod Rodericus filius dictæ Christinæ dictas Terras habeat et teneat hereditarie et quod idem Rodericus tenetur maritare filiam vel filias predicti Roderici avunculi sui si quam vel quas legitimas habuerit cum quadringentis marcis sterling : Et si contigerit humanitas de prædicto Roderico prædictæ Christianæ Ita quod successio præ-dictarum terrarum ad ipsum pervenire non poterit, filia vel filiæ predicti Roderici filii Alani post patrem suum hereditabit in terris predictis et si dictus Rodericus filius Alani nullum heredem super-

Haddington's Collections.

stitem habuerit volumus quod dictæ terræ cum pertinentiis ad
predictam Christianam et heredes suos ex tunc de dono nostro
libere reverentur.

In cujus Rei testimonium &c. &c.

REX EDWARDUS RATIFICAT INDENTURUM INTER EDWARDUM DE
BALLIOLO, SUUM PSEUDOREGEM SCOTIÆ ET JOHANNEM
DE INLULIS. 1336.

Rex omnibus ad quos &c. salutem.   Inspeximus quasdam
litteras indentatas factas inter magnificum principem Dominum
Edwardum regem Scotorum illustrem consanguineum nostrum
carissimum et Johannem de Insulis in hec verba

. Hec indentura facta apud villam de Perth die Jovis xij die
Septembris anno domini millesimo trescentesimo quinto inter
excellentissimum principem Dominum Edwardum Dei gratia
regem Scotorum illustrem ex una parte et Johannem de Insulis ex
altera parte testatur quod dictus dominus rex concessit quantum
in se est predicto Johanni pro bono et laudabili servitio sibi
impenso ac in futuro impendendo per se et heredes suos

Insulam de Ysle
Terram de Kentyre
Terram de Knappedoll
Insulum de Githe
Dimidium Insule de Dure
Insulam de Golwonche
Insulam de Mulle
Insulam de Sky
Insulam de Lewethy
Terram de Kenalbadon et de Ardinton

tenenda eidem Johanni heredibus et assignatis suis Concessit
etiam dictus dominus rex eidem Johanni wardam de Loghaber
usque ad legitimam etatem filii et heredis Domini David de
Strabolgy ultimi comitis Atholle'. Pro quibus quidem conces_
sionibus predictis prefatus Johannes de Insulis obligat se et
heredes suos esse ligios homines et fideles dicto domino regi et
heredibus suis imperpetuum et gravandi omnes suos inimicos et
rebelles quibuscumque diebus et locis et omnibus quibus eos
gravare poterit et se et suos ac heredes ejus quoscumque Et pro
securitate omnium premissorum fideliter complendi præstetur
sacramentum corporale per dictum Johannem super sanctum

eukaristiam calicem altaris et missale Item vult et concedit dictus Johannes quod si predictus dominus rex obsidem vel obsides ab eo voluerit habere pro majori securitate faciendum consanguineum vel consanguineos suos minoris etatis sibi propinquiores dicto nomino regi reddendos cum tempus opportunum advenerit quia dictus Johannes filium nec heredem a corpore suo nondum habet legitime procreatum quod compaternitas ejusdem heredis profato Johanni concedatur.

Nos autem omnia et singulas in litteris predictis contenta pro nobis et heredibus nostris quantum ad nos pertinet acceptamus ratificamus approbamus et confirmamus sicut littere predicte plenius testantur.

In cujus &c.

T. R. apud Aukland quinto die Octobris.   Per ipsum regem.

SAVLUS CONDUCTUS PRO JOHANNE DE INSULIS
EDWARD III. 1336.

Rex universis et singulis vicecomitibus ballivis ministris et Rotuli Scotiæ. aliis fidelibus tam infra libertates quam extra tam in Scotia quam in Anglia ad quos &c. salutem.   Sciatis quod cum nobilis vir Johannes de Insulis ad nos et Edwardum regem Scotorum illustrem consanguineum nostrum carissimum sit venturus suscepimus ipsum Johannem et homines de familia sua et servientes suos ac equos hernesia et alias res suas veniendo ad nos et ad dictum consanguineum nostrum ubicumque fuimus ibidem morando et exinde redeundo in protectionem et defensionem nostram specialem necnon in salvum et securum conductum nostrum &c.   Sicut in aliis literis de salvo conductu usque ad festum Sancti Andree proximum futurum duratur.

T. R. apud Aukeland quinto die Octobris   Per ipsum regem.

SALVUS CONDUCTUS PRO JOHANNE DE INSULIS CUM REGE
ANGLIÆ VEL SECRETARIIS EJUS TRACTATURO. 1337.

Rex universis et singulis admirallis vicecomitibus majoribus Rotuli Scotiæ. ballivis ministris magistris et marinariis navium ac omnibus aliis fidelibus suis ubicunque in dominiis nostris existentibus sive in mari sive in terra tam infra libertates quam extra ad quos,

32

&c., salutem. Cum nobilis vir Johannes de Insulis infra
regnum nostrum Angliae vel terram nostram Hiberniae seu ad
partis dominii nostri in Scotia cum sexaginta aut quatuor
viginti vel centum hominibus equitibus ad tractandum nobiscum
seu aliis fidelibus et sectariis nostris quos ad hoc debut
avimus sit venturus. Suscepimus ipsum Johannem et omnes
predictos equites ac eorum servientes necnon magistros et
marinarios navium eos ducentium ac easdem naves veniando infra
regnum nostram et partes predictos et aliunde infra dominium
nostrum tam per terram quam per mare ibidem morando et exinde
redeundo in protectionem et defensionem nostram specialem necnon in salvum et securum conductum nostrum. Et ideo vobis
sub forisfectura vite et membrorum et omnium aliorumque nobis
forisfacere poteritis mandamus districtius injungentes quod eidem
Johanni vel equitibus predictis aut ipsorum servientibus magistris
et marinariis navium ecs ducentium veniendo infra predicta
regnum terram et partes ac aliundo infra dominium nostrum
predictum sive per terram sive per mare ibidem morando et
exinde redeundo sicut predictum est in personis equis hernesiis
aut aliis rebus suis non inferatis seu quantum in vobis est ab
aliis inferri permittatis injuriam molestiam dampnum impedimentum aliquod seu gravamen sit eis potius salvum et securum
conductum cum per districtus vestros transitum fecerint habere
factum quotiens per ipsum Johannem vel ex parte sua fueritis
requisiti. Et si quid eis forisfectum fuerit id eis sine dilatione
facta emendari. In cujus, &c., usque ad festum Pentecostes
proximum futurum duratum.

   T. R. apud Aldermanston tertio die Decembris.

Per ipsum Regem.

COMITI SARISBURIÆ COMMITTITUR POTESTAS TRACTANDI CUM
JOHANNE DE INSULIS. 1337.

cotiæ.	Rex universis presentas litteras inspecturis salutem. Sciatis
quod nos de fidelitate probata et circumspectione provida dilecti
et fidelis nostri Willelmi de Monte Acuto comitis Sarisburiæ
intime confidentes ad tractandum et concordandum nostro nomine
et pro nobis cum nobile viro Johanne de Insulis super alligantiis
et federibus inter nos et ipsum ineundis et super aliis omnibus et
singulis que nostrum et nostros concernere potuerunt commodum
et honorem et ea que sic tractata et concordata fuerint quacunque

firmitate vallanda ac omnia alia et singula facienda que in
præmissis et circa ea oportuna fuerint etiam si mandatum exigant
speciale eidem comiti tenore presentium plenam committimus et
concedimus potestatem. Promittentes pro nobis et heredibus
nostris nos ratum et gratum habituros et effectualiter impleturos
quicquid per prefatum comitem tractatum concordatum vallatum
et actum fuit in premissis vel aliquo premissorum Et literas
dicti comitis in hac parte factas et contenta in eisdem acceptabi-
mus et ea faciemus per nostras patentas literas securiori modo quo
fieri potuerit confirmare In cujus &c

Per ipsum regem

Datum apud Redyng quarto die Decembris

REGIS EDWARDI EPISTOLA BLANDILOQUA JOHANNI DE INSULIS DIRECTA. 1337.

Rex nobili et potenti viro Johanni de Insulis amico suo Rotuli
carissimo salutem et sincere dilectois affectum Ex testimonio
laudibili collateralis nostri præcipui Willelmi de Monte Acuto
comitis Sarisburiæ et aliorum nostrorum fidelium recepimus et
operis evidentia id ostendit quod constanter in fidelitate nostra
presistitis et emulorum nostrorum malitiam multiplicitir refrenatis
de quibus quantas possimus grates vobis referimus speciales
gerentes in votis exceptam gratitudinis vestre constantiam cum
ea que regiam decet munificentiam retributionis exuberantia
permiare adeo quod debebitis merito contentari. Velitis igitur
petimus penes nos continuare benivolentiam quam cepistis tract-
antes cum prefato comite cui velud secretario nostro confidentissimo super quibusdam vobis exprimendis aperuimus plenissime
mentem nostram ac credentes eidem in dicendis ex parte nostra
velud prelatis ab ore nostro Nam revera quicquid pro nobis
vobis discerit vel præmiserit plene faciemus et implebimus et
multo plus prout excrescens vestra constantia id exposcet Ad
hec pro vobis ad veniendum cum sexaginta octoginta vel centum
comitibus secure infra regnum nostrum Angliæ et terras nostras
Hiberniæ et Scotie illuc tute morando exinde libere redeundo
literas nostras fieri fecimus de conductu quas prefato comiti
fecimus liberari.

Datum apud Redyng quarto die Decembris Et erat clausa.

CHARTER BY DAVID II. TO JOHN OF ISLA, LORD OF THE ISLES.
1344.

Scot-
Parlia-
.
Apud Are XII. Die Junii A.R. XV. Dauid Dei gracia rex
Scottorum omnibus probis hominibus locius terre sue clericis et
laicis salutem Sciatis quod super finali concordia inter nos et
Johannem de Yle consanguineum nostrum carissimum habito
prius diligenti tractatu communique utilitate regni nostri ac
tranquillitate eiusdem premises dedimus concessimus et hac
presenti carta nostra confirmavimus eidem Johanni pro homagio
et servicio suo omnes et singulas insulas et terras subscriptas
videlicet totam insulam que vocatur Yle insulam de Geday,
insulam de Jura insulam de Colinsay cum omnibus aliis minutis
insulis ad dictas insulas pertinentibus insulam de Mule cum suis
minutis insulis insulas de Tirayd et de Colla cum suis minutis
insulis insulam de Lewes cum suis minutis insulis totam terram
de Morimare cum pertinenciis totam terram de Louchabre liberam
et exemptam ab omni actione vel clameo cuiuscumque terram de
Glenchomyr cum pertinenciis et custodias castrorum nostrorum de
Kerneborgh Iselborgh et Dunchonall cum terris et minutis insulis
ad dicta nostra pertinentibus tenendas et habendas omnes terras
et insulas predictas cum custodiis castrorum predictorum eidem
Johanni et heredibus suis de nobis et heredibus nostris in fœdo et
hereditate libere, quiete plenarie integre et honorifice cum aduo-
cationibus ecclesiarum cum aucupationibus piscationibus et
venacionibus vnacum aeriis falconum et omnimodis aliis libertatibus commoditatibus ayfiamentis et iustis pertinentiis in omnibus
et per omnia tam non nominatis quam nominatis ad predictas
terras et iusulas spectantibus, seu juste spectari valentibus in
futurum quoquo modo : Faciendo nobis et heredibus nostris
predictus Johannes et heredes sui servicia, tam per mare quam per
terram, de omnibus et singulis terris et insulis predictis debita et
consueta tempore recolende memorie domini patris nostri ;
volumusque quod dictus Johannes et heredes sui terram de
Louchabir et omnes alias terras et insulas predictas habeant,
teneant, et possideant in eadem libertate in omnibus sicut liberius
teneri consueverunt tempore domini patris vel temporibus aliorum
predecessorum nostrorum regum Scocie.

In cuius rei testimonium &c.

SALVUS CONDUCTUS PRO JOHANNE DEL ISLE MILITE,
CAPTIVO PRINCIPIS WALLIÆ. 1357.

Rex universis et singulis vicecomitibus ballivis ministris et Rotuli Scotiæ. aliis fidelibus suis ad quos &c. salutem. Sciatis quod suscepimus in protectionem et defensionem nostram Johannem del Isle militem de partibus Scotie prisonarium Edwardi principis Wallie filii nostri carissimi et quatuor equites de comitiva sua eundo ad partes Scotie pro redemptione sua querenda et ipsum Johannem cum dictis quatuor equites pro se in Anglia cum redemptione prædicta redeundo. El ideo vobis mandamus quod eidem Johanni aut dictus quatuor equitibus &c. *prout in similibus.* In cujus &c. per unum annum duratur.

T. R. apud Westminster xvj. die Decembris   Per ipsum regum

CONFIRMATION BY DAVID II. OF THE CHARTER OF
JOHN OF THE ISLES—JULY 4, 1363.

David dei gratia Rex Scottorum omnibus &c. Sciatis nos Macdonald
Collections. approbasse &c. amnes donationes et concessiones factas vel concessas per quoscunque vel quascunque dilecto consanguineo nostro Johanni de Insulis de quibuscunque terris tenementis amnis redditibus et possessionibus quibuscunque justis cum pertinenciis. Tenendas at habendas dicto Johanni et heredibus nostris et de aliis capitalibus dominibus foedi dictarum terrarum annuorum reddituum et possessionum predictarum a deo libere et quicte in omnibus et per omnia sicut in cartis sive literis quas idem Johannes inde habet plenius continutur. Salvo servicio nostro. In cujus rei &c. Test. &c.

Apud Edijnburgh quarto die Julij Anno regni nostri Tricesimo quarto.

CARTA JOHANNIS DEL YLE. 1372.

Robertus Dei gracia, etc. Omnibus, etc. Sciatis nos dedisse Reg. Mag. Sig. concessisse et hac presenti carta nostra confirmasse dilecto filio nostro Johanni del Yle omnes et singulas terras tricentarum mercarum que fuerunt quondam Alani filii Rodorici infra regnum nostrum videlicet terras de Modoworth Arrassug Morcovyr Knodeworte Ouyste Barreh Rumme Egge et Hyrce cum pertinenciis tam

infra partes insularum quam in magna terra Tenendas et habendas
eidem Johanni heredibus suis et suis assignatis de nobis et
heredibus nostris in feodo et hereditate per omnes rectas metas
et divisas suas cum omnibus et singulis libertatibus commoditatibus aysiumentis et justis pertinenciis suis quibuscunque ac dictas
terras spectantibus seu aliquo modo spectare valentibus in futurum
adeo libere quiete plenarie integre et honorifice in omnibus et per
omnia sicut dictus quondam Alanus filius Roderici dictas terras
cum pertinenciis aliquo tempore liberius quiecius plenius et
honorificencius justo tenuit seu possedit Faciendo nobis et heredibus nostris predictus Johannes et heredes sui servicia de predictis
terris cum pertinenciis debita et consueta In cuius rei tetimonium
huic presenti carte nostre nostrum precepimus apponi Siggillum
Testibus etc. Apud Sconam tempore parliamenti nostri ibidem
tenti nono dei Marcii anno Regni nostri secundo.

DEATH OF RANALD MACRUARI. 1346.

Wyntoun's
Chronicle.

Qwhat was thare mare ? The King Daïvy
Gaddryd his ost in full gret hy ;
And wyth thame off the north cuntré
Till Saynt Johnystown than come he.
Raynald off the Ilys than,
That wes commendyt a gud man,
Come till hym at that rade to be.
The Erle off Ross wes thare allsua,
That to this Raynald wes full fa ;
Tharefore he gert hym swa aspy
In till Elyhok that nwnry,
Quhare that he wes lyand then
He gert sla hym and his scïvyn men ;
And to Ross wyth his menyhé
Agayne in hy than turnyd he.

CONFIRMACIO BEGINALDY DE INSULIS. 1372.

Reg. Mag. Sig.

Rex, etc. Omnibus, etc. Sciatis nos approbasse ratificasse et
hac presenti carta nostra pro nobis et nostris heredibus inper-
petuum confirmasse donacionem illam et concessionem quas
dilectus filius noster Johannes de Yle fecit Reginaldo de Yle filio

suo de Insulis, terris et castris infrascriptis videlicet De terra de
Mudewort cum castro de Elantirym de terra Arrasayk de terra de
Morowore et de terra de Chudeforde de insula de Egge de insula
de Rume de insula Huwyste cum castro de Vynvawle de insula de
Barre et de insula de Herce cum omnibus aliis minutis Insulis ad
dictas Insulas pertinentibus de tribus unciatis terre de Swynwort,
et de Lettirlochette de duabus unciatis terre de Ardegowar de una
unciata terre de Hawlaste cum advocacionibus ecclesiarum
earundem terrarum et sexaginta mercatis terre in partibus de
Lochabre videlicet De decem et septem denariatis terre de Loche
de dimidia davata terre de Kylmauld et de una davata cum
dimidia de Locharkage in extentam quadringentarum et viginti
mercatarum terre Tenendas et habendas prefatas terras insulas
cum castris predictis eidem Reginaldo et heredibus suis masculis
de corpore legitime procreandis de prefato . . Johanne de Yle et
heredibus suis per omnes rectas metas et divisas suas adeo libere
quiete plenarie integre et honorifice in omnibus et per omnia sicut
carta prefati . . Johannis de Yle prefato Reginaldo filio suo exinde
confecta in se justo continet et proportat salvo servicio nostro . .
In cujus rei etc. Testibus etc. Apud Arnele primo die . .
Januarii anno regni nostro secundo.

_____

CARTA JOHANNIS DEL YLE DE INSULA DE COLOWSAY. 1376.

Robertus dei gracia Rex Scottorum omnibus probis hominibus Reg.
tocuis terre sue salutem. Sciatis nos dedisse &c. dilecto filio
nostro Johanni del Yle insulam de Colowsay cum pertinenciis que
fuit euisdem Johannis et quam ipse Johannes nobis sursum
reddidit et resignavit Tenendam et habendum eidem Johanni et
dilecte filis nostre Margarete sponse sue eorumque alteri diucius
viventi ac heredibus dicti Johannis legitimis inter ipsos legitime
procreatis seu procreandis quibus forte deficientibus heredibus
dicti Johannis legitimis quibuscunque de nobis et heredibus nostris
in feodo et hereditate adeo libere et quiete in omnibus et per
omnia sicut dictus Johannes, dictam Insulam cum pertinenciis de
nobis ante huiusmodi Resignacionem liberius et quiccius iusto
tenuit sue possedit Faciendo inde servicia debita et consueta.
In cuius rei etc. Testibus etc.

Apud Strivelyne secto die Junii anno regni nostri sexto.

CHARTER BY ROBERT II. TO JOHN OF ISLA OF THE LANDS OF
LOCHABER—6TH JUNE 1376.

Macdonald
Collections.

Robertus dei gratia Rex Scottorum omnibus probis hominibus
tocuis terre salutem. Sciatis nos dedisse Concessisse et hae
presenti carta nostra confirmasse dilecto filio nostro Johannie del
Yle totas terras de Lochabre cum pertinenciis infra vicecomitatu
de Invernys que fuerunt ipsius Johannes et quas ipse Johannes
nobis rursum reddidit et resige navit Tenendas et habendas eidem
Johanne et dilecte filie nostre Margarete sponse sue eorumque
alteri diucius vivanti ac heredibus inter ipsos legitime procreatis
quibus forte deficientibus heredibus dicti Johannis legitimis
quibuscunque, de nobis et heredibus nostris in foedo et hereditate
adeo libere et quiete in omnibus et per omnia sicut dictas
Johannes dictas terras cum pertinenciis de nobis anti hujusmodi
resignationem liberius quiccius juste tenuit seu possidet. Faciendo inde servicia debita et consueta. In cujus rei, &c.
Testibus, &c.

Apud Strivelyne sexto die Junii anno regni nostri sexto.

CHARTER BY DAVID II. TO JOHN OF ISLA AND MARGARET HIS
WIFE OF THE LANDS OF BUCHANAN—6TH JUNE 1376.

Macdonald
Collections.

David dei gracia Rex Scottorum omnibus probis hominibus
Sciatis nos dedisse concessisse et hac presenti carta nostra confirmasse Johanni de Yle et Margaret de Vaus spouse sui totam
terram nostram de Buchanne cum pertinenciis infra vicecomitatu
de Strivlyne Tenendam et habendam eisdem Johanni et Margaret
et heredibus suis inter ipsos legitime procreatis seu procreandis de
nobis et heredibus nostris in foedo et hereditate per omnes rectas
metas et divisas suas et cum omnibus aliis et singulis libertatibus
etc. ad dictam terram spectantibus etc. Quibus vero heredibus
inter dictos Johannem et Margaretam procreatis seu procreandis
forte deficientibus volumus quod dicta terra de Buchanne cum
pertinentiis ad nos et successores nostros libere revertatur.
Faciendo nobis et heredibus nostris dictus Johannes et Margareta
et heredes sui supradicti, servicium de predicta terra debitum et
consuetum, Revocatione nostra de eadem facta non obstante. In
cujus rei etc. Apud Strivelyne sexto die Junii anno regni nostri
sexto.

SALVUS CONDUCTUS PRO DONALDO, FILIO JOHANNIS DE INSULIS, CLERICO. 1378.

Rex per literas suas patentis per sexcennium suscepit in Rotuli salvum et securum conductum suum ac in protectionem et defensionem. R. speciales Donaldum filium Johannis de Out Isles in Scotia Clericum Veniendo in regnum Angliæ per dominium et protestatem R. tam per terram quam per mare usque Villam Oxoniæ ibidem in universitate studendo morando et exinde ad propria rediundo. Dum tamen idem Donaldus quicquam quod in regni R. seu corone prejudicium sedere potuerit non attemptit seu attemptare faciat quovis modo.

T. R. Apud Westminstrem primo die Augusti. Per Concilium.

SALVUS CONDUCTUS PRO HUGONE OF THE OUTE ISLES. 1382.

Rex per literas suas patentes per unum annum duraturam si Rotuli treuge inter ipsum it illos de Scotia nuper inite per tantum tempus duraverint suscepit in salvum et securam conductum suum ac in protectionem et defensionem suas Speciales Hugonem of the Oute Isles de Scotia veniendo pro quibusdam negotiis suis expediendis cum sex equitibus in comitiva sua ad quascumque et partes regni nostri Angliæ sibı placuerit ibidem morando et exinde ad partes Scotie redeundo necnon equos bona et hernesia sua quicumque.

T. R. Apud Westminstrem xxj die Octobris.

EPISCOPO SODORENSI DATUR POTESTAS TRACTANDI DE CONFEDERATIONIBUS CUM FILIIS JOHANNIS, NUPER DOMINI INSULARUM. 1388.

Rex omnibus ad quos &c. salutem. Sciatis quod nos de Rotuli fidelitate circumpectione et industria venerabilis prioris Johannis episcopi Sodorensis plenam et solidam fiduciam reportantis eidem episcopo ad tractandum cum strenuo viro Godfrido filio Johannis de Yle nuper domini Insularum prope Scotiam ac sibi ad herentibus et alligatis seu ad hoc per eundem Godefridum deputatis mandatum sufficiens habentibus super quibuscumque ligis confederationibus et amicitiis inter nos subditos nostros regna et dominia nostra quecumque ex una et ipsum Godfridum subditos suos terras et dominia sua quecumque ex altera parte etiam de modo forma et quantitate auxilii subventoribus seu subsidii hinc inde tempore necessitatis mutuo ministrandi et de complicationibus inter subditos predictos hinc inde in mercimoniis et aliis licitis secure faciendis. Necnon super omnibus et singulis articulis quantumcumque specialibus que ligas confederationes seu amicitias inter nos et ipsum Godefridum firmandas concernere potuerunt quovis modo cum eorum incidentibus emergentibus dependentibus et connexis certaque omnia et singula nomine nostro facienda exercenda et expienda que in hoc casu necessaria fuerint seu quomodolicet opportuna et ad nos et concilium nostrum de premissis cum sic tractata fuerint et expurgisse certificanda ut tunc de hujus tractatu per idem concilium nostrum plenius avisati eidem sicurius et consultius imposterum annuere valimus prout de deliberatione avisamento et assensu ejusdem concilii nostri fore viderimus faciendam plenam tenore presentium concedimus et conmitimus potestatem. In cujus rei testimonium has literas nostras patentes fieri et sub magni sigilli nostri testimonio fecimus consignari.

T.R. Apud Westminstrem xiiij die Julii.   Per Consilium.

Consilis litere regis patentes designuntur eidem episcopo ad tractandum cum strenuis viris.

Donaldo filio Johannis de Yle nuper domini Insularum predictarum et Johanne fratre ejusdem Donaldi.

T. ut supra.   Per Consilium.

CHARTER BY GODFREY MACDONALD, LORD OF UIST, TO THE MONASTERY OF ST JOHN'S, INCHAFFRAY. 1389.

Insule rum.   Godfridus de Insula dominus de Wyst salutem in visceribus Saluatoris. Nouerit vniuersitas vestra nos[r] dedisse concessisse ac presenti [Carta] Confirmasse pro salute anime nostre et nostrorum predecessorum in honore sancte trinitatis et beate Marie Virginis gloriose monasterio Sancti Johannis euangeliste in Insula Missarum et conuentui ejusdem in puram et perpetuam elemosinam Capellam Sancte trinitatis in Wyst et totam terram de Karynch et quatuor deniaratas terre in Ilara inter Husabost[1] [et] Kanerrach cituatas sicut melius liberius honorificentius et utilius Cristina filia Alani

---

[1] Here Kirkibost Island is probably meant.

bone memorie vera heres et Reginaldus dictus Mc Rodry verus
dominus et patronus dictam capellam cum prefatis terris dictis
monasterio et conuentui contulerunt Nos vero volentes colla-
tionem et donationem eorundem firmam ac stabilem permanere
eosdem per presentes affirmamus ratificamus approbamus ac
innouamus et sub ea forma videlicet quod noster diiectus ac
specialis dominus Thomas sepedicte monasterij canonicus nomine
dicti monasterij dictam capellam cum prefatis terris et omnibus
suis pertinentiis integre pacifice et quiete possideat ac plenarie.
In cujus rei testimonium sigillum nostrum presentibus apponi
fecimus apud castrum nostrum de Elane tyrim vij die mensis
Julij anno domini millesimo CCC^{mo} octogesimo nono.

CHARTER BY DONALD OF ISLA, LORD OF THE ISLES,
- TO LACHLAN MACLEAN OF DOWART. 1390.

Noverint universi ad quoram noticiam presentes Litere perven- Reg.
erint Nos Donaldum de Ile Dominum Insularum Dedisse concessisse et hac presenti carta nostra confirmasse dilecto nostro et
fidelissimo alumpno et familiori Lachlano Makgilleone Constabu-
lariam et custodiam castrorum nostrorum de Kernaborg et Ileborg
unacum minutis Floda et Lunga et quatuor denariate de
Tressones et denariate de Calwogray et denariate de Arneanboge
et obulatum de Bedich necnon et officium Sragramanach et
Armanach in Insula de Hy cum omnibus libertatibus commoditatibus fructibus et pertinentiis quibuscunque ad dictum
castrum seu ad dictas terras aut dicta officia spectantibus
seu spectare valentibus in futurum Habendas et tenendas de
nobis et heredibus nostris eidem et suis heredibus libere plene
pacifice quiete et hereditarie in pascuis planis pratis memoribus
aquariis venationibus piscariis et ceteris circumstanciis quibuscunque prout melius liberius plenius quiescius et honorificeneins
aliqua constabularia seu alique terre aut officia poterint dari seu
litesis aut carta confirmari In cujus rei testimonium Sigillum
nostrum presentibus est appensum apud Ardchoranis duodecimo
die mensis Julii anno Domini millesimo tricentesimo nonagesimo.

SALVUS CCNDUCTUS PRO JOHANNE DE INSULIS ET DONALDO
FRATRE SUO. 1400.

cotiæ.   Rex universis et singulis admirallis &c. salutem Sciatis quod
cum nobilis vir Johannes de Insulis dominus Dunwage et de
Glynns et Donaldus frater ejus non valiant ut asserunt proptu
viarum discrimina et frequentis inimicorum suorum invasiones pro
conclusione cujusdem tractatus inter nos et prefatos Johannem et
Donaldum de ligeantia et retinentia suis ineunda ad nostram pro
voto presentiam personaliter declinare ac eo pretextu carissimo et
fideli consanguinio nostro Henrico de Percy comiti Northumbriæ
constabulario Angliæ qui pro celeriori expeditione negotii predicti
vel apud villam nostram de Karliolo vel apud Cokermouth
adventam ipsorum Johannis et Donaldi expectabit ad tractandum
et concordandum cum eisdem super premisses omnibus et singulis
plenam tenore literarum nostrarum commiserimus potestatem.
Nos ut iidem Johannes et Donaldus ad atteram villarum predictarum ex causis premissis salvo et secure venire ibidem morari
et exinde ad partes suas proprias redire valiant providere Volentes
suscepimus ipsos Johannem et Donaldum infra regnum nostrum
Angliæ usque atteram villarum predictarum ex causis promissis
veniendo ibidem morando et exinde ad partis suas proprias
redeundo cum quadraginta personis equitibus aut peditibus in
eorum comitiva nec non equas bona res et hernesia sua quecumque
in salvum et securum conductam nostram ac in protectionem
tuitionem et defensionem nostras speciales. Et ideo vobis mandamus quod ipsos Johannem et Donaldum infra dictum regnam
nostrum usque ad alteram villarum predictarum ex causis premissis veniendo ibidem morando et exinde ut permittitur ad partes
suas proprias redeundo una cum personis predictis necnon equos
bona res et hernesia sua predicta manuteneatis protegatis et
defendatis non inferentes eis seu quantum in vobis est ab aliis
inferri permittentes injuriam molestiam dampnum violentiam
impedimentum aliquod seu gravamen. Et si quid eis in personis
aut rebus suis forisfecturum seu injuratum fuerit id eis sine
delatione factum corrigi et debite reformari In cuijus per unum
annum duraturum.

T. R Apud Westminstrem quinto die Februarii.

DE TRACTANDO CUM DONALDO DE INSULIS. 1400.

Rex, Universis & Singulis Admirallis &c. ad quos &c. Salutem. Rymer's
Fœdera.
Cum Nobilis Vir, Donaldus de Insulis, & Johannes Frater ejus, infra Regnum nostrum Angliæ, cum Centum Equitibus, ad Tractandum Nobiscum seu aliis Fidelibus & Secretariis nostris, quos ad hoc deputaverimus, sit venturus, suscepimus ipsos Donaldum & Johannem, ac Equites prædictos, necnon eorum Servientes, Magistros & Marinarios Navium eos Ducentium, ac easdem Naves, veniendo infra Regnum nostrom prædictum, tam per terram, quam per mare, ibidem morando, & exinde redeundo, in protectionem & Defensionem nostram specialem, necnon in salvum & securum Conductum nostrum, &c. ut in similibus de Conductu Literis.

In cujus &c. per dimidium Annum duraturas
Teste Rege apud Wesmonasterium secundo die Junii
Per ipsum Regem &c. Concilium.

INTERFECTIO SUMERLEDI.
QUOMODO A PAUCISSIMIS INTERFECTUS SIT SUMERLEDUS SITEBI, THE KING, CUM SUO IMMENSO EXERCITU.

David rege, mortis lege, clauso in sarcofago, Appendix to
Fordun's
Chronica
Gesta Scott-
orum.
Fraus Scottorum infestorum propalatur ilico.
Galiensis, Argaidensis freti vi Albanica,
Sæviebant, et cædebant justos manu impia
Justiruunt atque luunt impiorum furias
Sævientes, destruentes urbes et ecclesias.
Pace fracta, vi redacta, fortes tradunt debiles,
Hostes cædunt atque ledunt igne, ferro, flebiles.
Debachantur et vastantur orti, campi, aratra ;
Dominatur et minatur mites manus barbara.
Glasguensis ictus ensis læsus fugit populus.
Marcus vero, sparso clero, solus sistit querulus,
Infra duros templi muros casus ferens asperos ;
Ibi flebat, et lugebat dies olim prosperos.
Sed modestus et honestus Herbertus episcopus
Condolebat, et mœrebat, secum longe positus ;
Kentegernum, ut supernum regem oret, obsecrat,
Pro suorum captivorum spe, ac hostes execrat ;
Cum oraret, et spiraret precum in discrimina,

Et effectu, non defectu, carerent precamina,
Cœpit sanctos Scotticanos verbo parvipendere,
Et beatum Kentegernum pie reprehendere
His sopitis et oblitus est clamorem præsulis ;
Nam, post multum tempus, ultum revocat episcopum
Ut saanctorum Scotticorum deleret opprobium.
Venerandus et laudandus senex mox episcopus
Jam perfecto, spreto lecto, perrexit quantocius ;
Et nocturnum et diurnum iter quasi juvenis,
Diligenter et libenter carpebat cum famulis ;
Sed cum iret, et nesciret cur tam erat avidus
Ite quia, cum Helia, inspiratur celitus ;
Quod probavit qui rogavit illum cito regredi,
Liberare et salvare se a manu invidi
Sunnerledi, fraude fœdi, hostis atrocissimi,
Conspirantis, anhelantis in ministros Domini ;
Qui repente, cum ingente classium satellite,
Applicatur, et minatur regnum totum perdere.
Hæc cum iret et audiret, spiritu ingemuit,
Quis nunc ire, aut redire, inquiens, me arguit,
Salomonem ac tyronem bellicosum advocat,
Et Heliam, qui per viam illum saepe adjuvat.
Festinemus, adjuvemus desolatos patriæ.
Et oremus, et obstemus illorum miseriae.
Debet doctor atque rector pugnare pro patria.
Properemus, et pugnemus, nostra est victoria ;
Quia Deus semper meus, non hasta nec gladio,
Suum gregem atque plebem tuetur in prælio.
Resistentes, audientes adventum episcopi,
Ut dracones, et leones, fiunt audacissimi ;
Quanquam ille, atque mille, Sumerledus, hostium
Contra centum innocentum prompti sunt ad prœtium,
Accurerunt, et fecerunt in phalanges impetum
Perfidorum Argaidorum infaustorum militum.
Audi mira ; quia diva diris erant prælia.
Imyriceta. et spineta, verticem moventia,
Thymus usta, et arbusta, rubi, atque filices,
Timebantur, et rebantur hostibus ut milites ;
In hac vita, non audita erant hæc miracula.
Umbrae thymi atqui fimi extant propugnacula
Sed in prima belli rima, dux funestus cecidit ;
Telo laesus ense caesus, Sumerledus obiit ;

Atque unda furibunda ejus sorbet filium,
Ac multorum fugatorum vulneratos millium.
Nam, hoc truce strato duce, fugam petunt impii,
Tam in tesris, quam in aquis, trucidantur plurimi ;
Cum in undis Sanguibundis naves vellent scandere,
Catervatim, alternatim, suffocantur reumate.
Facta strage atque clade perfidorum millium,
Nullus læsus neque cræsus erat expugnantium ;
Sic detrusis et delusis hostium agminibus,
Kentegernum omne regnum laudat altis vocibus.
Caput ducis infelicis Sumerledi Clericus
Amputavit, et donavit pontificis manibus ;
Ut suevit, pie flevit, viso hostis capite,
Dicens Sancti Scotticani sunt laudandi utique,
Et beato Kentegerno tradidit victoriam,
Cujus semper, et descenter, habete memoriam.
Hoc quod vidit et audivit Willelmus composuit,
Et honori et decori Kentegerni tribuit.

LINES ON SOMERLED. 1164.

Sowyrle off Argyle that yhere
Till hym gadryd a gret powere,
As twelff yhere he oysoyd in bataill
Hys Lord to warray and assaylle,
The King that wes off Scotland :
Than wyth a gret ost off Ireland,
And off other steddis sere,
That by him ware lyand nere,
At Renfrewe arrywyd swne.
That were swa at the last wes dwne,
That he, and his swne bath was
Left dede slayne in to that plas.j
And mony wyth thame in that sted
Thare than were slayne
And lefft for dede.

Wyntoun'
Chronicle.

COMPERIT Sᴿ JOHNE PERSOUN CHANTER OF CATHNES SCRIPTOR
ET PROCURATOR FOR YE McKY AND GAVE IN THIS
CHARTER UNDERWRITTEN AND DESIRIT YE SAMYN TO
BE TRANSUMPIT AND COPYIT . . OF THE WHILK TENOR
FOLLOWS :—

Dom.
cilii.

Sciant omnes presentes et futuri qnod nos Donaldus de Ile
dominus Insularum dedimus concessimus et presenti carta nostra
confirmarimus nobili viro Angusio eyg de Strathnavir et Nigello
filio suo senior inter Ipsum et Elizabetam de Insulis sororem
nostram procreato et ipsius filii heredibus masculis de suis corpori
legittime procreandis. Et si contingat dictum filium sine heredibus
masculis de eius corpore legitime procreandis de hac vita migrare
alteri filio supervenienti qui successive supervenire (superiori)
contingat de suis germanis fratribus et illius superinentibus filii
heredibus masculis de eius corpore legitime procreandis. Terras
de Strathalgadill et ferancestgraiyges habenda et tenenda per suas
rectas metas et antiquas fines in hereditatem et fœdum de nobis
et heredibus nostris sibi et Supradicto suo filio et illius filii
heredibus masculis ex eius corpore legittime procreandis. Reddendo inde nobis et heredibus nostris dictus Angusius et eius
filius ut supradictum et ipsius filii heredes masculi de eius corpore
procreandi eorum homagium familiaritatem et suitium contra
omnes huius vite mortales dolo et fraude remotis up per ipsius
Angusii patentes terras nobis inde factas plenius continetur
solvendo &c. nobis et heredibus nostris prefatus Angusius et eius
filii seu heredes predicti wardam et releviam quotiens fuerit
debitum et solvi consuetum nos vero et heredes nostri predictas
terras de Strathalgadill et ferancestgrayges concidimus dicto
Angusio et heredibus suis supradictis in planis pasturis campis et
nemoribus stagnis rivis aquis molendinis venacionibus piscariis
cum ceteris aliis emolumentis et pertinentiis sicut melius plenius
liberius et honorificentius certe in hereditate solent dari seu literis
confirmari. In cuius Rei Testimonii sigillum nostrum presentibus
apponi fecimus. Data apud Insula Marcage (marg. note "or in
Arcaig) Octavo die mensis Octobris Anno domini millesimo Quad-
rengentesimo hijs testibus Lauchlano Makgillane et Roderico
Mackloid cum duobus aliis.

DE TRACTANDO CUM DONALDO DE INSULIS. 1405.

Rex, Venerabili in Christo Patri I. eadem gratia, Episcopo de Doun infra Terram nostram Hiberniæ, ac, Dilecto Armigero nostro, Janico d'Artasso, Salutem. Sciatis quodkos (de fidelitate et circumspectione vestris plenius confidentes) assignavimus vos ad conveniendum. Omnibus viis et modis, licitis et honestis, quibus melius, pro Honore et Commodo nostri, ac Populi Regni nostri Angliæ, necnon dictae Terrae nostrae Hiberniæ, juxta sanas Discretiones vestras, sciveritis seu poteritis, Cum Donaldo de Insulis Chivaler, et Johanne Fratre ejus, super finale Pace, Allegantia, et Amititia, inter nos, et ligeos nostros Regni et Terrae nostrorum prædictorum, et præfatos Donaldum et Johannem, et Subditos suos omnium et singularum Insularum suarum, tam pes Terram, quam per Mare, habena, et Tractandum, Ipsoque Donaldum et Johannem super Modo et Forma Pacis, Alligantiæ, et Amicitiæ, quibus ipsi nobis cum habere, et tenere, et firmare intendunt, Audiendum, Et ad Nos de Tractatu et Auditu hujusmodi, necnon de toto Facto vestro in hac parte, cum præsens Mandatum nostrum fueritis executi, in propria Persona nostra, ubicumque fuerimus, sub Sigillis vestris, distincte et aperte certificandum, una cum hoc Brevi, Ut nos, super hiis, juxta avisamentum Concilii nostri, in hac parte, ordinare valeamus quod, pro Honore et Statu nostri, ac Regni, et Terrae nostrum prædictorum, fore viderimus faciendum ; Et ideo vobis Mandamus quod circa Præmista diligenter intendatis, et ea faciatis et exequamini in forma prædicta :

In cujus &c.

Teste Rege apud Bisshopesthorp juxta Eborum decimo sexto die Septembris.

Rymer's Fœdera.

GAELIC CHARTER BY MACDONALD, LORD OF THE ISLES, TO BRIAN VICAR MACKAY, OF LANDS IN ISLA. 1408.

AN AINIM DE AMEN.

A TAIMSE Macdomhnaill ag bronnagh agas tabhairt en mhairg deg go leth dfcaramn uaim pfhein agas om oighribh do Bhrian Bhicaire Mhagaodh agus da oighribh na dhiaigh go siorthuighe suthain ar son a sheirbhise . . . damh pfcin agas air chonghioll go tteobhraidh se fein agus iadsan damhsa agus dom oighribh am dhiaigh go bliadhnamhail ceithre ba ionmharbhtha chum mo

Register House, Edinburgh.

thighe agus a cas nach biadh na bath soin ar faghail bhearadh an
Brian huas agas oighriogh dhomhsa agas dom oighribh am dhiaigh
da mharg agas da fhichit marg ar son nambo cceadna ataimse
dom cheanghal fein fein agas ag ceanghal moighriogh um dhiaigh
go deiriogh an bheatha na fearainn soin moille re na dthoruibh
mara agas tire do sheasamh agus do chonghbhail don mbhrian
bhiccaire Mhagaodh huas agas da oighribh go siorthuighe na
dhiaigh mar an cceadna . agas as iad so na fearainn thugas dho
fein agas da oighribh go brach iadhon Baile bhicare Machaire
Learga riabhoige . Ciontragha . Grastol . Tocamol . Wglasgog .
Da ghleann astol . Cracobus . Cornubus . agas Baile Neaghtoin.
Agus ionnas go mbiaidh brigh . neart . agas laidireacht ag an
mbrontanas so bheirim uaim . ceanglam aris me fein agas moigh-
roigh go siorthuighe fo ccunsag so do sheasaibh agas chonghbhail
don mbhrian reimhraite agas da oighribh na dhiaigh go deiriogh
an bheatha . le cuir mo laimhe agas mo sheala sios an so a laithair
na bfhiaghain so so sios . agas an seiseamh la do misna bealtuine
agas an bhliadhan so do bhreith Chriosta Mile . ceithre ced . agas
a hocht.

McDOMHNAILL.

EOIN à MACDOMHNAILL
   chomhartha

PAT : III M'ABRIUIN
   chombartha

FFRCOS MACBETHA

AODH X M'CEI
   chomhartha

Translation of Gaelic Charter.

In the name of God. Amen.

I, Macdonald, am granting and giving eleven marks and a half of
land from myself and from my heirs to Brian Vicar Mackay and
to his heirs after him for ever and ever, and for his services . . .
to myself and to my father before me ; and this on covenant and
on condition that he himself and they shall give to me, and to my
heirs after me, yearly, four cows, fit for killing, for my house.
And, in case that these cows shall not be found, the above Brian
and his heirs shall give to me, and to my heirs after me, to the
end of the world, these lands together with their fruits of sea and
land, to defend and maintain to the above Brian Vicar Mackay,
and to his heirs for ever after him in like manner. And those are
the lands I have given to him and to his heirs for ever,—namely,
Baile Vicar, Machaire, Learga—riabhoighe, Ciontragha, Grastol,

Tocamol, Ugasgog, the two Gleanastol, Cracobus, Cornubus, and
Baile Neaughtoin. And in order that there may be meaning,
force, and effect in this grant, which I give from me, I again bind
myself and my heirs for ever under covenant this to uphold and
fulfil to the aforesaid Brian and to his heirs after him to the end
of the world by putting my hand and my seal down here, in the
presence of these witnesses here below, and on the sixth day of the
month of Beltane, and this year of the birth of Christ, one
thousand four hundred and eight.

MACDONALD.

John λ Macdonald.

Pat : III M^cᴀBrian.

Fergus MacBeth.

Hugh X Mackay.

DE TRACTANDO CUM DONALDO DE INSULIS. 1408.

Rex, Dilectis et Fidelibus suis, Christophero de Preston Chivaler,
et Janico D' Artasse Salutem.

Sciatis quod nos (de Fidelitate et Circumspectione vestris
plenius confidentes) Fecimus, Ordinavimus, et Constituimus vos
Deputatos nostros et Commissionarios speciales,

Dantes Vobis plenam, Fenore Praesentium, Potestatem,
Auctoritatem, et Mandatum Speciale Convendiendi et Tractandi,
nomine nostro, cum Donaldo de Insulis, et Johanne Fratre ejus
super Pace finali. Alligantia, et Amicitia,

Inter Nos et quoscumque Ligeos et Subditos nostros et prae-
fatum Donaldum et Johannem et Subditos suos universos habendis
et pro perpetuo duraturas,

Et nos et Consilium nostrum, super Modo et Forma Pacis,
Alligantiae, et Amicitiae, quibus ipsi vobiscum nomine nostro sic,
pertractare voluerint, et quid per hujusmodi Tractatum affectare
intendunt, de tempore in tempus, certificandi,

Ut Nos, habita inde Intelligentia et communicatione cum
Concilio nostro praedicto, ulterius inde fieri valeamus quod pro
Commodo et Honore nostro et nostrorum fore viderimus
faciendum,

Et ideo 'vobis mandamus quod circa Praemissa diligenter
intendatis in forma supradicta.

In cujus &c, quamdiu nobis placuerit duraturas,
Teste Reg apud Leycestre viii. die Maii
                                        Per ipsum Regem.

BROSNACHADH-CATHA DO MHACDHOMHNUILL ILE, ARDFHLATH
  INNSEGALL, LATHA CATH-GHARIACH A CHAIDH A CHUR
  ANNS A BHLIATHNA 1411.   LE LACHLUNN MOR MAC
  MHUIRICH ALBANNAICH, SEANACHAIDH CHLOINN DOMH-
  NUILL.

A

A Chlannaibh Chuinn, cuimhnichibh
Cruas an am na h-iorghuill,
Gu arinneach, gu arronach,
Gu àrach, gu allonta,
Gu athlamh, gu arronta,
Gu allmhara, gu arachdach,
Gu anmhorach, gu aoininntinneach,
Gu àrmeineach, gu anamanta,
Gu ascaoineach, gu airfideach,
Gu altuidh, gu anabarrach,
Gu ainmeineach, Angathlonnach,
Gu ainneartach, gu ainsgianach,
Gu ainteasach, gu anmhorach,
Gu armleonach, gu acfhuinneach,
Gu armchreuchdach, gu aigeannach,
Gu àillghiosach, gu agarach,
Gu àghmhor, gu abarach,
Gu airbheartach, gu athbhuilleach,
Gu aindligheach, gu athmhilleach
Gu ainmeil, gu allail,
Gu àrdanach, gu athsheallach,
Gu aonghuthach, gu aonchridheach,
Aonghneitheach, Allbhuadhach.

B

Gu beotha gu barrail,
Gu brighmhor, gu buadhach,
Gu borbanta, gu buanfheargach,
Gu builleach, gu buillsgeanach,
Gu borb, gu beothail,
Gu beumlannach, gu beumbhuilleach,

Gu bunanta, gu beumach,
Gu beachdaidh, gu beucach,
Gu blaghach, gu buadhail,
Gu boisgeanta, gu buaircasach,
Gu bagarach, gu buaidhghuthach,
Gu bunntuineach, gu buansheasmhach,
Gu ballsgiorrail, gu buaidhlarach,
Gu barrachdail, gu beumnach,
Gu beurtha, gu buadhmhor,
Gu baganta, gu bàdhach,
Gu biorganta, gu brasbhuilleach,
Gu barrcaideach, gu barantail,
Gu beo iunntinneach, beofhradharcach,
Buaidhchathach, bunailteach, buanlaith'reach.

C

Gu calma, gu curanta,
Gu crodha, gu cruadalach,
Gu cathbhuadhach, gu creuchdarmach,
Gu cruaidhlamach, gu corrghleusach,
Gu conspullach gu còmhragach,
Gu ciorusgrach, gu conusgrach,
Gu colganta, gu cathmhor,
Gu cuilbheireach, gu cruaidhlannach,
Gu cncadhach, gu caithreamach,
Gu cathchridheach, gu ceannspreathach,
Gu ceannasach, gu cùramach,
Gu craobhach, gu cliuiteach,
Gu cumhachdach, gu confhadach,
Gu claoidhbhuilleach, gu colgarra,
Gu cruaidhbhuilleach, gu casbheumach,
Gu coimheach, gu coirbte,
Gu cubhaidh, gu cudthromach,
Gu curaideach, gu cunbhalach,
Gu coinntinneach, gu cnagach,
Gu cruaidhchridheach, gu corrach,
Cràdhach, collaideach, creachmhor.

D

Gu dian, gu dùr,
Gu dàsanach, gu deagh fhulangach,
Gu dàna, gu disgir,
Gu dìoganta, gu dìchoisgte,

Gu deinteach, gu dlubhuilleach,
Gu dearglamhach, gu doruinneach,
Gu doiligh, gu dolubaidh,
Gu drochmheinneach, gu dubhailceach,
Gu deacarach, gu doirtfhuileach,
Gu deifireach, gu deannalach,
Gu dichiollach gu deurasach,
Gu dearg lasrach, gu dioghaltach,
Gu deistinneach, gu diubhalach,
Gu dimeasach, gu diongach,
Gu dealaidh, gu deaghbhuilleach,
Gu deonach, gu dùrachdach,
Gu durga, gu danarra,
Gu duranta, gu dalma,
Gu durganta, gu dorrda
Dochasach, dochiosaichte,

E

Gu euchdach, gu easguinn,
Gu carailteach, gu eudnamhach,
Gu eachruidheach, gu eagsamhlaidh,
Gu eudmhor, gu euchdghniomhach,
Gu eangnamhach, gu eighmhor,
Gu eatròcaireach, gu earghnaidh,
Gu eathlamhach, gu eagmhaiseach,
Gu eisgeartha, gu ealdhanach,
Gu ealamh, gu eireachdail,
Gu eachtrannach, gu eadarbhuaiseach,
Gu eagnaidheach, gu earbsach,
Gu eisimpleireach, easgaidh, eascairdeach.

F

Gu friotach, gu furachair,
Gu fiachmhor, gu fuileachdach,
Gu freachnamhach, gu frinneasach,
Gu feargloisgeach, gu fuathmhorach,
Gu fuadarach, gu fuathach,
Gu fealltach, gu fradharcach,
Gu fortail, gu fuathasach,
Gu farranta, gu foirneanta,
Gu frithir, gu feumail,
Gu fearail, gu flathmhaiseach,

Gu friodhail, gu fiorghleusda,
Gu fiorghlan, gu faramach,
Gu frithloisgeach gu fionnghaileach,
Gu faicilleach, gu fulangach,
Gu fraochmhor, gu foghainteach,
Gu fiadhaich, gu fiadhanta,
Gu foighidneach, gu faimeachail,
Gu foillghuineach, gu gaobharach,
Gu fuathchridheach, gu fuaimneach,
Gu farasda, gu fearrdha,
Gu fnghantach, gu foghluimte,
Gu foirneartach, gu feargach,
Gu flathail, furanach, furbanach.

G

Gu gruamach, gu grimeil,
Gu gràineil, gu gaisgeil,
Gu gleusda, gu geinneil,
Gu gasda, gu guineach,
Gu golghaireach, gu griongalach,
Gu griosnamhach, gu geurlamhach,
Gu glansgathach, gu geurlannach,
Gu goinlamhach, gu garbhchreuchdach,
Gu gaorrghonach, gu gaoirghulach,
Gu graisneach, gu glaodhmhor,
Gu gusmhor, gu guaismhor,
Gu goimhchridheach, gu guaisbheartach,
Gu glanchosgrach, gu gearrghuarsgrach,
Gu gramail, gu greannach,
Gu grinneasach, gu gradcharach,
Gu gearrbhuilleach, gu gniomhlochdach,
Gu gangaideach, gu geurchuiseach,
Gu goirtchathach, gu geurshaighideach,
Gu grioghanach, greadanach, gartmhor.

I

Gu inntinneach, gu ionbhuadhach,
Gu iomghonach, gu iomdheargach,
Gu iomshniomhach, gu imaithbhiorach,
Gu innleachdach, gu inncalta,
Gu iolachdach, gu idnearach,
Gu iogarnach, gu iolghuthach,
Gu iolghairdeach, gu iolbhuadhach,

Gu iolghonach, gu iolghneach,
Gu iollagach, gu imaithfearach,
Gu imeasarganach, gu imraiteach,
Gu imbhuilleach, gu imseach,
Gu imsgatach, gu iorguilcach,
Gu iunnsaidheach, gu ionnradhach,
Gu inghreimach, gu imluagail,
Gu itealach, gu iulmhor,
Gu imchubhaidh, gu iullagach,
Gu iriseach, gu iardhalta.

L

Gu laomsgirra, gu lanealamh,
Gu labanach, gu lanchrodha,
Gu làidir, gu lochdmhor,
Gu leoghanta, gu lamhdheargach,
Cu laochail, gu ladurna,
Gu lomsgarach, gu lomsgathach,
Gu lòghmhor, gu leirsgriosach,
Gu luathbhuilleach, gu luathchleasach,
Gu laochlamhach, gu luidheachanach,
Gu leacanta, gu loinnearach,
Gu lanneuchdach, gu loisgeanta,
Gu lamhlotach, gu liobhara,
Gu leonchraiteach, gu luaimneach,
Gu lanuchathach, gu lomarra,
Gu lamsgiorrail, gu lamhsgathach,
Gu leumnach, gu lasanta,
Gu leanailteach, gu leadrach,
Lotach, leirsineach, luailteach.

M

Gu mear, gu meanmnach,
Gu morchridheach, gu mearrganta,
Gu milcanta, gu maoimanta,
Gu meaghlach, gu mirechathach,
Gu meaghrach, gu mirunach,
Gu mòreuchdach, gu mothachail,
Gu measara, gu misneachail,
Gu mòrlotach, gu mòralach,
Gu mòrphronnach, gu mòrghairdeach,
Gu mòrurranta, gu mòrthaitneach,
Gu mòrainmeil, gu mòriorgantach,

Gu mòrinnleachdach, mòrchliutach,
Gu mishathsach, gu maitheasach,
Gu millteach, gu marbhtach,
Gu mòrsgriosach, gu mòrshuileach,
Mearchruadalach, mòrchuiseach.

N

Gu neimhneach, gu namhaidail,
Gu niata, gu nuadarra,
Gu neoeagalach, gu neoeisleanach,
Gu neoiochdmhor, gu neomheata,
Gu nuallghuthach, gu nochdlannach,
Gu neomhathach. gu neosgàthach,
Gu neo-iochd'ranach, gu neothròcaireach,
Gu nathairneimhcach, gu ncartmhor,
Gu neimheil, gu neulfheargach,
Nàmhaidcach, neoghioragach, neochearbach.

O

Gu oirdheirc, gu òglaochail,
Gu ollabhar, gu osnadhach,
Gu oscach, gu oscaradh,
Gu orbheartach, gu orbhuadhach,
Gu onorach, gu oufhadhach,
Gu òrdail, gu òrchiseach,
Gu òirncalta, gu òrloinneach,
Gu oilthreabhach, gu oirchilleach,
Gu oireil, gu oirfheadhnach,
Gu oidmhuinteach, gu oscaradh,
Gu olfhuileach, oilbheumach.

P

Gu prop, gu priomhurlamh,
Gu prosda, gu prionnsail,
Gu praidhinneach, gu preachanach,
Gu peirseach, gu preabanach,
Gu pronntach, gu painntireach,
Gu prosnadhach, gu pribbarrach,
Gu piolaisteach, gu peannaideach,
Gu praisbhallach, gu puinneanach,
Gu piollach, gu peilghuineach,
Gu parraicideach, gu porncimheach,
Gu plosgarnach, pleasganach,

R

Gu ruaimneach, gu rioghail,
Gu robhorb, gu rannphairteach,
Gu rathail, gu ruisceanta,
Gu ruireachail, gu rotach,
Gu riaghailteach, gu reubach,
Gu ruidigh, gu reachdail
Gu roinnphairteach, gu ruganta
Gu roghlic, gu rosgradharcach,
Gu rofhaicilleach, gu rannsachaidh,
Gu rothreun, gu reachdach,
Gu ringthach, gu ruatharach,
Gu riamhach, gu ribach,
Gu reublannach, gu roimheach,
Gu remeil, gu righfheinneach,
Gu robharail, gu roghasda,
Gu robhnadhach, gu ro-òirdheirc,
Gu roàghmhor, rodhian, roghleusta.

S

Gu sàrbhuilleach, gu socair,
Gu sobhuailteach, gu suilbhir,
Gu seunail, gu sàrbhuailteach,
Gu sanntach, gu suigeartach,
Gu siorbhualach, gu seimhidh,
Gu sgairteil, gu screitidh,
Gu sealgach, gu sracaireach,
Gu screideil, gu sgiamhach,
Gu sodhearbhta, gu sgiorrail,
Gu scealparra, gu sgealparra,
Gu sgathach, gu sgeilmeil,
Gu sadbhuilleach, gu saibhailt',
Gu sgairghreamach, gu smiorail,
Gu smuisghearrach, gu smiorchruadhach,
Gu sgairteil, gu smachdmhor,
Gu snaitheach, gu somulta,
Gu soibheusach, gu somhuinte,
Gu sgabullach, gu srollbhratach,
Gu spealanta, gu starbhanach,
Gu seannghlic, gu sgailcarra,
Gu seasmhach, gu soighneil,
Gu soghniomhach, gu scasgarach,

Gu saibhreach, gu saorghreasach,
Gu sgaiteach, gu sgiathach,
Gu suilfhurachair, gu saighidgheur,
Gu stuaghghreannach, gu stuthchruaidh,
Gu sluchach, gu slugach,
Gu sluaghmhor, gu sobhuadhach,
Gu sgapach, gu scanrach,
Gu sgarach, gu sgaoilteach,
Gu slacairteach, gu siansach,
Gu siosarnach, gu suughaothach,
Gu seideach, gu spuinneach,
Gu steallach, gu stròiceach,
Gu sgianach, gu spionach,
Gu sraoilleach, gu slighach,
Gu stalcarra, gu siorbhuanach,
Gu subhailceach, gu sracach,
Gu starach, gu streaugach,
Gu sonnta, gu smachdail,
Gu sona, subhach, seolta, suairce.

T

Gu treuntach, gu teinteach,
Gu togarach, gu tulchuiseach,
Gu troidfheargach, gu troidchathach
Gu teathfhuileach, gu traosgach,
Gu toirteil, gu treunchathach,
Gu turloisgeach, gu tearruiute,
Gu tarruigeach, gu treumbhuilleach,
Gu toirmisgeach, gu tostallach,
Gu tailceasach, gu teascaireach,
Gu teanailteach, gu tòireach,
Gu tartarach, gu trosgach,
Gu treunghreimeach, gu toirleanailteach,
Gu toibheumach, gu treunthonnach,
Gu truaghmheileach, gu tuineasach
Gu teaschathach, gu taitneach
Gu tartfhuileach, gu treunsgathach,
Gu trombuilleach, gu tion-sgnamhach,
Gu tuadhbhuilleach, gu tarbhach,
Gu trusganta, gu tiogaireach,
Gu treuntoisgeach, gu tochdfheargach,
Gu tochailleach, gu tollghonach,

Gu treachailleach, gu toichiosdalach,
Gu tormanach, gu tuiriosgach,
Gu teoma, gu tàbhachdach
Gu tàiceil, gu tromluidheach,
Gu treubhach, gu treiseil,
Gu toillteanach, gu turailteach,
Gu tùrail, tapaidh, tulgach, tionnsgnach.

U

Gu urlamhach, gu urmhaiseach,
Gu urranta, gu uraluinn,
Gu urchleasach, gu uaibhreach,
Gu uilfheargach, gu uaillfheartach,
Gu urchaideach, gu uamhasach,
Gu urrasach, gu urramach,
Gu urloisgeach, gu uainnhfhlochdach,
Gu uachdarach, gu uallach,
Gu ullamh, gu usgarach,
Gu urmhailleach, gu uchdarach,
Gu uidhimichte, gu ughdarach,
Gu upagach, gu uilefhradharcach,
Gu upairneach, gu urghleusach,
Gu urbhuilleach, gu urspeallach,
Gu urlabhrach, urlamhach, urneartmhor,
Gu coisneadh na Cathlàrach,
Ri bruidhne 'ur biùthaidh,
A Chlannaibh Chuinn cheudchathaich,
'Si nis uair 'ur n' aithneachadh,
A chuileanan confhadach,
A bheirichean bunanta,
A leomhainean langhasda,
Onnochonaibh iorrghuilleach,
De laochraidh chrodha, churanta,
De Chlannaibh Chuinn cheudchathaich,
A Chlannaibh Chuinn cuimhnichibh
Cruas an am na h-iorghuill.

CHARTER BY DONALD OF ISLA, LORD OF THE ISLES, TO HECTOR MACLEAN OF DOWART. 1409.

Noverint universi presentes et futuri nos Donaldum de Ile Reg. Dominum Insularum Dedisse concessisse et hac presenti castra nostra confirmasse dilecto nepoti nostro Hectori Makgilleone Domino de Doward Constabulario Castri nostri de Karnaborg et suis heredibus masculis eiusdem castra futuris Constabulariis de nobis et heredibus nostris terras Sex marcatarum de Tyrunghafeal in insula Cola loco victualium farine et casei ab incolis de Tyrnag ad custodiam dicti ejus castri Constabulario hactenis annuatim dari consueti Habendas et tenendas terras predictas sex marcatarum Tirunghafeal eidem Hectori et heredibus suis predictis de nobis et heredibus nostris per suas rectas metas et antiquos fines in campis montibus pratis planis et pascuis silvis et litoribus, stagnis rivis vinariis et molendinis ceterisque aquis dulcibus et amaris venationibus aucupationibus et piscationibus omnibusque aliis commoditatibus et pertinentiis ad terras predictas Tyrunghafeal de jure vel consuetudine ad presens spectantibus seu spectare valentibus quomodo libet in futurum libere quiete plene et honorifice sicut melius plenius et liberius et honorificentius aliqua porcio terre in regno Scotie datur a barone liberetenente in feodum seu carta confirmatur Quasquidem terras Sex marcatarum Tyrunghafeal nos et heredes nostri eidem Hectori et heredibus suis predictis contra omnes masculos et feminas warantazabimus imperpetuum poterimus et defendemus In cujus rei testimonium sigillum nostrum autenticum presenti carti apponi fecimus Datum apud castrum nostrum de Ardchoranis in festo omnium Sanctorum anno Domini millesimo quadringentesimo nono presentibus hiis testibus venerabili in propria persone Domino Michaele Dei gracia Episcopo Sodorensis in sacra theologia doctore discretis viris Magistris Malcomo et Nigello rectoribus ecclesiarum Sancti Columbe de Moyle et de Keneavadean Bachallariis in Decratis ac nobilibus viris Lachlano Makfingane et Roderico Maknele et multis aliis.

THE GENEALOGY OF SIOL CHUINN FROM CONN TO SOMERLED.

"An crann is dirich' ri sheanachas,
O na shiolaich e 'n Albainn,
MacGhillebhride nan Garbhchrioch,
Cholla 's Chuinn, righre Bhanbha."

I

The Book of Clanranald.

Somhairle,
Giollabrighde,
Giolla Adhamhnan,
Solomh,
Meargach,
Suibhne,
Niallghusa,
Gothfruigh,
Ferghus,
Maine
Earc
Carran
Eochaidh
Colla Uais
Eochach Duibhlein,
Cairbre Liffeachair
Cormac
Art
Conn Ceudchathach.

II

MS. 1450.

Somairle,
Gillebrigde,
Gilleeagan,
Solam,
Meargad,
Suibne,
Niallgusa,
Maine,
Gofrig,
Fergusa,
Erc,
Cartan,
Eathach Feighlioch,
Collad Uais,
Eathach Donilein,
Cairpre Liffechar,
Cormac Uilfata,
Art Ainfear Faulcha,
Conn Cead Fcaig.

III

The Books of Ballimote and Leccan.

Somairli,
Gillebrigde,
Gilleadamnan,
Solamh,
Imergi,
Suibhne,
Niallgusa,
Amaini,
Gofraidh,
Fergusa,
Erc,
Echach,
Colla Uais.

IV

MS. of Dean Munro, 1549.

Somerle,
Gillebryde,
Gilleadamnane,
Sella,
Mearshaighe
Swiffine,
Malheussa,
Eacime,
Gothefred,
Fergus,
Erich,
Cartayn,
Ethay,
Thola Craisme,
Ethay de Wiff Leist,
Frathrequerwy,
Cairpre Lissechuyr
Crorin weet Alada
Art Lermeche
Conn Chide Kakay.

V		VI	
Somerled,	MS. 1700.	Samhairle,	Keating's History of Ireland.
Gilbride,		Giolla Bride,	
Gileonan,		Giolla Adamhnan,	
Solaimh,		Solamh,	
Mergadh,		Mealbruidhe,	
Suibhne,		Suibhne,	
Nialgus,		Niallgus,	
Main,		Maine,	
Goffrie,		Goffra,	
Fergus,		Feargus,	
Eire,		Erc,	
Carthan,		Criomhthran,	
Eoghie Feligh		Eochaidh,	
Coll Uais,		Colla Uais,	
		Eochaidh Liffeachar,	
		Cormac Ulfhada,	
		Art Aonthir,	
		Conn Cead Cathach.	

CHARTER BY ALEXANDER OF ISLA, EARL OF ROSS, AND LORD OF THE ISLES, TO ALEXANDER M'CULLOCH. 1436.

Omnibus hanc cartam visuris vel audituris Alexander de Ile Comes Rossie Salutem in Domino Sempiternam, Noveritis Nos Dedisse concessisse et hac presenti carta nostra Confirmasse dilecto nostro armigero Alexandro M'Cullach omnes et singulas terras nostras de Scarvy, de Pladds, de Petnely, Petogarty, Balmaduthy (nunc Ballecuith) et Ballechory cum pertinenciis una cum officio balliatus Immunitatis de Tayne jacentes infra dictum nostrum Comitatum pro suo homagio et fideli servitio nobis impenso et heredibus nostris ac successoribus Comitibus Rossie imposterum impendendo Tenendas et habendas dictas terras et officium cum pertinenciis prefato Alexandro heredibus suis et suis assignatis de nobis heredibus nostris et nostris successoribus Comitibus Rossie imperpetuum in feodo et hereditate cum omnibus commoditatibus libertatibus et asiamentis ac justis suis pertinenciis quibuscunque per omnes rectas metas suas antiquas et divisas, in viis semitis boscis planis pratis pascuis et pasturis, in molendinis multuris et eorum sequelis in brasinis stagnis aquis et rivulis, in aucupationibus venationibus et piscationibus, in moris maresiis turbariis potariis et carbonariis cum libero introitu et exitu, cum curiis et escaetis

curiarum predictarum terrarum Reservatis nobis heredibus nostris
et nostris successoribus Comitibus escactis curiarum officii balliatus
dicti Immunitatis de Tayne prefatus vero Alexander heredes sui et
assignati possidentes in perpetuum dictas terras cum pertinenciis
cum omnibus commoditatibus tam non nominatis quam nominatis
una cum bondes et nativis ad dictas terras spectantibus seu juste
spectare valentibus in futurum, adeo libere integre plenarie et
honorofice bene et in pace sicut alique terre in comitatu nostro
dautur vel hereditarie concedentur Reddendo ex dictis terris cum
pertinenciis prefatus Alexander heredes sui et assignati uni
Capellano in ecclesia Sancti Monifacii Deo Servienti quinque
marcas usualis monete ad duos anni terminos viz. Pentecostes et
Beati Martini per equales portiones, ac faciendo nobis et heredibus
nostris et nostris successoribus Comitibus Rossie annuatim tres
sectas ad tria placita Capitalia tenenda apud Kynardy tantum pro
omni alio onere servitio vel demanda que de dictus terris et officio
exigi poterit vel requiri Et nos vero Alexander prefatus heredes
nostri et nostri successores Comites Rossie, prefatus terras cum
pertinentiis dicto Alexandro heredibus et suis assignatis, contra
omnes mortales warantizabimus acquietabimus et in perpetuum
defendemus. In cujus rei testimonium Sigillum nostrum appendi
fecimus apud castrum nostrum de Dingwale sexto die · mensis
Januarii anno Domini millesimo quadringentesimo tricesimo sexto
hiis testibus Hugone de Ross Domino de Balnagowyn, Donaldo de
Calder, Georgio de Munro de Foulis et Johanne M'Loyde cum
pluribus aliis in testimonium vocatis.

CHARTER OF CONFIRMATION FROM ALEXNDER OF ISLA, EARL OF ROSS AND LORD OF THE ISLES, TO SIR WALTER OF ., INNES, LORD OF THAT ILK. 1438.

Innes.   Alexander de Yle Dominus Insularum Comes Rossiae et
Justiciarius ex parte boreali a quae de Forth universis et singulis
hanc cartam visuris vel audituris salutem.   Sciatis nos approbasse
ratificasse et hac presenti carta nostra confirmasse donationem
illam et concessionem quam Dominus Johannes de Lindsay
Dominus de Byres fecit et concessit dilecto nostso consanguineo
Domino Waltero de Innes militi domino ejusdem de terris
baroniae de Aberkirder cum pertinentibus infra Vicecomitatum
de Banff. Tenendam et habendam dicto Domino Waltero et
heredibus suis cum omnibus et singulis libertatibus commodit-

atibus asiamentis et justis pertinentijs quibuscunque ad dictas spectantibus seu quomodo juste spectare valentibus in futurum adeo libere et quiete, plenarie integre et honorifice in omnibus et per omnia, sicut carta et evidentia dicti Domini Johannis de Lindsay eidem Domino Walteri de Lesly avi nostri facta quondam Domino Willielmo de Lindyssay de Byres consanguineo suo super dictas terras plenius continet et proportat. Et ut hec nostra confirmatio predictae cartae avi nostri robur virtutem et libertatem teneat, habent, et possident. In cujus rei testimonium sigillum nostrum presentibus apponi fecimus. Apud Castrum nostrum de Dingwall vicesimo secundo die mensis Februarii anno Domini millesimo quadringentesimo tricesimo Octavo. Testibus vener_ abilis viris Willielmo de Lesly Vicecomite de Inverness, Georgio de Munro Domino de Foullys, Willielmo de Urchard Willielmo de Calder, Hugone Le Rose, et Murchedo Revach Armigeris.

THE FOLLOWING PROCEEDS ON THE RESIGNATION BY JOHN ROSE IN FAVOUR OF HIS SON HUGH OF KILRAVOCK. 1440.

Magnifico et potenti domino ac domino suo praestantissimo **Family of** domino Alexandro comite de Rosse vester humilis Johannes de **Kilravock.** Roos de Kilrawak omnimodam reverentiam et honorem. In manus vestras ego Johannes predictus non vi aut metus ductus nec errore lapsus sed mera et spontanea voluntate nostra ac propria motu omnes et singulares terras meas baronie de Kylrawak cum pertinentiis jacentes infra vicecomitatum de Narne quas de vobis teneo in capite, in favorem dilecti filii mei Hugonis de Roos per fustem et baculum ac presentas meas literas patentes sursum reddo pure que simpliciter resigno ; salvis michi pro tempore vite mee le franktenement dictarum terrarum cum pertinentiis et sponse mee tertia parte ei spectante post mortem meam prout is de eisdem obierem vestitus et saisitus, ac totum jus et clameum quod ad proprietatem dictarum terrarum cum pertinentiis habui, habeo vel habere potero pro me et heredibus meis omnino quietum clamo in perpetuam . . . quod vos domine mi antedicto Hugonem filium meum antedictum de eisdem terris cum pertin- entiis investire valentis ; salvis mihi et sponse mee ut supra. Pro qua vero resignatione fienda in manibus vestris facio constituo et ordino nobiles viros Malcolmum McKyntosych ballivum de Badenach, Hectorem Tarlochson Senescallum de Urchard, Nigellum

M'Loide, Donaldum M'Loide, et Georgium de Munro . . . . .
actornatos . . . ad reddendum, &c. . . . In cujus rei
testimonium sigillum meum presentibus est appensum apud
manerium meum de Kylravok, vicesimo secundo die mensis Junii
anno Domini millesimo quadringentesimo quadragesimo.

CHARTOUR OF BAUDENYOCHT DALNAVERT AND KINRARACHE BE THE EARLE OF ROSSE. 1438.

ordon
ers.

Omnibus hanc cartam visuris vel audituris Alexander de Yla
comes Rossie eternam in Domino Salutem Noueritis nos cartas
Willelmi quondam comitis Rossie predecessoris nostri factas
cuidam Malmorano de Glencharny non rasas non abolitas non
cancellatas nec in aliqua sue parte suspectas vidisse inspexisse et
ad plenum intellexisse quarum tenor sequitur in hec verba
Omnibus hanc cartam visuris vel audituris Willelmus comes de
Ross salutem in domino sciatis nos dedisse concessisse et hec
presenti carta nostra confirmasse Malmorano de Glencharny duas
dauatas terre nostre in Badenach videlicet dauatam de Dalnafert
et dauatam de Kynrorayth cum omnibus suis pertinentiis et rectis
diuisis pro homagio et seruicio suo Reseruata nobis et heredibus
nostris nomine capitalis manerii una acra terre iacente iuxta le
stychan predicte ville de Dalnafert ex australi parte in qua situm
fuit manerium quondam Scayth filii Ferchardi Tenendas et
habendas dicto Malmorano et heredibus suis de nobis et heredibus
nostris in feodo et hereditate imperpetuum in pratis et pascuis (&c.)
Reddendo inde nobis et heredibus nostris ipse et heredes sui duas
marcas usualis monete annuatim Scilicet medietatem adfestum
Penthecostes aliam mediatatem ad festum Sancti Martini in yeme
et faciendo nobis et heredibus nostris ipse et heredes sui tres sectas
curie nostre infra dictum manerium terre ad tria placita capitalia
nostra ibidem tenenda cum nos ibidem sederimus et fornisecum
seruitium domini nostri regis quantum ad predictas duas dauatas
terre pertinet pro omnibus aliis seruitiis exactionibus et secularibus
demandis Nos vero Willelmus comes de Ross et heredes nostri
predicto Malmorano et heredibus suis predictas duas dauatas terre
in omnibus ut predicitur contra omnes homines et feminas
warantizabimus acquietavimus et imperpetuum defendemus In
cuius rei testimonuim huic carte sigillum nostrum apposuimus
hiis testibus domino Marca Dei gratia Abbate Noue Firme dompno

Mauricio de Belliloco monacho domino Willelmo de Mowbray
milite Johanne de Berclay Willelmo thane de Caldor Archibaldo
de Clunace et multis aliis Tenor secunde carte talis est Uniuersis
presentes litteras inspecturis Willelmus comes de Ross salutem in
domino Sciatis nos concessisse et feodifirmam dimississe Malmorano
de Glencharny totam terram nostram de Dalnafert in le Badenach
scilicet illam acram terre quam nobis reseruanimus in carta
infoedationis dicti Malmorani de eadem prout plenius in dicta
carta continetur Tenendam et habendam sibi et heredibus suis de
nobis et heredibus nostris ad feodifirmam imperpetuum Reddendo
ipse et heredes sui pro nobis et heredibus nostris duas marcas per
nos debitas superiori domino de la Badenach quas nobis et
heredibus nostris in carta infeodationis dicti Malmorani reseruamus
et soluendo ipsi et heredes sui sectatori nostro terrarum nostrorum
scilicet de Kynroreach et Dalnafert pro tribus sectis per nos debitis
ad tria capitalia placita de le Badenach per adnum dimidiam marcam
pro omnibus oneribus exactionibus et secularibus demandis. In cuius
rei testimonium presentibus sigillum nostrum apposuimus datum
apud Narn vicesimo secundo die mensis Nouembris anno Domino
millesimo tricentesimo tricesimo octavo. Quas quidem cartas in
omnibus punctis suis et articulis clausis conditionibus et circum-
stantiis uniuersis forma pariter et effectu nos Alexander comes
Rossie pro nobis heredibus nostris et successoribus comitibus
Rossie approbamus ratificamus et per presentes imperpetuum
confirmamus Saluis nobis seruitiis debitis et consuetis et faciendo
domino nostro regi fornisecum seruitium quantum ad dictas terras
pertinet. In cuius confirmationis nostre testimonium sigillum
nostrum appendi fecimus apud Kessok hiis testibus Celestino de
Insulis nostro filio Johanne M'Leoid de Glenelg Torquelo M'Leoid
de Leohos Johanne de Rosse de Balnagowin Georgio de Monro de
Fowlis Negello M'Leoid senescallo nostro et Negello Flemyng
secretario nostro cum multis aliis.

PRECEPT OF SASINE IN FAVOUR OF WILLIAM THANE OF CAWDOR,
BY ALEXANDER EARL OF ROSS, AND LORD OF THE ISLES.
1442.

Alexander de Ile, Earl of Ross, Lord of the Isles, and Justiciar Invernessiana,
of the part north of the water of Forth, to John Grant, Sheriff-
Depute of Inverness; Greeting: Since by inquest made by our
command and retoured to our chapel, it is found that the late

Donald of Caldor, father of William of Calder, bearer of these presents, died last vest and seized as of feu at the peace and faith of our Lord the King, of the land of the Thanage of Caldor, with the pertinents and the offices of Sheriff of Nairn and constabulary thereof, with the tax of bear and fish, together with the annual rent of six marks of Balmakath, and of the lands of Both and Banchre with pertinents, and of the lands of the half of Rate, together with the mill thereof, with pertinents lying in the Earldom of Moray, within the Sheriffdom of Nairn: And that the said William is lawful and nearest heir of his said late father, of said lands, annual rent and mill with the pertinents, and is of lawful age, and that the lands are held of us in chief: Therefore we command and charge you upon having seen these pertinents, to give without delay to the foresaid William, or his certain attorney, bearer of these presents, hereditary state and sasine of said lands, annual rent and mill with the pertinents, reserving the rights of parties as is the manner, for the doing of which we commit to you, in this part, by these presents, our plenary power and special mandate: And in testimony of said sasine, given by you, append your seal on the second tail after ours. Given under our seal at the burgh of Inverness, the seventeenth day of the month of August, in the year of the Lord 1442.

CARTA ALEXANDRI DE YLE COMITIS ROSSIE FACTA ALEXANDRI DE SETOUN COMITI DE HUNTLIE DE BARONIA DE KYNED-WARD 1442 VEL POTIUS 1442. FOL. R. 4. CARTULAR. ABERDON.

Omnibus hoc scriptum visuris vel audituris Alexander de Yle comes Rossie et Dominus Insularum ac Justiciarius extra Forth Eternam in Domino Salutam Noveritis nos Dedisse concessisse et presenti nostro scripto assignasse dilecto nostro Alexandro de Setoun militi Domino de Gordon, pro toto tempore vite sue, totam et integram baroniam nostram de Kynedward cum pertinenciis jacentem in Comitatu de Buchan infra vicecomitatum de Aberdeen unacum juri patronatiis ac donationis beneficiorum nobis in Episcopatu Aberdonensis spectantibus pro suo servitio et homagio nobis impensis et impendendis Tenendas et habendas dictas terras dicto baronie cum pertinenciis una cum jure patronatus et donationis beneficiorum dicte Alexandro de Setoun militi, cum curiis escaetis firmis redditibus que nobis pertinere dinoscuntur

quibuscunque temporibus, ac cum omnibus aliis commoditatibus
libertatibus et asiamentis ac suis justus pertinenciis quibuscunque
tam non nominatis quam nominatis ad dictam Baroniam specanti-
bus seu spectare valentibus quomodolibet in futurum durante
termino vite dicti Domini Alexandri militis ut prefertur. Insuper
Volumus et concedimus quod omnes tenentes dicte nostre baronie
obediant respondiant et intendant prefato Domino Alexandro de
Setoun durante dicto tempore sicut presentiam nostram haberent,
et sicut nobis facere deberent In cujus rei testimonium Sigillum
nostrum presentibus apponi fecimus apud Invernys quinto die
mensis Octobris anno Domini millesimo quadringentesimo
quadragesimo secundo. Scribitur in circumferentia Sigilli, S.
Alexan. de Yle Comitis Rossie ac Domini Insularum—In Sigillo
habet duas naviculas Scilicet Galeys et tres Leones insurgenter, in
circumferentia cum floribus.

CHARTER BY ALEXANDER EARL OF ROSS PENES MACKINTOSH
EX AUTOGRAPHO PROPRIO MACDONALD. 11th February, 1443.

Omnibus hanc cartam visuris vel audituris.

Alexander de Yle Comes Rossie et Dominus Insularum et Lochaber Eternam in domino salutem. Noveritis nos ex matura deliberatione Consilii nostri Dedisse concessi et hac presenti carta nostra confirmasse dilecto nostro Malcolmo McKintoch. *Macdonald Collections.*

Totas et integras terras nostras quadraginta marcarum infra scriptas viz. de Daliemeley Braenachan Tullocharder Invercuin Murbalgane, Glenglastour Kilkaraith Bothsyny Bothasky, Achadoire Collicharam, Bothynton Blairnafyngon, Bothynton moir Tranothan, Keppach Achamaddy Achadnacroise Breagach Inverrowaybeg, Bothlan Inverroymoir pro dimidia parte cum pertinentibus Jacentibus in dominio nostro de Lochaber infra vicecomitatem de Inverness. Pro suo fideli servitio nobis gratantes impendo et impendendo. Tenendas et Habendas totas et integras prenominatas terras ac pertinentes prefato Malcolmo et heredibus suis masculis de nobis et hereditate in perpetuam per omnes rectas metas suas antiquas et divisas in moras maresiis toftis planis viis semitis aquis pratis pascuis et pasturis molendinis multuris et eorum sequeles aucupationibus venationibus piscariis potariis turbariis carbonariis fabrilibus et brasinus ac curiis et curiarum (exitibus) Escketis et Blude wetis herezeldis mulierum

merchetis arriagiis et carriagiis omnibusque aliis commodicatibus
libertatibus, et asiamentio ac justis suis pertinentiis quibuscunque
tam non nominatis quam nominatis addictas terras cum pertinentibus spectantibus seu quomodolibet spectantibus valentibus in
futuram adeo libere quiete integre honorifice bene et in pace sicut
aliqua terra de dominio nostro Insularum datur et conceditur.
Faciendo inter nobis heredibus nostris et successoribus dictus
Malcolmus et heredes sui masculi servitium Warde et Relevii. Et
nos Alexander de Yle Comes ac Dominus prefatus heredes nostri et
successores predictas terras cum pertinentibus prefato Malcolmo
et heredibus suis masculis ut prefertur in omnibus et per omnia ut
predictum est contra omnes homines et feminas warantizabimus
acquietabimus et pro perpetuo defendemus.

In cujus rei testimonium sigillum nostrum appendi fecimus
apud Innerness Undecimo die mensis Februarij Anno Domini
millesimo quadringentesimo quadragesimo tertio Presentibus
ibidem Lachlano M'Gilleon Domino de Dowart Joanni Murchardi
M'Gilleon Domino de Canlochbouye Joanne Lachlani M'Gilleon
Domino de Colla Vylando de Chishelm, Georgio Munro domino de
Foulis et Nigello M'Loyd Consiliariis nostris pluribus aliis.

CONFIRMATION BY JAMES II. OF CHARTER BY ALEXANDER OF ISLA, EARL OF ROSS, AND LORD OF THE ISLES, TO JOHN SKRIMGEOURE.

Sig.   Apud Striveline 3 Nov. 1444.

REX confirmavit cartam Alexandri comitis Rossie domini
Insularum, &c., et baronis de Kincardin,—[qua concessit
JOHANNI SKRIMGEOURE militi, constabulario de Dunde,
heredibus ejus et assignatis, pro ejus fideli homagio et servitio,—
terras et villas cum annuo reditu et molendino subscriptis, viz., le
Bordland, cum duabus parkis muris circumdatis et castro ejusdem,
—salvo dicto comiti viridi monte infra dict. Bordland, pro curiis
ejus super eodem tenendis,—Wismanston, Fasdawach, Achkarny,
Balmakewin cum molendino ejusdem,—salvo jure ann, red. in
quantum tenetur D. Rob. de Levingstoun et heredibus ejus de
eadem villa de Balmakewin et molendino ejusdem,—Petgervy—
Salvo jure ann. red. in quantum tenetur ecclesie Cathed. de
Brechin,—le Muretoun, et ann. red. 20 sol. de Kirkhill, vic.
Kincardin.:—TENEND. a dicto comite de rege :—REDDEND. dicto

comiti et heredibus ejus wardam et relevium cum contigerint :—
TEST. Rob. episc. Cathanen. Alex. de Suthirland magistro ejusdem,
Finlao abbate de Fern et Malc. M‘Kintosch : Apud Invernys Oct.
10, 1444.

CHARTER OF THE BAILLIARY OF LOCHABER BY ALEXANDER
OF ISLA, EARL OF ROSS AND LORD OF THE ISLES, TO
MALCOLM MACKINTOSH. November 13, 1447.

Omnibus hanc Cartam visuris vel audituris Alexander de Yla **Macdonald**
Comes Rossie et Dominus Insularum, Eternam in Domino **Collections.**
Salutem, Noveritis Nos Dedisse concessisse et hoc presenti Scripto
nostro Confirmasse confidentissimo nostro consanguineo Malcolmo
MacIntosche presentium conservatori Totum et integrum officium
Ballivatus seu Senescallie omnium et singularum terrarum Dominii
nostri de Lochabber Tenendum et habendum dictum officium cum
omnibus et singulis pertinentiis ad dictum officium spectantibus seu
juste spectare valentibus quomodolibet in futurum dicto Malcolmo
MacIntosche ac omnibus suis heredibus de nobis et heredibus nostris
in feodo et hereditate in perpetuum, adeo libere pacifice bene et in
pace, sicut aliquod officium Ballivatus vel Senescallic in toto regno
Scotie alacui ballivo conceditur, seu pro perpetuo in Carta confirmatur.   Quod quidem officium ut prefertur Nos Alexander
Comes et Dominus antedictus et heredes nostri antedicto Malcolmo
et heredibus suis ut predicitur contra quoscumque mortales,
warrantizabimus acquietabimus et in perpetuum defendemus.   In
omnium premissorum testimonium Sigillum nostrum presentibus
appendi fecimus apud Castrum nostrum de Dingvale, decimo tertio
die mensis Novembris anno Domino millessimo quadringentesimo
quadragesimo septimo His Testibus Torquello MacLeoid Domino
de Leoghos, Johanne MacLeoid Domino de Glenelg, Celestino de
Insulis filio nostro naturali, Nigello Flemyng Secretario nostro et
Donaldo Judice, cum diversis aliis presentibus.

(Signed)   WILL. MacEWAN, N.P.

CHARTER BY JOHN, EARL OF ROSS, AND LORD OF THE ISLES,
TO THE MASTER OF SUTHERLAND. 1449.

To all who shall see or hear of this charter, John de Yle, Earl **Invernessiana.**
of Ross, and Lord of the Isles : Greeting eternal in the Lord :
Know all that we have given, granted, and by this our present

charter, confirmed to our beloved cousin, Alexander de Sutherland of Dunbeth, all and sundry the lands of Easter Kindeace, with the pertinents lying in our Earldom of Ross, within the Sheriffdom of Inverness, for his homage and faithful service: Which lands belonged to the late Thomas de Fentoune of Ogil, and which said Thomas . . . , resigned . . . . to be had and held the said lands of Easter Kindeace, with the pertinents, by the foresaid Alexander de Sutherland, his heirs and assignees, of us and our successors, Earls of Ross, in feu and heritage forever, by all right marches, ancient and devised, in woods and plains . . . . hunting, hawking, fishing, and fowling . . . . In testimony of which thing we have caused our seal to be appended to our present charter, at Inverness, the 13th day of the month of August, in the year of the Lord 1449, there being present—John Stewart, Lord of Lorn; Lachlan M'Gilleoin of Dowarde; John Murchardi M'Gilleoin of Fynschenys; John Lachlan M'Gilleoin of Colla; William, Thane of Cawdor; Master Thomas Lochmalony, Chancellor of the Church of Ross; Andrew Reed, Provost of the burgh of Inverness; and Alexander Flemmyng of Perth, with divers others called in testimony.

LITTERA JOHANIS COMITIS DE ROSS PENES ECCLESIAS INFRA SUAS BONDAS.

of   Johanne de Yle comes Rossie et dominus insularum universis et singulis ad quorum notitias presentes litteras pervenerint salutem in omnium salvatore.   Noverit universitas vestra nos dimisse, nec non per presentes libere quiete et pacifice dimittimus, venerabilibus et religiosis viris Abbati et conventui de Pasleto presentibus conservatoribus, ob reverentiam gloriam et honorem in Dei ac beatissimi Virginis Marie Matris ejus et Sancti Mirini omnicumque sanctorum, rectorias ecclesiarum Sancti Kylkeran et Colmaneli in Kyntire et Knapdale Ergadiensis diocesis per predecessores nostros eisdem, pro salute animarum ipsarum et nostra concessas temporibus retroactis sicut in cartas super hoc confectis plenius continetur permittentes eisdem Abbati et conventui dictas rectorias assedare et de eisdem libere disponere et providere futuris temporibus sicut eis melius videbitur expedire atque mandates firmiter et districte universis et singulis nostris hominibus quatenus prefatis domino Abbati et conventui aut eorum procuratoribus in hoc parte in assedatione dictarum ecclesiarum nullum impedimentum prestare presumat sub pena omniquam erga nostram donationem amittere poteruit quovismodo. In cujus rei testimonium nostrum sigillum presentibus est affixum. Datum apud Cleandaghallagan in Knapadal xxi° die mensis Maii anno Domini millesimo quadrigentesimo quinquagesimo quinto.

THE CLAN MACINNES.

The Clan MacInnes, associated in tradition with the early exploits of Somerled, are, according to the MS. of 1450, a branch of the Siol Gillevray. According to this MS. a certain Gillebride, *rig eilan*, or King of the Isles, lived in the 12th century, and was descended from a brother of Suibne, ancestor of the Macdonalds; and from Anradan, or Henry, the son of Gillebride, the same authority similarly traces the Macneills, Maclachlans, Macewens, and Maclaisrichs. The seat of this Gillebride's race (who must be carefully distinguished from the father of Somerled) seems to have been Lochaber. Dr Skene endorses this view, and calls this tribe Siol Ghillebride or Gillevray; and Hugh Macdonald says that in the time of Somerled the principal surnames in the country— that is of Morvern, Ardgour, and Lochaber—were the MacInneses and MacGillevrays, who were the same as the MacInneses. The MacInneses were of Ardgour and Morvern, and there is a castle at Kinlochaline said to have been built by a lady of the Clan MacInnes. It is thus evident that while the Clan MacInnes is of the Clan Cholla, they are not strictly of the Clan Donald.

PRECEPT OF SASINE TO WILLIAM THANE OF CAWDOR FOR LANDS OF BALMAKEITH BY JOHN OF ISLA, EARL OF ROSS, AND LORD OF THE ISLES. 1458.

Joannes de Ile comes Rossie ac dominus Insularum dilecto Thanes of nostro Willelmo Flemyng burgensi de Narn ballivo nostro in hac Cawdor. parte salutem. Quia concessimus per cartam nostram dilecto nostro Willelmo Thano de Caldor omnes et singulares terras nostras de Balmakayth jacentes in vice-comitatu nostro de Narn ut tenore carte nostre inde sibi confecte plenius continetur vobis precipuimus et mandamus quatinus prefato Willelmo vel suo certo actornato latori presentium saisinam et statim hereditarium per terram et lapidem visis presentibus tribuatis indilate. Saluo jure cujuslibet ut est moris. Ad quod faciendum vobis in hac parte nostram plenariam committimus potestatem et mandatum speciale ac in signum saisine per vos traditi sigillum vestrum in secunda cauda post nostrum penos predictum Willelmum pro perpetuo remansurum apponatis. Datum sub sigillo nostro apud castrum nostrum de Dingvale decimo nono die mensis Julii anno domini millesimo quadringentesimo quinquagesimo octavo.

PRECEPT BY JOHN OF YLE, EARL OF ROSS AND LORD OF THE ISLES, FOR INFEFTING THOMAS OF DINGWALE, HIS CHAMBERLAIN, AND THOMAS OF DINGWALE, JUNIOR, IN INCHEFUR. 18th February, 1462.

The Earls of Cromartie.

Johannes de Yle comes Rossie et dominus Insularum, principali balliuo nostro Rossia Johanni de Monro seu eius certo substituto Doucano de Monro, salutem : Et quia Robertus Johannis Dominus de Inchefur totas et integras terras suas de Inchefur cum pertinentiis in manibus nostris per fustem et baculum sursum raddidit, pureque et simpliciter resignauit ; quas quidem terras incontinente dedimus et concessimus ut de frauctenemento domino Tome de Dyngvale tunc subdecano Rossensi ac nostro tunc temporis camerario, et ut de feodo Thome de Dyngvale, heredibus suis, prout in eorum cartis latius continetur : Quare vobis et cuilibet vestrum precepimus, necnon et stricta preciendo mandamus, quatenus visis presentibus sasinam et statum hereditarium dictarum terrarum cum pertinentiis, ut de frauctene-mento dicto domino Thome de Dyngvale, et de feodo dicto Thome iuniori de Dyngvale, salus iure cuiuslibet, ut moris est, attribuatis, vel vuus vestrum attribuat : Et in signum sasine taliter per vos vel vuum vestrum eiis tradite tam de frauctenemento quam de feodo, sigillum vestrum antedicti Johannis in secunda cauda post nostrum appendatis : In cuius rei testimonium sigillum nostrum presentibus appendi fecimus apud manerium nostrum de Deluy, decimo octauo die mensis Februarii, anno Domino millesimo quadringentesimo sexagesimo secundo.

PRECEPT OF SASINE BY JOHN DE ILE, EARL OF ROSS AND
LORD OF THE ISLES, TO JOHN MUNRO OF FOWLIS. 21st
September, 1458.

Johannes de Ile comes Rossie ac dominus insularum dilecto **Family of**
nostro Johanni de Munro de Foulis ballivo nostro in hac parte **Kilravock.**
salutem. Quia concessimus per cartam nostram dilectis nostris
Mariote de Sutherlande et Willelmo de Caldor filio seu eorum
alteri diucius viventi et eorum heredibus inter se de corporibus
suis procreandis omnes et singulas terras nostras de Estirkyndes
cum pertinenciis iacentis in comitatu nostro infra vicecomitatum
de Inuernys ut tenore carte nostre inde eis confecte plenius continetur. Vobis precipimus et mandamus quatinus prefati Mariote
et Willelmo de Caldor vel suis certis procuratoribus, latoribus
presentium saisinam dictarum terrarum de Estir Kyndes per
terram et lapidem visis presentibus tribuatis inditate saluo jure
cuiuslibet ut est moris. Ad quod faciendum vobis in hac parte
nostram plenariam committimus potestatem et mandatum speciale
et in signum saisine per vos tradite sigillum vestrum in secunda
cauda post nostrum apponatis penes predictos imperpetuam
remansuram.

Datum sub sigillo nostro apud castrum nostrum de Dingvale
vicesimo primo die mensis Septembris anno domini millesimo
quadringentesimo octavo.

CHARTER BY JOHN OF YLE, EARL OF ROSS, AND LORD OF
THE ISLES, TO DONALD CORBATT, OF THE LANDS OF
ESTER ARDE. 12th April, 1463.

Omnibus hanc cartam visuris vel audituris Johannes de Yle **Cromartie**
Comes Rossie et dominus Insularum, eternam in Domino salutem: **Charters.**
Noveritis nos dedisse, concessisse, et hac presenti carta nostra
imperpetuum confirmasse dilecto nostro et natiuo armigero
Donaldo Corbatt, omnes et singulas terras nostras de Ester Arde
cum pertinenciis iacentes in dicto comitatu. Rossie infra vicecomitatum de Innernys: Quequidem terre cum pertinenciis
fuerunt quondam Johannis Tullach hereditarie, et quas idem
Johannes non vi aut metu ductus, nec errore lapsus, set mera et
spontanea sua voluntate, per fustem et baculum in manus nostras
resignauit; ac totum ius et clameum que habet, habuit, vel
habere potuit, pro se et heredibus suis omnino quitumclamauit
imperpetuum: Tenendas et habendas totas et integras pre-

nominatas terras de Ester Arde cum pertinenciis prefato Donaldo
Corbatt et heredibus suis; quibus deficientibus, quod absit,
Margarete Corbat filie dicti Donaldi et heredibus suis *inter ipsam
et prefatum Johannem Tullach* procreatis seu procreandis; de
nobis, heredibus nostris et successoribus comitibus Rossie, in
feodo et in hereditate imperpetuum, per omnes rectas metas suas
antiquas et diuisas, in boscis, planis, pratis, moris, marresiis,
pascuis et pasturis, petariis, turbariis, carbonariis, fabrilibus et
brasinis, viis, semitis, aquis, siluis, riuolis, et lacubus aucupacionibus, venacionibus, piscacionibus, cum vraik, waith et wair, cum
molendinis, multuris, et eorum sequelis, cum curiis et earum
*exitibus, herezeldis et mulierum merchettis, cum communi
pastura,* et libero introitu et exitu, ac cum omnibus aliis et
singulis commoditatibus et libertatibus, et asiamentis, ac iustis
suis pertinenciis quibuscunque, tam non nominatis quam
nominatis, tam subtus terra quam supra terram, tam prope
quam procul, ad predictas terras cum pertinenciis spectantibus
seu iuste spectare valentibus quomodolibet in futurum : adeo
libere, quiete, integre, plenarie, honorifice, bene et in pace, sine
renocacione aliquali : Reddendo inde annuatim prefatus Donaldus
et heredes sui, quibus deficientibus, quod absit, dicta Margareta et
heredes sui inter ipsam sepefatam Margaretam et prefatum
Johannem procreati seu procreandi, nobis, heredibus nostris et
successoribus, comitibus Rossie, tres sectas curie ad tria placita
capitalia nostra tenenda apud Kynnardy, tantum pro omni alio
onere, seruicio seculari, exactione seu demanda, que per nos,
heredes nostros, et successores comites Rossie exigi poterunt de
dictis terris cum pertinentiis vel requiri.   Et nos vero prefatus
Johannes comes Rossie, heredes nostri et successores, comites
Rossie, totas et integras prenominatas terras cum pertinenciis
prefato Donaldo, et heredibus suis, quibus deficientibus, dicte
Margarete et heredibus suis inter ipsam et dictum Johannem
procreatis seu procreandis, in omnibus et per omnia, ut predictum
est, contra omnes mortales homines et feminas varantizabimus,
acquietabimus, et imperpetuum defendemus : In cuius rei
testimonium sigillum nostrum presentibus appendi fecimus, apud
Tayne, duodecimo die mensis Aprilis, anno Domini millesimo
quadringentesimo sexagesimo tercio, coram hiis testibus, viz.,
venerabili in Christo patre *Finlaio abbate de Feru,* Willelmo
Thena de Caldor, milite, Johanne de Monro de Foulis, Colino
Laclanni McGillcoin ballivo de Mule, Johanne McGoyre de Wlua,
Thoma Monro nostro secretario, cum mulis aliis in testimonium
vocatis.

CONFIRMATION BY JAMES III. TO THOMAS, YOUNGER OF DING-
WALL, OF CHARTER BY JOHN OF ISLA, EARL OF ROSS,
AND LORD OF THE ISLES.

Apud Invernys, 14 Aug. 1464.

Rex confirmavit cartam Johannis de Yle, comitis Rossie et Reg. Mag. Sig.
domini Insularum,—[qua—de consensu et matura deliberatione
concilii sui—concessit THOME juniori DE DINGVALE—terras
de Usuy, in comitatu Rossie, vic. Invernys, in excambium terrarum tertie partis de Arkboll et terrarum de Inchfure, in maragio
de Delny :—TENEND. dictas terras de Usuy prefato Tho. de
Dingvale juniori, heredibus ejus masculis de corpore ejus legitime
procreatis et assignatis (ejus masculis) quibus quod absit deficientibus, Joh. de D. fratri ejus germano, et heredibus &c., et ipsis
quod absit dificientibus, validiori et digniori de cognatione de
Dingvale succedenti, ejusque heredibus masculis et assignatis :—
RESERVAND. dicto comiti et successoribus suis antiquum molen-
dinum tunc edificatum, cum consuetis antiqua crofta et tofta
ejusdem, cum consuetis multuris et sequelis dicti molendini
(multura et sequelis dicte Ville de Usuy tantummodo exceptis) :—
etiam quod liceret rivolo descendente de lacu de Usuy futuris
temporibus (uti) prout consuetum fuerat temporibus retroactis :—
RESERVAND. etiam *le fractenementum* dictarum terrarum de Usuy
Domino Tho. de Dingvale computori dicti comitis, tunc temporis
camerario suo tantummodo dum in humanis vixerit :—REDEND. 6
denarios nomine albe firme :—TEST. Donaldo de Insulis dom. de
Dunnowage et de Glynnys, Celestino de Insulis de Lochalch et de
Lochbryn, Lachlano M'Gilleoin dom. de Doward, Joh. de Munro
dom. de Foulis tunc temporis ballivo dicti comitis, Lachlano
juvene M'Gilleoin filio et herede dicti Lachlani M. de Doward,
Ranaldo Albo de Insulis fratre dict. Donaldi, Joh. Ranaldi Goffridi,
Joh. M'Geir de Ulva, Eugenio Donaldi Senescallo domus dicti
comitis, Hectore Torquelli Nigelli, Donaldo M'Duffee, et Tho. de
Munro Secretario dicti comitis :—Apud Dingvale, 12 Apr., 1463].

CARTA CONFIRMATIONIS JOANNIS DE ILE COMITIS ROSSIE AC
DOMINI INSULARUM SUPER TERRAS ABBACIE NOVE
FAIRNE. 2 Nov. 1467. EX APOGRAPHO CHARTACEO PENES
RODERICUM M'LEOD DE CATBOLE—1756.

Omnibus hanc cartam visuris vel audituris Johannes de Ile Macdonald
Comes Rossie et Dominus Insularum Eternam in Domino Salutem, Collections.
cum alias pie et recolende memorie magnificus ac potens Dominus

Farchardus quondam Comes Rossie et alii successores sui et antecessores nostri olim Comites Rossie, pro salute animarum suarum
antecessorum et successorum suorum, Deo omnipotenti beateque
virgini marie, Abbatique et Conventui Monasterii Nove Fernie per
prefatum Dominum Farchardum et antecessores nostros Comites
Rossie fundati et devote erecti Omnes et singulas terras suas infra
scriptas videlicet Terras Nove Fernie ubi dictum Monasterium
situatur cum ly Miltoun et Muldairg, Duas davatas terrarum que
nominantur Litill Rany et Mckill Rany, Duas davatas nuncupatas
Pitkery et Ballamochie, Tres davatas nuncupatas Wester Gany
Midill Gany et Eister Gany, Unam dimidiam davate nuncupate
Catboll-na-bryc; omnes et singulas terras et possessiones in
Westray, et Stracharron, videlizet, Terras de Downy in Westray,
Eister Ferne, et Wester Ferne, Laidehamoch, Innercharron cum
tota piscaria de la Bonach amante in Stracharron, Achnagart que
nunc nominatur Rulong, cum piscaria et passagio ejusdem; Auch-
nagullane et Brayliag—fudies cum Forrestis Alveyn et Salchy;
Necnon et usum lignorum et arborum per totum nostrum Comitatum Rossie; et presertim usum liguorum et arborum in parochia
de Kilmure Quem prefatus Farchardus quondam Comes Rossie
dicti monasterii primus fundator, eidem monasterio pia liberalitate
concessit, cum universis et singulis dictarum terrarum pertinentiis
jacentium in Comitatu nostro Rossie infra vicecomitatum de
Invernis; In puram et perpetuam elymosynam dedissent con-
cessissent et confirmassent per . . . . dederunt, conceperunt
pariter et confirmarunt prout in cartis et evidentiis dicti Domini
Farchardi Comitis et aliorum successorum suorum Comitum
Rossie, necnon in Bullis confirmationis premissorum Apostolicis
desuper dicto monasterio latius factis concessis et registratis
expressialius continebatur: Quequidem Charte et terrarum
evidentie tempore combustionis insignis Collegiate Capelle almi
confessoris Beati Duthaci de Taine, una cum aliis nonnullis
reliquiis et evidentiis adnichilate extiterunt prout informamur
pariter et combusta, &c. &c. . . .⁎ . Et ea que predicessores
nostri tam pie et devote concesserunt: Nec nos revocare set potius
augmentare et conservare intendimus et optamus Noveritis No's
eapropter Omnes et singulas illas antecessorum nostrorum
quondam Comitum Rossie donationes terrarum et possessionum
concessiones, largiationes dicto monasterio antiquitus factas et
concessas, et per abbatem et conventum ejusdem fuere habitas et
in presentiarum possessas, Ratificasse approbasse ac pro nobis et
heredibus nostris dicto monasterio in perpetuum confirmasse, nec

de novo noveritis nos ad instantiam venerabilis in Christo patris
Finlai permissione divina prefati Monasterii Novi Fernie abbatis
moderni et conventus ejusdem una cum matura deliberatione et
avisamento totius concilii nostri super hoc habitis, in laudem
gloriam et honorem omnipotentis Dei et gloriosissimi Virginis
Marie matris Domini nostri Jesu Christi patrone Monasterii predicti : nec non pro salubri statu nostro, et pro salute animi
quondam magnifici et potentis Domini Alexandri de Ile Comitis
Rossie, &c., patris nostri et Elizabeth sponse sue matris nostre,
pro saluteque anime nostre antecessorum et successorum nostrorum, in divini cultus continuum incrementum ac Monasterio
predicto, Dedisse concessisse et hac presenti carta nostra confirmasse Dei Omnipotenti Beateque virgini Marie Abbati et Conventui
Monasterii antedicti et successoribus suis, omnes et singulas terras
predictas de Nova Ferne cum le multoun et Muldarg, Duas
davatas terre de Pitkary et Ballemonchie, Tres davatas nuncupatas
Wester Gauy Mid Gauy et Eister Gauy, Duas davatas terrarum
que nominantur Litill Rauy et Mekill Rauy, unam dimidiam
davate nuncupate Catboll-na-Crey, omnes et singulas terras
predictas in Westray et Stracharroun, videlicet, Terres de Downy
in Westray, Eister Ferne et Wester Ferne, Laidelamoch Inner-
charroun, cum tota piscaria de le Bonach, amante in Stracharroun,
Achnagart, que nunc nuncupatur Ratony cum piscatura et
passagio ejusdem, Aconagullan et Bralugude cum Forrestis de
Alveyn et Salchy, nec non et usu lignorum et arborum per
universum nostrum Comitatum Rossie ad fabricam et reparationem
Monasterii predicti, et presertim usum lignorum et arborum in
parochia de Kilmure, cum universis justis pertinentiis ad prefatas
terras, &c. &c.   In quarum premissorum fidem et testimonium
Sigillum nostrum presentibus penes dictos Dominum Abbatem et
Conventum et successores suos perpetuis temporibus remansuris
duximus appendum Apud Castrum de Dingwall secundo die mensis
Novembris anno Domini millesimo quadringentesimo sexagesimo
septimo, Coram his testibus, videlizet.

CHARTER BY JOHN OF ISLA, EARL OF ROSS AND LORD OF THE
ISLES, IN FAVOUR OF HIS BROTHER CELESTINE.   25th
April, 1467.

Omnibus hanc cartam visuris vel audituris Johannes de Yle Macc
Comes Rossie et Dominus Insularum Eternam in domino Salutem Coll
Noveritis nos de consensu assensu et matura deliberacione tocius
nostri consilii dedisse concessisse et hac presenti castra nostra

imperpetuum confirmasse carissimo fratri nostro Celestino de
Insulis de Lochalche necnon et vicomiti de Innernys Omnes et
singulas terras nostras de Strathalmadale cum pertinenciis
Jacentes in comitatu Cathanie infra vicecomitatu de Innernys
Tenendas et habendas totas et integras terras prenominatas de
Strathalwadule cum pertinenciis prefato Celestino heredibus suis
et successoribus comitibus Rossie et dominus Insularum in foedo
et in hereditate imperpetuum per omnes rectas metas suas
antiquas et divisas. In boscis, planis, pratis moris marcsiis
pasturis et poscuis petariis turbariis carbonariis fabrilibus et
brasinis viis semitis acquis silvis Rivulis quercis virgultis et
lacubus ancupacionibus cum vrate vaith et vair cum molendinis
multuris et eorum sequelis cum curiis et earum excitibus herezeldis
et mulierum merchettis cum communi pasturi libero introitu et
exitu. Ac cum omnibus aliis et singulis commoditatibus libertatibus fertilitatibus et asiamentis.

Ac iustis suis pertinenciis quibuscunque tam non nominatis
quam nominatis tam subtus terra supra- terram tam prope
quam procul ad predictas terras cum pertinenciis spectantibus
seu justo spectare valentibus quomodlibet in futurum. Adeo
libere quiete integre plenarie honorifice bene et in pace sine
revocatione aliquali Reddendo inde annuatim prefatus Celestinus
heredes sui et successores nobis here dibus nostris et successoribus
comitibus Rossie et dominus Insularum unum denarium argenti
apud festum pentecostes super solum dictarum nomine albe firme
si petatur tantum pro omni alio onere servicio . . . exactione
seu demanda que pro nos heredes nostros et successores exigi
peterunt de dictis terris cum portinenciis quomodolibet vel requiri
Et nos vero prefatus Johannes Comes Rossie et dominus Insularum
heredes nostri et successores Comitis Rossie et domini Insularum
totas et integras prenominatas terras cum pertinenciis prefato
Celestino heredibus suis et successoribus in omnibus et per omnia
ut predictum est contra et adversus quoicunque mortales ,homines
et feminas varandizabimus et imperpetuum defendemus.

In cuius rei testimonium sigillum nostrum presenti carte
nostri appendi fecimus Apud Ayremore vicesimo quinto die mensis
Aprilis anno domini millesimo quadringentesimo sexagesimo
septimo Coram hijs testibus viz Donaldo de Insulis domino de
dunanowaige et de Glynnis Lachlanno McGilleoin domino de
dowarde Alexandro Johannis domino de Ardnamurchan Lachlano
Juveni McGilleoin Magistro de dowarde cum multis et diversis
aliis in fidem et testimonium omnium premissorum vocatis
specialiter et requisitis.

CONFIRMATION BY JOHN OF ISLA, EARL OF ROSS AND LORD OF
THE ISLES, OF THE LANDS OF INNERMERKY TO WILLIAM
OF CAWDOR AND MARIOT OF SUTHERLAND, HIS WIFE.
6th November, 1467.

Omnibus hanc cartam visuris vel audituris Johannes de Yle   Family of
comes Rossie et dominus Insularum eternam in Domino salutem.   Kilravock.
Sciatis nos proprie motu nostro ac consensu assensu et matura
deliberacione consilii nostri propter intimam dilectionem quam
habemus erga predilectum armigerum nostrum Willelmum
iuuenem de Caldor filium et apparentem heredem Willelmi Thani
de Caldor et Mariotam de Sutherland consanguineam nostrum
earum Sponsam priusdicte Willelmi dedisse et concessisse et hac
presenti carta nostra confirmasse prefatis Willelmi iuueni de
Caldor et Mariote de Sutherlande omnes et singulas terras nostras
de Innermerky cum pertinenciis jacentes in dominio de Badyenach
infra vicecomitatum de Innuerness. Tenendas et habendas totas
et integras prenominatas terras de Innermarky cum pertinenciis
suis uniuersis prefatis Willelmo et Mariote sponse sue et eorum
heredibus nostris et successoribus comitibus Rossie in foedo et
hereditate imperpetuum per omnes rectas metas suas antiquas et
diuisis . . . . Reddendo inde annuatim predicti Willelmus
de Caldor Mariota sponsa sua et eorum heredes inter se procreati
et procreandi unum par scrothecarum super solum dictarum
terrarum de Innermarky nomine albe firme si petatur tantum.
. . . Et nos vero prefatus Johannes comes Rossie . . . .
prefatas terras de Innermarky prefatas Willelmo et Mariote   . .
. . contra omnes mortales homines warrantizabimus . . . .
In cuius rei testimonium sigillum nostrum presentibus appendi
fecimus apud castrum nostrum de Dingvale VI die Novembris
A.D. millesimo quadringesimo sexagesimo septimo. Testibus
Celestino de Insulis de Lochailsch, Lachlanno McGilleoin de
Dowarde, Lachlanno iuuene M'Gilleoin senescallo domus nostre,
Johanne de Monro de Fowlis. Thoma de Dingvale subdecano
Rossensi camerario Lachlano McFynwyn de Myschenys et Ewgenio
Donaldi Lachlanni McGilleoin cum diversis aliis in testimonium
vocatis.

CHARTER OF JOHN, EARL OF ROSS. 1468.

Johannes de Ile Comes Rossie et dominus insularum dilectis   Thanes of
nostris consanguineis Domino Thome de Dynvale subdecano ac   Cawdor.
camerario nostro Rossensi necnon et Willelmo Flemyng burgensi

35

de Narne coniunctim et diuisim ballivis nostris in hac parte salutem. Et quia concepimus per mortem nostri compatris et consanguinei Willelmi Thani de Caldor bone memorie quod Willelmus de Caldor lator presentium est verus legitimus et propinquior heres dicti Willelmi quondam patris sui et omnibus et singulis terris cum pertinenciis quas dictus Willelmus pater suus tempore suo infra vicecomitatum de Narn possidebat unacum officio dicti vice-comitatus. Et quod dictus Willelmus est legitimi etatis Et quod dicte terre cum pertinenciis unacum dicto vice-comitatu de nobis tenentur in capite. Vobis igitur precipimus necnon et precipiendo mandamus coniunctim et diuisim quatinus visis presentibus sine quacunque dilacione saisinam et statum hereditarium dicti -vicecomitatus et dictarum terrarum cum pertinenciis infra dictum vicecomitatum jacentium prefato Willelmo saluo iure cuiuslibet et moris est attribuatis. Et in signum saisine taliter per vos vel aliquono vestrum in secundis candis seu canda post nostram presentibus appendatis. In cuius nostri precepti testimonium sigillum nostrum presentibus est appensum apud Killewnau in Kyntyr vicesimo septimo die mensis Marcii anno domini millesimo quadringentesimo sexagesimo octavo.

CONFIRMATION BY JAMES III: OF CHARTER BY JOHN OF ISLA, EARL OF ROSS AND LORD OF THE ISLES, TO THOMAS CUMING.

Reg. Mag. Sig.   Apud Edinburgh 11 Apr. 1474-5.

REX confirmavit cartam Johannis de Ile, comitis Rossie et domini Insularum ac baronie de Kynnedward,—[qua dictus comes confirmavit cartam Thome Cumyne de Pulllane,—TEST. Jac. episc. S. Andree, And. episc. Glasguen., David com. Crawfurdie, Jac. dom. Levinstoun, Gibb. dom. Kennedi, Jac. dom. Hamiltoun, Jac. Wrke, capellano :—Apud Insulam de But, 27 June 1461].

CHARTER BY JOHN OF ISLA, EARL OF ROSS AND LORD OF THE ISLES, TO JOHN DAVIDSON.

Macdonald Collections. Omnibus hanc cartam visuris vel audituris Johannes Comes Rossie et Dominus Insularum Salutem in Domino Sempiternam Noveritis nos pro nobis et heredibus nostris Dedisse consessisse et hac presenti carta nostra confirmasse dilecto nostro nativo armigero et alumpno Johanni Davidis filio et apparenti heredi Gibbonis Davidis presencium conservatori Omnes et singulas *terras nostras* de Grenane cum pertinenciis jacentes in comitatu de Carrik infra vicecomitatum de Ayir : Tenendas et habendas omnes et singulas terras de Grenane cum pertinenciis antedicto Johanni Gibbonis Davidis heredibus suis et assignatis infeodo et hereditate imperpetuum per omnes rectas metas suas antiquas et divisas In moris maresiis boscis planis pratis pacsuis et pasturis molendinis multuris et eoram sequelis aucupacionibus venaciopiscariis petariis turbariis carbonariis cum fabrilibus et brasinis cum calce et lapide cum curiis et curiarum exitibus ac earundem eschetis cum avaragiis et cariagiis bondagiis et custumnis cum bludwettis et herezeldis ac mulierum merchetis cum columbis et columbariis cum silvis virgultis aquis semitis stagnis rivolis ac cum omnibus aliis et singulis libertatibus commoditatibus et libertatibus et asiamentis ac justis suis pertinenciis quibuscunque tam non nominatis quam nominatis tam subtus terra quam supra terram tam prope quam procul ad dictas terras de Grenane cum pertinenciis spectantibus seu de jure aut consuetudine spectare valentibus quomodolibet in *futurum adeo libere quiete plenario integro honorifice bene et in* pace siue aliquo retinemento aut contradictione aliquali in futurum : Reddendo inde annuatim dictus Johannes Gibbonis Davidis heredes sui et assignati nobis heredibus nostris successoribus et assignatis de dictis terris de Grenane cum pertinenciis viginti libras monete regni Scotie ad usuales terminos videlicet decem libras monete Scotie ad festum peutecostes et decem libras monete Scotie ad festum Sancti Martini in yeme omni alio onere exercitio servicio exaccione seu consuetudine Sive demanda que de dictis terris de Grenane cum pertinenciis exigi *poterint aut requiri postpositis et* remotis. Et vos vero Johannes Comes Rossie et Dominus Insularum heredes nostri successores et assignati omnes et singulas terras prenominatas de Grenane cum pertinenciis antedicto Johanni Gibbonis Davidis suisque heredibus successoribus et assignatis in omnibus et per omnia sicut prius dictum est contra omnes mortales varantizabimus acquietabimus et imperpetuum defendemus. In cujus rei testimonium Sigillum nostrum presentibus affigi fecimus apud Killewnan in Kintyr secundo die mensis Aprilis anno *Domini* millesimo quadringentesimo septuagesimo quinto.

DEED BY DONALD BALLOCH, ACTING FOR JOHN, EARL OF ROSS AND LORD OF THE ISLES.

Macdonald
Collections. Omnibus hoc scriptum visuris vel audituris Donaldus de
Insulis Dominus de Glenys et de Dunnawak miles ac primus et
principalis conciliarius Magnifici et potentis Domini Johannis
Comitis Rossie ac Domini Insularum Salutem in Domino
Sempiternam, Sciatis nos illam donacionem seu concessionem
quas antedictus Dominus Comes fecit de terris de Grenane cum
pertinenciis jacentibus in Comitatu de Carric et infra vicecomitatum de Are Johanni Davisonn et heredibus suis prout in
cartis et evidenciis suis desuper confectis plenius continetur fuisse
ex concilio et consensu nostro Et predictam donacionem seu concessionem obligamus nos heredes et successores nostros ad
manutenendum fortificandum et defendendum prefato Johanni
et heredibus suis imperpetuum In cujus rei testimonium
Sigillum nostrum presentibus est appensum apud villam de
Erwyng octavo die mensis Octobris anno Domini millesimo
quadringentesimo septuagesimo quinto.

ARMORIAL BEARINGS OF THE LORDS OF THE ISLES.

The oldest Scottish authority on heraldry is Sir David Lindsay
of the Mount, Lyon King of Arms, whose collection of armorial
bearings is dated 1542. All authorities on Scottish heraldry are
agreed as to the value of this collection, and they look upon it'as
the only authentic source of information in regard to the armorial
bearings of Scottish families at that time. The impression on the
cover of our volume is taken from Sir David Lindsay's collection,
and represents a galley, or longfhada, with an eagle displayed,
and the fiery cross above the mast of the galley. Prior to the
time of Sir David Lindsay,'we have various seals preserved from
which alone correct data can be obtained as to the armorial
bearings, at different periods, of the Lords of the Isles. The
earliest description given of any seal of the Lords of the Isles is
that of the seal of Reginald, the son of Somerled. It was
probably attached to the Charter by Reginald to Paisley Abbey,
the date of which we have given as about 1180. In 1426,
Andrew Stuart, Prior of Paisley, caused a notarial transcript
of the charter of Reginald to Paisley Abbey to be made, on which
occasion the impression of the seal of the Lord of the Isles is

described in these terms:—"In the middle of the seal, on one side, a ship filled with men-at-arms, and on the reverse the figure of an armed man on horseback with a sword drawn in his hand." The next seal in order after that of Reginald is that of Angus Mor Macdonald of Islay, Lord of the Isles, formerly attached to a document in the Public Record Office, London, and dated 1292, now in the British Museum. On this seal there is no shield, but a design representing a galley on the sea with one mast, and cordage, and sail furled on square-yard, and four men sitting in her. The seal of Alexander, Lord of the Isles, still attached to the same document to which formerly the seal of his father, Angus Mor, was also attached, differs in some respects from that of the latter. In this seal it is interesting to find so early an indication of the Red Hand in the arms of the Family of Macdonald. It has the galley with two open hands, one on either side of the mast. The seal of Angus Og Macdonald, Lord of the Isles, adhibited to his letter to Edward I.—also preserved in the Public Record Office, and bearing the date of the year 1301—is described as being the same in all respects as that of his father, Angus Mor. The arms on Angus Og's tombstone, in Iona, are a ship with hoisted sails, a standard, four lions, and a tree. The other seals of the Chiefs of Macdonald which have been preserved are those of Alexander and his son John, Earls of Ross. The seal of Alexander is thus described by Laing:—"Couché. Quarterly; first, a galley, surmounted with an eagle displayed, for the Lordship of the Isles; second, three lions rampant, for Ross; three garbs, for Buchan; fourth on a bend cotised with six crosses, three buckles for Leslie; all within a double tressure flowered and counter-flowered. Crest, on a helmet, an eagle's head and wings. Supporters, two lions rampant, guardant, coné; the back ornamented with foliage." The arms of John—as represented on a seal adhibited to a document of the year 1476, shortly after his forfeiture as Earl of Ross—are thus described by Laing:—"A galley surmounted with an eagle displayed, all within a double tressure flowered and counter-flowered. On the dexter side of the shield is a mullet, and an eagle behind supports the shield in his beak." Impressions of the seals of Reginald, Angus Mor, and Alexander, Lords of the Isles, and of Alexander and John, Earls of Ross, are given in this volume. The other impressions of armorial bearings of the Lords of the Isles given are from the Sunderland Hall and Workman's MSS., neither of which is believed to be an authentic or reliable authority. We give these, not because we believe either to be an accurate representation of the arms of the Lords of Isles at any period, but because, on account of their uniqueness, and the sources from which they are derived, they might prove interesting to clansmen. Workman's is an illuminated MS. compiled by an unknown hand about the year 1565. It came into the possession of James Workman, a herald painter, in the year 1623. The Sunderland Hall MS. is of the time of James VI., previous to his succession to the English throne, and is now in the possession of Charles Scott Plummer, Esq., of Sunderland Hall. The armorial bearings of the Lords of the Isles given at p. 272, with the bears for supporters, are taken from Workman's MS.; while those at p. 208, with the headless supporters, are taken from the Sunderland Hall MS. The arms of the different branches of the Family of Macdonald will be given in another volume.

COMMISSION TO THE EARL OF LENNOX TO CARRY THROUGH THE FORFEITURE OF JOHN, EARL OF ROSS.

nald
ions.

In Dei nomine amen Per hoc presens publicum instrumentum cunctis pateat evidenter et sit notum quod anno Incarnacionis Dominice millesimo quadringentesimo secundum computacionem ecclesie Scoticane septuagesimo quinto die vero mensis Januarii nona Indictione nona Pontificatus que Sanctissimi in Christo patris et domini nostri Sixti divina providentia pape quarti anno quinto In mei notarii publici et testium subscriptorum presentia personaliter constitutus magnificus et potens Dominus Johannes Comes de Levinax Dominus Derulie ac Locum tenens Supremi Domini nostri Regis infra limites et bondas vicecomitatuum de Renfrew Aire Vigtone ac Senescallatus de Kirkcubricht et de le Nethirvarde de Cliddisdale ac vicecomitatus de Insularum de Bute et Arane pro executione processus forisfacture in parliamento ejusdem Supremi Domini Regis Juridice deducti super Johanne de Ile olim Comite de Rose et Domino Insularum proditore et rebelle pro suis proditoriis criminibus contra eundem Supremum Dominum nostrum et ejus regnum nequiter et proditorie comissis et perpetratis per literas dicti Domini Supremi nostri Regis sub suo sigillo Magno sigillatas specialiter factus et ordinatus vigore et auctoritate earundem litterarum recepit fidem et fidelitatem Juramentum ac homagium et ligianciam de futura fidelitate

observanda Supremo Domino nostro Regi a Johanne Davidsone
armigero tenente omnium terrarum de Grenane cum pertinenciis
jacentium infra vicecomitatum de Aire Johanni de Ile olim
Comiti de Rose et Domino Insularum : Ac etiam dictus Locum
tenens dictum Johannem Davidsone ut fidelum legium prefati
Supremi Domini nostri ad pacem ejusdem et sub ejus defensione
recepit secundum formam literarum Supremi Domini nostri
antedicti, quarum tenor de verbo in verbum sequitur et est talis :
Jacobus Dei gratia Rex Scotorum omnibus probis hominibus suis
ad quos presentes litere pervenerint Salutem Sciatis nos Fecisse
constituisse et ordinasse et tenore presentium Facimus Constituimus et ordinamus dilectum consanguineum nostrum Johannem
Comitem Levinax Dominum Derulie nostrum Locum tenentem
infra limites et bondas vicecomitatum nostrorum de Renfrew Aire
Vigtone ac Senescallatus de Kirkcubricht et de le Nethirvarde de
Cliddisdale ac vicecomitatus et Insularum de But et Arane pro
executione nostri processus forisfacture in nostro parliamento
Juridice deducti super Johanne de Ile olim Comite Rossie et
Domino Insularum nostro proditore et rebelle pro suis proditoriis
criminibus contra nos et regnum nostrum nequiter et preditorie
commissis et perpetratis et pro eisdem criminibus in dicto nostro
parliamento convicto et judicato : Dando et concedendo dicto
Johanni Comiti de Levinax Locumtenenti nostro plenariam
nostram potestatem et mandatum speciale dictum nostrum
processum forisfacture universis et singulis ligiis et subditis
nostris infra dictas limites et bondas ubi opus fuerit et sibi
videbitur expediens, Declarandom pronunciandum et proclamandum
Necnon terras redditus possessiones officia superioritates et
et proprietates quascunque dicto Johanni olim Comiti Rossie et
Domino Insularum pertinentes et que sibi ante dictam forisfacturam pertinuerunt in manibus nostris et in nostram regalem
proprietatem recipiendas et resasiendas ac etiam omnes et singulas
nostras ligios nunc cum dicto Johanne proditore existentes ac
temporibus retroactis sibi complices vel de eodem terras aut
redditus quoscunque in tenendriis possidentes premuniendo
mandando et stricte precipiendo ut nobis vel ipsi locumtenenti
indilati veniant nobis fidem et juramentum fidelitatis ac homagium
et ligianciam de futura fidelitate observanda faciendo dictosque
nostros ligios sibi Locumtenenti nostro venientes et fidelitatem
facientes infra terminos ac nostris instructionibus sibi deliberatis
contentos ad pacem nostram recipiendos Et ut nostros fideles
ligios defendendos necnon omnes et singulas inobedientes et

eidem Locumtenenti nostro ut premittitur non venientes Sive.
non parentes infra dictos terminos tanquam nostros proditores et
rebelles proclamandos et demandandos ac terras suas et possessiones
et bona eorum confiscandas et usui nostro eschaetandas et
applicandas eorumque districtus et fortalicia ut ipsi locumtenenti
videbitur expediens obsidendas necnon pro executione dicti
processus forisfacture omnes et singulos dictos nostros ligios et
infra limites et bondas predictas ad arma et exercitus infra
Sexdecim et sexaginta annorum etates convocandos et suscitandos
ordinaciones et Statuta condendos easdem exercendos et exequendos,
transgressores et delinquentes contra Statuta et ordinaciones
hujusmodi corrigendos castigandos et secundum qualitatem delicti
puniendos Constabularios marescallos et alios officiarios requisitos
et necessarios substituendos et deputandos, dictumque Johannem
olim Comitem proditorem et complices suos sibi adherentes
prosequendos et ad mortem invadendos, eundemque capiendo et
juxta tenorem Judicii super eo in dicto nostro parliamento dati
justificando ac terras et bona eorum devastandas et comburendas
Et generalaliter omnia alia et singula ad officium locumtenentis
pro premissis exequenda necessaria et opportuna facienda gerenda
expedienda et perimplenda ratum et gratum habentes et habituri
totum et quisquidem dictus noster Locumtenens aut Constabularii
Marescalli Officarii ministri aut servitores sui et
in premissis duxeruit vel duxerit faciendum Quare universis et
singulis ligiis et subditis nostris infra dictas limites et bondas
vicecomitatuum de Renfrew Air Uigtone Senescallatus de Kirkcubricht et de Nethirvarde de Cliddisdale ac vicecomitatus
Insularum de Bute et de Arane ceterisque quorum interest vel
interesse poterit stricte Precipimus et mandamus quatenus dicto
Locumtenenti nostro ac Constabulario Marescallis et officiariis suis
in omnibus et singulis premissa tangentibus prompte respondeant
pareant et intendant et cum eodem in burgis et extra burgos a
Sexdecem ad sexaginta annorum etates consurgant sub omni pena
quam erga nostram regiam incurrere poterint majestatem,
Presentibus pro nostra voluntate duranturis Datum Sub Magno
Sigillo nostro apud Edinburgh quarto die mensis Decembris anno
Domini m⁰ cccc⁰ lxxv⁰ et regni nostri decimo sexto." Et sic fuit
hujus modi literi tenor. Super quibus omnibus et singulis prefatus
Johannes Davidsone petiit a me notario infra scripto publicum et
publica instrumentum et instrumenta Acta fuerunt hoc in civitate
Glasguensi infra locum Mansionis Rectoris Glasguensis hora prima
postmeridiem vel escirca sub anno die mense Judictione et

Pontificatu quibus supra presentibus ibidem Reverendo in Christo
patre Augusio Dei et apostolice Sedis gratia Episcopo Sodorensi
Magistris Thoma Forsithe Willielmo Sympil vedaste de Murhede
Villielmo de Elphinstone Canonicis ecclesie Cathedralis Glasguensis,
Dominis Malcolmo Dirande rectore de Lochmaben Magistris
Patricio de Elphinstone Martino Rede David Blar de Adamtone
Roberto Sympil de Foulwode et Johanne Forsythe laicis cum
multis aliis ad premissa testibus vocatis pariter et rogatis.

Et Ego Johannes Aurifabri artium Magister Presbyter Glasguensis diocesis publicus Imperiali et regali auctoritatibus notarius,
Premissis, &c.

ARTICLES OF AGREEMENT BETWEEN JAMES III. AND JOHN,
LORD OF THE ISLES.

. . . . annem dominum Insularum obligari et per R e g i s t e r
presentes bona fide firmiter Obligo me et heredes meos linealiter House, Edin-
et recte vel ratione tallic discendentes . . . . mo principi burgh.
supremo que domino nostro domino Jacobo Tercio Scotorum
Regi illustrissimo suisque heredibus et successoribus Quia idem
Supremus Dominus noster post forisfacturam per eundem in suo
parliamento super me omnibusque meis terris possessionibus
redditibus officiis superioritatibus et bonis causantibus meis
demeritis juridice productum vero et ex gracia sua speciali michi
concessit hereditarie, omnes et singulas terras et . . . . .
michi ante dictam forisfacturam pertinentes, exceptis omnibus et
singulis terris tocius comitatus Rossie cum officio Vicecomitatus de
Iuvernes et Narne ac . . . . . Knapdale et dominii de
Kyntyre, cum castris et fortaliciis earundem, et aliis justis pertinenciis, proprietate et tenandria, Quod nec Ego nec her . . .
is nostro nomine impedimentum aut obstaculum faciam aut facient
dicto supremo Domino nostro Regi, aut Camerariis officiariis et
Ministris et tenentibus . . . . . . acone et assedatione
dictarum terrarum Comitatus de Ross, Dominorum de Knapdale
et Kyntire cum castris et officiis predictis, aut in levaco . . .
et proficuorum earundem cum pertinenciis sive aliquam per-
turbationem molestiam injuriam aut violenciam temporibus
futuris tenentibus et habitantibus dicta . . . . . . endam
vel impendent Et quod nunquam temporibus futuris nec Ego nec
heredes mei predicti, nec aliquis alius nomine vel ex parte aliquod
jus vel clameum directe vel indirecte publice vel occulte in vel ad

dictas terras cum pertinenciis aut dicta officia seu aliquam partem
earundem in proprietate vel tenandria prosequemur vel inde jus
aut clameum exigere aut vendicare valeam nec valeant Quas eciam
terras Comitatus · Rossie et Officia de Invernes et Narne predicta
ac antedictas terras dominiorum de Knapdale et Kintyre cum
castris predictis, cum tenentibus tenendriis et libore tenencium
serviciis ac omnibus suis pernentiis annexis et dependenciis a me
et heredibus meis eidem Suppremo Domino nostro Regi et successoribus Suis cum eisdem imperpetuum spectantes et remanendas
quitclamo et renuncio pro perpetuo per presentes Ita quod Ego et
heredes mei ab omni juris titulo tam petitorio quam possessorio
earundem Sim et sint exclusus et exclusi imperpetuum penitus et
omnius. In cujus rei testimonium presentibus Sigillum meum
appensum apud Edinburgh decimo quinto die mensis Julii anno
Domini millesimo quadringentesimo septuagesimo sexto.

CHARTER BY JAMES III. TO JOHN OF ISLA, LORD OF THE ISLES—15TH JULY 1476.

Sig.   Jacobus, Dei gracia, Rex Scotorum, omnibus probis hominibus
tocius terre sue, clericis et laicis, salutem.   Sciatis licet alias
in Parliamento nostro apud Edinburgh tento vicessimo septimo
die mensis Novembris anno Domini millesimo quadringentisimo
Septuagesimo quinto certos processus et judicia forisfacture contra
et adversus consanguineum nostrum Johannem de Ile, olim
comitem Rossie et dominum Insularum, pro suis proditoriis,
criminibus, demeritis, et transgressionibus contra nostrum regiam
majestatem et regnum nostrum perpetratis et commissio dedimus,
decrevimus, et promulgavimus ; nichilominus, ob requestam et
instanciam, carissime consortis nostre Margarete, Regine Scocie,
ac reverendorum et venerabilium patrum consanguineorumque
nostrorum episcoporum, prelatorum, comitum, et baronum ac
burgorum commissariorum regni nostri statuum in nostro parliamento tento apud Edinburgh decimo quinto die mensis instantis
Julii anno Domini millesimo quadringentesimo septuagesimo
sexto et ibidem die Lune primo die dicti mensis Julii inchoato
congregatorum nobis factas, ipsum consanguineum nostrum suis
mundanis· honoribus et dignitatibus ac bono fame sue persone ex
nostra gracia speciali restituimus, et per presentes restituimus,
omnem infamie notam quam propter premissa incidebat ab ipso
penitus auferendo : Preterea nos, attendentes et considerantes

propinquitatem sanguinis in qua ipse Johannes nobis attingit et nolentes eundem et heredes suos pro dictis criminibus et demeritis ab omnibus terris et possessionibus per ipsum et predecessores suos prius habitis et possessis omnino exhereditare, ipsum Johannem, cum consensu statuum dicti nostri parliamenti et ob requestam dicte carissime consortis nostre, dominum nostre parlia-menti et baronem de novo fecimus, ac presencium per tenorem facimus et creamus, dominum Insularum perpetuis futuris temporibus nuncupandum, ac eciam dedimus et concessimus, tenoreque presentis carte nostre nove infeodacionis damus et concedimus, eidem Johanni, nunc domino Insularum, pro suis fidelibus serviciis per ipsum suosque heredes et successores temporibus futuris nobis et successoribus impendendis omnes et singulas terras et subscriptas,—videlicet, terras insule de Ila cum pertinentiis; necnon terras omnium et singularum aliarum insularum que sibi Johanni ante dictam forisfacturam hereditarie pertinuerunt; ac eciam omnes et singulas terras de Morvarne Germorvarne . . . dominium de Lochabir . . . terras de Durwoin Glencoill . . . de Kinedward . . . ac terras de Grenane . . . que terre eidem Johanni ante dictam forisfac-turam in proprietate hereditarie pertinebant. Et super dedimus et concessimus, et presencium tenore damus et concedimus, hereditarie dicto Johanni, domino Insularum, omnes et singulas alias terras insulas et possessiones infra regnum nostrum ubicunque jacentes et existentes sibi ante dictam forisfacturam in proprietate pertinentes; necnon omnes libere tenentes et eorundem tenencium servicia que de predicto Johanne ante eandem forisfacturam in capitate tenuerunt,—exceptis tamen et reservatis nobis heredibus et successoribus nostris omnibus et singulis terris comitatus Rossie et terris dominiorum de Knapdale et Kintyre, cum tenentibus, tenandriis, et liberetenencium serviciis in proprietabis et tenandriis et aliis justis pertinenciis, unacum castris et fortaliciis dictarum terrarum ac officiis vicecomitatuum de Innerness et Narne et omnibus aliis officiis infra dictum comitatum et dominia predicta, quas et que nobis et successoribus nostris hereditarie reservamus ad memoriam delicti et transgressionis dicti Johannis: Tenendas et habendas omnes et singulas predictas terras insule de Ila et terras omnium aliarum insularum, terras de Morvarne Germor-varne, dominium de Lochabir, terras de Durwoyn Glencoill, terras do Kinedward, terras de Grenane, et omnes alias terras, insulas, et possessiones liberetenentes, et eorum servicia que sibi Johanni ante dictam forisfacturam pertinuerunt, exceptis omnibus et singulis terris comitatus Rossie terris dominiorum de Knapdale et

Kintyre cum tenentibus, tenandriis, et liberetenentium serviciis in proprietatibus et tenandriis et aliis suis justis pertinenciis, unacum castris et fortaliciis et officiis vicecomitatum de Innernes et Narne et ceteris officiis predictis nobis heredetarie prius reservatis predicto consanguineo nostro Johanni, domino Insularum, et heredibus masculis de corpore suo legittime procreandis; quibus forte deficientibus, Angusio de Ile, filio naturali dicti Johannis, et heredibus masculis de corpore ipsius Angusii legittime procreandis; quibus forte deficientibus, Johanni de Ile, filio eciam naturali dicti Johannis, domini Insularum, et heredibus masculis de corpore suo legittime procreandis; quibus deficientibus, veris legittimis et propinquioribus heredibus dicti Johannis, domini Insularum, quibuscunque de nobis heredibus et successoribus nostris in feode et hereditate imperpetuum per omnes rectas metas suas antiquas et divisas prout jacent in longitudine et latitudine, cum omnibus et singulis libertatibus commoditatibus, et asieamentis ac justis pertinenciis quibuscunque, tam non nominatis quam nominatis, ad dictas terras et insulas, cum pertinenciis spectantibus seu quovismodo juste spectare valentibus infuturum, et adeo libere, quiete, plenarie, integre, honorifice, bene, et in pace in omnibus et per omnia sicut idem Johannes, dominus Insularum, aut predecessores sui, dictas terras et insulas cum pertinenciis de nobis aut predecessoribus nostris ante forisfacturam ejusdem Johannis liberius tenuit seu possedit, tenuerunt seu possiderunt: Faciendo inde annuatim idem Johannes, dominus Insularum, et heredes sui masculi . . . nobis heredibus et successoribus nostris jura et servicia de dictis terris et insulis debita et consueta dicto eciam Johanne, domino Insularum, temporibus futuris pro perpetuo obediendo, subeundo, perimplendo, et observando per se suosque heredes et successores ac tenentes et inhabitantes dictas insulas et terras jura, leges et consuetudines regni nostri in omnibus et per omnia, sicut alii barones liberetenentes, et legei regni nostri jura et leges nostras subeunt, perimplent, et observant. In cujus rei testimonium . . . Apud Edinburgh, decimo quinto die mensis Julii anno domini millesimo quadringentesimo septuagesimo sexto, et regni nostri decimo sexto.

CHARTER BY JAMES III. TO JOHN OF ISLA, LORD OF THE ISLES.

nald
ions.
Jacobus Dei gracia Rex Scotorum dilecto consanguineo nostro Gilberto Domino Kennedy Ballivo nostro de Carric in hac parte specialiter constituto Salutem Quia Dedimus et concessimus

hereditarie dilecto consanguineo nostro Johanni Domino Insularum
terras de Grenane cum pertinenciis jacentes in comitatu de Carric
infra vicecomitatum nostrum de Are prout in carta nostra dicto
Johanni inde confecta plenius continetur Vobis precipimus et
mandamus quatenus dicto Johanni vel suo certo actornato latori
presencium sasinam dictarum terrarum cum pertinenciis secundum
tenorem dicte carte quam inde habet juste habere faciatis et sine
dilacione Et hoc nullo modo omittatis ad quod faciendum vobis in
hac parte nostram plenariam tenore presencium committimus
potestatem Datum sub testimonio magni sigilli nostri apud Edinburgh decimo octavo die mensis Julii anno regni nostri decimo
sexto.

CONFIRMATION BY JAMES III. OF CHARTER BY ALEXANDER
OF ISLA, EARL OF ROSS, AND LORD OF THE ISLES, TO
WALTER OGILVY.

Apud Edinburgh 4. Aug. 1476. Reg. Mag. Sig.

REX confirmavit cartam quondam Alexandri de Ile, comitis
Rossie, domini Insularum ac Justiciarii ex parte boreali aque de
Forth,—[qua concessit WALTERO OGILVY de Bewford et
omnibus heredibus ejus,—terrras de Thanistone, vic. Kincardin :
REDDEND. tantum quantum quondam Walt. de Lindesay tradere
solebat :—TEST. Alex. M'Cowlach de Pladdis, Geo. Munro de
Foulis, Wilando de Cheisholme, Nigello M'Leoid, et Nigello
Flemyng Secretario dicti com. :—Apud castrum de Dyngwele, 24
Oct. 1443].

CONFIRMATION BY JAMES III. OF CHARTER BY JOHN OF ISLA,
EARL OF ROSS, AND LORD OF THE ISLES, TO JOHN
DAVIDSON.

Jacobus Dei gracia Rex Scotorum Omnibus probis hominibus Macdonald
Collections.
tocius terre sue clericis et laicis Salutem Sciatis nos quandam
cartam feodifirme dilecti consanguinei nostri Johannis de Ila
Domini Iusularum factam et concessam dilecto nostro Johanni
Davidson filio quondam Gilberti Davidson de omnibus et singulis
terris de Grenane cum pertinentiis jacentibus in comitatu de
Carric infra vicecomitatum nostrum de Are, de mandato nostro
visam lectam inspectam et diligenter examinatam sanam integram
non rasam non cancellatam nec in aliqua sui parte suspectam ad

plenum intellexisse sub hac forma Omnibus hoc scriptum virsuris vel audituris Johanne de Ila et Domino Insularum Salutem in Domino Sempiternam Noveritis nos pro nobis et heredibus nostris assedasse allocasse et ad feodifirmam dimississe dilecto nostro nativo armigero et alumpno Johanni Davidson filio quondam Gilberti Davidson omnes et singulas terras nostras de Grenane cum pertinenciis jacentibus in comitatu de Carric infra vice-comitatum de Are Tenendas et habendas omnes et singulas terras de Grenane cum pertinenciis predicto Johanni et heredibus suis et assignatis de nobis heredibus et successoribus nostris in feodi-firma imperpetuum per omnes rectas metas suas antiquas et divisas In moris maresiis boscis planis pratis pascuis et pasturis molendinis multuris et eorum sequelis aucupationibus venationibus piscariis petariis turbariis carbonariis cum fabrilibus et brasiuis cum calce et lapide cum curiis et curiarum exitibus et earundem eschaetis cum aueragiis et cariagiis, cum bludewitis et herezeldis ac mulierum merchetis cum eschaetis cum columbis et columbariis, cum silvis virgultis aquis semitis stagnis rivolis ac cum omnibus aliis et singulis libertatibus commoditatibus asiamentis ac justis pertinenciis quibuscunque tam non nominatis quam nominatis tam subtus terra quam supra terram tam propequam procul ad dictas terras de Grenane cum pertinenciis spectantibus seu juste spectare valentibus quomodolibet in futurum adeo libere quiete plenarie integre honorifice bene et in pace sicut aliqua terra infra regnum Scotie secundum leges et consuetudines regni alicui ad feodifirmam allocatur seu ad feodifirmam dimittitur Reddendo inde annuatim dictus Johannes Davidson heredes sui et assignati nobis heredibus et successoribus nostris pro firmis dictarum terrarum de Grenane cum pertinenciis viginti libras usualis monete regni Scotie ad duos anni terminos consuetos videlicet penthecostes et Sancti Martini in hieme per equales portiones pro omni alio onere servicio exactione questione seu demanda que de dictis terris de Grenane cum pertinenciis per nos heredes nostros vel successores requiri aut exigi poterint seclusis postpositis et remotis Et nos vero Johannes de Ila et Dominus Insularum heredes nostri et succes-sores omnes et singulas prenominatas terras de Grenane cum pertinenciis predicto Johanni et heredibus suis et assignatis in omnibus et per omnia sicut premissum est contra omnes homines mortales warantizabimus acquietabimus et imperpetuum de-fendemus In cujus rei testimonium sigillum nostrum presentibus appendi fecimus apud Ila vicesimo die mensis Augusti anno Domini millesimo quadringentesimo septuagesimo sexto presenti.

bus Donaldo Ballache de Dunnowan Rollando Makclane de Dowart, Hectore Makclane de Canlochboye, Nigello McYlwride Archidiacono Sodorensi et Domino Jacobo Weyk clerico nostro et scriba cum diversis aliis."—Quamquidem cartam sive evidenciam feodifirme ac omnia et singula in easdem contenta in omnibus suis punctis et articulis condicionibus et modis ac circumstanciis suis quibuscunque forma pariter et effectu in omnibus et per omnia approbamus Ratificamus ac nomine tutorio carissimi filii nostri primogeniti Jacobi Ducis de Roithzay comitis de Carric et Domini Cunynghame pro nobis et successoribus nostris ut premissum ut pro perpetuo Confirmamus Salvo nobis ac dicto carissimo filio nostro primogenito heredibus et successoribus nostris wardis releviis maritagiis juribus et serviciis de dictis terris ante presentum confirmacionem nobis debitis et consuetis Et proviso quod per hanc nostram Confirmacionem nullum prejudicium generetur dilecte nostre consanguinee Elizabeth de Livingstoune sponse dicti Domini Insularum penes infeodacionem et donacionem dictarum terrarum sibi Elizabeth pro toto tempore vite sue factus In cujus rei testimonium presenti carta nostre confirmacionis magnum sigillum nostrum apponi precepimus Testibus reverentis in Cristo patribus Johanne Episcopo Glasguense Willielmo Episcopo Orchadense nostri Secreti Sigilli Custode dilectis consanguineis Andrea Domino Avandale Cancellario nostro Colino Comite de Ergile Domino Campbel et Lorne Magistro Hospicii nostri David Comite de Crawfurde Domino Lyndesay Jacobo Domino Hamyltone Johanne de Culquhone de eodem milite et Magistro Alexandro Inglis Cancellario Aberdonense clerico nostrorum Rotulorum et Registri apud Edinburgh ultimo die mensis Januarii anno domini millesimo quadringentesimo septuagesimo sexto, et regni nostri decimo septimo.

CHARTER BY JAMES III. TO JOHN OF ISLA, LORD OF THE ISLES.

Apud Edinburgh, 11 Aug. 1478.

REX concessit JOHANNI DE ILA, DOMINO INSULARUM— *Reg. M:* pro ejus fideli servitio, &c.—pro toto tempore ejus vite—terras subscriptas, viz.;—terras de Killowmane extendentes annuatim ad 12 merc.; terras de Owigill, Auchnaslesok, Achencork, et Kenochane, extend. annuatim ad 6 merc.; terras de duobus Knok-

renochis, Glemorele, Altnabay, Baduff, et Areskeauch, extend. ad
9 merc.; terras de duobus Tereferguse et Largbane, extend. ad
5 merc.; terras de Keynethane et Hening, extend ad 3 merc.;
terras de duobus Knokantis, et Calybole, extend. ad 6 merc.; de
le Lossit et Glenhawindee, extend. ad 5 merc.; de Ballegrogane et
Cregok, extenden. ad 4 merc.; de Catadill, Gertmeane, et Gartloskin, Bredelaide, et Keppragane, extenden. ad 8 merc.; de
Ballenabraide, extenden. ad 2 merc.; de Kilsolane, extend. ad 4
merc.; de Achuaclaich, extend. ad 2 merc.; de Lagnacreig, extend.
ad unam mercam; de Kerowsoyre, extend. ad unam merc.; de
Gartloskin, extend. ad unam merc.; de Glenranskill, extend. ad 3
merc.; de Glenvey, extend. ad 2 merc.; de Brownergyn, Drum-
trycnoch, Dalsmerill, Lagnadaise, et Enyngcokaloch, extend. ad 4
merc. cum dimedia; de Kildallok et Lonochane, extend. ad unam
mercam cum dimedia; de Ellerich, et Arenarroch, extend. ad 2
merc.; de Cralekill, Macherbanys, Darbrekane, et Clagkeile
extend ad 13 merc.;—acclamatas per Maknele, jacentes in dominio
de Kyntyre, vic Tarbart:—ac etiam concessit dicto Johanni, pro
toto tempore ejus vite,—terras subscriptas, viz.;—terras de Arymore, extend. ad 12 merc.; de Owragag, Achtydownegall, Scottomyl, Drummalaycht, Downskeig, le Lowb, Lemnamwk, Cartwaich,
et Tescard, extend. ad 21 merc.; de Barmore, Garalane, Achnafey,
Strondowr, Glenmolane, Glenraole, Largbanan, Barnellane, Howil-
drinoch, Glannafeoch, Ardpatrick, Ardmenys, Largnahowschine,
Forleyngloch, Crevyr, et Drummamwkloch, extend ad 31 merc.;
de Kilmolowok, extend. ad 4 merc.; de Drumdesok, extend. ad 4
merc.; de Clachbrek, extend. ad 2 merc.; de Barlonkyrt, extend.
ad 4 merc.; de Altbeith, extend. ad unam merc.; de Cragkeith,
extend. ad unam merc.; de Achetymelane, Dowynymultoch,
Renochane, Kilcamok, Gartnagrauch, et Ormsay, extend. ad 20
merc.; acclamatas per Maklane et Maknele, in dominio de Knapdale, vic. Tarbart.

CHARTER BY JAMES III. TO JOHN OF ISLA, LORD OF THE ISLES.

Sig. REX—quia in tenera etate sua post forisfacturam in Parliamento
super Johanne dom. Insularum productam, concessit eidem Joh.
terras et dominia subscripta, viz.;—terras de Ila, terras aliarum
insularum que dicto Joh. ante dictam forisfacturam pertinebant,
terras de Morwarne, Garmorwarne, dominium de Lochabir, terras
de Duroune, Glencoile, vic. Inverness; terras de Kynedward, vic.

Abirdene ; terras ; terras de Grenane, in comitatu de Carrik, vic.
Arc ; ac omnes terras, insulas, &c. infra regnum ubicunque,
unacum libertatibus, &c., quas idem Joh. de rege per donationem
habebat ;—tunc de novo post ultimam revocationem, concessit
dicto JOHANNI DOMINO INSULARUM et heredibus ejus
heredetarie dictas terras, &c. :—Exceptis et reservatis regi, &c.,
terris comitatus de Ross, terris dominiorum de Knapdale et Kintyr
cum tenentibus, &c., unacum castris, fortaliciis earundem, ac
etiam officiis vicecomitatus de Invernes et Narne, et certis aliis
officiis regi hereditarie prius reservatis :—TENEND. dicto Joh. et
heredibus ejus masculis de corpore ejus legitime procreatis, quibus
deficientibus, Angusio de Ila filio naturali dicti Joh., et heredibus,
&c. (ut supra), quibus def., legitimis et propinquioribus heredibus
dicti Joh. quibuscunque :—REDDEND. jura et servitia ante dictam
forisfacturam debita et consueta ;—ac etiam idem Joh. et heredes
sui, pro se, suisque tenentibus, successoribus, &c., obediendo et
observando jura, leges, et consuetudines regni in omnibus sicut
alii barones et liberetenentes et ligei faciunt et perimplent.

CONFIRMATION BY JAMES III. OF CHARTER BY JOHN OF ISLA,
LORD OF THE ISLES, TO ALEXANDER LESLY.

Apud Edinburgh, 4 Feb. 1478-9.

REX confirmavit cartam Johannis de Ila domini Insularum,—[qua Reg.
concessit et ad feodifirmam dismisit consanguineo suo ALEX-
ANDRO LESLY de Wardris, scutifero, regis receptori generali,
et heredibus ejus,—terras baronie de Kynedward, viz. terras
dominicales de Kynedwarde, vulgariter nuncupatas le Castletoun,
terras de Estirtiry, Kynnaroquhy, et Faithly, vic. Abirdene ;—
RESERVATIS dicto Joh. et heredibus ejus tribus mercatis dictarum
terrarum de Castletoun cum monte castri ejusdem ad faciendum
servitium pro dictis terris et baronia de K. debitum et consuetum ;
—TENEND. de dicto Joh. et heredibus ejus dominis Insularum
et baronibus de K. in feodifirma :—SOLVEND. annuatim 29 merc. ;
nomine feodifirme :—in super constituit dictum Alex. ballivum
suum dictarum terrarum :—TENEND. in feodo, cum omnibus
potestatibus &c., addictum officium pertinentibus :—TEST. Dominis
Colino comite Ergadie dom. Lorne et Campbell magistro hosp.
regis, Lachlano MakGilleoin de Doward, Hectore Makgilleoin de

36

Loichbowe, Wil. Makloid de Glennelg, Rory Makloide de Lewes, Alex. M'Cane de Ardnamercho, Malcomo Makneile de Geya, 22 Dec. 1478].

CONFIRMATION BY JAMES III. OF CHARTER BY JOHN OF ISLA, LORD OF THE ISLES, TO JOHN DAVIDSON.

Apud Edinburgh, 26 Jul. 1480.

Sig. REX—nomine tutorio filii primogeniti sui Jacobi, ducis de Rothissay, &c., confirmavit cartam Johannis de Ila et domini Insularum—[qua allocavit et ad feodifirmam dimisit nativo armigero et alumpno suo JOHANNI DAVIDSONE, filio quondam Gilberti D., heredibus ejus et assignatis—terras de Grenane, in comitatu de Carrik, vic. Are ; quas idem Joh. de Ila personaliter resignavit :—TENEND. de dicto Joh. de Ila in feodifirma :— REDDEND. annuatim pro firmis dictarum terrarum 20 libras :— TEST. Rollando Makclane de Dowart, Eugenio Makconnehill de Ardgour, M. Nigello Makkilbreid archdiacono Sodoren., et Dougallo Makgillaspik : Apud Ila, 6 Mar., 1478.]

CONFIRMATION BY JAMES IV. OF CHARTER BY JOHN OF ISLA, EARL OF ROSS, AND LORD OF THE ISLES, TO DUNCAN MACKINTOSH, CAPTAIN OF CLANCHATTAN.

Apud Edinburgh, 5 Jan. 1494.

Sig. REX confirmavit cartam Johannis de Ila, comitis Rosse, et domini Insularum,—[qua concessit consang. suo DUNCANO MAKKINTOISCHE, capitaneo de Clanchattane, et heredibus ejus,—terras de Keppach, Inverroygur, Achnacrose, duas Bointynnis, Bohene, Murvalgane, Tullach, Daildonedarg, Achderre, Inveroyg-minor, Mischoralich, Achynnellane, Leyndale, Cloynis, Glastormore, Nucomer, Leachturynnich, Cloynkallich, Stronenabay, Tornessa, Blarrobbir, duas Ratullichys, Achmesk, Inverglie, et Achrone, in dominio de Lochabbria, vic. Invernes ; unacum officio ballivatus dictarum terrarum, necnon officio ballivatus terrarum dicti comitis sibi reservatarum, viz. Achdrome, Glengarre, Lettirfinlai, et duarum villarum de Lanachynnis ;—pro ipsius heredumque ejus homagio et servitio fideli :—REDDEND. dicto comiti de terris de Inverroygur 2 mercas, cum servitio prius dicto :—Apud Urcharde, 14 Nov. 1466]

CONFIRMATION BY JAMES IV. OF CHARTER BY JOHN OF ISLA,
EARL OF ROSS AND LORD OF THE ISLES, TO HIS BROTHER,
HUGH OF SLEAT.

Apud Striveling, 10 Nov. 1495

REX confirmavit cartam Johannis de Yle, comites Rossie, et Reg. :
domini Insularum,—[qua, cum concensu concilii sui, concessit
fratri suo HUGONI ALEXANDRI DE INSULIS, domino de
Slete,—terras 30 mercarum de Skerehowg, 12 merc. de Beanbeacla,
denariatum de Gergremynis, 60 merc. ex parte borientali de Wist,
2 denar. de Scolpie, 4 den. de Gremynis, 2 den. de Talawmartin,
6 den. de Orvinsaig, dimed. den. de Waynlis, et dimed. den. de
insula Gillegerre, unacum terris 28 merc. de Slete, in dominio suo
Insularum : TENEND. dicto Hughoni et Heredibus ejus masculis
inter ipsum et Fynvolam Alexandri Johannis de Ardnamurchan
legitime sive illegitime procreatis, ac ipsorum legitimis heredibus,
quibus deficientibus, heredibus ejus masculis post mortem dicte
Fynvole inter ipsum Hugonem et quamcunque aliam mulierem de
consilio dicti Joh. necnon consiliis consanguineorum Suorum (viz
Donaldi de Insulis dom. de Dunnowaig et de Glynnis, Celestini de
Lochalche, Lachlanni M'Gilleoin de Doward, et Alex. Johannis de
Ardnamurchan), quibus deficientibus vel deficiente, tunc de
consilio ipsorum vel heredis ipsius deficientis electam, de dicto
Joh. :—TEST. Donaldo de Insulis dom. de Dunnowaig et de
Glynnis, Celestino de Insulis de Lochalch fratre dicti Joh.,
Lachlano M'Gilleoin dom. de Doward, Joh M'Gilleoin de Lochboyg,
Lachlano juvene M'Gilleoin Magistro de Doward, Wo M'Loyd de
Glennelg, Rodrico M'Leoid de Leoghiis, Alex. Johannis de Ardna-
murchan, Joh. Lachlani M'Gilleoin de Colla, et Tho. de Monro
secretario dicti Joh. de Yle ac rectore de Kilmanawik :—Apud
Aros, 28 June 1469.]

CONFIRMATION BY JAMES IV. OF CHARTER BY ALEXANDER OF
ISLA, LORD OF THE ISLES, TO MACNEILL OF BARRA.

Apud Striveling 12. Nov. 1495

REX confirmavit cartam quondam Alexandri de Yle, domini Reg.
Insularum, et magistri comitatus Rossie,—qua concessit alumpno
et armigero sue GILLEOWNAN RODRICI MURCHARDI
MAKNEILL, "conservatore presentium," ac omnibus et singulis
heredibus ejus masculis de legitimo thoro procreatis,—a dicto

Alex.,—terras totius insule de Barra,—pro ejus homagiis et servitiis, &c.:—Insuper concessit dicto Gill. et omnibus heredibus ejus masculis,—terras unciate de Baegastallis in Wist, in liberam et perpetnam hereditatem, viz, deficientibus vero ipso Gill. et ipsius legitimus heredibus de ejus corpore procreatis, tunc concessit dictas terras de Barra et Baegastallis diutius viventi de fratribus dicti Gill. inter predictum Rodricum Makneill et filiam Ferchardi Makgilleoin procreatis ; et def. omnibus his fratribus, concessit dictas terras dicto Rodrico et ipsius omnibus heredibus, in feodo, &c., modo et forma quibus supra:—Test. d. Angusio episc. Sodoren., M. Nigello Celestini bacallario utriusque juris ac rectore de Killecoman, Lachlanno M'Gilleoin, dom. de Doward, Joh. Murchardi Makgilleoin, Terleto Ferchardi Makgilleoin, Nigello Flemyn :—Apud Insulam S. Finlagani in Yle, in vigilia S. John Bapt. 1427].

CONFIRMATION TO BISHOP OF LISMORE BY JAMES IV. OF CHARTERS BY LORDS OF THE ISLES TO THE ABBEY OF SADDELL.

Apud Edinburgh 1 Jan. 1507.

. Sig. REX,—quia ipse et domini concilii inspexerunt evidentias per David Episcopum Lismoren. Ostensas, de nonnullis terris ABBACIE DE SAGADULL, infra dominium de Kintire, in puram elemosinam concessis, per reges Alexandrum, Robertum, David, et Robertum confirmatas, viz.—(1) Cartam Reginaldi filii Sorleti, qui se regem Insularum nominavit, dom. de Ergile et Kyntyre, dicti monasterii fundatoris,—de terris de Glensagadull, et de 12 mercatis de Baltebeam in dicto dominio ;—(2) aliam cartam ejusdem,—de 20 mercatis terrarum de Ceskene, in insula de Arane ;—(3) Cartam Roderici ejus filii,—de terris de Glentor-sadull et Ugladull in dominio de Kyntyre ; (4) Cartam Johannis dom. Insularum filii Angusii,—de 2 mercat. terrarum nuncup. Lesenmarg ;—(5) Cartam Alexandri dom. Insularum,—de 2 mercat. terrarum nuncupat. Cragvane, in insula de Giga, et de insula de Sanctbarre, apud Lochkilkerane ;—(6) Cartam Johannis dom. Insularum et Angusii ejus filii,—de terris de Knockantebeg, et 12 unciatis terrarum nuncupat. Kellipull.

CONFIRMATION BY JAMES IV. TO DAVID, BISHOP OF LISMORE,
OF CHARTER BY RODERICK, THE SON OF REGINALD.

Apud Edinburgh, 26. Sep. 1507.

Rex ad manum mortuam confirmavit novem cartas sibi et Reg.
dominus concilii per David episc. Lismoren productas, Ecclesia
Cathedrali et sedi Episcopali Lismorensi et prelatis ejusdem
concessas, viz,—

Cartam Rotherici, Reginaldi filii, dom. de Kyntire,—qua in
puram elemosinam concessit, ad serviendum ecclesie S. Johannis
in Kyntire,—5 denariatas terre, scilicet 3 de ecclesia S. Johannis
et de ecclesia S. Marie :—Test. Gilberto persona de Kilchiarane,
Eugenio Macgillemayrtin, Cristene Maccormoche, Gillefolane
decano de Kyntire, Mauricio persona de Chillmacdachormes.

CONFIRMATION BY JAMES IV. TO THE BISHOP OF LISMORE OF
A CHARTER BY JOHN OF ISLA, LORD OF THE ISLES, OF THE
PATRONAGE OF THE CHURCH OF KILBERRY.

Apud Edinr. 26. Sep. 1507.

Rex confirmavit &c—

Cartam Johanni de Ilay domini Insularum et patroni ecclesie Reg.
de Kilberry in Knapdaill,—[qua, in subsidium utilitatis ecclesie
Lesmoren., que parve importantie extitit, necnon relevationem
suam ydoneas personas presentare ignorantis,—cum consensu
Tho. Flemyng rectoris dicte ecclesie,—in puram elemosinam
concessit Roberto Lismoren. episc., et ejus successoribus, jus
patronatus dicte ecclesie :—Test. Alex. de Insulis de Lochage,
Celestino Eugenii, Martino Duncani :—Apud Arois, 6 Dec. 1492].

CHARTER OF MORTIFICATION TO THE BISHOP OF LISMORE
ANENT THE ABBEY OF SAGADULL, &c.

Jacobus Dei gracia Rex Scotorum Omnibus probis hominibus Reg.
tocius terre sue clericis et laicis salutem Sciatis quia nos et consilii
nostri domini inspeximus et ad plenum intelleximus nonnullas
evidencias autenticus coram nobis et ipsis per reverendum in
Christo patrem et consiliarum nostrum dilectum David Lesmoren-
sem Episcopum modernum pro ductas et ostensas per dominos
insularum . . . . abbacie se Sagadull situate infra dominum

nostrum de Kintire datas et concessis ut sequitur confectas et per
nobilisimos predecessores nostros Alexandrum Robertum David et
Robertum Scotorum reges . . . confirmatas (inter alias)
unam evidenciam per Alexandrum dominum Insularum de daubas
mercatis terrarum nuncupatarum Cragvan cum pertinenciis
jacencium in Insula de Giga et de insula de Sanct baroe cum suis
pertinenciis jacente apud Loch Kilkerane . . . .

Confirmation dated at Edinburgh 1 January 1507-8.

POEM ON THE LORDS OF THE ISLES BY O'HENNA. C. 1450.

The Book of Clanranald.

Ceannas Ghaidheal do Chlann Cholla, 's còir fhògradh,
'S iad a ris 's na cathaibh ceudna, flaithean Fodhla,
Ceannas Eiriun agus Albainn an fhuinn ghrianaich,
A ta aig an dream fhuilteach, fhaobharach, curaidhnean cliathrach.
Fhuair ceannas na h-aicme uile, Eoin a Ile.
Fhuair Alasdair, flath na feile, rath nan righre.
Domhnull, Eoin, agus dà Aonghus, bha fial, faoilidh,
Ceathrar a bhuinnig riar o righrean, 's do 'n gheill Gaidheil,
Somhairle nach do mheall a moladh, ceann nan curaidhean,
Ceathrar o Shomhairle suil ghorm, suas gu Suibhne,
Ceathrar sin nach foill an inbhe, 's còir an cuimhneachadh,
Seisear o Shuibhne, roimh-ràthmar, gu righ Colla,
Fion aca fo bhruaich Bhanna, a cuachaibh corra.
Nan àireamhainn na thainig uime do dh' uaislibh nan Gaidheal
Bheiream gach aon ghlùin naith gu Adhamh, ni fhuair aon fhear.
An so treis do ghinealach nan Gaidheal, mar a ghealladh,
An dream so ris nach còir coimeas, 's do 'n còir ceannas.

POEM ON THE MACDONALDS BY GILLECALLUM MAC AN OLLAIMH. C. 1493.

The Book of the Dean of Lismore.

Ni- h-aoibhneas gun chlann Domhnaill, ni comhrag bhi 'n an eugmhais,
A chlann do b 'fhearr 's a chruinne, gur dhiubh gach duine ceud,
Clann is saoire de 'r gheibh, an robh eangnath agus athais,
Clann do 'r mhoil na tirean an robh creidimh 'us cràbhath.
Clann chunbhalach chalm chrodha, clann bu luaithe an am throd,
Clann bu mhine am measg bheotha, 'us bu chalma a chog,

Clann bu lionmhor orra, do fhuair aithne 'us aireamh,
Clann nar chathaich air eaglais, clann le 'r am b'eagal an càineadh,
Gach aon an Albainn uaine, a chlann is cruaidh ghabh baisde.
Dh' an robh treas gach tire, seabhag fhial air ghaisge,
Chlann bu mho 'us bu mhear, clann bu ghrinn 'us bu réidh,
Clann do 'm b' fharsuinn cridhe, do b' fhearr foighdean 's feile,
Mic righ nior thoill an aor an robh diontachd a's troma,
Fir allda uailse on uair, an robh bronntachd 'us bochda,
Clann do'm b' fhearr fion 'us fasgath, clann do'm b' fhearr gaisge
    laimh,
Ole leam giorrad earuaidh, a bhith le 'r sniomhadh an snàth,
Nior b' iad na droch fhir mhiodhar, no na fir liomhara laga, '
Ri dol ann an ionadaibh ole, fir nach cruaidhe a chraig.
Clann gun uabhar, gun eucoir, 'n uair gheibh iad cudail chogaidh,
G'ar bhuineadh daoine uailse, agus 'g ar bhuineadh bodaich,
Mairg o 'r rug au dion mairg a dheilich r' an caidrimh,
Gun aon chlann mar chlann Domhnuill, saor chlann bu chomhrad
    aigne.
Gun aireamh air an urdail, gun chunntadh air an duaisibh,
Gun chrioch, gun tùs, gun deireadh, air cineach aig an uaislibh.
An toiseach chlann Domhnuill, do bhi foghlum 'ga àithneadh,
Agus do bhi 'n an deireadh, fion 'us eineach 'us nàire.
Air bhròn 'us air thursa, do ruigeas tuigse 'us foghlum,
Gach fhineadh orra ruigeas, ni h-aoibhneas gun chlann Domhnuill.
Bu treun gaoth an torrunn, fa 'n aicme chrionda chomhrad,
Ge taid an duigh fo dhimeas, ni h-aoibhneas gun chlann Domhnuill.
Na sloigh mhòr 'us an greann, am muirn, am meaghar s' am
    foghainteachd,
Ni còire bhi 'n an eugmhais, ni h-aoibhneas gun chlann Domhnuill.
Macan laimh a mhuime d' fhuair saoradh air gach doruinn,
Ge ta e dhuinne dileas, ni h-aoibhneas gun chlann Domhnuill.

Ni h-aoibhneas.

POEM ON JOHN, LORD OF THE ISLES. C. 1460.

Fior mo mholadh air Macdhomhnuill,
Curaidh le 'n ceanglam,
Curaidh gach còmhlainn, cridhe leomhain,
Lamh nach d' thugadh, guaire nan Gaidheal,
Aonfhear Ullaidh, tàth nam pobull,

The
Clan

Rosg le rugadh casg nan cogadh,
Grian nan Gaidheal, gnùis O' Cholla,
Fo bhruaich Bhanna, luath a longa,
Cuilein conbhaidh, chaisgeas foghaluidhen,
Cridhe cunbhalach, bile Bhanbha,
An tìr na deannal dearg na dheigh,
A bheart-bunaidh teachd o Theamhra,
Measgadh Meidhe, onchu Ile,
Freumh na feile, treun gach tìre,
Nior dh' eur aonfhear, no dàimh duilich,
Craobh fhial einich, o fhiadhan Oileach,
Nior dh' fhàs uime ach rioghainn agus righre :
Fuigheall fior , fior mo mholadh.

POEM ON THE MURDER OF ANGUS, SON OF JOHN, LORD OF
THE ISLES, BY JOHN OF KNOYDART. 1490.

of A chinn Diarmaid O'Chairbair, g'a leor airc agus tuaghal,
of Cha mhòr leam meud do dhocair, ge ta e cruaidh ri chuadh.
Cha truagh leam fo do ghruaidh ghreannaich; na gaoithe gleann-
aich
Cha truagh leum 'gad cheangladh, a chinn Diarmaid O'Charbair.
Mairg an smuain a bha am braghad, nach bu naimhdeas do
chairdeas,
Och is mairg 'n uair shaoilleadh teachd, a chinn Diarmaid
O'Charbair.
Do mhilleadh leat Righ Ile, fear imirt fhion 'us airgid,
Dha ta an trillis ùr earnach, a chinn Diarmaid O'Charbair.
Righ Ile nan corn cuachail, a chuireas onoir air chairdean,
Mairg a chreuchd a chneas neamhgheal, a chinn Diarmaid
O'Charbair.
Ionnmhuinn leam a bhos mhear nach doichleadh òr no argiod,
'Us le 'r b' annsa fleadh 'us fiadhach, a chinn Diarmaid O'Charbair.
Iarram air Righ nan Abstol an ti a phaisgeas le a fheartaibh,
D'a fhurtachd am feasd o phianaibh, a chinn Diarmaid O'Charbair
                                        A chinn Diarmaid.

POEM ON JOHN, LORD OF THE ISLES, AND ANGUS, HIS SON,
BY GILLECALLUM MAC AN OLLAIMH. C. 1480.

Thainig aobhar mo thuirse, cha leam chaidh a bhliathna so,   The Book of
Ni tuigse do neach nach tuig, mo thuirse theachd mar thainig,   the Dean of
Cia b' e neach nach tuigeadh sin, theachd comhlan do 'm chumha,   Lismore.
Na losta feuch o 'm chom, tuirse na creuchda ro gheibheam.
Is aoibhinn leam ge deacair roimhe, teughbhail air ghoirt na co ...
A ta am bròn gu 'm chradhadh fo 'm chlcibh, is mòr mo ghradh
      do 'n ...
Tha mo chridhe 'na dha leth, cha 'n ioghnadh e bhi briste,
Tha mo chorp gun fheoil gun fhuil, mar bhochd gun treoir ...
Cha 'n ioghnadh cumha dh' a meud, orm an deigh Mhic Mairirid,
A bhi cuimhneach air mhaith an fhir, cha 'n bheileamaid flath o
      dh' fhàg ...
Is truime dhuinne na dhol anmhuinn na dheigh 's an t-saoghal,
Mo chràdh a's d' fhuair air dhol as, an làmhach a fhuaireas o
      Aonghus,
Ge deacair leum dealach' ris, Mac Eoin a chomhraidh mhilis,
Is miosa e gun mhilleadh esan, gun bhi tilleadh gu 'innis.
Ge fada a bhitheam o m' àgh, us mo luchd tuaileis a 'm dheigh,
Do bu dheanadh mo rath ruinn, ceannach cha 'n iarradh orra ...
Cha 'n ioghnadh m' aigne do bhaithte, ri faicsinn tighearn eile,
Mi làn gun mo bhrigh gu trom, o ta mo righ gun anamin.
Do chràdhadh mo chridhe d' a éis, sgeul is furasd a fhaisneas,
Cha 'n 'eil fulachd air mo bhròn, do bhlagh cuiridh ...
Mòr mo bhròn us ni h-ioghnadh dhomh, cha tuirse ...
Dheargainn mo chridhe gu lom, gun sliòchd an Albain againn.
Nis o 's eigin domh triall, mo bhi aig càch fo ...
Ri luidhese do b' aithne dhol, á h-innse ald na h-Albainn.
Go do thriallaim is deacair leum, ge ta mar fhiachaibh orm,
Mo rùn do dhlù a mùghadh, cùl re 'm dhùthaich àm dheigh.
Is e an ni fa d' éirich dhomh, ar leam cha bheag an t-aobhar,
Gun mo ghaoil a theachd air ais, Ile air a leth taobh Innis.
Is trom na aghaidhsan, a lùth thainig dha aimsir,
A cnàmh' chridhe 's a cràdh' chorp, gun slighe aig cach d' a dhiolt.
Nior shaoileas duine ar domhainn, a mheud a rath air chean-
      sachadh.
Gur falamh oirn agus ort, mala le 'r h-oirnn a thigeadh.
O 's e ghuineadar a dhol, truagh nach amhuil a bhamar,
A Mhic Mhuire bhosgeal bhinn, gun duine a d' asgainn againn.
An aoin neach r' a aghaidh ghile, na gur gun dol 'n a dheigh,

37

Noch rath is fada no sin, de 'n mheud bha aig do mhuinntir.
Luchd caidrimh a chuil cam, air an aithnich cach an comunn,
An aigne do chaidh air ais, is truagh gach caidrimh as d' eugmhais.
Do bu dheacair coimeas rium, 'us do bhi o'm thighearn agam.
Caidreamh cochaill 'us daimh, aigne ro mhòr gun a laimh.
'N uair theid cach dha do'n òl, is e mo chuid de'n onoir,
Bhith fo bhròn gun deanamh mùgh, ag òl mo dhiol de chumha.
Taim anmhuinn gun dol tar éis, cha 'n anmhuinn cumha as m'
    eugmhais.
Cach aig do'n chumha mi, is pailte na dubha eile,
Iomadh neach romhainn rianh, do chur cumha fo dhimhiodh,
. na bhuin so dearbhar leam, ursgeul na 'r ghabh romham,—
Do chuala mi fad o shean, etc.—ut sequitur in alio loco.
Mac samhailt na brigh binn, daltan Chaoimh 'us Chonuil.

1700 MS. ON THE MARRIAGE OF JOHN OF ISLA.

The world is so malicious that some writters was pleased to
say, if the Lord of Lorne's Daughter had been married to John of
Iyla that Clanrannell would be Chief of the Macdonalds in Scotland and let those writters say what they please, Rannell is ye
first born all the world knows that the consent of both parties is
the Lawfull mariage whereas those writters says that John of
Iyla had taken the Lord of Lorne's Daughter upon a faithfull
promise to marry her ; and it is to be believed that Lorne would
not give his Daughter but upon that condition whereas he was a
powerfull man in that time and Long afterwards, moreover he
being come of the same family with John of Iyla furthermore the
same writters affirm that they lived peaessably together for the
space of seven years and that she Died in the same bed where she
begat her children.

1700 MS. ON THE MARRIAGE OF ANGUS OG.

Eneas Oge married O'Cahan's daughter, Conbuidghe O'Cahan,
Lord of Lemvady, and master of the whole County of Derry.
Her name was Any. Eneas Oge desired no portion, but so many
young gentlemen, and not two of them of one surname.

PRINTED BY THE NORTHERN COUNTIES NEWSPAPER AND PRINTING AND PUBLISHING
COMPANY, LIMITED, INVERNESS.

www.ingramcontent.com/pod-product-compliance
Ingram Content Group UK Ltd.
Pitfield, Milton Keynes, MK11 3LW, UK
UKHW020629130525
5885UKWH00003B/61